Rock Climbing the Wasatch Range

Bret Ruckman
Stuart Ruckman

GUILFORD, CONNECTICUT
HELENA, MONTANA
AN IMPRINT OF THE GLOBE PEQUOT PRESS

COVER: Jonny Woodward leading Dog Eat Dog, a three star 5.13d at the S-Curve Area in Big Cottonwood Canyon. See page 174.

Library of Congress Cataloging-in-Publication Data
Ruckman, Bret
Rock climbing Wasatch Range / Bret Ruckman, Stuart Ruckman
p. cm.
Includes index.
ISBN 978-0-7627-2730-8 (rev.)
1. Rock climbing—Wasatch Range (Utah and Idaho) Guidebooks.
2. Wasatch Range (Utah and Idaho) Guidebooks. I. Ruckman, Stuart
II. Title.
GV199.42.W16R82 1998
796.52'23'097922—dc21 98-29728
CIP

Manufactured in the United States of America
First Edition/Third Printing

WARNING:
CLIMBING IS A SPORT WHERE YOU MAY BE SERIOUSLY INJURED OR DIE. READ THIS BEFORE YOU USE THIS BOOK.

This guidebook is a compilation of unverified information gathered from many different climbers. The author cannot assure the accuracy of any of the information in this book, including the topos and route descriptions, the difficulty ratings, and the protection ratings. These may be incorrect or misleading and it is impossible for any one author to climb all the routes to confirm the information about each route. Also, ratings of climbing difficulty and danger are always subjective and depend on the physical characteristics (for example, height), experience, technical ability, confidence and physical fitness of the climber who supplied the rating. Additionally, climbers who achieve first ascents sometimes underrate the difficulty or danger of the climbing route out of fear of being ridiculed if a climb is later down-rated by subsequent ascents. Therefore, be warned that you must exercise your own judgment on where a climbing route goes, its difficulty and your ability to safely protect yourself from the risks of rock climbing. Examples of some of these risks are: falling due to technical difficulty or due to natural hazards such as holds breaking, falling rock, climbing equipment dropped by other climbers, hazards of weather and lightning, your own equipment failure, and failure or absence of fixed protection.

You should not depend on any information gleaned from this book for your personal safety; your safety depends on your own good judgment, based on experience and a realistic assessment of your climbing ability. If you have any doubt as to your ability to safely climb a route described in this book, do not attempt it.

The following are some ways to make your use of this book safer:

1. **CONSULTATION:** You should consult with other climbers about the difficulty and danger of a particular climb prior to attempting it. Most local climbers are glad to give advice on routes in their area and we suggest that you contact locals to confirm ratings and safety of particular routes and to obtain first-hand information about a route chosen from this book.

2. **INSTRUCTION:** Most climbing areas have local climbing instructors and guides available. We recommend that you engage an instructor or guide to learn safety techniques and to become familiar with the routes and hazards of the areas described in this book. Even after you are proficient in climbing safely, occasional use of a guide is a safe way to raise your climbing standard and learn advanced techniques.

3. **FIXED PROTECTION:** Many of the routes in this book use bolts and pitons which are permanently placed in the rock. Because of variances in the manner of placement, weathering, metal fatigue, the quality of the metal used, and many other factors, these fixed protection pieces should always be considered suspect and should always be backed up by equipment that you place yourself. Never depend for your safety on a single piece of fixed protection because you never can tell whether it will hold weight, and in some cases, fixed protection may have been removed or is now absent.

Be aware of the following specific potential hazards which could arise in using this book:

1. **MISDESCRIPTIONS OF ROUTES:** If you climb a route and you have a doubt as to where the route may go, you should not go on unless you are sure that you can go that way safely. Route descriptions and topos in this book may be inaccurate or misleading.

2. **INCORRECT DIFFICULTY RATING:** A route may, in fact, be more difficult than the rating indicates. Do not be lulled into a false sense of security by the difficulty rating.

3. **INCORRECT PROTECTION RATING:** If you climb a route and you are unable to arrange adequate protection from the risk of falling through the use of fixed pitons or bolts and by placing your own protection devices, do not assume that there is adequate protection available higher just because the route protection rating indicates the route is not an "X" or an "R" rating. Every route is potentially an "X" (a fall may be deadly), due to the inherent hazards of climbing – including, for example, failure or absence of fixed protection, your own equipment's failure, or improper use of climbing equipment.

THERE ARE NO WARRANTIES, WHETHER EXPRESS OR IMPLIED, THAT THIS GUIDEBOOK IS ACCURATE OR THAT THE INFORMATION CONTAINED IN IT IS RELIABLE. THERE ARE NO WARRANTIES OF FITNESS FOR A PARTICULAR PURPOSE OR THAT THIS GUIDE IS MERCHANTABLE. YOUR USE OF THIS BOOK INDICATES YOUR ASSUMPTION OF THE RISK THAT IT MAY CONTAIN ERRORS AND IS AN ACKNOWLEDGMENT OF YOUR OWN SOLE RESPONSIBILITY FOR YOUR CLIMBING SAFETY.

In memory of our dad, Stuart Allan Ruckman,
whose love of the mountains showed us the way.

Acknowledgements

The 1425 routes documented in this book represent thousands of hours of painstaking research, drawing, writing and compilation. We could never possibly do this alone. We've had to have help from dozens of kind individuals all along the way. In this nearly overwhelming go-round of guidebook mayhem, we owe many thanks to the following individuals who freely offered encouragement and enlightenment: (in no particular order) John Hansen, George Rosenthal, Chris Begue, Mark Bennett, Pat Maloney, Tim Wolfe, Steve Habovstak, Randy Kieliszewski, Nolan Wall, Tony Calderone, Jeff Baldwin, Kennan Harvey, Chris Harmston, Brian Smoot, Lange Jeffries, Drew Bedford, Jonny Woodward, Frank Delana, Douglas Heinrich, Gordon Douglass, Mindy Shulak, Craig Dillon, Shane Willet, James Garrett, Chad Zurinshas, Scott Keller, Dave Nix, John Laney, Hank Armantrout, The family of Doug Hall, Lee Cohen, Rick Reese, Tim Wagner, Lance Bateman, Kimber Almond, Bill Hunt, Dave Medera, Fred Henion, Eric Wright, Michael Pennings, Jim Reynolds, Lee Logston, John Barstow, Les Ellison, Tim Roberts, Emery Lortsher, Steve and Eva Kauffman, Bill Paton, Brian Mecham and Jon Ray.

We owe special thanks to Ron Stout, who endured all the darkroom printings and considerable rantings during this book.

Several guidebooks for Wasatch climbing have preceded this one. Rex Green, Dennis Turville, Dave Smith, Les Ellison and Brian Smoot, John Gottman, Gary Olsen and Tony Calderone— the authors of these books—provided the groundwork on which this one was written.

Finally, we'd like to thank our rock solid foundations—our families. The support of Kim and Fred Thalmann (and Hillary too!), Ivy Ruckman, Judy Ruckman and Libby Ellis, kept us motivated and focused. To Libby and Judy, who have been tested to the pinnacle of forbearance, there are no words of gratitude strong enough. We can simply say THANK YOU!

Table of Contents

Chris Harmston leading the Question Mark Wall Route, Lone Peak.

photo: Kennan Harvey

ABOUT THIS BOOK

The climbing areas in this book describe rock climbing in the Wasatch Range around Salt Lake City. Included is climbing in both Big and Little Cottonwood Canyons, as well as a number of other canyons and climbing areas in the region.

HOW TO USE THIS BOOK

The climbs in the areas described in this book are presented as topos. The form of these is pretty standard to all U.S. climbing guides and is outlined on page 8. Please send any corrections, new route information and general comments to the authors, in care of The Globe Pequot Press, P.O. Box 480, Guilford, CT 06437.

CONSERVATION

In the past, climbers have been a select few, and, in general, have held a common commitment to preservation. As rock climbing has grown in popularity and now is practiced by a broader segment of the population, not all of its participants share in this commitment. The canyons surrounding Salt Lake City now are overused. This is evidenced by increased damage to plants and trees, erosion problems, the presence of litter and human waste, disfiguring fire pits and graffiti, and unsafe water—the whole gamut of ills one associates with urban encroachment. Climbers should be leaders in the fight to save our canyons since we use—and sometimes abuse—them as much as anyone. Climbers are responsible for the ridiculously steep trails leading to the cliffs (erosional nightmares)—for overbolting, mutilating trees, strewing tape wads and Powerbar wrappers, leaving chalk, tangled masses of ugly slings on rock faces—and on and on.

What can we do? A few positive steps have been taken—like building gentler trails to the cliffs, and platforms on the steep slopes beneath popular routes. Although apparently damaging at the outset, this practice will prevent erosion over the years and will funnel climbers onto one path. When scrambling up talus, climbers should remember that such slopes generally are more stable near their margins; it is less damaging to travel on the edges. Climbers should pick up their own litter, bury excrement far away from heavily-traveled areas, and minimize their impact on plant and animal life wherever possible. The thoughtful climber also will take time to pick up litter left behind by others. Bolts and chains, when possible, should be camouflaged with colors that match the rock. When a sling is left behind, remember that earth-tone colors are preferable to neon eyesores. Chalk should be used sparingly (consider colored chalk), and climbers should remember that blaring boom boxes can ruin the outdoor experience for others.

The period of March 1 to July 31 is when raptors do their nesting. If you see an active nest on your intended climb during this nesting season, please choose a different route, one that is at least several hundred feet away, or consider coming back after July 31 when the young have fledged and left the nest.

Let's not trash the beautiful Wasatch. The canyons are our gift to cherish, our responsibility to preserve.

ACCESS

Unknown to most climbers visiting Little Cottonwood Canyon, the land that stretches from the Church Buttress up to and including the Gate Buttress is owned by the Church of Jesus Christ of Latter-Day Saints. This area has been the subject of enforced closures off and on, with the most recent closure occurring in 1987. The closures primarily were due to liability fears of the church leaders, fears that result from the litigious nature of today's society.

In the spring of 1988, the LDS church entered into negotiations with the U.S. Forest Service to assure climber access to the area. These efforts were instigated by local climbers Ted Wilson and Rick Reese, and Forest Service official Doug Abromeit. The church's willingness to enter into negotiations can be traced to Utah's Limitation of Landowner Liability Act, which will help protect the church from any financial liability resulting from a lawsuit involving climbing activities. Technically, the church land is still closed, but without enforcement. Climbers therefore are urged to use the utmost care when climbing on this private property and to take full responsibility for their actions. If climbing near The Fin or Gargoyle Wall, do not use the access road leading to the church vaults, even if it means a few extra feet of bushwhacking. Further discussions of access are in the LCC introduction.

– Allen Sanderson, American Alpine Club Access Committee

ETHICS

Historically, a strong ethical ideal of establishing routes from the ground up has prevailed in the Wasatch. Many first ascents involved bold exploration of virgin rock with little assurance of success. While a route completed in this style still is the best received by the climbing community, rappel-placed bolts now are generally accepted if well thought out and have shown their merits with the creation of many excellent new lines.

In our 1991 WASATCH NORTH guidebook we had designated how the bolts on a route were originally placed— on lead or on rappel. We inserted an R&D (rappel and drill) after a route listing, if it were established in this style. In this edition we have omitted the R&D designation, but hope that climbers understand the travails the early pioneer climbers went through.

When you clip a bolt, do you consider how it was originally placed? Probably not. You simply clip and go. The leader of the first ascent might have had a much different experience than you're having, however. Barely balancing on a sloping chickenhead, twenty feet above his last protection, the trembling leader would carefully pull out the heavy drill and hammer and begin to tap a hole. 20-30 minutes later, with quivering leg muscles, the leader could pound the bolt into the hole, clip-in and breathe a temporary sigh of relief. This is how nearly all face routes were established prior to 1986, and as a result, there just weren't that many bolts around. Few people had the strength or nerves for the task.

Since then, rappel-bolting by hand and rappel-bolting with power drills has, with numerous exceptions, become the norm. These techniques make bolting a much easier proposition, and bolts have proliferated like never before. Too easy in fact. Bolts are cropping up all over the place. So if you're considering bolting a "new" route, do some research to make sure the route hasn't already been done clean of bolts. Also try to evaluate the quality of the route—is it worth the time, expense and permanent alteration of bolting? If you are replacing old ¼ inch bolts with ⅜ or ½ inch new ones, think before you drill! Replace the old bolt with a new bolt. You are not the one to decide whether a route needs additional bolts, or whether the bolt-line needs to be straightened out. That is the decision of the first ascensionists. Consult with them before you get trigger-happy and start spraying bolts everywhere. Some routes are monuments to the boldness of their creators. Don't erase history with knee-jerk justifications for why a route needs more bolts. If it could be led thirty years ago with hiking boots and no bolts or chalk, then it doesn't need to be bolted now. The Salt Lake locals agree that it is absolutely taboo to add additional bolts to established routes, to cut or destroy foliage or to create new holds (chipping, enhancement, bolting on modular holds, etc.). Please abide by these standards.

Remember, no power drills in Wilderness Areas.

BOLT REPLACEMENT

Many of the bolts in the Wasatch are over thirty years old and have long since lost their reliability. Thankfully a group of climbers have taken on the huge and often expensive task of replacing these old time bombs. On most of the high quality popular routes in the area the bolts have been upgraded, thanks to the dedicated efforts of the following individuals: Rebecca Barry, Drew Bedford, Tony Calderone, John Hansen, Doug Heinrich, Pete Lenz and James Preziosi.

PROTECTION

The gear needed for a given climb is only occasionally specified in this guide. Climbers should carry RP's(micro nuts), nuts (at least a full set), cams and TCUs, quickdraws, over-the-shoulder runners, extra carabiners and maybe some hexentrics or tri-cams. On modern sport routes, quickdraws usually will suffice. Care must be taken here, as some routes may appear to be all bolt-protected, but in fact require some gear. In most instances, we try to mention the protection needed on these climbs. Keep in mind that old fixed pins and bolts always are suspect. In particular, be wary of pins in the quartzite, as there seems to be more shifting in quartzite than with other rock types. Bolt counts on a guidebook topo are not always accurate. Be prepared.

RATINGS

It is assumed the climber is aware of the current rating system (Yosemite Decimal System). On the topos, the fifth-class denotation is omitted (e.g. 5.6 becomes .6). Beware of the discrepancy in the ratings found in this book. Each area has its idiosyncrasies with regard to ratings and protection. We undoubtedly incorrectly identify the ratings of certain routes. Furthermore, we frequently have relied solely on the first ascensionist's ratings, so never take this guidebook to be definitive or infallible. Use it as a reference, as the climbing aid it is intended to be. Route lines on photos and topos are drawn to the best of our knowledge, but they, too, may not be strictly accurate.

Grade ratings*

grade

I. One to three hours

II. Three to four hours.

III. Four to six+ hours.

IV. Full day. There is only one of these listed in the book—The Ventral Fin.

V or VI. Multi-day routes. No such animals in the Wasatch.

Aid Ratings*

A0 "French free". Grabbing protection etc, but no etriers.

A1 Easy aid. Straightforward, solid placements

A2 Moderate aid. Placements generally solid but possibly awkward and strenuous to place.

A2+Like A2, but usually several tenuous placements above good pro.

A3 Hard aid. Many tenuous placements in a row.

A3+Like A3, but with dangerous fall potential. Can take 3+ hours to lead one pitch.

A4 Serious aid. Lots of jeopardy. 60-100 foot fall potential. This is the hardest of the Wasatch aid routes—Tin Man A4.

A4+-A5 It only gets worse. Can you imagine? Thankfully none of these have been done (in the Wasatch) to tempt someone's fate.

*Source: *How to Rock Climb: Big Walls* by John Long and John Middendorf (Evergreen: Chockstone Press, 1994).

THE WEATHER AND THE CLIMBER

WINTER (December-February): When high-pressure systems settle into the Rocky Mountain region, the Salt Lake Valley is particularly prone to temperature inversions. These cold, dark, smoggy periods may be escaped neatly by climbing above the inversion layer. With solar absorption on a sunny day, several cliffs offer good climbing. In Big Cottonwood Canyon (BCC), we suggest the following: Aquaworld, the Margin for Air Wall (afternoons), Power Plant Wall, Savage Arena (afternoons), Bumble Bee and Psychobabble Walls, the Choss Garden (afternoons), and the Upper S-Curve area. In Ferguson Canyon, the Guano Roof and Heart Wall warm up in mid-afternoon. Anything in Little Cottonwood Canyon (LCC) from the Egg down to the Bong Eater can be climbed on warm days in the winter. Be prepared for snowy, mucky approaches.

SPRING (March-May): Most of the rock is warm enough to climb, with the exceptions of routes at high elevations and on north-facing cliffs. Finding dry rock is another variable: keep in mind that April is the wettest month of the year. The spring allows good climbing in the Wasatch, although the fall, as a rule, is more stable.

SUMMER (June -August): The creative climber can find plenty of climbing, even on the hottest days. All north-facing stuff is ready for climbers. Ferguson Canyon is like a swamp cooler in summer, providing comfortable climbing. The complex cluster of crags in BCC offer many shady nooks, like the Narcolepsy Area and Storm Mountain Picnic Area's North Face, The Millstone, and The Pile. In Little Cottonwood Canyon the Green A Gully, Freedom Wall, the Hellgate Cliffs, Coalpit, Pentapitch and Industrial Walls, and the bouldering are also quite pleasant. Lone Peak, Hogum Fork, and Big Willow Cirque are primed for climbers. The long south-facing routes in LCC and Bell's Canyon should be avoided on very hot days.

FALL (September-November): The best time of year to climb in the Wasatch is in the autumn. The temperatures generally are perfect for all lower elevations, including Bell's Canyon.

CAMPING AND AMENITIES

Ample campsites are available in Big and Little Cottonwood Canyons, but aren't always convenient to the best climbing. There is a uniform seven-day limit, and none of the areas offer showers. Call 1-800-280-CAMP for campground reservations in the Salt Lake vicinity.

Big Cottonwood Canyon

Camping:

In Big Cottonwood Canyon, check out Spruces Campground, located 9.8 miles up the canyon. It offers 121 campsites (97 non-reservation) at $11 per night. Also in Big Cottonwood Canyon is Redman Campground, located 13.2 miles up-canyon a half-mile past the last entrance to Solitude ski resort. Redman offers 50 sites at $11 per night.

Gas/Groceries/ATM Machines:

At the mouth of BCC is the intersection of Wasatch Blvd. and Fort Union Blvd. A 7-11 store on the southwest corner of this intersection sells gas and has an automatic teller machine (ATM). Driving south on Wasatch Blvd. from this intersection will bring you to the next stoplight, at the corner of Wasatch Blvd. and 7800 South. Turn right here and one block west there is a Smith's grocery store and an ATM.

Little Cottonwood Canyon

Camping:

In Little Cottonwood Canyon, the Tanner's Flat Campground always has been a favorite. It is 4.1 miles up LCC, costs $11 per vehicle and has 38 sites available. Also in LCC is the Albion Basin Campground, at the absolute end of the road in the heart of the Alta ski resort. The first vehicle is $11 per night, with 26 sites available. This campground really cools off at night and is open only in the warmest months.

Gas/Groceries/ATM Machines:

Two options exist depending upon which way you are traveling. From the mouth of the canyon, highway 209 (see overview map, page 12) bends to become 9400 South and heads west towards Sandy. Along the north side of 9400 South at roughly 2000 East is a Smith's supermarket with a drive-through ATM, and an Amoco and 7-11 for gas, both with ATM machines. The second option from the mouth of the canyon is to follow highway 210 north (Wasatch Blvd.) towards Salt Lake. At the corner of Wasatch Blvd. and 7800 South, turn left. One block west, at the corner of 7800 South and 3500 East is a Smith's supermarket and an ATM machine. Continuing north on Wasatch Blvd. towards Salt Lake brings you to the next intersection which is at the mouth of Big Cottonwood Canyon. A 7-11 here sells gas and has an ATM.

If you desire more natural foods check out:

Wild Oats at: 1) 4695 S Holladay Blvd.
2) 2454 S 700 E
3) 812 E 200 S

Good Earth Natural Foods at 7206 S 900 E

Parley's, Millcreek and Neff's Canyon/Mt. Olympus

Camping:

There is no camping available in these areas.

Gas/Groceries/ATM Machines:

Central to all these climbing areas is the Olympus Hills Shopping Center, a bustling strip mall located at roughly 4000 S and Wasatch Blvd. Here you'll find a Dan's supermarket, two banks with ATM machines and two gas stations. There is also an Einstein's Bagels and a Rocky Mountain Pizza restaurant.

EMERGENCY SERVICES

Dial 911 from any phone for emergency service. Phones are located at the mouth of each of the Cottonwood Canyons in the commuter parking lots.The list below is the nearest hospital to each respective climbing area.

City Creek Canyon:

LDS Hospital at 8th Ave. and C St. **321-1101** or

University Hospital at 50 North Medical Dr. **581-2121.**

Parley's, The Reef, Millcreek and Neff's Canyon/Mt. Olympus:

St. Mark's Hospital at 1200 E 3900 S **268-7129.**

Big Cottonwood and Ferguson Canyon:

St. Mark's Hospital located at 1200 East 3900 South **268-7129.**

Cottonwood Hospital located at 5770 South 300 East **262-3461.**

Little Cottonwood Canyon, Bell's, Big Willow Areas:

Alta View Hospital located at 9660 South 1300 East **567-2600.**

Lone Peak (from Alpine):

American Fork Hospital located at 170 North and 1100 East **763-3300.**

LOCAL EQUIPMENT RETAILERS

Black Diamond

2084 East 3900 South, Salt Lake City.

(801) 278-0233

IME

3265 East 3300 South, Salt Lake City.

(801) 484-8073

REI

3285 East 3300 South, Salt Lake City.

(801) 486-2100

Wasatch Touring

702 East 100 South, Salt Lake City.

(801) 359-9361

LOCAL GUIDE SERVICES

Exum Utah Mountain Adventures

Black Diamond Center

2092 E 3900 S, Suite B

Salt Lake City, Utah 84124

(801) 272-7338

CLIMBING GYMS

Rockreation

2074 East 3900 South, Salt Lake City.

(801) 278-7473

Wasatch Front Climbing Gym

427 W. Universal Circle (9160 S.), Sandy.

(801) 565-3657

SHOWERS

LITTLE COTTONWOOD AREA:

Alta Canyon Sports Center, 9565 South Highland Drive (the corner of 9400 South and Highland Drive.) Showers cost $3.20 (actually the price of a swim), and their hours are M-F: 6am to 10pm, Sat.: 7 am to 8 pm. Sun: 12 to 5. (801)942-2582. This is the closest place to shower for LCC.

BIG COTTONWOOD AREA:

Cottonwood Heights Recreation Center, 7500 South 2700 East. Their hours are 5 am to 10 pm and showers cost $4.00 (the price of a swim). (801)943-3160. This is the closest place for BCC.

BETWEEN THE COTTONWOOD CANYONS AND LONE PEAK:

Mountain Shadows RV Park, 13275 South Minuteman Drive, Draper. (801)571-4024. Showers cost $3.00.

DOWNTOWN:

Campground VIP Salt Lake City, 1400 West North Temple. (801)328-0224. Showers cost $3.00. Located near downtown—freshen up before a night on the town.

HOSTELS

There are two hostels in the Salt Lake area that are frequently used by climbers and skiers; however, neither is particularly close to the crags. The Avenues Hostel is located at 107 North "F" Street (801) 359-4525. The Ute Hostel is located at 21 East (between State and Main) and 1160 South (801) 595-1645.

RESTAURANTS NEAR THE CANYONS

Fairly close to BCC and LCC canyons are restaurants galore. Below is a partial list from an unofficial climbers' survey of recommended dining near Big and Little Cottonwood Canyons. Within the actual canyons most of the ski resorts offer year-round dining—just take your pick. One particular favorite is Silver Fork Lodge in BCC (801) 649-9551 located just down canyon from Solitude Ski Resort. They offer breakfast, lunch and dinner at affordable prices in a great location.

Fong Ling Restaurant (Chinese)
8657 South Highland Drive
944-8765

Pomodoro Restaurant (Italian)
2440 East Fort Union Blvd.
944-1895

La Salsa (burritos, etc.)
7190 South Union Park Avenue
567-9100

Carl's Cafe (homestyle breakfast)
2336 East 7000 South
943-5138

Giardino's (Italian)
3698 East 7000 South (Ft. Union Blvd.)
943-8199

Lone Star Taqueria (killer burritos, etc.)
2265 East Fort Union Blvd.
944-2300

Hoppers Grill and Brewing Co.
Corner of Fort Union Blvd. (7145 S.) and 900 East
566-0424

Cottonbottom (pub, garlic burgers)
2820 East 6200 South
273-9830

REST DAY DIVERSIONS

Obviously there are a-million-and-one things you can do, but we'd like to make one suggestion. The old original road up LCC is great walking, running or mountain biking terrain. It starts at the Temple Quarry Nature Trail area at the mouth of the canyon and follows LCC creek for several miles up the canyon. The path leads one past boulders with old temple quarry drill holes, past two bouldering areas (The Swamp and The Hidden Forest), and continues up through beautiful, verdant areas to a terminus somewhere near Hogum Fork.

Topo Legend

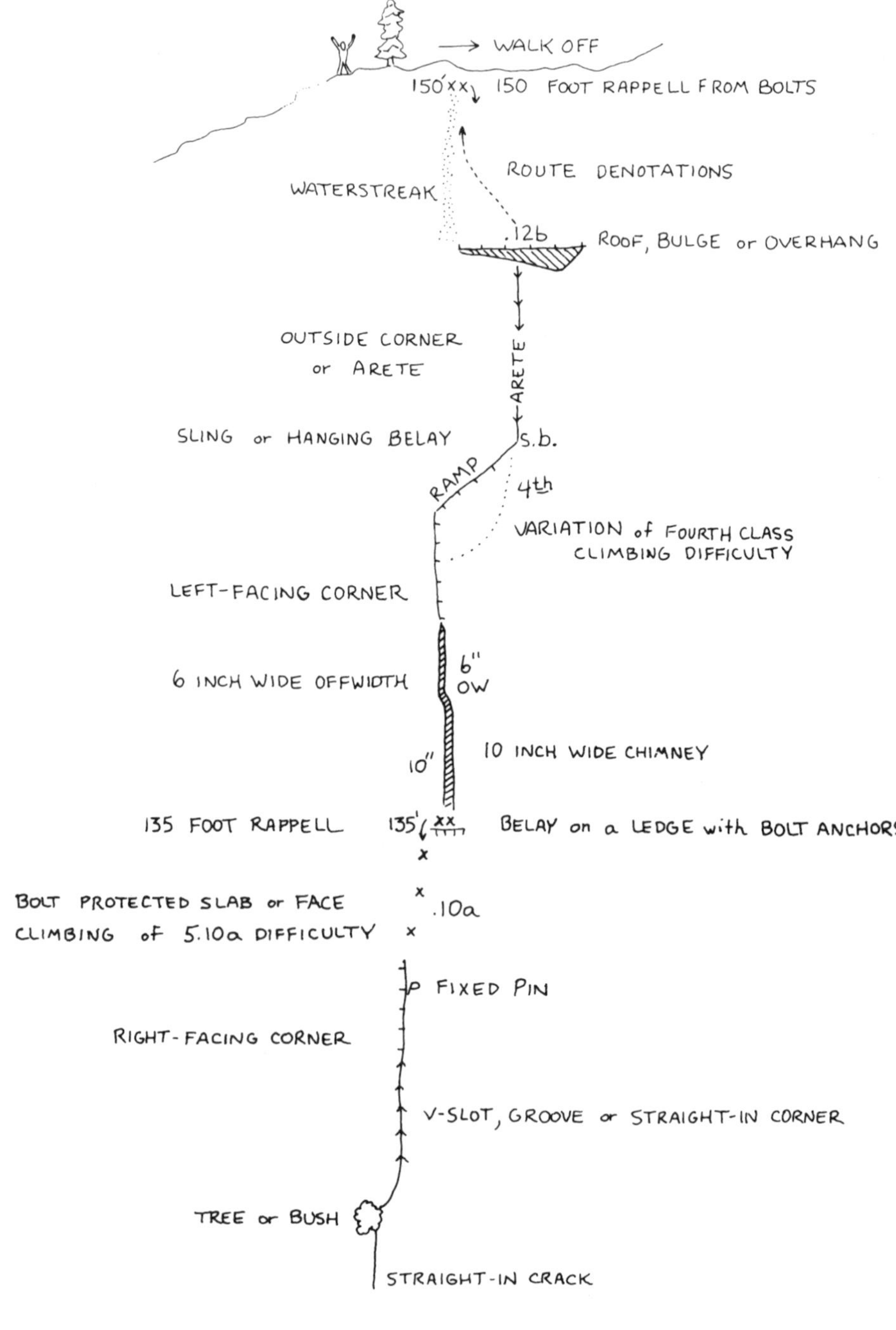

WALK OFF
150'xx
150 FOOT RAPPELL FROM BOLTS
ROUTE DENOTATIONS
WATERSTREAK
.12b
ROOF, BULGE or OVERHANG
OUTSIDE CORNER
or ARETE
ARETE
SLING or HANGING BELAY
s.b.
RAMP
4th
VARIATION of FOURTH CLASS
CLIMBING DIFFICULTY
LEFT-FACING CORNER
6"
OW
6 INCH WIDE OFFWIDTH
10"
10 INCH WIDE CHIMNEY
135 FOOT RAPPELL
135'
xx
BELAY on a LEDGE with BOLT ANCHORS
.10a
BOLT PROTECTED SLAB or FACE
CLIMBING of 5.10a DIFFICULTY
FIXED PIN
RIGHT-FACING CORNER
V-SLOT, GROOVE or STRAIGHT-IN CORNER
TREE or BUSH
STRAIGHT-IN CRACK

ABBREVIATIONS AND SYMBOLS USED

3rd ....third class (usually unroped) climbing or hiking.

AKA ....also known as.

FA ....first ascent.

FFA ....first free ascent.

FN ....fixed nut.

KB ....knife blade piton.

LA ....lost arrow piton.

lb ....lieback.

ow ....offwidth.

QD ....quickdraw.

R ....runout or restricted protection.

s.b. ....sling belay or hanging belay.

TR ....toprope problem.

TCU ....three-cam unit.

X ....obscenely poor protection, i.e. a very serious fall could occur.

— ··· — ......stream.

★ ....route of fair quality.

★★ ....pretty darn good—do it.

★★★ ....an exceptional route; a definite must-do.

A CONSOLIDATED WASATCH CLIMBING HISTORY

Although always in the shadows of Yosemite, Eldorado Canyon and the Tetons, the Wasatch has a robust climbing history of its own. Stretching over seven decades, the history may be divided into five eras—the early days (pre-1960), the Alpenbock Club period, the Lowe era, the years of the nut, and now, the modern era. Hundreds of climbers have contributed to the Wasatch climbing scene, either by first ascents or by exhibiting unusual climbing abilities. Perhaps as important are the host of climbers who frequent slide shows, equipment shops and bouldering sessions—the ones who make "the scene" by their enthusiasm. Although every contributor can't be acknowledged in a guidebook, the "stand outs" from each of these eras warrant mention.

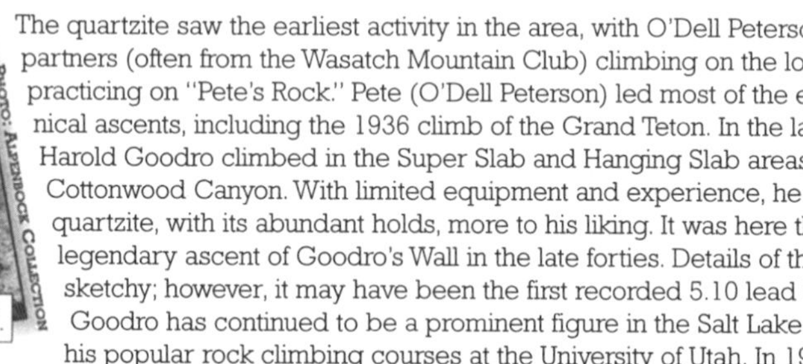

Rich Ream leading the first ascent of Schoolroom, 1964.

The quartzite saw the earliest activity in the area, with O'Dell Peterson and various partners (often from the Wasatch Mountain Club) climbing on the local peaks and practicing on "Pete's Rock." Pete (O'Dell Peterson) led most of the early WMC technical ascents, including the 1936 climb of the Grand Teton. In the late thirties, Harold Goodro climbed in the Super Slab and Hanging Slab areas of Little Cottonwood Canyon. With limited equipment and experience, he soon found the quartzite, with its abundant holds, more to his liking. It was here that he made his legendary ascent of Goodro's Wall in the late forties. Details of the ascent are a bit sketchy; however, it may have been the first recorded 5.10 lead in the country. Goodro has continued to be a prominent figure in the Salt Lake area, notable for his popular rock climbing courses at the University of Utah. In 1958, Tom Spencer and partners made their foray into the Lone Peak Cirque, where they made several impressive first ascents. The Open Book route was their classic ascent; the Left Thumb, their most difficult.

The Alpenbock Club dominated the scene from 1960 to 1964, a time when the major lines in Little Cottonwood were established—routes like The Coffin, Wilson-Love Route on The Sail, the S-Crack on The Thumb, Variety Delight on The Egg and Schoolroom on the Gate Buttress. Among active club members were Larry Evans, Curt Hawkins, Milt Hokanson, Bob Irvine, Dick Ream, Rick Reese, Court Richards, Ralph Tingey, Dick Wallin, Ted Wilson and Dave Wood. Visiting climbers Fred Beckey, Layton Kor and Royal Robbins added several difficult routes in LCC, often with members of the Alpenbock. The ascent of The Robbins' Route on The Thumb established 5.10 in LCC. In a bold two-day effort in 1962, Fred Beckey and Dan Davis tackled the Question Mark Wall on Lone Peak, traveling up the most formidable rock in the Cirque.

George Lowe of Ogden, Utah, began climbing at Tahquitz Rock in California and became an excellent free climber. He brought his skills back to the granite of LCC and began an impressive list of first free ascents and first ascents that left others in awe. Mark McQuarrie, a young and inspired Alpenbock member, teamed up with George Lowe for the first free ascent The Coffin in 1964. The pair then went on to make a landmark ascent of the Dorsal Fin in 1965. Not following any crack systems for the first 1-½ pitches, the Dorsal Fin required bolt protection on one of the most exposed positions in LCC. It seems fair to say that this route was ten years ahead of its time, requiring the expertise and cool-headedness that established George Lowe as one of the best free climbers in the country. Free ascents of the S-Matrix, the S-Direct, Bong Eater, Mexican Crack, The Green Adjective, the Undone Book, and many others are to his credit, and climbers still exude accolades over his gifted abilities. Cousins Jeff and/or Greg accompanied George on several of these climbs and made first ascents of their own. Jeff Lowe climbed the Ross Route in 1968, now rated 5.11a, and Greg Lowe free-climbed the steep crack portion of the S-Crack's third pitch, rated 5.11d. This Lowe predominance lasted nearly a decade, from 1964 to 1974. George commonly underrated his routes, adding to the pervasive opinion that Lowe routes were indomitable.

Photo by John Barstow

John Stratton aiding the Schoolroom Roof, 1975.

Between 1974 and 1985, referred to here as "the nut era," more and more climbers became involved in the sport—and the records began to tumble. Kim Miller was one of the first to do rapid repeats of the hardest routes in LCC. A very adept face climber, Kim displayed a confidence that few had seen before. He climbed these routes often, as if they were trivial, and by doing so broke through the Lowe ceiling. Mark Ward and others joined Kim on these escapades, and together they added a bold new route on a slab left of the Dorsal Fin: Intensive Care. This climb ushered in the

5.11 standard. Brian and Jonathan Smoot, teenagers at the time, climbed a new route on The Fin, capturing a brilliant line left of the Dorsal Fin. Also at this ripe, young age Brian added Split Finger (5.11c). Les Ellison came onto the scene with a fervor for first ascents. He found many fine lines, with the pinnacle of his FA expertise being his routes on the Middle Bell Tower—Arm and Hammer and Butcher Knife. Merrill Bitter, a five-foot, seven-inch power package, showed immediate aptitude for the sport, and although he did not particularly seek out new routes, he made his mark with repeats of the hardest, soloing unbelievable challenges and climbing more hard pitches in a day than most climbers could in a month. Merrill engendered both Bitterfingers and Mother of Pearl. While going to medical school at the University of Utah, Steve Hong showed his mastery of crack climbing with the long-awaited ascent of The Coffin Roof on his second try. Steve went on to climb routes that made him truly an apotheosis to local climbers, for how could one climb 5.13 and succeed at medical school at the same time? The Slash, Trinity Left and Fallen Arches were his "biggest and baddest" in LCC, with hundreds more climbed in Canyonlands.

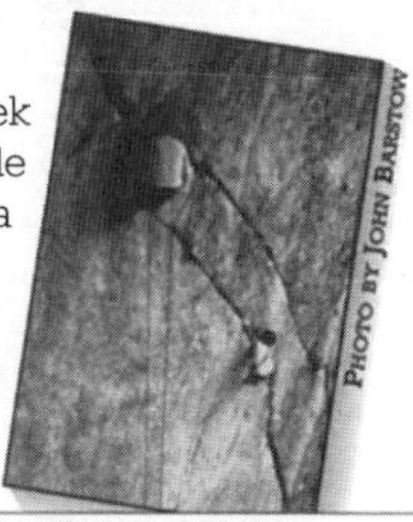

Steve Hong and Steve Carruthers on the FFA of the first pitch on Fallen Arches, 1983.

Between 1986 and the present, the ethical parameters have expanded to allow rappel-placed bolt routes. The crowning achievements during this period are more difficult to determine, as toprope rehearsal often relegates the first ascent to a lower status than onsight repeats. However, routes have been established during this time that took a creative eye to see, and standards have been pushed as never before. Merrill Bitter, Drew Bedford, Dana Hauser, Stuart Ruckman, John Storm and others developed routes that show the merits of intelligent rap-bolting, making steep faces possible that would not be protectable by traditional methods.

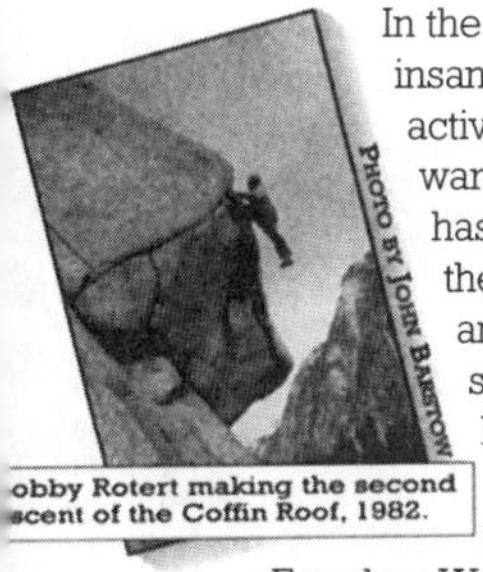

obby Rotert making the second scent of the Coffin Roof, 1982.

In the 90's, with new routes becoming increasing difficult to find, and sometimes insanely arduous to approach, a group of climbers have none-the-less stayed very active, and their perseverance has paid off. Topping the expense list for fixed hardware and tackling the most labor intensive projects, the ever-active James Garrett has contributed many new routes. Hell Raiser/Till Hell Freezes Over, Little Hellion, the Black Streak, the Swiss Edge and the aid lines Stratosphere and Batman are among many others. For two decades Brian Smoot has sought out new routes and some of his most recent creations are great additions. These include The Final Link, Tingey's Torture, The Answer and Questionable Connection. Tony Calderone has pushed the limits of slab climbing further and further with The Schoolroom Streak, Talus Food and Benson Bolt. His development of the Freedom Wall opened a neat new area. Chad Zurinshas and Fred Henion are to thank for the wonderful new limestone area, The Chadbourne Crag, which will guarantee new fun and fitness for those who visit frequently. Steve Habovstak, Randy Kieliszewski and Eric Klement have been the primary figures in the development of the Humane Society Wall, the Above and Beyond Area and Aguaworld, finding some pretty darn good stuff. The long and illustrious climbing career of Jonny Woodward has now made its mark in the Wasatch with the establishment of the hardest route in this book—Dog Eat Dog (5.13d)—and the offwidth testpiece Trench Warfare (5.12d). Tim Wagner has pursued aid climbing and has repeated most of the areas most demanding lines. He added Skin Man (A3+) to the list of Black Peeler aid challenges. Jim Reynolds had the vision and determination to create eleven new Little Cottonwood routes with his find, The Industrial Wall. Others deserving mention here are: Jon Ray, Ray Dahl, Scott Keller, Kent Wheeler, Pat McInerney, Kimber Almond, Dave Medera, John Hansen, Lance Bateman, Ben Folsom, Cameron Lawson, Shane Willet, Bill Hunt, Lange Jeffries, Jeff Baldwin, Hank Armantrout, Mike Friedrichs and Chris Harmston, who have all left their mark with excellent new routes.

Drew Bedford on Meat Puppet, 1988.

In our attempt to condense, we undoubtedly have left out the accomplishments of "key" climbers. Our hope is that their routes are nonetheless recorded in this guide. In the end, the lively, colorful oral history—climbers swapping stories—may be the more enduring record.

Wasatch Area
Overview Map
North to
Ogden
Rotary Park
City Creek Canyon
215
Salt Lake
International
Airport
State
Capitol
"B" Street
15
South Temple
80
West to
Wendover
500 South
400 South
University
of Utah
600 South
East To Park City
and Evanston
Foothill
Blvd.
80
State Street
700 East
1300 East
Groceries/ATM
Parleys Canyon
Gas
80
Salt Lake City
215
Grandeur Peak
Church Fork
3300 South
Exit 3
3900 South
Exit 4
Millcreek Canyon
15
Groc./ATM
Hospital
Gas
4500 South
Exit 5
Neffs Canyon
215
Mt. Olympus
Van Winkle Expressway
Tolcat Canyon
State Street
Wasatch Blvd
Mill B
N. Fork
Exit 6
Mule
Hollow
Exit 302
215
Fort Union Blvd.
7200 South
Gas
Stairs
Broads
Fork
Mill B
S. Fork

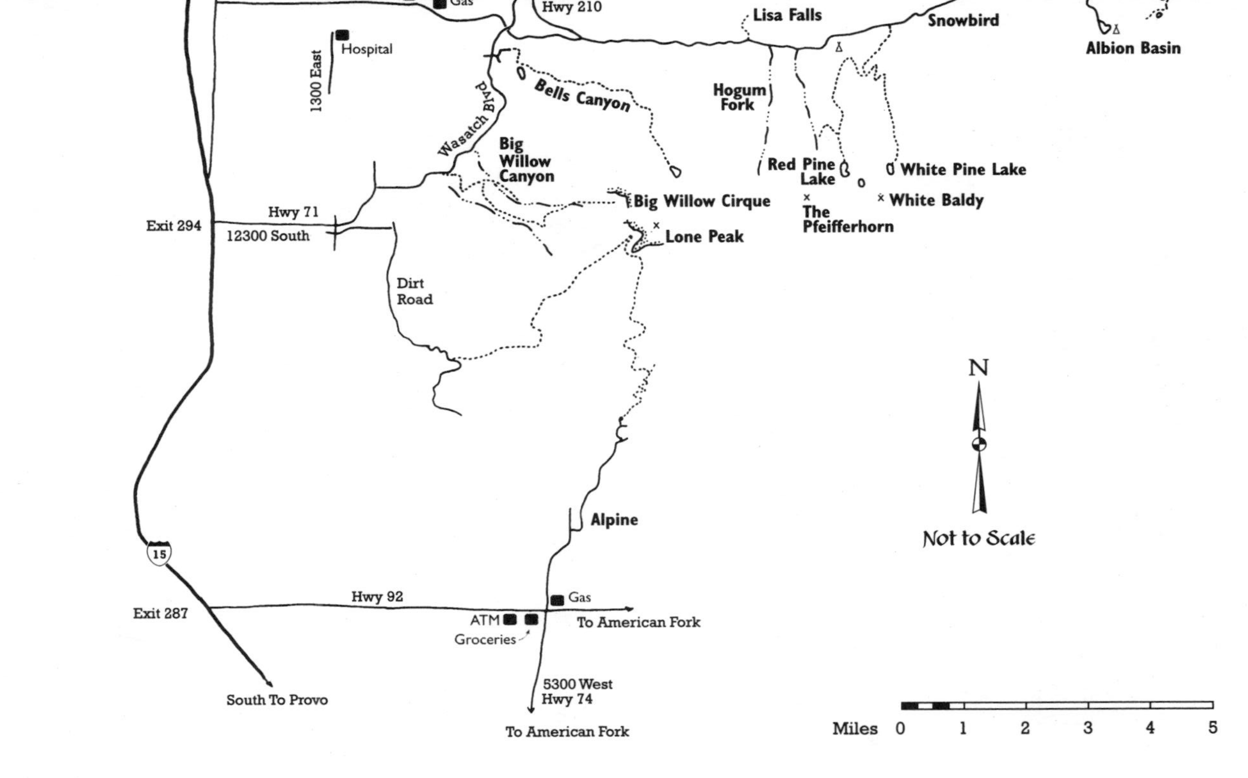

Gas
Hwy 210
Lisa Falls
Snowbird
Albion Basin
Hospital
1300 East
Wasatch Blvd
Bells Canyon
Hogum Fork
Big Willow Canyon
Red Pine Lake
White Pine Lake
Big Willow Cirque
The Pfeifferhorn
White Baldy
Lone Peak
Hwy 71
Exit 294
12300 South
Dirt Road
N
Alpine
Not to Scale
15
Hwy 92
Gas
Exit 287
ATM
To American Fork
Groceries
5300 West
Hwy 74
South To Provo
To American Fork
Miles 0 1 2 3 4 5

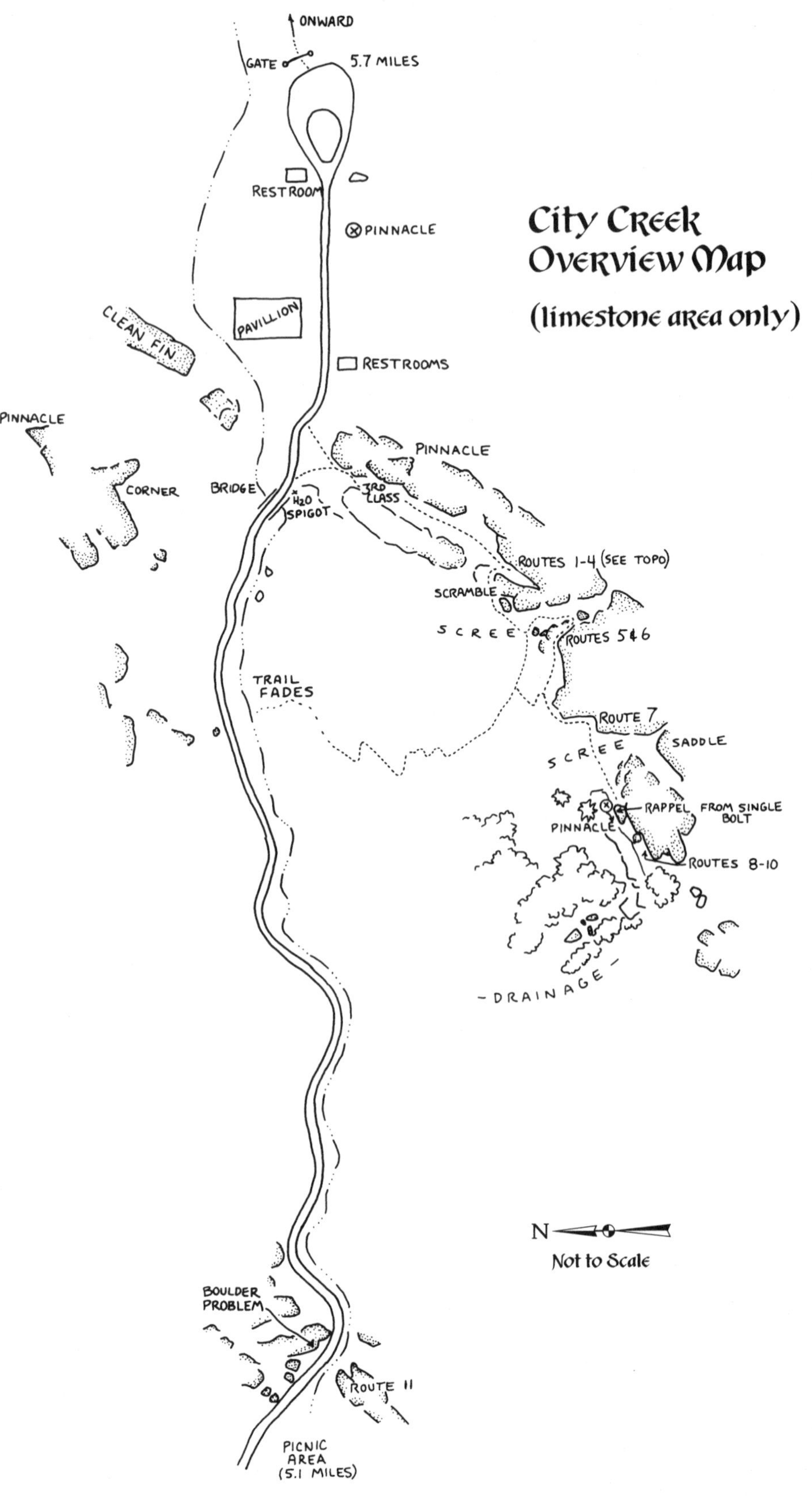

ONWARD
GATE
5.7 MILES
RESTROOM
PINNACLE
City Creek
Overview Map
(limestone area only)
CLEAN FIN
PAVILLION
RESTROOMS
PINNACLE
PINNACLE
CORNER
BRIDGE
H2O
SPIGOT
3RD
CLASS
ROUTES 1-4 (SEE TOPO)
SCRAMBLE
SCREE
ROUTES 5&6
TRAIL
FADES
ROUTE 7
SADDLE
SCREE
RAPPEL FROM SINGLE
BOLT
PINNACLE
ROUTES 8-10
DRAINAGE
N
Not to Scale
BOULDER
PROBLEM
ROUTE 11
PICNIC
AREA
(5.1 MILES)

City Creek Canyon

City Creek Canyon is a gem for Salt Lake hikers, bikers and runners. Close enough to downtown, it allows urbanites a place to escape for lunch-hour runs, evening bike rides, or a quick walk between errands, all within shouting distance of a pleasant stream and a canopy of trees. Perhaps the greatest irony of City Creek Canyon, a drainage that is minutes from the State Capital, is the untrampled nature of the surroundings. Upper City Creek today is one of the least damaged of all the Wasatch Front canyons, due in large part to the reservation system and the relative difficulty of motorized travel. For climbers, City Creek is far from a Mecca, but a few worthy limestone and cobble routes exist, and a good day of climbing here is possible, even if it's just for the scenery and a picnic afterwards. Lange Jeffries, who has probably spent more time than anyone thrashing through City Creek brush looking for new routes strongly recommends wearing helmets while climbing in City Creek.

GENERAL: Strict travel restrictions are enforced in City Creek Canyon year round. Foot traffic is allowed every day of the year. From the end of May to the end of September, bikes are allowed on odd numbered days, and cars are allowed on even numbered days. From October through the end of May, there is simply no driving up City Creek Canyon. During the summer, if you plan to drive, the fee is two dollars, and you can make reservations ahead of time (especially important on holidays) by calling 483-6797 or you can pay at the gate at the mouth of the canyon. You can also reserve a picnic table in the canyon or receive additional information by calling this number.

HOW TO GET THERE: Exit I-15 at the 600 South exit, the exit that leads to downtown Salt Lake. Drive east on 600 South to State Street. Turn left (north) on State Street and drive to South Temple. Turn right (east) and follow South Temple to "B" Street. A left turn (north) will lead up "B" street to an intersection with 11th Avenue. Cross 11th Avenue and follow the one way loop road known as Bonneville Blvd. Turn right on Canyon Road, which leads to the mouth of the canyon and the gate across the road. From here, walk, bike or drive to picnic area 5 (about ½ mile) for the shoreline crag (no topo, not on overview) or continue to the end of the road at Rotary Park (about 5.7 miles) to the limestone crags.

APPROACH: The easiest approach to the limestone crags is shown on the overview map, page 14. The approach begins just above the bridge, which is 200 feet down canyon from the pavilion. On the right (west) side of the wall nearest to the road is a corridor. Scramble up this corridor, passing one third-class section to reach routes 1-4. A ledge system west of the these routes allows access to a scree slope and an upward march to reach routes 5-7. Walk west along the base of this wall, cross a steep scree slope just below a saddle, and you'll encounter another corridor, blocked by a large chockstone. A short rappel from a single bolt deposits you at the base of routes 8-10.

For The Shoreline crag, see approach information included with the route descriptions.

DESCENT: All routes can be descended with one rope from anchors at the top of each climb.

THE CORRIDOR

1. MYSTIFY 5.12a ★★
Cryptic moves on a bouldery bulge are hard to read. The rest of the route is really good, cruiser climbing.
FA: Drew Bedford.

2. PROJECT
Expect this one to weigh in at 5.14.

3. PROJECT
Futuristic—one bolt, so far.

4. REMEDY 5.12c ★★
Sharp, thin and sustained. It might be a good idea to stick clip first bolt.
FA: Drew Bedford.

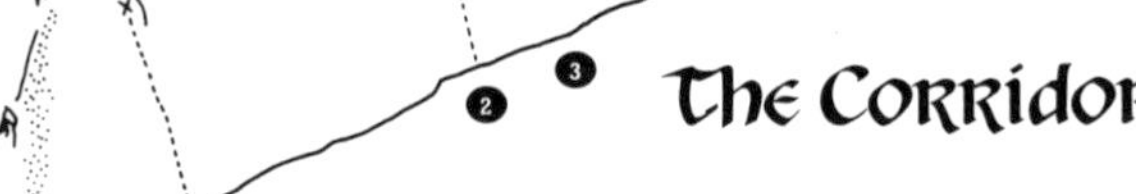

THE TOWER (no topo)

See overview page 14.

5. JIG ON THE RIG 5.12c ★★
A steep, overhanging line that tackles the undercut corner of the buttress. Seven bolts lead leftward to chains.
FA: Drew Bedford and Lange Jeffries.

6. JIGGING THE PIG 5.12a ★★
The arête just right of Jig On The Rig. Climb to that route's first bolt, then move right to the arête.
FA: Drew Bedford and Stuart Middlemiss, 1997.

7. CALIFORNIA CRACK 5.11d ★
A series of pins and bolts up a smooth face, topped by a cool pine tree.
FA: Lange Jeffries.

THE TUNNEL (no topo)

See overview page 14.

8. FROG AND THE PRINCESS 5.9
At the upper end of the corridor on the south-facing wall. A short face protected by three bolts leads to anchors.
FA: Lange Jeffries, 1996.

9. UNFINISHED 5.10
Two rap hangers and two bolts near the top of the tallest formation on the south side of the corridor are all that exist of this project.

10. ERROR OF WAYS 5.10a

This route is located at the lowest end of the corridor on the north face. Follow the crack, which is protected by one pin and four bolts to bolt anchors.

FA: Lange Jeffries, 1996.

11. CREEKSIDE MANOR 5.10a ★

Located at the next picnic area down canyon (roughly a half mile) from the end of the road at Rotary Park (see overview map, page 14). Facing west, this climb can be found on a small formation residing next to the creek. It's a good choice on a hot day. A crack threads its way up the face, protecting well with stoppers and cams, to a two-bolt anchor. (As of this writing, this was destined to be bolted.)

FA: Lange Jeffries, 1991.

SHORELINE CRAG (no topo)

One thing is for sure—The Shoreline Crag will never become the most popular climbing destination in the Wasatch. What isn't for sure is whether the first ascentionists were crazy for developing such wild-looking rock, or whether they were visionaries. You decide.

The Shoreline Crag is an overhanging conglomerate wall, full of quartzite "cobbles," pockets, and caves. The climbing and appearance of the cliff are similar to the super-popular Maple Canyon. While most climbers agree that the City Creek cobbles aren't quite in the same league as Maple, few people complain after a day at The Shoreline. Lee Logston, one of the areas chief developers, offers a few words of advice: "The rock is more solid than it looks, but if a hold doesn't have chalk on it, be careful. Also, climbing after a rainstorm is definitely not advised."

APPROACH: Walk up from the main road from the gate at the mouth of the canyon to picnic area number five. Across from this site is a trail that leads up and left (west) through the trees. Follow this path to a junction with the footpath that parallels the road. Turn right (east) and walk upcanyon to another junction at a power pole. Take the left fork and walk up into the trees. At the fifth switchback, follow a faint path towards the gully. March a short ways up the side of the gully to a rocky impasse which guards the base of the wall. Scranble up the slope to the right (east) of this cleft to access the ledge system at the start of the routes. A fixed hand line makes traversing this ledge system more secure. Flat locales at either end of the fixed line provide good hang-out spots. Approach time is about 25 minutes.

DESCENT: Lower off anchors at the top of each route with a single rope.

Routes are listed left to right. A boulder traverse on the wall just right of Shit Fly is a popular warmup.

1. THE SYNDROME 5.10a ★

The far left line has some big cobbles and a more forgiving angle. Five Bolts.

FA: Lee Logston, 1997.

2. UNKNOWN 5.12a ★

The steep stuff to the right of The Syndrome. Start left of the cave on the left side of the wall. Five Bolts.

FA: Unknown.

3. BRINE SHRIMP 5.12c/d ★

Rig a belay in the middle of the hand line, and climb pockets up the bulge overhead. Five bolts

FA: Unknown.

4. MUD PUPPY 5.12d/13a ★

Starts with some amazing cobbles, turns to pockets, then joins the Brine Shrimp anchors. Seven bolts.

FA: Lee Logston, 1997.

5. BLACK FLY 5.12c/d ★

A direct line up the steepest stone. Many two finger pockets and dishes. Six bolts.

FA: Lange Jeffries, 1997.

6. BIG BOSS GROOVE 5.11c ★

Lots of big holds with some space between them. Seven Bolts.

FA: Lange Jeffries, 1997.

7. SHORELINE 5.12c ★★

The most popular line on the wall. Slippery sloping cobbles that pack a big wallop. Seven bolts.

FA: Lange Jeffries, 1997.

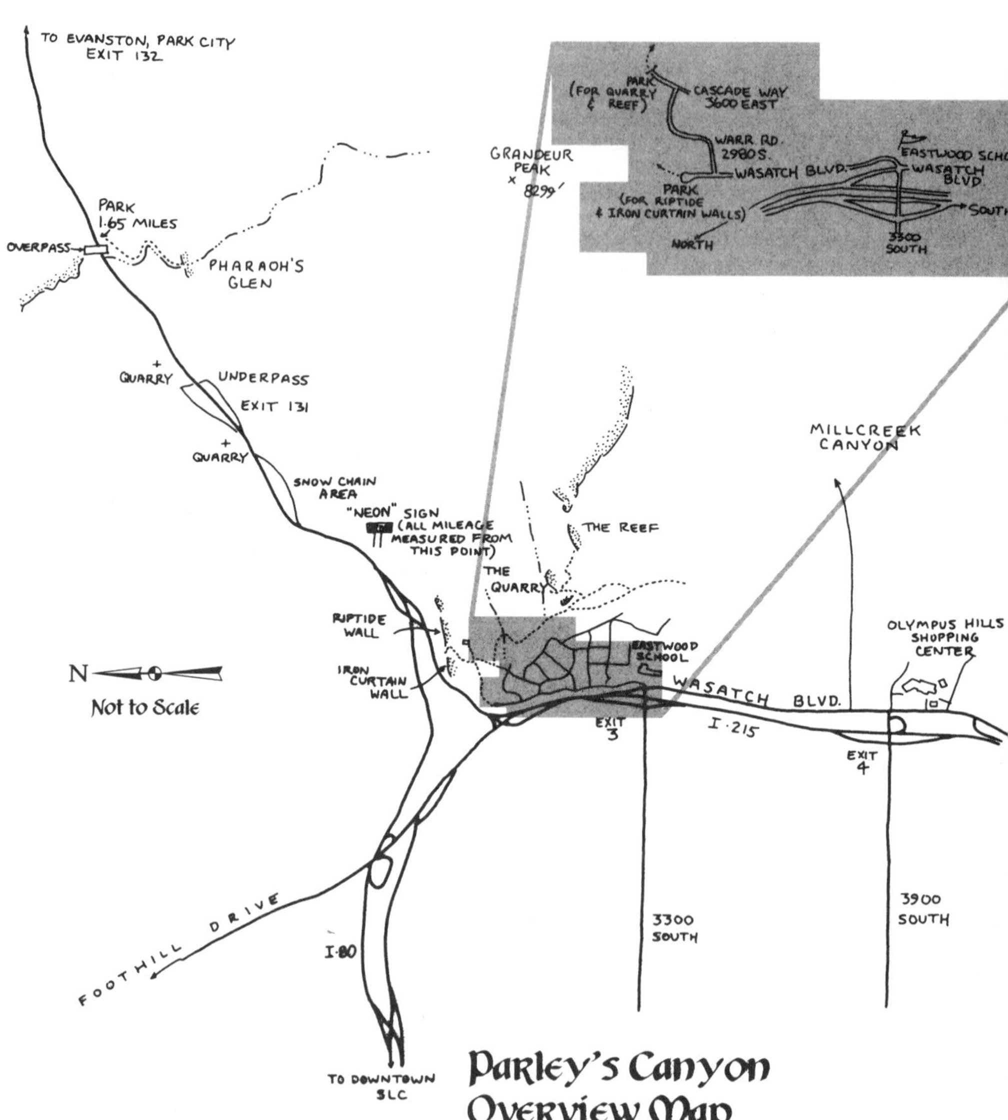

Parley's Canyon Overview Map

Parley's Canyon

Better known as a thoroughfare between Park City and Salt Lake City, Parley's Canyon has been ignored by climbers in the past, despite a few prominent outcrops of limestone and quartzite. Recently, however, climbing has become extremely popular on the quartzite slabs at the mouth of the canyon. Parley's forms the northern boundary of Grandeur Peak, a popular hiking destination with great views of the city, and even better views of the bigger mountains to the south. Although both Parley's and Grandeur Peak are connected by bands of limestone and quartzite, the similarity for climbers is in the access. The approaches to the Irontide Area and the Quarry and Reef areas are within a neighborhood block of each other.

HOW TO GET THERE: From I-15 turn east on I-80. I-80 leads directly into Parley's Canyon where the Pharaoh's Glen Area is found. The Irontide and Grandeur Peak areas are accessed by turning south off I-80 onto I-215, and making a quick exit on 33rd South. See individual approach descriptions from here.

PARLEY'S CANYON—IRONTIDE AREA

These two walls offer numerous routes within minutes of the city. Their northerly aspect makes for tolerable temperatures even in the summer heat. Aside from the aesthetics, climbing at either the Riptide or Iron Curtain Walls is very fun, and generally well protected.

APPROACH: From the 3300 South and I-215 interchange, drive east on 3300 South, through the stoplight, until it bends left (north) and joins Wasatch Blvd. Follow Wasatch Blvd. north to the end of the road (about 2900 South). Park here and walk up the dirt road that climbs the hill by the power poles. Continue up the road until a trail from the north intersects, just before you reach a building surrounded by a chain link fence. This trail leads to some square boulders, then bends east, skirts the top of The Iron Curtain Wall, and descends a steep slope to the base of the routes. The Iron Curtain Wall is to the west, the Riptide Wall to the east. See overview on page 18.

DESCENT: With one rope, you can lower or rappel off anchors at the top of each route.

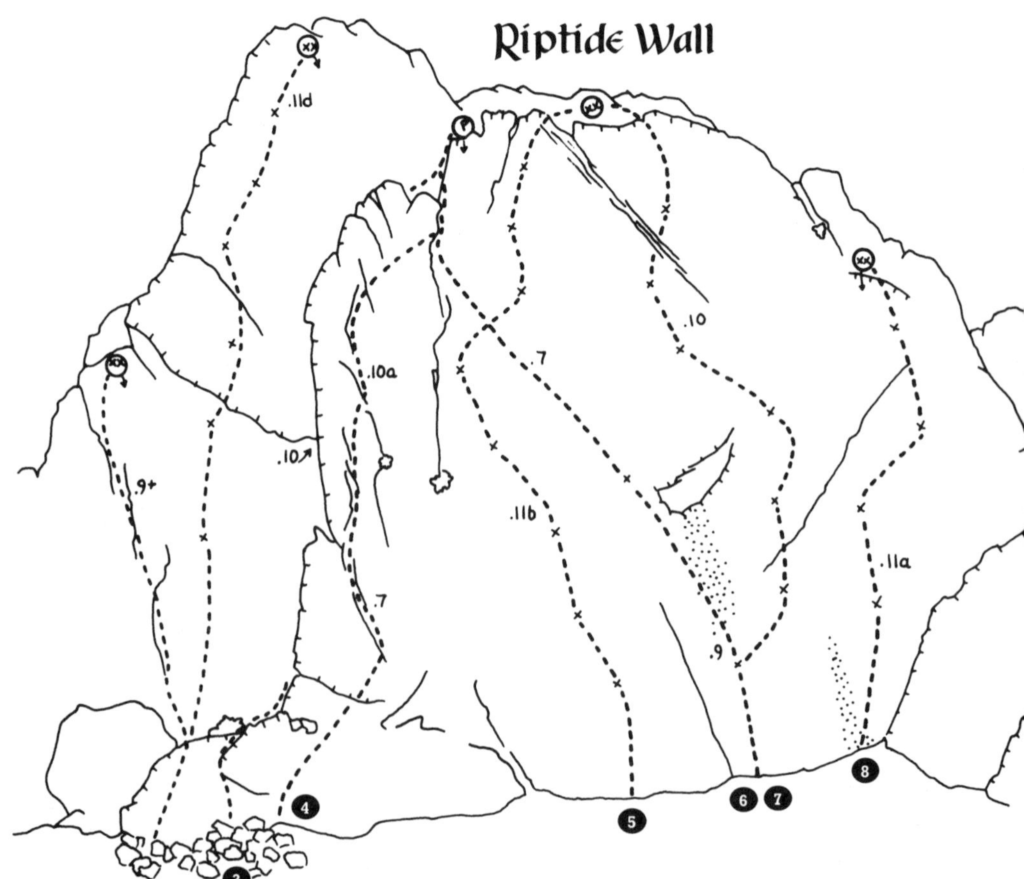

RIPTIDE WALL

Several routes require gear on this wall.

1. 'LECTRIC GRANNY 5.9+
Two short cracks with several tricky moves.
FA: Brian and Vicki Smoot, 1989.

2. ASTROPROJECTION 5.11d ★★
The Parley's test piece. One needs to be a master of thin edging to stick to this mirror. The arête to the left is off limits.
FA: Brian Smoot, 1989.

3. DIRTY ROTTEN HORROR 5.10
The name says it all. Bring gear.

4. EDGE OF THE SEA 5.10a ★★
Cerebral moves link together the nice cracks just right of the arête. Camming devices seem especially helpful.
FA: Brian and Jonathan Smoot, 1989.

5. CROSSCURRENT 5.11b ★★
Good, fun moves down low lead to steeper climbing above. Another equilibrium test.
FA: Brian Smoot, 1989.

6. RIPTIDE 5.9 ★★
A sweeping leftward traverse that links together many of the main features of the wall, eventually joining the top of Edge of the Sea, so be sure to bring gear.
FA: Brian and Jonathan Smoot, 1989.

7. FEEDING FRENZY 5.10 ★
Continuous climbing that starts out fun and ends that way. Could be a pump for the portly.
FA: Brian Smoot, 1989.

8. WHERE THERE'S A DRILL, THERE'S A WAY 5.11a ★
Short but very thin moves mark the crux of this slick route.
FA: Brian and Jonathan Smoot, 1989.

THE IRON CURTAIN WALL

This is the larger, more westerly wall. It has a greater number of climbs, with the longest route reaching up 110 feet. All routes on this wall protect with bolts and fixed pins.

THE IRON CURTAIN WALL ROUTES

9. PICK-POCKET 5.8 ★
Short, with some touchy friction moves.
FA: Vicki and Brian Smoot, 1989.

10. MUTATION 5.9
FA: Brian and Vicki Smoot, 1989.

11. MOTLEY CRUISE 5.9 ★
A crescendo of head-banging moves.
FA: Jonathan and Brian Smoot, 1989.

12. UP IN A FLASH 5.8 ★★
This is a good route for fledgling leaders to flash. The hard climbing ostensibly is in the first 20 feet, but one last move awaits.
FA: Brian and Vicki Smoot, 1989.

13. GOTTA BE TALL OR ELSE YOU'LL FALL 5.9 ★★
Well traveled. An undertaking that really isn't that height dependent.
FA: Brian and Jonathan Smoot, 1989.

14. PERESTROIKA 5.10 ★★
The initial moves have dropped many. The climbing continues above, staying left of the corner and turning a small roof.
FA: Brian and Jonathan Smoot, 1989.

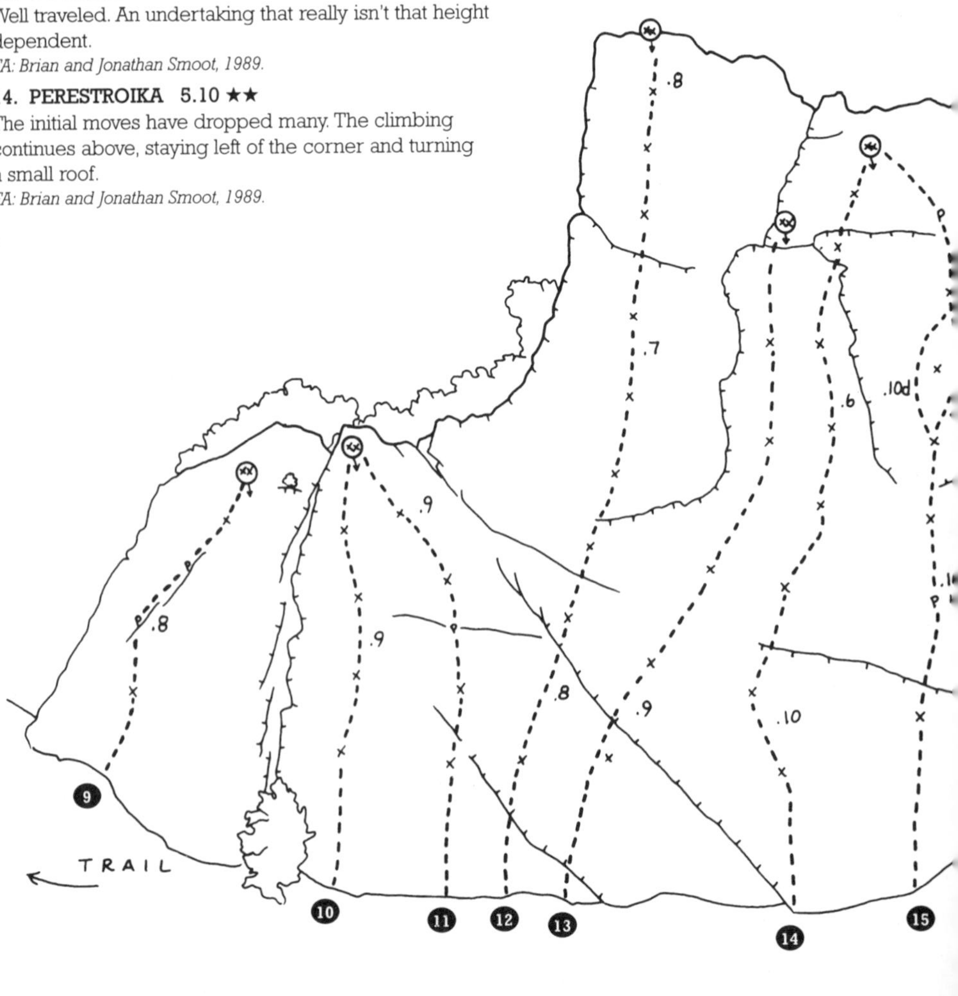

15. IRON CURTAIN 5.10a/5.10d ★★★

Another fallen barrier. Perhaps the most popular climb on the wall. Shorter people may have trouble clipping into the pin that protects the crux. The climbing remains satisfying to the end.

FA: Brian and Jonathan Smoot, 1989.

16. OUT OF TOUCH 5.9+ ★

Three cruxes give this route character. A pumped climber literally will be "out of touch" on the challenging final roof.

FA: Brian and Vicki Smoot, 1989.

17. ONE WITH THE ROCK 5.11c ★★

A successful ascent requires zen-like powers: the sequence is far from obvious.

FA: Brian Smoot, 1989.

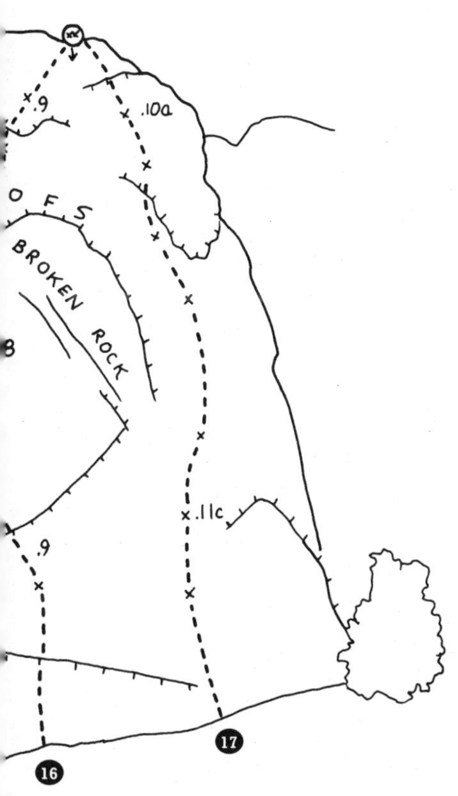

PARLEY'S CANYON—PHARAOH'S GLEN

Amid the cars, the freeway, and the drone of commuters racing up and down Parley's Canyon is an oasis, a small spot of Shangri-la that is hard to believe exists. This is Pharaoh's Glen, a cascade over sandstone, untrampled by the masses, blocked by private land. Access to this area is touchy at best. The wall is on Forest Service land, and the following approach crosses private property to reach the public land. The residents that live here are under no obligation to allow hikers or climbers, and you will pass very close to their trailers. This privilege may be denied at any time.

APPROACH: Park on the south side of I-80, just past an overpass, 1.65 miles up canyon from the neon sign. This is the overpass between Exits 131 and 132. A dirt road leads back to the overpass, then heads south into the canyon. Make sure you do not block this road, as this will anger the residents. Walk up the dirt road, past the gate, and follow the road as it winds around, eventually coming to a five way fork. Take the second left fork, the one that leads towards the mountains and the water. Walk up this road and take a path that branches off to the right and follows the small creek. This path leads to the base of the wall. Again, be respectful of the private land—people live here. See overview on page 18.

DESCENT: One rope allows escape from routes 1 and 2, while route 3 is descended via a walk off.

1

PHARAOH'S GLEN ROUTES

1. BILL'S FAIRWELL EPIC 5.9+
Follow four bolts and a pin up the best looking part of the face.
FA: Bill Foster, Tim Broughton, and Bob Dawson, 1991.

2. FLAKEY 5.6
Start on the right side of the wall and climb to a single bolt. Above, a leftward shuffle gains a series of flakes and cracks, and the anchors atop Bill's Fairwell.
FA: Doug Fuller and Pete Lenz, 1991.

3. GASTRONOMY CRACK 5.8
The corner on the wall to the right of the cascade has a crack which can be followed to the top of the wall.
FA: Tim Broughton et al, 1991.

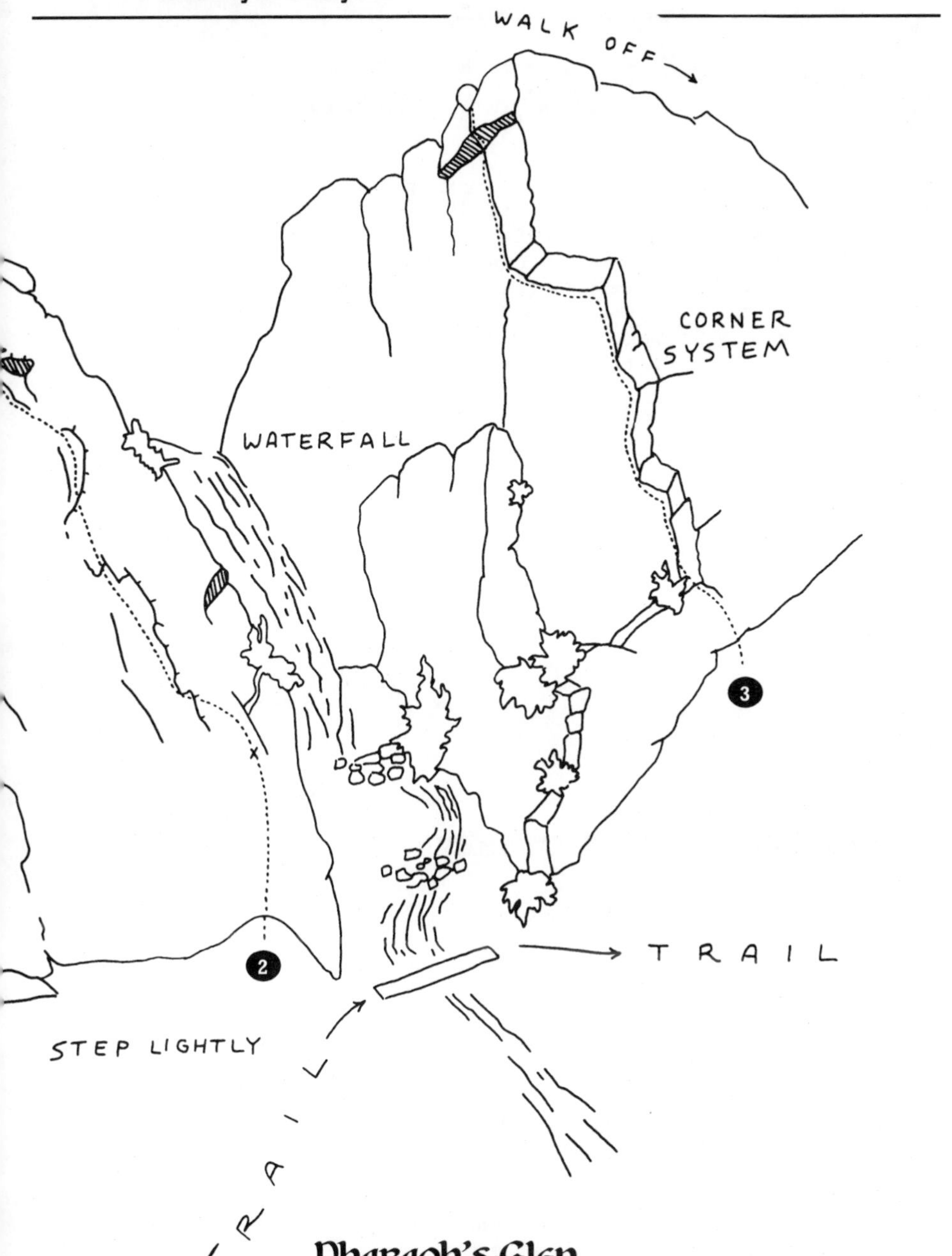

Pharaoh's Glen

Grandeur Peak

When looking up at the west slopes of Grandeur Peak, the mountain between Parley's Canyon and Millcreek Canyon, the most prominent feature is the limestone "hogback" that twists its way up the hillside. Formed eons ago by some ocean or lake, this formation is best seen while driving east on 3300 South. The size and shape of the walls have caught climbers eyes for years, however, to date the only reported routes are concentrated at the lowest point of the limestone outcrop, where the north face bulges like a potbelly. Below the limestone, hidden from view, a small quarry with a limited amount of broken quartzite provides easy-access climbing. In general, the routes at The Reef and The Quarry are short, bouldery, and sometimes sharp, but always worthwhile.

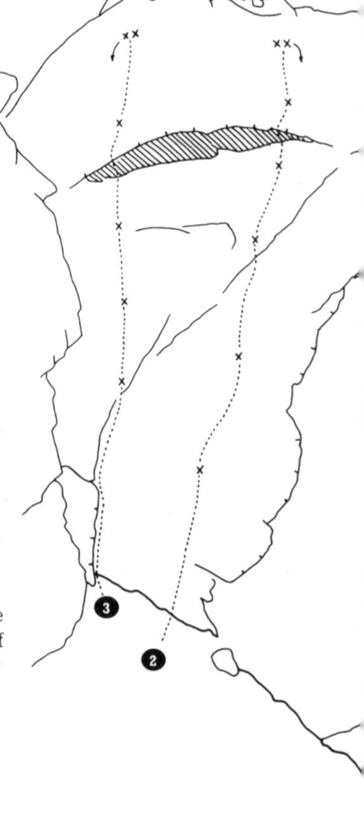

GRANDEUR PEAK—THE QUARRY

Loose rock and a lack of definitive lines have kept most climbers away from The Quarry. More recently, several bolted climbs have been added, and cleaned, and the Quarry has gained a notch of popularity. If you're a connoisseur, this isn't the place for you. However, if you can enjoy the sense of movement, despite some suspect holds, you will most likely appreciate The Quarry, despite its shortcomings. The north-facing aspect of The Quarry, and the close proximity to the city are the main draw.

APPROACH: From the 3300 South and I-215 interchange, drive east on 3300 South, through the stoplight, until it bends left (north) and joins Wasatch Blvd. Follow Wasatch Blvd. north to Warr Road (2980 South). Turn right and drive uphill to Cascade Way (3600 East). Turn left and park near the end of the road. Please take care not to block the residents' driveways or interfere with the ability of cars to turn around, even if it means parking downhill and walking a few extra feet. A dirt road begins just past the gate and forks immediately. Follow the right fork. The road climbs steeply, then levels out, splitting again. Take the right fork again and continue south, above the neighborhood, to yet another fork in the road, below a rubble strewn slope. Follow the left branch here. About 300 feet along this road, a small trail cuts uphill and north across the slope, to join the remnants of an old dirt road that leads into the drainage. The trail to The Reef cuts up from here, while the trail to the Quarry is straight ahead. The Quarry is the scruffy looking series of slabs and walls at the very back of this drainage. The routes are described as they are encountered, from lowest to highest—west to east. See overview on page 18.

DESCENT: With one rope, you can lower or rappel off anchors at the top of each route.

THE QUARRY ROUTES

1. THE ROOF ROUTE 5.10 ★

You'll see a very large roof on the first rock worth climbing. Two bolts protect the cool sequence of moves out the roof, which is climbed at the thin splitter crack. The lower-angled face above is considerably easier, until the last bolt. Chains at the top provide a handy exit. Not on topo.

2. QUADRATIC EQUATION 5.9

Mostly good edges lead to a small roof, where suddenly all the holds lean the wrong way.

3. QUADRAPHONIC 5.8

The corner to the left is more of a black hole than any help. Some slopers and some good edges—you never know which.

GRANDEUR PEAK—THE REEF

The Reef is the lowest limestone outcrop on the "hogback" formation that twists up Grandeur Peak. The limestone here is compact, solid and very sharp. Initially, The Reef was home to one crack climb and several toprope problems. Then four routes were added, creating sharp, yet popular leads. History from here grows murky, but the bolts soon diss-appeared. After a time they were replaced, then chopped again. For several years The Reef was back to its original toproping self. Over the past year, the bolts have been replaced, although in new locations, creating altogether different climbs. For now, the bolts seem to be secure, and leading at The Reef is possible once again. Bolts at the top of most routes simplify toproping and a bouldering traverse, albeit stout, provides a warm-up. Tape is recommended.

APPROACH: Follow the approach to The Quarry. Just before you reach The Quarry, turn south and follow a path that heads up the slope to the ridge. Continue on this trail which switchbacks up the hillside, avoiding the brush, to The Reef, the lowest limestone outcrop. See overview on page 18.

DESCENT: With one rope, you can lower or rappel off anchors at the top of each route.

THE REEF ROUTES

1. REEF ON THIS 5.11b ★

The most popular climb on the wall. A series of leftward moves leads to a devious crux.

2. NUMBER TWO 5.10 ★

Although short, you might feel like you just topped out after a longer pitch.

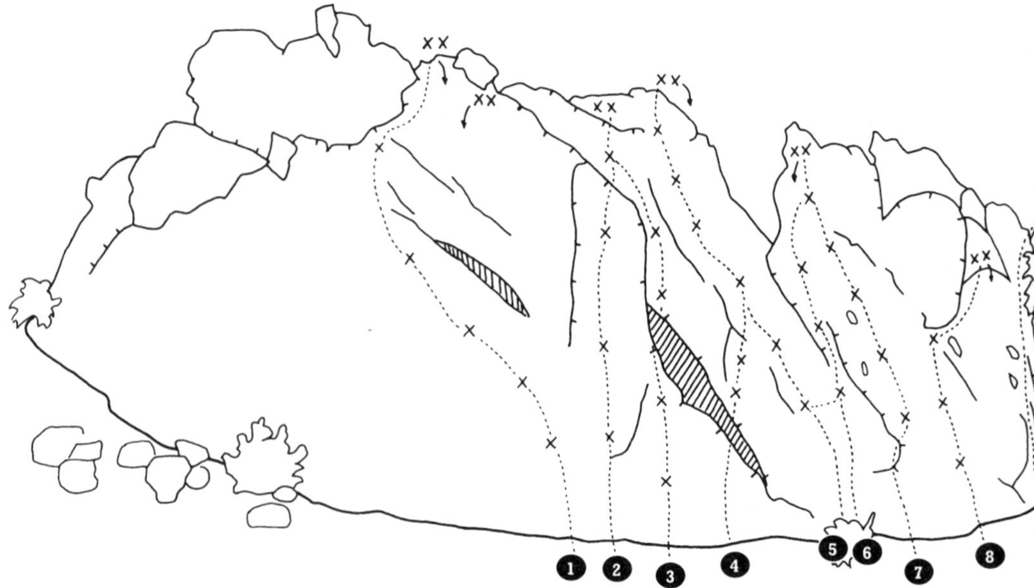

THE REEF ROUTES

3. NUMBER THREE 5.?
A hard start.

4. PROJECT X 5.?
Direct start to November Sun.

5. NOVEMBER SUN 5.12c ★
Super tweaky moves with hard core foot work.
FA: Ben Folsom, 1994.

6. NUMBER SIX 5.12c
Squeezed.

7. LEVIATHAN 5.12a ★
Climb pockets past five bolts on a convex face.
FA: Drew Bedford, 1990.

8. PROJECT Y 5.?
Three bolts worth of bouldery holds.

9. DEER SKULL CRACK 5.10d ★
A deceptive route that follows the short corner/ crack system near the right side of the wall. A selection of gear is needed.
FA: Drew Bedford and Les Ellison, 1983.

The next three routes climb the formation 200 feet above (east) of The Reef. Walk up to its west face from The Reef, then walk down the scree to reach the northwest face.

10. PROJECT
This climbs the overhanging south face of "the cave" located on the west face of this fin.

11. POCKET ROCKET 5.8 ★
Climb the edge and face where the formation turns from west to north-facing. The route follows 10 bolts, the last two of which are hidden. There is a two-bolt anchor.

12. ROCKET SCIENCE 5.8
This short four-bolter is located 100 feet left of Pocket Rocket.

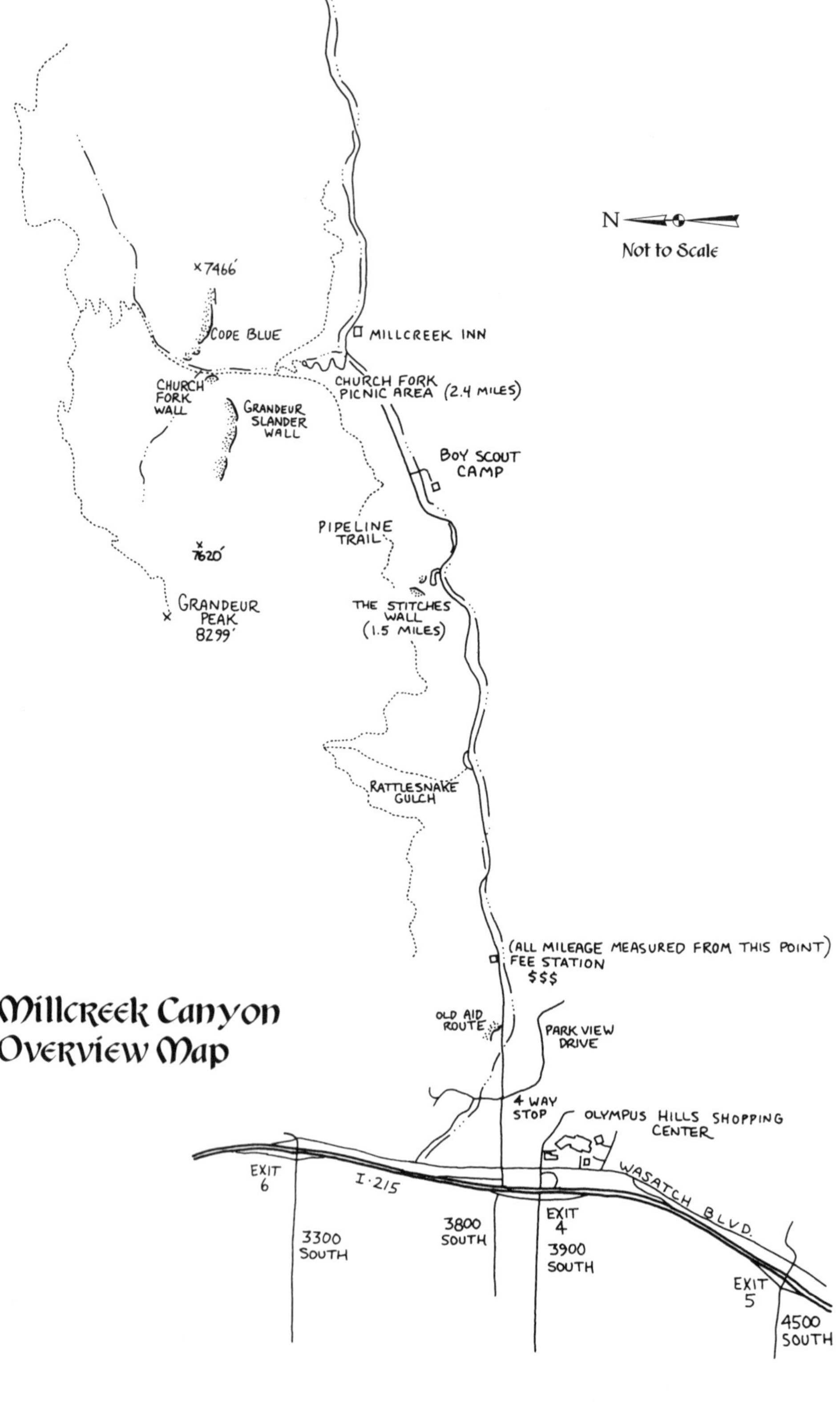

Millcreek Canyon Overview Map

Millcreek Canyon

Millcreek Canyon has a long and rich history with Salt Lakers. The early pioneers found Millcreek to be among the most heavily wooded canyons in the Wasatch, and years ago, many sawmills were established in this area. Much later, Millcreek became the center of the Scouting universe for resident Boy Scouts. At about the same time, the shady stream and tree lined picnic grounds made Millcreek the picnic capital of the Salt Lake area. Overuse, however, began to turn the once lush canyon bottom into a dusty, trampled mess. In recent years, efforts to revegetate the banks of the stream, limit the number of people using the picnic sites, and increase awareness as to the fragility of the canyon, have begun to turn Millcreek back into what it once was—a wooded canyon full of promise. Today, a series of well maintained trails beckon the hiker, mountain biker, and trail runner. The picnic tables that once lured the valley's residents to an evening barbecue still exist, only now they look less tired, and the area feels less crowded.

Millcreek Canyon also has an abundance of rock. Unfortunately, much of that rock is suspect. Faces that from a distance look promising, turn out to be loose and crumbly upon closer inspection. Luckily, good rock does exist. The areas described in this section seem to be anomalies: the rock is solid and good climbing is possible.

HOW TO GET THERE: From the north, exit I-15 on I-80 East. Follow I-80 to I-215. Drive south on I-215 to the 3900 South Exit. Exit here, then turn east towards the mountains and drive under the freeway to Wasatch Blvd. Make a left (north) onto Wasatch Blvd, then follow Wasatch Blvd. to 3800 South and turn east. This road leads into Millcreek Canyon.

From the south, exit off I-15 onto I-215 East. Follow I-215 to the 3900 South Exit. This exit's directly onto Wasatch Blvd. Drive north on Wasatch Blvd. to 3800 South and turn east. This road leads into Millcreek Canyon.

Mileage is measured from the fee station, where it costs $2.25 per vehicle. An annual pass may also be purchased. This is one of the few canyons in the Wasatch where dogs are allowed. Individual approach descriptions are described with each wall.

MILLCREEK CANYON —THE STITCHES WALL

This projection of limestone hosts two worthy routes and a bit (or is it bite?) of sharp rock.

APPROACH: A parking lot with a gate on the north side of the road is located 1.5 miles up canyon from the fee station. Park here and walk up the steep, loose slope to the north, aiming for a fin-like face 300 feet above the road. The two semi-popular routes face east. See overview on page 30.

DESCENT: Anchors at the top of the routes provide a speedy exit with one rope.

1. UNKNOWN

Climb the crack past a pin on the short west face.

2. ITCHY STITCHES 5.9+ ★

Sharp rock is in the majority, but hopefully stitches won't be necessary. Climb past four bolts to the highest point of the wall. A short but popular climb.

FA: Zach Hawkins and Shane Collard, 1990.

3. MR. MILKBONES 5.9- ★

Climb the cracks and weaknesses to the right of Itchy Stitches. Gear is necessary, and again, beware of sharp rock.

FA: Zach Hawkins, 1990.

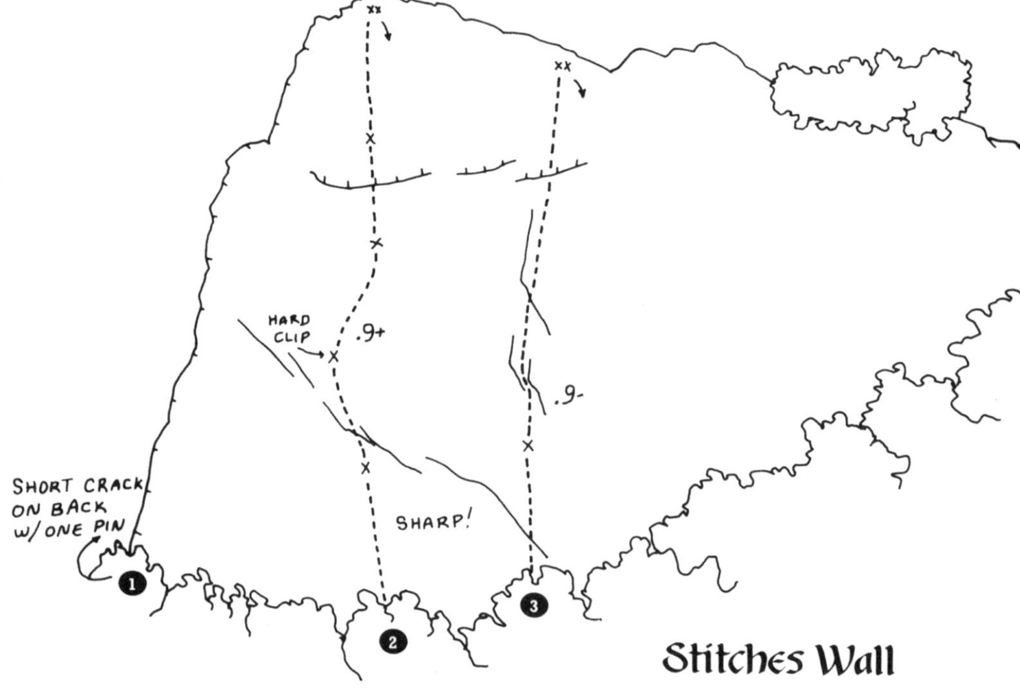

MILLCREEK CANYON —CHURCH FORK WALL (no topo)

The Church Fork Wall is a rounded facade of limestone positioned right next to the Church Fork hiking trail. Although one lead has been established, toproping is the main activity here, and a selection of hardware is needed to rig anchors. The lead, and all the top rope problems are harder than they appear. This area is usually cool and shady. See overview on page 30.

APPROACH: Drive up canyon 2.4 miles from the fee station to the Church Fork Picnic Area. Drive, or walk if the gate is closed for the off-season, through the picnic ground to the end of the road and the start of the hiking trail. Follow the trail for a tenth of a mile to the junction with the Pipeline Trail. Continue up Church Fork on the Grandeur Peak Trail for a rough quarter of a mile to a smooth, grey limestone wall on the west side of the trail.

DESCENT: Walk off to the west, or lower off the chain anchors at the top of Bohemian Crystal with a single rope.

1. BOHEMIAN CRYSTAL 5.10a ★
Follow weaknesses and overlaps on the left side of the broad east face. All bolts.
FA: James Garrett and Thomas Etzler from Bohemia, 1991.

MILLCREEK CANYON —GRANDEUR SLANDER WALL (no topo)

This wall is the lowest end of the major band of limestone that runs west from Church Fork, up towards the summit of Grandeur Peak. Although it can be seen from the vicinity of the Millcreek Inn, the best view is from the top of the Church Fork Wall. See overview on page 30.

APPROACH: Follow the approach to the Church Fork Wall. Scramble around the right (north) side of the wall to gain the top. Look southwest and you'll see a large band of rock—this is what you're heading towards. Trudge up and west through the brush, picking up the occasional deer trail to the base of the wall.
DESCENT: Lower off chains with one rope.

1. NEURO DEFICITS 5.11c ★★
Start to the right of a long roof. Climb into a scoop, then traverse left above the roof to chains. All bolts.
FA: James Garrett and Will Gilmer, 1991.

MILLCREEK CANYON —CODE BLUE WALL (no topo)

This wall is located at the lowest end of the limestone cliffband that runs east from Church Fork, up towards Church Fork Peak. It can be easily seen through the trees when looking east from the Church Fork Wall, and is distinguished by the large roof that caps the top of the cliff. See overview on page 30.

APPROACH: Perhaps the name of the wall is a reference to the approach, which requires persistence in the face of unruly brush. Follow the approach to the Church Fork Wall. Continue walking up the hiking trail for 200 feet, then dive into the brush and make your way directly to the first (lowest) rock outcrop. Pass this on the left (north) and continue upwards, following an increasingly better trail that reaches the base of the wall.

DESCENT: Anchors at the top require an 80 foot rappel to reach the ground.

1. CODE BLUE 5.10b
Climb the lower angled rock left of the big roofs. Steep climbing gives way to better pockets and edges. Expect some choss.
FA: James Garrett, 1993.

Neff's Canyon and Mount Olympus Overview Map

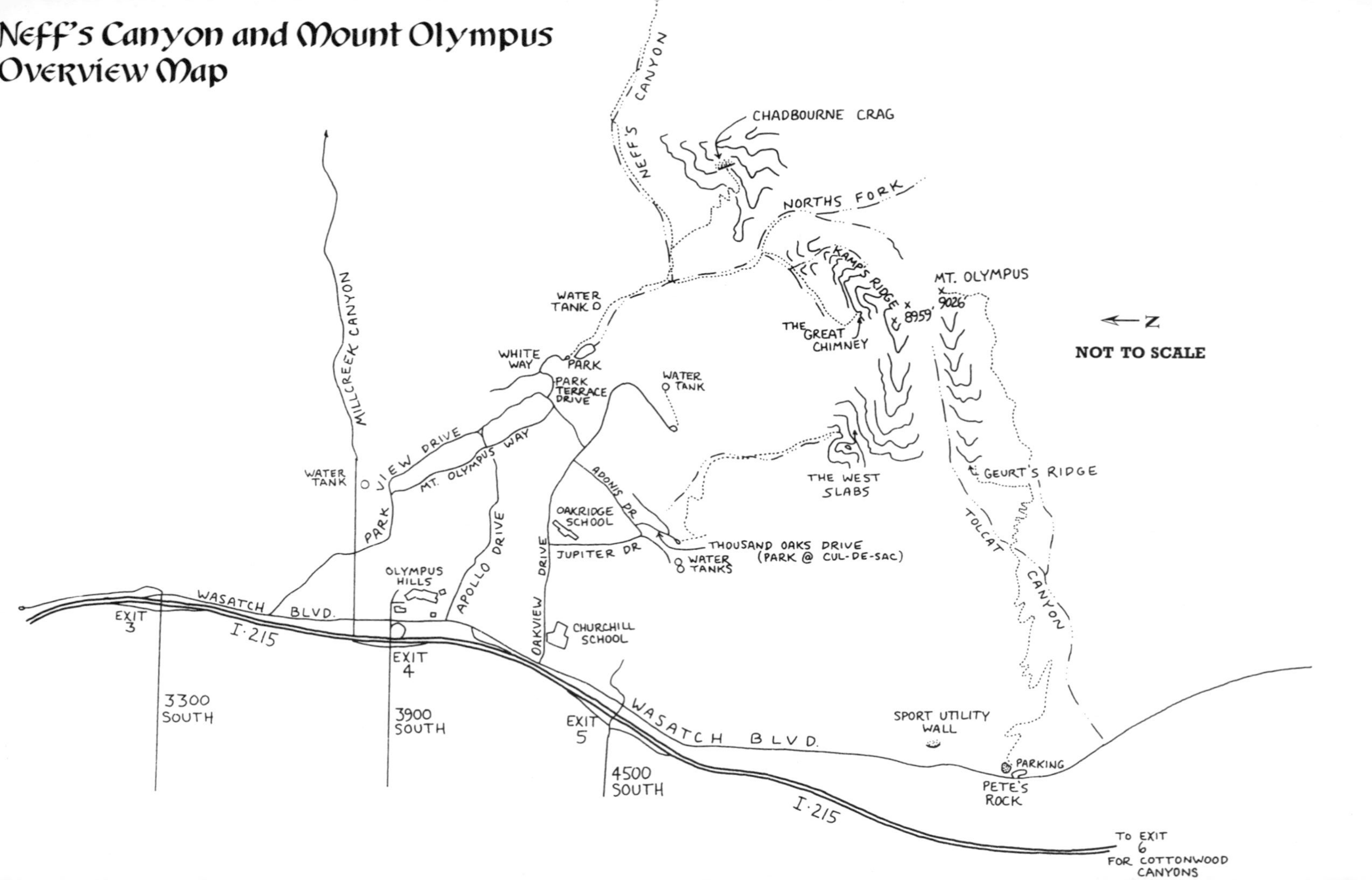

Neff's Canyon

Neff's canyon and the north face of Mount Olympus are two of the most rugged, least visited ramparts in the Wasatch range. Neff's canyon is most known to a small group of cavers, since hidden among its brush and thick trees is a cave that drops 1170 feet below the surface. Mount Olympus is best known among hikers for the short and steep summit trail that offers great views of both the Big Cottonwood Peaks and the city. However, where climbers want to go, visitors are few, the terrain is rugged, the views are striking, and the climbing is challenging.

HOW TO GET THERE: From the north, exit off I-15 onto I-80 East. Follow I-80 to the junction with I-215. Follow I-215 South to the 3900 South Exit. Exit here, turn east towards the mountains and drive to Wasatch Blvd. For the Chadbourne Crag, Kamp's Ridge and The Great Chimney, turn left (north) on Wasatch Blvd. For the West Slabs and Geurt's Ridge, turn right (south) on Wasatch Blvd. See individual cliff descriptions for the approach information from Wasatch Blvd.

From the south, exit off I-15 onto I-215 East. Follow I-215 to the 3900 South Exit. This exits directly onto Wasatch Blvd. Follow the directions above from here.

NEFF'S CANYON —THE CHADBOURNE CRAG

The canyon system to the left (north) of the Mt. Olympus massif is Neff's Canyon, which consists of North's Fork, Thomas Fork and the main Neff's Canyon. In April of 1996 Chad Zurinshas was skiing between North's Fork and Thomas Fork and saw a limestone cliff that showed great potential for steep, pocketed routes. He came back the next day and began developing the crag and it has become an exciting new addition for the Salt Lake hardcores (knuckleheads?).

APPROACH: From Wasatch Blvd. (about 3500 East), turn east on 3800 South, the road that leads to Millcreek Canyon. Follow 3800 South to the four way stop. Here, turn right onto Park View Drive (3700 East). Follow Park View Drive as it climbs uphill towards Mount Olympus to an intersection with Park Terrace Drive (4175 East). Turn left and drive to White Way (4275 South). Turn right and drive up to the trailhead at the end of White Way. Park here.

Walk up the main Neff's Canyon trail/road past a water tank to a fork in the trail at the first stream crossing (about three quarters of a mile.) Take the left branch (don't cross the stream here) and continue up to another stream crossing in a flat area with maple trees. Take the right branch of another split in the trail, and when the trail starts a gradual descent, look for a small limestone boulder on the left. Straight across the trail from this boulder is a faint path which leads up to the crag. It begins with a straight upward grunt through the brush and then zig-zags through the pine covered slope above. Tremendous views of Mt. Olympus are your reward at the top of the zig-zags. The trail then starts a leftward (northeasterly) traverse over to the crag. This approach will take most people about 1 hour and 15 minutes.

DESCENT: All routes can be descended from anchors with one rope. However, a 60m rope is needed to descend Four Deep in the Hoopti and Beckey Route.

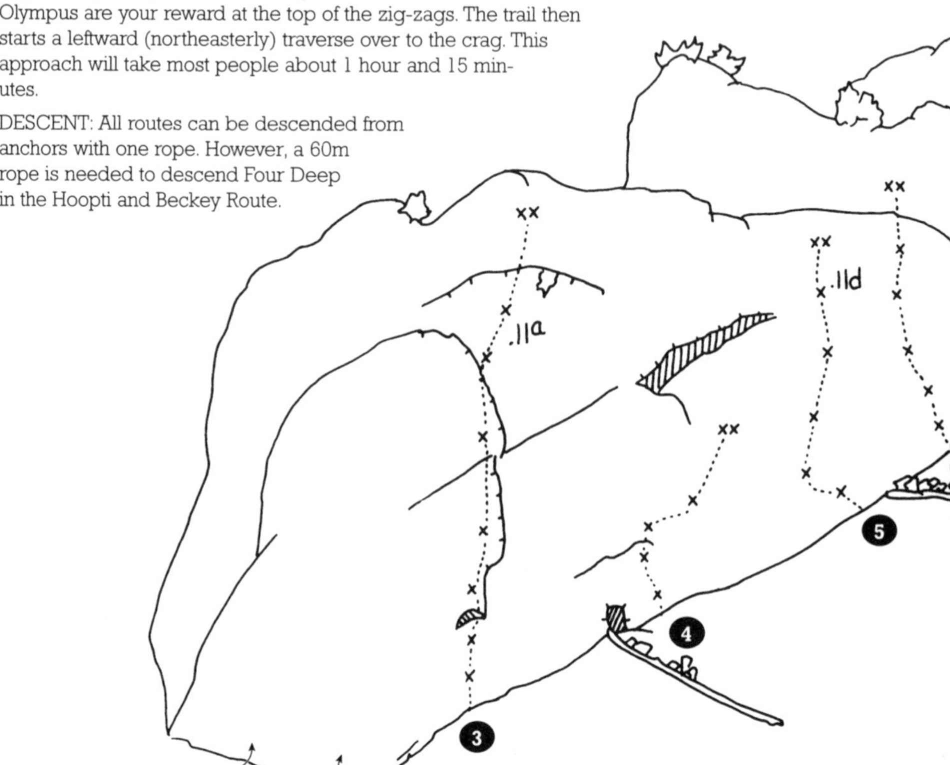

The Chadbourne Crag

THE CHADBOURNE CRAG ROUTES

1. PROJECT
The lowest route on the wall. A tentative name has been suggested: The Low Route.

2. POINT MAN 5.11b ★
Good rock, good pockets.
FA: Chad Zurinshas

3. FEATURE ATTRACTION 5.11a ★
The most popular warm-up on the wall. Hellgate-like.
FA: Fred Henion, 1996.

4. BENSON BOLTS 5.10a
Should clean up with a few more ascents.
FA: Unknown

5. VAGRANT CIRCLE 5.11d ★
Stick clip the first bolt and crimp at the end.
FA: Chad Zurinshas and Scott Lockhart, 1996.

6. LITTLE BUDDY 5.10d
Again, this route should clean up with traffic.
FA: Unknown

7. HALF CAB 5.12b ★
Crimpers at the end.
FA: Chad Zurinshas

8. THE CLAM 5.12c ★★
Stick clip the first bolt. Great moves between good pockets. Almost three stars.
FA: Fred Henion, 1996.

9. PISTON BULLY 5.12b/c ★★★
Groom the rugged start and enjoy the upper section.
FA: Chad Zurinshas and Scott Lockhart, 1996.

10. FOUR DEEP IN THE HOOPTI 5.13b
(Project.) A long, right-trending, 12 bolt affair.

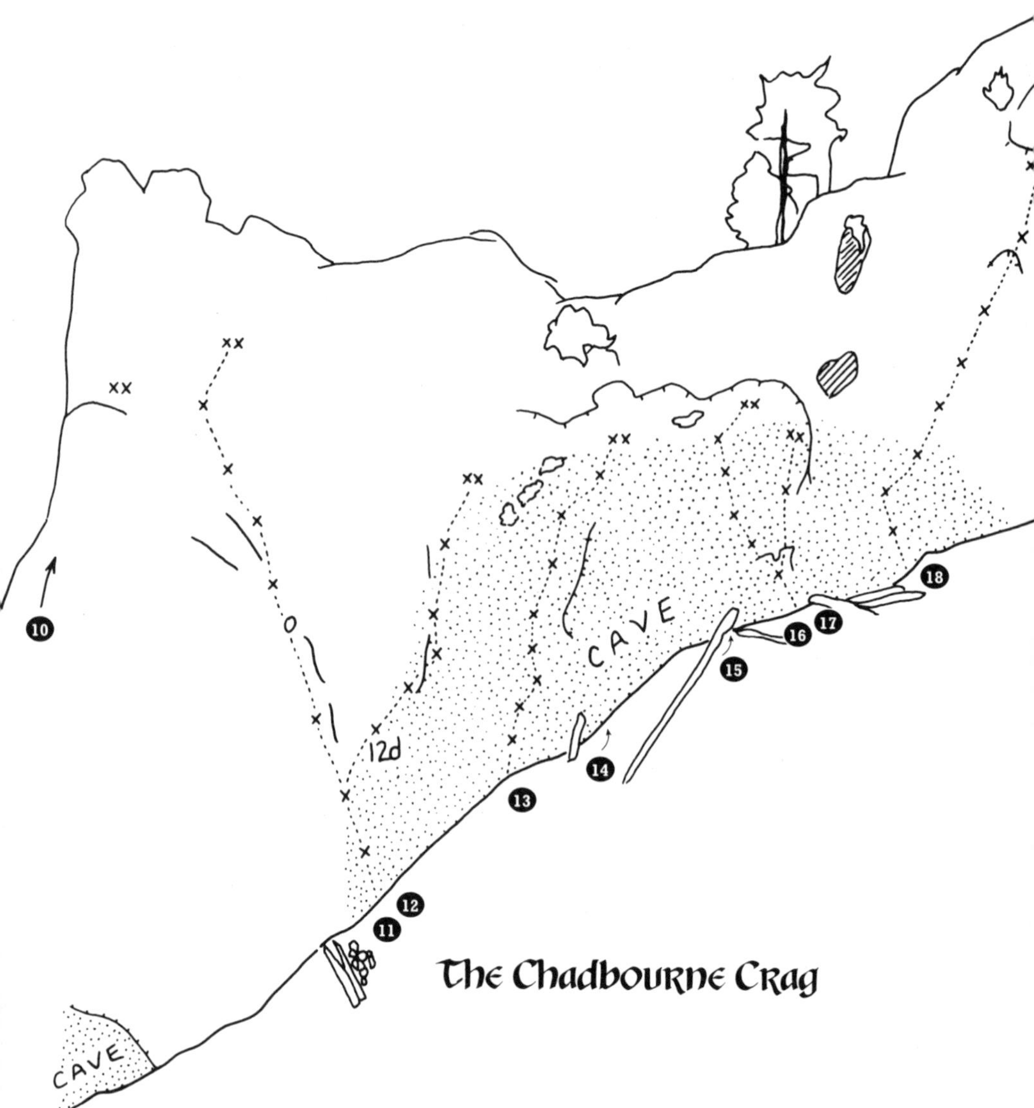

The Chadbourne Crag

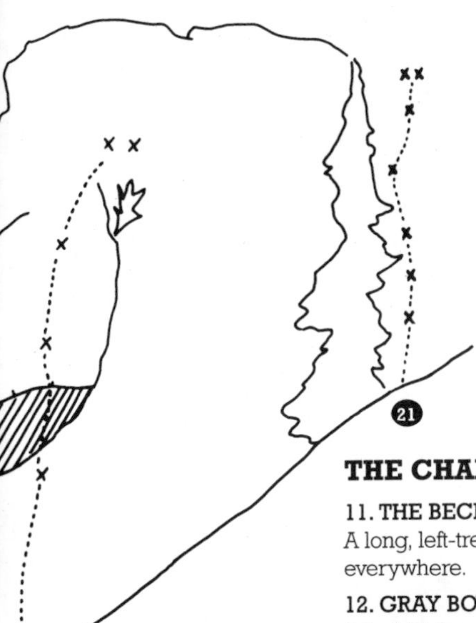

THE CHADBOURNE CRAG ROUTES

11. THE BECKEY ROUTE 5.12 (Project.)
A long, left-trending affair. Every crag needs a Beckey Route—he was everywhere.

12. GRAY BOY 5.12d ★★★
A butt-kicker at the bottom, but "tonka" holds up high. Stick clip the first bolt.
FA: Chad Zurinshas, 1996.

13. INTERSTATE 5 .13c?
(Project.) Looks stellar.

14. PROJECT

15 BEAM AND COKE 5.12d ★★★
Arguably the best line on the wall.
FA: Chad Zurinshas, 1997

16. SLICE OF PIE 5.12 ?
Climb to the first bolt on Inconthievable, then move left to join Beam and Coke.

17. INCONTHIEVABLE 5.12b ★
Good rock graces the crux. This route may punish shorter climbers.
FA: Fred Henion, 1997.

18. NO MANS LAND 5.12b ★★
A burly jug haul.
FA: On sight, Scott Lazar, 1996.

19. PROJECT

20. PROJECT 5.12?

21. GLITTER NIGHT 5.10b ★
The rightmost climb with 7 bolts. This is a good warm-up climb.
FA: Fred Henion, 1996.

Mount Olympus

Perhaps one of the most impressive peaks seen from Salt Lake City is Mount Olympus, with its sheer quartzite north face, rugged ridges and deep gullies. A well maintained hiking trail ascends the west slope of Mount Olympus, providing hikers with a beautiful walk in a federally-designated wilderness area minutes from downtown Salt Lake. The north face looks ominous and more suited to the mountain goats that walk the ledges here. On closer inspection, though, you'll find that the north face reclines at a kind angle, allowing moderate routes in a scenic environment. All four routes are long and mostly require a full day. In addition, these are mountaineering routes—loose rock, route finding problems, and difficult protection are part of the experience. Climbers need to be prepared for these difficulties and more. Helmets on Mount Olympus should be considered mandatory equipment. Winter climbs of these routes are possible; however, avalanche awareness and evaluation skills must be high, while the avalanche conditions must be very low. O'Dell Peterson, active in this area in the 30s, teamed up in the 40s with Harold Goodro for more serious roped climbs.

MOUNT OLYMPUS—KAMP'S RIDGE

This ridge is named for Bill Kamp, who made several early ascents. From the valley, this ridge is the left skyline, dropping from the north summit into Neff's Canyon. The Great Chimney cuts a notch in the ridge near the summit. It is a long climb, between 8 and 10 pitches, in addition to considerable scrambling.

APPROACH: Follow the approach to the Chadbourne Crag to reach the trailhead parking area. Follow the Neff's Canyon trail which joins a dirt road that passes a large water tank. After three-quarters-of-a-mile, the road forks, with the left route heading into Neff's Canyon and the right following North's Fork. Go right and follow the trail as it becomes faint and wanders among the many stream beds. After another half-mile, the North's Fork trail begins heading east, and a smaller drainage/gully comes in from the right. This drainage leads up to The Great Chimney (the trees open enough in several places to see Kamp's Ridge and The Great Chimney beyond).

Turn south and follow a faint trail that meanders through the brush, in and out of the drainage. After several hundred yards the drainage forks. The smaller, left fork climbs up over a series of slabs. The right fork is more prominent, leading up into the pine trees and The Great Chimney beyond. For Kamp's ridge, scramble up the left fork, passing the largest slab that blocks the gully on ledges to the left. Continue up the gully above this impass several hundred feet to the base of the ridge, which is quite unobvious from this point, and usually requires some scrambling to locate. Continue scrambling in and around the ridge crest until you feel the need to rope up. The hike takes around one-and-a-half hours. See overview on page 34.

DESCENT: From the north summit of Olympus, scramble down into the next gully to the east. Follow the left (west) side of the gully until cliffs force you over to the east side. This gully leads back to the slab impass described in the approach.

1. KAMP'S RIDGE III 5.6 ★
Climb the ridge for several pitches to a vertical section that can be passed on the north face. Continue up the ridge above to the top of The Great Chimney. From the chimney, an exposed traverse on a ledge system on the North Face past a pine tree is a must. This balancey rightward shuffle leads to a crack that gains the ridge again. Continue along the ridge to the north summit.

MOUNT OLYMPUS —THE GREAT CHIMNEY

This route climbs the dark slash of rock which begins as a notch on the left skyline and runs down the North Face. A repertoire of climbing techniques are called into play over the course of six pitches. Helmets are strongly recommended on this route. In the late summer, raspberries can be found in the gully below The Great Chimney.

APPROACH: Follow the approach to Kamp's Ridge, but instead of following the left fork in the drainage, continue up the more prominent right fork. This is the easiest, though more brushy approach to The Great Chimney. Follow this drainage uphill until the gully below The Great Chimney joins from the left (east). Turn left and scramble up this gully to the base of the chimney. The approach takes two hours and is very steep. See overview on page 34.

It is also possible to approach via a small gully between the two drainages. This involves some scrambling, a bit of route finding, and a quick descent on an exposed ledge at the top of the gully, but avoids the brush.

DESCENT: Follow the descent described for Kamp's Ridge.

2. THE GREAT CHIMNEY II 5.7 ★★
The chimney itself is four LONG pitches. Bolts have been added at the top of each pitch to provide secure belays for winter and spring ascents. Unfortunately, these aren't always in the best location for summer belays. The third pitch used to be the crux, involving several chockstones and some delicate chimney work, but rockfall in recent years has turned a relatively benign chockstone on the last pitch into a tricky overhang. From the notch, an exposed traverse on the north face, past a pine tree to a vertical crack, is loads of fun. This eventually gains the ridge again and the summit beyond.
FA: O'Dell Peterson, Harold Goodro and Lee Steorts.

MOUNT OLYMPUS —THE WEST SLABS

These slabs begin in a gully on the right side of the north face, and continue straight up to the skyline ridge. Clean and exposed, they offer an ideal combination of length and difficulty.

APPROACH: From Wasatch Blvd. (about 3365 East), turn east on Oakview Drive (4275 South). This road is immediately north of a pedestrian overpass that crosses Wasatch Blvd. Follow Oakview Drive uphill and make a right turn on Jupiter Drive (3735 East). Follow Jupiter Drive to Adonis Drive (4505 South) and turn left. Drive a short distance to Thousand Oaks Drive (4500 S) and turn right. Continue up Thousand Oaks Drive, continuing straight ahead at the sharp left turn, to a cul-de-sac above two water tanks, and park. A dirt road begins here and heads south. Walk up this road about 200 feet, and look for a less defined dirt road heading off to the left (east). Follow this less traveled road uphill. Just before a black, metal fence blocks the road, turn right and head steeply uphill on a faint trail. This trail eventually meets a level

1
2
OLYMPUS HILLS LANES
COFFEE SHOP

MOUNT OLYMPUS

1. KAMP'S RIDGE III 5.6 ★
2. THE GREAT CHIMNEY II 5.7 ★★
3. THE WEST SLABS III 5.5 ★★★

path from the left (east). At the time of this writing, there was an old water pipe across the steep trail here. Turn left and follow the path as it descends back down to join the continuation of the same dirt road that you were on before. From here, the road switchbacks up the slope and ends at some water-collecting gizmos. Traverse east through the brush to the stream bed which descends from the base of the wall. Head up the gully to reach the lowest point of the slabs. The approach takes approximately one and a half hours. See overview on page 34.

DESCENT: The west ridge of the North Face is the best descent route. A few moves of exposed scrambling are involved near the top of the ridge. After reaching the shoulder below the West Ridge, either descend down the gully to the west of the ascent gully (brushy), or scramble east, following the base of the slabs, to reach the start of the climb. From here, continue back down the ascent gully.

It is also possible to continue along the ridge from the top of the climb to the north summit, and descend via the Kamp's Ridge descent. A considerable amount of scrambling is involved this way, not to mention an additional trek through the neighborhood to get back to your car.

3. THE WEST SLABS III 5.5 ★★★
The face can be climbed almost anywhere, but the simplest route seems to begin at the low point of the slabs. This route climbs for two pitches to reach a good ledge. Climb directly above this, following the path of least resistance and taking advantage of all possible protection. The face becomes lower-angled above, and ultimately, after 10 to 12 pitches if you belay the whole face, the ridge is gained. The climbing stays interesting for the entirety, with exposure that just keeps increasing. After the first two pitches, the climb remains at 5.4.

MOUNT OLYMPUS —SPORT UTILITY WALL

Vertical to slightly overhanging, The Sport Utility Wall is the best (biggest) chunk of quartzite in the next major outcrop north of Pete's Rock. Easy access and decent climbing make these routes a justifiable stop among the Wasatch circuit.

APPROACH: Drive along Wasatch Blvd. to roughly 5300 South (.4 miles north of the parking for Pete's Rock). From the road the approach looks deceptively straightforward. However, a shattered slab makes a direct scramble to the base a bit scary. The best approach is up a gully about 120 feet south of the wall. Scramble up the gully to its top. Then walk north along a big, downsloping ledge to the base of the wall. See overview on page 34.

SPORT UTILITY WALL ROUTES

1. BLAND CHEROKEE 5.10a

A truckload of sloping holds and an off balance roof will put miles on your rig.

FA: Toby Weed, Eric Cylvik and Brian Eagan, 1996.

2. WRANGLER GIRLS 5.9 ★

Cruise up the center of the wall on mostly good holds.

FA: Kamet Erickson and Brian Eagan, 1996.

3. STRANGE ROVER 5.8 ★

A variation that connects Wrangler Girls to the upper part of Hiditaka Suzuki's Sidekick. A long runner is needed.

FA: Kamet Erickson, 1996.

4. HIDITAKA SUZUKI'S SIDEKICK 5.10c ★

Steeper than it first appears. Climb past several roofs on the south-facing prow. The first bolt is easier to clip from the right.

FA: Brian Eagan and Kamet Erickson, 1996.

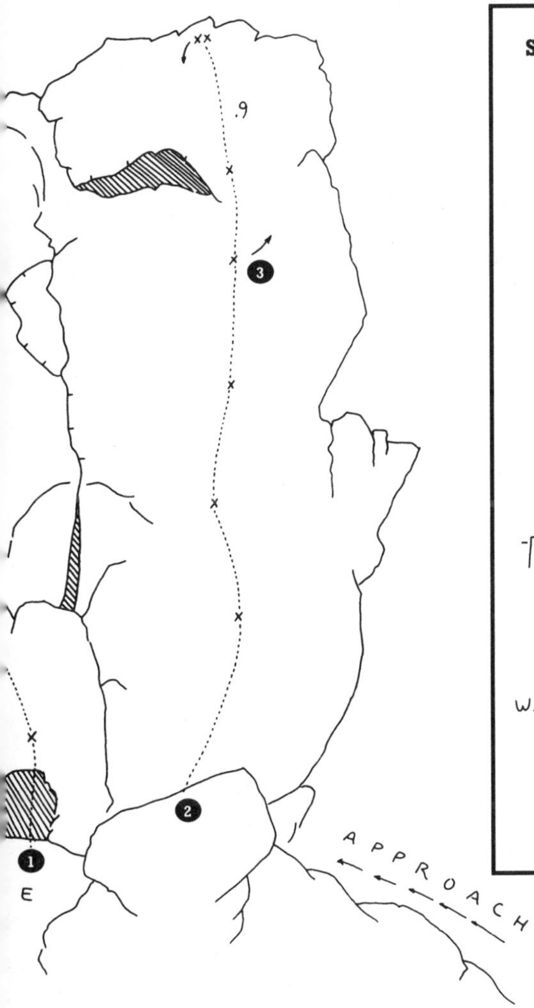

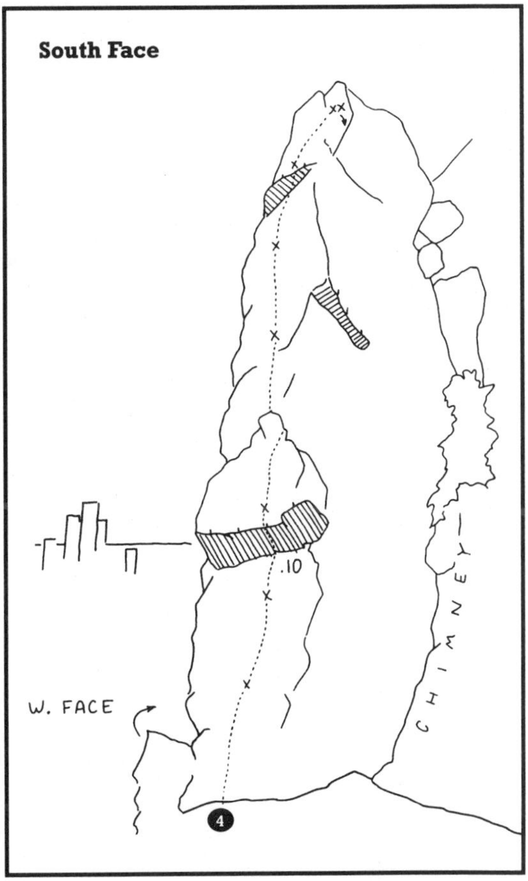

South Face

Sport Utility Wall

MOUNT OLYMPUS—GEURT'S RIDGE

This wonderful ridge climb ascends the rocky rib that descends west from the south summit of Mount Olympus. In addition, this route has the benefit of having a slightly less troublesome approach than the other Mount Olympus routes.

APPROACH: Follow Wasatch Blvd. to Pete's Rock located roughly at 5500 South. Pete's is the quartzite outcrop with a row of numbers painted along its base. Park in the parking area just east of the boulevard. This is the start of the Mount Olympus Trail. Follow the hiking trail which climbs steeply above Pete's Rock at first, then makes a big switchback to the north. Several more swithcbacks lead to a stream crossing. Above this is the notorious "Blister Hill." Luckily the trail switchbacks up this slope now, rather than the straight-up trail that used to exist. Just before the top of Blister Hill, stop and look east towards the summit, which is hidden from view. It's possible to plot a course from here, diagonalling up and left (north) above a little cliffband, across an open slope and to the rounded ridge that obscures the summit from your view. Once the ridge is gained, follow it more or less directly upwards to gain the base of Guert's Ridge. Expect some brush! The rope-up spot varies for each party, depending on your ability and comfort level. The approach takes a good two hours, and is steep. See overview on page 34.

DESCENT: From the summit, scramble south to the saddle, and follow the well worn trail back to the parking area.

4. GEURT'S RIDGE II 5.5 ★★

The route is straightforward in concept—simply follow the ridge crest to the south summit. Towers, notches, and a few overhangs create obstacles, and each impasse must be dealt with differently. Most parties rappel off the backsides of these towers. Since route finding is part of the fun on this ridge, little detail will be included. Enjoy!

FA: Irene Geurts, O'Dell Petersen and Harold Goodro, early 40's.

MOUNT OLYMPUS—PETE'S ROCK

This quartzite outcrop has played an active role in the history of Salt Lake climbing. The Wasatch Mountain Club began climbing on Pete's Rock in the 1930's, practicing for longer mountain routes. Harold Goodro started calling the outcrop Pete's Rock after O'Dell Peterson, who was a major motivator for climbers during the 30's. The name stuck, and generations of rock enthusiasts have learned to climb or practiced their techniques on this highly-accessible rock.

APPROACH: Follow Wasatch Blvd. to roughly 5500 South. Pete's is the quartzite outcrop with a row of numbers painted along its base. Park in the parking area just east of the boulevard. The approach from the parking area to the base of the wall takes about twenty seconds. See overview on page 34.

Toproping is the main activity here, with numbers painted on the rock to give reference to the difficulty. Number 1 supposedly is the easiest, and 15 the most difficult. Bring some gear to set up the topropes (two ropes may be needed for some routes). A good boulder traverse exists as well, staying one to three feet off the deck. A couple of scary boulder problems on the lowest west face also are worth noting.

An outcrop 300 feet above and right of Pete's Rock offers a good traverse and some short topropes. This is best approached by walking up the Mount Olympus Trail.

PETE'S ROCK

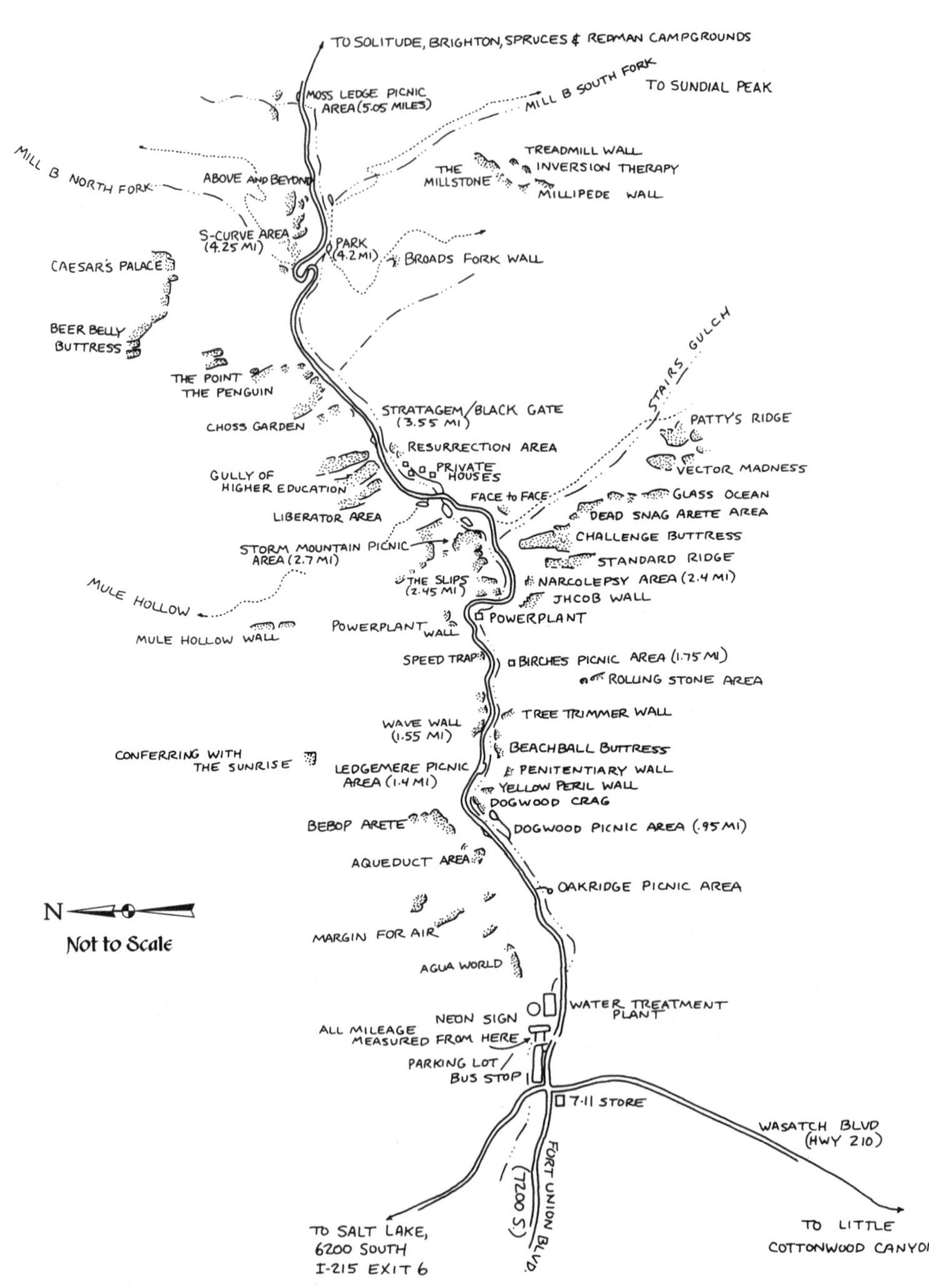

Big Cottonwood Canyon Overview Map

Big Cottonwood Canyon

The curving and complex Big Cottonwood Canyon (BCC) sees year-round popularity and holds an endless array of recreational opportunities. The alpine skiing is great at both Brighton and Solitude ski resorts—thus far they have avoided the "shopping mall mayhem" of many modern resorts. For the free heelers, BCC is a favorite, with loads of tours that have marvelous glade skiing, open "shots" and vistas. Climbing, hiking, mountain biking, picnicking, fishing—whatever your pleasure, you likely will find it in BCC.

At first glance, a climber might dismiss the cliffs of BCC as unworthy—they look broken, small and inconsequential. Surprisingly, the routes are fun. They offer a full spectrum of difficulties, with quality routes from 5.4 to 5.13. Once the newcomer experiences these routes, the scruffy cliffs will be seen in new light.

In recent years, BCC has been explored like never before. In an earlier guidebook, Wasatch Quartzite, the sage Harold Goodro said this about the unclimbed rock in BCC: "One has to drive up Big Cottonwood Canyon in summer, preferably in a convertible or jeep with the top down, to realize there are many climbs yet to be attempted ... many have never yet been considered by the climbing fraternity." With generally short approaches, these climbs were shuffled into the category of "things to do someday." Well, someday has arrived, and energetic climbers now are scouring the canyon for new routes. The once-ignored walls suddenly have named routes—creations of the late '80s that have proliferated into the '90s.

Climbing on quartzite takes some getting used to. Slippery holds form at odd angles, and unique body positions are often called into play to utilize these holds. However, the positive side to all these features is often "holds galore." Beginning climbers like the quartzite because of the abundant grips, and hone-masters can climb the overhangs for the same reason. Another aspect of the BCC experience that takes some getting used to is the routes that belie their true nature—they are steeper than you think, and uninitiated leaders can easily "fall" into this trap. The protection here can be funky, as well. Quartzite rarely allows a good pin, and hand-drilling bolts can be laborious, bordering on ludicrous, because of the hardness of the rock. Therefore, before the availability of power drills, many bold routes were led, often times with poor or difficult-to-place protection. The result is that some Big Cottonwood routes require expertise with nutcraft. Bold routes characterized the harder grades until power drills entered the scene. Nowadays, the more recent lines are generally protected by bolts, or by bolts interspersed with natural gear.

Unfortunately, history has been lost on many BCC routes, either from non-documentation of the early climbing that took place throughout the canyon, or from careless bolting of purportedly "virgin" rock. Please do your homework before drilling a "new" route, and remember that adding bolts to an existing line is not accepted by the Wasatch climbing community. Plenty of well-protected routes line the walls of BCC, so if you don't feel comfortable leading a route as is, please save it for another day, and allow others to experience the route in its original form. However, power drills have enabled bolt protection where it was practically impossible before, and constructive, thoughtful use has resulted in numerous exciting and worthwhile routes.

BCC offers more shady crags than Little Cottonwood Canyon, making it a good choice for summer. Several crags bode well for winter climbing as well, resting high on the south faces of the canyon. Especially popular among the novice climbers is the Storm Mountain picnic area, where a picnic can follow an afternoon of pleasant climbing.

HOW TO GET THERE: From the north, follow I-15 to the I-80 East Exit. Follow I-80 east toward the mountains to the I-215 South Exit. Exit off I-215 at the 6200 South Exit. From here signs will lead you to the mouth of Big Cottonwood Canyon.

From the south, exit off I-15 at the I-215 East Exit. Follow I-215 to Exit 6, the 6200 South exit. From here signs will lead you to the mouth of the canyon.

Individual cliff approaches are described with each cliff.

The routes in BCC will be listed in the order they are reached when driving up the canyon. All mileage is measured from the large lighted sign (herein referred to as "neon") sign which posts road conditions located near the mouth of the canyon.

AGUAWORLD

This is the first large quartzite wall on the north side of the canyon. Positioned above the wooden aqueduct and facing towards the sun all day, Aguaworld is the perfect cool weather crag. As with most Big Cottonwood Walls, this area suffers from a lack of clean, unbroken rock and sweeping lines. However, the climbing here is good, and should, as the saying goes "clean up after a few more ascents." The climbs themselves tend to be in the vertical realm with slightly overhanging bulges and roofs. Bring along a full rack—not all of the climbs are bolted.

APPROACH: Park at a pullout on the right (south) side of the road, .75 miles up canyon from the neon sign. A small talus slope meets the road to the north, and is split by a trail. Follow the trail as it heads up a slope, then turns west and parallels the power lines. At a group of large boulders on the right side of the trail, turn right (north) and walk up the slope to reach the top of a mine tailing. The brush free approach drops off the backside of the mine dump and gains a talus slope which can be followed uphill to the wooden aqueduct and the base of the wall. See overview on page 48.

DESCENT: Except for The Snatch/Scavenger link-up, and Four Twenty, both of which require a walk-off, all routes can be rappelled from anchors at the top of each route.

Gordon Douglass keeps cool on Minimum Security, Penitentiary Wall.

photo: Ruckman.

AGUAWORLD ROUTES

1. THE SNATCH 5.8
Climb the obvious chimney/corner system at the far west end of the wall. Belay at a large block.
FA: Unknown.

2. SCAVENGER 5.9
This is the second pitch of The Snatch. Climb up and right to a corner, which passes by a large bird's nest, then up to a chimney. Either follow the chimney or traverse out to the arête and up to the top.
FA: Steve Habovstak and Randy Kieliszewski, 1996.

3. DROP TEST DUMMIES 5.11d ★
This one can be hard to spot. Start 15 feet west of the small point/overhang of rock nearest the aqueduct. Scramble up ledges to the base of a small corner. Climb the corner and the overhanging crack above (good gear). Easier climbing leads up the crack to the belay.
FA: Steve Habovstak and Randy Kieliszewski, 1996.

4. THE GEARHUNTER 5.11b ★
Set your sights on the crack and corner system directly above the point of rock that comes closest to touching the aqueduct. This thin crack requires small to medium gear. The crack treads slightly right then meets a corner. Pump up the corner to the chains.
FA: Steve Habovstak and Randy Kieliszewski, 1996.

5. AQUA VELVET 5.11b ★
Follow the prow through enduring overhangs. All bolts.
FA: Steve Habovstak and Eric Klement, 1995.

6. T.H.C. 5.12a ★★
After bolt three, move right, stemming and laying away the corner to a ledge. Launch up the smooth face above on gradually bigger holds. All bolts.
FA: Steve Habovstak and Eric Klement, 1995.

The following routes, with the exception of Golden Finger are located on what is known as the Power Hits Wall.

7. SMOKE 'EM IF YOU GOT 'EM 5.12a ★★
A mixed bolt and gear route that dispenses with the ominous alcove via a boulder move, then roughly parallels the prow formed by the chimney—a 1 1/2" cam is handy for this stretch. Above, turn the roof and follow bolts to the belay.
FA: Randy Kieliszewski and Steve Habovstak, 1996.

8. BURN TOUGH 5.11d ★★
Pull the big alcove, then blaze past bolts and overhangs to a desperate exit. All bolts.
FA: Randy Kieliszewski, 1996.

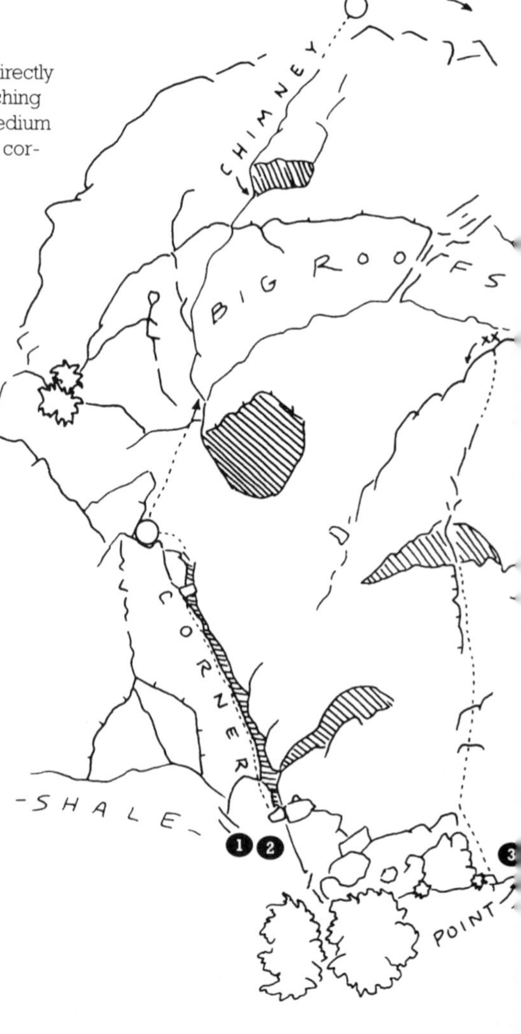

9. RESIN HARDMAN 5.10c R ★★

Traverse left along a diagonal crack, then pull straight up to a ramp. From the ramp, a series of up and left shuffles gains a flake-like system that turns the roof and joins the belay anchors on Burn Tough. A second pitch wanders the upper face, aiming for a two-bolt belay.

FA: Steve Habovstak, Randy Kieliszewski and John Ray, 1995.

10. PIPE DREAMS 5.10a R ★

Climb straight up a small, thin corner. The headwall atop the corner requires some vision.

FA: Randy Kieliszewski and John Ray, 1996.

11. FOUR TWENTY 5.9+

Wander up the face to the right of the Pipe Dreams' corner.

FA: Randy Kieliszewski and Steve Habovstak, 1996.

12. GOLDEN FINGER 5.11 TR

Several hundred yards east of Aguaworld, the aqueduct goes under a chunk of rock with a steep face. A top rope is easy to set up.

FA: Randy Kieliszewski, Steve Habovstak and John Ray 1996.

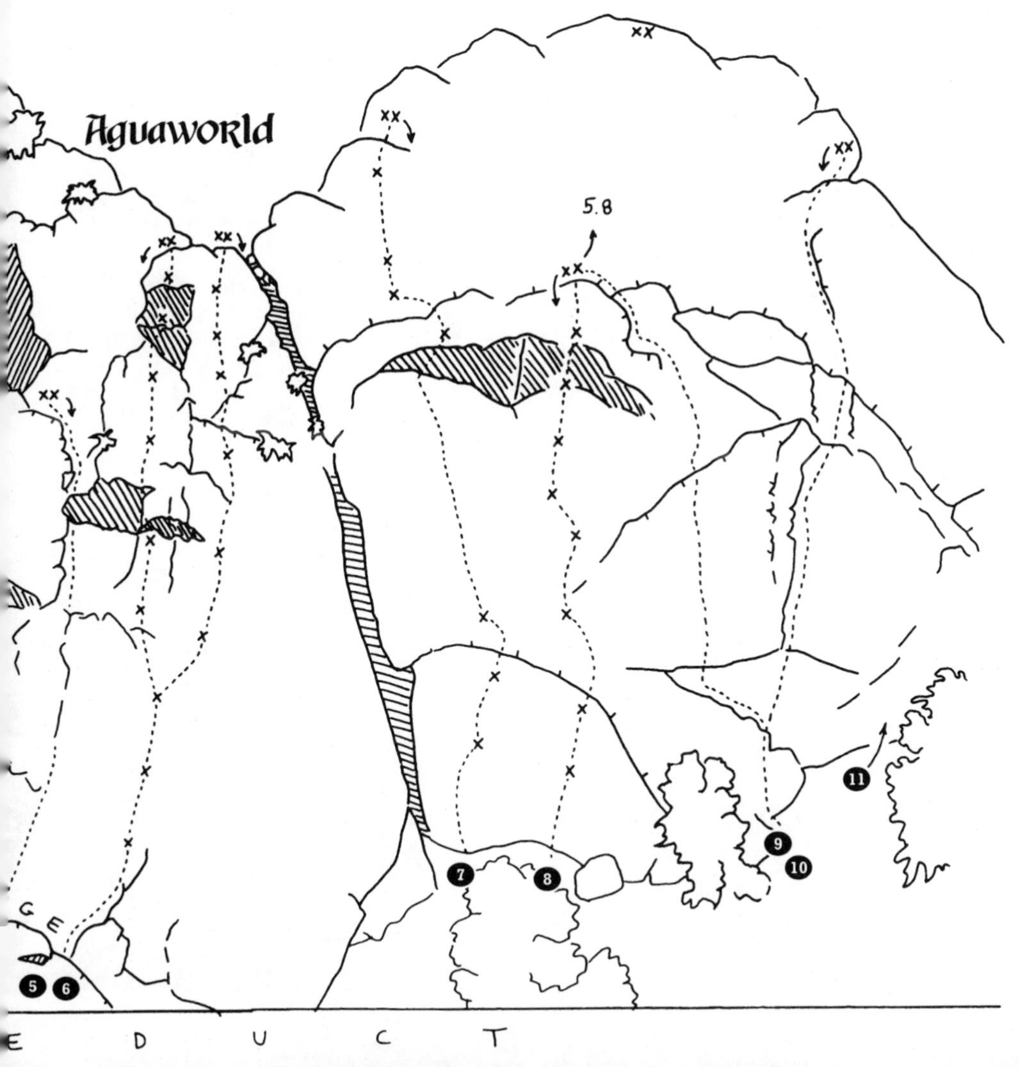

MARGIN FOR AIR WALL AND ENVIRONS

This wall has a rotten appearance, however excellent climbing exists. Steep and pumpy, and peppered with roofs, the Margin For Air Wall rests high on the canyon flank, basking in afternoon and evening sun. A long approach and some flaky rock are the drawbacks to this wall.

APPROACH: Follow the approach to Aguaworld. From the base of the Aguaworld wall, carefully walk east on the aqueduct (this is considered trespassing) until you come to a rock protrusion that the aqueduct sneaks under (route number 12 at Aguaworld). Continue 150 feet further, jump off the aqueduct, and head up the talus to the base of the cliff. Most brush can be avoided with this path. See overview on page 48.

DESCENT: Walk off to the north for Margin For Air, or downclimb and make an eighty foot rappel from two bolts at the top of Air of Supremacy.

MARGIN FOR AIR WALL AND ENVIRONS ROUTES

1. MARGIN FOR AIR 5.10a ★★★
4. FLYING HIGH AGAIN 5.10c R ★

4

MARGIN FOR AIR WALL AND ENVIRONS ROUTES

1. MARGIN FOR AIR 5.10a ★★★

Start 25 feet left of Air of Supremacy. Begin off a sloping ramp and climb a face directly to the diagonalling crack. This face does, in fact, have protection. Climb the crack leftward through airy bulges and escape right near the top (or continue the leftward trend). Bring about eight full-length runners to help alleviate rope drag.

FA: Bret Ruckman and Gary Olsen, 1984.

2. PROFIT MARGIN 5.9+ ★

This follows corners and roofs left of the bolted Air of Supremacy. Once again, rope drag can be a problem, so bring lots of runners. Some loose rock.

FA: Drew Bedford and Conrad Anker.

3. AIR OF SUPREMACY 5.11d ★★★

Expect big-time air on this classic passage. Bring 2 and 2-1/2" cams for the roof, as well as a few nuts.

FA: Bret and Stuart Ruckman, 1990.

4. FLYING HIGH AGAIN 5.10c R ★

Roughly 300 feet east of the Margin For Air Wall is a steep and obvious corner that faces the road. This is just less than a mile up BCC. Approach as for Margin For Air, and traverse east to this climb. Bring small to medium-sized gear.

FA: Doug Heinrich and Conrad Anker, 1987.

The true meaning of roadside climbing. The now closed Wave Wall in its heydey.

photo: Gary Olsen.

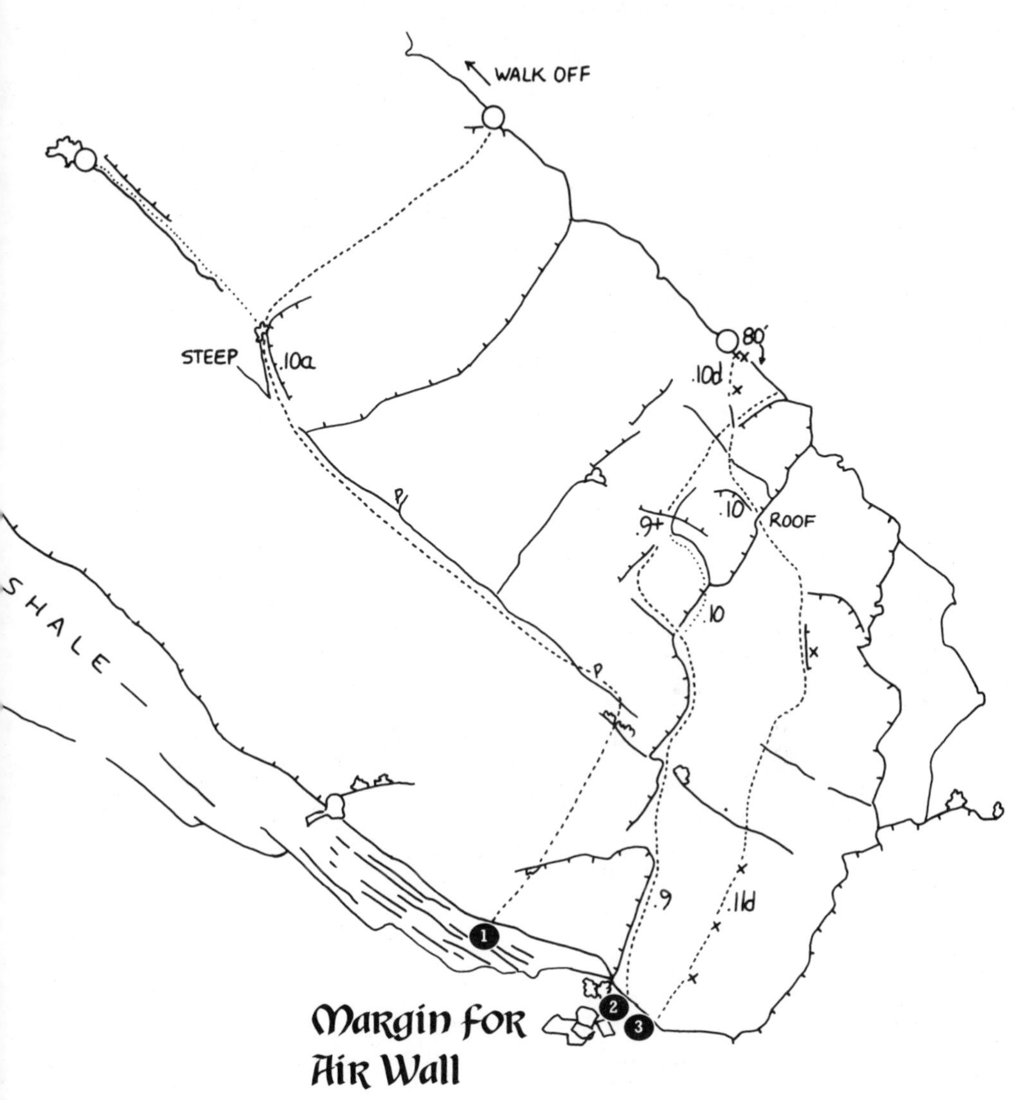

Margin for Air Wall

THE AQUEDUCT AREA

Ten years ago, this area was lush and green, complete with running water, moss, and the feeling that this was a secret oasis. Now, after repair of the leaking aqueduct above, only the dead cottonwood trees are left as vestiges of a more fertile past.

APPROACH: Park 1.0 miles up-canyon from the neon sign. Walk up a good trail that begins on the west side of a clearing/scooped-out area next to the road. After 100 feet, traverse west past a small ridge, then follow the trail straight up to a rock outcrop. Traverse west under the outcrop, then straight up again to reach the base of the wall. Watch for poison ivy. See Overview on page 48.

DESCENT: Rappel off all routes on this wall with one rope.

The Aqueduct Area (south face) routes

1. PANDORA'S BOX OF HOLOCAUSTS 5.12a ★

A steep, four bolt route, located 150 feet west of Aquaduct, directly under the wooden aqueduct.

FA: Ray Dahl and Tony Calderone, et. al. 1995.

2. AQUADUCK 5.10d R ★★

Down low on the south face is a large roof. Aquaduck climbs the smooth face to the left of this roof. It looks horrible, but for the competent leader, it is well worth the effort. The protection, although perfectly adequate, is pumping to place.

FA: Merrill Bitter, et. al. 1984.

3. TERRA NOVA 5.11b ★

New ground. Another pumper climb. Turn the big roof and face the bemusing moves above.

FA: Bret and Stuart Ruckman, Gary Olsen, 1985.

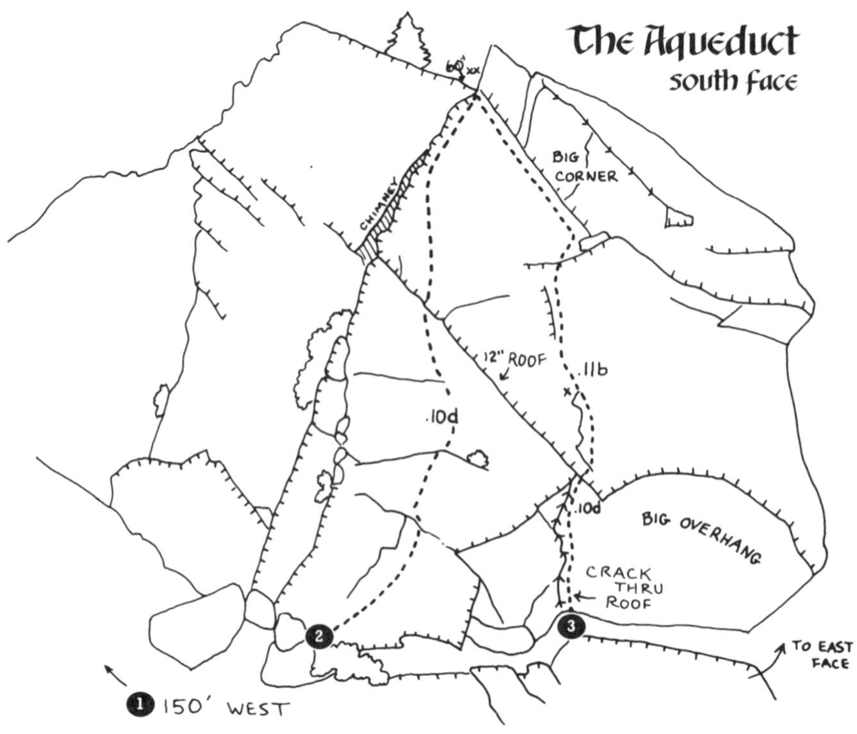

The Aqueduct Area (east face) routes

4. LIP SERVICE 5.9- ★

A thin, shallow crack leads to the first bolt, while big holds lead past three bolts above. Bring small to medium nuts.

FA: Libby Ellis and Stuart Ruckman, 1989.

5. SUBTERRAINIAN 5.11a ★

An unfinished route that climbs the face between Lip Service and Double Standard.

6. DOUBLE STANDARD 5.9 ★

Start below the boulder. Stem and jam the fine cracks above. Good protection and interesting moves.

FA: Stuart Ruckman and Libby Ellis, 1989.

7. SOCKDOLLAGER 5.9 ★

Step directly off the boulder and climb the nice right-leaning hand crack.

FA: Stuart Ruckman and Libby Ellis, 1989.

8. STRAIGHT TALK 5.10a

Short. Climb the right-most crack on the east face, avoiding the wide section by tricky face climbing.

FA: Stuart Ruckman and Libby Ellis, 1989.

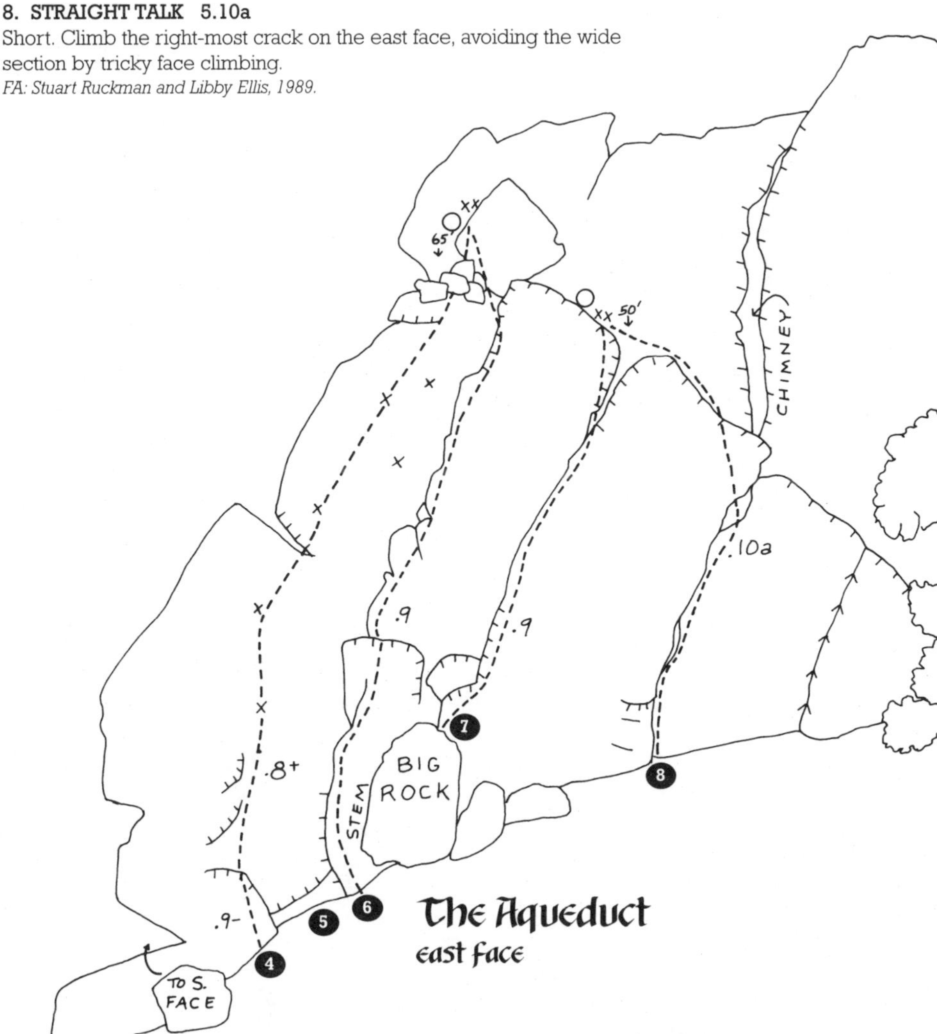

ART MAJOR WALL

This wall is short, but offers shady climbing and a good pump. Bring a selection of small gear.

APPROACH: Not actually on the Aqueduct Wall, this wall is located 200 feet to the east. Follow the approach to the Aqueduct Area's East Face. Continue up the gully past Straight Talk, and scramble up the broken rock underneath the Aqueduct. Walk east along the top of the Aqueduct (this is considered trespassing) 200 feet to a steep wall and gully on the left (west). Walk a bit further, then jump off the aqueduct and backtrack to access the wall. See overview on page 48.

DESCENT: Belay at the top of the routes and downclimb to the east to reach the Aqueduct.

Art Major Wall routes

1. COLOR ME WILD 5.11c ★
Climb the left line, past three fixed pins. Move left toward the top, onto better holds.
FA: Bret and Stuart Ruckman, 1988.

2. ART NOUVEAU 5.11a ★
The line in the center. Near the top, diagonal left toward the top of Color Me Wild.
FA: Stuart and Bret Ruckman, 1988.

3. TROMPE-L'OEIL 5.11b ★
Easier done than said. This climb is located about three feet right of Art Nouveau. A series of holds leads rightward. Climb up to a bolt and pump it out to the top. The longest route on the wall.
FA: Stuart and Bret Ruckman, 1988.

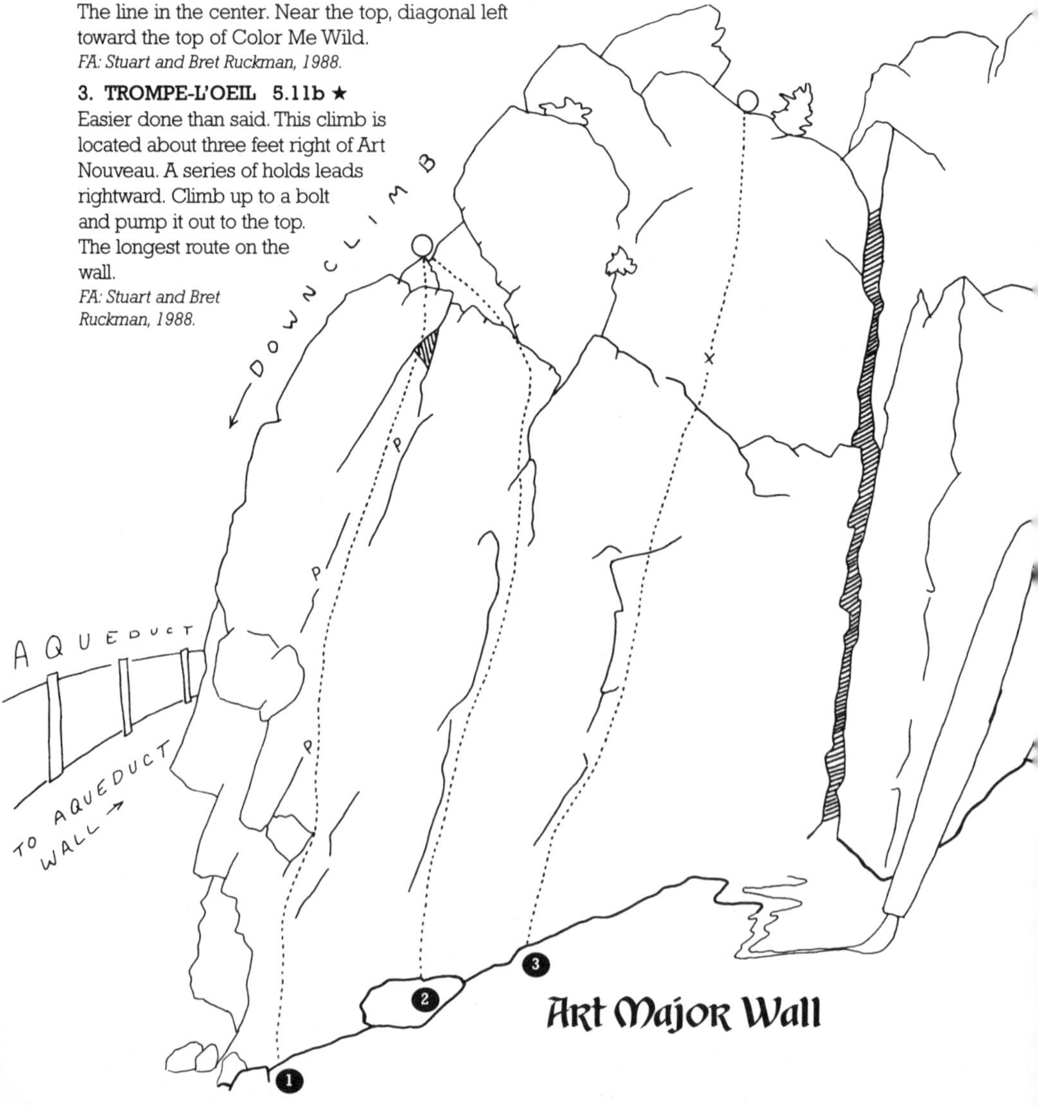

Karl Munge edging on the Glass Ocean.

photo: Ruckman.

DOGWOOD CRAG

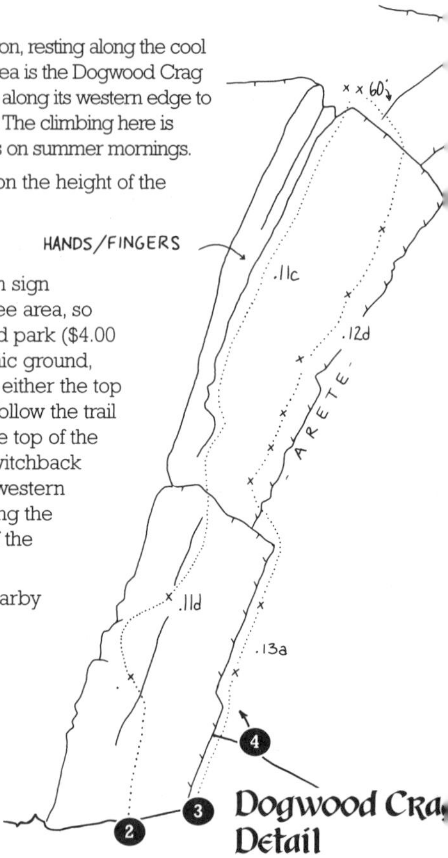

The Dogwood Picnic Area is located roughly one mile upcanyon, resting along the cool banks of the Big Cottonwood stream. Just beyond the picnic area is the Dogwood Crag which rises out of (or nearly out of) the stream and leans back along its western edge to an angle that makes the slick, water polished holds climbable. The climbing here is popular due in part to the quick approach and the shady walls on summer mornings.

APPROACH: Two approaches are used here, depending on the height of the stream. If the stream is low, park off the road at a pullout 1.15 miles up canyon from the neon sign and cross the stream directly over to the routes. During highwater, use the following approach: .95 miles up canyon from the neon sign is the Dogwood Picnic Area. This is a U.S. Forest Service fee area, so either park on the road and walk in ($2.00), or drive in and park ($4.00 per vehicle). From the far eastern parking area in the picnic ground, amble east along a trail that parallels the stream. To reach either the top of the wall, or routes 1 to 7 at the eastern end of the wall, follow the trail that leads uphill at the end of the chain link fence. From the top of the wall, keep walking east and you'll eventually be able to switchback down to the base of the routes. To reach the routes at the western end of the wall, routes 8 to 12, continue straight ahead along the trail that follows the river until it drops down to the base of the wall. See overview on page 48.

DESCENT: Not every route has anchors at the top, but nearby anchors make it possible to rappel easily from the top. Walk-offs, though not fashionable, are easy as well.

Dogwood Crag routes

1. LIFE DURING WARTIME 5.8 R ★
Climb the smooth north-facing slabs eight feet left of This Ain't No Party.
FA: Stuart Ruckman, 1984.

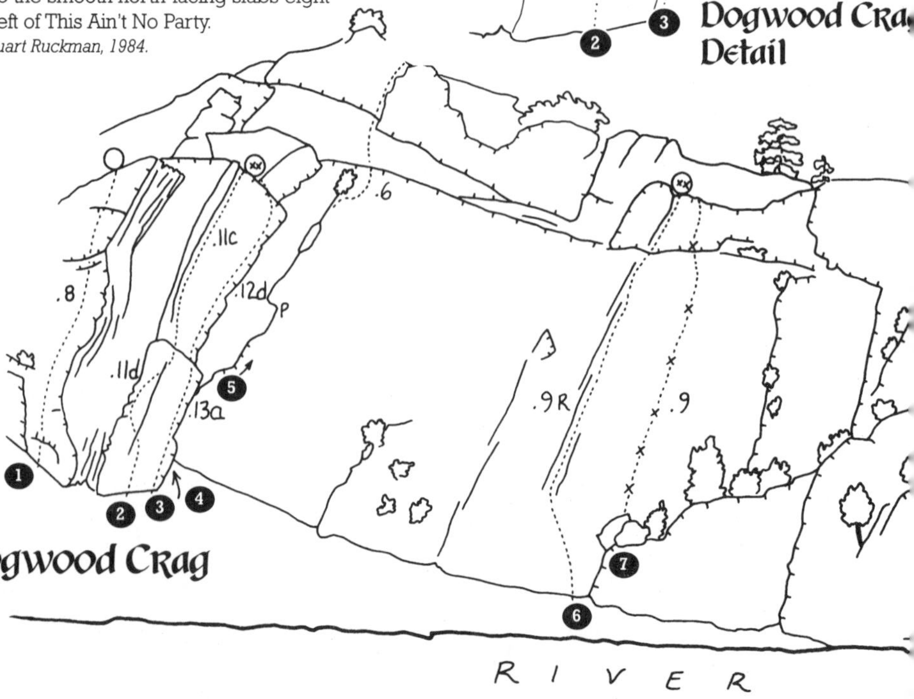

2. THIS AIN'T NO PARTY, THIS AIN'T NO DISCO 5.11d ★★

On the lower block, climb up the radically-overhung face, making a few moves on the left edge, then continue up the crack and face to a big ledge. Above, climb the pumping upper crack. A 2" cam is handy here, as well as other hand and finger sized protection.

FA: Bret Ruckman and Gary Olsen, 1984. FA: (not using the left edge, 5.12b) John Storm, 1988.

3. CROSS-EYED AND PAINLESS 5.13a ★★★

With long reaches and dynos, esoteric sequences and a classic arête, is it any wonder this route has such mass-a-peel? Follow eight bolts up the ominous edge for 60 feet. Some climbers just climb the upper arête, which is rated 5.12d.

FA: Stuart Ruckman and Gordon Douglas, 1989.

4. LITTLE CREATURES 5.11c ★★

The relentless flake on the left wall of the cavern right of Cross-eyed and Painless. A pump from the word go. Bring a healthy supply of pro up to 2 inches.

FA: Conrad Anker and Doug Heinrich, et al, 1986.

5. LITTLE CRITTERS 5.6

Follow a crack and flake system on the slab that rises out of the "cave".

FA: Unknown.

6. HYPER-GAMMA SPACES 5.9 R ★

Follow a thin crack up an exceedingly smooth face 30 feet right of Cross-Eyed and Painless. Bring micro nuts.

FA: Gary Olsen and Bret Ruckman, 1984.

7. A MODEST MAN FROM MANDRAKE 5.9 ★

Climb the smooth face past six bolts and turn an overhang near the top.

FA: Stuart and Bret Ruckman, Libby Ellis, 1990.

8. THE LION OF ZION 5.6

FA: Unknown.

9. I THINK I'M GOING BALD 5.9- ★

From the right side of the wall climb out left above the river and past six bolts. Great rock.

FA: Stuart Ruckman and Theron McNeely, 1990.

10. HAVEN'T A CLUE 5.8 ★

More slippery, rounded stuff. Clip the first bolt on I Think I'm Going Bald, then march up and right.

FA: Shane Willet and Mike Carnahan, 1991.

11. ON THE SKIDS 5.8 ★

Again, climb past six bolts on a fun face. Start where the water last touches the cliff on its right side.

FA of bolted line: Stuart Ruckman and Theron McNeely, 1990.

12. TAKE ME TO THE RIVER 5.7

Tricky protection.

FA: Bret Ruckman and Merrill Bitter, 1983.

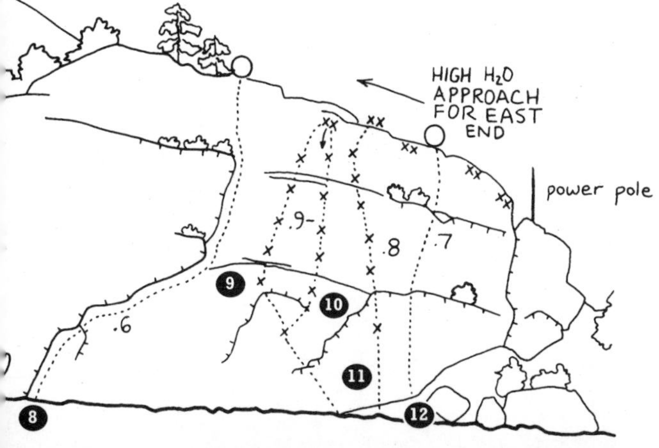

The following routes are not on the Dogwood Crag, instead they are located north of the low water parking area.

13. BEBOP ARETE 5.10

This is located above the parking for the Dogwood Crag's low-water approach, about 1.15 miles up BCC. The major cliff on the north side is mostly low-angled, with a plethora of roofs. This route apparently follows the right arête of this buttress for several pitches. Little else is known.

FA: Jim Dockery and Lynn Wheeler, mid 70s.

14. ALPENBOCK ROUTE 5.6

Also in this area is a climb done by the "Bock Bunch." The following is an excerpt from the Alpenbock scrapbook: "... We did about 50 feet of class 2.3978 scrambling. This brought us to a large grass-covered ledge where the prospects of loafing seemed far more attractive than climbing the somewhat ominous-appearing pitch ahead of us. After some rather clever cowering movements by Bob and Ted, Milt, whose cowering prowess [sic] had been dulled by the long evening at the Hacienda, bravely started up what was to be the toughest pitch of the day. A strenuous start, combined with some real muscle antics required to pass the last 15 feet, would put the grading scale at about 5.6."

FA: Bob Springmeyer, Milt Hokanson and Ted Wilson, 1964.

YELLOW PERIL WALL

From the Ledgemere picnic area look southwest. You'll see an uncompromisingly smooth quartzite slab that faces up canyon. This is the Yellow Peril Wall. Small holds on excellent rock are the featured attraction.

APPROACH: Park 1.4 miles up canyon from the neon sign at the Ledgemere Picnic Area. Park alongside the road to avoid the parking fee, or pay $2.00 and park in the picnic area parking lot. From here, simply cross the bridge, walk west to the last picnic table and cruise up the short hill to the base. See overview on page 48.

DESCENT: An easy walk-off to the north is advised.

Yellow Peril Wall routes

1. DOUBLE TROUBLE 5.?

Climb the chimney that forms the left side of the wall.

FA: Unknown.

2. CATCH THE WAVE 5.9- R ★

Climb the left edge of the face. Unfortunately, there are more holds than protection.

FA: Drew Bedford and Kevin Gheen, 1985.

3. BUCKETS TO BANGKOK 5.12a R/X ★★★

Well-respected but not well-protected. Usually toproped. RP's essential, especially for a critical, blind placement.

FA: toprope, Merrill Bitter.

FA: Paul Smith and Pokey Amory, 1984.

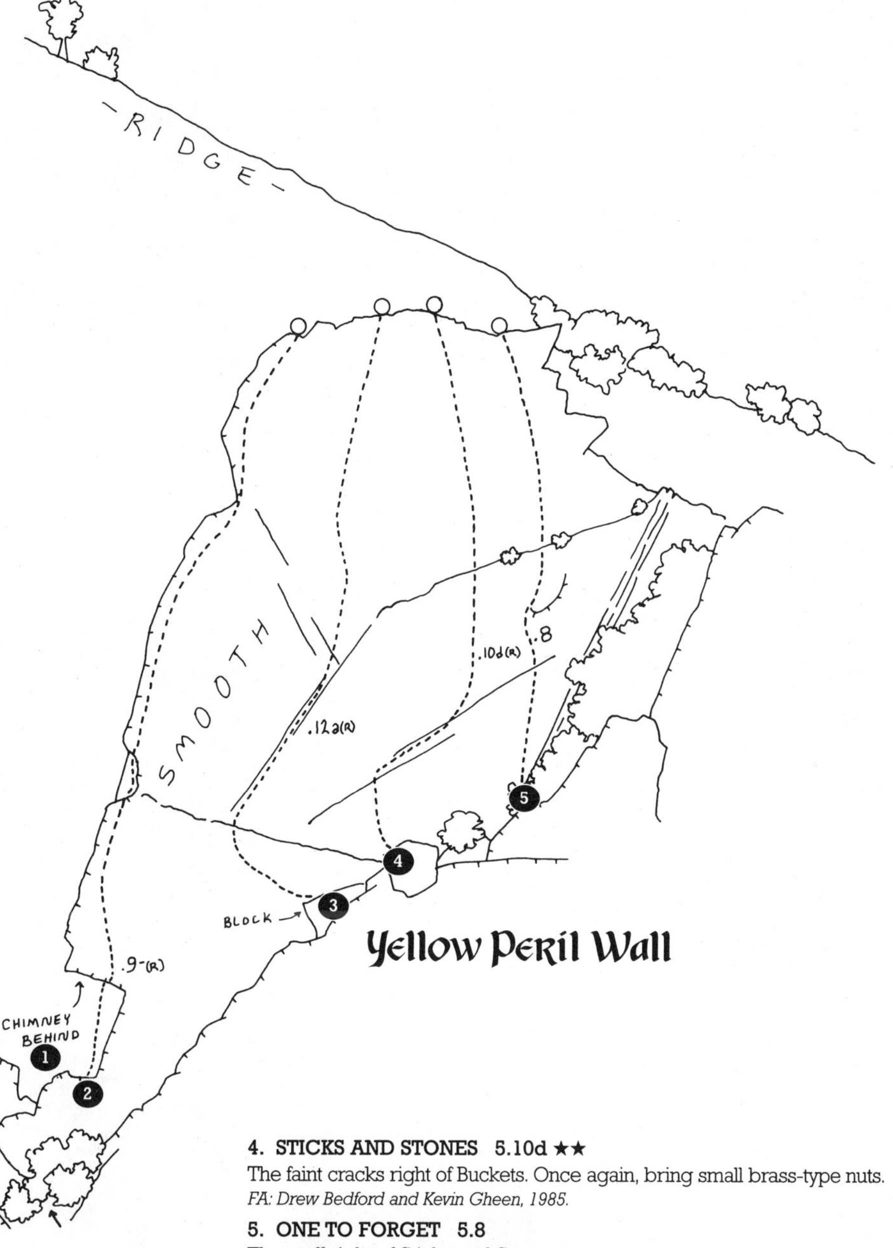

4. STICKS AND STONES 5.10d ★★

The faint cracks right of Buckets. Once again, bring small brass-type nuts.

FA: Drew Bedford and Kevin Gheen, 1985.

5. ONE TO FORGET 5.8

The stuff right of Sticks and Stones.

FA: Gary Olsen and Bret Ruckman, 1984.

6. DISHES TO DETROIT 5.12? ★

This route is located about 200 feet south and uphill of the Yellow Peril Wall, on a steep, north-facing fin of rock hidden among the brush. Follow the line of bolts to a two-bolt anchor. Bad feet make for hard moves and a hard clip.

FA: Unknown.

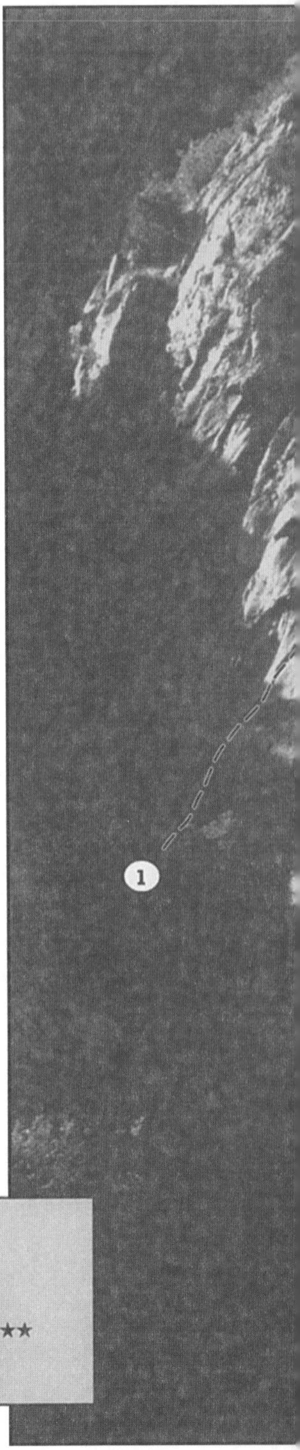

PENITENTIARY WALL

The smooth quartzite slabs up the hill and south (behind) the Ledgemere Picnic Area, offer superb rock and challenging climbing. Thin cracks and seams split the faces, and most routes link these weaknesses. Square edges are the rule, but the occasional slick friction move is thrown in for good measure. In general, expect small protection that is tricky to place, but solid once secured. All of the routes were established from the ground up.

APPROACH: Park 1.4 miles up canyon from the neon sign at the Ledgemere Picnic Area. Park along the side of the road to avoid the parking fee, or pay $2.00 and park in the picnic area parking lot. From here, simply cross the bridge, walk west until you reach a talus slope descending from the hill behind a picnic table. Walk up this slope, staying near the left margin, until a gully that leads up to the base of the wall is met. Scramble up this gully. See overview on page 48.

DESCENT: There should be slings around flakes at the top of most routes which allow one rope rappels.

1

Penetentiary Wall Routes

1. REHABILITATION 5.7 ★
3. LIFE SENTENCE 5.10a R ★★
12. MINIMUM SECURITY 5.10a R ★★
14. JAILBAIT 5.9+ ★★

14
12

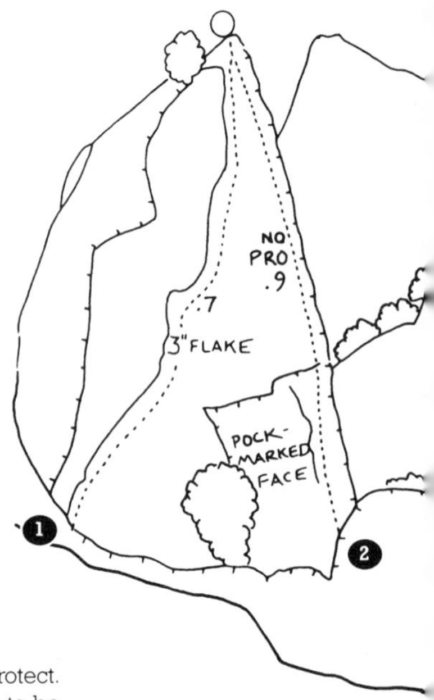

PENITENTIARY WALL ROUTES

1. REHABILITATION 5.7 ★
The hollow flake on the far left-hand slab.
FA: Chris Pendleton, Gary Olsen and Bret Ruckman, 1984.

2. DECEPTION 5.9 ★
Unprotected climbing on the right edge of Rehabilitation.
FA: Mark Bennett and Gary Olsen, 1985.

3. LIFE SENTENCE 5.10a R ★★
The most prominent of the slabs, this continuous route utilizes incipient cracks for protection and thin, clean edges for holds. Several sets of micro nuts are useful.
FA: Bret and Stuart Ruckman, Gary Olsen, 1984.

4. JACK THE RIPPER 5.12a R ★★
A direct start to Life Sentence. Desperately thin, and murder to protect. A hand-placed knifeblade 12 feet up in a horizontal crack seems to be the ticket.
FA: Drew Bedford, 1986.

5. CELL LIFE 5.11a TR ★★
The sharp right edge of the Life Sentence slab. Intricate and balancey. If you don't discover a secret, this is 5.12a.
FA: Stuart Ruckman, 1987.

6. STICKY ZIPPER 5.9+
One foot to the right of Cell Life, on the west-facing offset, is a nice crack.
FA: Drew Bedford and Kevin Gheen, 1985.

7. CLIMB AND PUNISHMENT 5.9- ★★
The most obvious of the cracks on the Penitentiary Wall, splitting the small slab. Tricky moves lead to secure hand jams. The cell-block rappel is at the terminus of the crack.
FA: Stuart and Bret Ruckman and Gary Olsen, 1984.

8. CLIMBS AND MISDEMEANORS 5.10c TR ★
Climb Tax Evasion until you can move left and onto the face. Fifteen feet of arête climbing finishes things off. Like Cell Life, there is a trick.

9. TAX EVASION 5.7 ★
A right-facing corner five feet right of Climb and Punishment. Bring hand-sized Friends.

10. POSSESSION 5.7?

11. SPEED IS OF THE ESSENCE 5.7 ★
The six-inch crack in a left-facing corner is best liebacked.
Probable FA: Stuart and Bret Ruckman, 1985.

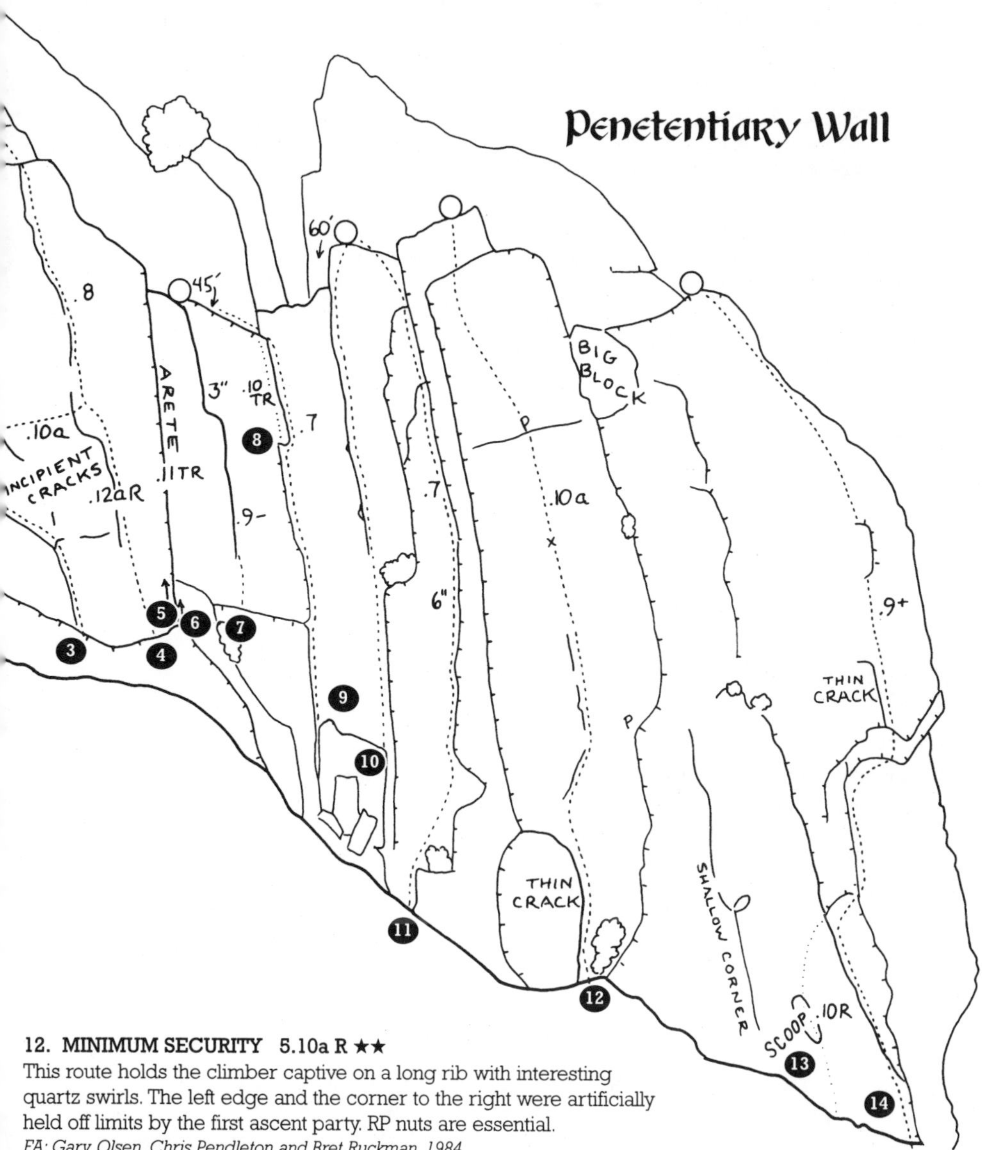

12. **MINIMUM SECURITY 5.10a R ★★**
This route holds the climber captive on a long rib with interesting quartz swirls. The left edge and the corner to the right were artificially held off limits by the first ascent party. RP nuts are essential.
FA: Gary Olsen, Chris Pendleton and Bret Ruckman, 1984.

13. **S&M 5.10c R**
Dice up through the "silica snakes," joining Jailbait 20 feet up.
FA: Chris Pendleton and Gary Olsen, 1984.

14. **JAILBAIT 5.9+ ★★**
The upper part of the route, above the overlaps, is a brilliant shield of the finest quartzite.
FA: Gary Olsen, Bret and Stuart Ruckman, 1984.

CONFERRING WITH THE SUNRISE

This climb is located on a prominent arête way up high on the north side of BCC, above the Ledgemere picnic area.

APPROACH: Park at the Ledgemere Picnic Area, 1.4 miles up canyon from the neon sign. Looking north, you can see this wall and its impressive arête. The approach is the path of least resistance and requires about one hour.

DESCENT: Two ropes are required for the descent off of a two-bolt anchor.

1. CONFERRING WITH THE SUNRISE 5.11b ★★

This climb faces southeast (hence the name), and climbs the right side of an obvious, dark arête. It is a long climb for BCC (90 feet). Climb 20 feet to a horizontal crack, above which is a bolt. Two more bolts define the route. Superb RP and small wired placements (bring two sets) protect the climbing between the bolts. No topo.

FA: Merrill Bitter and Jeff Baldwin, 1989.

BEACHBALL CRAG

This small yet popular wall is split by several cracks and rises directly out of the stream. North facing and cool, this is a good choice in the summer.

APPROACH: Park 1.5 miles up canyon from the neon sign. The easiest approach is to simply hop rocks across the stream to reach the base of the wall. During high water, park 1.4 miles up canyon at the entrance to Ledgemere Picnic Area. From the parking area at Ledgemere, cross the upper bridge and walk east to the uppermost picnic area. A trail here leads east along the river to the base of the wall. See overview on page 48.

DESCENT: Walk off all routes to the east or west, with the western option being preferred.

Beachball Crag routes

1. BREAKING THE LAW 5.10 R

Follow incipient cracks through the overlap to the top. Protection is marginal.

FA: Doug Heinrich and Todd Evans.

2. ACROSS FROM THE WAVE 5.7 ★

Climb the nice crack to the top. Small camming devices are useful. In high water, a rightward traverse can be made to reach the crack.

FA: Dana Hauser and Merrill Bitter, 1987.

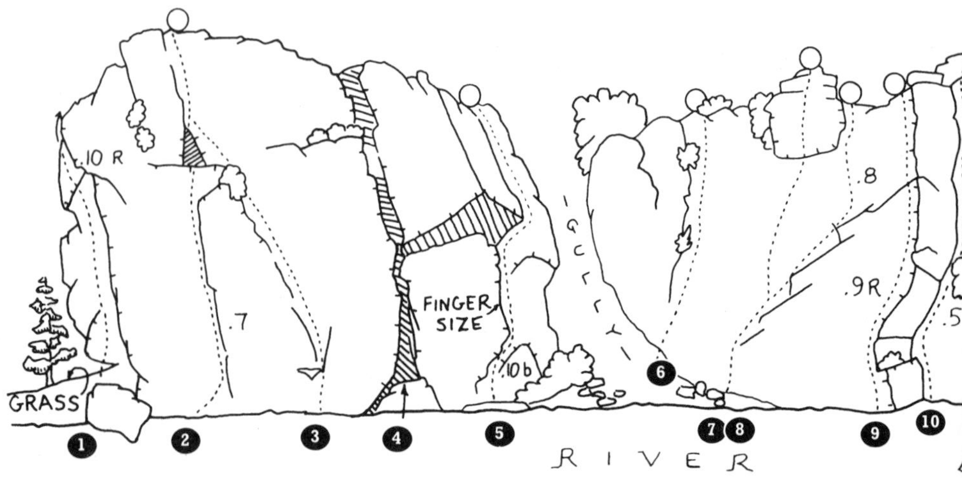

3. BUDDHA BABIES ON THE BEACH 5.6 ★
A thin, clean crack that joins Across From The Wave near the top.
FA: Tony Calderone and Kathy Lagerquist, 1992.

4. RUBBLE WITHOUT A CAUSE 5.5
Handjams, cobwebs and a wide section.
FA: Unknown.

5. SPF 25 5.10b ★
A hard crank at the start. Hidden buckets ease the pain.

6. WATERFRONT 5.5
Short.
FA: Ray Dahl, 1994.

7. HIS FEET SMELL 5.10c
The crux is a hard reach over the overhang.
FA: Riccardo Olliveri and Paul Overall, 1993.

8. REACH THE BEACH 5.8 ★
Climb good cracks on compact rock.
FA: Kevin Griffith

9. SNEAK-A-PEAK ARETE 5.9- R ★
A scary undertaking that climbs the arête. The rock is great but the protection is lacking.
FA: Fred Henion

10. MASTERS OF THE OBVIOUS 5.5 ★
The Beachball classic. A straightforward corner.
FA: Unknown.

11. RIP'S ROOF 5.8 ★
A mini-climb that pulls the roof via a nice hand crack.

12. OUTSIDE, IT'S AMERICA 5.12a ★
The roof daunts many. Two bolts. U2 may be a victim.
FA: Gordon Douglass and Stuart Ruckman, 1988.

13. RED ARGYLE 5.5 ★
An obligatory Beachball tick-off.

14. BEACH BLANKET BINGO 5.4
A ridiculously short route. Its best purpose is as an approach to the top of the wall.

Beachball Crag

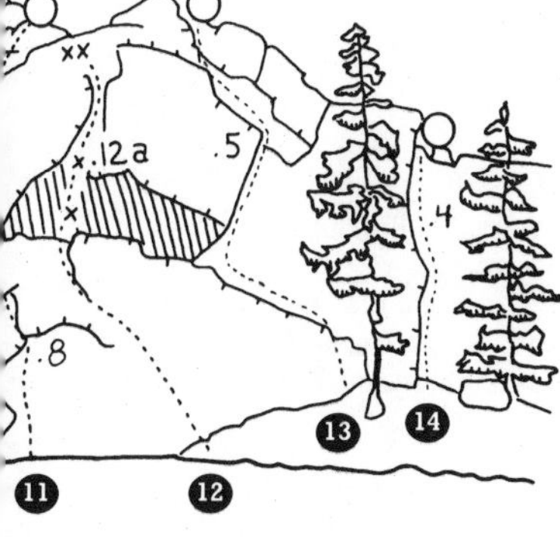

THE WAVE (no topo)

Located 1.55 miles up canyon from the neon sign, The Wave is on the north side of the road, practically overhanging the pavement. Eleven very popular routes graced this rock until the fall of 1990, when all the bolts were removed by Utah Power and Light. After years of lambasting climbers, the authorities got fed up and took action to ensure the cliff's closure for the future. Today the Wave Wall is most popular for a bouldering traverse that graces the overhanging wall and provides a quick pump with zero approach. Please resist the temptation to toprope on this wall. Not only will the authorities become angry, but you may become a hood ornament for a passing vehicle if you pop off. See overview on page 48.

TREE TRIMMER WALL (no topo)

This broken wall rises out of the water and sports two routes on its east face.

APPROACH: Park in a pullout on the south side of the road 1.6 miles up canyon from the neon sign (this is just past The Wave wall). Cross the river to gain the base of the wall. During high water, this approach is impossible. No Topo.

DESCENT: Walk off.

1. LAWNMOWER MAN 5.6
Start a few feet uphill from the wide crack that splits the east face. A thin crack that starts with a few good moves leads to a hole, then moves left to thrash through the tree and the broken rock above.
FA: Ray Dahl, Brian Pyper and Steve Adamson, 1994.

2. NOTHING BUT ROCK 5.8 ★
Follow the arête left of the wide crack. Some runouts on good rock.
FA: Steve Adamson, Ray Dahl and Brian Pyper, 1994.

Rolling Stone area

ROLLING STONE AREA

East facing and split by several prominent cracks, the Rolling Stone Area sits alone along the edge of a huge talus slope. Bring along a quiver of tricks that includes both crack and face technique. Crowds are never a problem here.

APPROACH: The approach can be described in one word—talus. Park at the Birches Picnic Area, 1.75 miles up canyon from the neon sign. Cross the bridge and walk to the restrooms in the picnic area. Just down canyon from the restrooms is a picnic table with some talus behind it. Walk up this talus slope which will lead to bigger and bigger expanses of talus. Generally, walk upwards and slightly west until the wall appears on the right (west). See overview on page 48.

DESCENT: A sixty foot rappel off the top of Paint It Black will reach the ground.

Rolling Stone routes

1. PAINT IT BLACK 5.11b/c ★

Follow five bolts up the center of the face. The overhanging headwall may leave you seeing black. The first clip is strenuous.

FA: Scott Keller and Tony Calderone, 1995.

2. THE LOST ART OF MANLINESS 5.10b ★★

Mostly hand jams in the prominent crack that leads to a ledge. A fine finger crack finishes this route off nicely.

FA: Tony Calderone and Scott Keller, 1995.

3. RUBY TUESDAY 5.10a ★

A variation. Climb The Lost Art of Manliness to the ledge. An easy move right reaches the base of a wider crack that splits its way to the top of the wall.

FA: Scott Keller, 1994.

4. BEAST OF BURDEN 5.7

A thin crack in the corner starts licheny, moves into some bushes, and finishes clean.

FA: Scott Keller and Tony Calderone, 1995.

5. BARRACUDA 5.10c

This route is located 75 feet down the talus from the other climbs. Two bolts followed by a broken crack. Blowing the second clip would be very bad.

FA: Scott Keller and Tony Calderone, 1995.

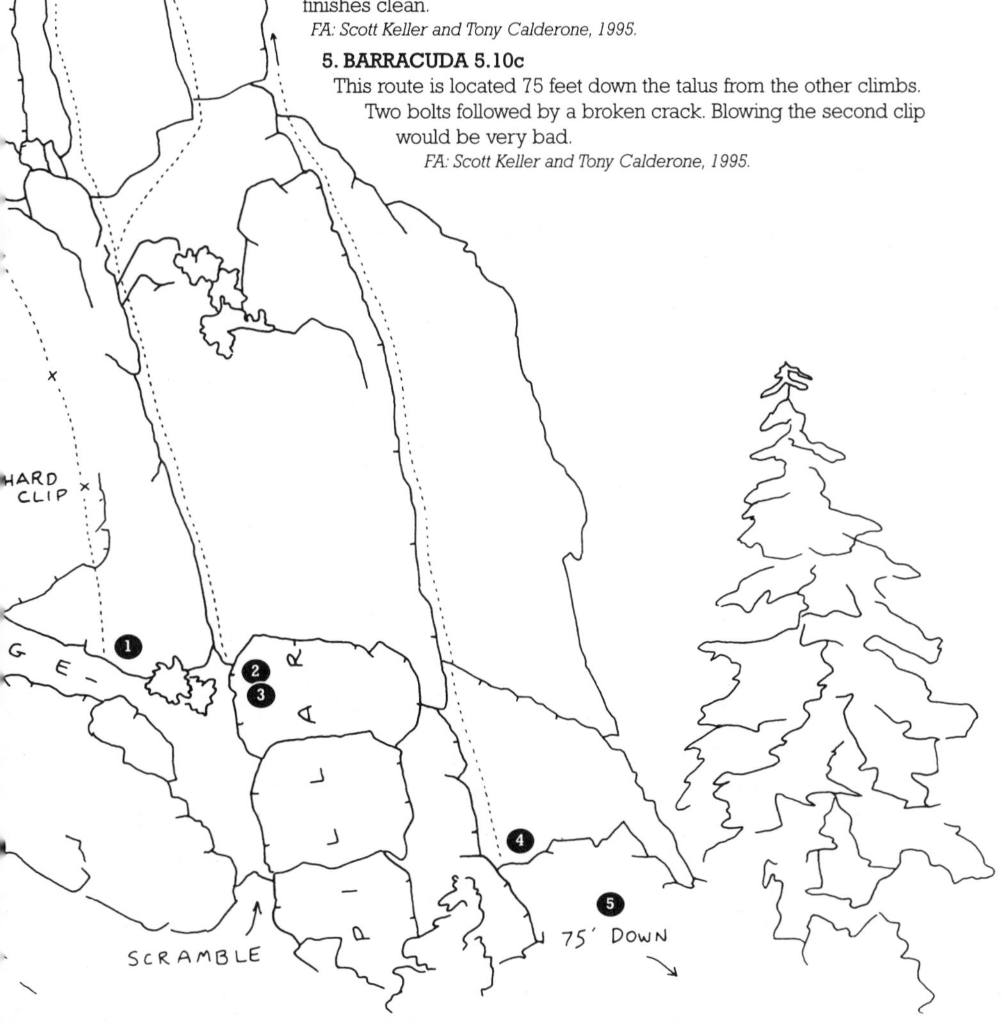

THE SPEED TRAP

Zero approach and overhanging climbing have made this wall very popular.

APPROACH: Park 1.75 up canyon from the neon sign, at a large pullout that is directly across the road from the entrance to the Birches Picnic Ground. Walk up the road from the pullout to some large boulders, and follow a trail through the shale scree to the wall. The overhanging east face houses the routes. See overview on page 48.

DESCENT: It is possible to lower off all the routes here, although many climbers walk off Neon Leon, or use long runners on its anchors.

THE SPEED TRAP ROUTES

1. NITROUS OXIDE 5.12a ★
Big pulls, steep stone.
FA: John Laney and Brent Christianson.

2. SPEED RACER 5.12b/c ★
Start on Nitrous Oxide, finish on Speed Trap.
FA: John Laney and Brent Christianson.

3. NEON LEON 5.10a ★
Angle left past three bolts to the south arête, which is climbed past one more bolt to the top.
FA: Jim and Tomi Howe, 1990.

4. MACH 5 5.11d ★
Start on Speed Trap and finish on Nitrous Oxide.
FA: John Laney and Brent Christianson.

5. SPEED TRAP 5.12b/c ★★
Blitz up the face protected by five bolts.
The intriguing crux is at the top.
FA: Steve Carruthers and Jim Howe, 1990.

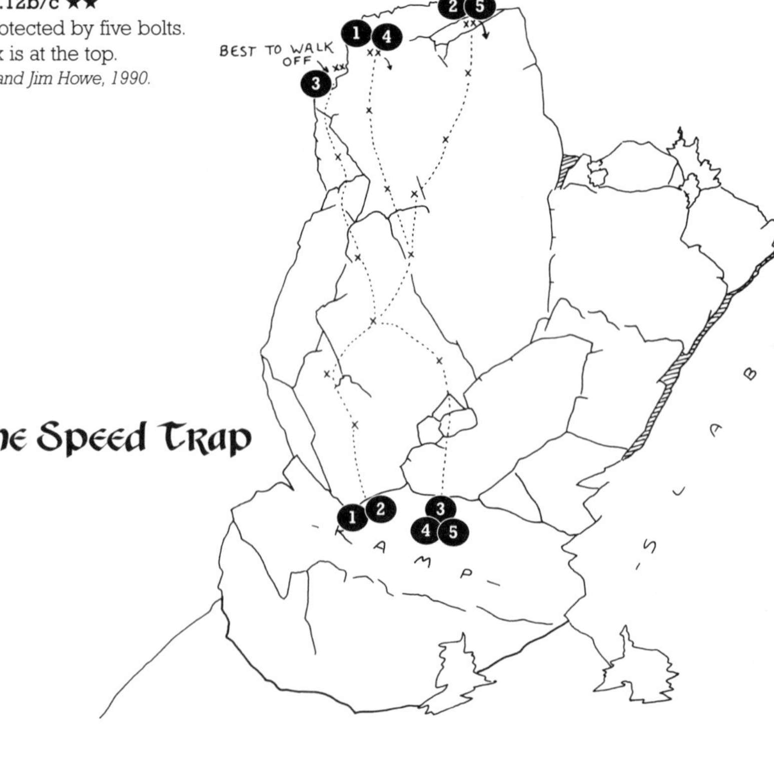

POWER PLANT WALL

North of the Stair's Station Power Plant, is a "grotty-looking" cliff which offers five routes. Despite the appearance, sections of these two walls have good stone, and the angle of these routes is certainly deceptive.

APPROACH: Park 2.05 miles up canyon from the neon sign. This parking is 200 feet beyond the power plant at a pullout on the right side of the road, just before the steep and sharp right turn. Cross the road and bushwhack (or find a faint trail) up to the cliff. Approaching from the right is recommended. See overview on page 48.

DESCENT: For routes 1 and 2, rappel from the top. To descend from routes 3 through 5, walk off the ledge system to the west.

WAVEBREAK WALL ROUTES

1. JAGGED EDGE 5.8 ★★
Climb the arête on the left side of the cliff.
FA: Brian, Vicki and Jonathan Smoot, 1989.

2. WAVE BREAK 5.11a R
A fin of rock that looks like a breaking wave. Climb the overhanging east face with dubious protection. RP's are welcomed.
FA: Stuart Ruckman and Bret Ruckman, 1986.

POWER PLANT WALL ROUTES

3. PIPELINE SEQUENCE 5.10 R ★★
The line up the middle of the steep south face.
FA: Bret Ruckman and John Storm, 1986.

4. STEEPNESS 5.10d ★★
The route follows the obvious line of bolts to the left of an arête.
FA: Brian Smoot, 1989.

5. IPECAC CRACK 5.10d
Five feet right of the prominent chimney system is a finger/hand crack. A definite anti-classic.
FA: Bret and Stuart Ruckman, 1986.

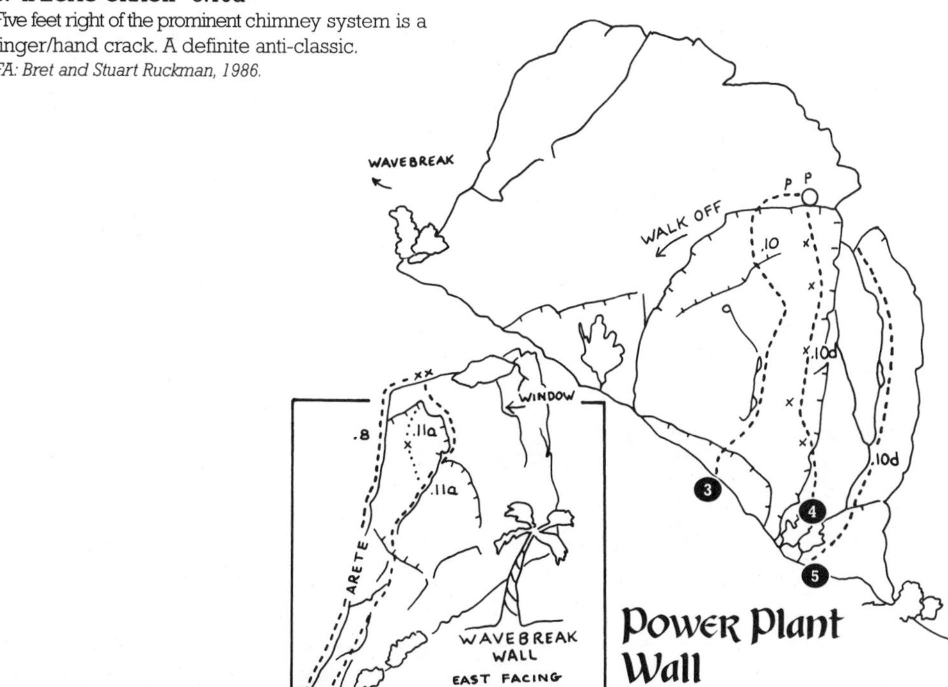

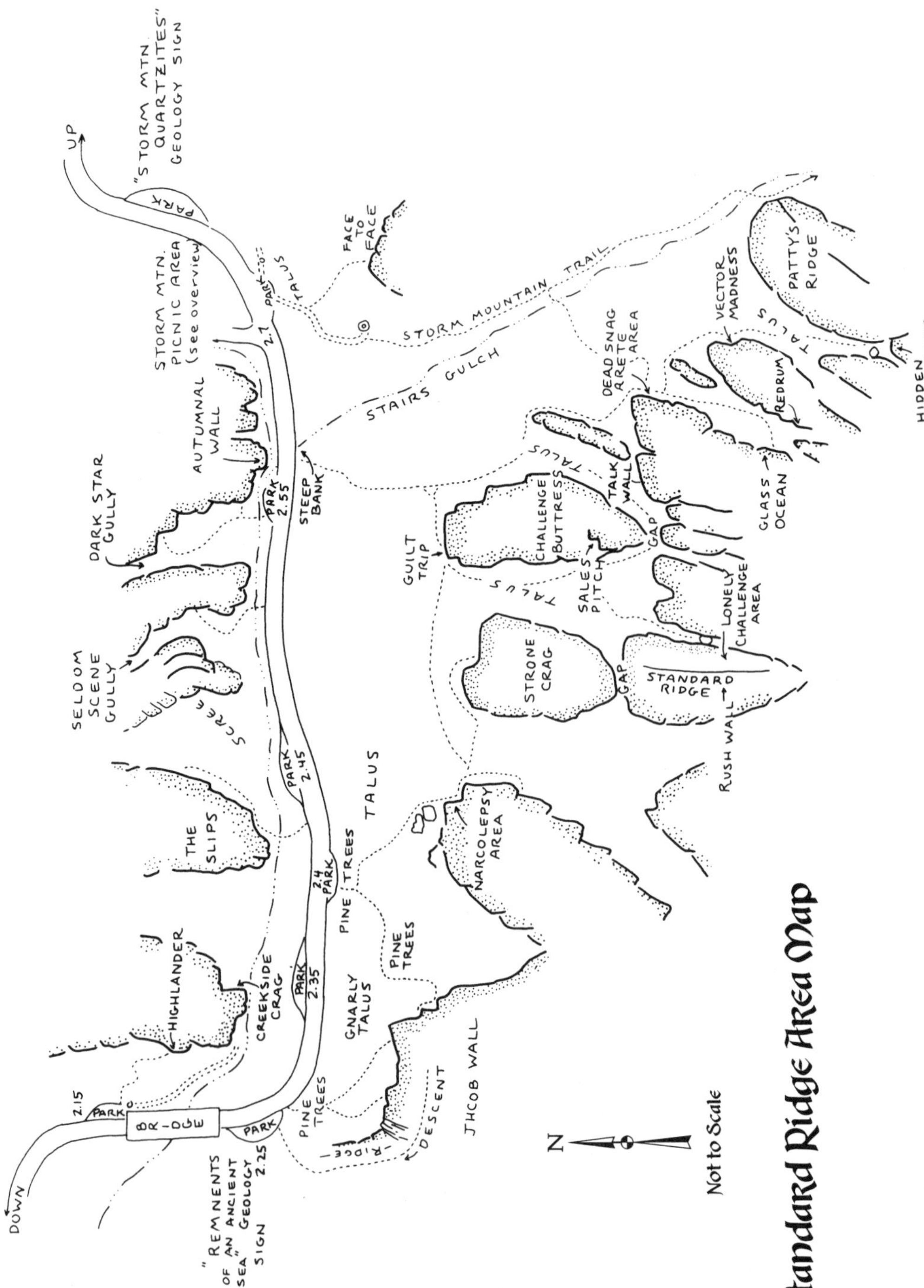
Standard Ridge Area Map
Not to Scale
N
UP
DOWN
"STORM MTN. QUARTZITES" GEOLOGY SIGN
"REMNENTS OF AN ANCIENT SEA" GEOLOGY SIGN
STORM MTN. PICNIC AREA (see overview)
FACE TO FACE
TALUS
STORM MOUNTAIN TRAIL
STAIRS GULCH
DEAD SNAG ARETE AREA
VECTOR MADNESS
PATTY'S RIDGE
REDRUM
HIDDEN
GLASS OCEAN
TALK WALL
GAP
CHALLENGE BUTTRESS
SALES PITCH
GUILT TRIP
LONELY CHALLENGE AREA
STANDARD RIDGE
RUSH WALL
STRONE CRAG
NARCOLEPSY AREA
STEEP BANK
AUTUMNAL WALL
DARK STAR GULLY
SELDOM SCENE GULLY
SCREE
THE SLIPS
HIGHLANDER
CREEKSIDE CRAG
PARK 2.15
BRIDGE
PARK 2.25
PARK 2.35
PARK 2.4
PARK 2.45
PARK 2.55
PARK 2.7
PARK
PINE TREES
GNARLY TALUS
JACOB WALL
DESCENT
RIDGE

STANDARD RIDGE AREA

The Standard Ridge Area is a complex cluster of high quality crags located between the "Remnants of the Ancient Sea" geology sign and the Storm Mountain Picnic Area. Some of the finest rock in the canyon is found here. In addition, every type of climbing is represented among these walls, from multiple pitch crack climbs, to short, powerful sport routes. The crags themselves are oriented in every direction of the compass—early spring through late fall, you're guaranteed to find sun or shade, whichever you prefer. Bolts or gear routes, roadside approach or quiet solitude, it's hard to go wrong climbing along the margins of this half-mile stretch of road.

HIGHLANDER

West facing and overhanging, this wall is quite obvious from the road. Closer inspection reveals a shorter than expected wall sitting atop a slab. The one route here is certainly worthwhile, however, as is the bouldering that can be found in the area.

APPROACH: Park 2.15 miles up canyon from the neon sign. This big pullout is on the east side of the road at the lower end of the bridge. A trail begins about twenty feet up canyon from the end of the cement barricade, between two Box Elder Trees, and meanders southeast through the brush to the base of the wall. It is worth finding this path, as the surrounding brush is quite thick. See overview on page 76.

DESCENT: Lower off chains at the top of the route with one rope.

1. THE HIGHLANDER 5.12a ★
Scramble up easy rock to reach a belay bolt. More scrambling leads to the first bolt, then big holds on an overhanging wall lead out into space.
FA: Shane Willet, Steve Habovstak and Paul Moore, 1993.

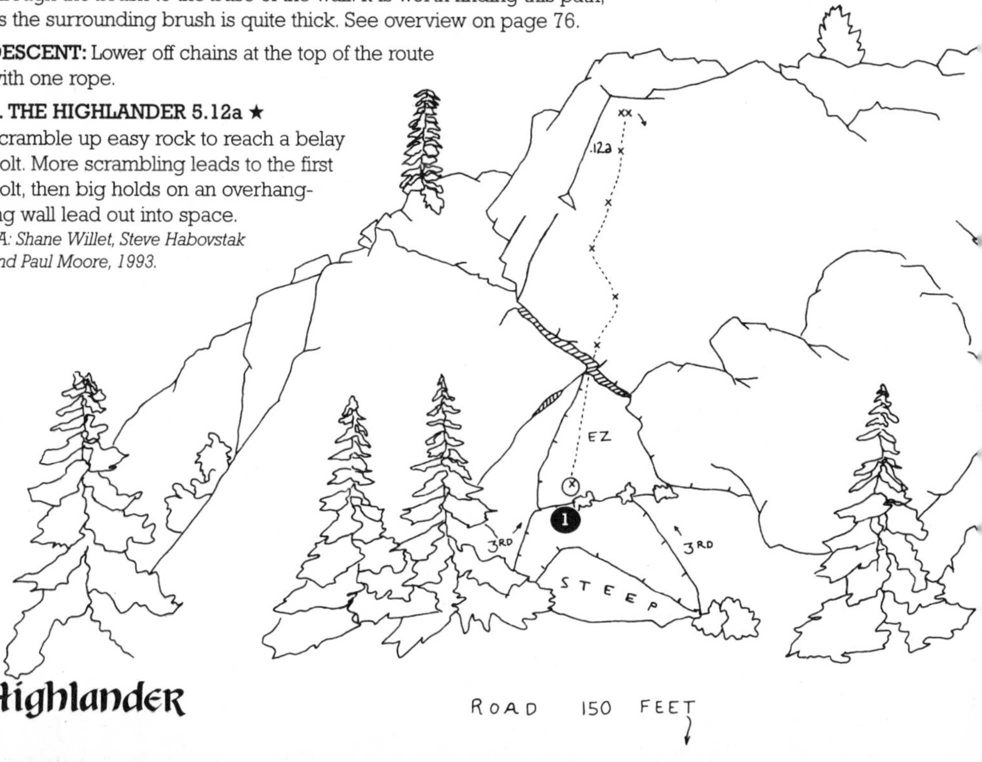

Highlander

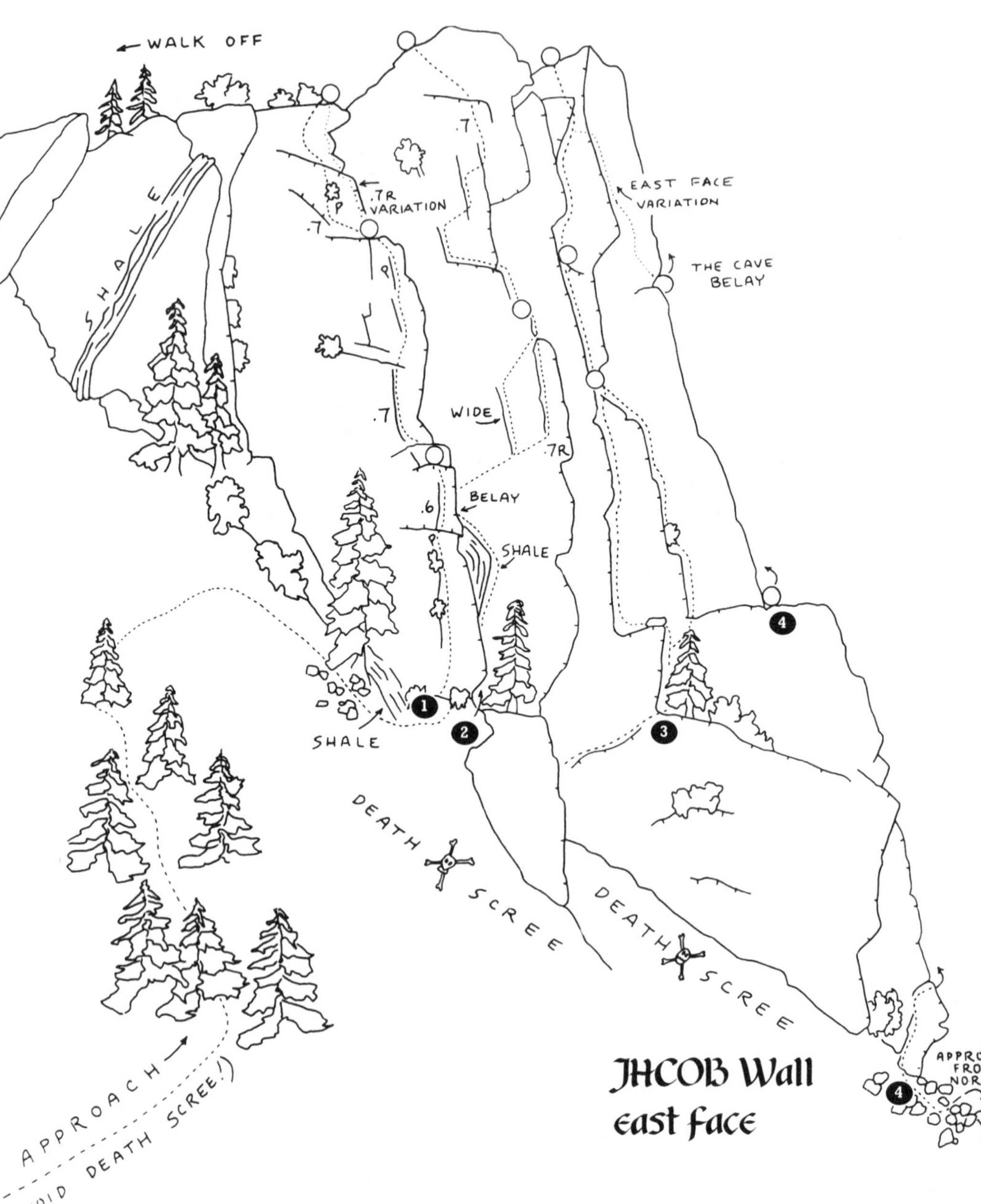

JHCOB Wall
east face

JHCOB WALL

Sometimes called the Jacob wall. JHCOB is an acronym for Jesus H. Christ on a Bicycle. The wall is located directly above the large turn in the road just past the "Remnants of an Ancient Sea" geology sign. Some of the routes on this wall are among the canyon's finest, offering crack systems and a multitude of square edges. However, because of abundant loose rock, a helmet is advised.

APPROACH: For routes 4 to 13, park 2.25 miles up canyon at the pullout marked by the geology sign. All rocks dislodged on the approach and the climb could potentially strike the road, so be extremely careful. From the parking area, walk up canyon on the road for roughly 200 feet, then walk up the talus slope to reach the wall. For the routes east of the Outside Corner, routes 1-3, park as for the Narcolepsy Area. Walk up the stable talus directly above the parking area, then cross one particularly nasty scree slope up high and walk down 60 feet to the climbs. See topos of the wall and overview on page 76.

DESCENT: A hike west from the routes (watch for snakes) along a path lands one at the top of the shale layer. A final steep scree slope drops one back to the parking at the geology sign. Many climbers bring their tennis shoes on the climb to use for the descent

The routes are described left to right.

JHCOB Wall routes

1. SECOND EAST FACE 5.7 ★★
Great cracks in perfect quartzite. Small camming devices are useful. RP's are needed for the final arête variation.

2. FIRST EAST FACE 5.7 ★
Watch for loose rock. Four pitches of disconnected cracks.

3. THE INSIDE CORNER 5.5
Not recommended. Pass the large summit overhang by traversing right on a detached block that accesses an easy crack leading to the top.

4. OUTSIDE CORNER 5.7 ★★
One of the best of its grade in BCC. Take the north face variation on the last pitch for a real thrill. See topo of the north face, on following page.

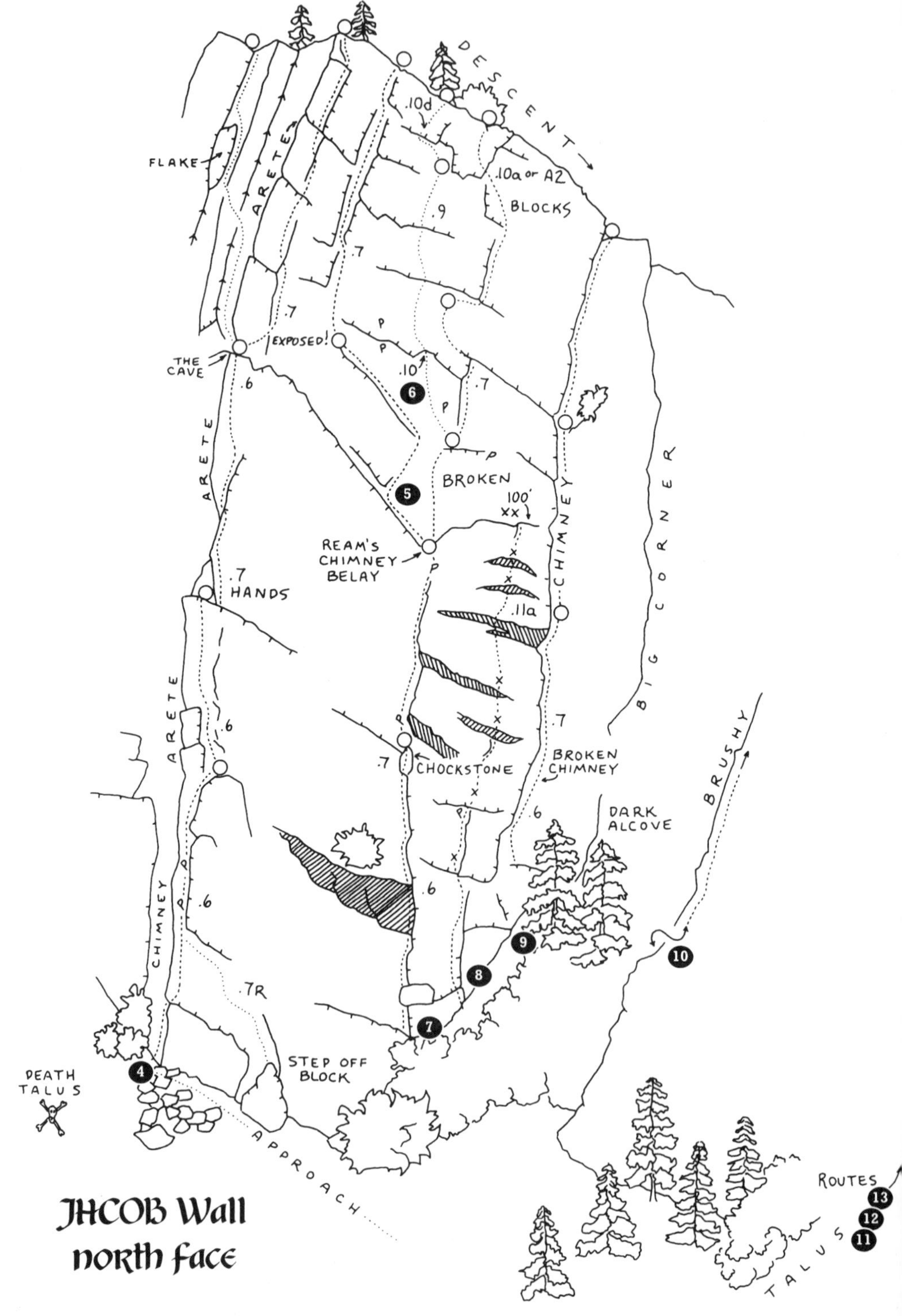

JHCOB Wall north face

JHCOB Wall routes

4. OUTSIDE CORNER 5.7 ★★

One of the best of its grade in BCC. Take the north face variation on the last pitch for a real thrill.

5. REAM'S CHIMNEY 5.7 ★

Climb Straight Up for the first 1-1/2 pitches and traverse left into the chimney system that defines the left side of the big overhang guarding the wall at two-thirds height. A chimney through an overhang on the final pitch is the crux.

FA: Rich Ream and Ted Wilson, 1961.

6. ON THE ROCKS VARIATION 5.10d

Climb the Straight Up route until the third pitch, then branch off left and climb a hand-sized roof crack, the dicey face above, and two more roofs above to the top.

7. STRAIGHT UP II 5.7 A1 or 5.10a

Start in a left-facing corner system 40 feet right of Outside Corner. Climb this for two fairly evident pitches. Then move right, climb up to the roof and traverse left on a six-foot ledge. Work up and left into an alcove and belay. Traverse right (west) 10 feet and climb up to blocks. Aid or hard free climbing straight above the blocks captures the top. Bring small protection.

FFA: Les Ellison and Terry Lein, 1978.

8. WEED KILLER 5.11a ★★

A long pitch that turns roof after roof after roof. In addition to the bolts, you'll need wireds, TCU's, camming devices, and long runners to reduce rope drag. A 60 meter rope or two ropes are needed for the descent.

FA: Andy Ross, Scott Carson and Paul Ross, 1996.

9. DEEP DARK CRACK 5.7

You'll do yourself a big favor by avoiding this route .

10. PEDESTAL 5.6

Low aesthetics. See Deep Dark Crack.

FA: Harold Goodro, Dale Green and Ed Reed, early '50's

JHCOB WALL ROUTES

The following routes are located on a small, overhanging block. This wall is not actually on the JHCOB Wall, rather it sits at the top of a talus slope to the west of the main wall. Approach from the talus 200 feet up canyon from the geology sign.

11. PROJECT

12. OSIRIS 5.13b ★★

A modern classic with a name that is a reflection of the past. Supremely good climbing. A little longer and this would get three stars.
FA: Jeff Baldwin, 1996.

13. WHIPLASH 5.12a or 5.12c ★

This route got its name from an auto accident witnessed during the first ascent – and because of the whiplashing you get when falling off. There are two variations; the right path is easier.
FA: Stuart Ruckman and Gordon Douglass, 1989.

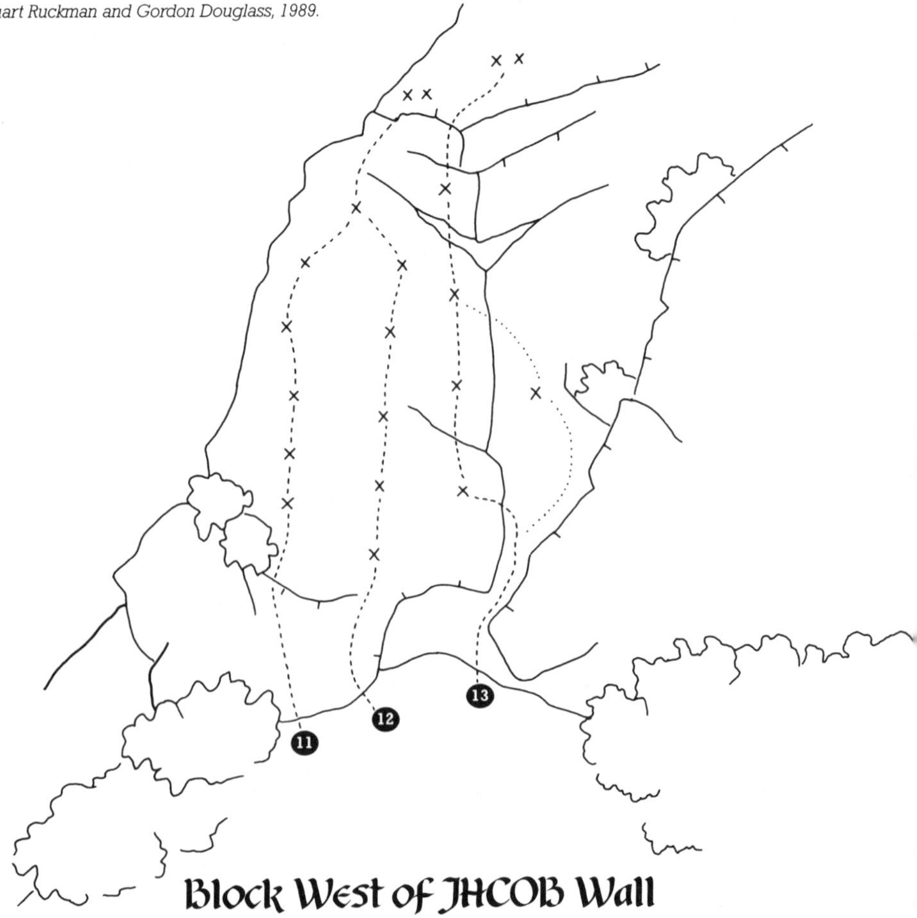

11 12 13

Block West of JHCOB Wall

CREEKSIDE WALL

This smooth section of cliff juts abruptly out of the stream. Vertical cracks and water-polished holds provide the features for the seven routes here. Located across the river from the JHCOB Wall, this east-facing cliff is recommended as a summer and autumn crag, as the usual approach requires a stream crossing.

APPROACH: Park 2.35 miles up canyon from the neon sign. Walk down the embankment and cross the stream on rocks to reach the wall. Another possible approach requires parking down canyon at a pull-out on the east side of the road just below the bridge. Scramble along the old dirt road that parallels the stream and ends at the west end of the wall. See overview on page 76.

DESCENT: A 40-foot rappel from the top of Alien provides escape for routes 1-4. For routes 5-7 make a 60 foot rappel from a two pin one bolt anchor.

CREEKSIDE WALL ROUTES

1. ISOGRAM 5.9- ★★
The straight-in finger crack on the south side is very good and best done during low water.
FA: unknown.

2. ALIEN 5.10a R ★
Climb the left arête. This has sketchy protection.
FA: Drew Bedford, Pokey Amory, Jamie Cameron and Conrad Anker, 1986.

3. CHUTES AND LADDERS 5.11 R
Take this game seriously. Long, dangerous runouts.
FA: Boone Speed and Chris Lacock.

4. RAISIN BRAN 5.9 R ★
Climb the zig-zag crack up the center of the face, ending at a mahogany tree. The pro is thin and sparse from mid-height to the top. Bring brass-type nuts.
FA: Conrad Anker, Pokey Amory, Drew Bedford and Jamie Cameron, 1986.

The next three routes are on the south-facing slab, which is the next buttress east of Creekside Crag.

5. THIEVES' REPRIEVE 5.9 R ★
The leftmost route includes one bolt and some difficult-to-protect territory.
FA: Scott Unice and Julie Gustin, 1990.

6. FACE THE FAX 5.8 ★
The romp up the center part of the slab, past one bolt and one pin to the anchor atop Thieves' Reprieve.
FA: Scott Unice and Julie Gustin, 1990.

7. INTERN'S BURN 5.6
The chossy crack 10 feet right of Face the Fax.
FA: Scott Unice and Julie Gustin, 1990.

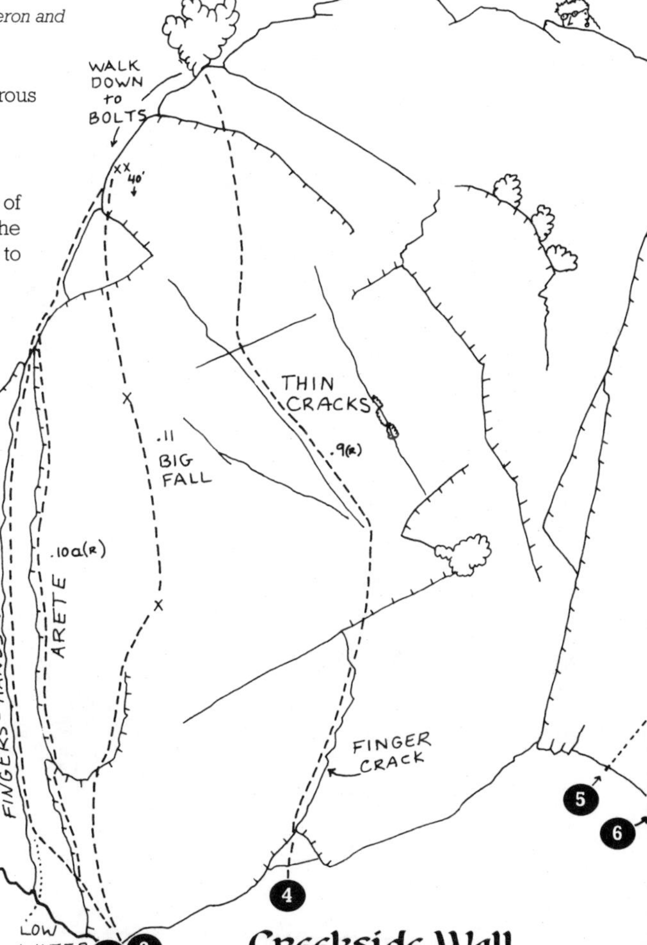

NARCOLEPSY AREA

This crag is almost hidden by pine trees and rests just up canyon from the JHCOB wall on the right (south) side. Within its 100-foot breadth are eleven routes; three others are nearby. The rock quality is tops and the routes linger at vertical or just less than vertical. Most of the wall remains shady throughout the day.

APPROACH: Park 2.4 miles up canyon from the neon sign. A trail heads into a grove of pine trees that sit between two talus slopes. Follow the trail as it heads up and east to the large talus slope running directly down from the Narcolepsy Area. Skip up this shifting hill to the base of the climbs. See overview on page 76.

DESCENT: It is easy enough to walk off all the routes here, but most climbers opt for a sixty foot rappel from the tops of Up a Cliff Without a Ladder, Dreamscape, or Dream Slate.

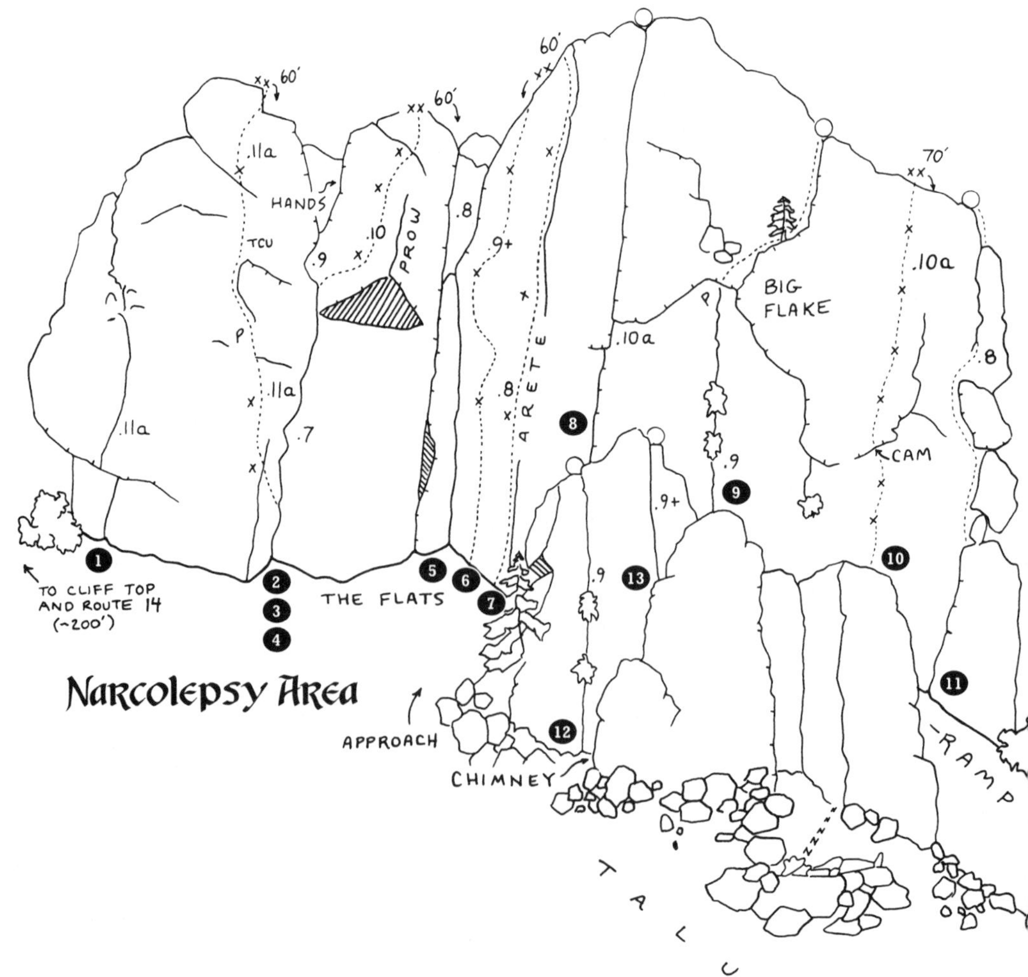

NARCOLEPSY AREA ROUTES

1. ETHIOPIAN KID 5.11a
A crack on the left side of the cliff. The first 20 feet are good and hard, but the crack emaciates, and shattered face climbing prevails.
FA: Bret and Stuart Ruckman, 1985.

2. UP A CLIFF WITHOUT A LADDER 5.11a ★★
This fine face is protected with bolts, TCUs, nuts and pins. A 1/2-inch TCU fits a horizontal seam at two-thirds height.
FA: Bret and Stuart Ruckman, Gordon Douglass, 1986.

3. CHIMNEY SWEEP 5.9+
The chimney system between the two main faces.
FA: Stuart and Bret Ruckman, Gordon Douglass, 1986.

4. MR. SANDMAN 5.10 ★
Jog right about two thirds of the way up Chimney Sweep and climb up the left side of a hanging prow past three bolts.
FA: Gordon Douglass and Stuart Ruckman, 1989.

5. NARCOSIS 5.8
The large chimney at the left side of the Dreamscape wall.

6. DREAMSCAPE 5.9+ ★★
The bolt-protected face that is east-facing.
FA: Stuart, Judy and Bret Ruckman, Gordon Douglass, 1986.

7. NARCOLEPSY 5.8 R ★★
Three bolts.
Follow the apparent edge to a good ledge.
FA: Bret and Judy Ruckman, 1985.

8. INVOLUNTARY RELEASE 5.10a ★★
Thin cracks 4 feet right of Narcolepsy. Micro nuts are key for protection.
FA: Chris Pendleton and Bret Ruckman, 1985.

9. SUTURE FANCY 5.9
A good crack and flake system splitting the center of the north face.

10. DREAM SLATE 5.10a ★★
Thin edges make for enjoyable face climbing. A medium sized camming unit protects the space between the second and third bolts.
FA: Mark Sargent and Mike Kurlich, 1993.

11. TURN OF THE SENTRY 5.8 ★
Climb the hand cracks and blocks near the far west edge of the wall.

12. ANURESIS 5.9 ★
The left crack on somewhat shattered rock.
FA: Fred Thalmann and Frank Ray, 1986.

13. DON'T JUMP BACK CRACK 5.9 ★
Try the right crack without chimneying. Good finger locks on the upper half.
FA: Jim Booth and Lenny Nelson, 1964.

14. NO DOZE 5.10a ★
No Doze, a thin, right-leaning crack splitting a short face is 200 feet above Narcolepsy. It is best viewed from the top of Narcolepsy.
FA: Stuart and Bret Ruckman, 1985.

SALT LAKE SLIPS

High caliber rock, lots of square edges, and moderately difficult bolted routes—it's no wonder that this area is so popular. Add to the mix a comfortable angle and an easy approach and you've got a winner. Facing east, the main wall catches morning sun, while the south face is always shaded and cooled by the river.

APPROACH: Park 2.45 miles up canyon from the neon sign at small pull-outs on either side of the road. This is just up from the Narcolepsy parking, so it can get crowded here. Depending on where you park, walk up or down the road until you are directly across from the wall. Drop down over the embankment to the river. Cross the river on rocks, or if the water is high, use the rope traverse or a log bridge, both of which seem to come and go. Across the river, a good trail leads easily to the base of the wall. See overview on page 76.

DESCENT: All routes can be descended with one rope from anchors at the top of each climb, except for Abracadabra, Senseless Banter and Forgotten Ambition, which require a walk off, or at least a walk to the north to gain the top of the second pitch of Italian Arête, where anchors and two rappels with one rope make it possible to reach the ground.

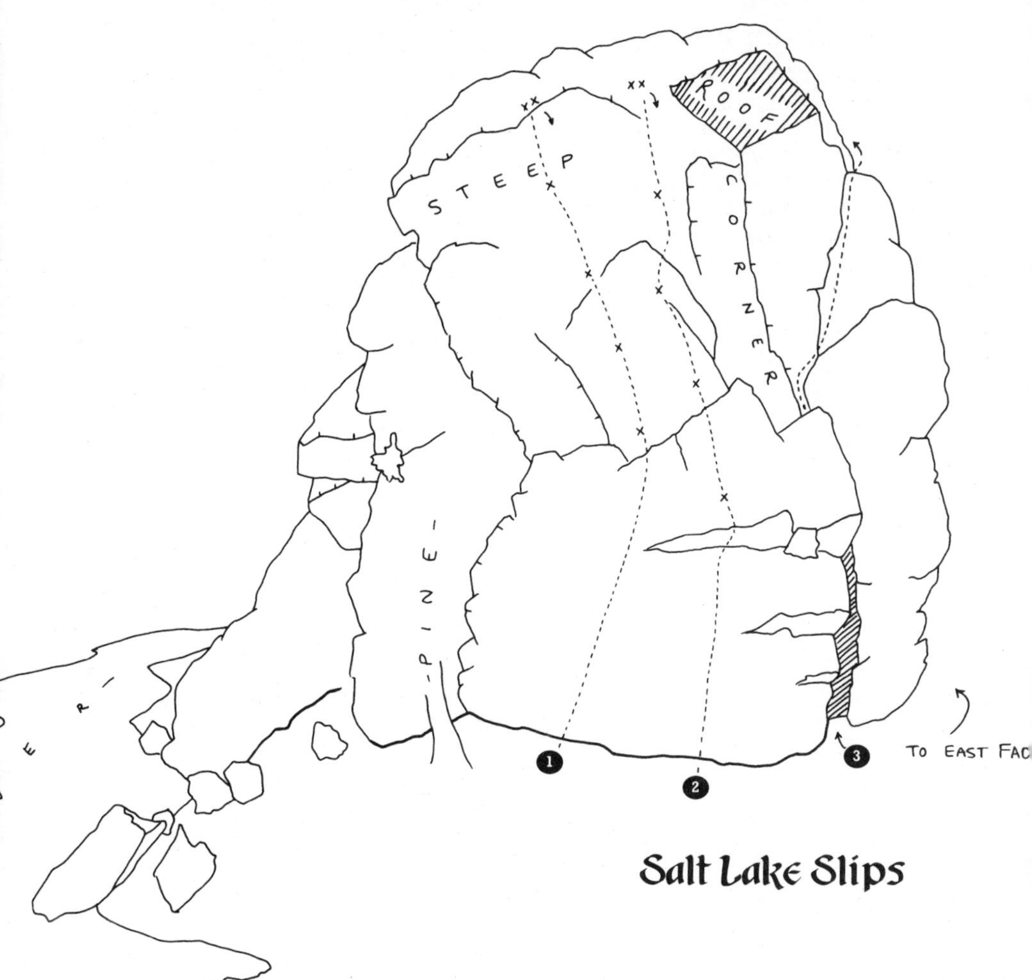

Salt Lake Slips

SALT LAKE SLIPS ROUTES

1. SALEM'S LOT 5.10c ★

Steep pulling up the most overhung part of the south face. Some holds seem possessed, insisting that they lean the wrong way.

FA: Shane Willet and Mike Carnahan, 1992.

2. WITCHHUNT 5.10a ★★

Prolonged moves, good holds, steep rock.

FA: Shane Willet and Mike Carnahan, 1992.

3. ABRACADABRA 5.5

Start up the chimney, then move right to a hand crack on the face. Follow the crack around the corner and face climb to the top.

FA: Unknown.

SALT LAKE SLIPS ROUTES

4. SENSELESS BANTER 5.9+ ★

This route climbs thin cracks up to a solitary bolt in the middle of a triangular-shaped face. A crack above leads past an ugly pin to the top. Bring a standard rack with an emphasis on the small stuff.

FA: Scott Unice and Julie Gustin, 1990.

5. FORGOTTEN AMBITION 5.9

Follow thin seams in a smooth, dark face 20 feet left of the Italian Arête. Meander past a small pine tree to a bolt, then up the face above to a small right-leaning corner. This leads to the top. A standard rack is sufficient.

FA: Scott Unice and Julie Gustin, 1990.

6. ITALIAN ARETE 5.6 ★★

Two pitches, although only the first is commonly climbed. The line is hard to miss—follow the arête to the ledge.

FA: Tony Calderone, 1992.

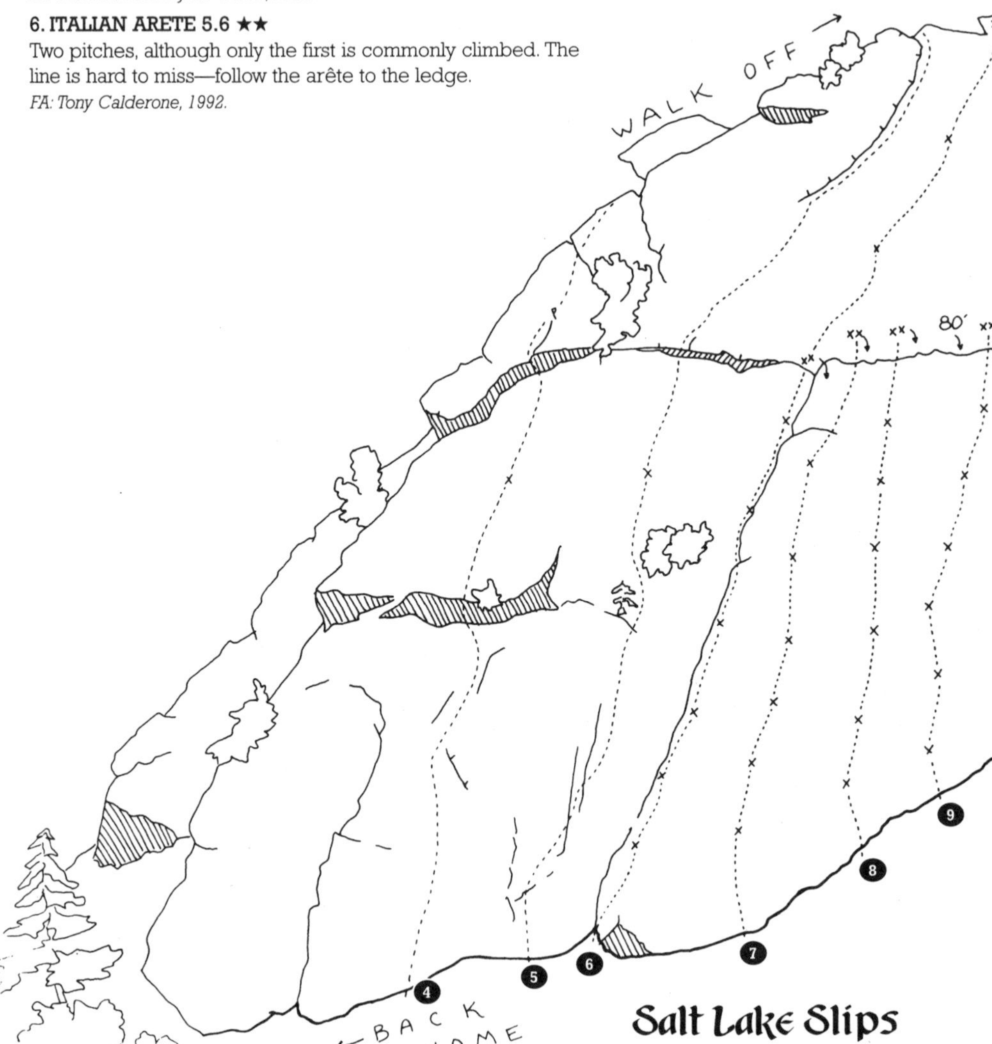

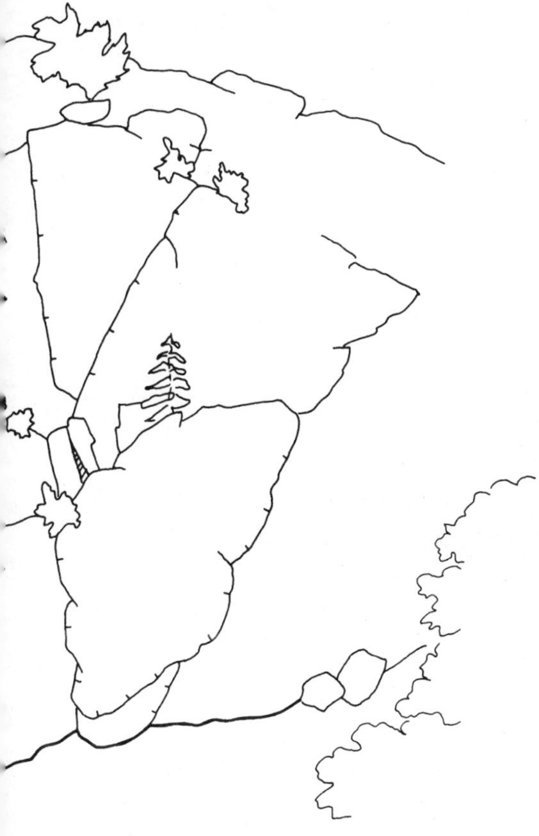

7. ENTRE NOUS 5.8+ ★★

Eighty feet of edging on the face just right of the arête.

FA: Stuart Ruckman and Libby Ellis, 1989.

8. THIEVING MAGPIE 5.7 ★★

More clean, crisp edge climbing, this time with a thin crux.

FA: Paul Hodges and Ray Dahl, 1992.

9. ROLL THE BONES 5.6 ★★

It's action, reaction, random interaction... A fine line of continuous edges and deliberate moves on a shield of quartzite.

FA: Ray Dahl and Paul Hodges, 1991.

Hidden Fortress
Buena Vista Wall
Glass Oc
Area
Patty's
Ridge
Redrum Wall
Vector
Madness
Dead Snag
Arête Area
Face to Face
Area

STANDARD RIDGE AREA OVERVIEW
(See overview on page 76.)
Lonely Challenge Area
Standard Ridge
Talk Wall
Strone Crag
Challenge Buttress (east face)

STANDARD RIDGE

This ridge is located between the Narcolepsy Area and the Challenge Gully. The ridge has three main faces—the west, which is broken and shattered up to the point that it begins to overhang at the Rush Wall, the north, known as the Strone Crag, and the east face, which is the smooth Lonely Challenge Wall. These many faces have one common link—quality routes on very good rock.

APPROACH: There are two separate approaches, depending upon which wall is the final destination. See the individual wall descriptions for the approach information. See overview on pages 76 and 90.

DESCENT: In most cases, rappel the route. However, for the Standard Ridge route, a scramble east to Stair's Gulch is recommended.

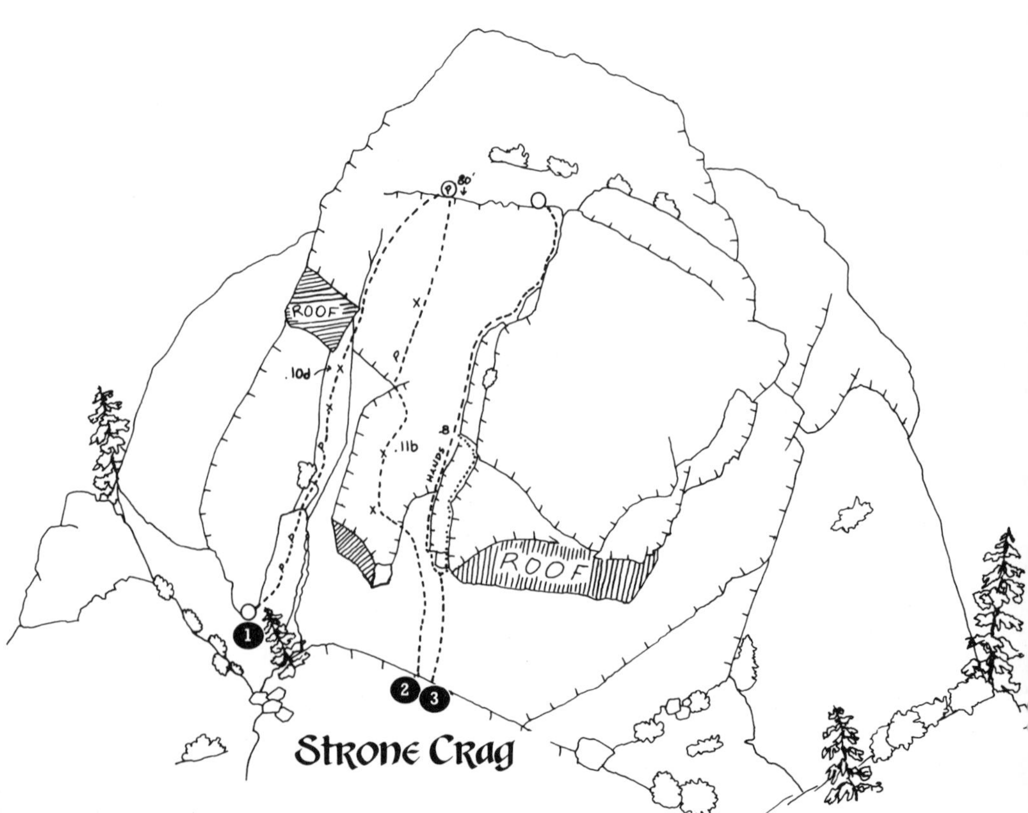

STANDARD RIDGE NORTH FACE —STRONE CRAG

The north side of the Standard Ridge has a steep face with a prominent roof band on its right side.

APPROACH: Approach as for the Narcolepsy Area. Walk east past the routes there and follow a trail east that crosses the talus and reaches the north end of the Standard Ridge. Some scrambling gains the base of the routes. See overview on pages 76 and 90.

DESCENT: An eighty foot rappel from the top of Le Rap Et Tap reaches the ground.

STRONE CRAG ROUTES

1. REAR-VIEW MIRRORS 5.10d
Thin face climbing up the smooth, east-facing section of the Standard Ridge. The route is divided in the middle by a big crack.
FA: Stuart Ruckman, 1987.

2. LE RAP ET TAP 5.11b ★★
Start a few feet left of Wealth of Nations in an open corner. Move past a loose block (a small micro nut works well here) and climb past three bolts and one pin to the top. The weird start is more than compensated for by superb face climbing.
FA: Dana Hauser, Jim Hall and Scott Carson, 1987.

3. WEALTH OF NATIONS 5.8 ★★
The left-facing corner system on the left side of the roof band. Fun route.
FFA: Dave Smith, 1970's.

4. STANDARD RIDGE II 5.6 ★★
The ridge crest runs from the Strone Crag all the way up to the top of the Lonely Challenge Wall, and above. Access this crest by starting on the northeast corner of the buttress in a corner system, or climbing the east or west faces via more broken rock. The other vertical section, near the top of the Lonely Challenge Wall, can be bypassed on the west. Descend off the east side, eventually joining the Stair's Gulch trail.

STANDARD RIDGE WEST FACE —RUSH WALL

Well up the Standard Ridge Route is a small overhanging wall with superb rock. This wall faces west and is split by a right-leaning hand and finger crack.

APPROACH: The best approach is from the talus gully on the west side of Challenge Buttress. Approach as for the Challenge Buttress West Face. Continue up the talus gully. About two-thirds of the way up this gully, walk through a gap in the right (west) wall to gain the west face. Scramble up fourth-class rock to the base of the overhanging wall. See overview on page 76.

DESCENT: Two bolts at the top of La Villa Strangiato provide a handy rappel with a single rope.

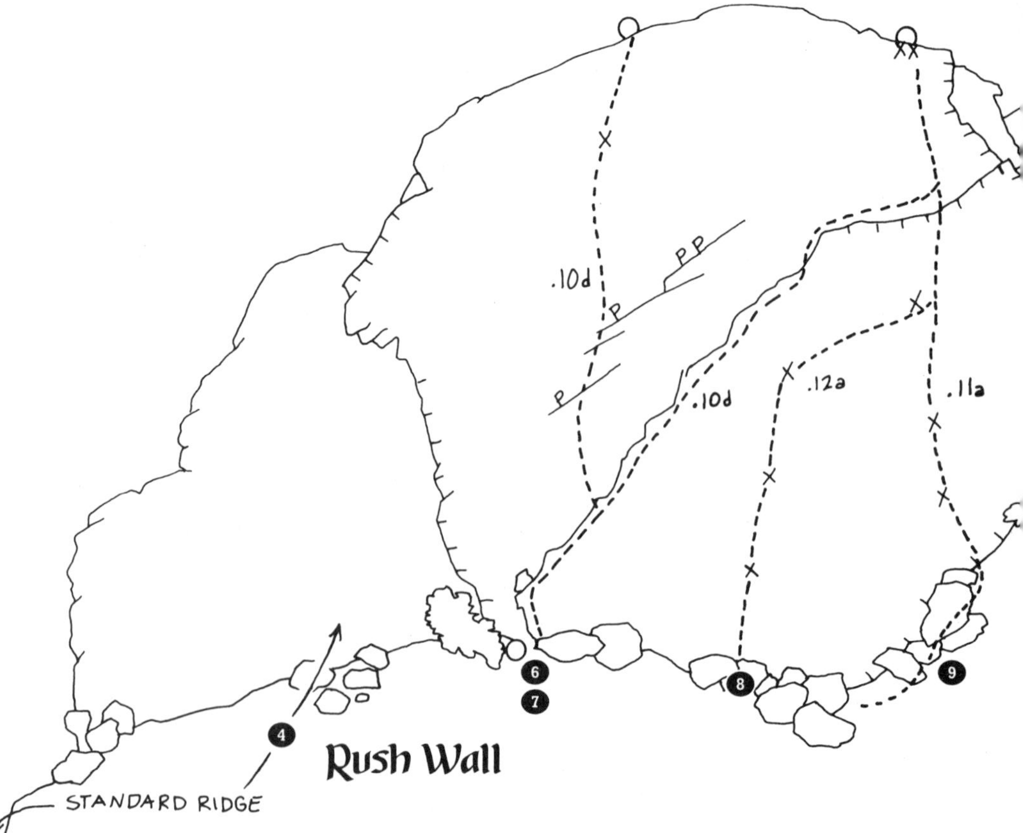

RUSH WALL ROUTES

5. MSR BREAKDOWN 5.11a ★

This route isn't located on the Rush Wall, but is found along the approach. Climb a hand-and-finger crack in the north face above the gap that you pass through en route to the Rush Wall.

FA: Drew Bedford and Doug Heinrich, 1986.

6. NEW WORLD MAN 5.10d ★★

Climb La Villa Strangiato for 10 feet, then cut left and up past some old fixed iron. Exit past a bolt. Bring a couple mid-sized nuts for a belay 15 feet back from the rim.

FA: Stuart and Bret Ruckman, 1990.

7. LA VILLA STRANGIATO 5.10d ★★

This crack is elegant and strange. Bring along 1 1/2 and 2 inch camming devices.

FA: Stuart and Bret Ruckman, 1990.

8. RUSH 'N BRAVADO 5.12a ★★

If you're poised for a pump, try this beautiful route. Bring a few mid-sized nuts for protection above the fourth bolt.

FA: Bret and Stuart Ruckman, 1990.

9. 2112 5.11a ★★

The "dike-like" feature on the right side is loads of fun. Protection as for Rush 'N Bravado.

FA: Stuart and Bret Ruckman, 1990.

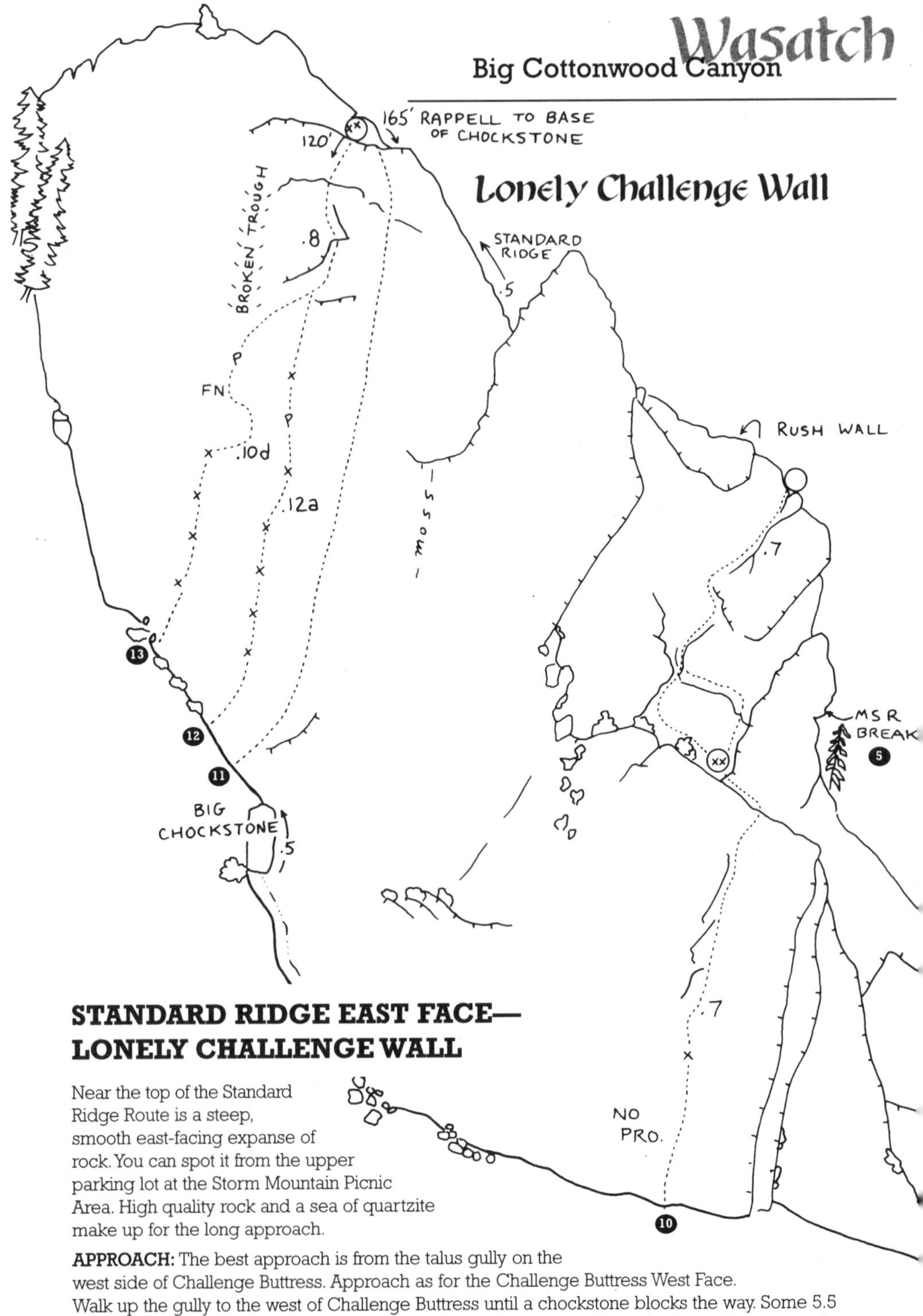

STANDARD RIDGE EAST FACE—LONELY CHALLENGE WALL

Near the top of the Standard Ridge Route is a steep, smooth east-facing expanse of rock. You can spot it from the upper parking lot at the Storm Mountain Picnic Area. High quality rock and a sea of quartzite make up for the long approach.

APPROACH: The best approach is from the talus gully on the west side of Challenge Buttress. Approach as for the Challenge Buttress West Face. Walk up the gully to the west of Challenge Buttress until a chockstone blocks the way. Some 5.5 climbing (usually wet) leads past the chockstone. Just above, you'll see the bolts. Stinging nettle and ferns populate the angled base. See overview on pages 76 and 90.

DESCENT: If you want to avoid the downclimb past the chockstone, a rappel from the two-bolt anchor at the top of Zen And The Art reaches the base of the chockstone (165+ feet.)

LONELY CHALLENGE WALL ROUTES

10. BROKEN DREAMS 5.7 ★

A two pitch flight of fancy that features one protection bolt, some good rock, a little bad rock, a nice crack, and widely spaced protection that requires creativity to secure.

FA: Brian Smoot and Jonathan Smoot, 1995.

11. LONELY CHALLENGE 5.8 R ★

Climb the face 20 feet right of Zen and the Art for 165 feet. Bring pins for protection.

FA: Stuart and Bret Ruckman, 1984.

12. ZEN AND THE ART 5.12a ★★

A Big Cottonwood thin face test piece. Adhere to the wall 10 feet right of Lone Man Running. Climb on small holds past six bolts—one hard to clip—and one pin. Bring a selection of small gear for the runout (but easy) upper face. Two ropes required for the descent.

FA: Stuart and Bret Ruckman, 1990.

13. LONE MAN RUNNING 5.10d ★★★

Climb the left bolt line on the smooth face. Bring a selection of small gear for the runout (but easy) upper face. Two ropes are needed for the descent.

FA: Bret and Stuart Ruckman, 1990.

Merrill Bitter throwing a little dynamic on Crosseyed and Painless, Dogwood Crag.

photo: Jeff Baldwin.

CHALLENGE BUTTRESS

The Challenge Buttress is a complex cluster of outcrops and gullies that are difficult to see from the road. It is located 200 yards east of Narcolepsy Area and 100 yards east of Strone Crag. It is the first crag west of Stair's Gulch. The routes are described from left to right.

APPROACH: Park 2.55 miles up canyon from the neon sign. This pullout is on the north side of the road (at the south end of the Dark Star Gully) about 100 yards down canyon from the Storm Mountain Picnic Area. Scramble up the steep embankment just above the road on the west side of Stair's Gulch stream. A trail from here leads through the trees up to the crag, where it forks. The left fork leads to the Challenge Buttress East Face and the Talk Buttress beyond. The right path leads to the Challenge Buttress West Face, the Sales Pitch Area, and the Lonely Challenge Area. See overview on pages 76 and 90.

DESCENT: Most of the routes have anchors at the top where single rope rappels reach the ground. With the exception of Lateral Force and Falling Apart At The Seams, which require different walk offs, the remaining routes without anchors at their finish can be descended by walking north towards the northeast corner of the buttress, where a chimney provides a quick down climb to the ground.

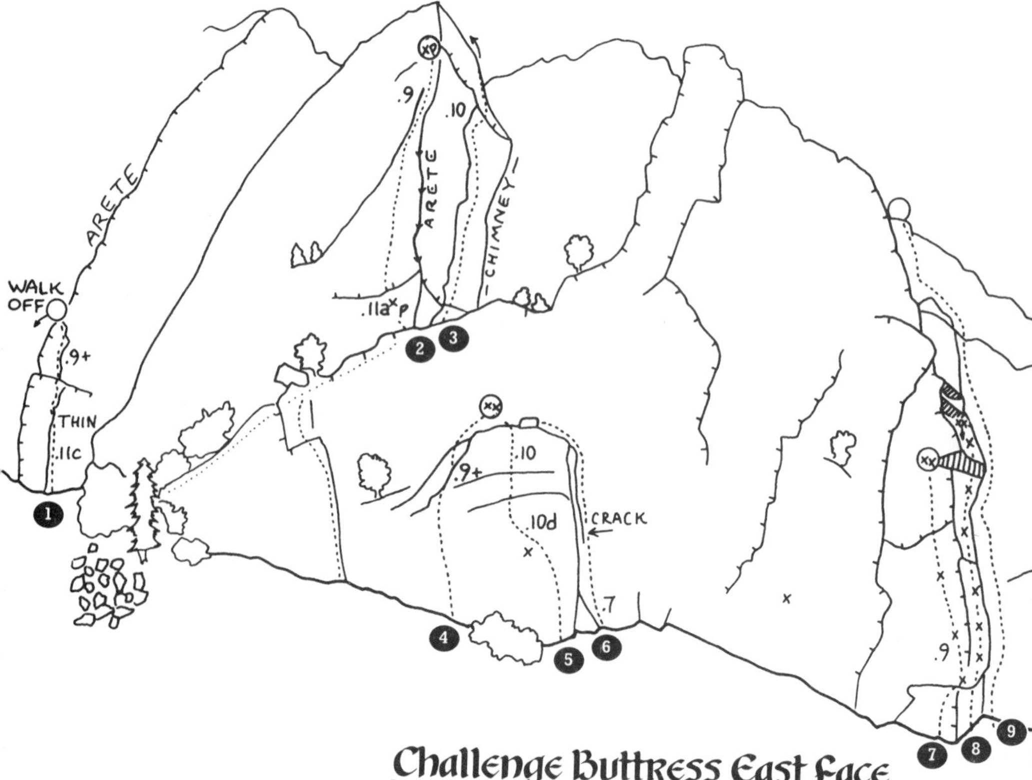

Challenge Buttress East Face

CHALLENGE BUTTRESS EAST FACE

1. PUMP UP THE JAM 5.11c

The north-facing crack 100 feet left of Deltoid Force. Shattered rock and hard-to-place gear.

FA: Stuart and Bret Ruckman, 1990.

2. DELTOID FORCE 5.11a ★★

Traverse along a ledge from the south to reach the base. Crank a heinous move past a bolt, and stem a fold of beautiful quartzite to a ledge with rappel anchors.

FA: Stuart Ruckman and Gary Olsen, 1986.

3. LATERAL FORCE 5.10c R

Climb a crack in the north face 10 feet to the right of Deltoid Force. RP's and TCU's are helpful.

FA: Gary Olsen, Stuart and Bret Ruckman, 1986.

4. TEFLON TECHNIQUE 5.9+ ★

Skid up the face 10 feet left of Touch of Teflon. Brass-type nuts are needed.

FA: Merrill Bitter, et al, 1989.

5. TOUCH OF TEFLON 5.10d ★

Climb up the teflon-smooth face directly to a bolt. The upper face protects with small to medium sized nuts.

FA: Stuart Ruckman and Libby Ellis, 1988.

6. DAILY DIATRIBE 5.7

A short hand and finger crack that protects well.

FA: Unknown.

7. CORAL BELLS ARETE 5.9 ★★

Pull an overhang and follow bolts up the arête to a two-bolt anchor. Bring a few nuts.

FA: Pat Contor, Gary Taylor, and Kevin Sweeny, 1988.

8. CHAMBERED NAUTILUS 5.10a ★

Six bolts' worth of roof-turning that's guaranteed to twist the forearms.

FA: Shane Willet and Mike Carnahan, 1995.

9. BIRTH SIMULATOR 5.6

Dirty, vegetated, and lichen covered.

FA: Tony Calderone, 1992.

10. STRONG PERSUADER 5.8 R

Climb the face immediately left of the corner on Leftoverture.

FA: Stuart Ruckman and Gordon Douglass, 1987.

11. LEFTOVERTURE 5.9 ★

Climb the right-facing corner until it ends, then continue to the top.

FA: Stuart Ruckman and Gordon Douglass, 1987.

12. OVERTURE 5.10a R ★

Branch right off of Leftoverture and figure out some tricky moves by a pin.

FA: Stuart Ruckman and Gordon Douglass, 1987.

13. RASPBERRY RIPPLE 5.10a ★

Great rock. Gear is needed after the third bolt. Weird bolt placements.

FA: Pat Contor, Gary Taylor and Kevin Sweeney, 1988.

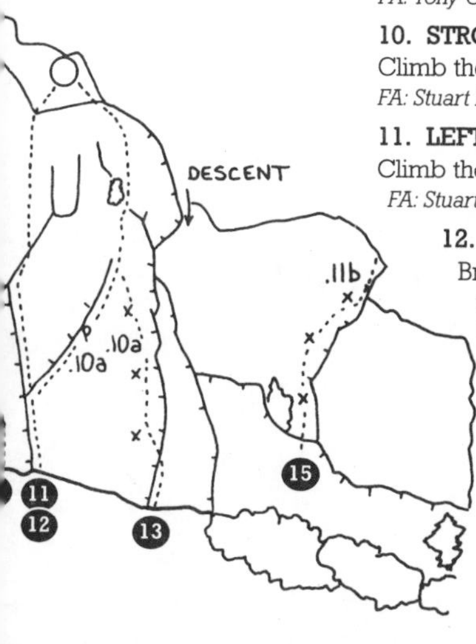

CHALLENGE BUTTRESS NORTH FACE

These routes are located near or climb across the large roof.

14. ON A WHIM 5.8-
Super short crack on a north-facing wall left of Tuff'n Up. Not on topo.
FA: Ray Dahl and Kelly Amott, 1990.

15. TUFF 'N UP 5.11b ★★
Follow three bolts and a series of holds trending to the right. It is slightly easier (but not as fun) if you don't complete the rightward traverse in its entirety.
FA: Stuart and Bret Ruckman, 1986.

16. TUFF ENOUGH 5.8 ★
A fun crack 25 feet left of Guilt Trip. Not on topo.
FA: Stuart Ruckman, 1986.

17. GUILT TRIP 5.10d ★★
Force the roof (2 bolts) and enjoy the steep face above.
FA: Bret and Stuart Ruckman, 1986.

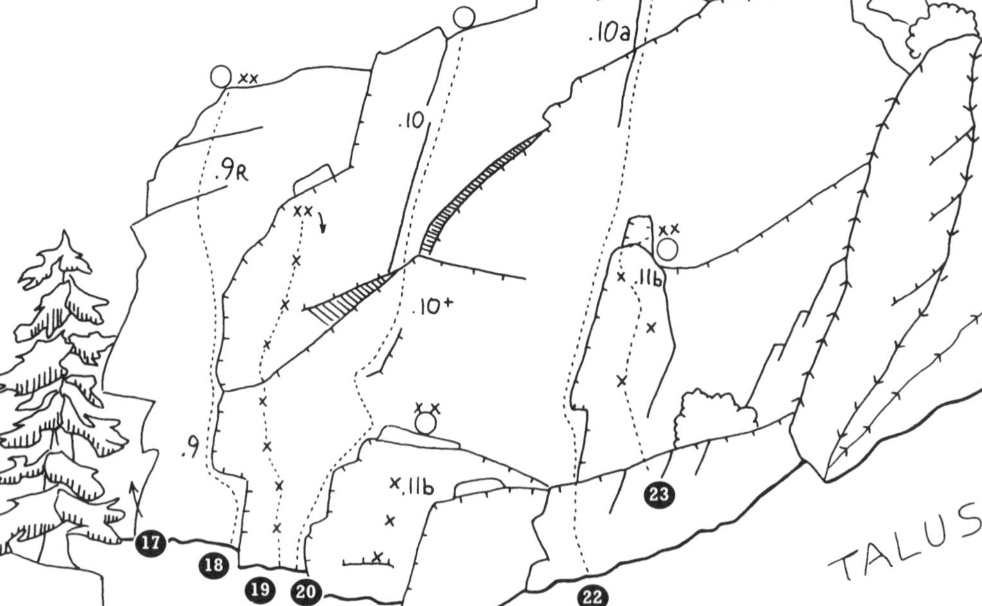

Challenge Buttress West Face

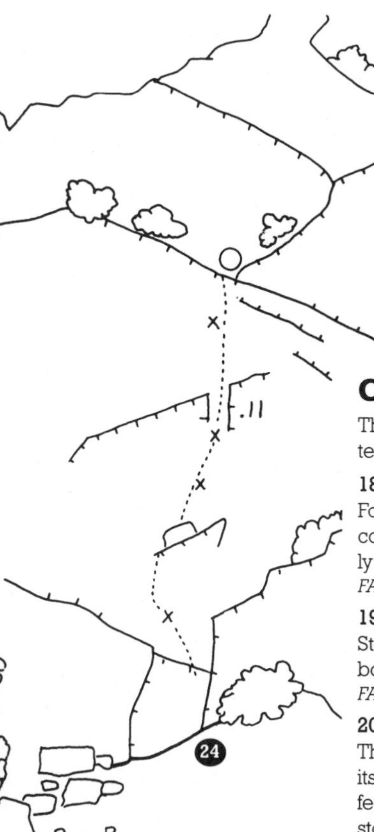

CHALLENGE BUTTRESS WEST FACE

The rock on this side of the Challenge Buttress is more shattered than the East Face, but also steeper.

18. FLAMIN' FREDDIE 5.9 R ★★

Follow a left-facing dihedral to a continuously difficult face. The composed leader will enjoy the upper face, protected primarily with RP's. Superb Rock.

FA: Stuart Ruckman and Fred Thalmann, 1986.

19. HOLLOW MAN 5.9 ★★

Steep to slightly overhanging rock separates the men from the boys.

FA: Mark Nakada, Shane Willet, Mike Carnahan, 1995.

20. PINS AND KNICKERS 5.11a R ★★

The pins-and-knickers crowd will delight over this route with its lack of fixed protection. Start up the left-facing dihedral 10 feet right of Flamin' Freddie. Bring RP's and small to medium stoppers.

FA: Stuart Ruckman, Gordon Douglass, Eric Stroud, and Libby Ellis, 1987.

21. WINKY AND WAXMAN GO BOLTING 5.11b ★

Three bolts protect this short yet popular overhanging block.

FA: Merrill Bitter and Robyn Waxman, 1987.

22. SPLIT SEAM 5.10a R ★★

An archetypal BCC climb – hard to discern and hard to protect. Climb the corner left of Diminishing Returns and up the overhanging crack to the top.

FA: Gary Olsen and Steve Britt, 1985.

23. DIMINISHING RETURNS 5.11b ★★

A crowd pleaser, with well-protected climbing. A stopper helps protect the initial moves.

FA: Stuart Ruckman and Gordon Douglass, 1987.

24. FALLING APART AT THE SEAMS 5.11b ★★

This hard to see line starts off a ledge 200 feet up hill to the south of Diminishing Returns. Traverse left to a bolt and pump it out to ledge. Climb up into a weird slot past two more bolts and unravel the crux. More strenuous moves lead to the top. The bolts were added by the first ascent party to replace several sketchy pins.

FA: Stuart Ruckman and Fred Thalmann, 1986.

CHALLENGE BUTTRESS—SALES PITCH AREA

A prominent corner topped by a roof is the main feature on this wall. Located about 300 feet up the Challenge Buttress scree gully from Falling Apart at the Seams. See overview on page 76.

25. DON'T JUDGE A BOOK BY ITS COVER 5.9+ R ★

A north-facing corner arching to the right leads to an undercling, and then the top. Bring RP's and small TCU's for the sparse protection.

FA: Bret and Stuart Ruckman, 1986.

26. SALES PITCH 5.10d ★★

Climb the compact face right of Don't Judge A Book past four bolts. A small TCU is helpful near the top. Also, a 2-1/2" cam is advised to back up the single-bolt anchor.

FA: Bret and Stuart Ruckman, Libby Ellis, 1990.

27. POKEY'S OVERHANG 5.10b ★

A slippery hand-crack problem.

FA: Pokey Amory and Bret Ruckman, 1986.

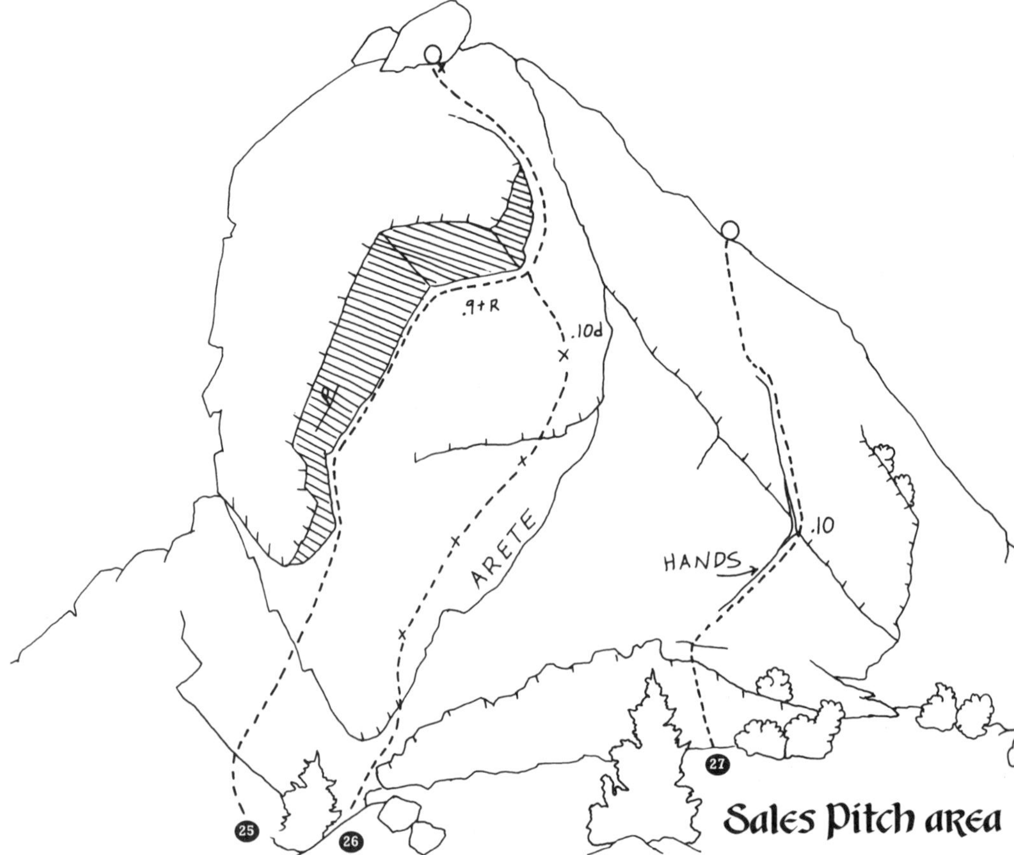

TALK BUTTRESS

This north-facing cliff, with its two prominent right-angling cracks, lies between the Dead Snag Arête and The Challenge Buttress East Side. Quiet and shady, this is a good wall to visit if the crowds are getting you down. See overview on pages 76 and 90.

APPROACH: Follow the approach to the Challenge Buttress East Face. From there, simply continue up the talus gully to this wall which sits at the head of the gully.

DESCENT: Walk off to the west for routes 2 and 4. For route 1, scramble down the ledge and make some tricky moves (best to belay) to reach the start of route 2.

1. EMPTY RHETORIC 5.10c R ★
Climb the thin crack rising from beneath the chockstone on the far left side of the buttress.
FA: Bret and Stuart Ruckman, 1990.

2. LOOK WHO'S TALKING 5.8 ★
Start off of a chockstone and climb the right-leaning dihedral/crack in one long pitch.
FA: unknown.

3. TALKING TOUGH 5.9 ★★
Climb the face in between the two prominent crack systems, crossing Look Who's Talking above the overhang. Good rock. Bring some medium to small pieces.
FA: Bret and Stuart Ruckman, 1990.

4. NOTALOTATALK 5.8 ★★
Lieback a flake and join a nice right-slanting crack to a good ledge.
FA: unknown.

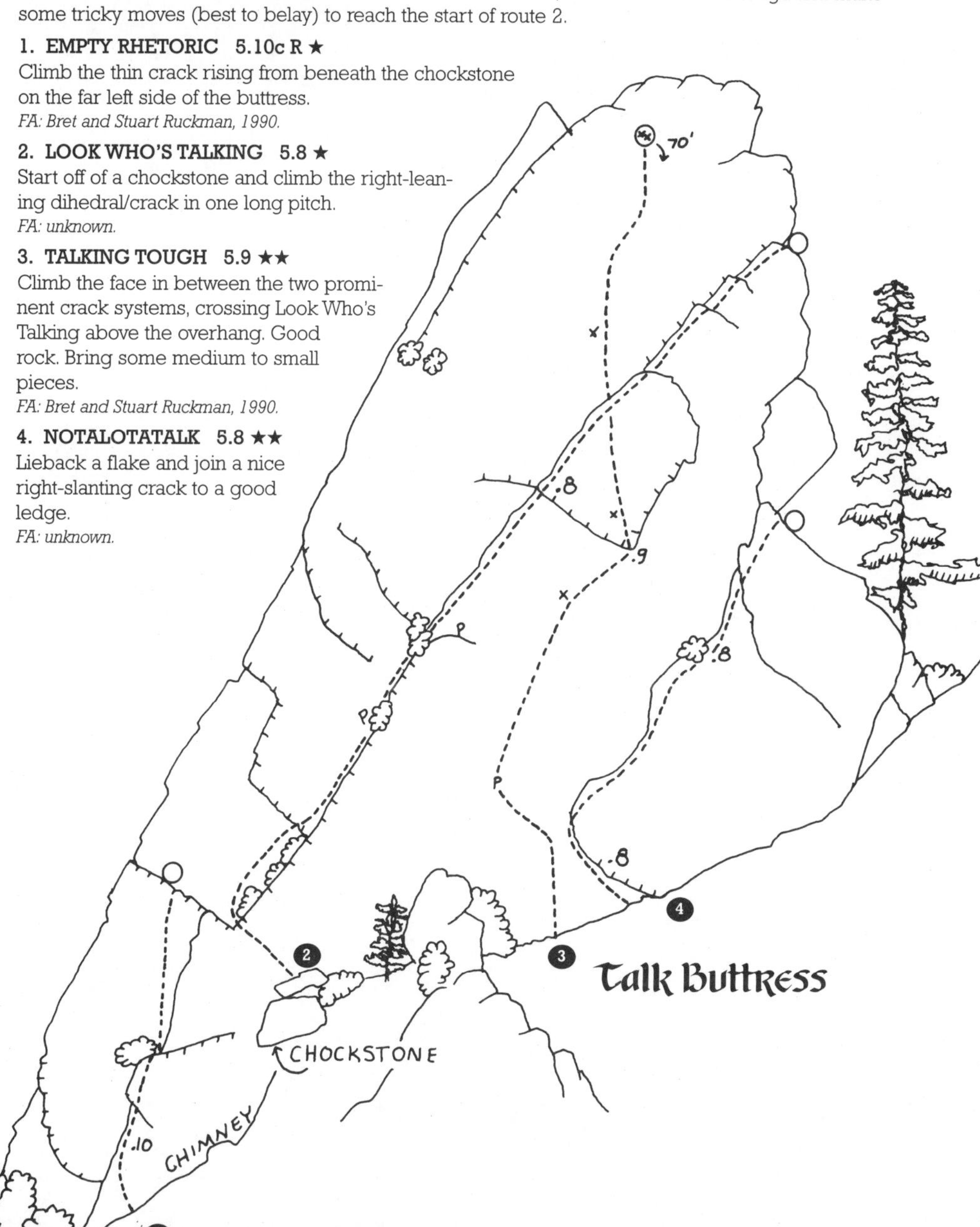

SELDOM SCENE GULLY

When driving up canyon from the JHCOB Wall to the Storm Mountain Picnic Area, you may notice a series of gullies on the left (north) side of the road. These gullies run north and south, from the Storm Mountain "Island" to the Big Cottonwood stream. The first gully is the Creekside Crag, the second is The Slips and the third, The Seldom Scene Gully. West facing, these routes cross broken looking rock that forms the east side of the gully.

APPROACH: Park 2.55 miles up canyon from the neon sign at the mouth of the canyon. There is a pull-out on the north side of the road. In low water, simply walk down the road 150 feet from the parking, hop the rocks across the stream, and walk up the gully to the routes. A longer approach is involved in the spring runoff season. Follow the approach information for the Storm Mountain Island North Face. From the amphitheater, walk north along a good trail that switchbacks up the hill to the west of the baseball diamond to a pass with a powerline pole. From the pass, continue walking up and south until a trail cuts off to the right (southwest). This trail will deposit you near the head of a gully that drains towards the stream. This first gully is the Dark Star Gully. Walk west several hundred more feet to reach the top of the Seldom Scene Gully. Scramble down the gully to reach the routes. See overview page 76.

Seldom Scene Gully

The magnificent backdrop at the Hellgate Cliffs. Climbing Mon Ami.

photo: Craig Dillon.

SELDOM SCENE GULLY ROUTES

1. LUNAR CLIPS 5.11b ★

Featured face climbing leads to a barren arête.

FA: Randy Kieliszewski and Steve Habovstak, lunar eclipse, 1994.

2. LAST CALL 5.10d ★

Harder than it looks. Small to medium gear protects the flake on the upper face.

FA: Randy Kieliszewski and Jon Ray.

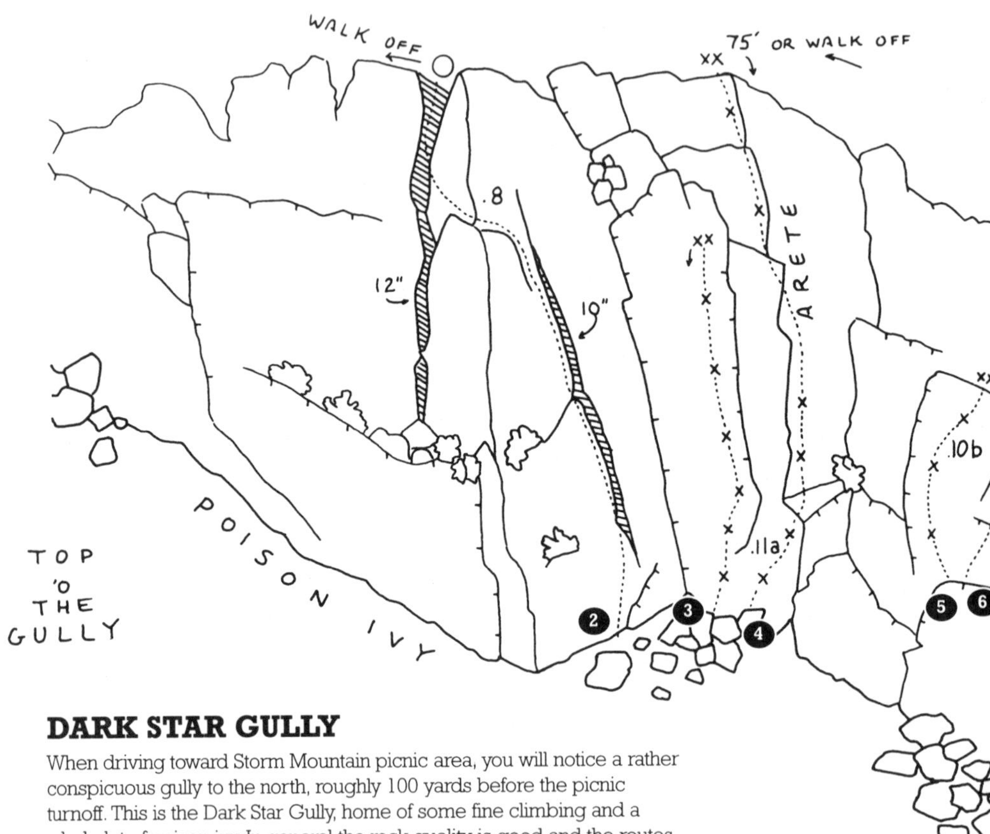

DARK STAR GULLY

When driving toward Storm Mountain picnic area, you will notice a rather conspicuous gully to the north, roughly 100 yards before the picnic turnoff. This is the Dark Star Gully, home of some fine climbing and a whole lot of poison ivy. In general the rock quality is good and the routes are steep—a nice combination.

APPROACH: The best approach is possible during low water. Simply park 2.55 miles up canyon from the neon sign at a pullout on the north side of the road, right where the Stairs Gulch stream crosses under the main highway. From here hop rocks across the stream to reach the route of choice. A longer approach is involved in the spring runoff season. Follow the approach information for the Storm Mountain Island North Face. From the amphitheater, walk north along a good trail that switchbacks up the hill to the west of the baseball diamond to a pass with a powerline pole. From the pass, continue walking up and south until a trail cuts off to the right (southwest). This trail will deposit you near the head of a gully that drains down towards the stream. This is the Dark Star Gully. The routes are on the west-facing wall of the gully. Beware of poison ivy, especially in the lower reaches of the gully. See overview on page 76.

DESCENT: For route 2, simply walk to the top of the gully and back down. Routes 3-6 and route 8 can be rappelled. Routes 9 to 12 require a quick walk off down the gully to the east.

DARK STAR GULLY ROUTES (upper wall)

1. DARWIN 5.9 ★

A steep, south-facing route located just above the stream on the wall that forms the west margin of the gully. Small to medium sized gear protects the crack that leads up to the first bolt. Cool edges pass one more bolt and reach the top.

2. THE BIRDS 5.8

Climb the fat crack left of Karmic Whiplash. A hand traverse left into another crack concludes the show.

FA: Stuart Ruckman, 1985.

3. KARMIC WHIPLASH 5.12b ★★

Steep and tricky, but it's all there. Have Fun!

FA: Douglas Heinrich and Kevin Fosburg, 1996.

4. THE WRAITH 5.11a ★★

Great climbing on a west-facing arête near the head of the Dark Star Gully. An apparition of a famous old climber was seen on the first ascent, prompting the name. A 1 1/2" camming unit protects the mid-section.

FA: Stuart Ruckman, Doug Heinrich and Bob Ingall, 1989.

5. SPRING INTO ACTION 5.10b ★

Climb an arête past 3 bolts to chains. Being tall helps mitigate the crux.

FA: Todd Evans and Drew Bedford, 1989.

6. SPRING FLING 5.9 R ★

Obvious thin crack right of Spring Into Action.

FA: Andy Marker and Doug Heinrich, 1989.

7. ARTIST'S RENDITION 5.8

Climb the short hand crack.

FA: unknown.

Dark Star Gully upper wall

DARK STAR GULLY ROUTES (lower wall)

8. GUNS AND BULLETS 5.11d ★

Have your guns loaded for this short standoff. Three bolts up the steep face left of Headbanging Dudes.

FA: Boone Speed, 1989.

9. HEADBANGING DUDES 5.10

Named for the hard-rockers that used to hang out in the Storm Mountain parking lot. A crack on a prow of rock, the route is clearly visible from the road. Guns and Bullets is two feet left.

FA: Scott Carson and Todd Cozzens, 1986.

10. WINKY WALKS THE DOG 5.11d R

Climb the face seven feet right of Headbanging Dudes. Led from the ground up.

FA: Merrill Bitter and Paul Lanz, 1987.

11. BLACK HEART 5.10d X

Climb the face left of the right-facing corner to a ledge, and continue up the face to the top. #1 RP's are critical.

FA: Merrill Bitter and Paul Lanz, 1987.

12. SHIBUMI 5.11a R ★

Hand traverse right to reach cracks six feet right of the prominent corner that houses a bush. Climb the faint cracks on great rock. Micro nuts and tri-cams are indispensable. Lead from the ground up.

FA: Stuart Ruckman and Merrill Bitter, 1987.

13. DARK STAR 5.11 R

A short one-bolt route on the offshoot piece of rock right on the stream. Micro nuts are needed.

FA: Merrill Bitter and Paul Lanz, 1987.

Dark Star Gully lower wall

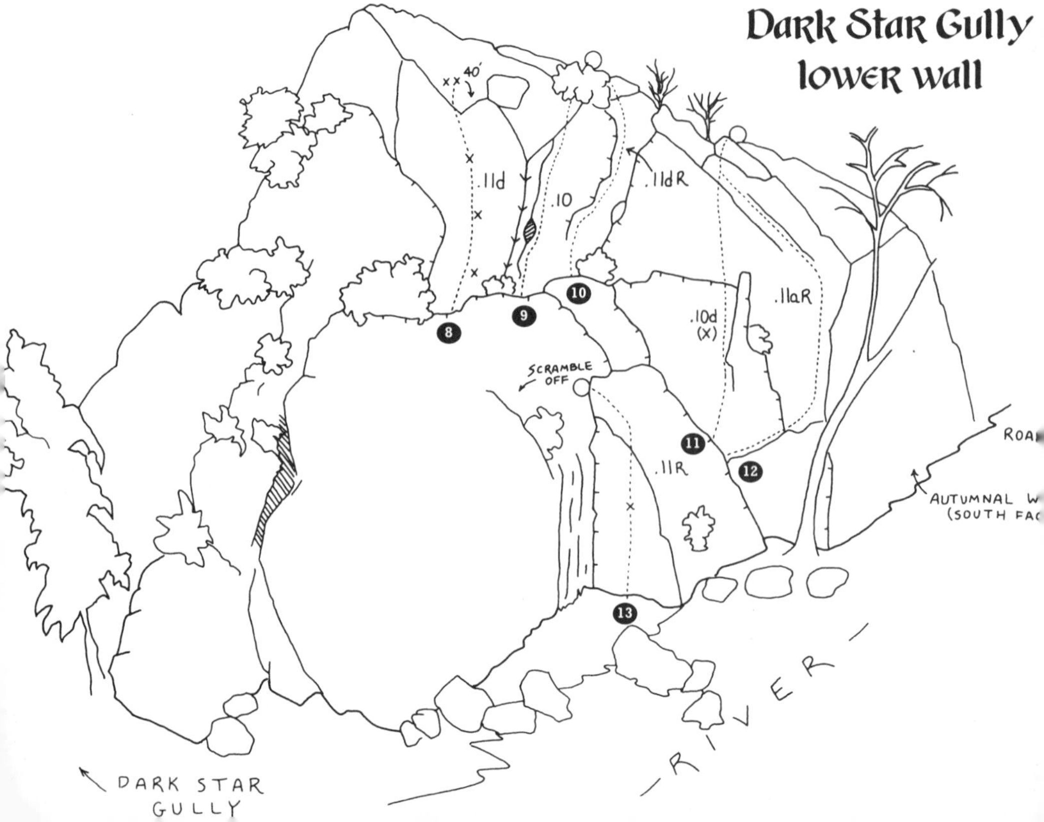

AUTUMNAL WALL

Autumnal Wall is the right facet of the Dark Star Gully (the southern end), located right over the stream and only 30 feet from the road. These routes face the highway and are characterized by steep cracks and water polished holds. The climbs are best done in the summer and autumn when the stream is low.

APPROACH: Park 2.55 miles up canyon from the neon sign at a pullout on the north side of the road. Walk up the road a short bit and hop rocks across the stream to the base of the wall. This wall is only accessible during low water. See overview on page 76.

DESCENT: Walk down the gully to the east from the top of the climbs.

AUTUMNAL WALL ROUTES

1. STAY LEFT FOR NUMBERS 5.10a ★
Climb up a dihedral to the right of a three-stalked tree. Diagonal up and left to a headwall. Look for an undercling to gain the face above. TCU's are needed.
First reported ascent: Pokey Amory and Conrad Anker, 1986.

2. O.F.R. 5.9+ R ★
The climb was named for the old fixed rings that serve as protection. Climb straight up to a roof with poor protection, and then head straight out rightward on bulge above these old fixed pins. Bring TCU's.
First reported ascent: Conrad Anker and Pokey Amory, 1986.

3. MISTER ED HAS HAY 5.8 ★
Deceptively easy and fun. This climbs a blunt arête, after negotiating the slippery rock below. Use TCU's.
First reported ascent: Pokey Amory and Conrad Anker, 1986.

4. SHARK BAIT 5.8 ★
Bring some cams to protect this tasty morsel – an obvious crack just left of the right edge.
First reported ascent: Doug Heinrich, Pokey Amory and Conrad Anker, 1986.

5. LONE SHARK 5.6 ★
This is the slippery corner five feet right of Shark Bait.
First reported ascent: Doug Heinrich.

6. EAST OF AUTUMN 5.7
The upper left-leaning crack creates a few worthy moves.
FA: Ray Dahl and Peter Jones, 1991.

7. SORCERER'S APPRENTICE 5.8 ★
Three bolts, a roof, and a few square holds thrown in, provide the magic on this route.
FA: Ray Dahl and Paul Hodges, 1991.

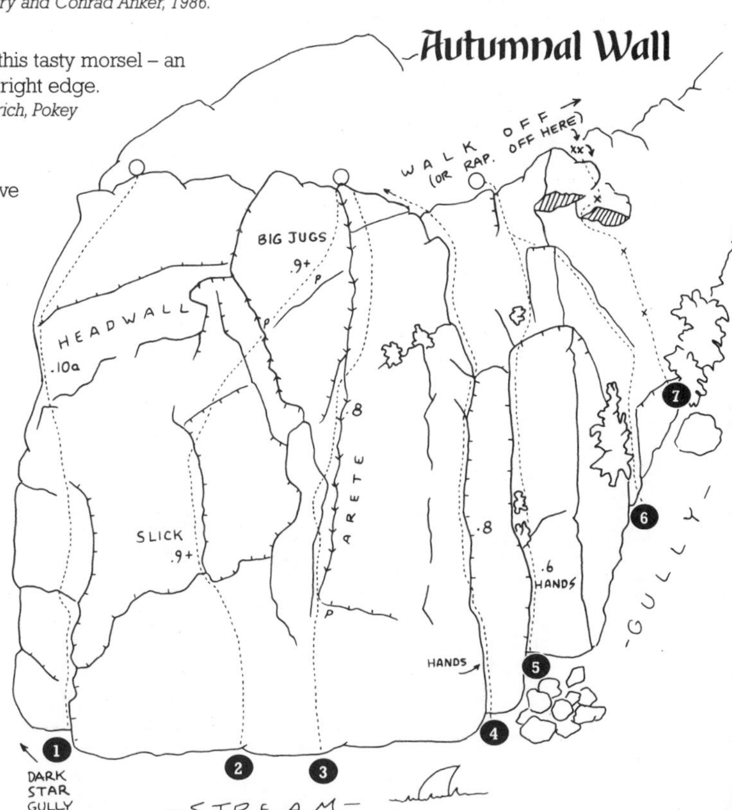

80'
80'
60'
60'
.6
.6
.5
.5
.5
.4
.6
.5
.6
.6
.6
.6
arete
1
2
3
4
5

THE DEAD SNAG AREA

This large, east-facing wall rests at a kind angle and offers many fine routes on excellent quartzite. A short approach, longer routes, and moderate grades have made this area popular. The lines follow clean crack systems, however, face climbing predominates, due to the square holds that abound.

APPROACH: Park 2.7 miles up canyon from the neon sign. This is directly across from the entrance to the Storm Mountain Picnic Area. Eighty feet up canyon from the Storm Mountain Picnic Area sign, a dirt road heads right (south west) towards a talus slope. Walk up this road, skirting underneath the talus, past some water pipes, for a short quarter mile. The trail levels off and immediately the surrounding brush opens up to a good view of the Dead Snag Area. Stop here. A trail cuts off right (west), descending through the brush to the stream. Cross the creek at the easiest point, then walk up stream roughly thirty feet to catch the trail on the other bank. This meanders through the trees to reach the base of the wall. The start of Steort's Ridge is a bit inobvious. It begins a few feet left of a prominent arete that forms the edge of a large, broken right-facing corner. See overview on pages 76 and 90.

DESCENT: Three one-rope rappels are possible from the top of the East Dihedrals. An alternate descent involves some scrambling, but only one short rappel. From the top of the routes, walk south along the prominent ledge system. Scramble down and around the corner as the ledge narrows to a pine tree. A sixty-foot rappel reaches the ground. See photo.

THE DEAD SNAG AREA ROUTES

1. TIGER'S DEN 5.8? ★

A fun looking route that liebacks up a pillar at the base of the wall, then follows a right-diagonaling crack and corner system. A solitary bolt protects the face above the roof.

2. EAST DIHEDRALS 5.6 ★★

The long right-facing corner system near the center of the face.

3. JIG'S UP 5.6 ★★

Thin crack climbing on good rock are the attractions on this route.

FA: Ted Wilson and Milt Hokanson, 1961.

4. STEORT'S RIDGE 5.6 ★★★

Exciting arête climbing. Start near the left edge of a broken right-facing corner (30 feet left from the point where the wall turns from east- to north-facing).

FA: Lee Steorts and Harold Goodro, late 40s.

5. NORTH DIHEDRALS 5.6 ★

The last few moves of this climb are the exciting crux. Start in a broken, vegetated inside corner, 20 feet left of the point where the wall turns from east- to north-facing.

6. AD LIB 5.10a ★

This route climbs a short, thin right-diagonalling crack on the smooth north face. Climb the crack, which features ever-increasing difficulty, to a two-pin anchor. Not on topo.

FA: Stuart Ruckman and Libby Ellis, 1986.

7. NORTH RIDGE 5.5

The north face of the Dead Snag Area turns into a chimney where it meets a second, smaller east face. This route climbs the right weakness of this east-facing wall. Broken and vegetated. Not on topo.

GLASS OCEAN AND ENVIRONS

The Glass Ocean rests above and south of the Dead Snag Arête area. Its east-facing walls are comprised of excellent rock, and feature a certain solitude. Face climbing prevails, but several clean, parallel cracks also divide the wall. Bring a rack of gear to supplement the bolt protection.

APPROACH: Approach as for the Dead Snag Arête area. When you reach the Dead Snag Wall, turn south and head up the talus slope into a gully. The left (east) side of this gully offers a brush-free approach. Cut across the talus to reach the base of the Glass Ocean. See overview on pages 76 and 90.

DESCENT: The descents vary from two rope rappels to walk offs. See the topo for specific information.

GLASS OCEAN AND ENVIRONS ROUTES

1. ATLANTIS 5.10a ★
Thin face climbing is protected by two bolts and some natural gear.
FA: Pat Contor, Gary Taylor and Kevin Sweeny, 1988.

2. GET THE NET 5.10d ★
A two pitch route that dives head first into the stormy terrain on the wall's left side. Atlantis makes the best first pitch, and a 160 foot rappel is necessary for the descent. A light rack will help take the bite out of the cracks and corners between bolts.
FA: Brian Smoot and Glen Henshaw, 1994.

3. HIGH DIVE 5.9+ ★★★
Don't bellyflop on this elegant route, which follows thin cracks to the very summit, and tops out next to the "diving board." Bring those small nuts and TCU's. Rappel 165+ feet.
FA: Pat Contor and Gary Taylor, 1988.

4. LORD OF THE LONG ARMS 5.9+ ★
This favors long reaches, but short folks seem to do fine. This is a good start to High Dive.
FA: Pat Contor, Gary Taylor and Kevin Sweeny, 1988.

5. DELTA "Y" 5.10a
A very short arête problem.
FA: Pat Contor, Gary Taylor and Kevin Sweeny, 1988.

6. TSUNAMI 5.10b ★
A much longer, more direct start to High Dive.
FA: Pat Contor and Gary Taylor, 1992.

7. NORTHWEST PASSAGE 5.10c ★★
Start on Glass Ocean. At the ledge after the first two bolts, step left and surf the face above, turning a small roof before a two-bolt belay. The second pitch climbs some scrappy rock, crosses High Dive, and finishes on the spectacular upper face.
FA: Pat Contor and Gary Taylor.

8. GLASS OCEAN 5.8 ★★
Smooth as glass, vast as an ocean. The upper face is beautiful and continuous.
FA: Pat Contor and Gary Taylor, 1988.

9. LEFT TRIBUTARY 5.10d ★
Flow to the left of the bolts for a hard-to-decipher short route, or continue up Glass Ocean for a longer route.
FA: Pat Contor and Gary Taylor, 1988.

10. RIGHT TRIBUTARY 5.11a ★
Follow a thin crack to the second bolt of Left Tributary, then stay right of the boltline.
FA: Pat Contor and Gary Taylor, 1988.

11. SAIL AWAY 5.7 ★

More broken, yet still enjoyable climbing on the right side of the wall. One frictiony bulge is the apparent crux.

FA: Pat Contor and Nancy Cohn, 1992.

12. THE PANE 5.12c ★

A two-bolt line on a smooth south-facing wall to the right of Right Tributary. There is a lot of climbing packed into this short route, and if you master the one-finger hold, you can be crowned the King of Pane.

FA: Gary Taylor, 1988.

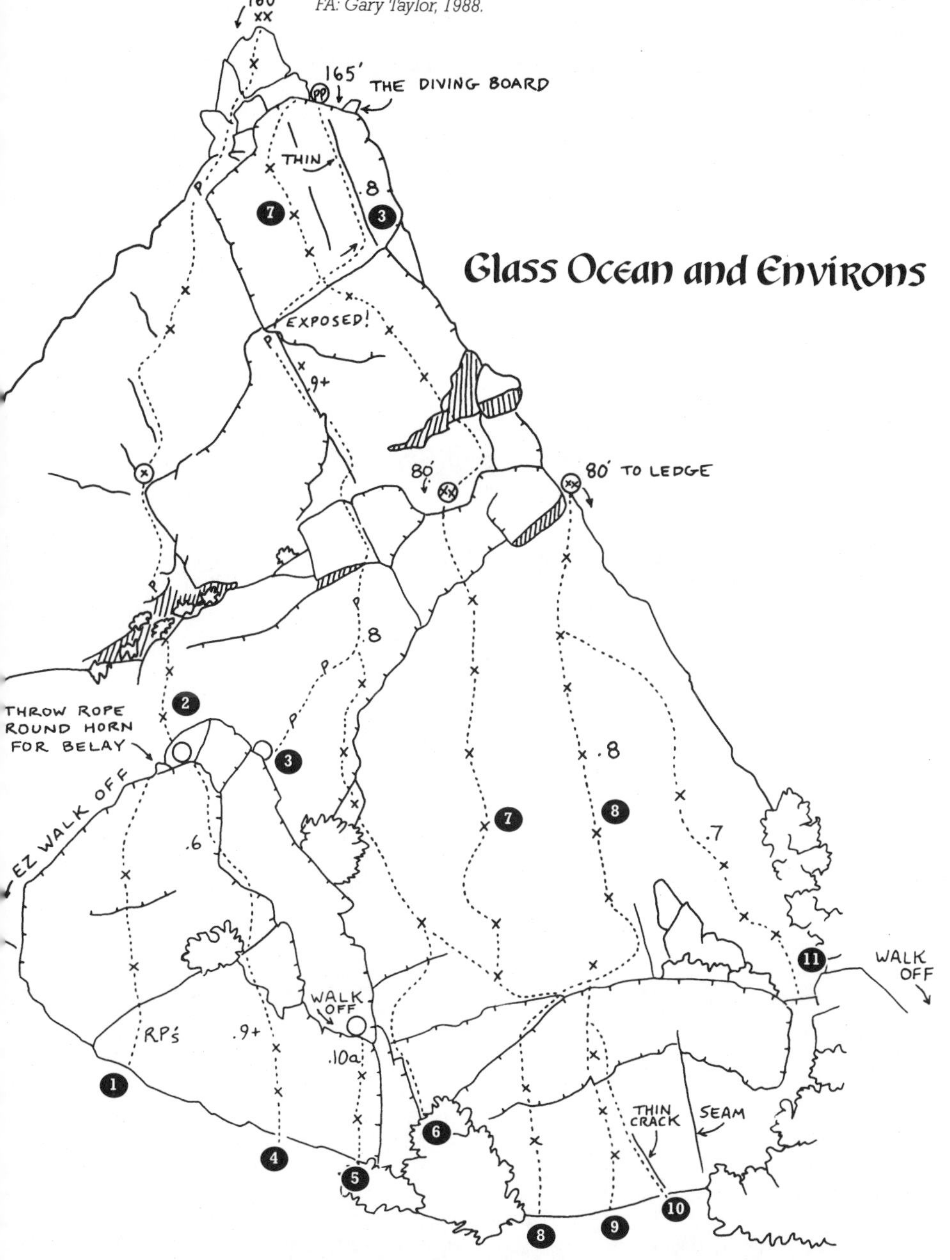

REDRUM (no topo)

A west-facing wall that is characterized by a series of right-leaning corners and aretes. The close proximity to the Glass Ocean Area is an extra bonus.

APPROACH: From the base of the Glass Ocen Wall, walk across the talus to the east side of the gully. Jog down a bit, crossing underneath the small rock formation that forms the east wall of the Glass Ocean gully. Then walk directly east across the next talus slope to reach the wall. See overview on pages 76 and 90.

DESCENT: Walk off to the south.

1. REDRUM 5.10c ★
Tricky moves past the first bolt are followed by balancey climbing past two more bolts to a ledge. Four more bolts lead up the slightly overhanging headwall.
FA: Pat Contor and Gary Taylor.

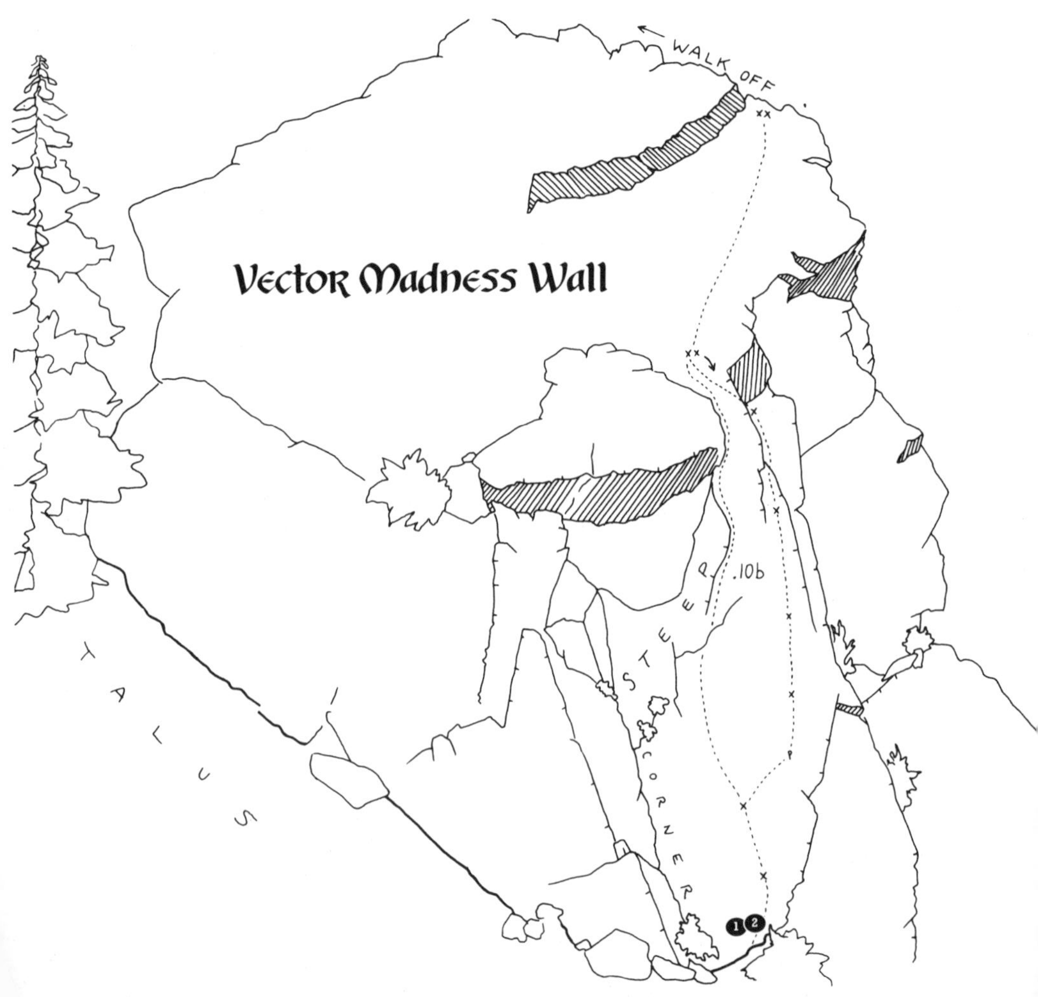

VECTOR MADNESS WALL

A fairly isolated area, the Vector Madness Wall is a large chunk of quartzite east of the Glass Ocean Area. A large roof is the most prominent feature, shadowing the northeast face of the wall. Both routes climb the steep terrain near the roof.

APPROACH: Approach as for the Dead Snag Arête. If you take a breather before dropping down to the stream crossing, the Vector Madness Wall can be seen to the southeast of the Dead Snag Area. It can be identified by the roof on the northeast side, the sloping west face and its position in the middle of two talus slopes. From the base of the Dead Snag area, continue up the gully toward the Glass Ocean a short distance, traverse east underneath the left wall of the gully, and reach a pine slope that leads (mostly brush free) to the base of the wall. The two routes are just uphill from the overhang, on the east face. See overview on pages 76 and 90.

DESCENT: Walk off to the south, or make a one rope rappel.

VECTOR MADNESS WALL ROUTES

1. VERTICAL COMPONENT 5.10b ★

Stemming, jugs, and only one hand jam are required in the obtuse corner that splits the center of the wall.

FA: Gary Taylor and Pat Contor.

2. VECTOR MADNESS 5.10d ★★

Start right of a licheny corner and climb the steep wall past several pins and bolts. Above the bulge, the angle eases and the original route continued to the top (bring a small selection of gear). Now, most parties rappel from the anchors added by the first ascent party.

FA: Pat Contor and Gary Taylor, 1989.

BUENA VISTA WALL (no topo)

A two pitch climb up a sharp ridge is the attraction here.

APPROACH: Follow the Vector Madness approach. Continue hiking upwards along the east side of the Vector Madness Wall. Just above the top of the wall the talus forks into two gullies. Take the right fork. A sharp knife-edged ridge sits above and right (south) of the top of the Vector Madness wall. From the fork, continue up more talus and scree to reach the ridge. See overview on page 90.

DESCENT: Although it is possible to make a 160 foot rappel, this requires two ropes, so most parties simply walk off.

1. RIDGE WITH A VIEW 5.8 ★
Start near a six inch crack just left of the arete. Follow this crack directly to a belay ledge, passing two protection bolts along the way. From the belay, traverse left to a crack that leads up to a roof. Traverse right at the roof and follow the ridge to the top.
FA: Unknown.

HIDDEN FORTRESS (no topo)

Remote. This tower-like wall sees little sun and even less traffic. For those souls willing to endure a lengthy approach through shifting talus, a fine route awaits.

APPROACH: Follow the Vector Madness approach. Continue hiking upwards along the east side of the Vector Madness Wall. Just above the top of the wall the talus forks into two gullies. Take the smaller, left fork. Continue up the gully, passing a very nice seep, to a large chockstone which blocks the entire gully. Scramble past the chockstone, and the north-facing Hidden Fortress will be right in front of you. See overview on pages 76 and 90.

DESCENT: Two rappels can be made with a single rope.

1. HIDDEN FORTRESS 5.11b ★
This one can be hard to spot . Follow eight bolts just left of the center of the face to a two-bolt belay. The cracks above lead to the top (bring gear) and two one-rope rappels reach the ground.
FA: Gary Taylor and Pat Contor.

PATTY'S RIDGE (no topo)

Named for Patty Parmelee, this dark quartzite ridge rises at a 45 degree angle from the Stair's Gulch stream.

APPROACH: Follow the approach to the Dead Snag Arete Area up to the point where that approach drops down to the creek from the main hiking trail. From here continue hiking up the Stair's Gulch Trail to the last ridge on the right. See overview on pages 76 and 90.

DESCENT: Walk off south into the gully.

1. PATTY'S RIDGE 5.5 ★
Climb the right-facing corner immediately left of the arête to a level spot and belay. Scramble up to the base of the next steep section. Climb corners and cracks near the arête to the top.

FACE TO FACE (no topo)

A small but worthwhile destination for those shade seekers in the summer. It can be seen rising above a talus slope to the southeast of the Storm Mountain Picnic Area parking lot.

APPROACH: Park 2.7 miles up canyon from the neon sign. This is directly across from the entrance to the Storm Mountain Picnic Area. Eighty feet up canyon from the Storm Mountain Picnic Area sign, a dirt road heads right (south west) towards a talus slope. Walk up this road, then amble up the talus, angling right, until it is possible to traverse across to the base of the routes. Routes are described from left to right. See overview on pages 76 and 90.

DESCENT: Walk off to the west.

1. THE FACADE 5.?
This right-diagonalling crack is 15 feet to the left of an acute corner/chimney system. Climb this crack to a ledge, and then climb the double cracks above.

2. BABY FACE 5.?
Climb the hand crack at the back of the big, acute corner.

3. FACE TO FACE 5.9 R ★
Start 15 feet right of Baby Face at the left side of the most prominent section of light brown rock. Climb a thin crack that diagonals right to the center of the face and a bolt. Continue up the center of the face to a nice ledge and chains.
FA: Stuart Ruckman and Libby Ellis, 1987, sans bolt.

4. AMBER LIES 5.11b ★
Climb the bolted arête just right of Face to Face. A fixed stopper and three bolts protect the inobvious moves. Bring a few pieces of natural gear.
FA: Scott Unice and Julie Gustin, 1990.

Storm Mountain Island area overview map

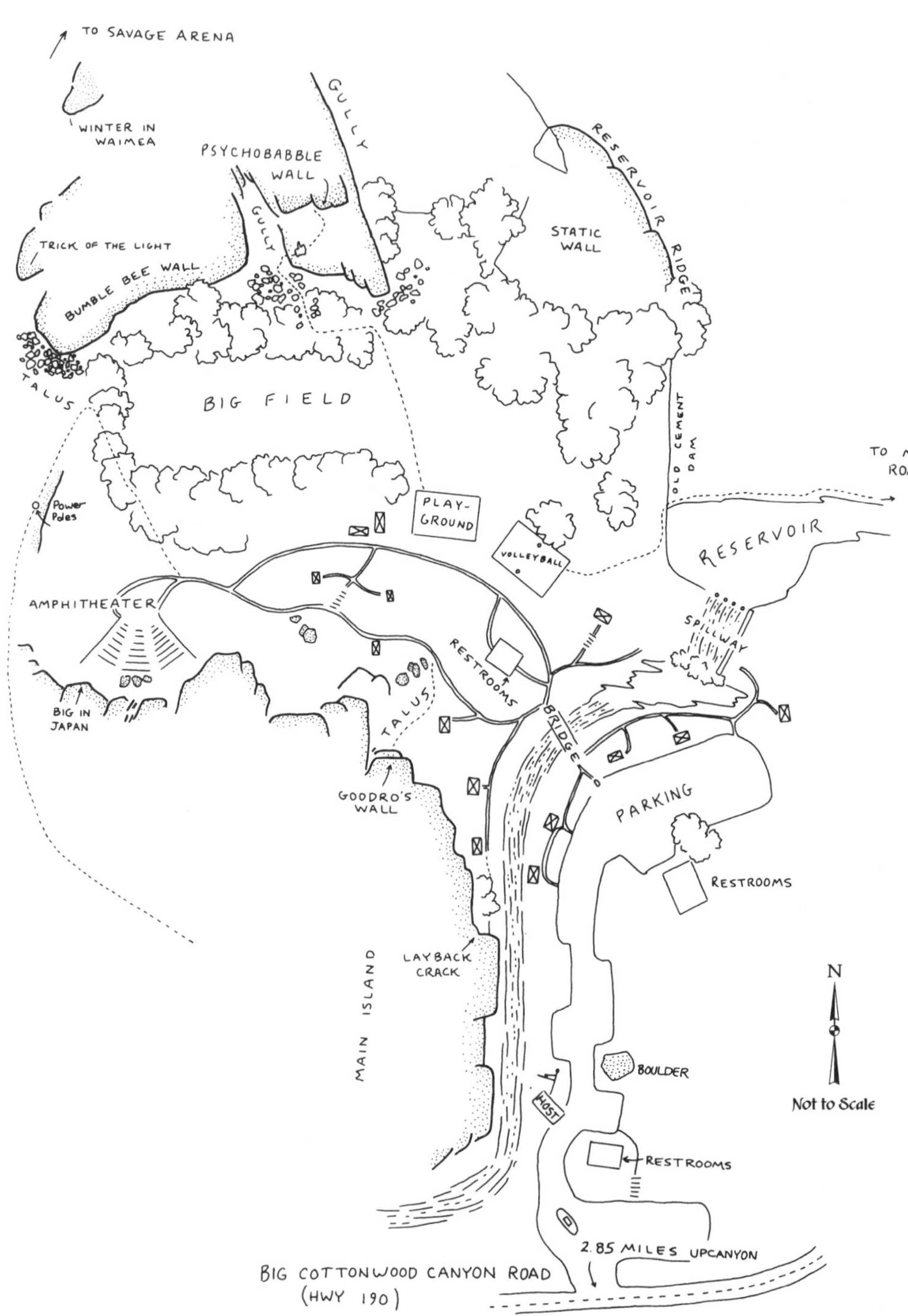

STORM MOUNTAIN PICNIC AREA

Immensely popular for both climbers and picnickers, the Storm Mountain Picnic Area is a pleasant destination with spectacular views. Climbing here ranges from delightful 5.4 cracks to 5.13 overhanging desperates, and everything in- between. A multitude of walls means that climbing is possible almost year round, since the walls face every direction, including cool north faces and heat infused south faces. Historically, the Storm Mountain Picnic Area used to be the site of the infamous Wasatch Mountain Club's Thursday evening burgers and beer social. Climbers would race to the cliffs after work, with Goodro's Wall being the most sought after climb. Around sunset, for a dollar, you could get a fresh-off-the-grill burger and an icy beer. Now relegated to the history books, these burgers and beer evenings were once the main way to meet and socialize with other climbers.

This oasis among the cottonwoods is a U.S. Forest service fee area, and you can park inside the picnic area for four dollars per car, or park on the main highway and walk in for two dollars per person. All the approaches are quite straightforward and are described in detail at the beginning of each wall. See overview on page 48 and Storm Mountain overview on page 118.

STORM MOUNTAIN ISLAND—EAST FACE

The "island" is a blob of quartzite bounded by a large field, or baseball diamond on the north, the Storm Mountain Picnic Area on the east, and the Big Cottonwood Creek and highway on the south. It has been a principal climbing area in Big Cottonwood Canyon from the beginning, and offers a good selection of moderate to extreme routes on good rock. During spring high-water periods some of the climbs on the south end are hard to access.

APPROACH: Park 2.85 miles up canyon from the neon sign. Walk or drive to the parking area near the spillway of the dam, and cross the river on the bridge. For routes 1 through 4, turn left just after the bridge and follow the paved path past two picnic tables near the river. Continue along the edge of the water until a ledge system is reached that allows a southward traverse to the base of the routes. For the Goodro's wall area, routes 5 through 9, turn left after the bridge, then take the right fork until the trail passes several small boulders between two picnic tables. Turn left (south) and march up the talus to an easy third class corner which accesses the routes. See Storm Mountain overview page 118.

DESCENT: Except for Goodro's Wall, Six Appeal and Six Pence, all routes reach the top of the "island." To descend, walk off west, then follow one of the paths that heads down to the north. The main trail can be picked up here, near the powerline, and followed back to the bridge across the stream. For Goodro's, Six Appeal and Six Pence, simply lower or rappel off the chains at the top of each route.

EAST FACE ROUTES

1. NICE LITTLE CRACK 5.5 ★
This climb is behind a box elder tree on the left side of wall. Climb a thin crack up and over a roof. Fun.

2. STORM MOUNTAIN STUPOR 5.5 ★
Swagger up the left-facing corner with double cracks.

3. LE CREME DE SHORTS 5.9 ★★
North-facing steep finger/hand crack.

4. LAYBACK CRACK 5.5 ★★
The major right-facing corner system. Two pitches, with the crux being the first 30 feet.

Routes 5-8 and 10 see topo on page 124.

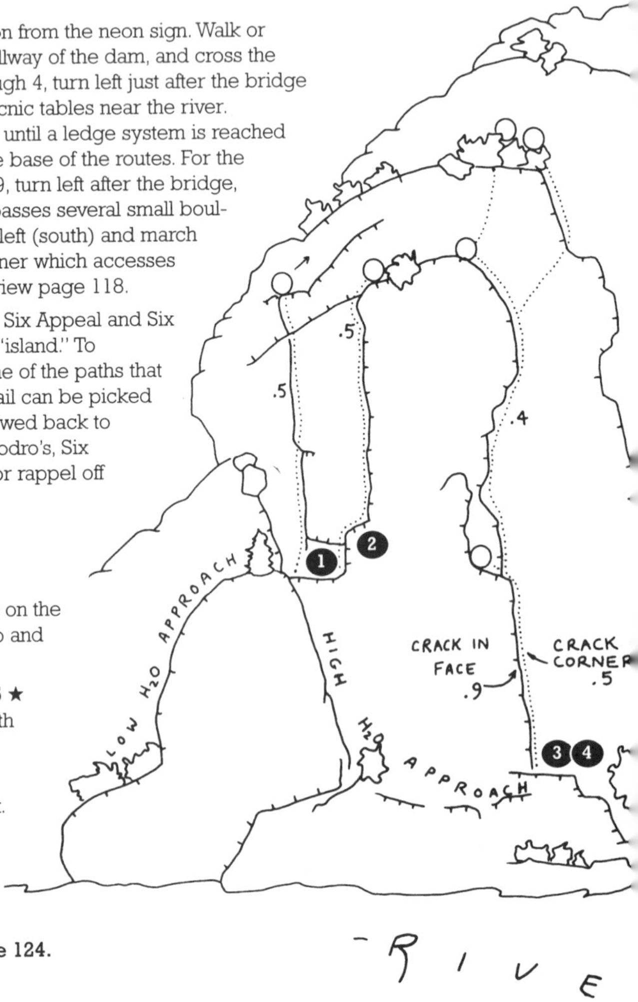

Storm Mountain Island
East Face

8. SIX APPEAL 5.6 ★★

Popular.

FA: Vicki and Brian Smoot, 1989.

9. EPIC WALL 5.5 ★

Look for a mahogany tree on the skyline. Climb up to it in two pitches; the first has many variations.

11. BOLT ROUTE 5.4

The first sport route in the region! Climb the over-bolted face to a ledge. A second pitch (gear needed) gains the top of the "island".

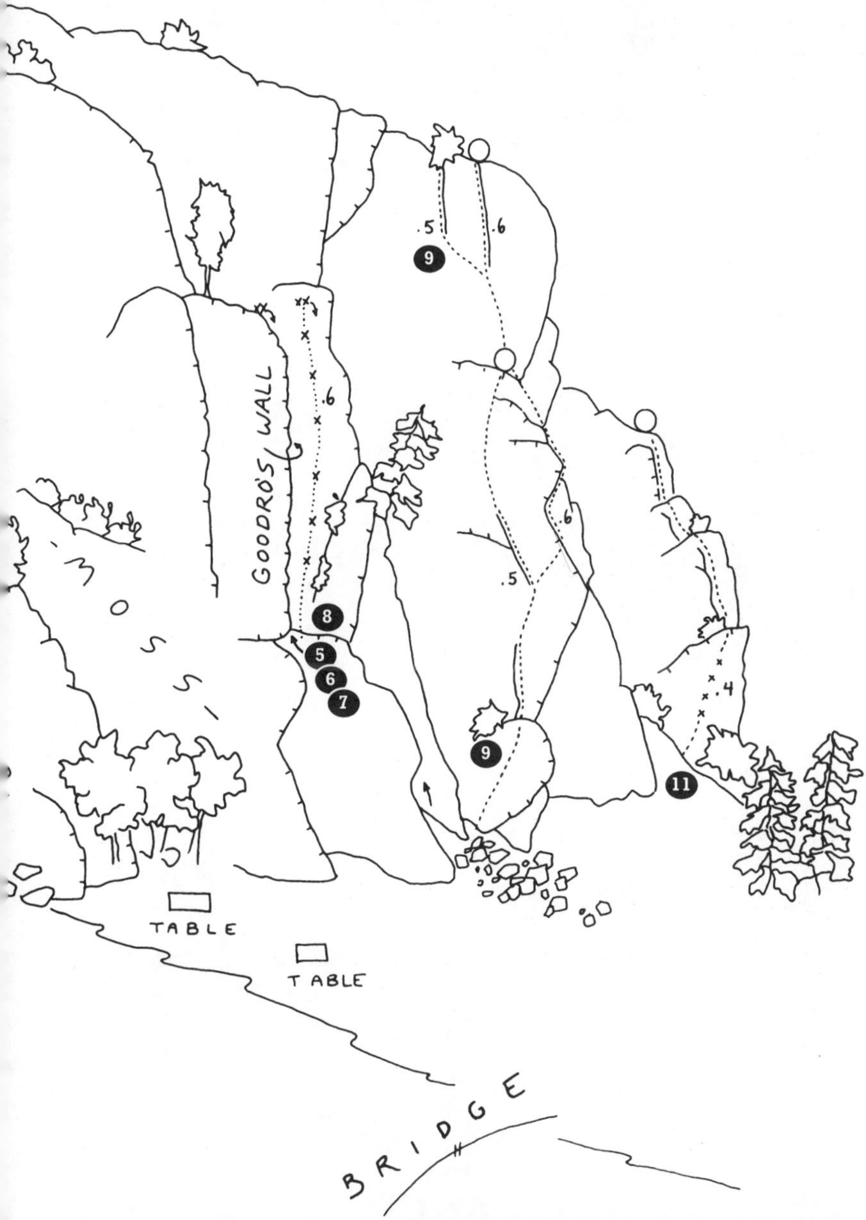

Storm Mountain—North Face

5. GOODRO'S WALL 5.10c ★★★
12. THE FLAKE 5.5 ★
13. PADDED CELL 5.12a or 5.12c ★★
16. THIN SLICE OF TIME 5.10c ★
17. BIG IN JAPAN 5.12b ★★

13
12
16
17

STORM MOUNTAIN ISLAND— NORTH FACE (LEFT SIDE)

Shady, even in summer. These routes sit just above the amphitheater.

APPROACH: See the approach for the East Face. Continue walking past the cut-off for Goodro's Wall, until the amphitheater is reached. Walk up the stairs to the base of the routes. See Storm Mountain overview page 118.

DESCENT: Lower off chains for all of these routes except for Amphitheater Overhang Left, where you just jump off after the hard bit, and The Flake and Bolt Route where a walk off west meets the main trail near the power line, and a switchback below the power line brings you back to your packs.

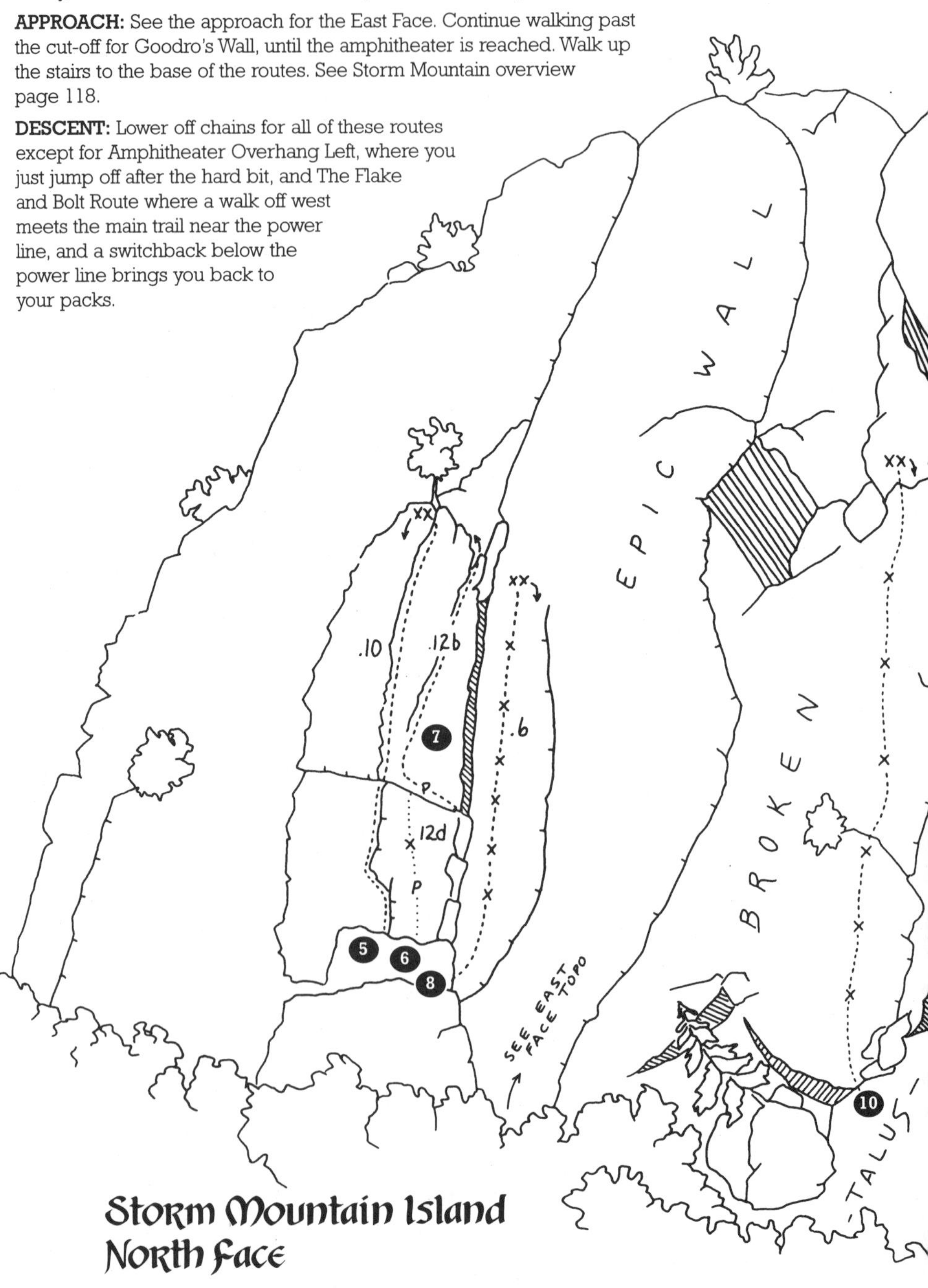

Storm Mountain Island North Face

STORM MOUNTAIN ISLAND—NORTH FACE (LEFT SIDE) ROUTES

5. GOODRO'S WALL 5.10c ★★★

Possibly the best route in BCC. Named after the vibrant and always youthful Harold Goodro, who led this circa 1949. Climb the slightly overhung wall via a magnificent crack. Bring gear to 2 inches.

6. CLOSING THE GAP VARIATION 5.12d ★

Sickly hard. The direct start to Generation Gap.

FA: Drew Bedford, 1989.

7. GENERATION GAP 5.12b ★

Whistle your way up the crack to the right of Goodro's. Bring micro nuts.

FA: John Storm, Stuart Ruckman and Gordon Douglass, 1988.

8. SIX APPEAL 5.6 ★★

Popular.

FA: Vicki and Brian Smoot, 1989.

10. SIX PENCE 5.6 ★

Edges and ledges, smears and no fears. Well protected, popular climbing.

Storm Mountain Island North Face

STORM MOUNTAIN ISLAND— NORTH FACE (RIGHT SIDE) ROUTES

12. THE FLAKE 5.5 ★

Climb the left-facing corner above a pine tree, 20 feet left of Amphitheater Overhang. The conclusion of the second pitch is an exposed mantel, if you refrain from clipping the Padded Cell anchors.

13. PADDED CELL 5.12a or 5.12c ★★

The left variation is the easiest. The smooth face above the Amphitheater Overhang will drive you stark-raving mad.

FA: Drew Bedford, 1987.

14. AMPHITHEATER OVERHANG LEFT 5.12d ★

Throw an unbelievable dyno to the lip.

FA: Royal Robbins, 1964.

FFA: Jim Karn or Steve Habovstak, 1988.

15. AMPHITHEATER OVERHANG RIGHT A1

Mostly fixed.

16. THIN SLICE OF TIME 5.10c ★

Climb the ragged-looking slices right of the Amphitheater Overhang. Link the upper portion with the cool cracks above Big in Japan. Small micronuts and TCU's are especially useful.

FA: Lynn Wheeler.

17. BIG IN JAPAN 5.12b ★★

Brief, but good grief! It is best to make the first clip off the ramp to the right. Almost three stars.

FA: Drew Bedford and Dana Hauser, 1987.

STORM MOUNTAIN PICNIC AREA—SAVAGE ARENA

The Savage Arena is reached via a long approach, but the area offers four neighboring routes of unfeigned difficulty. Good rock and overhanging stone are the draw, but afternoon sun and incredible backdrop views also add to the overall experience.

APPROACH: See the approach information for Storm Mountain Island East Face. Cross the bridge and walk straight ahead to the playground. Walk across the large field aiming for the north west corner. Skirt around the west end of the Bumble Bee Wall on talus, and continue uphill. By hugging the scattered cliffs on the right, sometimes even scrambling among them, the approach stays brush free. From the Bumble Bee Wall, it's about 600 vertical feet until you reach the southwest-facing overhanging cliffs. See Storm Mountain overview on page 118.

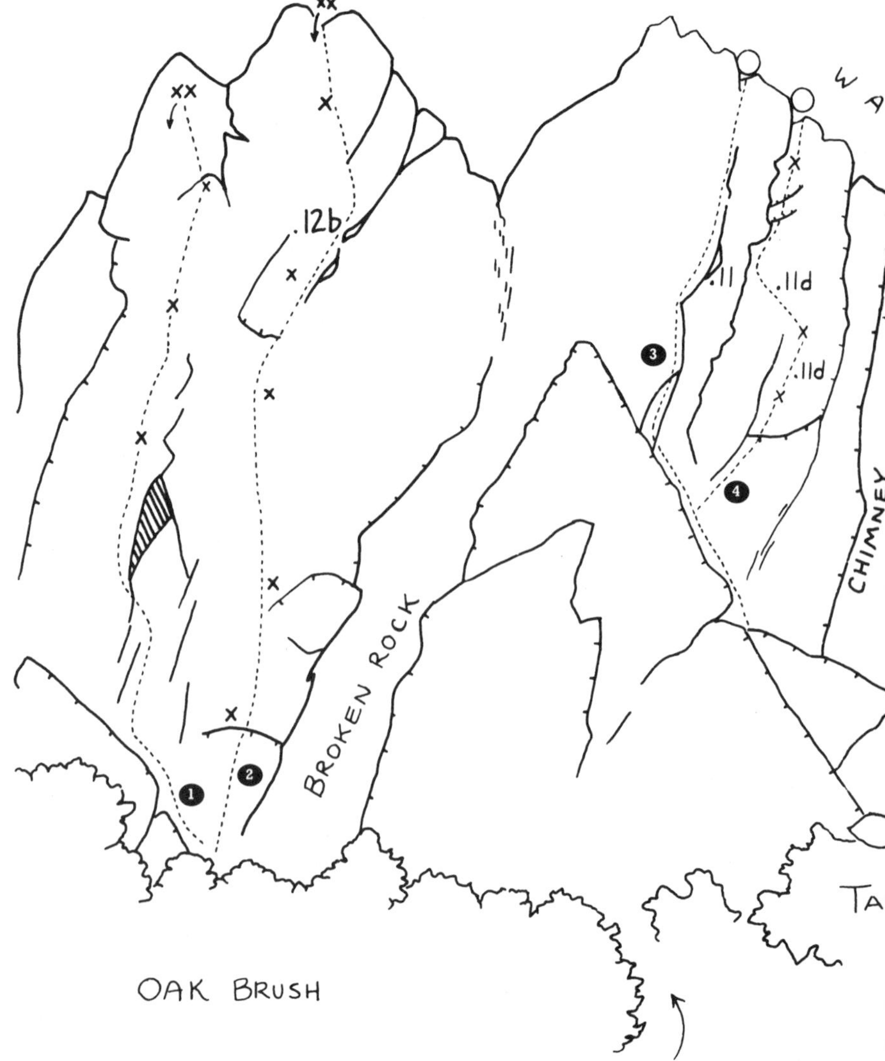

SAVAGE ARENA ROUTES

DESCENT: Routes 1 and 2 can be lowered off of with a single rope. Routes 3-5 are descended quickly with a short walk to the south.

1. CHOSS-A-GO-GO 5.11 R ★
Shattered rock and several less than ideal gear placements lead to the first bolt. From here everything improves.
FA: Dale Goddard, 1992.

2. SAVAGE DANCE 5.12b ★★★
A savagely pumping fandango of overhanging face.
FA: Merrill Bitter, 1986.

3. RUNNING FROM THE SUN 5.11 ★★
The good, overhanging crack left of Slap or Flap. Bring wireds, brass nuts and camming devices.
FA: Merrill Bitter and Paul Lanz, 1986.

4. SLAP OR FLAP 5.11d/.12a ★
Climb the right edge of the overhanging wall that rises 60 feet right of Savage Dance. A traverse left at mid-height leads to more weaknesses (especially in your arms). Bring wireds and brass-type nuts.
FA: Dana Hauser and Tom Carruthers, 1987.

5. LONG FOR MIDGETS 5.11d ★
A crack 40 feet down hill and right of Slap or Flap. Again, bring brass-type nuts and wireds.
FA: Merrill Bitter and Paul Lanz, 1986.

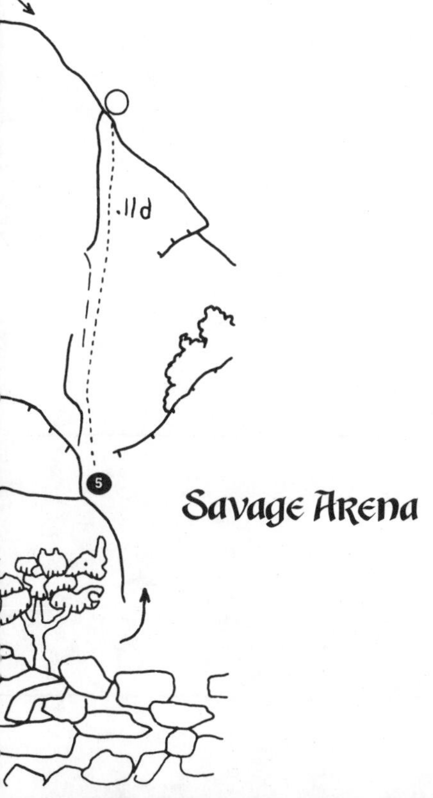

Savage Arena

BUMBLE BEE WALL ROUTES
13. PERSEVERANCE BULGE CRACK 5.9 ★★
PSYCHOBABBLE WALL ROUTES
1. THE ENEMY WITHIN 5.12a ★★★
Savage Arena
Bumble Bee Wall
Psychobabble Wall
1
13

Static
Wall
Reservoir Ridge

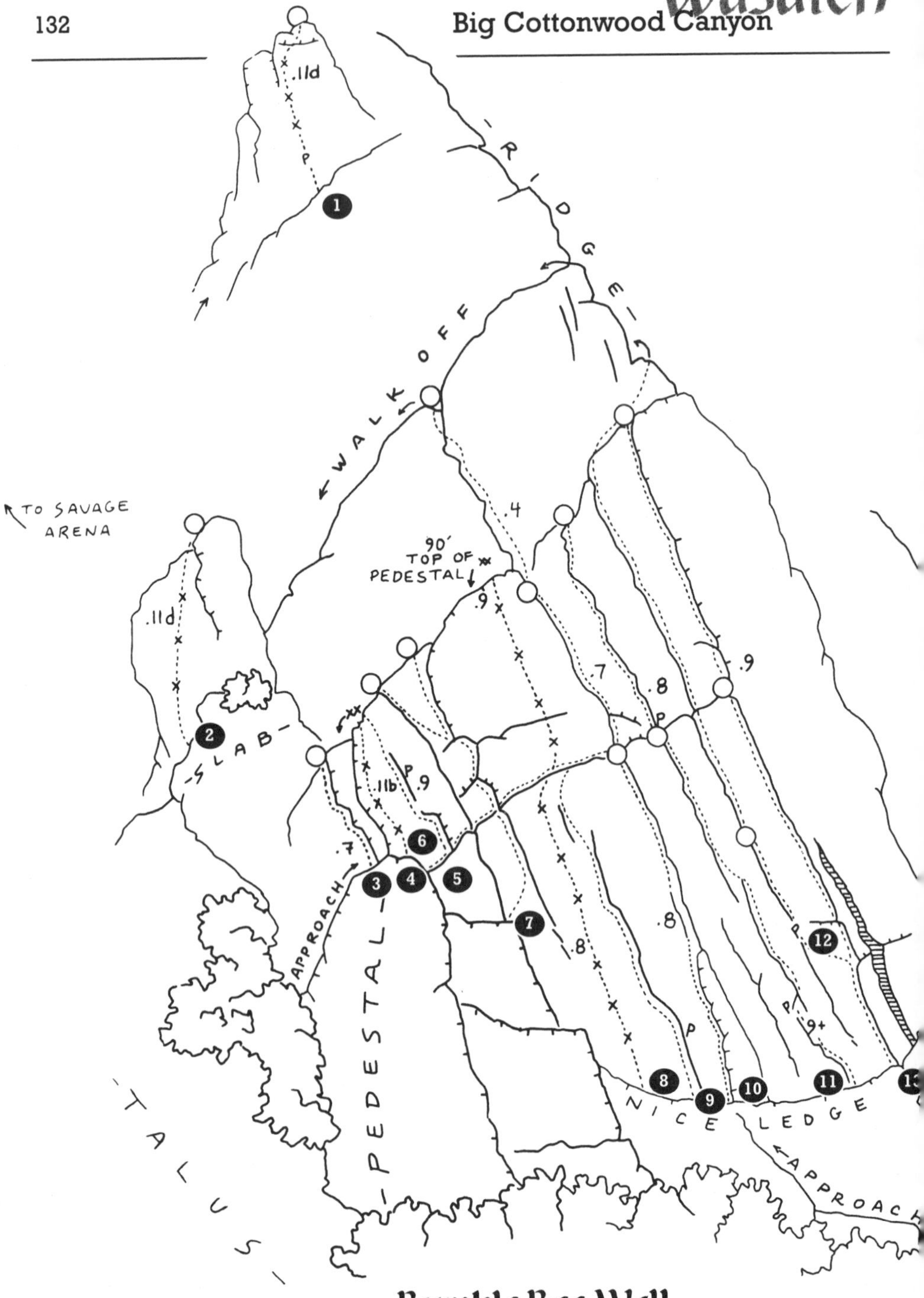

Bumble Bee Wall

STORM MOUNTAIN PICNIC AREA—BUMBLE BEE WALL

If you are standing in the playground at the Storm Mountain Picnic Area, Bumble Bee Wall is the large south-facing cliff to the northwest. Expect two long pitches, and deceptively difficult and steep climbing. Some routes have better rock quality than others. Generally, the climbs follow strata layers and diagonal to the left. Routes 1 and 2 are west of the main wall and are short, pumpy face climbs.

APPROACH: See the approach information for Storm Mountain Island East Face. From the parking area near the spillway, cross the bridge and follow the path to the playground. Walk northwest across the big field and enter the trees. At the base of the wall, a short section of scramblling on ledge systems will bring you to a nice ledge below the main wall. See Storm Mountain overview on page 118.

DESCENT: Routes 1,2, 4, and 5 can be descended with a one rope rappel. Route 8 requires a 60 meter rope or two ropes to rappel from its anchors. All other routes can be descended by a walk off to the west. See topo for specific descent information.

BUMBLE BEE WALL ROUTES

1 TRICK OF THE LIGHT 5.11d ★
This three-bolt route is found along the approach to the Savage Dance Arena. Exciting exit moves.
FA: Paul Lanz, 1987.

2. WINTER IN WAIMEA 5.11d ★
Five bolts and a searing pump.
FA: Paul Lanz, 1987.

3. MERCY STREET 5.7+ ★
Climb a 30-foot hand crack on the left side of the buttress.

4. MERCI-BUCKETS 5.11b ★
Climb a little left-facing corner and follow bolts to a bucketed finish.
FA: Stuart and Bret Ruckman, 1990.

5. CHARLIE'S TRAVERSE 5.6 ★
Traverse a ledge system rightward to gain The Bee Pitch.
FA: Dick Bell, Ben Peterson and John Paup, early 60's.

6. MERCY ME 5.9
An ancient pin marks the route. Climb the overhanging wall 20 feet right of Merci-Buckets.

7. UPCHUCK 5.10a ★
Start up a hand crack, intersect Charlie's Traverse, continue up a hand crack through a roof. Either stem the right corner above or escape left to easier climbing and better rock. This is an 85-foot route.

8. FOWL PLAY 5.9 ★
A bolt protected line that climbs the wall in one long pitch. The quality of this route should improve with more traffic.
FA: Brian Smoot and Glen Henshaw, 1995.

9. CHECK POINT CHARLIE 5.9+
Start just left of The Bee Pitch and climb up thin weaknesses to join Charlie's Traverse.

BUMBLE BEE WALL ROUTES

10. THE BEE PITCH 5.8 ★★

The slightly overhung direct start to Charlie's Traverse.
FA: Dave Wood and Bob Irvine, 1961.

11. SIN NOMBRE 5.9+ ★★

Nice cracks between Rotten Roost and Perseverance Bulge Crack. Climb a short, overhanging finger crack and continue to a fixed belay. The second pitch mostly is hand cracks, and medium-sized nuts work well (or medium cams).
FA: Unknown.

12. ROTTEN ROOST 5.8? R

The exact location of this route is unclear. Start just left of Perseverance Bulge Crack and traverse left to gain the crack?
FA: Dave Wood and Bob Irvine, 1962.

13. PERSEVERANCE BULGE CRACK 5.9 ★★

A hard route with tricky bulges, usually done in two long pitches. Bring some big protection. This is the obvious crack/dihedral on the east end.
FA: Rich Reese and Milt Hokanson, 1961.

The amazing Goodro's Wall. Douglas Heinrich making it look easy. Storm Mountain Picnic Area.

photo: Ruckman.

walk off
.10
.11b
.12a/b
.10a
.11c
P #2 Friend
.10 d
P
.11b
.12a
.10
83'
1
2
3
4
5
6
7

STORM MOUNTAIN PICNIC AREA —PSYCHOBABBLE WALL

From a distance this wall appears insignificant and broken. At the base of the routes, however, the wall has a different character: overhanging and solid. Each climb is unique, and techniques as varied as overhanging arête climbing, pumper crack moves and thin face problems are employed on this wall.

APPROACH: Follow the approach information for Storm Mountain Island East Face. After crossing the bridge, walk straight ahead to the playground. From there, walk north across the field to an open area in the trees with a steep trail. Walk up this trail for twenty feet, turn left (west) and walk along another trail for fifty feet, then turn right (north) and walk up talus to the gully west of the Psychobabble Wall. Walk up this gully a bit, to a break in the cliff by a Box Elder tree. From here some moderate scrambling leads to the base. See Storm Mountain overview page 118.

DESCENT: With a single rope you can lower off from anchors at the top of each route.

PSYCHOBABBLE WALL ROUTES

1. THE ENEMY WITHIN 5.12a ★★★
An endurance extravaganza up the left edge of the Psychobabble Wall. Six widely spaced bolts protect.
FA: Stuart Ruckman and Gordon Douglass, 1987.

2. THE EYE OF THE ENEMY VARIATION 5.11b ★★
Avoid the cruxes of both routes, making a fine 5.11. Bring small to medium nuts and TCU's.
FA: Stuart and Bret Ruckman, 1990.

3. EYE IN THE SKY 5.12a/b ★★★
A route up the stellar face left of Psychobabble. Bolts mixed with nut placements (bring RP's), and TCU's provide (barely) adequate protection.
FFA: Paul Smith, Pokey Amory and Jim Karn, 1986.

4. PSYCHOBABBLE 5.10b/c ★★★
Climb the leftward-diagonalling crack in the center of the face for 25 feet, traverse left 8 feet, then continue up the corners to the top. A bit of mumbling is to be expected.
FA: Bret Ruckman, Chris Pendleton and Gary Olsen, 1984.

5. PSYCHOSTEMATIC 5.10a ★★
A study in opposition. Stem up the corner to the right and avoid the leftward traverse.
FA: Bret Ruckman and Paul Shelton, 1986.

6. REBEL YELL 5.11c ★★
Don't "Idol" too long or you'll run out of gas. An awkward, troubling arête right of Psychostematic. Bring a 2" cam and several medium nuts.
FA: Conrad Anker and Doug Heinrich.
FFA: Merrill Bitter, 1987.

7. ROCK CAPADES 5.10d ★★
Futz with micro nuts in the corner six feet right of Rebel Yell. A really good route.
FA: Kevin Gheen and Tom Carruthers, 1984.

8. EYES WITHOUT A FACE 5.11a ★★
The rightmost crack has moves and protection that could stump a myopic leader. Again, micro nuts are deemed prudent.
FA. Merrill Bitter, Lynn Watson and Steve Carruthers, 1984.

9. UNWORTHY OF TITLE 5.7
Six feet of interesting climbing at the top.

STORM MOUNTAIN PICNIC AREA —STATIC WALL

The routes here are located in an alcove near the descent for the Reservoir Ridge. A peaceful location with a short approach, this wall enjoys considerable populartity. In winter, a three pitch ice climb forms just left of Transformer (see page 139).

APPROACH: Follow the approach information for Storm Mountain Island East Face. After crossing the bridge, walk straight ahead to the playground. From there, walk north across the field to an open area in the trees with a steep trail. Walk up this trail for twenty feet, until it levels out. Turn right (east) and angle upwards following the talus along the left side of a broad gully. When possible, cross to the right side of the gully, which ends at a flat spot at the base of a steep, water-streaked wall. Transformer climbs to the right of the water streaks. See Storm Mountain overview on page 118.

DESCENT: You can lower off all the routes in this area, but Transformer requires a 180 foot rope, or two ropes.

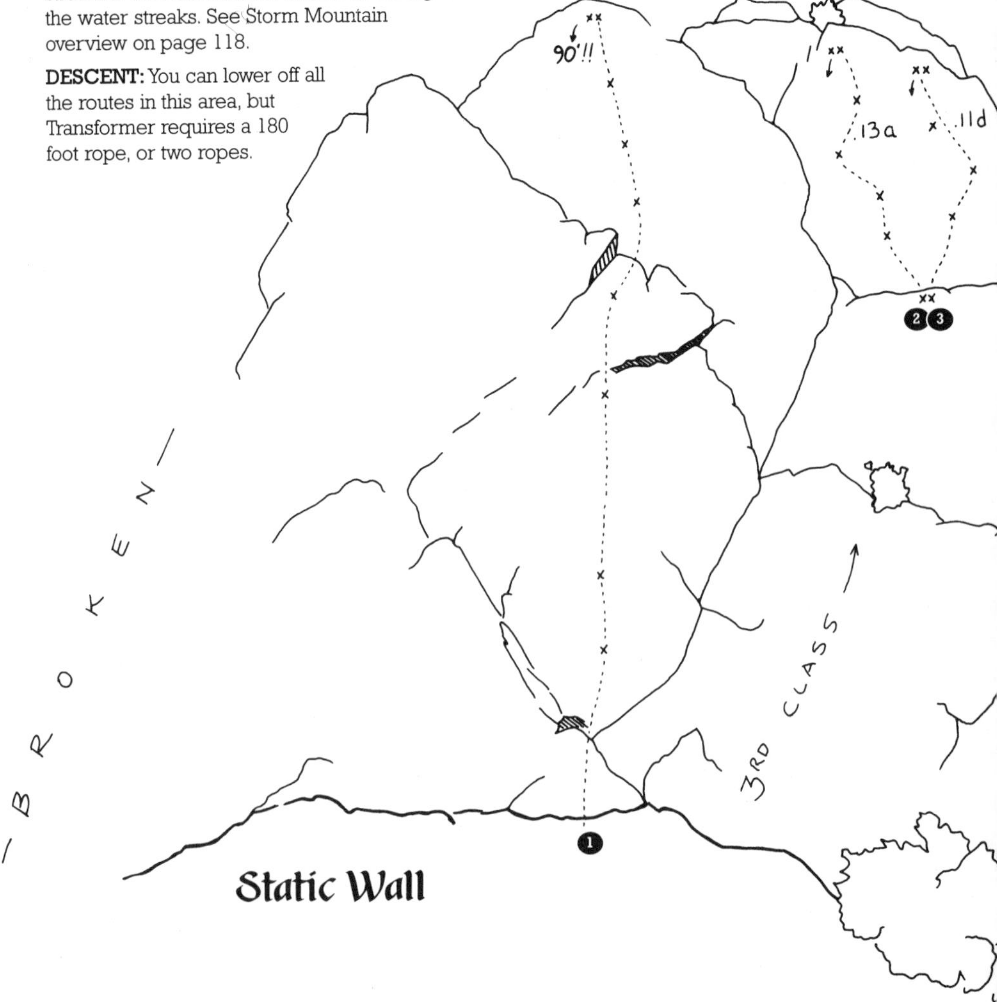

STATIC WALL ROUTES

STORM MOUNTAIN FALLS—MIXED ICE ROUTE
The 3-pitch ice climb just left of Transformer. This route usually sports thin ice and requires some mixed climbing.

1. TRANSFORMER 5.8 ★★
Vertical climbing with physical moves, protected by widely spaced bolts.
FA: Brian Smoot and Sam Carter, 1994.

2. SPINNING IN THE DRAIN 5.13a ★
After a few attempts, most climbers' forearms get spun down the drain. Although short, Spinning requires execution of a difficult sequence that eludes many.
FA: Stuart Ruckman, 1988.

3. ALL STATIC AND NO DYNAMIC 5.11d ★
Despite the name, a little dynamic action might be in order. Three bolts protect this furious fling.
FA: Merrill Bitter, 1987.

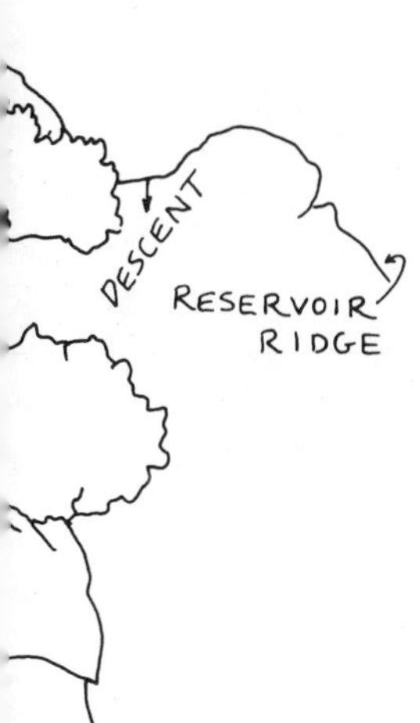

STORM MOUNTAIN PICNIC AREA —RESERVOIR RIDGE

This rib of rock climbs upwards from reservior level to meet the Static Wall. It is located immediately north of the concrete dam at the west end of the reservoir.

APPROACH: Follow the approach information for Storm Mountain Island East Face. After crossing the bridge, turn right and follow the path that climbs the hill to the reservoir. Walk north along the reservoir to the rock rib at the end of the concrete. See Storm Mountain overview page 118.

DESCENT: Descend to the west by down-climbing cracks and ramps that are not too easy. Some exposed sections.

RESERVOIR RIDGE ROUTES (no topo)

1. RESERVOIR RIDGE 5.4 ★★
A fun, three-pitch ridge climb with exposure, great rock, and only the occasional tricky move. The east face of this ridge is the site of a 5.5 climb with several variations, and considerable topropping.

Mule Hollow Wall
—Sea of Glass Wall
1. THE GROUND GLASS 5.6 ★★
2. SEA OF GLASS 5.9+ R ★
3. GLASNOST 5.8 R
—Descent Gully routes
4. PAT'S ARETE 5.7 R
5. DELUSIONS OF GRANDEUR 5.10d ★★
6. KIM AT THE GYM 5.10d ★
—Main Wall
7. EXPLORIEN 5.8 ★★
8. SOUTH CORNER ROUTE 5.5 R ★
9. LEFT OF CENTER ROUTE 5.5 R ★★★
10. THE CENTER FACE 5.6 R ★★★
11. JAM CRACK ROUTE 5.6 ★★★
12. HIGH ON CRACK 5.8+ ★
13. PINNACLE ROUTES 5.5 ★
14. YOU'RE ON YOUR OWN 5.10c ★★
60'
90'
.5
150'
60'
90'
.9+ R
.8 R
.6
1
2
3
4
5
6
7
8

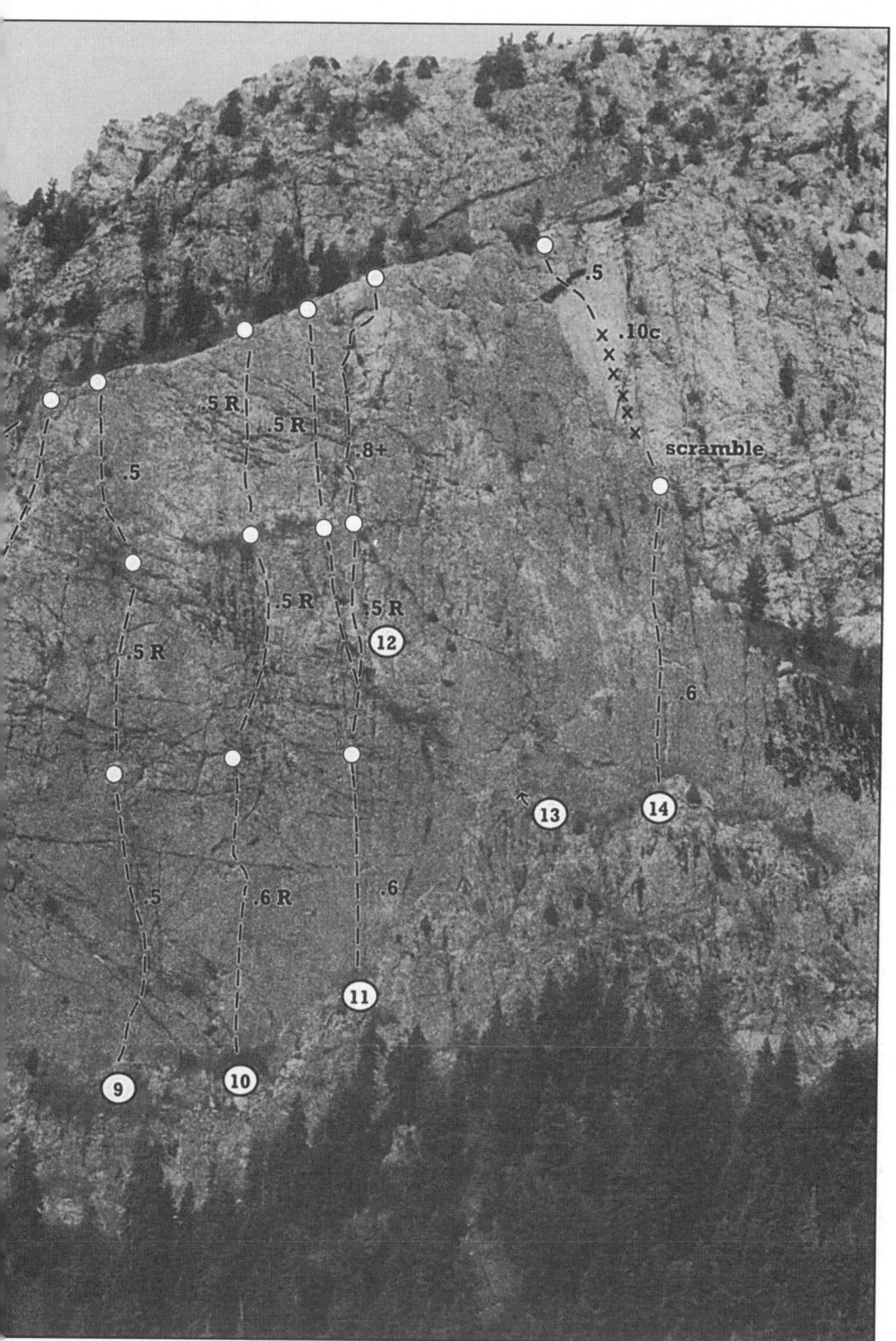
.5
.10c
scramble
.5 R
.5 R
.8+
.5
.5 R
.5 R
12
.5 R
.6
13
14
.5
.6 R
.6
11
9
10

MULE HOLLOW WALL

Located three-quarters of a mile up Mule Hollow Gulch, this large, east-facing wall sports some of the best quartzite in the Wasatch. At its highest point, the wall stands nearly 500 feet tall. The first pitches are close to vertical, and bucket holds are standard issue. Seemingly remote, the Mule Hollow Wall is a great place to escape crowds and enjoy quality multi-pitch routes.

APPROACH: Park at a pullout on the left (west) side of the road 2.95 miles up canyon from the neon sign. This parking area is .2 miles beyond the Storm Mountain Picnic area, just after the road crosses the Big Cottonwood stream. Follow the hiking trail in the narrow canyon bottom northward for roughly three-quarters of a mile. The trail stays in the canyon bottom, near the stream, and in Spring, parts of the trail become stream beds. The trail crosses the stream many times and the turn-off to the wall is tricky to locate. Avoid cutting up the slope towards the wall too soon. Just the same, walking too far up the trail, then cutting up to the wall results in heinous brush as well. Take the time to locate a small talus field that spills from the west and barely reaches the trail. At the time of this writing, this was just before the tenth stream crossing (the trail goes from the west to east bank here) and directly across from a slope of shale. Ahead are two large boulders, one forming the left (west) bank of the stream and another up the slope. These boulders are just up canyon of this talus field. Scramble up this talus and walk through the pines directly above. After a steep couple hundred feet, a larger talus field will be gained. About 300 feet above this is the descent gully for the main Mule Hollow routes. Watch for snakes! Approximate approach time: 45 minutes to one hour. See overview on page 48.

DESCENT: Two descents are possible, one a walk off and one involving two rappels with rockfall hazard. For both options, walk south along the top of the wall. Resist the temptation to rappel from fixed anchors found near the top of the South Corner Route, as the anchors on this rappel are very sketchy. Continue south along ledge systems at the top of the wall to the large gully that forms the southern terminus of the cliff. The first descent rappels the first gully to the south, the one that looks "semi-reasonable" and has a pine tree with slings at its top. Two 60-foot rappels are involved. The first is off a big pine tree and the second is off two fixed pins. Take great care with rockfall, especially on this second rappel.

A second descent that avoids the rappels is to climb a mossy 10-foot wall directly behind the first rappel tree mentioned above, and traverse south to another gully that can be followed down to the base of the routes. This descent route avoids the rockfall hazards of the rappel gully and is highly recommended.

MULE HOLLOW WALL —SEA OF GLASS WALL

This wall is down and south of the descent gully. Very smooth in appearance, the wall actually offers more holds than you would think. The base is flat and pleasant. See topo page 140.

1. THE GROUND GLASS 5.6 ★★
Climb the long finger crack 20 feet right of the left-hand edge of the Sea of Glass Wall. Excellent protection on the first pitch leads to a ledge on the left, about 130 feet up. Continue up the thinning crack on good holds and widely-spaced protection.
FA: Stuart Ruckman, 1990.

2. SEA OF GLASS 5.9+ R ★
The route, at the right side of the smoothest section of the face, is a leftward-arching seam near the center of the wall. Follow the seam as it widens into a crack, and end above a large bush at a three-pin belay. Rappel the route (150 feet). Bring small nuts, micro nuts, etc.
FA: Pat Maloney and Ted Coletti, 1989.

3. GLASNOST 5.8 R
This basically tackles the smooth rock 25 feet right of Sea Of Glass. Rappel Sea of Glass. Bring RP's and small tri-cams.
FA: Bret Ruckman and Fred Thalmann, 1990.

MULE HOLLOW WALL —DESCENT GULLY

At the base of the rappel descent gully are several steep crack climbs. See topo page 140.

4. PAT'S ARETE 5.7 R
Climb the runout arête left of Delusions to its belay.
FA: Pat Maloney and Ted Coletti, 1989.

5. DELUSIONS OF GRANDEUR 5.10d ★★
Climb the north-facing, right-angling finger crack at the base of this gully. The belay is around the corner to the left after 60 feet.
FA: Pat Maloney and Ted Coletti, 1989.

6. KIM AT THE GYM 5.10d ★
Climb the south-facing crack directly across the gully from Delusions (5.10d). The second pitch follows the 90-foot, left-leaning, south-facing crack 30 feet up the gully from the top of the first pitch (5.9). Descend the rappel gully. Small to medium nuts are called for.
FA: Bret Ruckman and Fred Thalmann, 1990.

MULE HOLLOW WALL —MAIN WALL

This is the 500-foot main section of rock, with a ledge at its base. See topo page 140.

7. EXPLORIEN 5.8 ★★

A mostly bolt protected face climb that bee-lines to the top of the "pinnacle" on the left side of the main wall. Although not absolutely necessary, most parties bring gear that includes stoppers and a few camming devices. Start twenty feet right of the arête, and make two 180 foot rappels to get off, or finish on the South Corner Route.

FA: Brian Smoot and Mark Galbraith, 1996.

8. SOUTH CORNER ROUTE 5.5 R ★

This route follows a right-facing corner for one pitch to the top of a conical-shaped "pinnacle" near the left side of the main wall. Two more pitches stay near the left-hand arête reaching to the top of the wall.

9. LEFT OF CENTER ROUTE 5.5 R ★★★

Climb up the numerous cracks that are above a left-diagonalling brushy ledge and alcove. Start to the left of the vegetation and join the cracks for some fun bucket-pulling. Three long pitches reach the top, with the second ending at a brushy ledge at two-thirds height. The last pitch follows a three- to four-inch crack directly above the ledge.

10. THE CENTER FACE 5.6 R ★★★

Climb a thin crack 75 feet left of the Jam Crack Route. This crack is directly below the middle of the treed ledge at two-thirds height. Angle left, following the protection, to a tricky 5.6 section below a ledge. Two more pitches above, all on excellent rock, complete the climb. Some hidden pockets on the last pitch are a real surprise. Do not pass up any protection opportunities.

11. JAM CRACK ROUTE 5.6 ★★★

This is the prominent crack on the right end of the cliff, 100 feet left of the pinnacle. The first pitch is great climbing and sports bomber protection. The second and third pitches get easier and have more difficult pro.

12. HIGH ON CRACK 5.8+ ★

A variation that climbs the wide crack to the right of the second and third pitches of the Jam Crack Route. Large cams are needed.

FA: Tony Calderone and Kathy Lagerquist, 1992.

13. PINNACLE ROUTES 5.5 ★

Three routes have ascended this formation. Climb the face directly above the pinnacle – or the crack to the right (by the bush) – or the crack even further right. Three pitches lead to the large ledge system at the top of the cliff.

14. YOU'RE ON YOUR OWN 5.10c ★★

As the name suggests . . . This route climbs the extremely smooth, inset face on the north (right) end of the main wall. From a ledge 100 feet right of the top of the pinnacle, climb a shallow corner system (5.6) for 135 feet to the large, brushy ledge near the base of the second pitch. Scramble up this ledge and belay off the first bolt. Seven bolts, TCU's, tri-cams, RP's and a host of other goodies protect this long pitch on very good rock. Angle left at the top for the belay.

FA: Pat Contor and Susan Ashley, 1988.

THE LIBERATOR GULLY (no topo)

One-half mile up canyon from the Storm Mountain Picnic area, on the north side of the road, are three steep parallel gullies. The Liberator is the west-most of these three—the one that begins as a dark shale band with quartzite underneath. It's a safe bet that crowds won't be a problem on these routes. The rock quality, however, is good.

APPROACH: Park at a small pullout 3.1 miles up canyon from the neon sign. This pullout is .45 miles above the Storm Mountain Picnic Area and .1 mile below the large turnaround area that serves as parking for the Gully of Higher Education. Bushwhack directly up the gully (unpleasant), staying close to the right hand (east) wall. The Liberator resides on a smooth south-facing wall capped by a leftward-leaning roof. See overview on page 48.

DESCENT: A one rope rappel from a two-bolt anchor at the top of The Liberator is the easiest way down..

1. WAR PAINT 5.7
Climb the V-slot corner-and-crack 15 feet left of The Liberator. Some slippery stems provide entertainment.
FA: Stuart Ruckman and Libby Ellis, 1990.

2. SCARS 5.11 TR ★★
Climb the arête between The Liberator and War Paint on small, sharp edges. Start eight feet left of The Liberator.
FA: Stuart Ruckman, 1990.

3. THE LIBERATOR 5.10a ★★
Climb directly up the center of the face, past six bolts on excellent rock, to a two-bolt rappel. Devious.
FA: Libby Ellis and Stuart Ruckman, 1990.

RESURRECTION AREA (no topo)

Once a popular crag, this area is unfortunately located on private property. The landowners, concerned over liability issues, have closed this crag to climbing. Please respect their wishes.

GULLY OF HIGHER EDUCATION

Graduates of this gully will be skilled in navigating steep rock with an abundance of features, only a few of which are positive enough to call holds. Protected by everything from all-bolts to tiny RPs, the leads here run the gamut from knee-quaking to awe-inspiring. A bachelor's degree is usually awarded for the successful completion of Trail of Tiers. A master's degree goes to those bold students who lead Dr. Luval Goes to Harvard, and a doctorate degree is endowed to the few stunned graduates of Ms. Luval Cranks A Thesis.

APPROACH: Park at a large parking area on the left (north) side of the road 3.25 miles up canyon from the neon sign. This parking is .55 miles up canyon from the Storm Mountain Picnic Area. Walk down canyon from the parking area, past the large pine trees to an unstable talus slope descending from the gully. Tromp up the scree until the west-facing routes are reached. The first routes encountered require about five minutes, the furthest, fifteen or more minutes. The routes are described from the top of the gully to the bottom (north to south). See overview on page 48.

DESCENT: Routes 6-10 can be descended with a single rope from anchors at the top of each route. The remaining climbs require a walk off. Routes 2-5 can be descended to the east via some downclimbing.

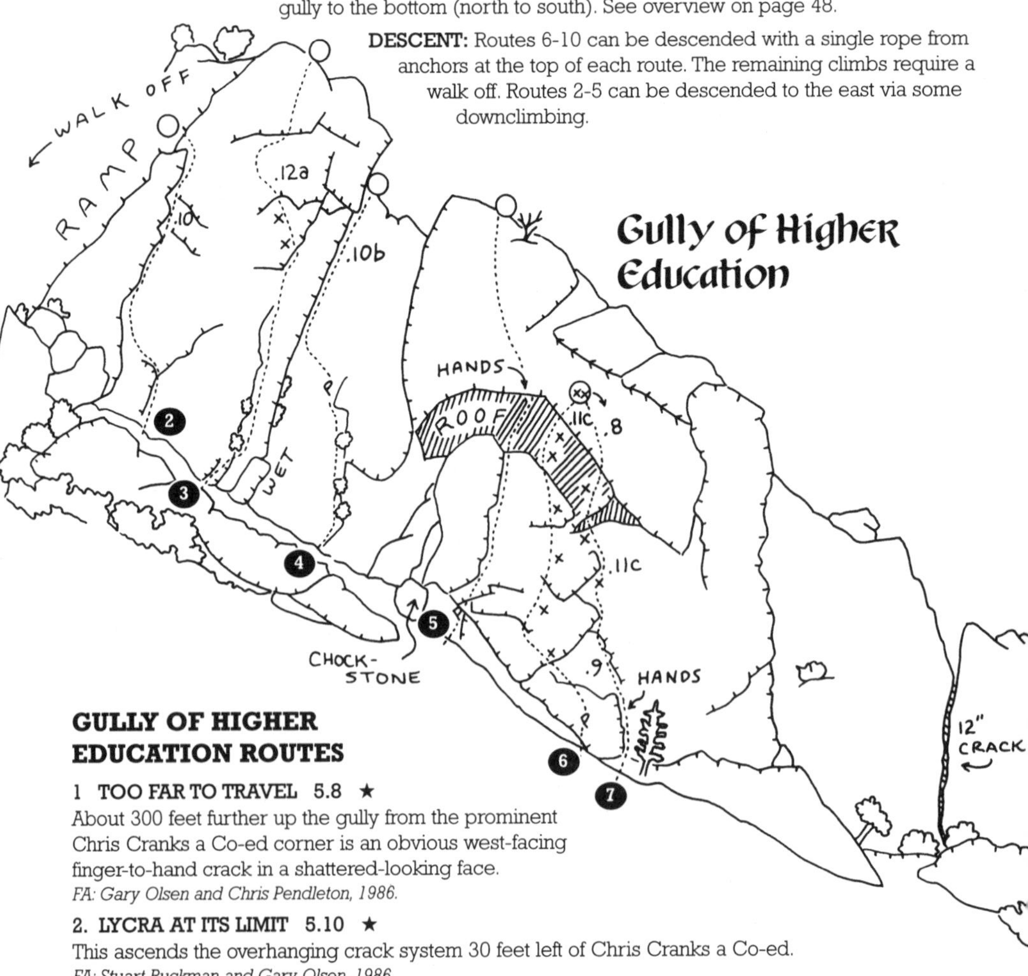

GULLY OF HIGHER EDUCATION ROUTES

1 TOO FAR TO TRAVEL 5.8 ★

About 300 feet further up the gully from the prominent Chris Cranks a Co-ed corner is an obvious west-facing finger-to-hand crack in a shattered-looking face.

FA: Gary Olsen and Chris Pendleton, 1986.

2. LYCRA AT ITS LIMIT 5.10 ★

This ascends the overhanging crack system 30 feet left of Chris Cranks a Co-ed.

FA: Stuart Ruckman and Gary Olsen, 1986.

3. MS. LUVAL CRANKS A THESIS 5.12a R ★★

A higher cognizance is needed to keep it together on this route. Start five feet left of Chris Cranks a Co-ed. Bring loads of micro nuts and extra guns. Two bolts are well hidden from below.

FA: Merrill Bitter and Stuart Ruckman, 1986.

4. CHRIS CRANKS A CO-ED 5.10b ★
The only real obvious feature in this gully is a right-facing, right-leaning corner. This route climbs the corner, but usually starts to the right to avoid a wet section at the base of the corner.
FA: Gary Olsen and Chris Pendleton, 1986.

5. DR. LUVAL GOES TO HARVARD 5.11d R ★
Another Bitter tribute to RP's and loved ones. On the lower section of the gully, just before a chockstone blocks the way, is a roof with a crack in it. Agilely move up to the roof, being wary of poor protection. The roof itself protects better. Micro nuts and one fixed pin are needed, as well as medium sized camming units. Led from the ground up.
FA: Merrill Bitter and Stuart Ruckman, 1986.

6. TRAIL OF TIERS 5.11c ★★
Work up over tiered roofs, past one pin and six bolts. Neat "headrests". A TCU works well on the hand traverse at the start.
FA: Stuart and Bret Ruckman, 1990.

7. ACADEMIA NUT 5.11c ★
Climb up a left-angling corner, above a juniper tree, 30 feet downhill from the chockstone. Bring a #3 Friend and RP's for the easier bottom section. The first roof is a brain-teaser.
FA: Bret and Stuart Ruckman, 1990.

8. THE PROFESSOR 5.12c ★★
This is the south-facing shield of iron-clad quartzite, 15 feet to the left of Big Man On Campus and The Graduate. Five bolts protect this studious lead.
FA: Stuart and Bret Ruckman, 1990.

9. BIG MAN ON CAMPUS 5.9+
This is located on the first good west-facing stuff in the gully. Climbs a balancey crack and turns the roof to the left. Short.
FA: Stuart Ruckman and Libby Ellis, 1990.

10. THE GRADUATE 5.9- ★
Climbs the right bolt line and turns the roof on the right. Short.
FA: Stuart Ruckman and Libby Ellis, 1990.

11. MR. B CRANKS A FECES 5.11b/c ★
This south-facing wall is located 200 feet from the road, near the bottom of the gully. A left-slanting finger crack leads to broken face.
FA: Drew Bedford, 1987.

12. B.S. 5.9
20 feet right of Mr. B. Cranks A Feces. Climb a short crack and face.
FA: Gary Olsen, solo, 1986.

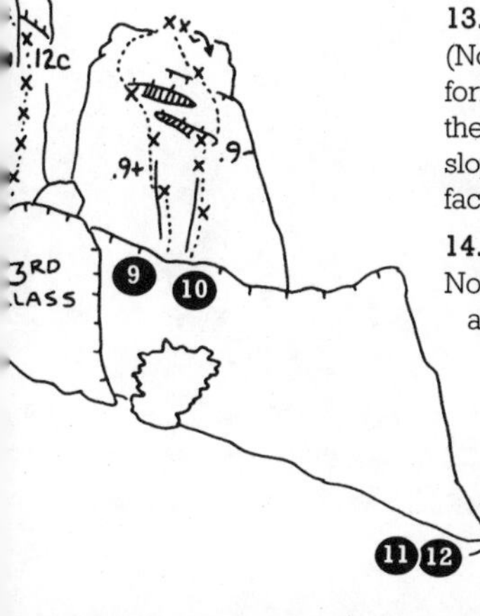

13. MCKINLEY'S CRACK 5.7 ★
(Not on topo) This fine crack is located on the west face of the wall that forms the left side of the Gully of Higher Education. From the base of the Gully of Higher Education, walk down the road 100 feet to a talus slope. March up up this talus 100 feet to the obvious crack splitting the face on the right.

14. LYCRA EATER 5.10 ★ (Not on topo.)
Not really a part of the Higher Education Gully, this route faces the road and is located on the east side of the Higher Education massif, and is approached by walking 200 feet directly above the parking area. Climb a leftward-arcing hand crack, just right of a "cave."
FA: Drew Bedford and Conrad Anker, 1987.

STRATAGEM (no topo)

This tiny crag is popular for bouldering. Eliminate problems are the rage on the short overhanging walls at the base of the crag. One leadable route is here, as well. Stratagem rests a mere 50 feet from the road, on the north side, just right of a black iron fence.

APPROACH: Park 3.55 miles up canyon from the neon sign (about 1.5 miles up the BCC road from Storm Mountain Picnic Area). See overview on page 48.

DESCENT: Two bolts at the top provide handy rappel or top rope anchors with a single rope.

1. STRATAGEM 5.10d ★
Glide up through a series of roofs, staying in the main corner system, and turn the final crux roof out right. One relic pin under the top roof and two pins at the top provide the only fixed gear. Bring nuts, tri-cams and small TCU's.
FA: unknown; FFA: Joe Schnebly, 1965.

Kris Petriega on the relentless Inversion Therapy. Millstone Area.

photo: George Rosenthal.

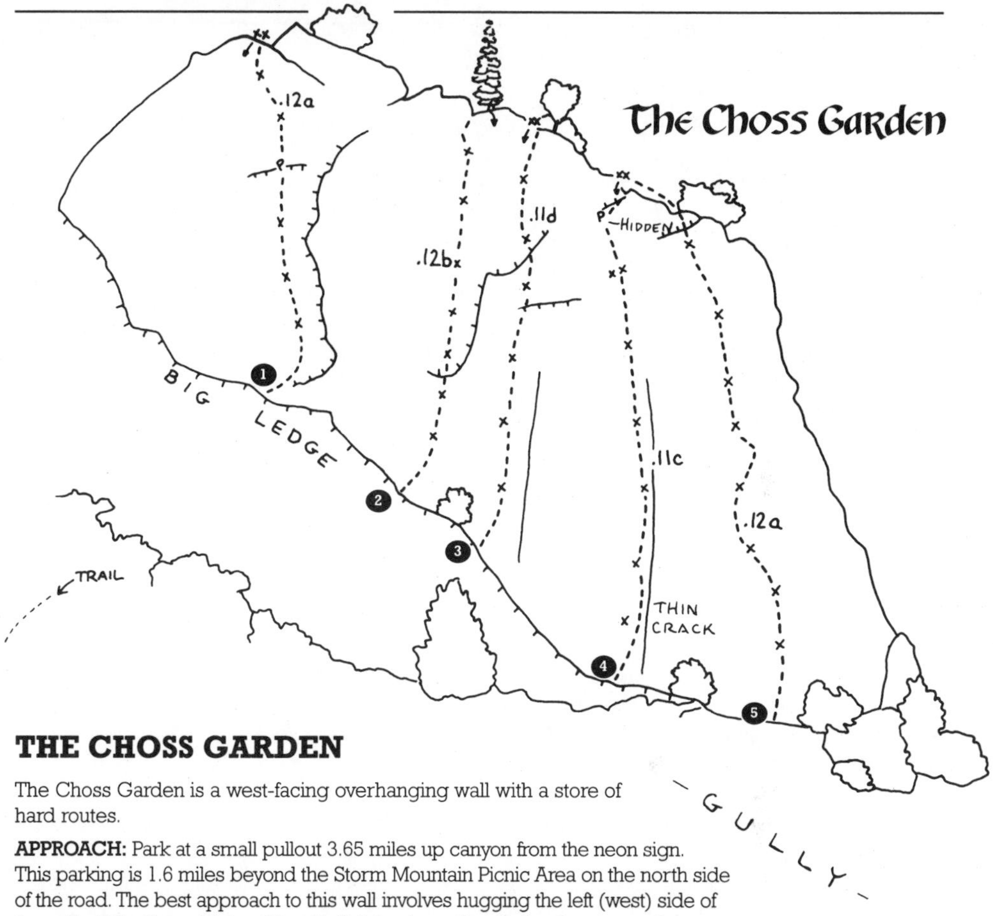

THE CHOSS GARDEN

The Choss Garden is a west-facing overhanging wall with a store of hard routes.

APPROACH: Park at a small pullout 3.65 miles up canyon from the neon sign. This parking is 1.6 miles beyond the Storm Mountain Picnic Area on the north side of the road. The best approach to this wall involves hugging the left (west) side of the gully (following a faint path) until slightly above the climbs, then traversing east over to them. The approach takes about 15 minutes. See overview on page 48.

DESCENT: It is possible to rappel off all the routes here with a single rope.

CHOSS GARDEN ROUTES

1. PITBULLS ON CRACK 5.12a ★
This is the left bolt line, which lies immediately left of a prominent corner system. Less than perfect rock.
FA: Bret and Stuart Ruckman, 1990.

2. THE BENEFACTOR 5.12b ★★
Tie on a burly pump. Greatly improved rock above the third bolt. Almost three stars.
FA: Bret and Stuart Ruckman, 1990.

3. UP IN ARMS 5.11d ★
After a 5.10 face, engage the crux bulge with its airy moves.
FA: Bret and Stuart Ruckman, 1990.

4. TOUCHY SUBJECT 5.11c ★★
Six bolts and one hidden pin protect continuously difficult face climbing.
FA: Bret and Stuart Ruckman, 1990.

5. DEPTH OF FIELD 5.12a ★★
The most popular line on the cliff. Fantastic wandering on the right side.
FA: Stuart and Bret Ruckman, 1990.

THE PENGUIN (no topo)

The Penguin is a pinnacle located on an east-facing wall that forms the left side of a broad, shallow gully. Located along the approach to the Beer Belly Buttress, The Penguin takes about 15 to 20 minutes to reach. This small pinnacle is hard to discern until you get close to it. See overview on page 48.

APPROACH: Follow the approach to the Beer Belly Buttress. Keep an eye out for this east-facing wall which is on the west side of the approach gully.

DESCENT: Anchors at the top make a quick single rope rappel possible.

1. TOTALLY GILLIGAN 5.6
The south face has a thin crack that turns a small roof.
FA: Pat Contor, 1987.

2. THE PENGUIN 5.10a
Two bolts and a pin protect this short route on the west face.
FA: Pat Contor, winter 1987.

THE POINT (no topo)

Located along the approach to the Beer Belly Buttress, The Point takes about 20 minutes of walking to reach. The Point is an interesting corridor of steep quartzite 500 feet above The Penguin. Its routes are about 40 feet high, and the rock is less metamorphosed than the typical BCC rock. If you are seeking solitude, The Point is hard to beat. Don't miss the formation, though, or you'll end up at Beer Belly Buttress.

APPROACH: Follow the approach to the Beer Belly Buttress. You will pass right by The Point en route to Beer Belly. See overview on page 48.

DESCENT: Anchors at the top of most of the routes allow easy single rope rappels.

1. POINT BLANK 5.11b ★
As the name implies, blank climbing on a 80-degree slab is the agenda. This route is located on the farthest uphill and west-facing side of the formation. There are five bolts.
FA: Stuart Ruckman and Gordon Douglass, 1990.

2. POINT OF CONCEPTION 5.10a R ★
Steep climbing on the west face, 20 feet left of Point of View. Climb past a pin into a hueco and continue straight up. Bring RP's.
FA: Bret and Stuart Ruckman, 1990.

3. POINT OF VIEW 5.11b ★★
Glide up the bolt line just left of the arête. If you persevere on the sloping holds, you may capture The Point a vue. Five bolts protect the climb.
FA: Stuart Ruckman and Gordon Douglass, 1990.

4. POINT OF IGNITION 5.11b ★
Flame directly up the prow on mostly good holds. Once again, five bolts mark the route.
FA: Gordon Douglass and Stuart Ruckman, 1990.

5. COUNTERPOINT 5.10d ★
Within the corridor itself, on its west-facing wall, is a face leading to a thin crack. This route sports three bolts.
FA: Stuart Ruckman and Gordon Douglass, 1990.

Steve Kauffman throwing back Miller Time, The Millstone.

photo: Ruckman.

3
1
2
4
5
BEER BELLY BUTTRESS ROUTES
1. LUMINOUS ANIMALS 5.11b ★★★
2. PERSPECTIVE CONTROL 5.10d ★★
3. KEY WAY 5.11a ★
PINNACLE AREA ROUTES
4. KRONENBORG ARETE 5.9 R ★★
5. KATIE'S FOOD 5.9/5.10 ★
THE MAIN FACE ROUTES
6. RIBBON IN THE SKY 5.10c ★★★
7. WHIP-POOR-WILL CRACK 5.11a ★★★
8. FRACTURE ZONE 5.10 ★★
9. SIX-PACK CRACK 5.8 ★★
10. 12 OZ. CURL 5.10d ★★
11. JUDE THE OBSCURE 5.8

6
7
8
9
10
11

BEER BELLY BUTTRESS

The best view of this buttress is from along the road just past the parking area for Mule Hollow wall, and in the Gully of Higher Education vicinity. If you look way up high and to the left (north), you'll see a smooth-looking set of west-facing slabs. This is the Beer Belly Buttress, the ultimate misnomer for an area with a horrendous approach. This collection of walls holds many surprises. The routes are some of the best in BCC—featuring long pitches, great rock, stupendous views and total isolation.

APPROACH: Park 3.9 miles up canyon from the neon sign. A lone pine tree right next to road at the lowest, most eastern edge of a gully marks the inobvious start. By linking up scree/talus slopes in the gully, angling slighting left, you'll reach The Penguin, which usually requires a bit of a traverse left (west) to reach. From The Penguin, walk up and right (east) to access The Point. If this linking of talus is followed, most brush can be avoided. Once 200 yards beyond The Point, start a rightward traverse to the Beer Belly Buttress. This is probably an hour-and-a-half approach, ending at roughly a 9000-foot elevation—and is arduous, to say the least. See overview on page 48.

DESCENT: The descent from the routes on the main Beer Belly face can be accomplished with an 80-foot rappel off the right shoulder from the top of 12 oz. Curl, or a 160-foot rappel off Ribbon in the Sky. Simultaneous rappelling escapes the Beer Belly Pinnacle. Routes 1-3 are descended by traversing to the top of Beer Belly Buttress and utilizing one of the rappels there.

The following three routes are on the spectacular south-facing fins above and north of the Beer Belly Pinnacle.

BEER BELLY BUTTRESS ROUTES

1. LUMINOUS ANIMALS 5.11b ★★★

The left of the two major fins. Pump it out up the steeeep face. Take gear, for sure. A crack above provides an optional second pitch.

FA: Pat Contor and Gary Taylor, 1988.

2. PERSPECTIVE CONTROL 5.10d ★★

The right of the two major fins. Climb the left arête past six bolts. RP's, TCU's and tri-cams should supplement the rack.

FA: Pat Contor and Kevin Sweeny, 1988.

3. KEY WAY 5.11a ★

A variation to Perspective Control. Traverse right at the ledge, and climb the south face past two bolts. There are some awkward moves. Bring RP's.

FA: Pat Contor and Gary Taylor, 1988.

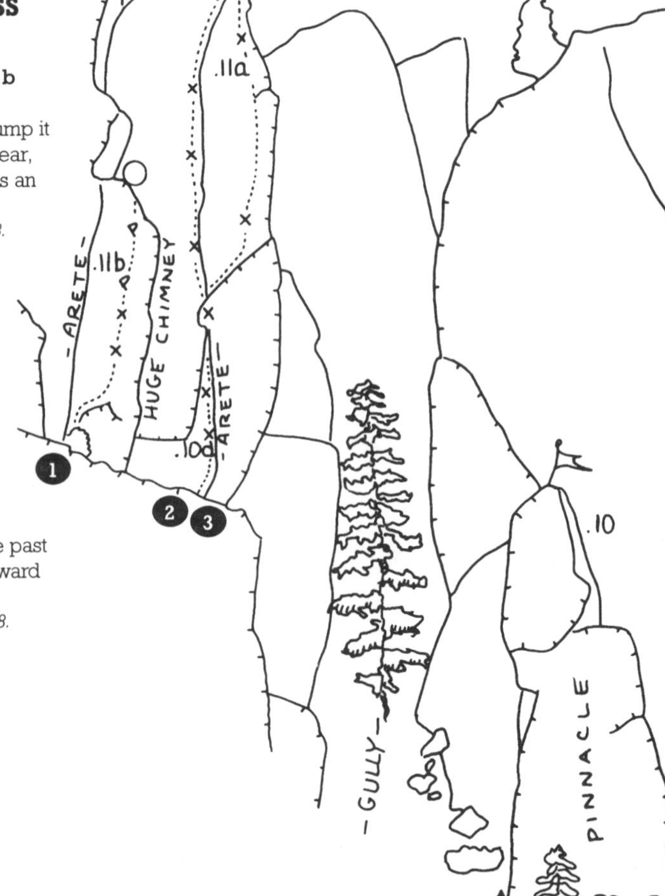

BEER BELLY PINNACLE AREA

This pinnacle is just west of the main Beer Belly Face. Simul-rappels are required for descent.

4. KRONENBORG ARÊTE 5.9 R ★★
Climb the southwest arête of the pinnacle. The first move is the crux—groundfall potential.
FA: Pat Contor and Kevin Sweeny, 1988.

5. KATIE'S FOOD 5.9/5.10 ★
Climb a nice crack on the pinnacle's north face.
FA: Pat Contor and Kevin Sweeny, 1988.

THE MAIN BEER BELLY FACE

This is the middle of three west faces – the one that looks the best.

6. RIBBON IN THE SKY 5.10c ★★★
Climb the 140-foot face on the left side of the main face. This route features some of the best quartzite in the canyon. Take gear from micro nuts to a 2- 1/2" cam. Two ropes are needed for the rappel (or rappel off of 12 Oz. Curl with one rope). Protection is tricky to find, but adequate.
FA: Pat Contor and Gary Taylor, 1988.

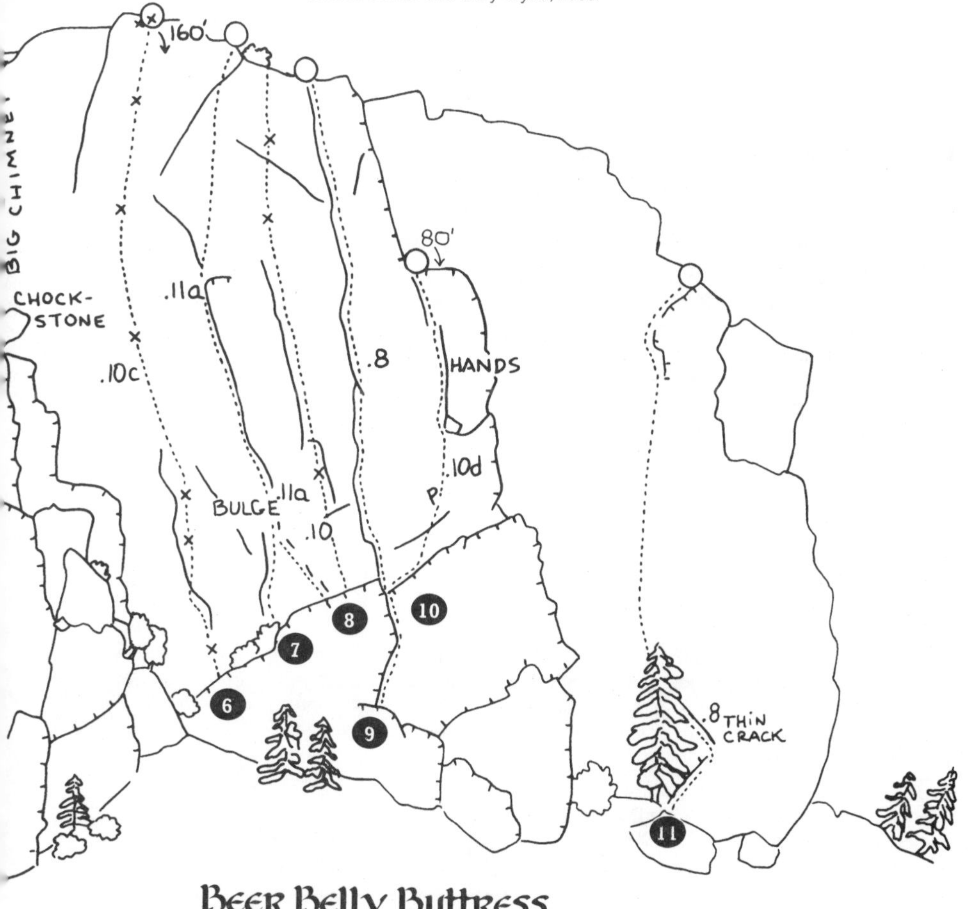

Beer Belly Buttress

BEER BELLY BUTTRESS ROUTES

7. WHIP-POOR-WILL CRACK 5.11a ★★★

This is a series of hairline cracks on excellent rock left of Six-Pack Crack. Tired legs might suggest Contor Line as a more apropos name. Bring brass tyoe nuts and several of the smallest TCU's. Once the crack dissipates, continue straight up, using horizontal cracks for protection.

First top-roped: Dana Hauser

FA: Pat Contor and Kevin Sweeny, 1988.

8. FRACTURE ZONE 5.10 ★★

Perhaps 10 feet left of Six Pack Crack is another thin seam. Three bolts and thin, imaginative gear protect this.

FA: Pat Contor and Kevin Sweeny, 1988.

9. SIX-PACK CRACK 5.8 ★★

This is the main feature on the wall—a crack system in the middle. It starts in a right-facing corner and continues up hand/fist cracks for a full rope length.

FA: Chris Pendleton and Bret Ruckman, 1985.

10. 12 OZ. CURL 5.10d ★★

Immediately right of the end of the first dihedral on Six Pack Crack are thin cracks leading up to a tight hand crack. Pumping moves by the pin.

FA: Bret Ruckman and Chris Pendleton, 1985.

11. JUDE THE OBSCURE 5.8

On the recessed face just south of the main face is a wall with many cracks. This route starts directly behind the pine tree. Move up a rightward-diagonalling weakness for 10 feet, then traverse 15 feet left on a thin crack. Improvise the rest.

FA: Bret and Judy Ruckman, 1985.

CAESAR'S PALACE (no topo)

Remote and uncrowded, this area is a complex series of outcrops, gullies, and fins of rock. Although a ton of rock exists, only a few adventurous souls have made the trek to this area. If you've got a craving for exploration and the unknown, this is a good place to satisfy the appetite.

APPROACH: Park 4.2 miles up canyon from the neon sign. A small road comes in from the right (east) and leads to the parking lot for the Lake Blanche and Broad's Fork trailheads. While standing at the Broad's Fork trailhead, look north and slightly west. A giant rock formation resembling a poor person's Devil's Tower looms to the west of the Mill B North Fork drainage. This formation is known as Caesar's Palace. The approach is rough, sometimes brushy, and long. The path of least resistance seems to follow the west ridge of Mill B North Fork. Eventually a traverse west to avoid brush gains a series of broken slabs and grass. Above this section, another westward traverse allows access to a gully topped by a huge chockstone. This chockstone guards the base of the South Face of Caesar's Palace. Walk to the east from the chockstone to access the East Face route, west to find Edge of Hell.

DESCENT: See the individual route descriptions.

1. EAST FACE 5.7 ★

A route has been reported on the east face. Wander up good rock for a full 165 foot pitch. Walk off.

FA: Brian Wieland and Scott Keller, 1994.

2. EDGE OF HELL 5.11a ★★

Not located on the Caesar's Palace formation. This route is found roughly a thousand yards west of Caesar's Palace and at the head of a significant gully between Beer Belly Buttress and Caesar's Palace. Climb a very nice finger crack on the formations east side. One fixed pin and gear up to two inches protects the lead, while a 65 foot rappel gets you back down to the ground.

FA: Scott Keller and Brian Wieland, 1994.

3. IDES OF MARCH 5.11b/c TR ★

Top rope the face to the left of the Edge of Hell.

FA: Scott Keller and Brian Wieland, 1994.

Gina Sorensen leading Right Pile.

photo: Lee Cohen.

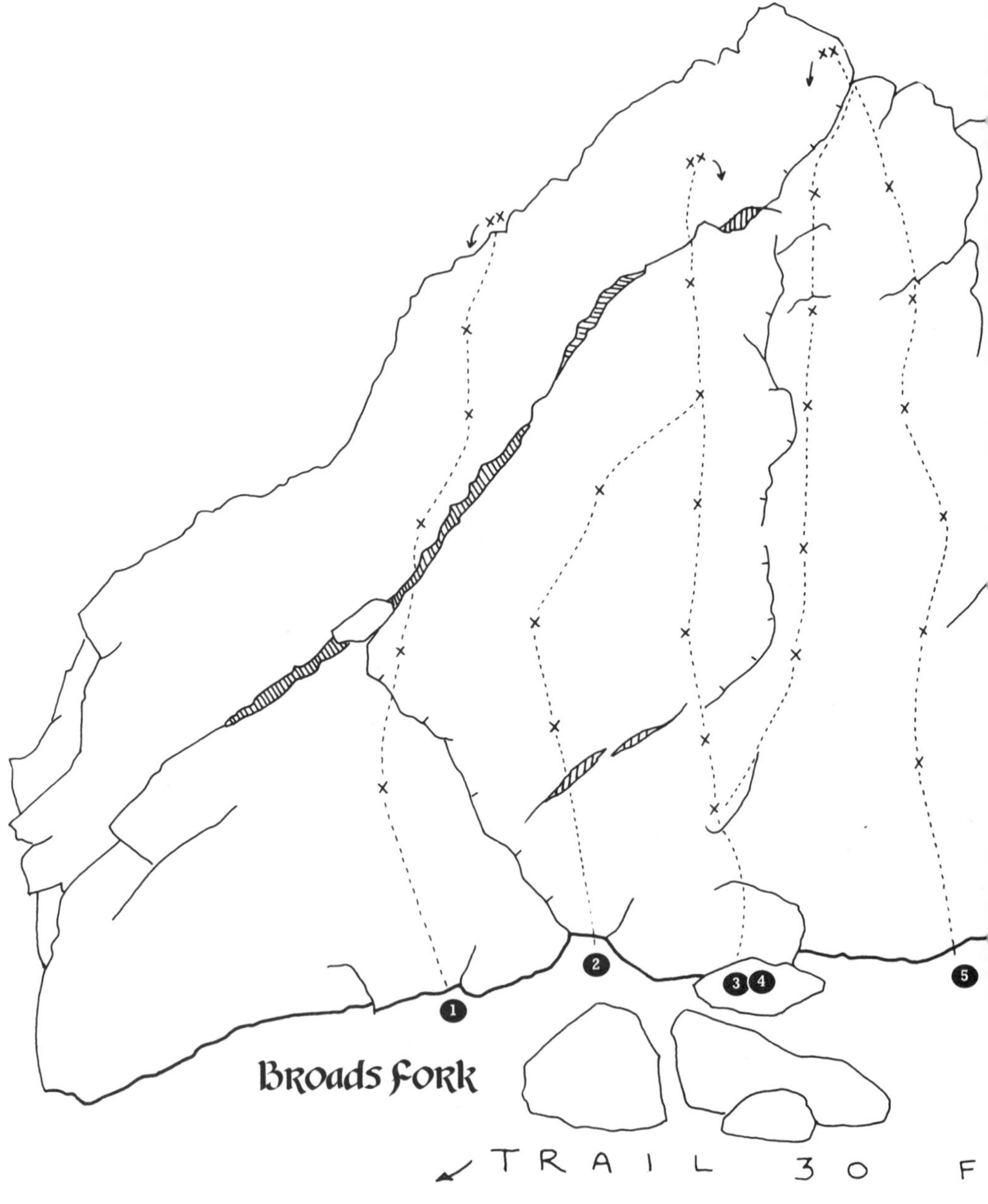
1
2
3
4
5
Broads Fork
TRAIL 30 F

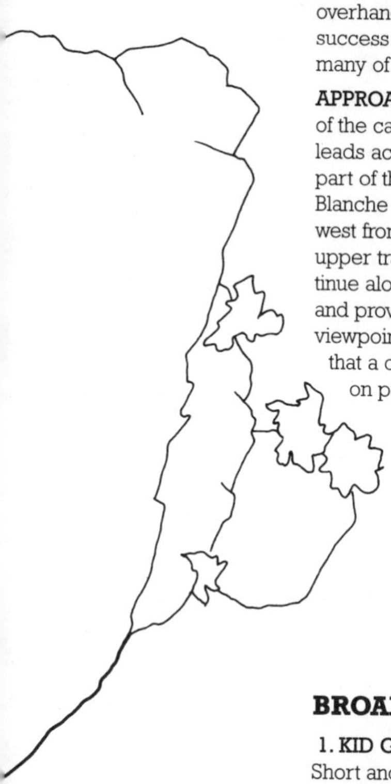

BROAD'S FORK

This small wall offers shady climbing and a relatively easy approach, that is just long enough to keep the crowds at bay. All of the routes overhang, and require the power necessary for steep stone. However, success at Broad's Fork is assured more by finesse than brawn, since many of the holds are inobvious or angled inconveniently.

APPROACH: Park 4.2 miles up canyon from the neon sign at the mouth of the canyon. A small spur road joins the highway from the right, and leads across a bridge to a small parking lot. This road is at the lowest part of the "S-Curve". Parking here is for the Broad's Fork and Lake Blanche Trailheads. Walk up the Broad's Fork Trail, the trail that heads west from the south end of the parking lot. The Broad's Fork Trail is the upper trail, not the lower path which follows the stream. Basically, continue along the hiking trail which starts out steep, then rounds a ridge and provides a good view of Big Cottonwood Canyon. Shortly after the viewpoint the trail enters the Twin Peaks Wilderness, and shortly after that a dark crag appears on the right. This is the place. See overview on page 170.

DESCENT: Lower off anchors at the top of every route with one rope.

BROAD'S FORK ROUTES

1. KID GLOVES 5.10b ★

Short and steep, this turns the overhang on the left side of the wall.
FA: Stuart Ruckman and Fred Henion, 1991.

2. BROAD EXPECTATIONS 5.12c ★

Cross some difficult territory above the firepit until it is possible to join Plimsol Line for more hard moves.
FA: Brent Jeffry and Jeff Twait, 1996.

3. PLIMSOL LINE 5.12b ★★

A burly pull-down that seems to climb the underside of a ship's prow.
FA: Stuart Ruckman, 1991.

4. MISERY 5.11b ★

The overhanging corner system that fuels big stems.
FA: Fred Henion and Stuart Ruckman, 1991.

5. DUMB BROADS 5.11d ★★

The best line on the cliff. Continuous climbing through a sea of overhanging quartzite.
FA: Bret Ruckman and Stuart Ruckman, 1991.

THE MILLSTONE AND ENVIRONS

The first huge slab on the west side of the Lake Blanche Trail has a broad, vertical southeast face. This face offers a high concentration of quality vertical to overhanging routes that are mostly bolt protected. Expect sun in the mornings, shade in the afternoons and dramatic views of the upper cirque from atop the climbs.

APPROACH: 4.2 miles up canyon from the intersection at the mouth of the canyon, a small spur road comes in from the right and leads to a parking lot at the trailheads for the Broad's Fork and the Lake Blanche Trail. Park here and walk up the spur road toward the Lake Blanche Trail. The trail begins three hundred feet down canyon from the end of the road, right where the road crosses the creek. The main hiking trail follows the west side of the creek for a quarter mile to a bridge. The climbers trail to the Millstone doesn't cross the bridge, instead it stays on the right (west) side of the creek. Follow this path as it parallels the stream, climbs a short, steep bank, then continues paralleling the stream from the slopes above.

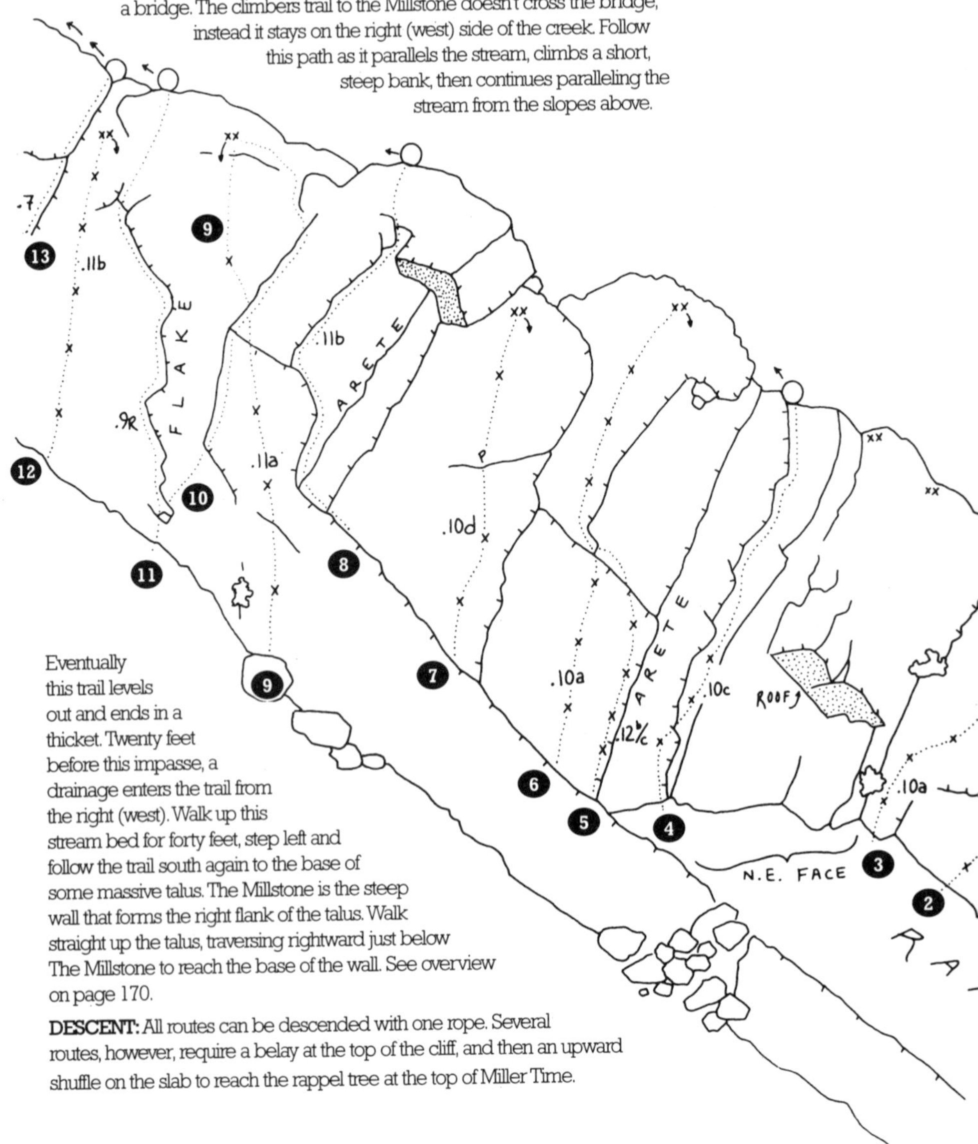

Eventually this trail levels out and ends in a thicket. Twenty feet before this impasse, a drainage enters the trail from the right (west). Walk up this stream bed for forty feet, step left and follow the trail south again to the base of some massive talus. The Millstone is the steep wall that forms the right flank of the talus. Walk straight up the talus, traversing rightward just below The Millstone to reach the base of the wall. See overview on page 170.

DESCENT: All routes can be descended with one rope. Several routes, however, require a belay at the top of the cliff, and then an upward shuffle on the slab to reach the rappel tree at the top of Miller Time.

THE MILLSTONE

The routes are described from right to left on the cliff.

1. INTELLIGENT LIFE FORM 5.8 ★
Walk across a 5.2 slab to the base of the route.
FA: Brian and Jonathan Smoot, 1990.

2. TIE DIE 5.10c ★
FA: Keith Maas, Jim Haisley and Eric Wood, 1990.

3. PRIVATE HELL 5.10a ★
Insecure.
FA: Brian Smoot and Bret Ruckman, 1990.

4. BLOCKBUSTER 5.10c ★
This is the only route completed on the severely overhung northeast face. Three bolts protect the initial moves, then small gear protects the remainder.
FA: Jim and Tomi Howe, 1989.

5. CALLING ALL KARMAS 5.12b ★
A difficult, balancey start to Angle of Repose.
FA: Tim Roberts, 1995.

6. ANGLE OF REPOSE 5.10a ★
The bolt line six feet left of the arête between the northeast and southeast faces.
FA: Tomi and Jim Howe, 1990.

7. PERSONAL JESUS 5.10d ★
This line is 20 feet left of Angle of Repose.
FA: Jim Howe and Keith Maas, 1990.

8. MILLING ABOUT 5.11b ★★
The right-facing, right-slanting corner with a 1-½" crack. Strenuous and Canyonlands-esque.
FA: Stuart Ruckman and Gary Olsen, 1987.

9. ERASERHEAD 5.11a ★★
The steep and continuous face just left of Milling About. Bring a few small pieces for the crack.
FA: Keith Maas and Gordon Douglass, 1989.

10. PENCILNECK 5.10c ★
Follow the thin crack up and across Eraserhead, eventually sharing its belay. Bring small gear.
FA:Jim Haisley and Jim Howe, 1989.

11. HOLLOW EXCUSES 5.9 R ★
The flake system, one of the main features on the southeast face, has scary moves and pro.
FA: Gary Olsen and Stuart Ruckman, 1987.

12. AGAINST THE ESTABLISHMENT 5.11b ★
Many climbers encounter an impasse in the vicinity of the third bolt.
FA: Brain Smoot and Kevin Florendo, 1990.

13. BUSH DOCTOR 5.7
FA: Tomi Howe, Tracy Maas and Barbara Bean, 1989.

he Millstone (lower)

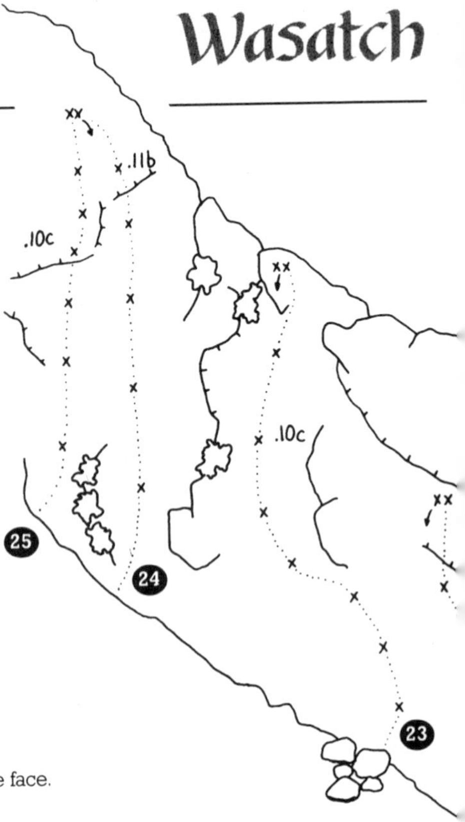

.11b
.10c
.10c
25
24
23

THE MILLSTONE ROUTES

14. MORONS OF THE MILITIA 5.10b TR ★
Climb the face between Bush doctor and Miller Time.
FA: Jonny Woodward, Robert Raker, 1996.

15. MILLER TIME 5.10c ★★
Hold off on the celebration until you've diced through the technical crux.
FA: Jim Haisely and Keith Maas, 1989.

16. EARTHLING 5.11a ★
Very delicate and strange.
FA: Brian Smoot and Bret Ruckman, 1990.

17. MOONWALK 5.11d ★★
The line of bolts just left of a large flake midway up the face. Deceptively steep and continuous.
FA: Jim Haisely and Keith Maas, 1989.

18. STRONG ARM WITH THE LADS 5.11a ★★
HH Overhangs galore.
FA: Jim Howe, Jim Haisely and Keith Maas, 1989.

19. STONE GROUND 5.11b ★★★
The thin crack system offers unique holds and brilliant climbing. Reachy and pumpy.
FA: Keith Maas and Eric Wood, 1989.

20. THE MAIZE 5.12a ★
A bifurcation of Stone Ground. Traverse left into no man's land after the second bolt.
FA: Jim Haisley, Keith Maas and Jim Howe, 1989.

21. THE ODD GET EVEN 5.11b ★★
Some sort of vindication? Five bolts of steepness just beyond a left-facing corner identified by a bush.
FA: Stuart and Bret Ruckman, 1990.

22. STICK FIGURE STAYS HOME 5.11a ★
Pump first, then pay. Some flexi-flakes grace the top.
FA: Jim Howe and Keith Maas, 1990.

23. CAT JUGGLING 5.10c ★
One of the longest on the Millstone.
FA: Brian and Jonathan Smoot, 1990.

24. LEAD BALLOON 5.11b ★
Increasingly hard to a wicked crux.
FA: Brian Smoot and Kevin Florendo, 1990.

25. YUPPIE LOVE 5.10c ★
This is 70 feet up from Stick Figure. The bulge is a blast.
FA: Keith and Tracy Maas, 1990.

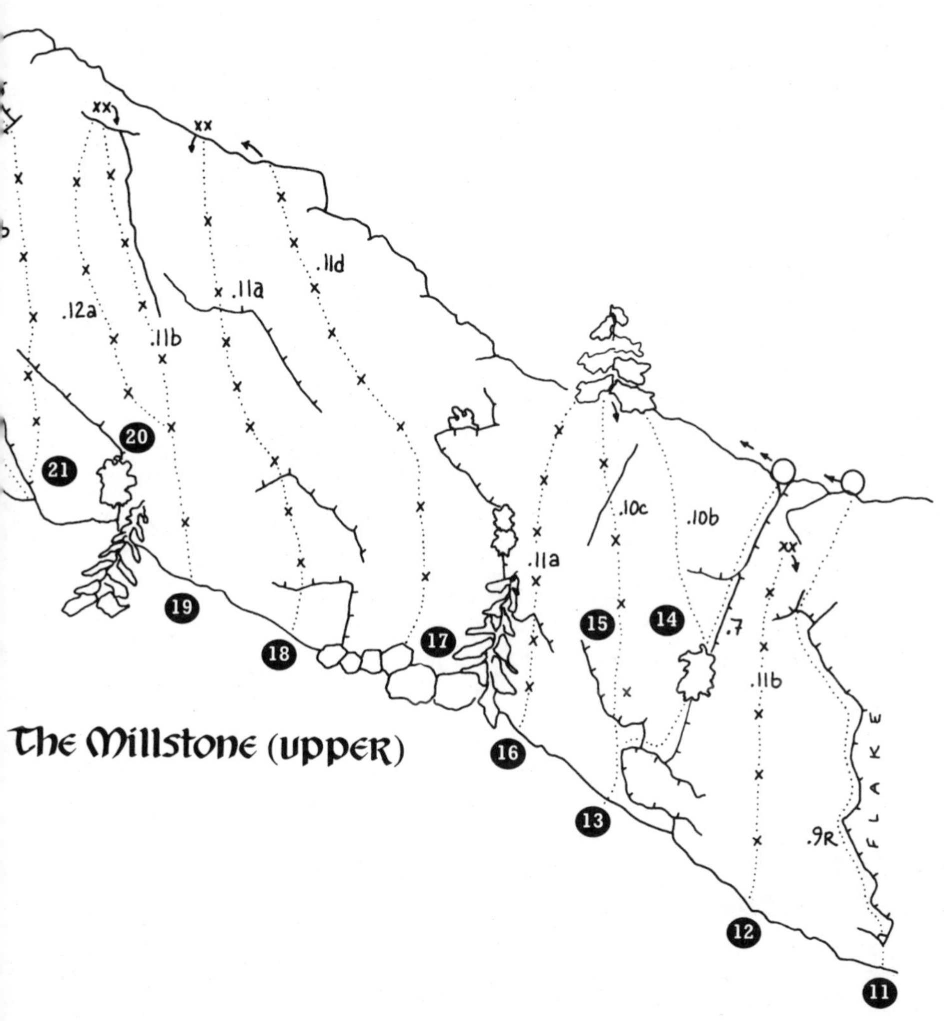

The Millstone (upper)

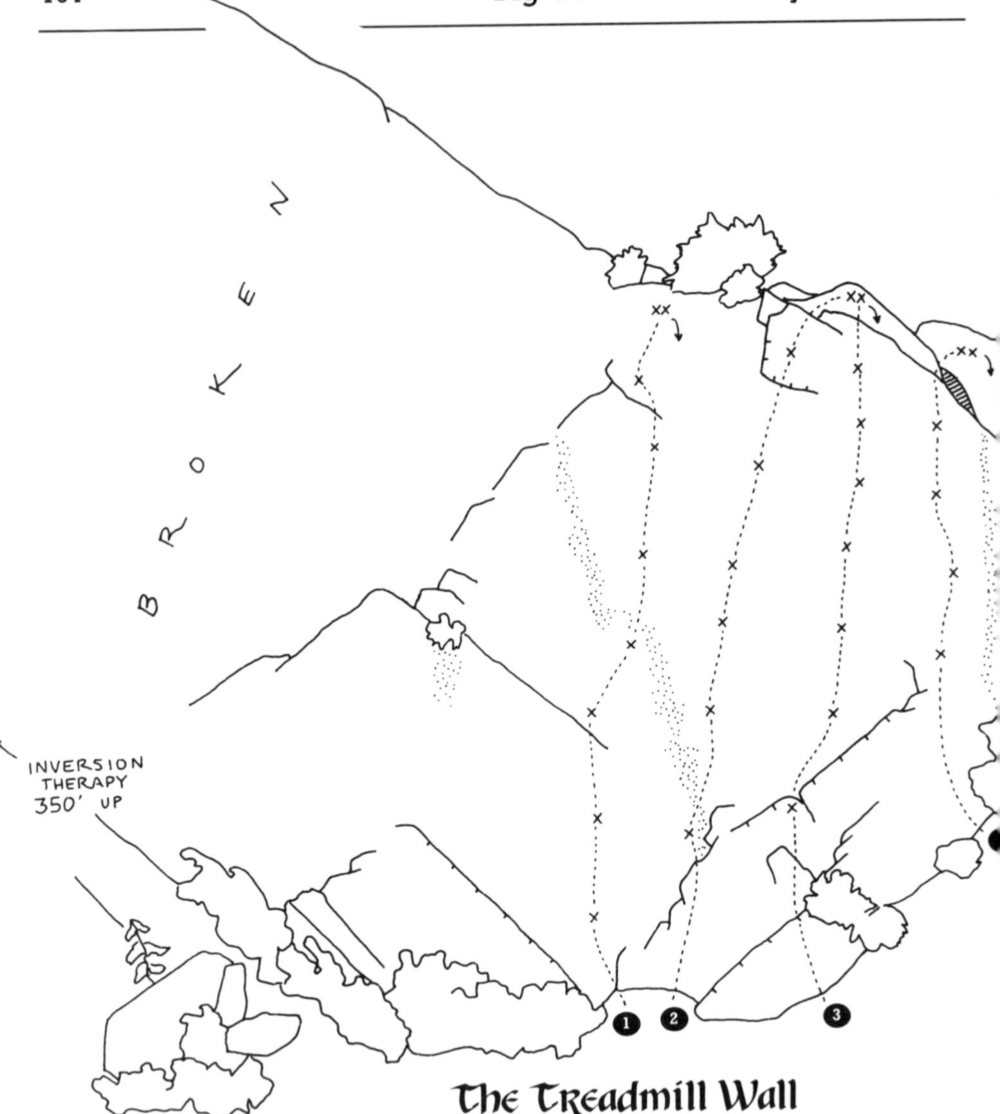

MILLSTONE AREA —THE TREADMILL WALL

The routes on this wall cover more broken terrain than the routes on The Millstone, but they are also more overhanging.

APPROACH: Follow the approach to the Millstone. From the route Yuppie Love, traverse south about 200 yards across the talus slope.

DESCENT: You can lower off all routes with one rope.

THE TREADMILL WALL ROUTES

1. JVS 5.11a ★★

A medical acronym that stands for Jamaican Vomiting Sickness, which hopefully you won't contract while in the throws of this steep lead.
FA: Tim Wolfe.

2. ANGINA 5.10d ★★

Steep, good-hold climbing that will surely quicken the pulse.
FA: Tim Wolfe.

3. TREADMILL 5.11a ★★

Seven bolts lead to chains. Overhanging with big holds that just keep coming at you.
FA: Keith Maas and Eric Wood, 1990.

4. DNR 5.11b ★

A potential heartbreak awaits at the finish. Another medical acronym which means Do Not Resuscitate.
FA: John Werner, Susan Wolfe, Tim Wolfe.

MILLSTONE AREA —INVERSION THERAPY

A wall with a single, huge roof that sits 350 above The Treadmill Wall.

APPROACH: Follow the approach to the Millstone, and then follow the approach to The Treadmill Wall. From The Treadmill Wall, walk south along the base of the cliff to the steep pine covered slope. Hoist yourself up this slope, paralleling the rock outcrop on the right, to reach the base of a wall with a distinct overhang.

DESCENT: Rappel off with one rope.

1. INVERSION THERAPY 5.11b ★★

After the initial crux, it is just a matter of inverted endurance.

FA: Tim Wolfe and George Rosenthal, 1995.

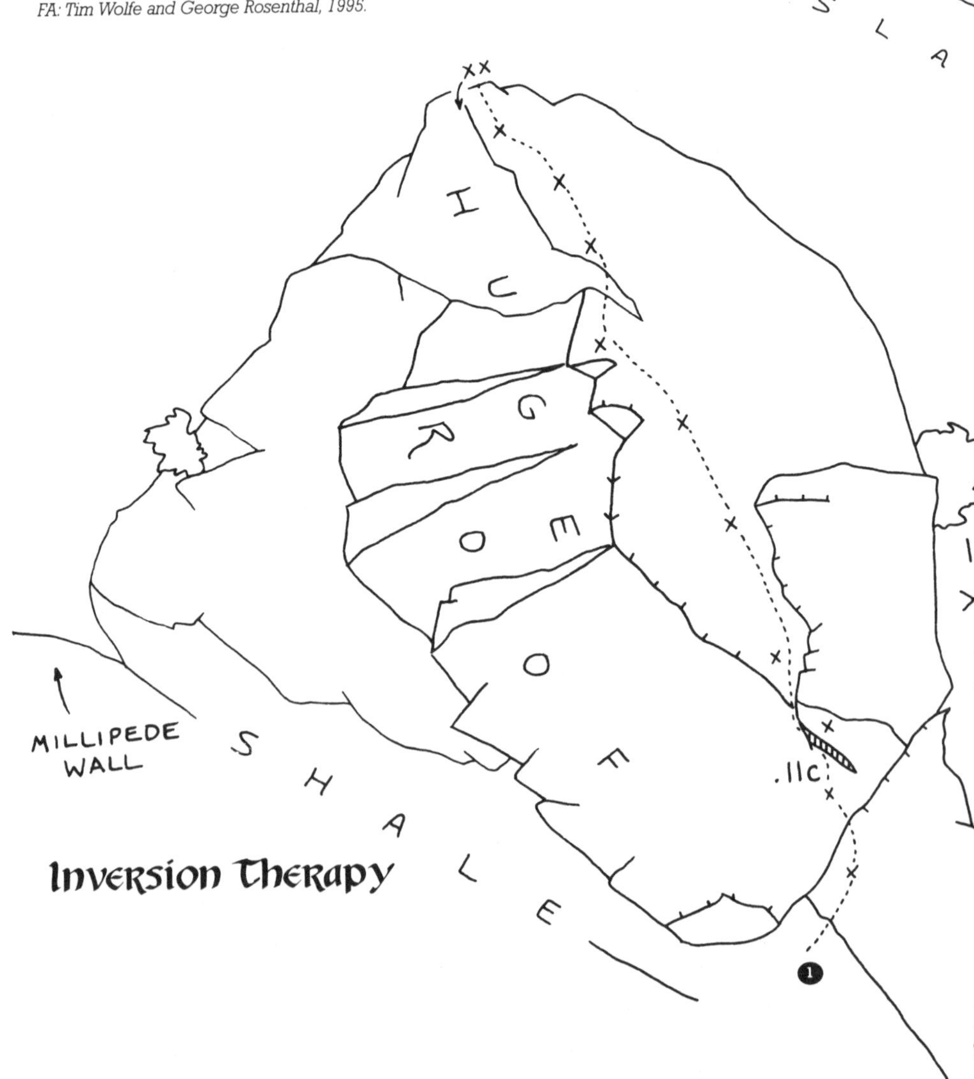

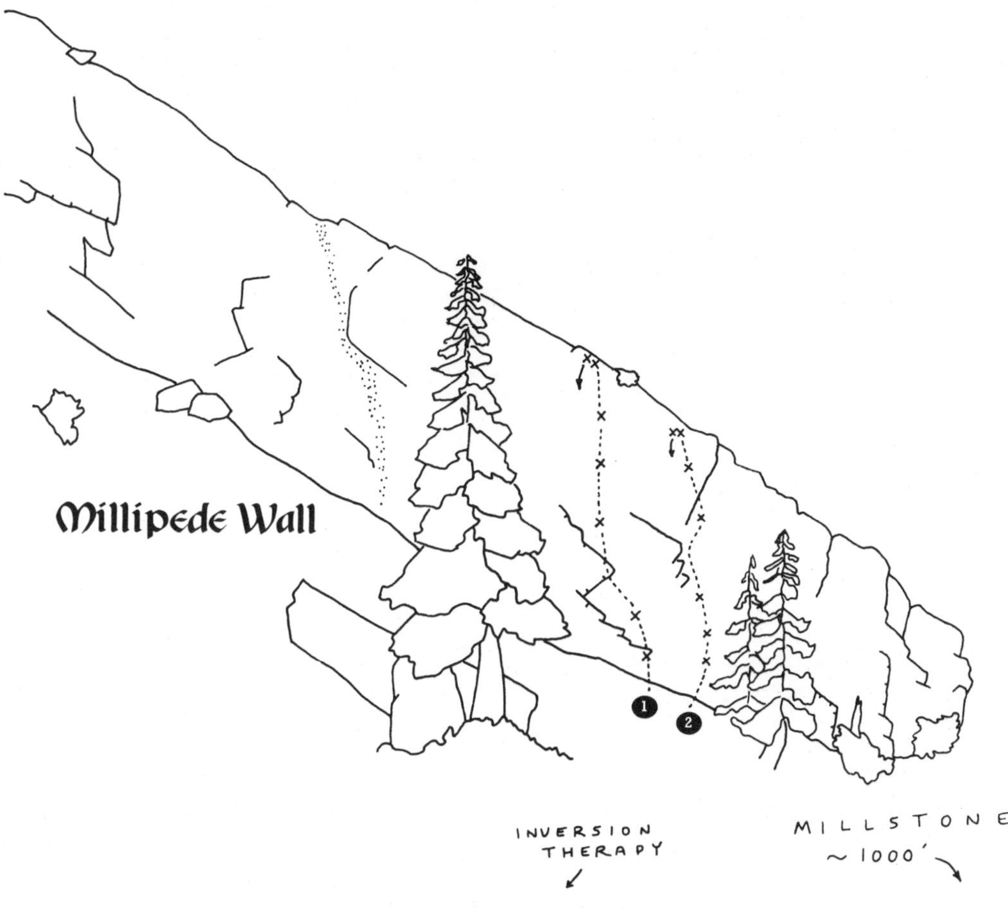

MILLSTONE AREA —MILLIPEDE WALL

The wall of a million steps. Small, with a sheer face, the Millipede wall hosts two routes and an ungainly approach.

APPROACH: Follow the approach to The Millstone. From The Millstone, there are two approaches. The first is to cross over to The Treadmill Wall, but instead of dropping down to the wall, turn west and head up the long slope, to reach the Millipede Wall. The second approach is to walk over to the Treadmill Wall, then up to Inversion Therapy, then up again to the next cliff band above Inversion Therapy. A lower angled ramp is reached just before this next wall turns steep. Carefully scramble up this ramp to the crest of the cliff, then walk across the slope to the base of the Millipede Wall.

EADMILL WALL 50' DOWN

DESCENT: Rappel or lower off the two routes here with a single rope.

1. RUMOR MILL 5.10?
Five bolts and a medium size camming unit protect this lead.

2. MILLENNIUM 5.10?
Thin, technical climbing on the right side of the wall. Bring some gear.

SUNDIAL PEAK

The beautiful Lake Blanche and environs wouldn't be the same without Sundial Peak as a backdrop. This aptly-named feature sits at the heart of the Twin Peaks Wilderness Area, and has been a destination for climbers since the brothers O'Dell and Rodell Petersen made an early ascent in the 40s. Harold Goodro and Jim Shane added a route in the late 40s, and renewed interest in the mid-seventies by Larry and Steve Swanson resulted in the ascents of several more lines. Unfortunately, like the snows that accumulate at the base of the Sundial, the details of these ascents have melted away. All we can do now is ponder what it must have been like in the forties to undertake a climb up the steep face of this peak. The route descriptions that follow are vague, reflecting the fact that endless possibilities exist for every Sundial route, and most parties get off route anyhow. The protection is sparse and thin crack protection is necessary. A sense of adventure, confidence in placing protection, and good route finding skills are all basic requirements for climbing here. Expect a full day's outing when climbing on Sundial Peak. The Sundial, as seen from lake Blanche, is the logo of the Wasatch Mountain Club—an organization that works hard to protect these fragile mountain environments. Please do your part to minimize impact.

APPROACH: Drive up BCC 4.2 miles to the first switchback of the S-curve. The road branching off to the right leads to a parking lot and the trailhead to Lake Blanche. A three-mile hike following a good trail is required to reach the lake, and a half-hour scramble reaches the base of Sundial, the prominent summit south of the lake.

DESCENT: The descent can be accomplished by continuing south on the Sundial ridge (toward the true summit) until downclimbing to the east looks feasible. Another option is descending a gully just north of the final ridge to the summit and dropping west.

SUNDIAL PEAK ROUTES

1. NORTH FACE 5.6-5.9 ★

Many variations are possible on the north face. Most of the routes seem to start on the right (west) half of the face and climb for two pitches to reach the large ledge half way up the wall. Many of these so called "lines" offer holds, but only difficult, thin protection. Don't pass gear placements here. The overhang above the large ledge can be passed on either the left or the right.

2. THE ELEVENTH HOUR 5.8 ★★

A four pitch route that climbs on or near the ridge separating the north and east faces. The first pitch starts on the north side of the Sundial and ascends a broken face above a bush to a small ledge about 60 feet up. The second pitch follows quality cracks past a tree and then upwards to the large ledge. A scramble right along the ledge leads to the base of a sizable 5.8 corner on the west face. Belay at the top of the corner on a ledge with two boulders. The memorable fourth pitch climbs an exposed finger crack to a mantle, followed by a traverse. A 5.6 lieback finishes things off.

3. SOUTH OF THE CORNER 5.7 ★

A variation start to either of the above routes. The first pitch climbs just south of the NW corner of Sundial Peak. The second pitch can follow a more direct line above (more difficult), or traverse south towards a corner system, which can be followed, more or less, to the large ledge half way up the wall. Finish via a North Face Route, the last two pitches of The Eleventh Hour, or your own creation.

Sundial Peak

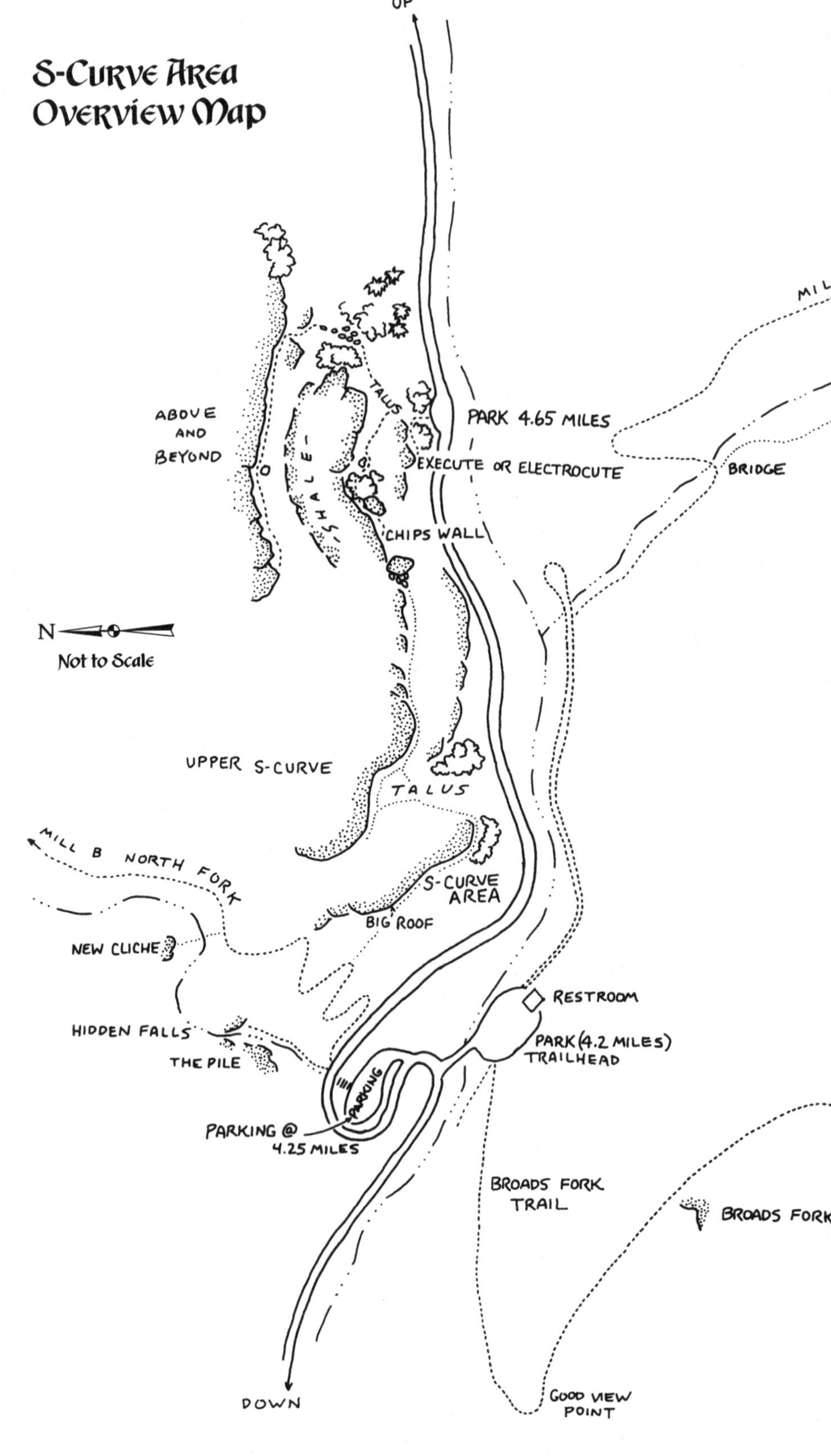
S-Curve Area
Overview Map
UP
N
Not to Scale
ABOVE AND BEYOND
SHALE
TALUS
PARK 4.65 MILES
EXECUTE OR ELECTROCUTE
BRIDGE
CHIPS WALL
UPPER S-CURVE
TALUS
MILL B NORTH FORK
S-CURVE AREA
BIG ROOF
NEW CLICHE
RESTROOM
HIDDEN FALLS
PARK (4.2 MILES) TRAILHEAD
THE PILE
PARKING
PARKING @ 4.25 MILES
BROADS FORK TRAIL
BROADS FORK
DOWN
GOOD VIEW POINT

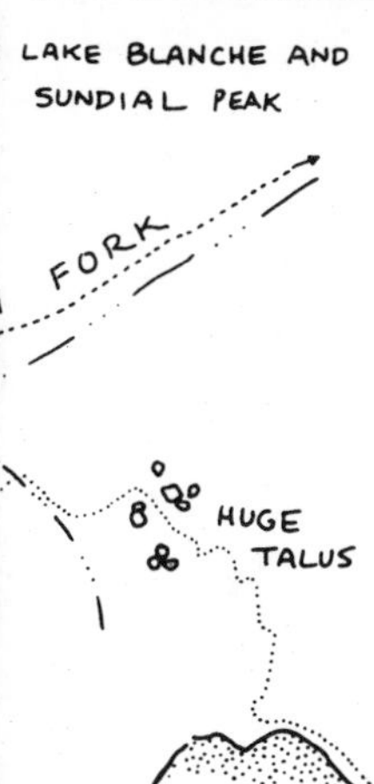

S-CURVE AREA

Bolt protected climbing has made the S-Curve Area into a vastly popular climbing locale, with plenty to choose from in a variety of grades. Overhangs pervade this area, and most of the routes tackle them in some capacity. Even the huge overhang at the left end of the wall now sports three routes.

APPROACH: Park 4.25 miles up canyon from the neon sign. There is a small parking lot between the turns of the big S-curve in the road, and additional parking on the right side of the first curve. Stairs lead from the parking area to the road at the top of the S-curve. Cross the highway. For the routes at The Pile, routes number 1 through 7, continue straight ahead on a path that follows the small creek. After one hundred feet the climbs will be obvious on the left (west) side of the creek.

TO TWIN PEAKS

Follow the hiking trail right (east), to reach the S-Curve Area. At the end of the third switchback, continue straight ahead on a climber's trail to reach the base of the wall. See overview on facing page.

DESCENT: Except for two routes, the Alpenbock Route and Très Facile, all routes in this area can be descended using one rope. Several routes require two rappels. See topo for specific descent information.

S-CURVE AREA—THE PILE

The Pile is unbelievably popular, due to its 20-second approach, cool temperatures and bolt-protected overhanging climbing. Simply walk up the Hidden Falls trail, the path that follows the stream, and the routes will be evident. See overview on page 170.

THE PILE ROUTES

1. GOMER PILE 5.10a ★
Golly! Five bolts of befuddleness on the walls left side.
FA: Unknown.

2. LEFT PILE 5.12b ★★
Cling tight to the series of hard moves that lead to a final crux. Most climbers log some air time on this ruthless route.
FA: Merrill Bitter and Mike Beck, 1989.

3. PILE SURGERY 5.12a ★
A variation that climbs past the first two bolts on Left Pile, then traverses right past a bolt to finish on Right Pile.
FA: Nolan Wall and Tyler McMillen, 1996.

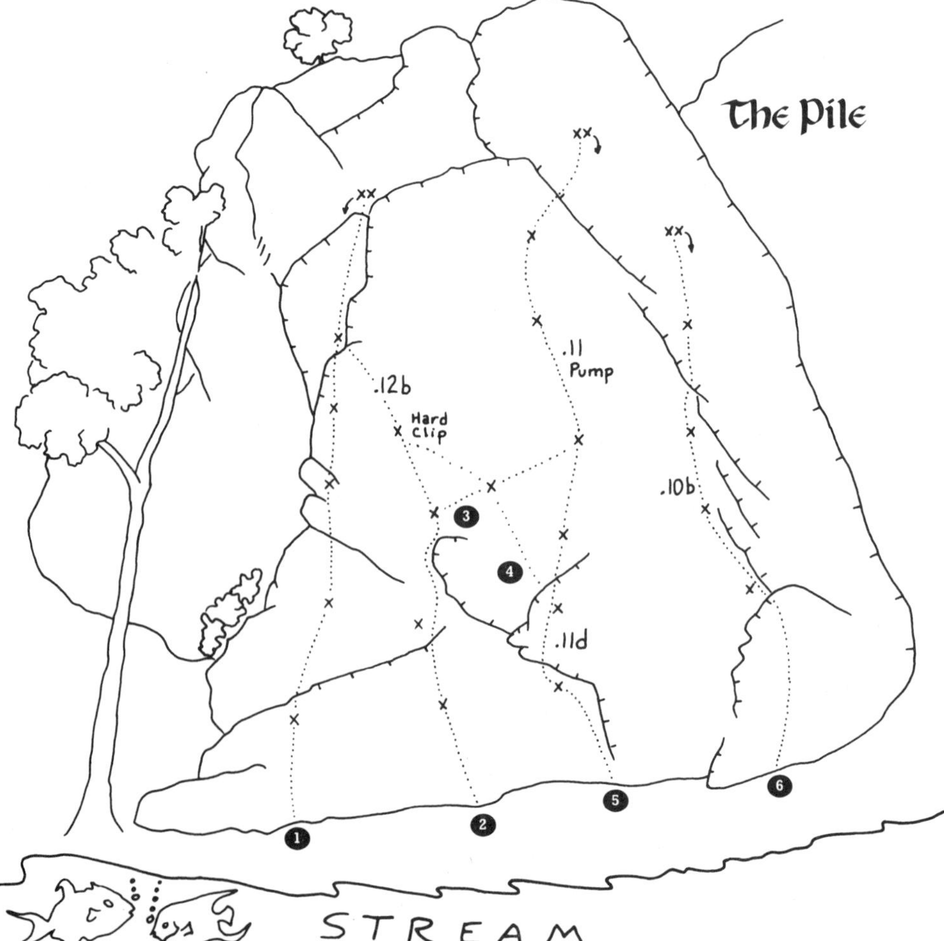

THE PILE ROUTES

4. COMPILED 5.12b ★

Another variation on a theme. Climb up to the second bolt on Right Pile, then traverse left past a bolt to link up with Left Pile.
FA: Nolan Wall and Tyler McMillen, 1996.

5. RIGHT PILE 5.11d ★★

This line offers big holds, but continuously steep climbing. The holds are all there, but are the arms?
FA: Merrill Bitter and Mike Beck, 1989.

6. DOG PILE 5.10b ★

The right-most line is shorter than the others, but still sports pumper climbing with good holds.
FA: Steve Bullock, 1990.

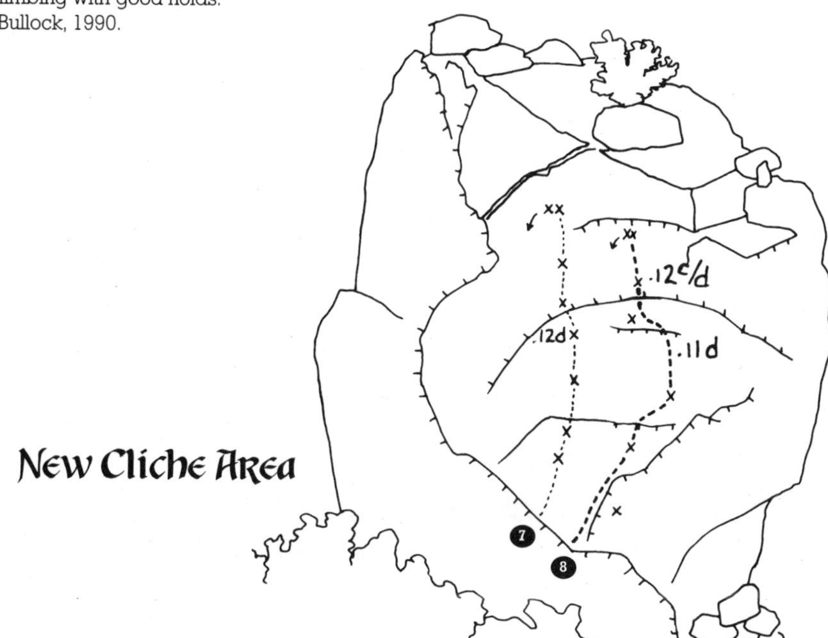

S-CURVE AREA—NEW CLICHE AREA

A lone, south-facing overhang is the attraction here. Both routes climb like long boulder problems, with technical moves and hard lock-offs. In the fall, this wall basks in the sun, surrounded by fire-yellow cottonwood trees. A diamond in the waste, these routes are well worth the 10-minute walk.

APPROACH: Approach as for the S-Curve Overhang Area, but instead of taking the climbers trail over to the S-Curve Wall, continue uphill on the Mill B North Fork Hiking Trail. New Cliche is located on a small formation with a large scooped-out roof, just north of the final switchback. From a level spot on the trail, descend to the stream, hop across, and stroll to the base of the wall. See overview on page 170.

NEW CLICHE AREA ROUTES

7. KISS IT GOODBYE 5.12d ★★

Lack of finger strength may prove to be the kiss of death on this extended boulder problem.
FA: Jeff Baldwin and Liz Hastings, 1993.

8. NEW CLICHE 5.12c/d ★★

Do opposites attract? Climb the roof via a series of shrinking holds.
FA: Stuart Ruckman, Gordon Douglass and Eric Stroud, 1988.

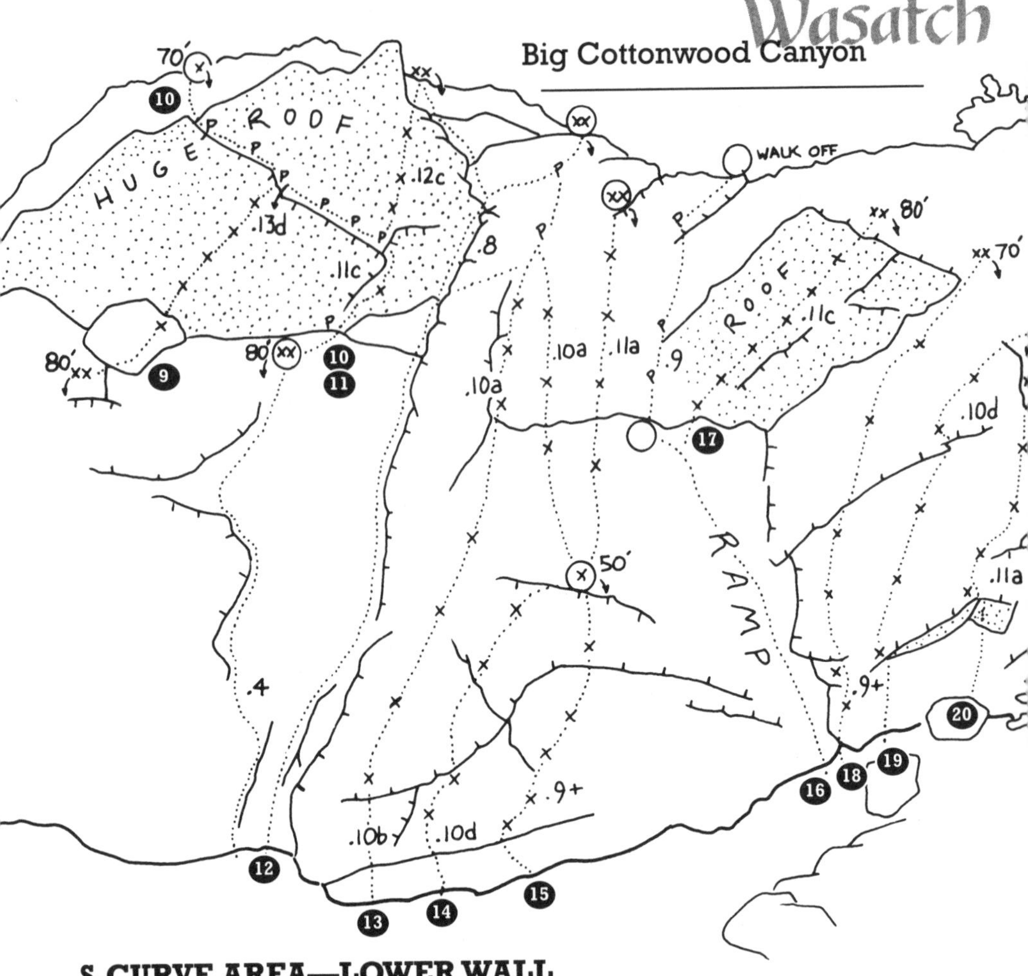

S-CURVE AREA—LOWER WALL

This is the main wall, the one with the obvious overhang at its west end.

APPROACH: See the Approach and Descent information at the beginning of the S-Curve Area section. See overview on page 170.

LOWER WALL ROUTES

9. DOG EAT DOG 5.13d ★★★
Big pulls off bad slopers. Big Cottonwood's reigning top dog. Jump off at the ramp on the S-Curve Overhang route.
FA: Jonny Woodward, 1995.

10. S-CURVE OVERHANG 5.11c ★★
This is one of the most unique routes around. After establishing oneself on the ramp, a mind-blowing leftward shuffle finishes with a 5.10a move. A free rappel lands one back at the belay. Bring long runners, and some gear to protect the reach to the first pin.
FA: Bret and Stuart Ruckman, 1989.

11. HIGH LIFE 5.12c ★★
Exposed and pumpy, steep and strenuous—finish this one, and you'll be leading the good life.
FA: Jonny Woodward, 1995.

12. OLD ROUTE 5.8
This climbs the corner to the right of the prominent S-Curve Overhang, then traverses right underneath the roof and above a steep wall. Above the roof, the route splits. Whether you go right or left, gear is needed.

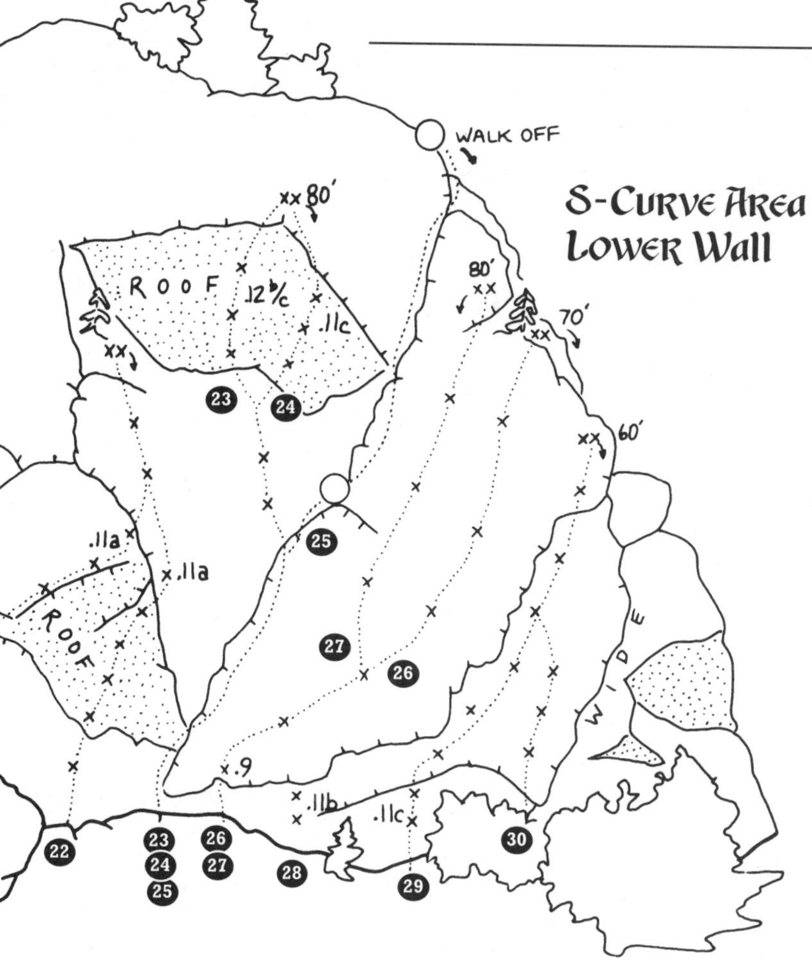

13. MELTING POINT 5.10b ★

A strenuous start (harder for shorter folks) leads to easier climbing above. It finishes near the blunt arête to the right of Old Route.

FA: Brian and Jonathan Smoot, 1990.

14. CLASTIC CLING 5.10d ★

The bouldering start is difficult and the upper headwall is wicked fun. The optional belay is recommended – or use long runners to reduce rope drag.

FA: Brian Smoot and Stuart Ruckman, 1990.

15. IONIC BONDING 5.11a ★★

Big jug climbing on a steep wall provides a pump for the first pitch. Exposed and tricky moves on the headwall above complete this popular route.

FA: Brian and Jonathan Smoot, 1990.

16. ALPENBOCK ROUTE 5.9 ★

This starts in the corner between Ionic Bonding and Red Light District. Climb the low-angled corner, angling left to a steep wall with several pins, just right of Ionic Bonding. Climb past the pins and move right to the top. Bring a selection of gear.

17. MASS WASTING 5.11c ★★

Belay at the sixth bolt on Ionic Bonding to start. A hard roof problem that requires big guns. Long runners are handy for the bolts above the roof.

FA: Brian Smoot and Lynn Ross, 1990.

LOWER WALL ROUTES

18. RED LIGHT DISTRICT 5.9+ ★
Turns a funky roof and continues up the face to the left of Madison Avenue. The climbing is deceptively difficult.
FA: Brian and Vicki Smoot, 1990.

19. MADISON AVENUE 5.10d ★★
Strenuous climbing that is enjoyed by many.
FA: Stuart Ruckman, Gordon Douglass and Eric Stroud, 1989.

20. CITY SLAVE 5.10d ★
Bound to the city? A roof problem.
FA: Eric Stroud, Stuart Ruckman and Gordon Douglass, 1989.

21. TIMES SQUARE 5.11a ★
An overhanging corner leads to a tricky lip sequence. Very steep.
FA: Stuart Ruckman and Gordon Douglass.

22. BLACK MONDAY 5.11a ★★★
You could be a victim of jug abuse. Big holds on a steeeeep wall.
FA: Gordon Douglass and Stuart Ruckman.

23. THINK TANK 5.12c/d ★
A deranging sequence out the roof above Black Monday. A necessary dyno leaves many mystified.
FA: Brian Smoot, 1990.

24. GAS CHAMBER 5.11b/c ★
The right route on the upper roof. Strenuous, as usual.
FA: Brian and Jonathan Smoot, 1990.

25. TRES FACILE 5.6 ★
A nice corner that starts a bit wide. Good protection.

26. CHORUS LINE 5.9 ★
A roof sequence leads to a nice, sweeping upper face.
FA: Stuart Ruckman and Brian Smoot, 1990.

27. CHOIR BOY 5.9 ★
Climb the center of the face after the third bolt on Chorus Line.
FA: Shane Willet, Mike Carnahan, 1995.

28. SKID ROW VARIATION 5.11b ★
A difficult roof start with a long reach.
FA: Brian Smoot and Stuart Ruckman, 1990.

29. CROSS TOWN 5.11c ★★
Classic. Hard and devious climbing follows the overhanging rib to a big jug finish.
FA: Stuart Ruckman and Gordon Douglass, 1990.

30. BOURBON STREET 5.10d ★
A direct start to Cross Town.
FA: Shane Willet, Mike Carnahan, 1995.

Paul Hodges taking a stroll on Madison Avenue, S-Curve Area.

photo: Jeff Baldwin.

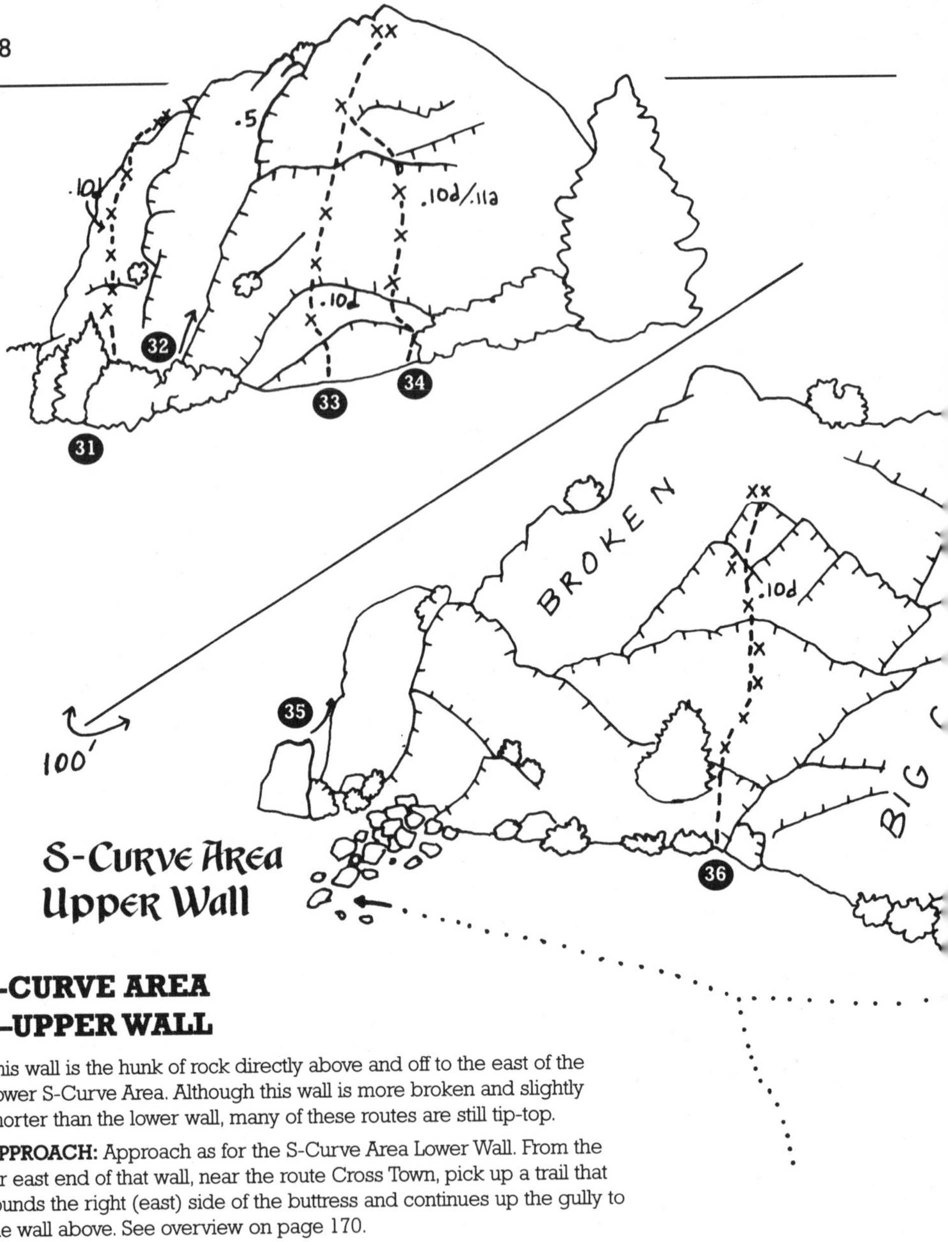

S-Curve Area
Upper Wall

S-CURVE AREA —UPPER WALL

This wall is the hunk of rock directly above and off to the east of the Lower S-Curve Area. Although this wall is more broken and slightly shorter than the lower wall, many of these routes are still tip-top.

APPROACH: Approach as for the S-Curve Area Lower Wall. From the far east end of that wall, near the route Cross Town, pick up a trail that rounds the right (east) side of the buttress and continues up the gully to the wall above. See overview on page 170.

DESCENT: With the exception of Little Feet and Skyscraper, all routes can be descended from fixed anchors with a single rope. For those two routes, walk off to the west.

UPPER WALL ROUTES

31. DEVIOUS DOGS 5.11a
Pretty contrived.
FA: Brian and Jonathan Smoot, 1990..

32. LITTLE FEAT 5.5 ★
Climbs the lower-angled west-facing wall 15 feet right of Devious Dogs. Good protection and rock. Walk off west.
FA: Brian and Vicki Smoot, 1990.

33. BEWARE OF DOG 5.10d ★
Most people unleash a dyno at the start.
FA: Jonathan and Brian Smoot, 1990.

34. GIVE THE DOG A BONE 5.11a ★
The final moves on the bulge can throw you for a loss.
FA: Brian and Jonathan Smoot, 1990.

35. GRAVY TRAIN 5.5
Climb the west-facing wall 50 feet right of Give The Dog A Bone. Start at a wide crack in a small alcove. Follow the line of protection, which leads to an exciting roof. Standard rack. Walk off west.
FA: Brian and Vicki Smoot, 1990.

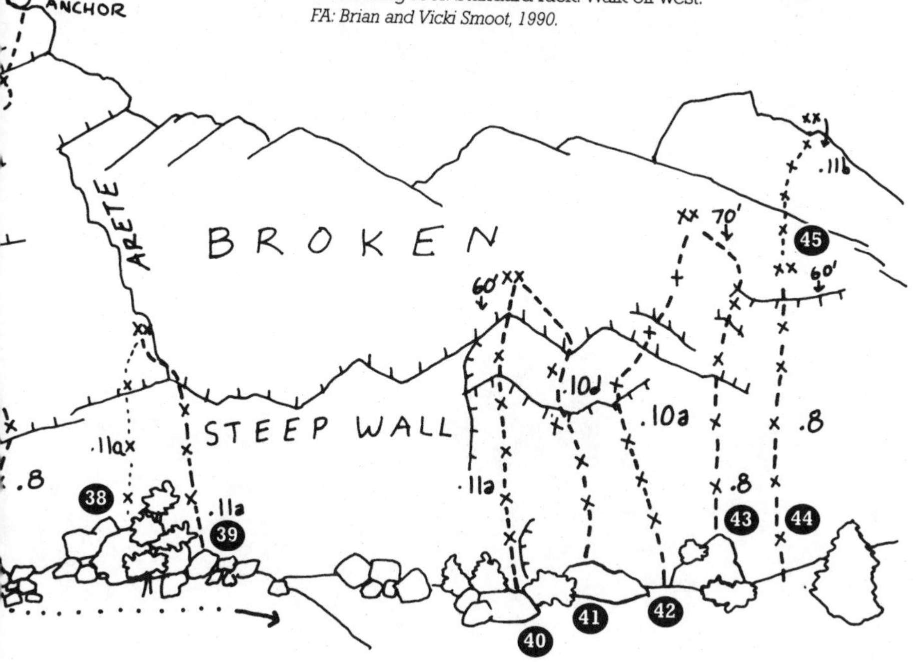

36. BITE THE WALL 5.10d ★
Start behind the piñon pine. The best holds are sometimes hard to find.
FA: Brian Smoot, 1990.

37. SKYSCRAPER 5.8 ★★
A long (165 foot) lead with an airy finish. Bring some small nuts, long runners and TCU's. Walk off west from the top.
FA: Brian Smoot and Rich Carlston, 1990.

38. GET A LIFE 5.11a ★
Bouldery moves, orange rock, not a bad life.
FA: Unknown.

39. GET A GRIP 5.11a ★
The initial moves leave many gripless.
FA: Brian and Jonathan Smoot, 1990.

40. MEGALOPOLIS 5.11a ★★
The left arête of this overhanging section is packed with fun moves.
FA: Gordon Douglass and Stuart Ruckman, 1990.

Jurgen Grunewald leading Black and White John and Mary. The Dihedrals.

photo: Kennan Harvey.

S-CURVE UPPER WALL ROUTES

41. TEAMING METROPOLIS 5.10d

This is the line up the center. There is a trick to the final moves.

FA: Gordon Douglass and Stuart Ruckman, 1990.

42. URBAN SPRAWL 5.10a ★★

Big holds on the right side. The key word here is fun.

FA: Stuart Ruckman and Gordon Douglass, 1990. .

43. CLEAN UNDERWEAR 5.9 ★

This is the line of mostly good holds right of Urban Sprawl.

FA: Brian and Jonathan Smoot, 1990.

44. GERONIMO 5.8 ★

Many bulges.

FA: Brian, Jonathan and Vicki Smoot, 1990.

45. HIGH DIVE 5.11b ★

The roof above Geronimo.

FA: Brian and Jonathan Smoot, 1990.

Chips
Wall
1
2
5
U.P.&L.
Wall
1

Above and Beyond
7
8
13
14
17
Approach
CHIPS WALL
1. CHIPS AND SALSA 5.10a ★
2. NEW MEXICAN CRACK 5.9 ★
U.P. & L WALL
1. NEVER ENOUGH 5.11d ★
ABOVE AND BEYOND WALL
5. DO OR DIVE 5.10d ★★★
7. THE HORSE'S MOUTH 5.10 ★
8. RANDY'S POLKA 5.11d ★★
13. RAPTORS ROOST 5.9
14. HARI 5.10d ★★
17. THE LEAK 5.10 ★★

U.P. & L. WALL

More of an overhang than a wall, this south-facing cove is easily seen from the road. The single route derives its name from a close proximity to the overhead powerlines.

APPROACH: Park on the north side of the road at a small pullout 4.65 miles up canyon from the neon sign. A small talus slope resides just left (west) of several pine trees. Walk up the talus for 60 feet, until a wall on the left (west) joins the talus. Bushwack along the base of this wall for 100 feet to the bottom of the roof-like wall. A nice mahogany tree sits at the base. See overview on pages 170 and 182.

DESCENT: Lower off anchors at the top of the route with one rope.

1. EXECUTE OR ELECTROCUTE 5.11 ★
This route climbs the left margin of the wall past three bolts and some steep overlaps.
FA: Randy Kieliszewski and Steve Habovstack, 1994.

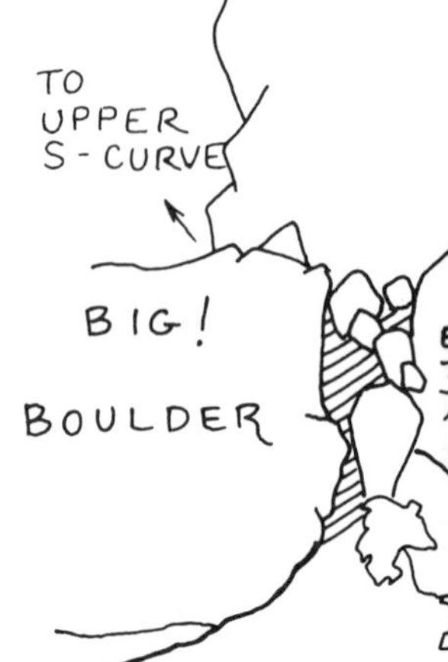

CHIPS WALL

This wall, actually the continuation of the Upper S-Curve Area, is a broad expanse of quartzite, divided by a headwall that separates broken rock on the lower face and clean, compact rock on the upper half. Perfect for spring and fall climbing—the southern exposure bakes the wall in the midday sun.

APPROACH: Park on the north side of the road at a small pullout 4.65 miles up canyon from the neon sign. A small talus slope resides just left (west) of several pine trees. Walk up the left side of the talus for 150 feet, until it is possible to traverse up and left (west) on a broad ramp system that is the same height as the powerlines. Pass by a large boulder at the top of the ramp, then Bushwhack west, following the base of the wall for 300 feet, to a giant boulder that blocks further passage. The Chips Wall is directly above. It is also possible to follow the approach information for the Upper S-Curve Area, then walk east 200 feet from Geronimo along the base of the wall. At the big dropoff, downclimb 30 feet and you're at the Chips Wall. See overview on pages 170 and 182.

DESCENT: Rappel 75 feet from anchors at the top of the route.

CHIPS WALL ROUTES

1. CHIPS AND SALSA 5.10a ★

A direct blast up the wall, that starts at a flake 30 feet east of the large boulder. Some fixed gear at the headwall protects the crux, but the mouth-watering stuff is on the upper face. Add a few extra small nuts to the rack.

FA: Randy Kieliszewski and John Higgins, 1992.

2. NEW MEXICAN CRACK 5.9 ★

Easy climbing leads to a possible belay near a bush. From here, let 'er rip, diagonally up and left, following a series of thin cracks to join the upper part of Chips And Salsa. Many small nuts are needed.

FA: Randy Kieliszewski and John Higgins, 1992.

ABOVE AND BEYOND WALL

The Above and Beyond Wall is a long fold of rock punctuated by scattered roofs and split into three distinct sections by broken chimneys.

APPROACH: Park on the north side of the road at a small pullout 4.65 miles up canyon from the neon sign. A small talus slope resides just left (west) of several pine trees. Walk up the left side of the talus for 150 feet, then angle up and right through the brush, skirting the wall that blocks upward progress on the right (east). Continue straight up through the oak and talus to a clearing with a moss covered slab above. Traverse left (west) around the slab, and scramble to the base of the wall. See overview on pages 170 and 182.

DESCENT: All routes, except for Kari and Above and Beyond, which require two ropes to descend, can be rappelled with one rope.

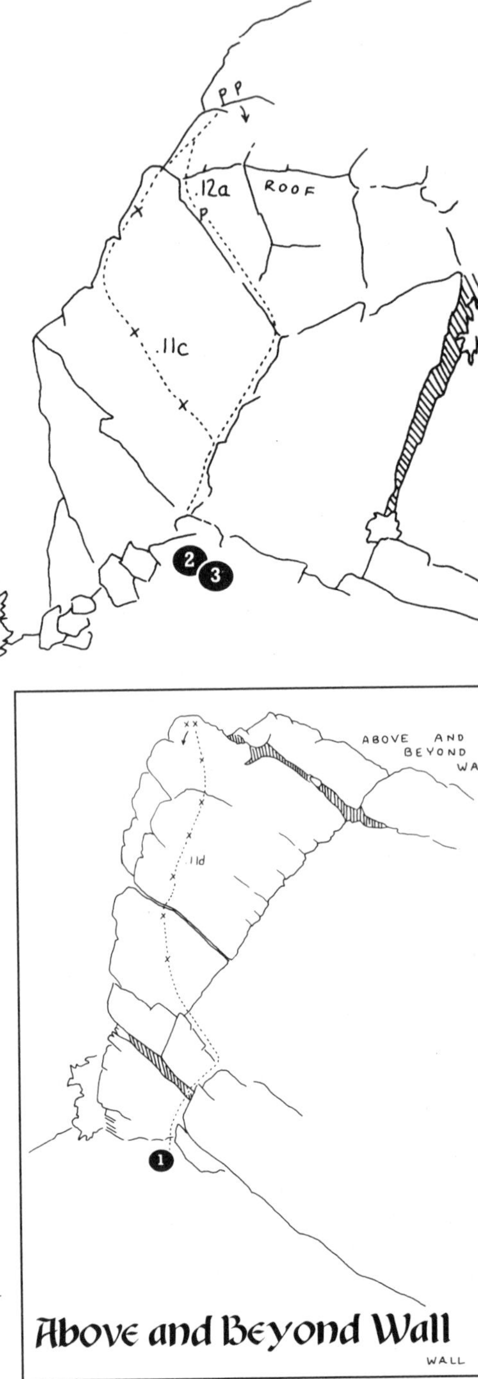

ABOVE AND BEYOND (WEST) ROUTES

1. NEVER ENOUGH 5.11d ★
This is the first route you'll encounter, and is located below the main wall, just west of the approach. Deceptively overhanging climbing and wicked moves may leave you saying "enough is enough." Small TCU's or wired nuts provide optional protection for reaching the first bolt.
FA: Randy Kieliszewski, 1993.

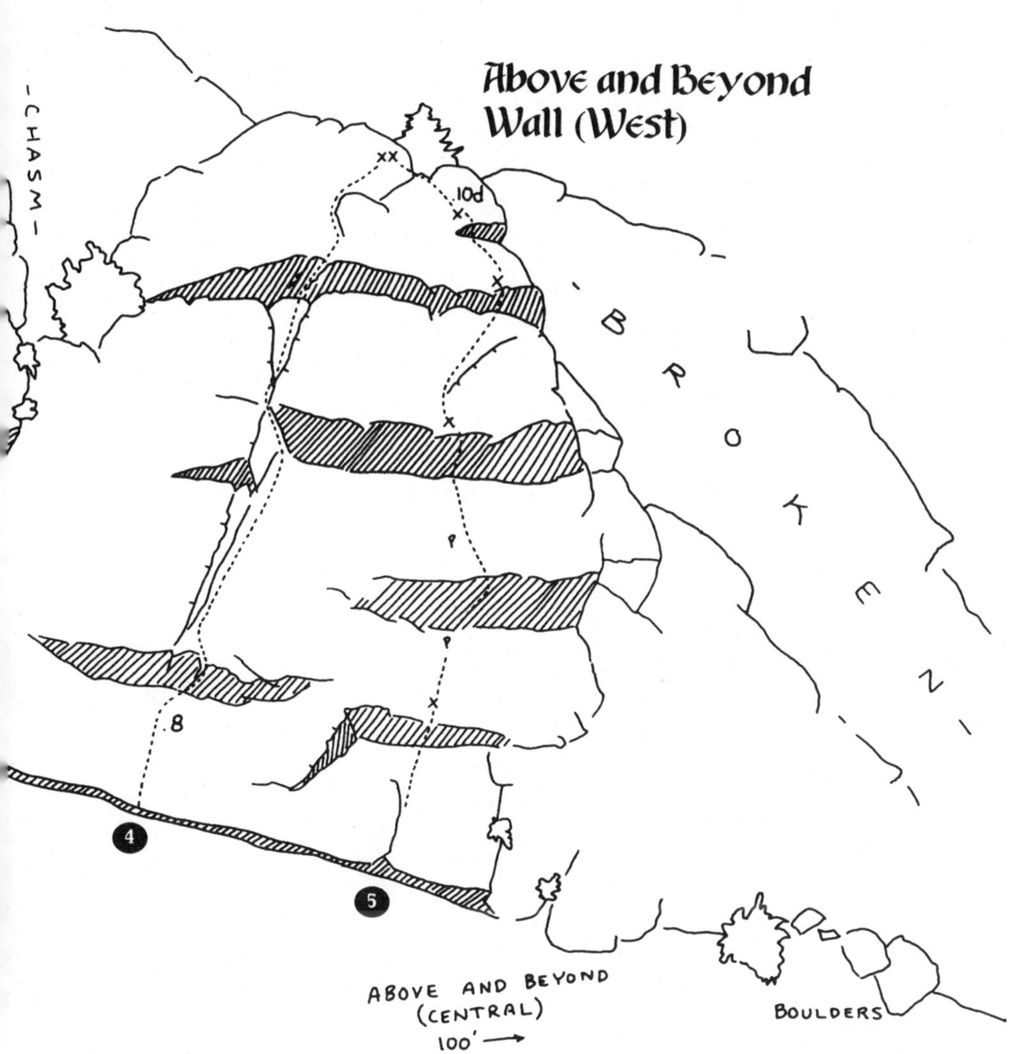

2. GET BENT 5.11c
Climb across some wild colored rock that is unfortunately of poor quality. Footholds are critical but very difficult to utilize.
FA: Steve Habovstak and Scott Ford, 1992.

3. FINGER TWINKIES 5.12a
Good gear in the corner protects super thin moves out the seam. Turning the lip is not a fun filled treat.
FA: Steve Habovstak and Eric Klement, 1992.

4. OSCILLATION 5.8
Broken cracks and corners with a bouldery start.
FA: Unknown.

5. DO OR DIVE 5.10d ★★★
Roofs galore. Luckily, you can catch rests under each roof. Long reaches to blind holds on an upside down staircase.
FA: Steve Habovstak, Randy Kieliszewski, and Eric Klement, 1992.

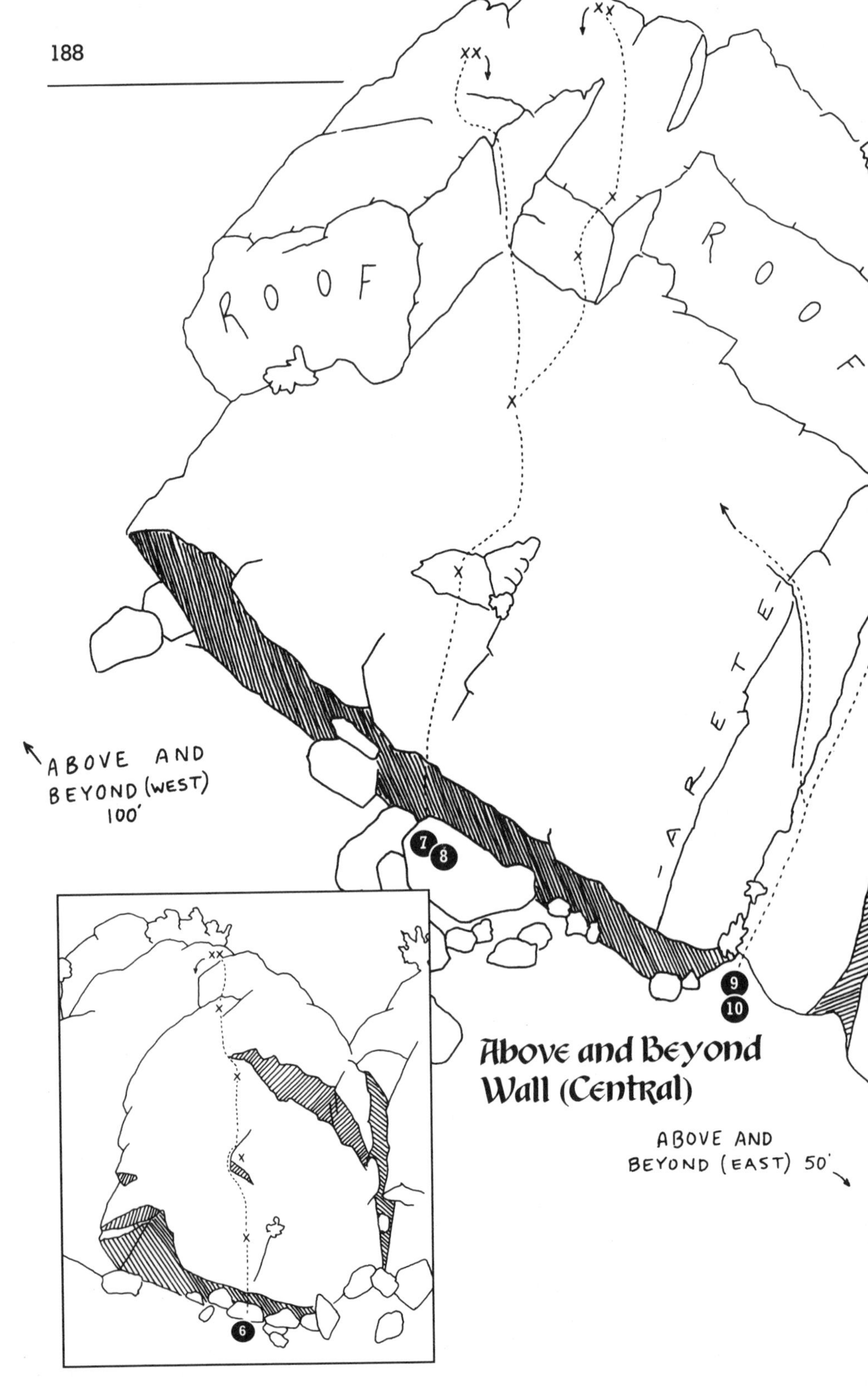

Above and Beyond Wall (Central)

ABOVE AND BEYOND (CENTRAL) ROUTES

6. ASCENT OF A MAN 5.10 ★★

A series of steep sidepulls and layaways lead thankfully to better holds.
FA: Randy Kieliszewski and Steve Habovstak, 1994.

7. THE HORSE'S MOUTH 5.10 ★

Climb Randy's Polka to the second bolt, then move left and follow an overhanging handcrack that splits the corner.
FA: Steve Habovstak, Eric Klement, and Randy Kieliszewski, 1992.

8. RANDY'S POLKA 5.11d ★★

Several hidden pockets make the roof possible. The problem is figuring out how to use them.
FA: Randy Kieliszewski and Steve Habovstak, 1992.

9. DIAGONAL FINGER CRACK 5.12a

Just as the name says, only on flakey rock. Good protection.
FA: Steve Habovstak and Randy Kieliszewski, 1992.

10. WAVY GRAVY 5.11 ★

The corner overhangs in two ways. The consequence is forearms that feel like gravy. A variation second pitch, called the Gravy Train, has been climbed, linking Wavy Gravy and the final crack of Horses Mouth.
FA: Randy Kieliszewski and Steve Habovstak, 1992.

Chris Harmston hand traversing the flake on Touch Up. Perhaps Area.

photo: Kennan Harvey.

ABOVE AND BEYOND WALL EAST ROUTES

11. NO U TURNS ALLOWED 5.10a ★

Start at the bottom of a seam that turns into a four inch crack. The first ascent party climbed the nice rock just left of this wide crack, eventually traversing right to meet Tombstone. Thin gear if you stay left, some wide stuff if you continue up the main crack.

FA: Randy Kieliszewski and Jami Mueller, 1993.

12. TOMBSTONE 5.10a ★

Pulling the roof is the crux, but the face above is the most fun.

FA: John Higgins and Randy Kieliszewski, 1993.

13. RAPTORS ROOST 5.9

Climb up to, and then follow the prominent right-leaning corner in the middle of the face. Although the corner is a seam, gear is available in the cracks that split the left-hand wall of the corner. A series of long, rightward wanderings gain the anchors at the top of Hari.

FA: Randy Kieliszewski and John Higgins, 1993.

14. HARI 5.10d ★★

Two bolts near a lighter colored face mark the start. Tricky moves on downsloping holds pass the two bolts, then easier climbing up cracks and corners lead to a belay. TCU's are handy.

FA: Randy Kieliszewski and Steve Habovstak, 1993.

15. KARI 5.12 ★★

Four bolts worth of wild prow climbing. Two ropes are needed for the descent.

FA: Steve Habovstak and Randy Kieliszewski, 1993.

16. ABOVE AND BEYOND 5.11d ★★

A diagonal crack splits the upper face. Traverse out this crack, armed with some large camming devices and large forearms. Big exposure.

FA: Steve Habovstak and Randy Kieliszewski, 1993.

17. THE LEAK 5.10 ★★

Climbs up the most aesthetic rock on the wall. Several twenty foot runouts are made less formidable with some optional gear, like TCUs.

FA: Steve Habovstak, Randy Kieliszewski, and Eric Klement, 1993.

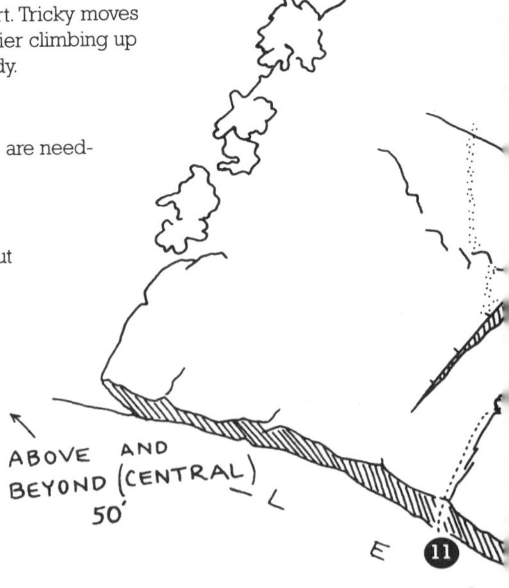

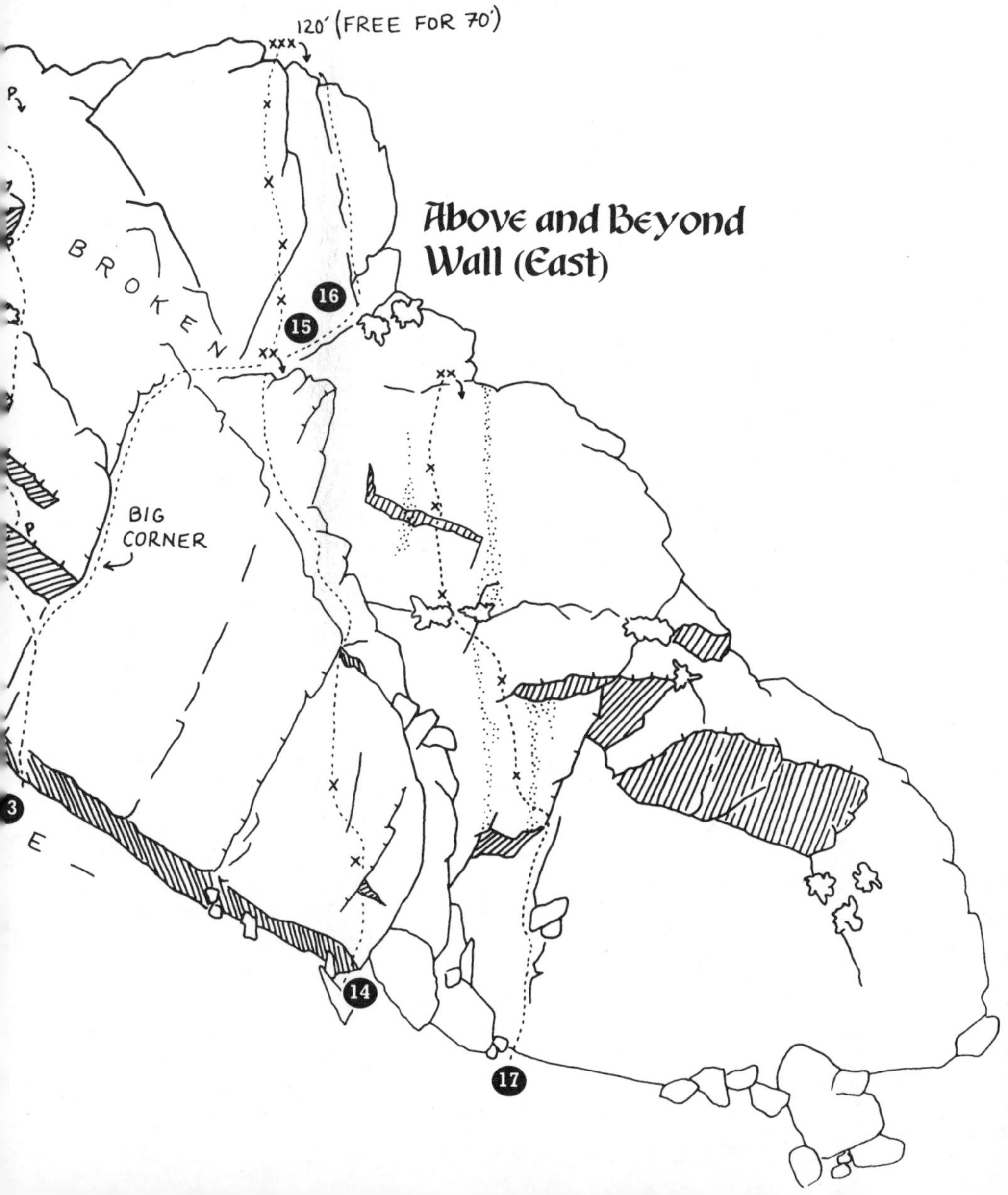
120' (FREE FOR 70')
Above and Beyond Wall (East)
BROKEN
BIG CORNER
16
15
14
17
3

MOSS LEDGES AREA

A beautiful picnic area surrounded by trees, water and rock greets the traveler who stops to explore this drainage. The rock here is divided by numerous horizontal cracks. These rifts provide hand and foot holds as well as protection.

APPROACH: Park at the picnic area on the north side of the road 5.05 miles up canyon from the neon sign. Walk up the trail that leads to the picnic area, walk to the final picnic table and look up. See overview on page 48.

DESCENT: Descend from fixed anchors with one rope.

MOSS LEDGES AREA ROUTES

1. THE RAW AND THE COOKED 5.11a ★★
Bolts, nuts and small- to mid-sized cams protect the left-hand line, which makes its way up the mildly-overhanging wall.
FA: Bret and Stuart Ruckman, 1989.

2. WIENIE ROAST 5.10d ★★
Start up the easy face, then work into a little corner. Launch out left—up the prow—and continue on overhanging rock to the belay ledge. Bring mid-sized nuts and cams. Originally led without bolts, they were later added by the first ascent party.
FA: Stuart Ruckman, Gary Olsen and Bret Ruckman, 1986.

3. SUNDAY BRUNCH 5.10c ★
Climb a short easy pitch above the last picnic table, then blast out the exposed diagonalling hand crack to a belay 20 feet to the left.
FA: Bret and Stuart Ruckman, Gary Olsen, 1986.

4. MAGGOT 5.10a ★
This route is located up the Moss Ledge canyon near a waterfall. Continue up the drainage beyond the last picnic table, following a series of trails that crisscross the stream. Eventually the canyon boxes out at the waterfall. 100 feet below the waterfall, behind a large pine tree on the west side of the stream is a steep wall with four bolts and some tricky moves.
FA: Cory Andersen and JP Gambatese, 1992.

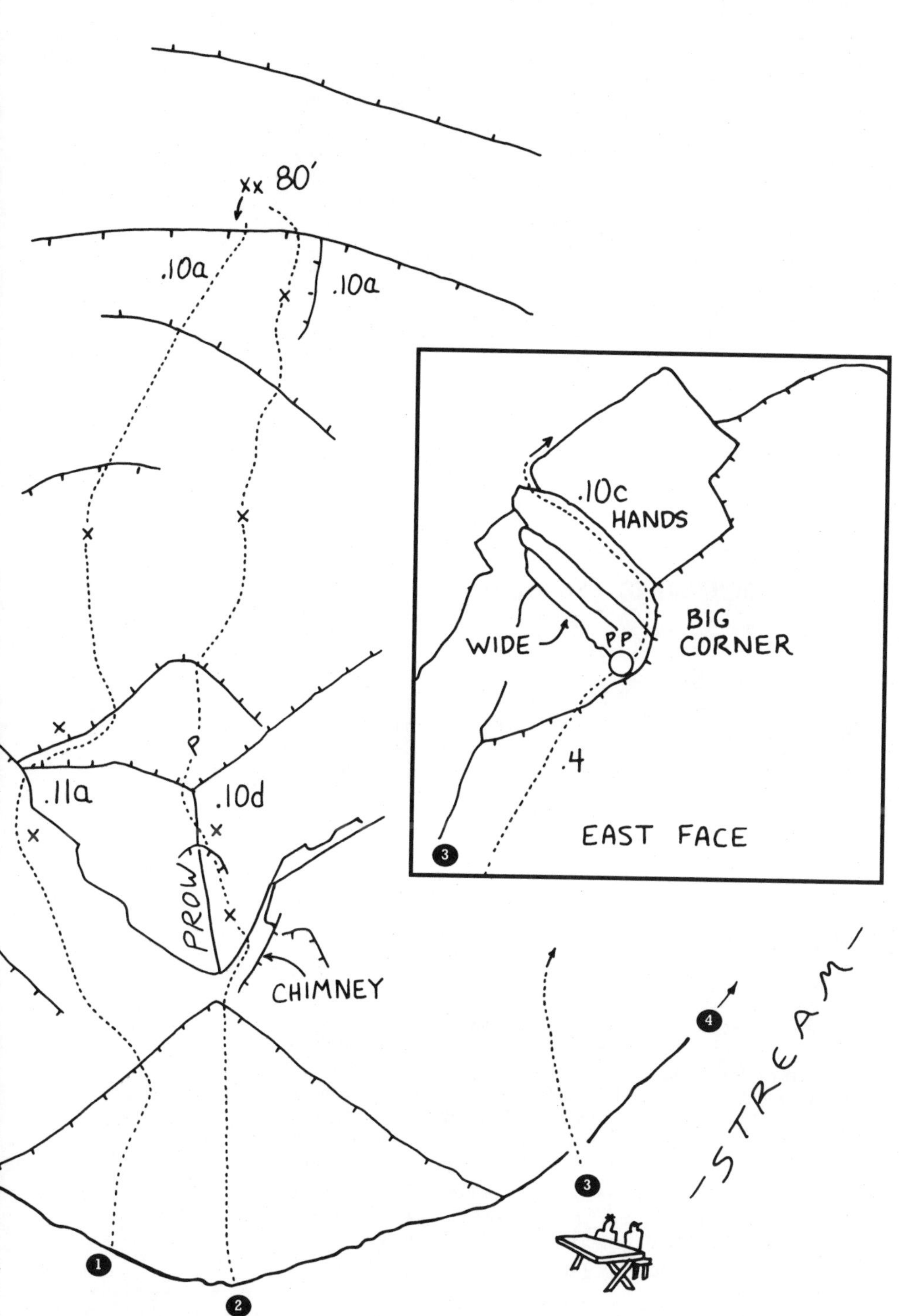
XX 80'
.10a
.10a
.11a
P
.10d
PROW
CHIMNEY
.10c
HANDS
BIG
CORNER
WIDE
PP
.4
EAST FACE
3
1
2
3
4
STREAM

LONE PINE WALL (no topo)

With the shortest approach in the canyon and a southerly aspect, the Lone Pine Wall could be a popular Big Cottonwood attraction. The shattered rock and short routes have limited appeal, however, and the proximity to the road deters most climbers. But if you're short on time, and craving a gear route or two, this might just be the wall for youi.

APPROACH: Park at a pullout on the north side of the road 5.45 miles up canyon from the neon sign. The wall is hard to miss—a large solitary pine tree guards the base of the wall, and the routes climb the short face west of the tree.

DESCENT: Lower off anchors at the top of each route with one rope.

1. PUMP FOR THE PLUMP 5.9-
Start at a right-leaning, thin seam/corner system 40 feet down canyon from the big pine tree. This seam is left of the more obvious corner near the center of the wall. Climb up the seam, angling right near the top, to gain a short corner that leads to the ledge. Bring along that thin stuff.
FA: Tony Calderone and Dave Strampe, 1993.

2. DREAMBOAT ANNIE 5.7
Start 10 feet down canyon from the pine tree, near the right side of an overhang. Climb the corner to the right of the overhang on big holds. Angle up and left to reach the chains.
FA: Tony Calderone and Dave Strampe, 1993.

RED ROCK WALL (no topo)

The Red Rock Wall is a large, south-facing wall directly across from the popular Cardiff Fork. Prominent from the road, and dotted with overhangs, the wall looks promising. However, poor rock quality has limited climbing activity here to just one recorded climb.

APPROACH: The easiest approach is to park in a pullout 8.7 miles up canyon from the neon sign. This pullout is at the upper edge of a slope of pine trees. Hike upwards through the pines, then thrash to the base of the wall.

1. RED ROCK 5.9 R/X
Runout and loose, this route climbs the path of least resistance to the top of the wall. The exact location of this climb is unknown.
FA: Jim Edwards and Cory Andersen, 1995.

BRIGHTON BOWL AREA (no topo)

Cool and scenic, the Brighton Bowl is a popular hiking area, and several trails access the fields of stunning wildflowers that bloom in late summer. Climbers will most likely notice that the rock type in Big Cottonwood Canyon switches from quartzite to granitic. This granite has been the scene of exploration for many years, as evidenced by the old pitons found here and there. Since mid-summer exploration is one of the main attractions, little has ever been recorded. The following is a very brief mention of seven small crags that have worthwhile climbing. On a hot day in the valley, go explore and see what hidden gems can be found.

- There are several easily-toproped boulder problems just below the Girl Scout Camp by the picnic grounds; most are 5.9 or harder. To approach: park in the SE corner of the upper Brighton parking lot, at the trailhead for the Brighton Lakes trail, but don't follow the trail, instead follow a footpath that leads to several picnic tables. Follow this trail (which avoids the Girl Scout Camp), walk past the picnic tables, and you'll see the two boulders.

• Just above the top cabins of the Girl Scout Camp on the north end is a 25 to 30 foot face with two parallel cracks. The left crack is slightly overhanging and is supposed to be 5.11; the right is easier, around 5.10.

• A trail goes up the left (south) side of the talus from the Girl Scout Camp. At the top of the talus are two east-facing walls with many cracks, most of which look climbable. Tentative ratings are: bolt ladder, A1; pin crack, 5.10c; just right of the pin crack, 5.11 A1?; and on the right side, 5.9.

• Follow the east-facing walls around to the right (north) to some north-facing dihedrals. These climbs are shorter than the east-facing walls—and generally are easier. All of the obvious lines have been done and range from 5.9 to 5.6.

• Further to the west are some nice-looking arêtes that could yield some good climbing.

• About 200 yards south of the east-facing walls is a north-facing, bright rust-colored wall with a thin right-slanting crack (5.10d).

• Further up above the east and north-facing walls are more crags, many of which have manky fixed pins that were put in years ago. Rumor has it there is a two-pitch route in this vicinity. See for yourself.

SHIVA WALL (no topo)

With a view that overlooks the Brighton Bowl, the Shiva Wall is worth the hike just for the atmosphere, especially during the peak wildflower season. Facing north and sandwiched between Lake Martha and Lake Catherine at an elevation of 9800 feet, the Shiva Wall is ideal during the hottest summer months.

APPROACH: Park at the very end of the Big Cottonwood Road, at the trailhead for the Brighton Lakes Trail. This well traveled path leads to Lake Mary, Lake Martha, Lake Catherine, and eventually to Catherine's Pass at the head of Big and Little Cottonwood Canyons. Walk up the trail past Lake Mary, the first and largest of the three Brighton Lakes. The trail continues along the eastern shore of Lake Mary and after a short distance, reaches Lake Martha. At the first major switchback above Lake Martha, step off the main hiking trail and continue traversing uphill in a southerly direction. Cut across the scree slope and walk up the small ridge that descends from the base of the cliff.

1-5. UNNAMED 5.9-5.11 ★
Four to five routes have been climbed here, most on top rope. A large "turtle" shaped block sitting on top of the wall provides a convenient anchor, if you have several twelve foot runners

Ferguson Canyon Overview Map

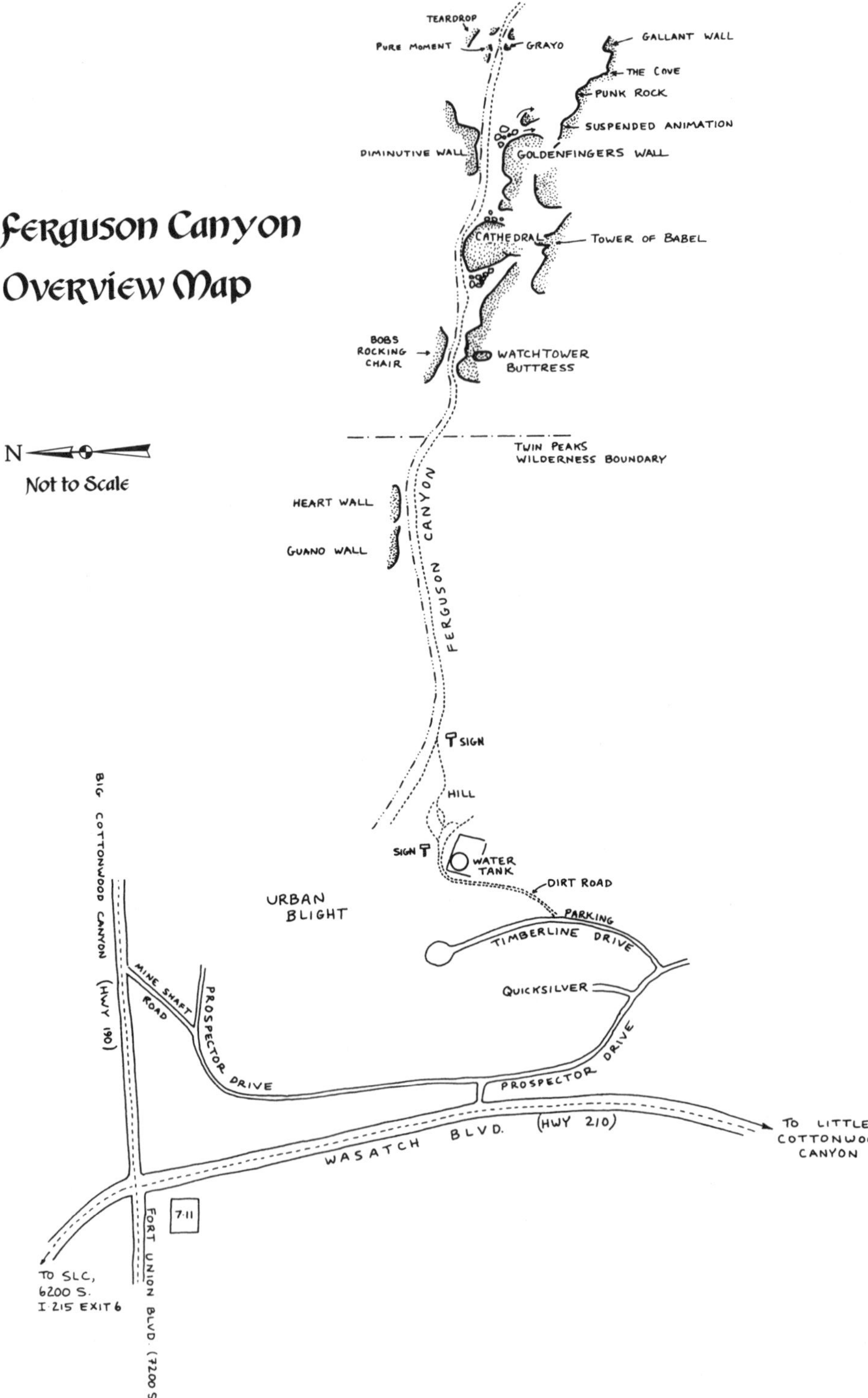

Ferguson Canyon

Just south of the mouth of Big Cottonwood Canyon is a smaller drainage that descends steeply from Storm Mountain and ends at a sub-division strewn alluvial fan. This narrow and rugged canyon was supposedly the home of the lost Ferguson gold mine, where a large vein of gold was found. Local history has it that the miners went to seek advice from Brigham Young concerning their find, and Brigham, fearing an influx of "gentiles" of California gold rush proportions, told them to close the mine and never tell of its whereabouts. The location of the mine has been a mystery ever since.

Today, the area is a gold mine for climbers, especially in the heat of summer. Its north-facing walls, rising above the creek, stay refreshingly cool when other areas are sizzling. Located on the contact zone between the granite and the much-older quartzite, the rocks and minerals found here are unusual. The granite is characterized by horizontal offset seams, large crystals and enticing overlaps that beg to be climbed. The routes are all short, averaging 50 feet in length, but are steeper than most of the granite areas to the south. In the summer, this unique grotto appeases most who pass through it, whether for a picnic or a pump!

Perhaps the most obvious feature upon entering this lush climbing area are the signs of tremendous overuse and abuse. Trampled vegetation, chopped down trees, fire pits, spray painted graffiti—all the negatives of encroaching urbanization are apparent. To be sure, not all of this spoilage is at the hands of climbers, but since we are such a visible user group, most of it is attributed to climbers by unknowing officials. Please, do more than your part to clean up after others, stay on trails, avoid eroding soil, and if you see others mistreating this wilderness area, let them know, politely, how you feel. Ferguson Canyon and the Twin Peaks Wilderness Area are a gift to us and to future generations—let's not pass along an abused hand-me-down.

HOW TO GET THERE: Follow the How To Get There information for Big Cottonwood Canyon. From the intersection of Wasatch Blvd. and Fort Union Blvd. at the mouth of Big Cottonwood Canyon, drive a quarter-mile south along Wasatch Blvd. to Prospector Drive (7535 South). Prospector is on the east side of Wasatch Blvd. Turn onto Prospector and drive up the hill to the south, past Quicksilver, then turn left on Timberline (7780 South). Park at a gate that blocks access to a dirt road on the east. This dirt road leads up to a white water tower, where it turns into a trail that descends down to the canyon bottom. See overview on page 196 for the on-foot approach. See individual cliff approaches for additional approach information. The approach time for most climbs is about 20 minutes.

The routes are listed in the order that they are reached as one walks up the trail. This order is counterclockwise, from the south side going up canyon to the north side going down canyon. All of the routes in Ferguson Canyon are within the Twin Peaks Wilderness Boundary. Therefore, no power drills are allowed.

THE WATCHTOWER

The first buttress on the south side of the canyon is the most popular wall by far. To say that there is a high concentration of quality routes on this buttress is an understatement. The Watchtower embodies the quintessence of the Ferguson experience—steep, shady stone, horizontal seams, and a roof (or two).

APPROACH: See overview on page 196.

DESCENT: Most routes have anchors at the top for a speedy, one rope rappel. Those that don't can be descended by a quick walk to the west. The Watchtower Proper is descended via a walk off to the west as well.

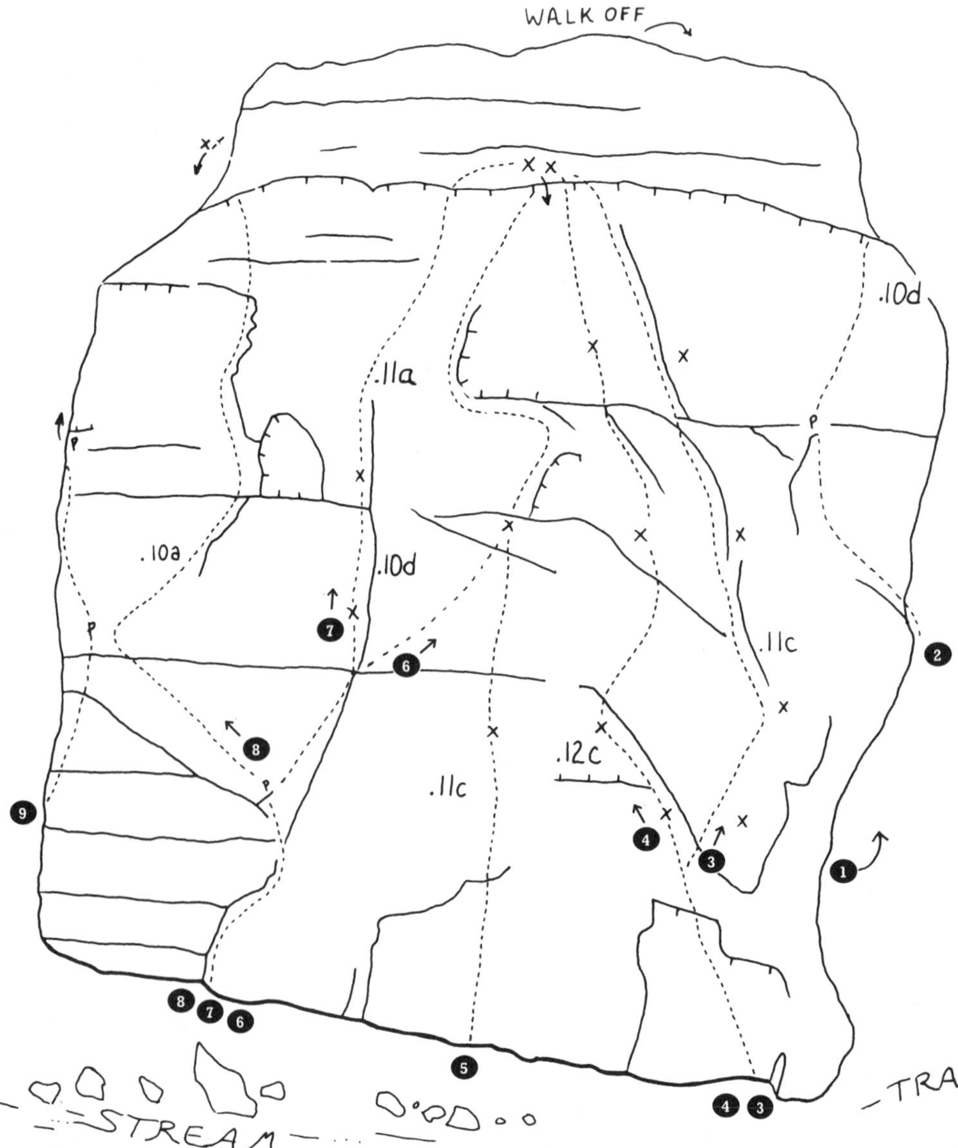

THE WATCHTOWER ROUTES

1. DOUBLE CROSS 5.8 ★

This climbs the right-facing corner right of the double crucifix.

FA: Les Ellison and Carl Buckland, 1982.

2. GO FOR THE ROSES 5.10d R ★

This is just left of Double Cross. The strenuous crack has an even harder exit move. No "guns," no roses.

FA: Les Ellison, 1982.

3. DARK ROSE 5.11c ★

This heinous seam lies eight feet left of Go For The Roses. Four bolts protect demanding moves.

FA: Drew Bedford and Hank Armantrout, 1983.

4. CROWN OF THORNS 5.12c ★★

From the initial ledge of Dark Rose, undercling left to a pocket, then up the crack to the top. The undeniable sequence is protected by four bolts.

FA: Eric Stroud and Gordon Douglass, 1988.

5. THE REVELATION 5.11b/c ★

A direct start to Invocation.

FA: Eric Stroud and Gordon Douglass, 1988.

6. INVOCATION 5.10d ★★

A thin, incipient seam is basically the line, and leads to the second bolt on The Revelation. TCU's are handy.

FA: Brian Smoot and Les Ellison, 1983.

7. THE DIRGE 5.11a ★★

A straight-up, two-bolt variant of Invocation. A gnarly mantle greets the weary climber at the top.

FA: unknown

8. FINAL PRAYER VARIATION 5.10a ★

About half-way up Benediction, escape right into a crack system.

FA: Bobby Rotert, 1982.

9. BENEDICTION 5.10d ★★

Fine face climbing on a "Gunks"-like, orange-colored wall. This is 15 feet right of the first bombay chimney (Outer Darkness) in the canyon.

FA: Les Ellison, 1982.

THE WATCHTOWER ROUTES

10. INNER LIGHT 5.7 R ★

An irresistible climb five feet right of the Outer Darkness chimney.

FA Unknown.

11. OUTER DARKNESS 5.3

The first big chimney on the south side of the canyon.

FA unknown.

12. ST. TERESA 5.10d R ★★

A small corner rising from the left wall of Outer Darkness. Try to do it without stemming to the right wall of the chimney.

FA: Les Ellison and Carl Buckland, 1982.

13. FISHLIPS 5.11d ★

The prow proper; a hard one to hold on to. Three pins protect barn-door layaways.

FA: Danny Kholert, 1986.

14. EXTREME UNCTION 5.10a ★★★

Bear hug the upside-down staircase to a stance, climb an easy face, then use extreme gumption to pass the tiered roofs. Classic.

FA: Les Ellison, Brian Smoot and Bill Robins, 1983.

15. LAST RITES VARIATION 5.9 ★

Escape right under the roof to the crack in the prow on Fishlips.

FA: Bobby Rotert, 1982.

16. THE CONFESSIONAL 5.6 ★★

Repent or perish! Climb the big cleft just left of Extreme Unction.

FA: Unknown

17. BROKEN SERENITY 5.9

Climb the broken face between The Confessional and Garden of Eden.

FA: Jeff Trauba, 1989.

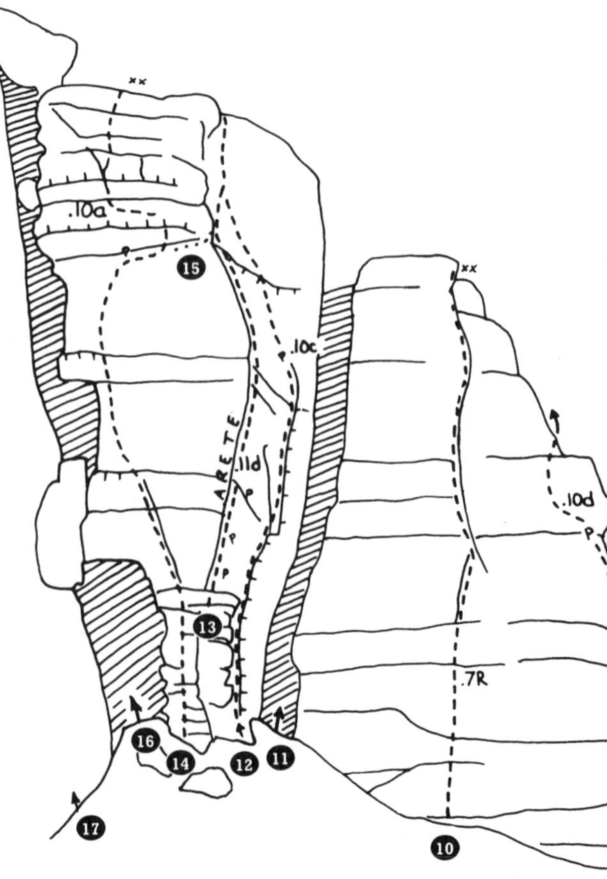

THE WATCHTOWER-PROPER

This is the tower-like formation that sits up above the Watchtower buttress. Because of the thick canopy of trees in the canyon bottom, it can be hard to spot from below. It can be approached by scrambling around the Watchtower buttress to the west, or better, by climbing one of the routes directly below the tower.

18. FAULTLINE VARIATION 5.9- ★
If the roof looks too intimidating, staying to the right the whole way is a reasonable option.
FA: Les Ellison and Ken Speirs, 1983.

19. BUCKLAND VARIATIONS 5.10d
The original route up the Watchtower.
FA: Les Ellison and Carl Buckland, 1982.
FFA: Bill Simmons, Mark Bennett and Bill Robins, 1985.

20. BATS IN THE BELFRY 5.10d ★★
Originally done in two short pitches to reduce rope drag. This line tackles the Watchtower with airy moves through the prominent roof and a breathtaking second-pitch arête.
FA: Bobby Rotert and Steve Carruthers, 1983.

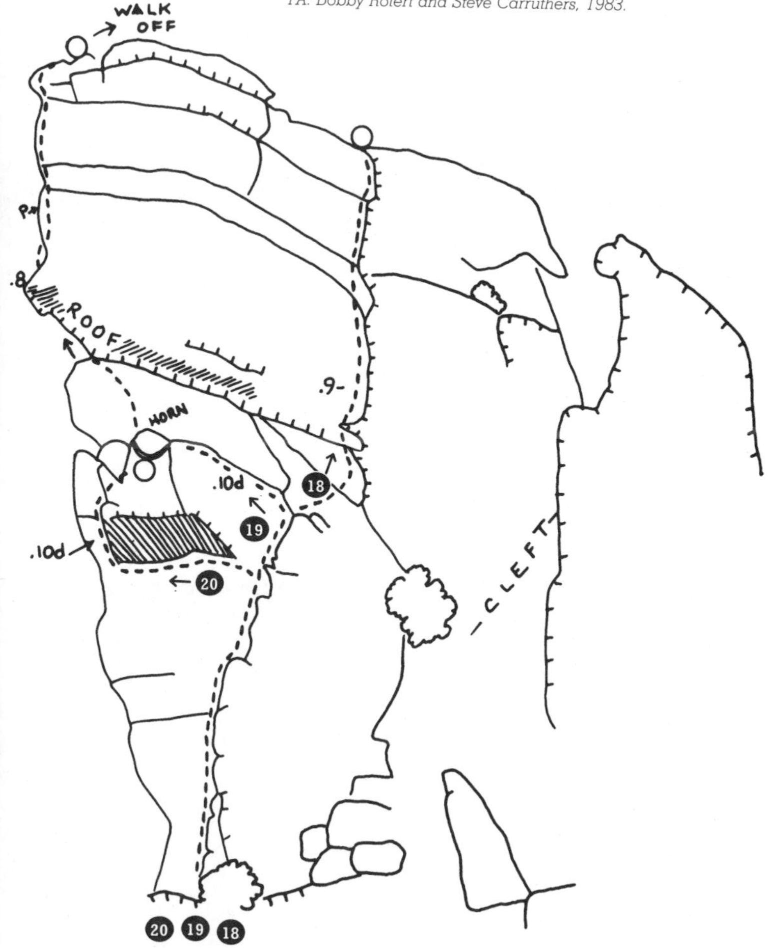

THE WATCHTOWER ROUTES

The following routes are back down at ground level.

21. GARDEN OF EDEN 5.8

This starts 15 feet left of The Confessional, up a maddening crack.

FA: Les Ellison and Carl Buckland, 1982.

22. BEEF JERKY 5.10c ★

Basically a boulder problem with some flare.

FA: Bobby Rotert and Merrill Bitter, 1982.

23. HUNGRY FOR HEAVEN 5.10c ★

The arête. The direct start is the intended line, but easier climbing to the left often draws the wavering leader.

FA: Tony Calderone and Kathy Lagerquist, 1992.

24. HOLY GRAIL 5.6 ★

A left-facing corner 15 feet left of Beef Jerky.

FA: Les Ellison, Gail Ellison and Michelle Slack, 1982.

25. THE ROSARY 5.10a ★

The wall just left of Holy Grail. The upper cracks are where it's at.

FA: Les Ellison and Carl Buckland, 1982.

26. SPIRIT PRISON 5.2

The chimney rising above the triple-trunked cottonwood tree.

FA: Hank Armantrout, 1983.

27. FIRE AND BRIMSTONE 5.10a ★

A good route on the recessed north-facing wall, 25 feet off the trail. Don't skip the left-slanting crack after the ledge.

FA: Brian Smoot, Hank Armantrout and Mark Smith, 1983.

28. FEELS LIKE NADINE 5.10a

A second pitch to Fire And Brimstone. The crux is protected by a bolt.

FA: Tony Calderone and Ken Grob, 1992.

29. HELLFIRE VARIATION 5.9+ ★

This is the most popular way to start Fire and Brimstone. Climb cracks five feet left of the start of Fire and Brimstone. The intimidated may continue right and skip the crux.

FA: Steve Carruthers, Les Ellison and Brian Smoot, 1983.

30. FORTRESS 5.11a ★★

Climb the more challenging cracks three feet left of Fire and Brimstone, joining that route for its final few feet.

FA: Mark Bennett, 1983.

31. JOHN DOE #2 5.?

Two bolts that don't seem to have a home.

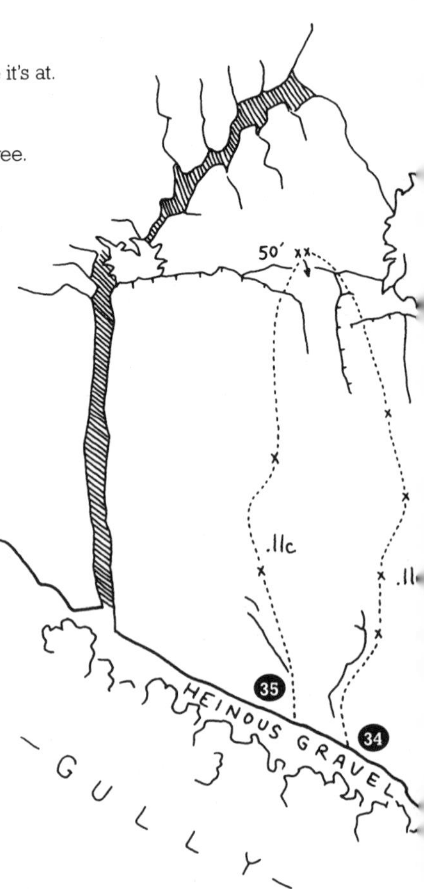

32. REACH THE BEACH 5.11a R

Begin 20 feet left of Fortress. Climb up the face, then finish up via the upper portion of Fortress.

FA: Scott Unice and Gordon Oakeson, 1988.

33. TOTAL X 5.?

A steep three bolt unknown. Go for it!

34. SCRATCHIN' FOR THE LOOMER 5.11d ★

This is the thin dihedral and face immediately right of Total Ramon. Stout.

FA: Drew Bedford, 1987.

35. TOTAL RAMON 5.11c ★★

Some sort of surfing lingo, dude. Climb a smooth wall on rounded patina holds. Steep, technical and hard. The bolts were placed on lead.

FA: Drew Bedford and Hank Armantrout, 1983.

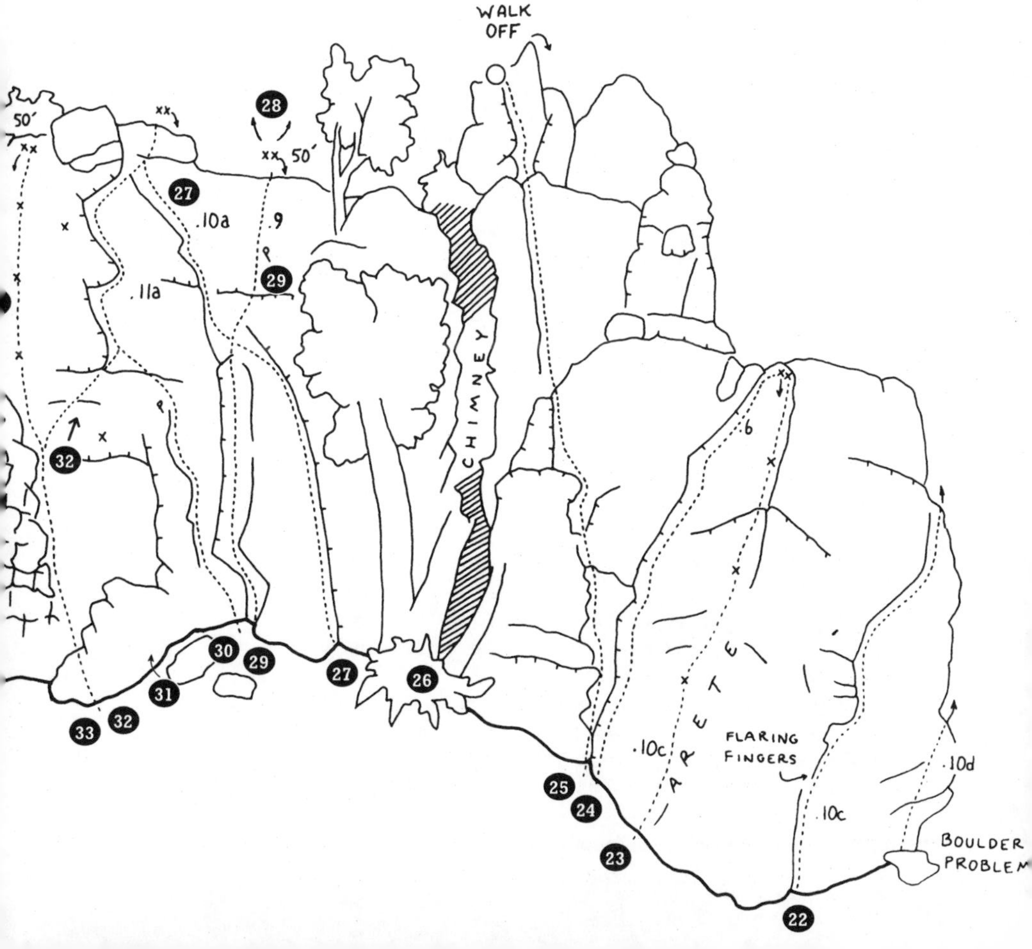

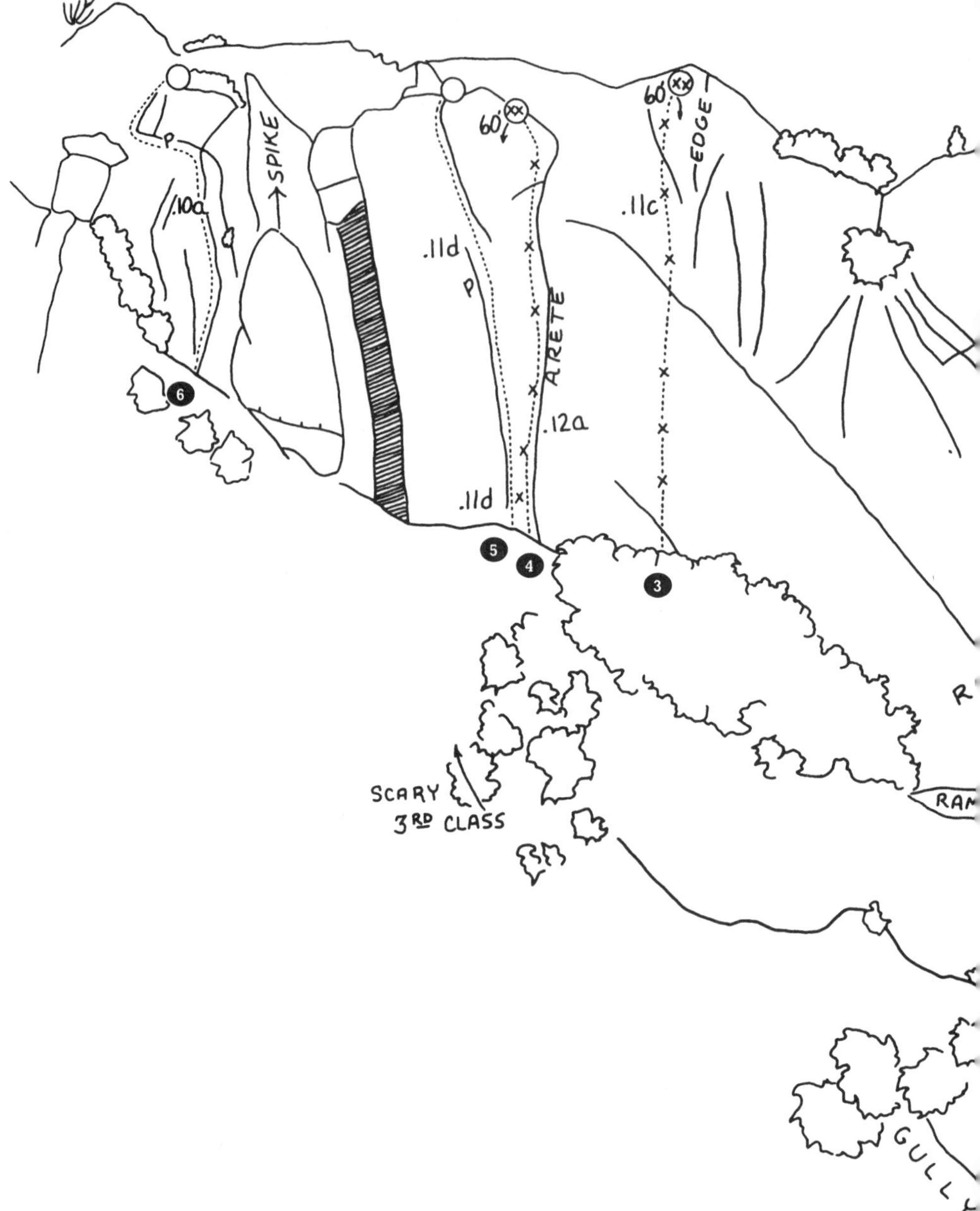

TOWER OF BABEL

This buttress lies between the Watchtower and The Cathedral, on the next tier above. Many of the routes here are worthy, sprinkled with square patina edges. However, the approach and descent are quite scary due to loose and sandy rock. Be careful!

APPROACH: The easiest approach is to follow a path up the gully just east of The Cathedral. This path flattens out and leads south then west to the base of routes 1-3. Access routes 4-6 where the path turns from south to west, via fifty feet of dirty third class scrambling. Take care here. See overview on page 196.

DESCENT: Carefully downclimb the approach.

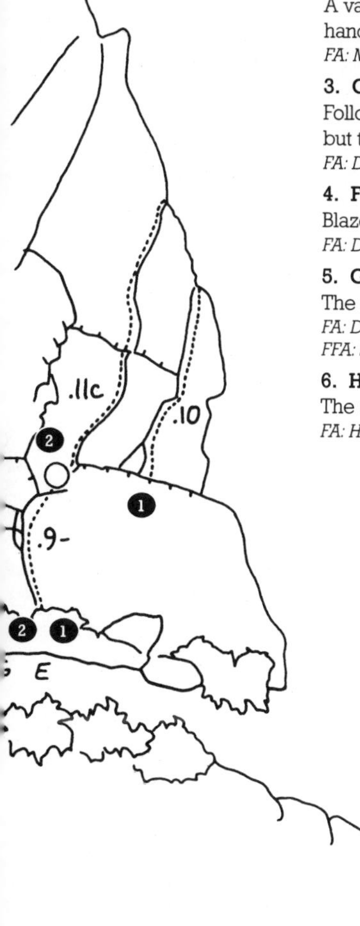

TOWER OF BABEL ROUTES

1. DELIRIOUS BUT NOT SERIOUS 5.10d ★
The rightmost of the two cracks rising on the right side of the Tower of Babel. Two pitches.
FA: Steve Carruthers and Pat Maloney, 1983.
FFA: Steve Carruthers and Les Ellison, 1983.

2. GRAVE MISGIVINGS (AKA MONTEZUMA'S REVENGE) 5.11 ★★
A variation to the second pitch of Delirious. The right-slanting finger to hand crack turns a desperate roof on a loose block.
FA: Mark Bennett, 1983.

3. CONCRETE JUNGLE 5.11c ★★
Follow the line of bolts right of Fuego. Some clips are in strange places, but the good climbing hardly makes you notice.
FA: Drew Bedford, Doug Heinrich and Todd Evans, 1989.

4. FUEGO 5.12a ★★★
Blaze up a bolt-protected arête just right of Pump or Jump. Superb.
FA: Drew Bedford and Doug Heinrich, 1989.

5. GET A PUMP OR JUMP 5.11d ★★
The overhanging crack in the center of the wall. Way pumper!
FA: Drew Bedford and Hank Armantrout, 1983.
FFA: Steve Hong, 1983.

6. HANK'S CRANK 5.10a
The crack on the left side of the wall, just left of the prominent spike.
FA: Hank Armantrout and Drew Bedford, 1983.

THE CATHEDRAL

Once past the Watchtower, the next obvious cliff on the right—the one with an overhanging north face—is The Cathedral. The best routes on this wall come to grips with this overhanging face in some way. Almost always shady, The Cathedral is good for summertime pulling down. In the fall of 1996 some bolt hangers had mysteriously vanished from this wall—beware.

APPROACH: See overview on page 196.

DESCENT: Many of the routes have fixed anchors at the top to allow a single rope rappel. Those routes that don't have fixed anchors can be descended by walking down the gully to the east.

The following routes are described counter clockwise.

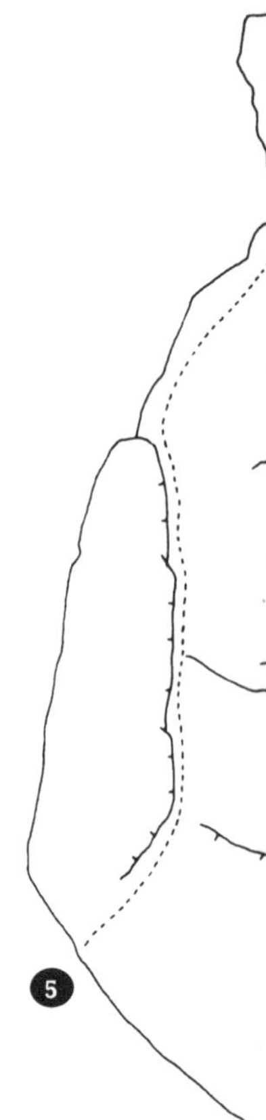

THE CATHEDRAL ROUTES

1. SON OF SLAB 5.12c ★★
Desperate, sequential climbing that is very good.
FA: Drew Bedford, 1994.

2. BRASS BUSTER 5.11d ★
This climb graces the west-facing side of the Cathedral. A rush on the strenuous overhangs.
FA: Rush Bowers and Kent Wheeler.

3. FEAST OF FRIENDS 5.9
The prominent pair of diagonal cracks on the west-facing side. Protection can be tricky. Bring small cams.
FA: Hank Armantrout and Bill Cramer, 1983.

4. ANASTASIA 5.10a
Climb up to a bolt and finish on some cracks.
FA: Jeff Baldwin,

5. CELESTIAL ASCENSION 5.7 ★
Fun route, bad name. Short.
FA: Brian Smoot, 1982.

UGLY GUANO-FILLED CHIMNEY

EZ

EZ

P

.10a

FLAKES

GULLY

1

1

2

3

4

The Cathedral N. Face

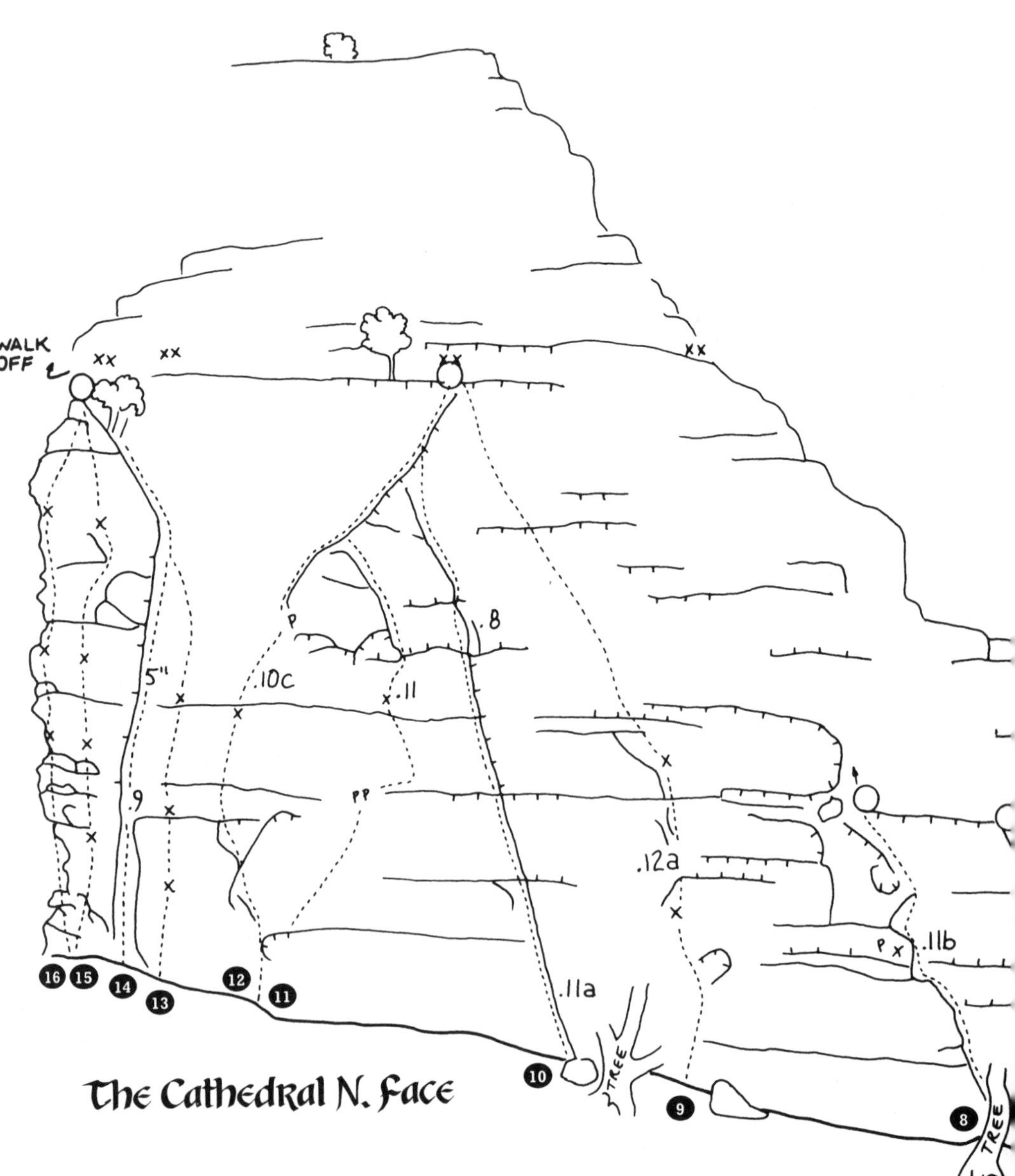

The Cathedral N. Face

THE CATHEDRAL ROUTES

6. DEVIL TREE 5.10a ★

The left-slanting crack on the west end of the north face. Deceptively difficult.

FA: Les Ellison and Kurt Ottmann, 1982.

7. TAINTED WORD 5.?

A single pin marks this route.

8. PAINTED BIRD 5.11b ★

The three-foot roof is the primary challenge.

FA: Les Ellison, 1983.

9. SWAMP COOLER 5.12a ★★

First led on manky protection, then done with almost no protection, and then retro-bolted by the first ascent party. This climbs through waves of overhangs just right of Oracle. A strange, but good, variation has been climbed starting near Devil Tree and making the boulder traverse left to Swamp Cooler, which is climbed to its finish. This is known as Turbo Cooler, and clocks in at 5.12c.

FA: Steve Hong and Steve Carruthers, 1983.

10. ORACLE 5.11a ★★

Defly maneuver the conspicuous crack rising out of the stream bottom, in the middle of the north face.

FA: Bret and Stuart Ruckman, Dec. 1980.
FFA: Bret and Stuart Ruckman, 1983.

11. IRON CROSS 5.11 ★

A long arm span and strong deltoids will expedite matters. Start 10 feet left of Oracle.

FA: Brian Smoot, Bill Robins and Les Ellison, 1983.

12. AFTERSHOCK 5.10c ★★

The moves past the bulge with a bolt are quite tricky. Good climbing.

FA: Steve Carruthers and Les Ellison, 1983.

13. SKINNY LEN CRIMPS 5.11a ★

The face with three bolts barely right of Mission Impossible.

14. MISSION IMPOSSIBLE 5.9 ★

Crack the code of the blocky fissure on the left side of the north face.

FA: Brian Smoot and Les Ellison, 1982.

15. NUPTIAL VOW 5.8

This route now has four bolts, placed by a clueless climber. Climb a crack 15 feet left of Mission Impossible. The route slithers over a roof and continues up a crack to the top.

FA: Les Ellison, Paul Scannel and Brian Smoot, sans bolts, 1983.

16. MONOGAMY 5.7

Another hapless route with three more bolts.

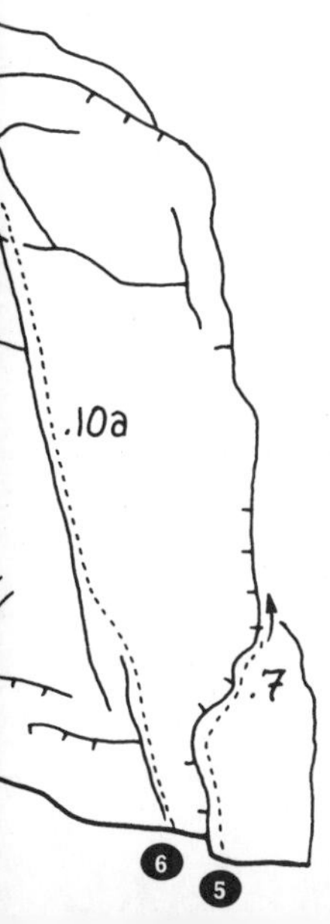

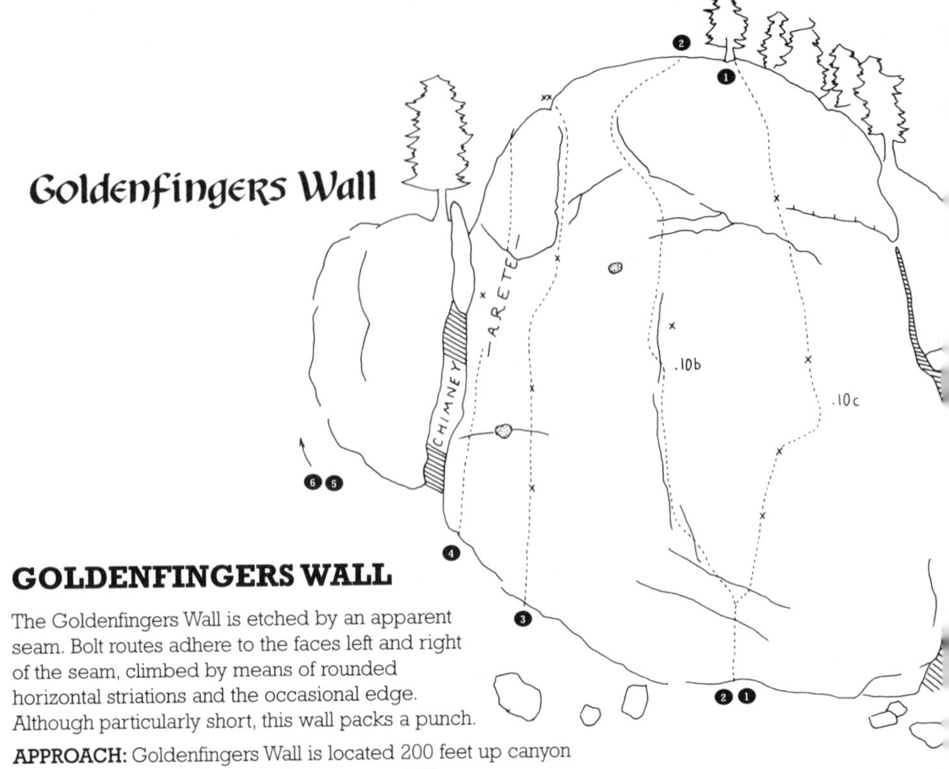

GOLDENFINGERS WALL

The Goldenfingers Wall is etched by an apparent seam. Bolt routes adhere to the faces left and right of the seam, climbed by means of rounded horizontal striations and the occasional edge. Although particularly short, this wall packs a punch.

APPROACH: Goldenfingers Wall is located 200 feet up canyon from The Cathedral. See overview on page 196.

DESCENT: It is easy to walk off the Goldenfingers Wall, but bolts at the top of Goldbagger can be rappelled with one rope.

GOLDENFINGERS WALL ROUTES

1. STONE THEY REJECTED 5.10c ★

Start on Goldenfingers and follow the line of bolts rightward to the top. Tenuous.

FA: Onsight solo, Gary Olsen, 1983. Unknowingly bolted later by another party.

2. GOLDENFINGERS 5.10b ★★

Climb the finger crack with a bolt just above its attenuation. Kind of hard to protect. Bring TCUs.

FA: Brian Smoot and Les Ellison, 1982.

3. GOLDEN OLDIE 5.11a ★

Thin, balancey clamboring that aims for the right edge of a flake.

4. GOLDBAGGER 5.10a ★

This route lays claim to the left arête.

FA: onsight solo, Gary Olsen, 1983. Bolt added unknowingly by another party.

5. GARDEN OF GORDON 5.6

Located near a hanging flake 30 feet left of Goldbagger. Climb just right of this flake and up the face on the right side of an arête, past a pin, to the top.

FA: Gordon Oakeson and Scott Unice, 1988.

6. ARÊTE JULIETTE 5.10a

Climb the hanging flake described in Garden of Gordon, and stay on the left side of the arête above, passing two bolts. The natural tendency is to go to the right side of the arête.

FA: Scott Unice, Julie Gustin and Gordon Oakeson, 1988.

ANIMATION WALL

At the top of the gully just east of the Goldenfingers Wall is an orange face divided by a slanting ramp. Two routes have been led. Both feature high quality rock and inobvious, wandering moves.

APPROACH: Thrash up the gully just east of the Goldenfingers Wall. See overview on page 196.

DESCENT: A 60 meter rope is needed to descend from the fixed anchors with a single rope, or rappel using two ropes.

ANIMATION WALL ROUTES

1. PVUSS 5.12b ★★★
Good rock, good moves, good luck! This route starts to the right of Suspended Animation, follows slim holds more or less straight up for three bolts, then traverses left, crossing Suspended Animation. Above the fourth bolt, continue straight up again to a pin and another leftward shuffle to a ledge. One more bolt protects the final section.
FA: Lance Bateman and Ben Folsom, 1993.

2. SUSPENDED ANIMATION 5.11d ★★
Start in the crack system on the left margin of the wall, climb past a pin and a bolt, then traverse right along the slanting ramp to a two-bolt belay on its far right side (5.11d). Next, climb up and left to a bolt, and begin a leftward traverse past a pin to gain a ledge with a bolt. Rising from the left side of this ledge is a thin crack system (with a pin), which is followed to the top (5.10). Take measures to reduce rope drag.
FA: Brian Smoot, Les Ellison and Paul Scannel, 1983.

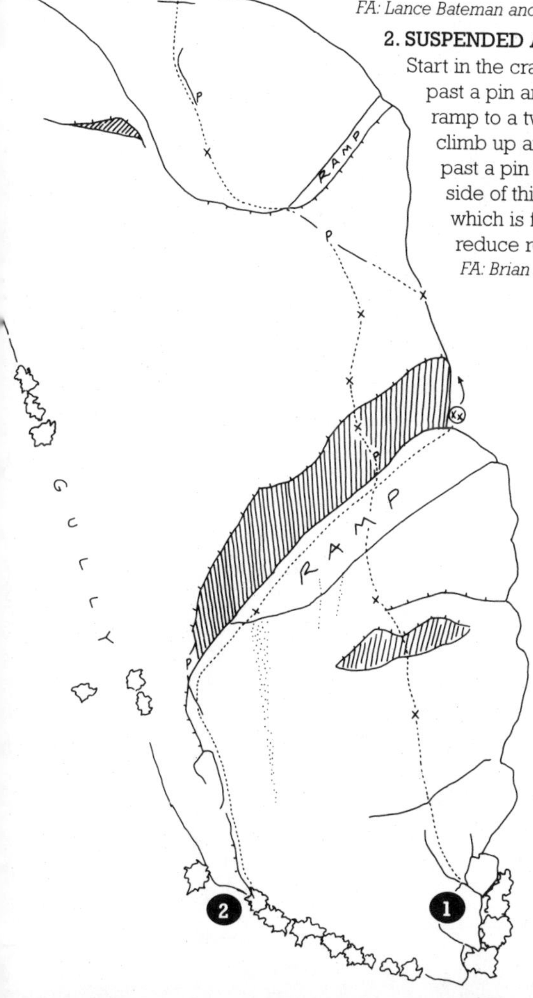

PUNK ROCK

This is a round blob of granite that sits east of the Animation Wall. Antithesis to the theme of the canyon, this is where the infidels climb.

APPROACH: 50 feet up canyon from the upper end of the Goldenfingers Wall is a rock formation dubbed the Drystone Wall. Claw your way up the gully just east of the Drystone Wall for awhile, until Punk Rock appears on the right. Thrash through scrub oak to its base. See overview on page 196.

DESCENT: Routes 1-4 can be descended from fixed anchors with one rope. Route number five is a walk off.

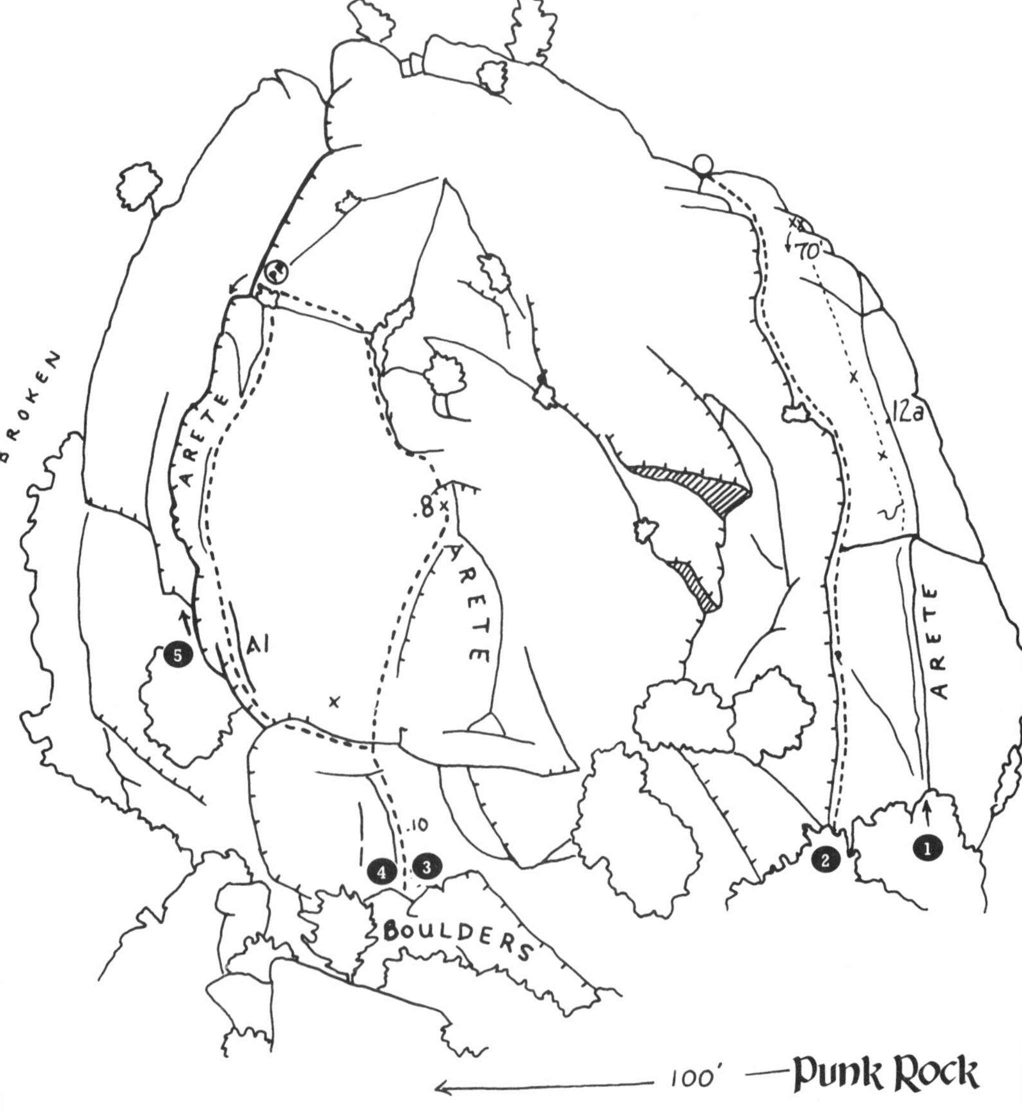

PUNK ROCK ROUTES

1. CAMANOE 5.12a ★★
The arête right of the Mr. Sandman corner. Starts with a crack on an arête, then strikes out left past two bolts. High quality.
FA: Jeff Baldwin, Hank Armantrout, and John Cronin, 1993.

2. MR. SANDMAN 5.10a
The left-facing corner system with one fixed pin.
FA: Bill Simmons and Skip Boissonault.

3. QUIET RIOT 5.10 ★
Climb cracks off of the boulder to a bolt, diagonal right to another bolt, mantel, then rock out.
FA: Drew Bedford and Doug Heinrich.

4. JOHNNY ROTTEN 5.10 A1
Step off the boulder, climb a one-inch crack, skip left and up using some aid, then dash to the top. Rappel off of a tree to the right.
FA: Drew Bedford and Pokey Amory, 1984.

5. DEAD AUSSIES 5.10a ★
Around the left side of Punk Rock is a dihedral crack with a small roof at the start.
FA: Drew Bedford, solo, 1984.

THE COVE (no topo)

This grey wall sits at the illusive dead-end to a steep and brush filled gully. The rock here is broken, and the climbing links up cleaner sections of rock between fissures and ledges.

APPROACH: Follow the approach information to Punk Rock. However, instead of traversing over to Punk Rock when the gully splits, continue left up the gully 200 feet to a dead end. This is The Cove. These climbs all face north. See overview on page 196.

DESCENT: Two ropes are needed to rappel these routes. Anchors at the top of each route provide a quick descent.

1. BIRD OF PARADISE 5.10d
A two-bolt line on the rightmost flank of the Cove ends at tree/bolt anchor. Climb a good crack up to the first bolt, then cast off, passing a thin crack via edges to reach the second bolt.
FA: Jeff Baldwin and Hank Armantrout, 1993.

2. MAROONED 5.10b R ★
Climb the face just right of the very back of The Cove. Work up onto a ramp, then up a face past a bolt, staying to the left of a Mahogany tree. Follow the dike to the top. 90+ feet long.
FA: Jeff Baldwin and Hank Armantrout, 1993.

3. THE TRAWLER 5.10b
Climb up a water polished face just left of the back of The Cove. Pass 5 pins to reach a horizontal crack for protection. Above, clip a bolt, turn the roof, then follow 2 more bolts up an arête to a 2-bolt anchor. 100+ feet long.
FA: Hank Armantrout and Jeff Baldwin, 1993.

THE GALLANT WALL

The fixed pins on this wall can be hard to see from below.

APPROACH: Follow the approach to The Cove. From there, hike uphill 250', scraping past the left (east) side of The Cove (a large pine tree) to this northwest facing wall. See overview on page 196.

DESCENT: Rappel off a tree at the top of the wall.

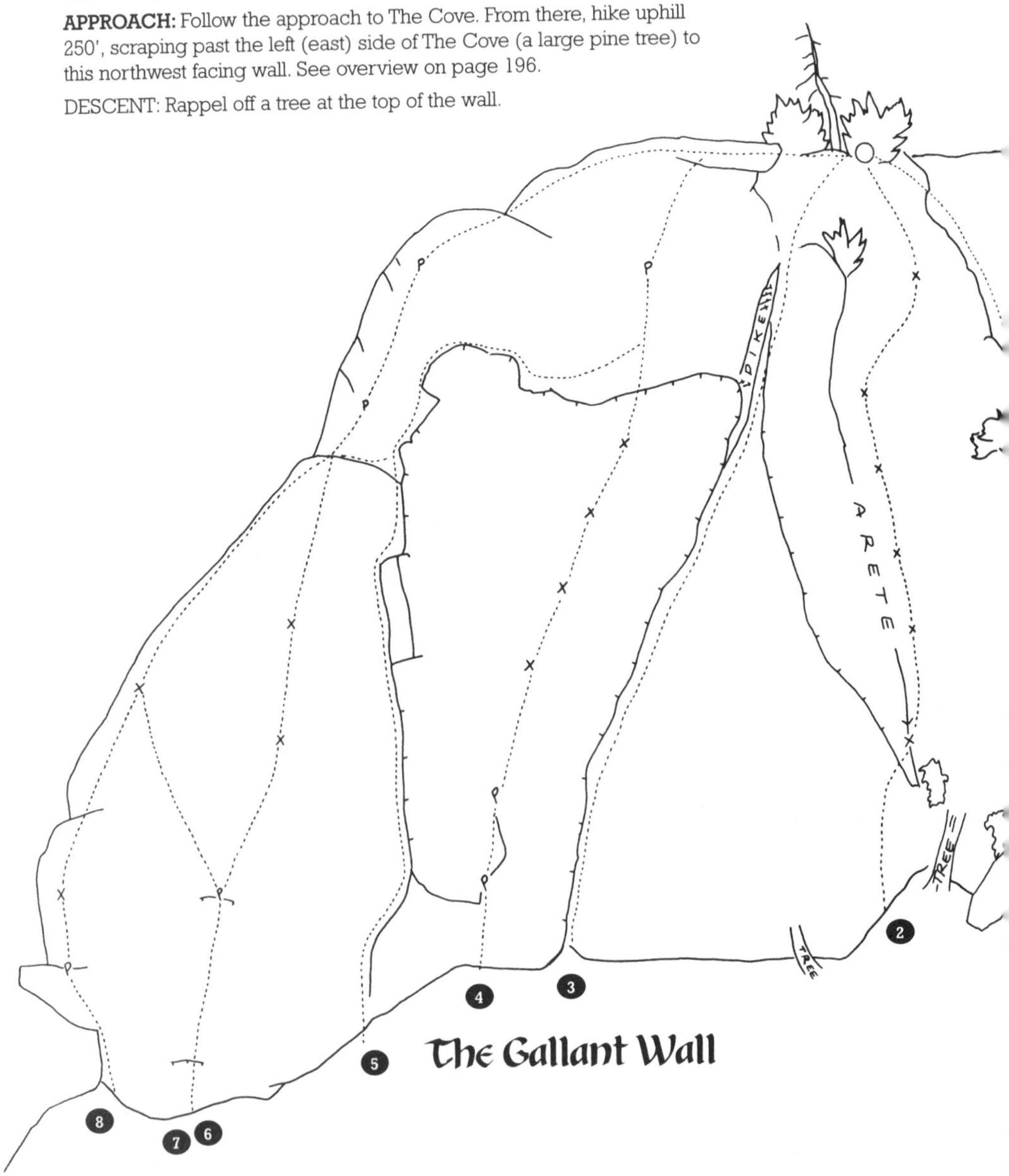

DIKE
ARETE
TREE
TREE
2
3
4
5
6
7
8

The Gallant Wall

THE GALLANT WALL ROUTES

1. RUN AGROUND 5.7

Climb to the right of two trees, move a bit left and follow the good cracks to the top.

FA: Hank Armantrout and Jeff Baldwin, 1993.

2. RED SKY AT NIGHT 5.11b ★★

Scurry up and right to clip the first bolt, then step down and around the arête to a stance. From here, edges and strenuous underclings blaze a line to the top.

FA: Jeff Baldwin, Hank Armantrout, 1993.

3. PRESIDING NYMPH 5.9 ★

A good, right-leaning crack splits the center of the face. Bring hand-sized protection.

FA: Hank Armantrout, Mike Mead, 1993.

4. PROJECT ROYAL SPAR 5.12?

Should be three stars when finished.

5. INLAND REFUGE 5.9

An easier crack leads to a ledge, followed by a few tricky face moves. A fixed pin protects the final section.

FA: Hank Armantrout and Jeff Baldwin, 1993.

6. CLOSE REACH 5.11b ★

Climb to the hidden pin on Scandinavian Tuna, then chase two bolts up and right to a hard mantle at the lip. Finish on Inland Refuge.

FA: Hank Armantrout and Jeff Baldwin, 1993.

7. SCANDINAVIAN TUNA 5.10b ★

The first pin is hidden. Once it is found, traverse left to the arête and a pin which can be backed up with a medium sized camming device. Blast up the arête, past one more fixed pin to the top.

FA: Hank Armantrout and Brith Otterud, 1993.

8. STONE CRAB 5.11b ★

A difficult direct start to Scandinavian Tuna.

FA: Jeff Baldwin, 1993.

GRAYO (no topo)

Grayo is located on the south side of the hiking trail about two minutes up canyon from Diminutive Rock. This climb is just below the point where the trail ascends a steep, dusty hill.

1. GRAYO 5.8 ★

Climb a short west-facing arête. Two bolts leads to chains.

FA: Jeff Baldwin, 1990.

2. UNKNOWN

One bolt protects the start to a L-facing corner 100 feet up canyon from Grayo.

TEARDROP AREA (no topo)

A series of broken, south-facing walls.

APPROACH: See individual route descriptions for approach information.

DESCENT: All routes can be rappelled with one rope from fixed gear.

1. PROJECT
75 feet right of Teardrop. 1 bolt, so far.

2. TEARDROP 5.11a ★★
Across the stream and up canyon 200 feet from Grayo, this south-facing route climbs up a black-streaked, 80 degree section of rock, past four bolts. Climb a little above the 4th bolt, place some gear and traverse right 15 feet (under the second roof) to the chain anchor.
FA: Jeff Baldwin, Merrill Bitter and Jeff Bergovoy, 1991

3. MINE SWEEPER 5.9
Climb a left-trending dike system (two feet left of Teardrop) to chain anchors.
FA: Jeff Baldwin, Hank Armantrout, 1993.

4. PURE MOMENT 5.12 ★★
Located directly across the stream from Grayo. Look for chains atop a roof. Start up a seam which leads to a roof. Place gear in a crack on the right side of this roof, but climb the "juggy"-looking left side of the roof. A TCU works in a hidden placement on the left side "jugs." There may be a moment of panic at the lip.
FA: Jeff Baldwin, Hank Armantrout and John Cronin.

DIMINUTIVE ROCK

Directly across the stream from the Goldenfingers wall is a lower-angled face that is quite short.

APPROACH: See overview on page 196.

DESCENT: A quick walk off is the usual descent.

1. SMALL POTATOES 5.8
FA: Bret Ruckman, 1990.

2. TWO-BIT GRIT 5.11
Analytical climbing past two bolts. The crack to the right is off route.
FA: Jeff Baldwin, 1988.

3. EXODUS 5.9
This is the two-bolt route on the right of the lower angled face directly above the creek.
FA: Colin Reynolds.

4. DRAW THE LINE 5.9
Friction past two bolts to a ledge.
FA: Hank Armantrout, Bill Cramer and Dave Casey, 1983.

5. f/8 5.8
Located 50 feet down and left of Draw the Line. Diagonal up and rightward for 90 feet. 5 bolts.
FA: Jeff Baldwin, 1988.

BOB'S ROCKING CHAIR (no topo)

Across the stream from the Watchtower is a scruffy buttress with a scary block on top (Bob's rocking chair). The following three climbs are found along the base, and are only 30 feet long.

APPROACH: See overview on page 196.

DESCENT: Routes 1 and 5 are descended with one rope from slings wrapped around tree branches. Routes 2-4 require a walk off to the east.

1. NEANDERTHAL OR NOT AT ALL 5.10a ★
Strenuous.
FA: Scott Unice and Gordon Oakeson, 1986.

2. JOINTED VENTURE 5.9-
Scramble over three blocks and up a right-facing flake system to a ledge (immediately below Bob's Rocking Chair). Walk off.
FA: Bill Cramer and Hank Armantrout, 1983.

3. SQUASH ROCKER 5.10a/b ★
Start 15 left of Neanderthal. Climb past one bolt, then traverse under a roof and climb straight up the face past another bolt to the top. Bring a 2-½" cam and small wireds.
FA: Scott Unice, Mike Grossman and Kristen Carrol, 1990.

4. BLIND MAN'S GLASSES 5.8
The hand crack in the left-facing corner, just left of Jointed Venture.
FA: Unknown.

5. ANONYMOUS 5.9
Climb the short face to a bolt, and lower off the tree.

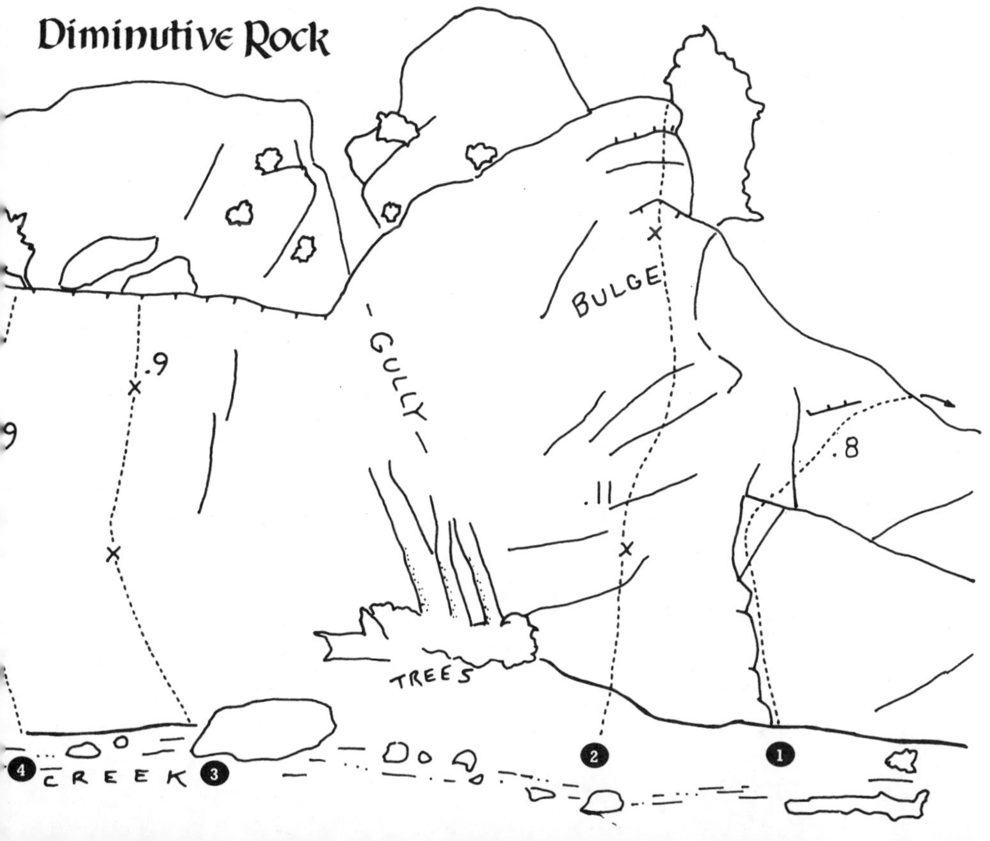

GUANO WALL

This is the first buttress in the canyon on the left (north) side. The Guano Wall has a roof band towards its bottom, which Delirium Tremens and Guano Roof fight their way over. The cliff receives abundant sun and can be climbed even in winter.

APPROACH: See overview on page 196. Bushwhacking and some third-class scrambling takes one to the start of the routes.

DESCENT: Anchors at the top of Guano Roof allow a quick, one rope descent.

1. GUANO ROOF 5.10d ★★
This route follows a hand crack that splits the roof at its western end, and the deceptive face above. Rope drag can be a problem.
FA: Steve Carruthers, Les Ellison and Brian Smoot, 1983.

2. DELIRIUM TREMENS 5.11a ★★
This follows the right-curving dihedral 10 feet right of Guano Roof. A drunken nausea might be felt on the second-pitch roof.
FA: Bob Rotert and Les Ellison, 1983.

3. TOTAL DELIRIUM VARIATION 5.9- ★
Move right and up from the first-pitch belay bolts of Delirium Tremens.
FA: Les Ellison, Brian Smoot and Steve Carruthers, 1983.

HEART WALL

Two routes of fair quality are found on this south-facing wall—the second buttress on the left (north) side of the canyon. On cold clear days, this wall remains in the sun.

APPROACH: See overview on page 196. Bushwhacking seems to be the only solution.

DESCENT: A walk off to the west and down the gully separating Heart Wall and Guano Wall seems to be the quickest.

1. NO GUANO ROOF 5.8 ★
The right-curving crack left of Meteor Shower.
FA: Blaine Sorenson, Steve Williams and Linda Sorenson, 1988.

2. METEOR SHOWER 5.8 ★
The easily-distinguished right-facing dihedral.
FA: Brian Smoot, Hank Armantrout and Les Ellison, 1983.

3. HEART ATTACK 5.4
Don't defibrilate on the exit.
FA: George Lowe and Les Ellison, 1983.

4. AORTA 5.7
FA: Hank Armantrout, Brian Smoot and Les Ellison, 1983.

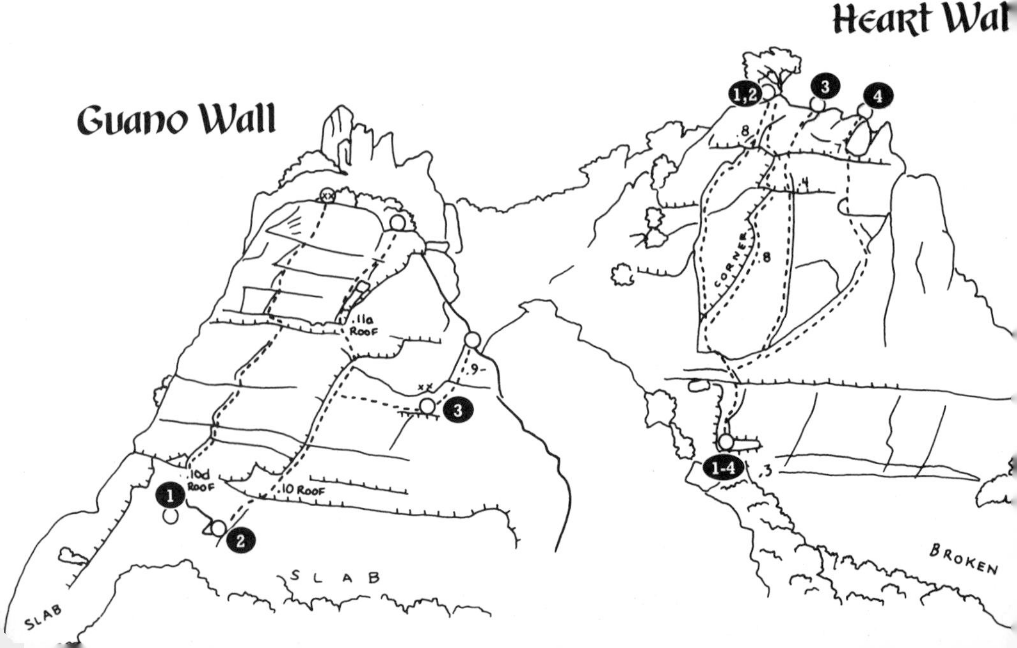

The Hound's Tooth

Overlooking the valley from its perch on the ridge between the North Fork of Deaf Smith Canyon and Ferguson Canyon, The Hound's Tooth is about as far away from the climbing scene as you can get in the Wasatch. The rock on the Hound's Tooth is gritty and few striking lines are immediately visible. Add a long, dry approach and you get a seldom visited, even more seldomly ascended rock formation. It is possible to scramble to the summit from the east.

HOW TO GET THERE: Follow the How To Get There information for Big Cottonwood Canyon. From the intersection of Wasatch Blvd. and Fort Union Blvd. at the mouth of Big Cottonwood Canyon, drive south on Wasatch Blvd. for a rough two miles to Golden Hills Avenue (8785 South). Turn east towards the mountains, then make a quick left on Alpen Way (3590 East), then a right on Escalade Avenue (8730 South). At the top of this street, turn left on Kings Hill Drive (3655 East), go up the hill and make a right on Golden Oaks Drive (8620 South). Park at the top of this street, where a chain link fence blocks the way.

APPROACH: A dirt road here heads south across the slope and provides the best starting point for a hike to The Hound's Tooth. Walk along the dirt road scouting for a less brushy location, and then point it upwards. The hike follows the ridge, weaving in and out of oak brush.

DESCENT: Scramble down the east face and return home via the hiking route.

1. WEST RIDGE II 5.6
At the base of the west ridge are a series of slabs that can be climbed for roughly 40 feet to steep, right leaning cracks. Follow the cracks until it is possible to ascend a steep chimney/gully that tops out on the crest of the ridge. Follow the ridge to the summit. Three pitches of flakey rock and poor protection.
FA: Unknown.

2. SOUTH FACE RAMP II 5.8 A3
Sketchy information on this route has been passed along from guidebook to guidebook. The route seems to follow a line up the south face to a large ramp located about two-thirds of the way up the formation. The route then climbs the ramp and the flakes above to the summit. It is unknown whether pins are needed.
FA: Chuck Satterfield and Dave Allen, 1965.

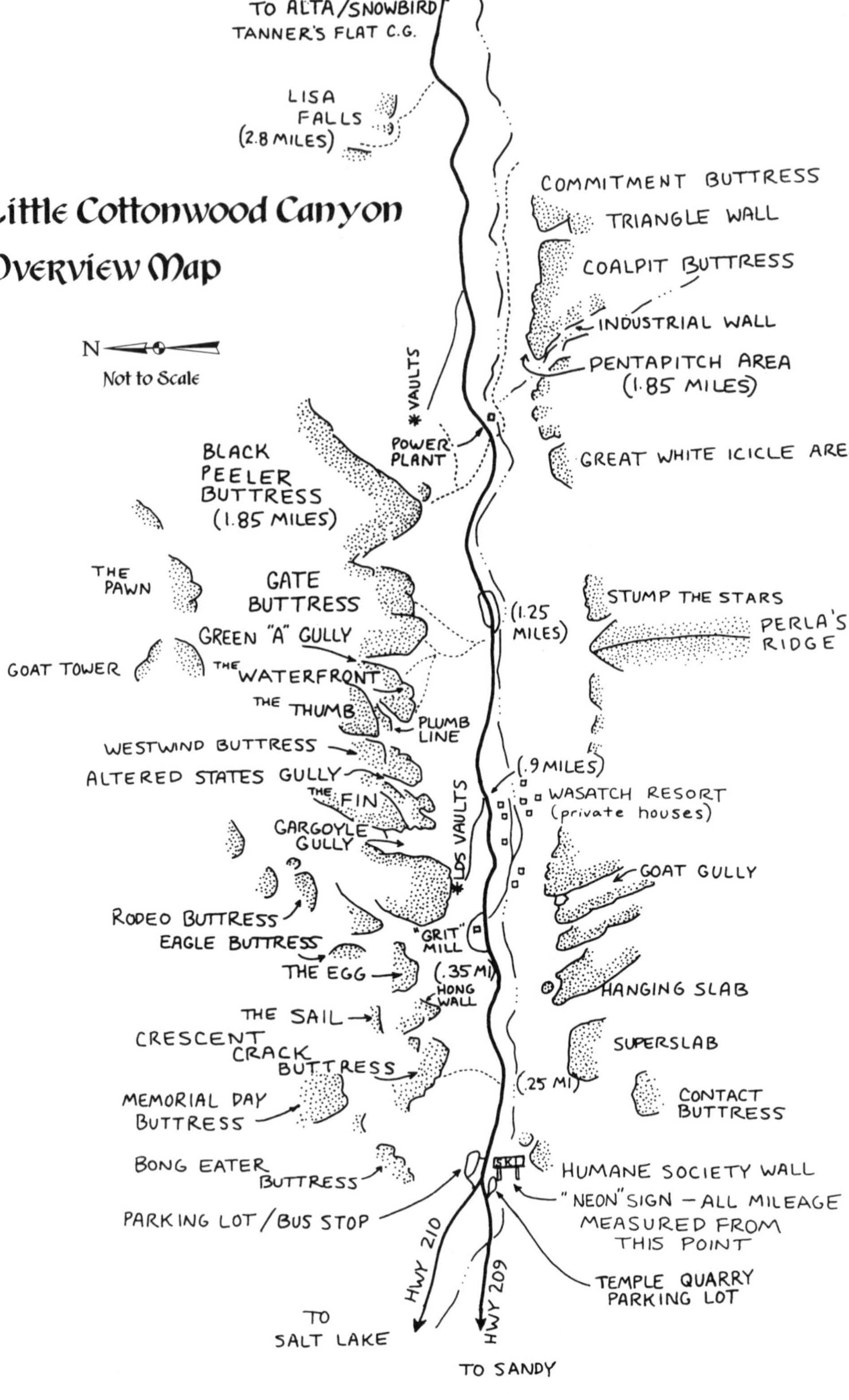
TO ALTA/SNOWBIRD
TANNER'S FLAT C.G.
LISA FALLS (2.8 MILES)
Little Cottonwood Canyon Overview Map
N
Not to Scale
COMMITMENT BUTTRESS
TRIANGLE WALL
COALPIT BUTTRESS
INDUSTRIAL WALL
PENTAPITCH AREA (1.85 MILES)
VAULTS
POWER PLANT
GREAT WHITE ICICLE AREA
BLACK PEELER BUTTRESS (1.85 MILES)
THE PAWN
GATE BUTTRESS
STUMP THE STARS
(1.25 MILES)
PERLA'S RIDGE
GREEN "A" GULLY
GOAT TOWER
THE WATERFRONT
THE THUMB
PLUMB LINE
WESTWIND BUTTRESS
ALTERED STATES GULLY
(.9 MILES)
WASATCH RESORT (private houses)
THE FIN
GARGOYLE GULLY
LDS VAULTS
GOAT GULLY
RODEO BUTTRESS
EAGLE BUTTRESS
"GRIT" MILL
THE EGG
(.35 MI)
HONG WALL
HANGING SLAB
THE SAIL
SUPERSLAB
CRESCENT CRACK BUTTRESS
(.25 MI)
MEMORIAL DAY BUTTRESS
CONTACT BUTTRESS
BONG EATER BUTTRESS
HUMANE SOCIETY WALL
SKI
"NEON" SIGN – ALL MILEAGE MEASURED FROM THIS POINT
PARKING LOT/BUS STOP
HWY 210
HWY 209
TEMPLE QUARRY PARKING LOT
TO SALT LAKE
TO SANDY

Little Cottonwood Canyon

Little Cottonwood Canyon (LCC) is a recreational haven. The U-shaped, glacially-carved valley is visited by hundreds of thousands of people each year—a small percentage of whom are climbers. Snowbird and Alta, bustling at the head of the canyon, maintain reputations as world-class ski resorts, and what the locals say is true: the snow dumps here. Usually it's the light, low-density stuff that provides fantastic backcountry skiing as well. Summer offers pleasant temperatures, scenic hikes (wildflowers galore in July and August), peak-bagging amongst bountiful 11,000-foot summits, festivals, concerts, tram rides—and, of course, rock climbing.

The rock climbing, for the most part, is on granite, with the limestone Hellgate Cliffs and Albion Basin Area being the main exception. The vast majority of the routes are on the north side, and in the lower third of the canyon. A potpourri of climbing styles comes into play here, but the rock lends itself predominantly to face climbing. Rock quality on the more popular routes is excellent, although flaky rock may be encountered on certain of the more obscure climbs.

In winter, the portion of LCC that gets the most sun reaches from The Bong Eater to The Egg. The high ridge to the south blocks most of the sun that bakes the Gate Buttress and environs in the summer months. In summer, for the climber chasing shadows, the Green Adjective Gully is good in the morning and The Dihedrals area is best in the evening. Other good summertime hangouts are the Pentapitch Area, Great White Icicle, and Albion Basin areas.

The modern climbing scene is a far cry from the happy-go-lucky, carefree days when climbers were a small user group. Today, land ownership in LCC is an important consideration for anyone planning to enjoy the rock. The LDS church owns property that stretches, roughly, from the "gritmill" below the church archives to up past the Gate Buttress. The Black Peeler Buttress and the Hellgate Cliffs also are on private land. (Most remaining cliffs of interest to climbers belong to the Forest Service.) There is no legal way to get to some routes on the south side of the canyon, where the Wasatch Resort makes access difficult. Unfortunately, too, parking is limited in LCC. Nonetheless, positive steps are being taken to preserve our crags. In 1984, a parcel of land in LCC was acquired by the Forest Service via a complex land exchange. In 1989, after the LDS Church posted No Trespassing signs, Ted Wilson and Rick Reese, representing the climbing community, successfully negotiated for continued access. Future climbing practices, in part determined by the courtesy and respect of regular users, potentially may be different from what this guidebook describes.

Ice climbing in the lower portion of the canyon deserves mention. Scruffy Band, an epithet that stuck, is just that—a smear of ice on the first granite outcrop on the south side of the canyon. It is intermediate to advanced territory, depending on ice conditions. The Great White

Burner
Buttress
Upper
Burner
Buttress
Bong Eater
Buttress

Memorial Day Buttress

Crescent Crack Buttress (West End)

BURNER BUTTRESS

UPPER BURNER BUTTRESS

BONG EATER BUTTRESS

MEMORIAL DAY BUTTRESS

CRESCENT CRACK BUTTRESS

Icicle, a superb five-pitch climb that is moderately difficult and almost always formed up, is 1.8 miles up canyon. The rock climb Disco Duck infrequently forms a thin shield of ice in winter and is aptly named Cold Duck. In Little Cottonwood Canyon, it is entirely possible to go ice climbing, rock climbing and skiing on the same day without leaving the canyon.

HOW TO GET THERE: From the north, follow I-15 to the I-80 East Exit. Follow I-80 east toward the mountains to the I-215 South Exit. Exit off I-215 at the 6200 South exit. From here signs will lead south, past the mouth of Big Cottonwood Canyon to Wasatch Blvd, and the road to Little Cottonwood Canyon.

From the south, exit off I-15 at the 90th South Exit. Follow 90th South as it bends and joins 9400 South at a stoplight. Continue east on 9400 South, and it will deposit you directly at the mouth of Little Cottonwood Canyon.

Individual cliff approaches are described with each cliff.

The routes in LCC are listed in a clockwise direction, beginning with the routes near the mouth of the canyon on the north side, and ending with the routes near the mouth of the canyon on the south side. All mileage is measured from the large lighted sign (herein referred to as the "neon" sign) which posts road conditions located near the mouth of the canyon.

BONG EATER BUTTRESS

On the north (left) side of Little Cottonwood Canyon, straight above the neon sign at the intersection of Highways 209 and 210, is a steep chunk of granite with an obvious dihedral. This dihedral is Bong Eater, the first significant outcropping of granite in the canyon.

APPROACH: Park in the bus stop/parking lot at the mouth of the canyon. From the very upper most (northeast) corner of the parking lot, follow a trail up the embankment. At the top of this first hill turn left and walk west on another path for 30 feet. A trail here heads uphill through the brush to the base of Bong Eater. It is also possible to follow the Crescent Crack trail to the Hand Jive area. Then hike up and west until thick scrub oak impedes progress. A faint trail leads west through smaller scrub and takes one to a quartzite talus slope. Travel down and over 200 feet to reach the base of Bong Eater. See overview on pages 220 and 222.

DESCENT: Descend all routes with an easy downclimb off the back side.

BONG EATER BUTTRESS ROUTES

1. DESPERADO 5.8
FA: Les Ellison and Kurt Ottmann, 1976.

2 PROWSER 5.12b ★★
Exhilarating moves up an incipient prow crack lead to vertical face climbing on microwafers. Micro nuts are handy.
FA: Mark Ward and Dave Houser.
FFA: Drew Bedford, 1988.

3. BONG EATER 5.10d ★★★
Strenuous. Save yourself for the pumping lieback (or offwidth) at the top. Big nuts or cams are needed at crux. (HAND EATER 5.10 ★★ is a difficult preamble to Bong Eater and climbs the flaring crack just to the right.)
FA: Warren Marshall and Lenny Nelson, 1964.
FFA: George Lowe and Pete Gibbs, 1974.

4. LIFE BY THE THROAT 5.12b ★★
Climb the east face past four bolts to the top. If the moves left leave you breathless, don't choke on the finish.
FA: John Storm, 1987.

The following routes are located on two walls above the Bong Eater Buttress. They are collectively known as The Burner Buttress.

5. DEATH FLAKE 5.8
Climb the deep chimney up and past a loose chockstone. For a second pitch, climb grooves up and slightly left to the top.
FA: Brian Smoot, 1979.

6. DREAD LOCKS 5.10d
An overhanging crack 25 feet right of Death Flake makes for challenging stuff. For the second pitch, climb up a face and join Death Flake.
FA: Les Ellison and Doug Moffat, 1977.

7. THE BURNER 5.10 ★★
This is a full-on fatty; bring large cams.
FA: Mark Ward and Kim Miller, 1976.

8. FIRESTARTER 5.9 ★
Another wide crack.
FA: unknown.

9. HOPSCOTCH 5.10a
Climb a nice crack in a small dihedral that slants right and joins a big dihedral. Thrash through some oaks and climb the gritty rock (crux) above.
FA: Tom Carruthers and Pat Maloney, 1982.
FFA: Tom and Steve Carruthers, 1982.

10. STASIS 5.10d
Climb up to and across the prominent left-slanting crack. Rotten rock.
FA: Dirk Tyler, 1980.

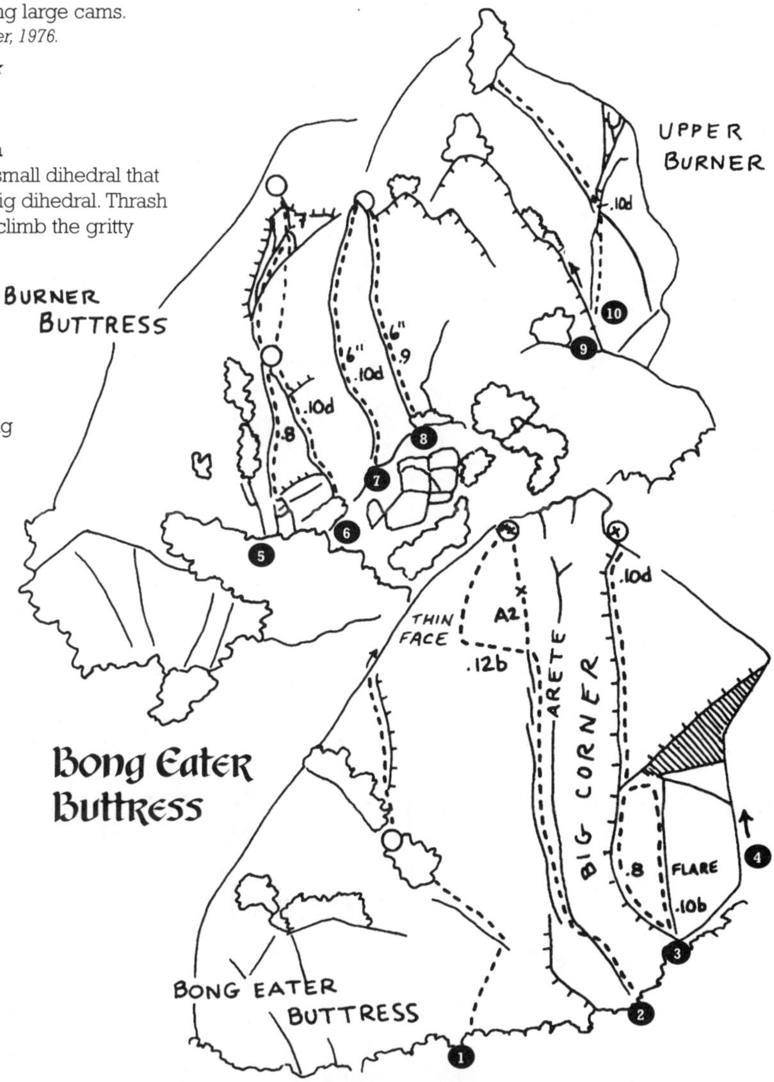

Bong Eater Buttress

MEMORIAL DAY BUTTRESS

The Memorial Day Buttress rests several hundred feet above the Bong Eater Buttress. Its south face is characterized by overhangs; its southwest, by slabs.

APPROACH: Follow the approach to the Crescent Crack Buttress and continue along its west margin. Once beyond the routes on the west side, trudge upward until the brush invades. Faint trails lead from here up to the base of Memorial Day Buttress. See overview on pages 220 and 222.

DESCENT: The walk-off descent is nasty, no matter which way you go. The west side is recommended.

MEMORIAL DAY BUTTRESS ROUTES

1. PRE-SCHOOL 5.9-
Climb the slab/cracks 30 feet left of Graduate School.
FA: Lenny Nelson, Bill Robins, 1987.

2. GRADUATE SCHOOL 5.10
This route is on the face left of the Woodberry Route, but the exact location is uncertain.
FA: Bill Robins and Thomas Koch, 1986.

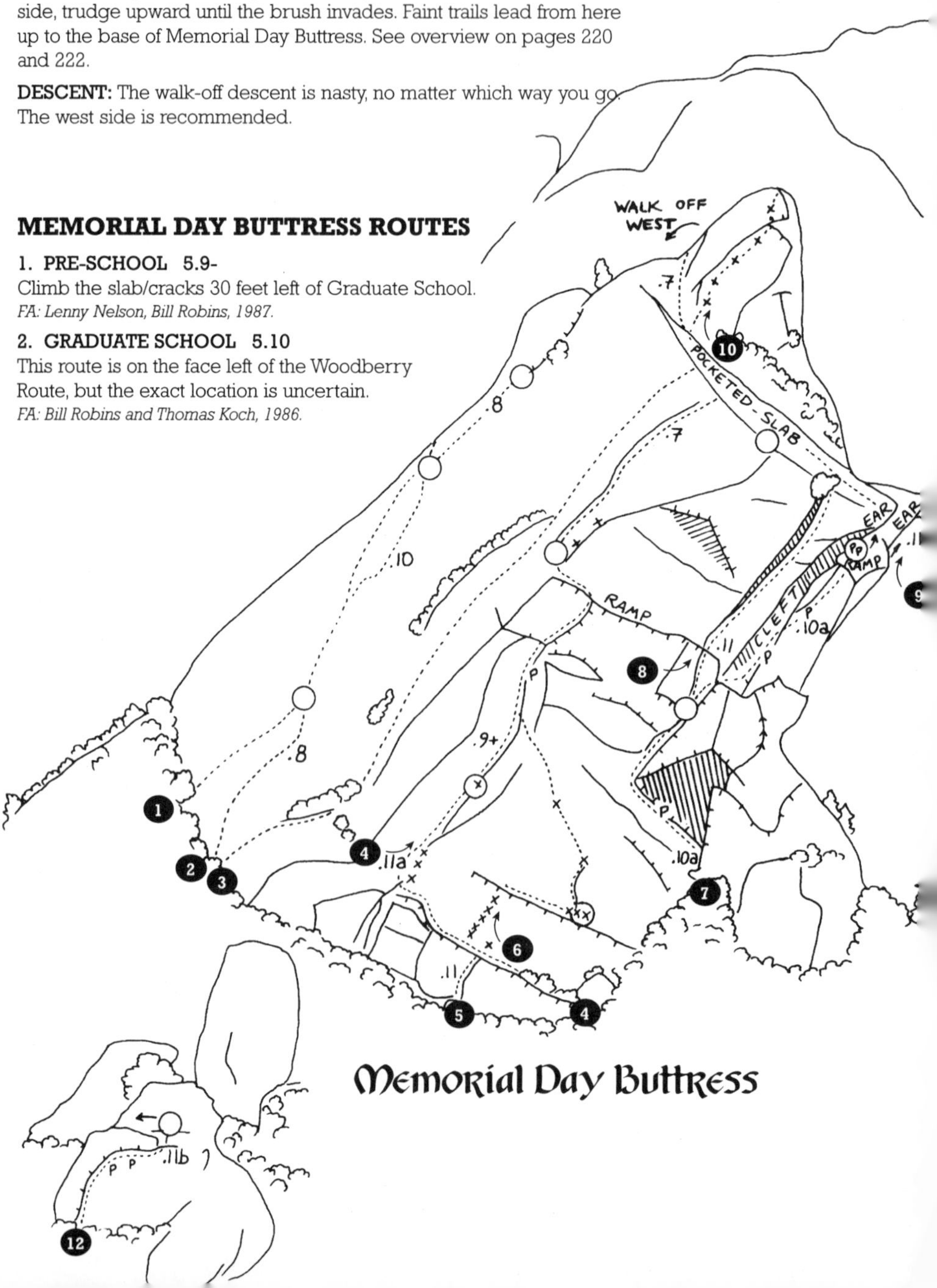

Memorial Day Buttress

3. WOODBERRY ROUTE 5.7
Ascend a series of dirty cracks and dihedrals on the right side of the southwest face.
FA: Paul Horton and Renny Jackson, 1974.

4. GRAND PINALLEY II 5.11a ★
In the middle of the buttress, between the southwest face and the south face, is an open book crack system. Bring plenty of small-to-mid-sized nuts and RPs/TCU's. The initial moves may be harder if you're shorter.
FA: Lynn Wheeler and Paul Horton, 1982.
FFA: Lynn Wheeler and Jay Anderson, 1982.

5. AGGRESSION 5.11c ★★
The finger crack 40 feet right of Grand Pinalley. Short but hard.
FA: Lynn Wheeler and Jay Anderson, 1983.

6. HEAVY METAL 5.10a A2
Above Aggression is a bolt ladder. Aid up this to a down sloping ramp and a belay. A seam above can be nailed to reach easier mixed climbing, eventually joining Grand Pinalley
FA: James Garrett.

7. MEMORIAL DAY ROUTE III 5.10d ★
The monumental line on the face climbs the left side of the diamond-shaped overhang and weasels right, avoiding The Mouth. Bring large nuts or Friends. The third pitch climbs a steep east-facing crack and face (5.10d).
FA: Dave Boyd and Dennis Turville, 1970.
FFA: Jim Donini and Mark Ward, 1978.

8. THE MOUTH VARIATION 5.11 ★
The big cleft left of the prow imparts brutal chimneying. Eventually, it meets the Memorial Day Route on the upper ramp. Bring large nuts or Friends.
FA: George Lowe and Lenny Nelson, 1970.
FFA: Ray Daurrelle and Bill Robins, sometime in the 1980s.

9. ROCK 'TIL YOU DROP VARIATION 5.11a ★
From the top of the second pitch of the Memorial Day Route, continue along a ramp to a mahogany tree and climb a steep and strenuous crack in a dihedral. One fixed pin.
FA: Doug Madera, Jeff Butterfield and Jeff Newsome, 1980.

10. EYEBROW 5.11a ★
A five bolt finish to the Memorial Day Route, guaranteed to open your eyes.
FA: Dave Anderson and James Garrett, 1993.

11. EL VIENTO ES FRIO 5.? A1+
An uncompleted aid route that climbs the east face of the wall. Walk up the gully to the east. The route starts across from a prominent pine tree. The first pitch climbs a crack up a steep wall to a sloping ledge. The second pitch follows a corner above the belay to a two-bolt belay below a series of roofs. The third pitch will go right and up, and eventually the route should join up with Eyebrow. Good cracks with easy nailing/nutting. Bring lots of KBs, LAs, TCUs, and a set of cams up to 3½ inches.

12. JUDAS PRIEST 5.11b ★★
This route is located well below the Memorial Day Buttress, on a small south-facing wall between The Burner Buttress and the Memorial Day Buttress. Climb a right-arching crack-and-corner system past some fixed protection to a funky crux that turns the overhang.
FA: Merrill Bitter, Bobby Rotert and Les Ellison, 1982.

10
23
CRESCENT CRACK BUTTRESS

THE SAIL

THE COFFIN

31

CRESCENT CRACK BUTTRESS ROUTES

10. MEXICAN CRACK 5.10a ★★★
23. THE GREAT CHOCKSTONE 5.7 ★
31. CRESCENT CRACK 5.7 ★★

CRESCENT CRACK BUTTRESS

The Crescent Crack Buttress is the first major rock formation on the north side of Little Cottonwood Canyon. The combination of varied climbing, reasonable approaches, and warm rock on sunny winter days make this area one of the canyon's main attractions.

APPROACH: Park .25 miles up canyon from the neon sign at the mouth of the canyon. A powerline crosses the road here, and wooden steps lead northward up a dirt bank and into the oak brush. Follow this trail as it meanders through the forest to a fork in the trail. In the spring of 1996 a torrential downpour turned the trail into a streambed at this point, making this junction a bit hard to find. For routes 1 to 41, take the left (west) fork of the trail at the junction. Crescent Crack is reached after roughly one hundred and fifty feet of mostly level walking. It begins as a double crack system leading up and left into a deep chimney. For routes in the Mexican Crack vicinity, routes number 8 to 12, continue up and left (west) on the trail for another one hundred and fifty feet. For the Hand Jive area, routes number 1 to 7, continue left (west), then up another one hundred and fifty feet.

To reach the Coffin Area routes 42 to 46, continue straight up the wash from the trail junction mentioned above, joining the talus and gully descending from the Coffin. March up this until it is possible to scramble left (west) over some ledges and broken rock to reach the base of the Coffin. See overview on pages 220 and 222.

DESCENT: Single rope rappels work for all the routes in this area with the exception of Crescent Crack, which is descended by climbing a chimney above the final belay, then traversing east into the gully below the coffin. This gully leads down to the trail junction described in the approach section.

CRESCENT CRACK BUTTRESS ROUTES (West Face)

1. CRACK IN THE WOODS 5.9 ★★
A good start to Hand Jive. Climb a thin crack to a ledge with bolt belay.
FA: Unknown.

2. CRANK IN THE WOODS 5.11d ★
Crank a killer move over a roof, and don't be dissuaded by the 5.9 runout above.
FA: Stuart and Bret Ruckman, 1989.

3. HAND JIVE 5.8 ★★
Belay atop Crack in the Woods. After down-climbing a chimney, span across to reach the face and climb up into a scabrous crack. Follow the crack to a bolt belay.
FA: Jack Roberts and Don McCarthy, 1976.

4. NO JIVE ARETE 5.11d ★
This long, featured face sports bolts and several thin moves.
FA: Kent Wheeler and Scott Lazar, 1995.

5. KUTCORNER 5.5
The corner that is mostly a chimney.

6. PARAPLEGIC WARD 5.9 A0 or 5.11
The right-slanting offwidth crack is the goal; getting to it presents a challenge. From the anchor atop Kutcorner, clip a bolt and pendulum or free climb to the crack.
FA: Mark Ward and Randy Wright, 1976.
FFA: Mark Bennett, sans bolt, mid '80s.

7. A KAT THAT GRUMPS 5.7
Climbs the face above Mexican Crack, joining Paraplegic Ward at the fixed belay.
FA: Kirsten Davis and Bill Robins, 1985.

8. ROTERT'S ROOTER 5.11d ★
Climb the short but d-d-desperate undercling/lieback crack to a stance.
FA: Bob Rotert, 1982.

9. SPANISH FLY 5.11c ★
A meandering route of extreme friction. Hint: don't try it on a hot day! The route starts just below Rotert's Rooter—climb out onto the face, then rejoin the arête to the top.
FA: Alan Bartlett, Dave and Tito Black, 1982.
FFA: Dave and Tito Black, 1984.

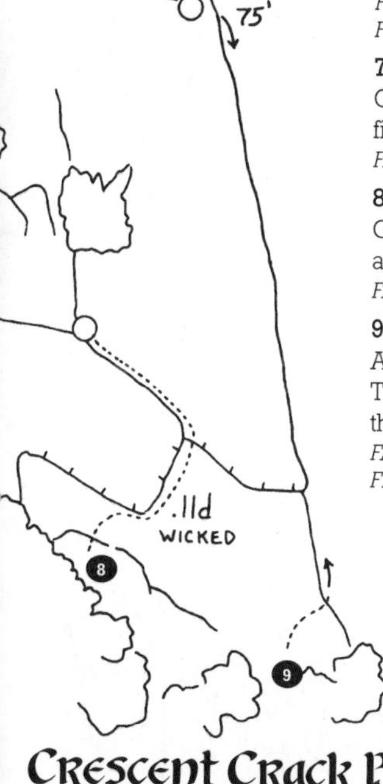

Crescent Crack Buttress (west face)

CRESCENT CRACK BUTTRESS ROUTES

10. MEXICAN CRACK 5.10a ★★★

One of the best offerings in the canyon consists of a tricky dihedral, tenuous double cracks and a primo diagonalling finger crack. Magnifico! An unprotected alternate start climbs the slab 10 feet left of the initial dihedral. The face directly below the anchors has been toproped at 5.12d.

FA: Pete Gibbs and George Lowe, 1970.

11. GRUNTING GRINGOS 5.11a

This leads to nowhere and has rotten rock.

FA: Brian Smoot.

12. LESS THAN ZERO 5.12a ★

Despite flaky rock and a bizarre line, this route gets attempted fairly often. Pull onto the left side of the arête after the sixth bolt, or you'll have nada chance. Stoppers are needed to protect the final crack.

FA: Stuart Ruckman, Gordon Douglass and Eric Stroud, 1988.

13. C.P.O.S. 5.11b ★

The crux is getting to the offwidth, which ultimately must be reckoned with. One bolt.

FFA: Steve Hong, Steve Carruthers and Lynn Wheeler, 1984.

14. SLAM, JAM, THANK YOU MA'AM 5.11d R ★

Awkward and insecure offwidth and liebacking describe this debauchery. Difficult protection. Camming units are useful.

FA: Merrill Bitter and Bret Ruckman, 1985.

15. INTERPLANETARY VOYAGE 5.11 ★

A mondo roof with an offwidth splitting it.

FA: Bill Simmons, Mark Bennett and Bill Robins, 1985.

16. JOURNEY TO THE MOON 5.10

The crack systems 10 feet right of Interplanetary Voyage.

FA: Mark Bennett and Bill Robins, 1985.

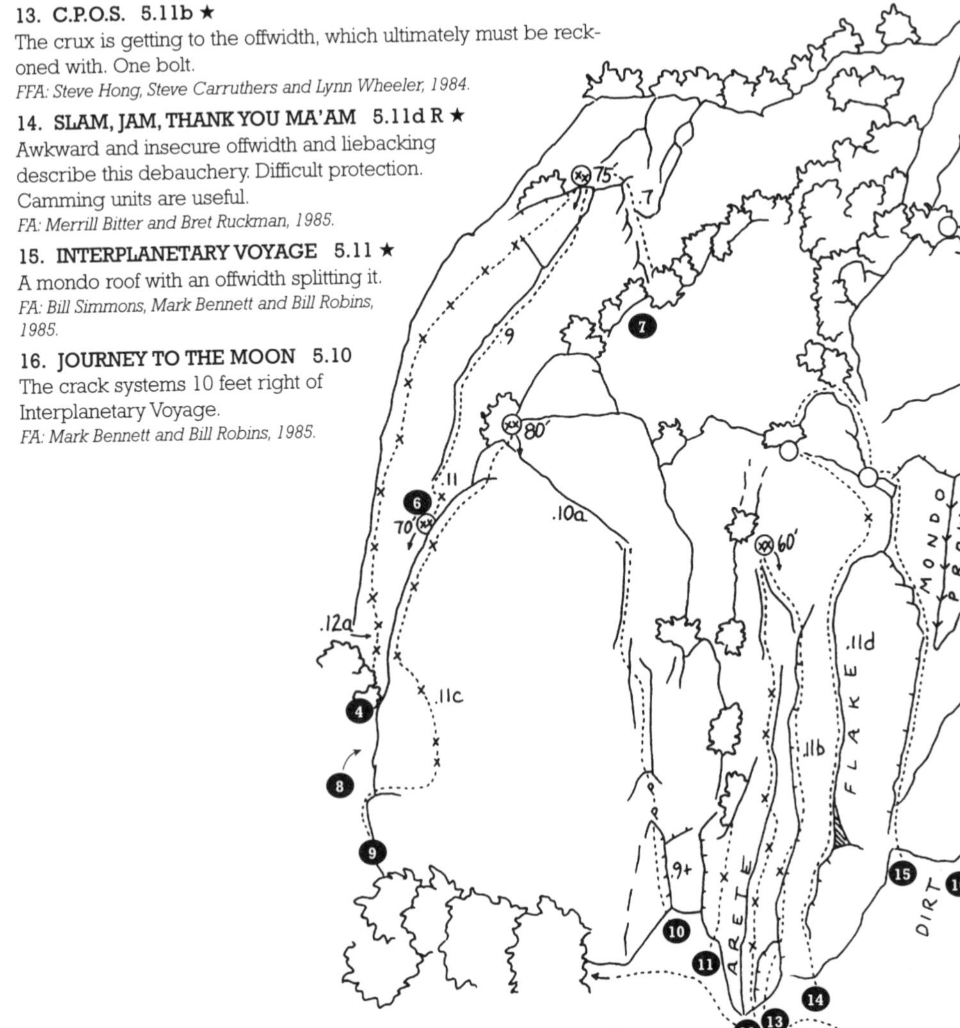

17. RE-ENTRY VARIATION 5.10d
Climb Journey To The Moon until you are above the roofs then traverse left and climb a crack to the top.
FA: Brian Smoot and Bill Robins.

18. E.V.A. VARIATION 5.10d
Follows flakes over a roof to the right of the second pitch of Journey To The Moon.
FA: Mark Bennett and Bill Robins, 1985.

19. BODY ENGLISH 5.9
The chimney between Journey to the Moon and Fairweather Variation.
FA: Larson and Bill Robins.

20. FAIRWEATHER VARIATION 5.10d
Starting 15 feet left of Rainy Day Blues, face climb up and right to meet that route.
FA: Mark Bennett and Bill Robins, 1985.

21. RAINY DAY BLUES 5.11a A0
This starts with a difficult flaring hand crack over an overhang. The second pitch has a pendulum.
FA: Mark Bennett and Bill Robins, 1985.

22. GET THE HEARSE 5.10a R/X
The small face 15 feet to the right of the hand crack on Rainy Day Blues.
FA: Bill Robins and Kirsten Davis, 1985.

23. THE GREAT CHOCKSTONE 5.7 ★
The first pitch is long, and mostly features chimneying. The second pitch has a short overhanging section.
FA: Larry Evans, Dick Ream and Rich Ream, 1965.

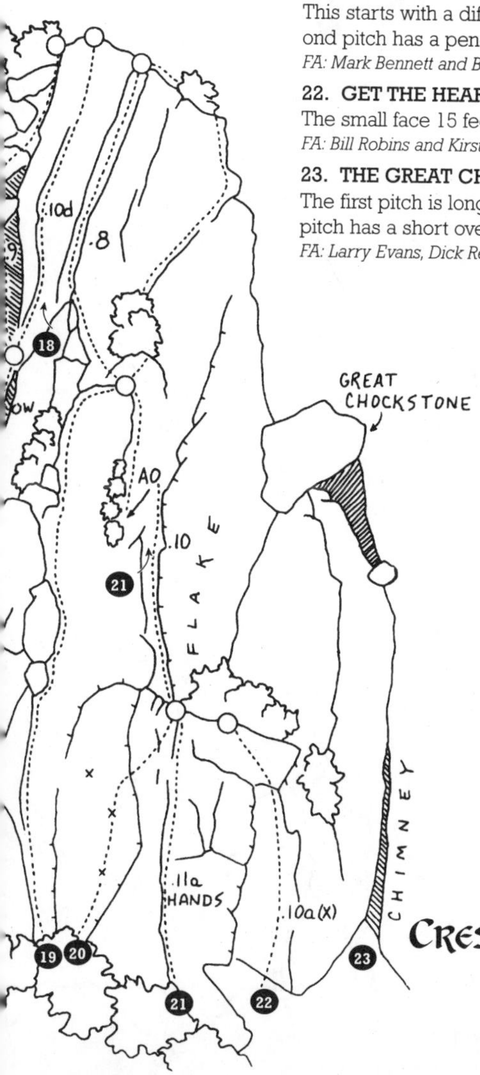

Crescent Crack Buttress

CRESCENT CRACK BUTTRESS ROUTES

24. KURT'S DEMISE VARIATION 5.7

Climb the slab to the right of The Great Chockstone first-pitch chimney, avoiding some of the chimneying. (Not on topo.)

25. NEPTUNE VARIATION 5.7

A dihedral above the last pitch of The Great Chockstone. A seemingly logical continuation.

FA: Ray Durrell and partner.

26. LAZARUS 5.8 ★

A fun and varied four-pitch outing.

FA: Rick Reese and Rich Ream, 1965.

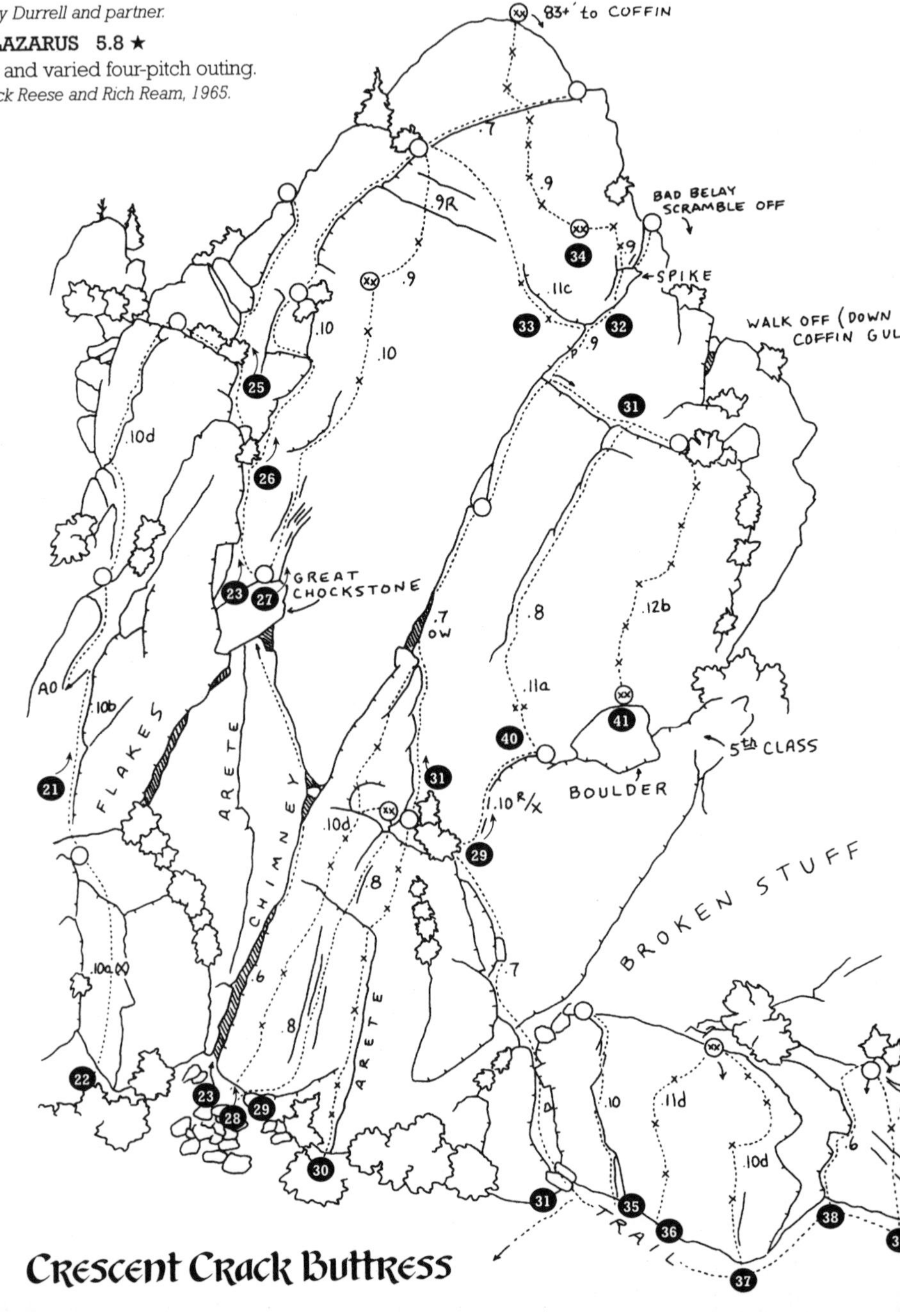

Crescent Crack Buttress

27. MISSING LINK 5.10 R ★★
An imaginative line that offers great climbing. Camming devices are helpful on second-pitch grooves.
FA: Les Ellison, Bret Ruckman and Gary Olsen, 1980.

28. WHO'S ON FIRST 5.10d ★
Thin face moves and tricky liebacking on good rock.
FA: John Maddux, John Hansen and Tony Calderone, 1995.

29. THE ROSS CONNECTION 5.10c R/X ★
By climbing cracks and grooves right of Who's On First, you can grab a nice 5.8 pitch that ends at the top of the first pitch of Crescent Crack. From here, an unprotected, tricky traverse right to a thin, short crack (and some manky protection) leads up to a chickenhead move and over to the Ross Route's first pitch.
FA: pitch one unknown
FA: pitch two Merrill Bitter and Bret Ruckman, 1981.

30. MULTIPLICITY 5.10c ★
Six bolts on the slab/arête.
FA of direct start: John Maddux and John Hansen, 1994..

31. CRESCENT CRACK 5.7 ★★
A quintessential climb for the intermediate leader. The chimney on pitch two is difficult to protect. Try to protect the second climber on the final sloping ramp.
FA: Rick Reese, Jim Gaddis, Wilf Bruschke, 1962.

32. CRESCENT CRACK DIRECT VARIATION 5.9- ★★
Continue straight up instead of traversing the down-sloping ramp. The exit is strange and the belay is tricky to establish.
FA: unknown.

33. GENUINE RISK 5.11c R ★
On the first ascent, the leader, in a hurry to get to work, rushed up the slab above the crux, not placing any bolts. As a result, the climb is quite runout. Hang a belay at the top of the down-sloping ramp of Crescent Crack, and strive to minimize rope drag.
FA: Mark Smith and Les Ellison, 1980.

34. FINAL LINK 5.9 ★★
A great addition, this slab pitch adds 130 ft. of fun climbing to the top of the Crescent Crack Buttress. An 83+ foot rappel off a pin/tree anchor takes one to the base of the Coffin. Some gritty rock, but cleaning up.
FA: Brian and Jonathan Smoot, 1996.

35. LUNGE OR PLUNGE 5.10b/c ★
Bring those micro nuts.
FA: Pat Maloney and Jim Mutscheller, 1980.
FFA: Ed Van Steenwuyk and Dana Hauser, 1982.

36. IF LOOKS COULD KILL 5.11d ★
Shiver up to the first bolt and continue on desperately thin friction.
FA: Neil Glad, 1987.

37. CLOSET LYCRA 5.10d/11a ★★
A small RP is a good first piece.
FA: Jim Reynolds and Jeff Cobabe, 1987.

38. SHORT CORNER 5.6

39. WATERSLIDE 5.9+
Getting to the first bolt is quite a quiver.
FA: Kent Jameson and Ken Gygi,1980.

40. ROSS ROUTE 5.11a ★
Named for Larry Ross, who was killed climbing Haystack Peak in the Wind Rivers. A difficult mantle leads to a moderate crack.
FA: Jeff Lowe and Larry Ross, 1968.

41. RAZORS EDGE 5.12b ★
6 bolts protect heinous slab work. Callous those fingertips—sharp edges.
FA: Kent Wheeler and Rush Bowers, 199?.

THE COFFIN

Routes 42 through 46 live on the Coffin Buttress, which forms the upper right side of the Crescent Crack Buttress, and can be identified as a mottled face split by a perfect crack and capped with a roof.
APPROACH: To reach the Coffin Area, continue straight up the wash from the trail junction mentioned in the Crescent Crack Approach secton, joining the talus and gully descending from the Coffin. March up this until it is possible to scramble left (west) over some ledges and broken rock to reach the base of the Coffin. See overview on pages 220 and 222.
DESCENT: One rope rappels are possible for all the routes on this wall.

THE COFFIN ROUTES

42. EXSQUEEZE ME 5.11d ★★
Ultra-thin face moves finish off this continuously difficult pitch.
FA: Dana Hauser, 1987.

43. THE COFFIN 5.9 ★★★
Not to be missed, The Coffin is the best 5.9 crack in the area. The first pitch's crux is very dependent on finger size, but the remainder of the route shows no favoritism. The start is somewhat runout and the first belay is at three bolts eight feet left of the roof.
FA: Court Richards and Jim Gully, Nov. 24, 1963.
FFA: Mark McQuarrie and George Lowe, 1964.

44. COFFIN ROOF VARIATION 5.12a ★★★
This is a sequential series of character-building finger locks and pinches out the 10-foot roof crack. Fight rope drag to the top, or down aid it.
Finger locks or wooden box!
FA: Unknown
FFA: Steve Hong, 1980.

45. RIGHTSIDE VARIATION 5.9 ★★★
Belay under the right side of the roof. The second pitch rambles up the corners above.

46. THE VIEWING 5.10a ★★★
Superb face climbing on the far right side of the Coffin face. Start traversing rightward, leaving The Coffin crack at the black spot on the right wall. Most parties rappel from the belay anchor (84 feet). Expect 20-foot runouts. Continuing up the crack above is 5.8.
FA: Stuart Ruckman and Gordon Douglass, 1987.

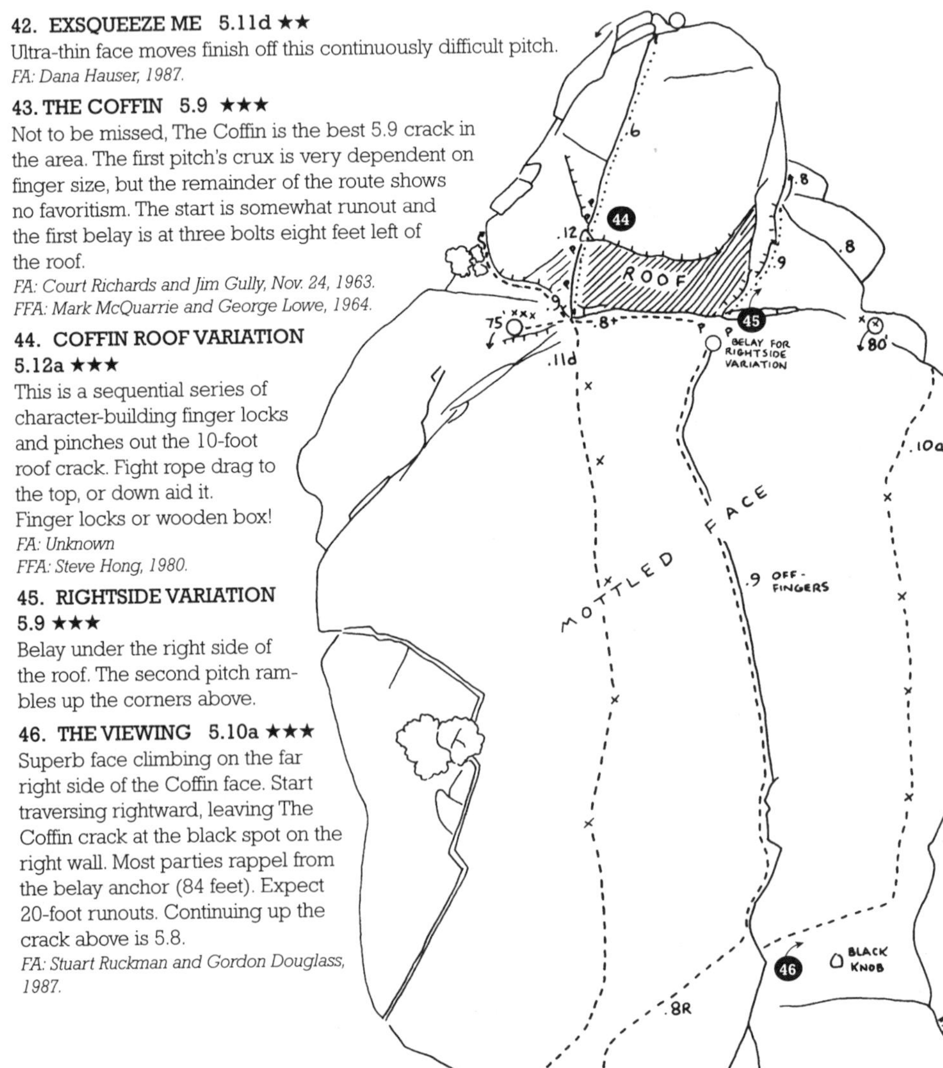

THE KEEL

The Keel is the broken, west-facing buttress of rock that descends directly beneath The Sail, forming the east wall of the gully that leads to The Coffin. See overview on page 220.

APPROACH: Follow the approach to the Coffin and look for these routes on the right (east) wall of the gully.

DESCENT: Walk off for most routes, except for Dumb Fun and Spotted Fever, where single rope rappels are possible.

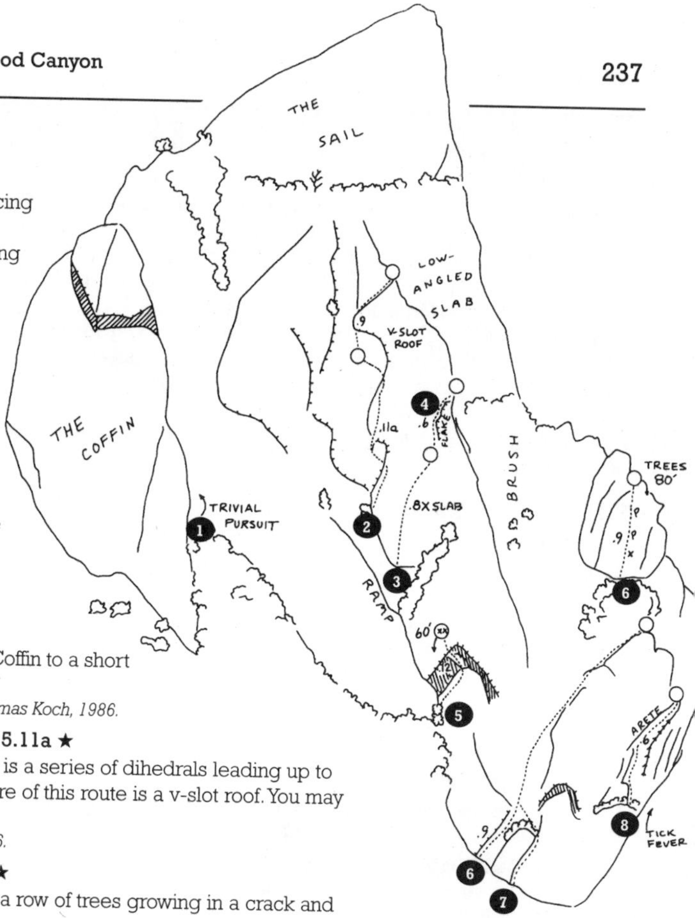

The Keel

THE KEEL ROUTES

1. TRIVIAL PURSUIT 5.9 R
Continue up the gully from The Coffin to a short slab with one bolt, and climb it.
FA: Bill Robins, Mark Bennett and Thomas Koch, 1986.

2. PETER'S FLIGHT SCHOOL 5.11a ★
The best-looking line on the cliff is a series of dihedrals leading up to the Sail. The distinguishing feature of this route is a v-slot roof. You may keel over at the base of the Sail.
FA: Thomas Koch and Bill Robins, 1986.

3. BARKING SPIDERS 5.8 X ★
Climb the runout slab just left of a row of trees growing in a crack and finish on Razor Flake.
FA: Thomas Koch and Bill Robins, 1986.

4. RAZOR FLAKE 5.6 ★
Best viewed from near The Coffin, this is a serrated flake high on the west-facing wall of the Coffin Gully.
FA: Rick Wyatt and Dave Jenkins, 1978.

5. DUMB FUN 5.12b ★★
The roof crack that angles leftward has a low-angled slab leading up to it. The moves out this roof are totally abstruse.
FA: Steve Hong and Karin Budding, 1984.

6. SPOTTED FEVER 5.9
One hundred feet up the hill from the furthest south point of the Keel is a small right-facing dihedral. Climb this and the cracks above to the top. The mottled slab residing above the Hong Wall forms a second pitch and ends on a pinnacle. This pinnacle was climbed eons ago and was coined Pimple Pinnacle. Bring runners to loop chickenheads.
FA: Chris Begue and Bill Robins, 1986.

7. YELLOW FEVER VARIATION 5.8
FA: Bill Foster and Bill Robins, 1987.

8. EVENING FUN 5.6
Climb cracks to a slab leading to the top.
FA: Thomas Koch and Bill Robins, 1986.

THE SAIL

The Sail rests high on Little Cottonwood's south face, above the Coffin and the Hong Wall. Basking in the winter sun, and the breezes of summer, The Sail is split by several fine cracks which prove to be longer than they appear from the base of the wall. A lengthy, loose approach discourages many; however, the climbing is good.

APPROACH: Follow the approach to the Hong Wall. From here, work your way up the steep, loose gully between the Hong Wall and The Egg. This leads to the east side of the Sail, where a bit more thrashing leads to the base of the wall. See overview on page 220.

DESCENT: Scramble off the west side. Some downclimbing will be encountered.

THE SAIL ROUTES

1. SPACELAND 5.11a
"Spaced-out" protection. Bring small wired nuts, RPs and TCUs. One bolt near the top.
FA: Les Ellison and Chris Abbott, 1977
FFA: Drew Bedford and Hank Armantrout, 1983.

2. BONG BONG FIRECRACKER 5.7 ★★
A continuously difficult route. Large nuts or medium-to-large cams are handy.
FA: Steve Ellsworth and Mark McQuarrie, 1964.

3. FUSE VARIATION 5.7
An exciting traverse left gains the next crack to the west.
FA: Kelly Stevens, Jim Mutscheller and Chris Pendleton

4. FLYING DUTCHMAN 5.10c ★★
A stout lead with some difficult protection.
FA: Jack Roberts, 1976.

5. REAM CRACK 5.7 R ★
The bottom squeeze is pitiless.
FA: Rich and Dick Ream.

6. WILSON-LOVE 5.8 ★★
Three 5.8 cruxes and a lot of continuous climbing in-between.
FA: Larry Love and Ted Wilson, 1962.

7. CASTAWAY 5.9+ R ★
Despite some gritty rock, this route offers good stuff. The first 20 feet are shared with the Wilson-Love route.
FA: Stuart Ruckman and Libby Ellis, 1989.

8. CASTAWAY DIRECT 5.10b R ★
An arête start to Castaway with groundfall potential.
FA: Unknown.

9. APPLE JELLY 5.8
Ascend the 30-foot crack on the east face.
FA: Hank Armantrout and Bill Cramer, 1981

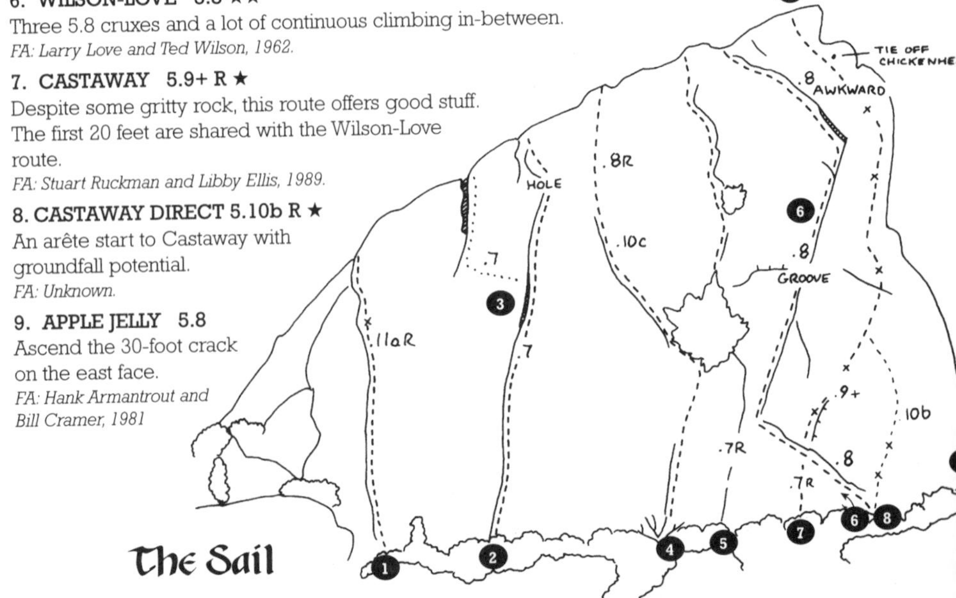

HONG WALL

Overlooked because of its rotten appearance, this wall remained untouched for years. The free climbing potential was finally recognized by the ubiquitous Hong/Budding team, which created three classic crack routes. The wall overhangs a good bit, routinely thwarting supposed 5.11 to 5.12 leaders .

APPROACH: Park .35 miles up canyon from the neon sign. Follow the steep trail which leads up the dirt embankment directly above the road. At the powerline pole, the trail forks. Take the left (west) fork, and continue to climb steeply through the trees. This trail leads along the overhanging west face of a large boulder, then up again to a junction with a trail leading up from the large spike-like boulder that sticks out prominently from the hillside. 50 feet above this junction is a fork. Take the left fork, which climbs initially like it's headed for The Egg, but then turns and traverses directly west to the base of the wall. See overview on page 220.

DESCENT: A single rope rappel is possible from anchors at the top of each route.

HONG WALL ROUTES

1. TICK FEVER 5.11a ★★★

One of the best cracks of this grade in the Wasatch. The start is way strenuous, but the double cracks at the top are the crux.

FA: Lynn Wheeler and Jeff Newsome, 1981.
FFA: Steve Hong and Karin Budding, 1983.

2. WING NUT 5.11c ★★

Starts hard, stays hard and sports cranker finger locks.

FA: Steve Hong and Karin Budding, 1983.

3. STREWN MASTERS OF GORE 5.12b ★★

If the name sounds gruesome, wait until you try the route. Expect power layaways and clutches with difficult clips.

FA: Steve Hong, Karin Budding and Steve Carruthers.
FFA: Steve Hong, 1984.

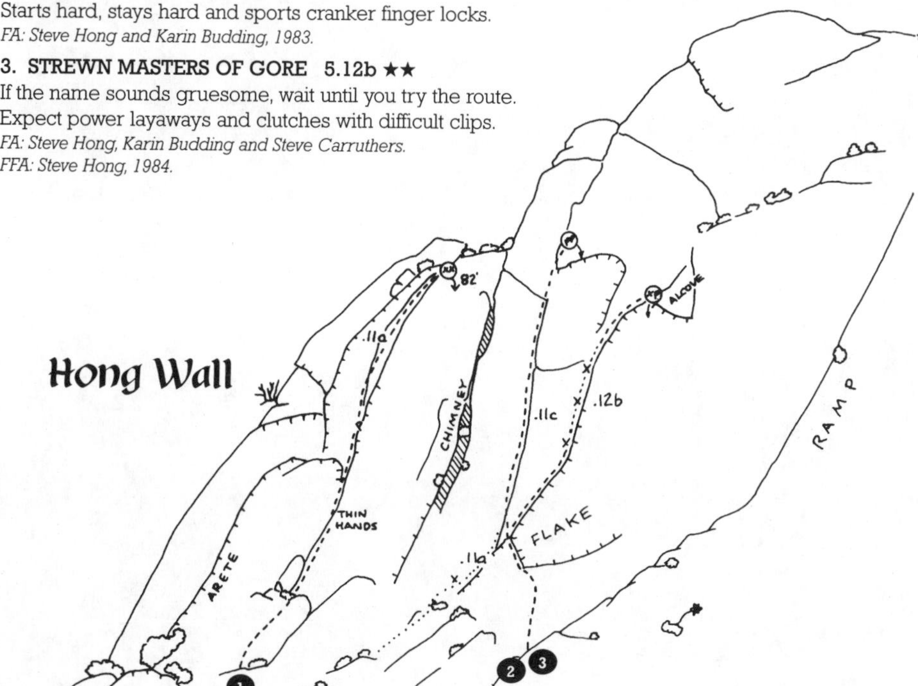

THE EGG
4
1

DRAGON ARCH AREA

7

THE EGG

4. VARIETY DELIGHT 5.7 ★

DRAGON ARCH AREA ROUTES

1. RODEO GIRLS IN BONDAGE 5.9+ ★

7. DRAGON ARCH 5.10 ★

THE EGG

The Egg is the brown-and-white mottled face prominent from the road just up canyon from the Crescent Crack parking. A popular cliff due to its plethora of holds and moderate angle, The Egg is particularly pleasant on cool days when the sun is shining. The cracks are often bottoming seams and can be difficult to protect.

APPROACH: Park .35 miles up canyon from the neon sign. Follow the steep trail which leads up the dirt embankment directly above the road. At the powerline pole, the trail forks. Take the left (west) fork, and continue to climb steeply through the trees. This trail leads along the overhanging west face of a large boulder, then up again to a junction with a trail leading up from the large spike-like boulder that sticks out prominently from the hillside. 50 feet above this junction is a fork. Take the right fork, which climbs uphill towards The Egg. 100 feet below the base of The Egg, the trail forks again. Follow the left fork (straight up), which leads to the base. Scramble up a gully/weaknesses to reach ledges at the start of the routes. See overview on pages 220 and 240.

DESCENT: Walk off west and skitter down scree to the base, or employ a two-rope rappel from the top of the first pitch of Variety Delight.

The Egg

THE EGG ROUTES

1. LEGGO MY EGGO 5.10a ★★
Bring eight quickdraws and one long runner for the tree. Long, with eggsasperating first moves.
FA: Stuart Ruckman and Libby Ellis, 1990.

2. LOW BROW 5.7 ★
This is the west-to-east girdle. Climb directly up to the left end of the traverse on Over Easy, traverse right to the first bolt on Huevos, join the belay of Lowe Blowe and make a hair-raising traverse right to the top of Groovin'. Two pitches. (Not on topo.)
FA: Les Ellison and Tom Loeff, 1982.

3. OVER EASY 5.7 ★
Start on Variety Delight and traverse left.
FA: Marshall Ralph, Mike Bogart and Karen Bogart.

4. VARIETY DELIGHT 5.7 ★
Delightful. The first pitch has tricky protection.
FA: Ted Wilson and Curt Hawkins, 1962.

5. HUEVOS RANCHEROS 5.7 R ★
Very runout, but still popular.
FA: Ed Webster, Sue Patenaude and Les Ellison, 1980.

6. LOWE BLOWE 5.9+ ★
The second pitch is awkward and continuous. Bring some large nuts or camming units.
FA: George Lowe and Eric Eliason, 1968.

7. JESUS OR JEOPARDY 5.10a ★
Interesting, but squeezed. Runner the third bolt long, or use double ropes.
FA: Colin Reynolds and John Gonthier, 1986.

8. GROOVIN' 5.8+ ★★
A popular romp following rightward trending grooves right of the main, mottled face.
FA: Les Ellison and Chris Noble, 1982.

9. GO VAN GOGH 5.9+ ★
The steep corner right of Groovin'. Tricky.
FA: Hank Armantrout and Bill Cramer, 1982

10. HIGH WIRE 5.9+ ★
This is the east-to-west girdle. Start in Go Van Gogh, traverse left from there, bisecting the first belay of Lowe Blow, the first bolt of Huevos and joining the traverse on Over Easy. Two pitches. (Not on topo.)
FA: Merrill Bitter, Les Ellison and Bob Rotert.

11. WINDJAMMER 5.10
This buttress is located above the Egg about 250 feet, and has a south-west face with an obvious crack (behind the pine tree). Climb this crack (5.10). Continue to the north behind the summit notch (5.8).
FA: Kent Jameson and Ken Gygi, 1982.

DRAGON ARCH AREA

This area is comprised of the more broken cliffs and corners located 200 feet to the east of The Egg.

APPROACH: Follow the approach described for The Egg. Follow the right fork in the trail 100 feet below the base of The Egg. This path leads to the east of The Dragon Arch Area and into a small gully. Walk up the gully, then traverse west on slabs at the very base of the wall. See overview on pages 220 and 240.

DESCENT: Most routes on this wall can be descended from fixed anchors with one rope. Those routes that top out require a walk off, which seems to be easier if you head to the west and aim for the gully to the west of The Egg.

DRAGON ARCH AREA ROUTES

1. RODEO GIRLS IN BONDAGE 5.9+ ★
Thrash up to flakes on the right wall of an ugly gully. From here, the route improves, following a knobby arête for two pitches.
FA: Brian Smoot and Bill Robins, 1985.

2. GRITISH DEAL 5.10d/11a
Climb out past two bolts on a leftward ramp to a crack. Follow the crack to another bolt, and then up to a two-bolt belay/rappel. Bring a large camming unit.
FA: Kyle Ricketts and Cary Siteman.

3. VALENTINE CRACK 5.8
Two pitches of wide cracks in a dihedral system. Bring large protection.
FA: Bob Irvine, Rick Reese and Ted Wilson, Feb. 14, 1963.
FFA: George Lowe and Rex Alldredge.

4. RALPH, HERB, BERT AND ERNIE 5.10
Start 50 feet right of the start to Valentine Crack and 25 feet left of Lunar Tick.
FA: Kirsten Davis, Lori Ness and Bill Robins, 1987.

5. LUNAR TICK 5.10c ★
Climb the orange-tinged west face, located 25 feet left of Dragon Arch. Start in a corner and follow 6 bolts to a two-bolt belay. Touchy friction with some grit. Climbed January 1st of 1990, this was most likely the first route of the 90's.
FA: Randy Kieliszewski and Jon Ray, 1990.

6. TWO HEADS ARE BETTER THAN ONE 5.9- ★
Climb a flake twelve feet left of Dragon Arch. Bring runners for tie-offs, and thin pro for the bottom.
FA: Michael Durvidge and Pat Contor, 1989.

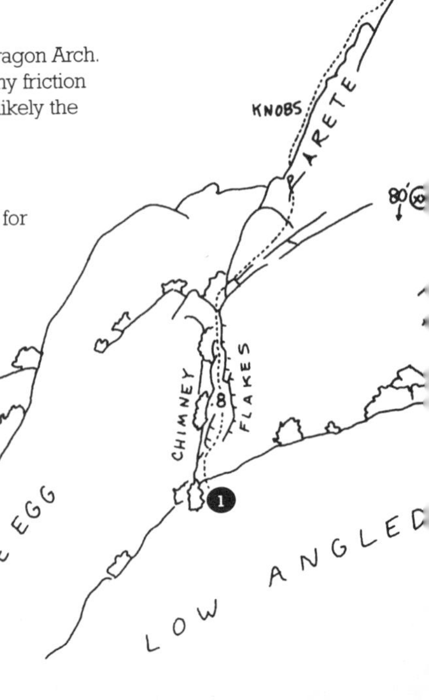

7. DRAGON ARCH 5.10 ★

The crack directly in the center of the south face, just left of a scary hollow flake, is the route. The second pitch is not recommended.

FA: Bill Robins and Thomas Koch, 1986.

8. HAIRSTYLES AND ATTITUDES 5.10a ★

On the east side of the "buttress" is a fine short corner. A third-class thrash through oak trees reaches the base—or better yet, climb the face just right of Dragon Arch, and then step right into Hairstyles And Attitudes. The second pitch is not recommended.

FA: Stuart and Bret Ruckman, 1980.

9. TOYMAKERS DREAM 5.11a ★

Climb the small corner 10 feet right of Hairstyles, past four bolts to the top. Thin gear is needed for the corner.

FA: Pat Contor and Lori Ness, 1988.

10. DANCING MOUNTAIN GOAT 5.11

If tenuous friction is your forte, try this two-pitcher. Located way above the Dragon Arch Area.

FA: Bill Robins and Thomas Koch, 1986.

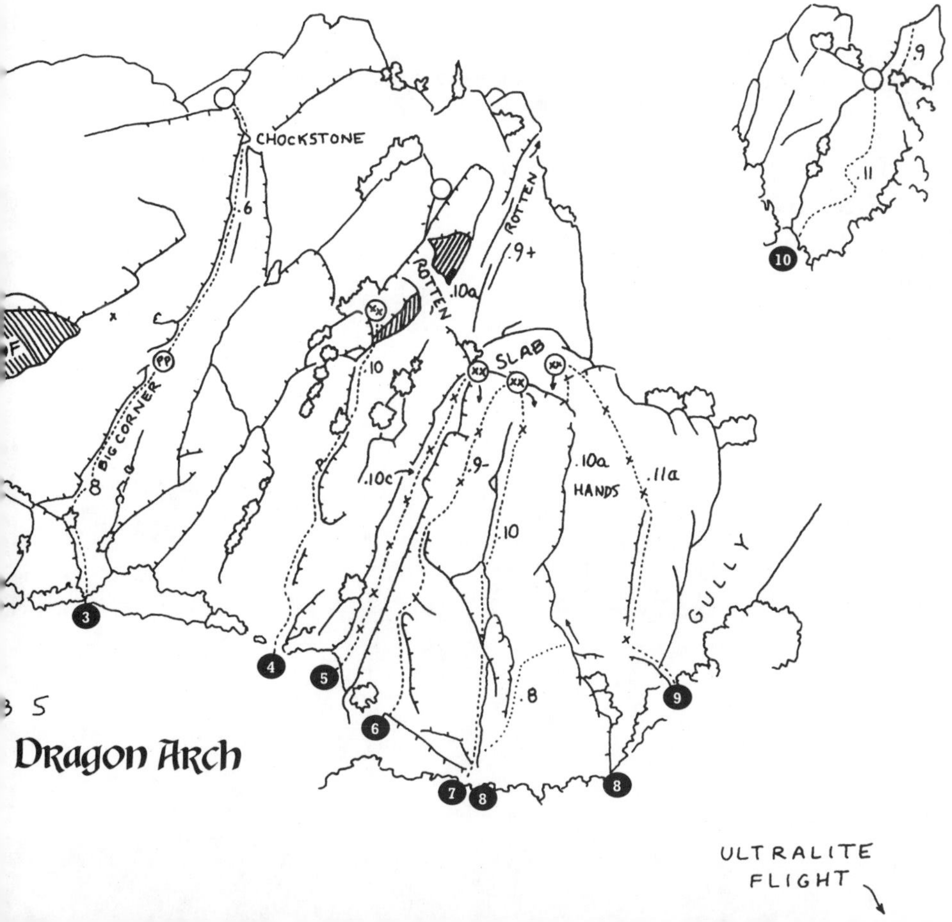
CHOCKSTONE
6
ROTTEN
ROTTEN
.9+
.10a
10
SLAB
BIG CORNER
8
.10c
9-
.10a
HANDS
.11a
10
GULLY
8
.9
.11
3
4
5
6
7
8
8
9
10
ULTRALITE FLIGHT

Dragon Arch

THE EAGLE BUTTRESS AND ENVIRONS

From the junction of the Little Cottonwood Canyon Road and the road that leads to the Wasatch Resort housing community, Eagle Buttress can be seen as the dark, sheer, east-facing wall located high in the gully that forms the west margin of the Church Buttress. See overview on page 220.

APPROACH. Park at the old gritmill, .55 miles up canyon from the neon sign, on the north side. These obscure climbs are most easily accessed from here. From the parking area, look for a tongue of rock that extends down and right (east) of the Dragon Arch area. Ultralite Flight resides at the lowest point of this tongue. The gully to the right of Ultralite Flight can be thrashed up to reach Mission to Moscow (the apparent, wide crack on the right), and the Eagle Buttress straight across the gully to the west.

DESCENT: With the exception of Ultralight Flight and Mission to Moscow, which can be rappelled from fixed anchors with one rope, walk-offs are the standard descent.

1. ULTRALITE FLIGHT 5.11d ★★
If you're seeking a pump, try this wicked overhang. Walk up hill and west about 10 minutes from the gritmill to access this south-facing roof. It liebacks past two pins to an abdominally pumping rest, and continues out awkward weirdness to a two-bolt belay. 40 feet.
FA: Merrill Bitter and Bret Ruckman, 1983.

2. MISSION TO MOSCOW 5.11a
This one is a hard-liner. A nice crack in a corner leads to an offwidth/chimney ending at a three-bolt anchor. This prominent right-slanting crack can be seen from the road.
FA: Hank Armantrout and Bill Cramer, 1982.

EAGLE BUTTRESS

This buttress is east-facing and has poor rock.

3. BETH ANN'S CRACK 5.10
This is the major line on the left side of this buttress. Climb the fat crack in the right-facing corner to a one-pin, one-bolt anchor. Bring 4" cams.
FA: Kelly Laakso and Bill Robins, 1987.

5. EIGHT BALL II 5.9 A0
The exact location of this route is unknown. There are, however, eight bolts on the first pitch.
FA: James Garrett, Thomas Etzler, Loren Glick, 1992.

6. X-ORCIST 5.11a A1
Climb through jumbled blocks, traverse up and left to some scrub oaks and belay (5.9). Continue left and gain the perfect, but rotten crack (some A1 through the bulgy section at the top of this crack) and thrash up the right-curving chimney to the top.
FA: Bill Robins and Thomas Koch, 1986.

Judy Ruckman climbs Hand Jive, Crescent Crack Area.

photo: Ruckman.

RODEO BUTTRESS
TURTLE BUTTRESS
7

NORTH BELL
RODEO BUTTRESS
3. COWBOYS DON'T CRY 5.10d ★★
TURTLE BUTTRESS
7. WET DREAM 5.10 R ★★

RODEO BUTTRESS AND ENVIRONS

The Lots of Balls slab is the low-angled, broken slab above the left (west) end of the Church Buttress. Rodeo Buttress is located above Lots of Balls slab, and Turtle and North Bell Buttresses are even closer to the ridge. The approach to these areas is arduous, bordering on comical. Slab climbing pervades. Expect a full day's outing.

APPROACH: Park at the gritmill, .55 miles up canyon from the neon sign. Hike up the gully just west of Church Buttress. Turn right at the base of Lots of Balls slab and you eventually will get to Rodeo Buttress. See overview on pages 220 and 248.

DESCENT: Walk off all the routes in this area.

RODEO BUTTRESS

The pine tree mentioned below can be reached by a fourth-class slab under the broad roof band.

1. SIDE SADDLE 5.9
Start at the pine tree and climb the slab above and left directly. Stay right of the chimney, following more slabs (3 bolts) and connect with a prominent right-diagonalling crack that leads up and out.
FA: Kirk Andriano and Bill Robins, 1987.

2. ROPING CHICKENS 5.10 ★★
Start at the pine tree, climb the crack to scrub oaks, hop onto a textured face and follow it past a bolt to a ramp and belay (5.9). Climb the slabs above, angling leftward to a bolt, then traverse right 40 feet to a bolt and join the trough a bit higher. Belay at the top of the trough (5.8). Climb the gritty face above to the top (5.10).
FA: Thomas Koch and Bill Robins, 1986.

3. COWBOYS DON'T CRY 5.10d ★★
Start at the right end of a barrier overhang. Climb grooves to a slab above and belay (5.9). Climb the steep groove past a bolt and belay on the left end of the next ledge (5.10d). Traverse left to a bolt, and smear up past a second bolt. Intersect Side Saddle and master one more face to a belay in a wind cave. Follow a thin crack directly left to scrub oaks and go on to the top (5.10d).
FA: Kirsten Davis, Thomas Koch and Bill Robins, 1986.

WORRY BUTTRESS

The south-facing blob called Worry Buttress is located 400 feet up from the bottom of Rodeo Buttress and on its east side. Route #4 climbs the smooth south slab.

APPROACH: Follow the approach described for Rodeo Buttress.

DESCENT: Walk off all routes.

4. WORRY JUST A LITTLE BIT 5.12a R ★
Climb the left side of this slab past three bolts (runout, but the crux is well-protected) to a belay on the right (5.12a). Smear up the face above past a bolt (5.9). The first pitch is continuously difficult.
FA: Thomas Koch and Bill Robins, 1986.

5. PICKPOCKET 5.11 X
Located 150 feet up and right from Worry are two parallel grooves in a south face. Climb the left groove as it eventually melds in to the right one. The protection is slim pickings.
FA: Brian Smoot and Bill Robins, 1987.

TURTLE BUTTRESS

This impressive buttress, with a series of water troughs striping the south face, is 600 feet above Rodeo Buttress. Rightward-diagonalling cracks and dikes form other weaknesses.

APPROACH: Follow the approach described for Rodeo Buttress.

DESCENT: Walk off all routes.

6. TURTLE SOUP 5.10d R ★★

Start up by a pin and 2 bolts (just right of a chimney with a chockstone), traverse right to gain a flake system, and belay in a nook (5.10d). Climb the water trough above (5.8 R). Turn the roof system on the left and wander to the top.

FA: Thomas Koch and Bill Robins, 1986.

7. WET DREAM 5.10 R ★★

This is located 40 feet to the right of Turtle Soup. Climb the chimney system to a belay on dikes (5.9). Climb up the face to the left of a roof. The trough will lead to a belay (5.10). Climb the trough above to join Turtle Soup (5.8 R).

FA: Thomas Koch and Bill Robins, 1986.

NORTH BELL

The North Bell is up and right of Turtle Buttress about 400 feet. (The longest approach in North America!?). A rotten, vertical 100-foot cliff forms the left side of the gully.

APPROACH: Follow the approach described for Rodeo Buttress.

DESCENT: Walk off all routes.

8. CHOCOLATE SUNDAY 5.10a R

Climb the curving crack system with two big mahogany trees, 10 feet right of Chocolate Channel. There are two pitches with bad bolts.

FA: Bill Robins and Kirk Andriano, 1987.

9. CHOCOLATE CHANNEL 5.11a X ★★

Climb past a pin and two bolts to a crack left of a steep trough and belay (5.10). Climb the steep trough past two bolts. Extremely hard, runout climbing leads to the left of the summit turret (5.11).

FA: Thomas Koch and Bill Robins, 1986.

10. THIS AIN'T NO CHOCOLATE 5.11d R ★★

Begin 20 feet left of Chocolate Channel. Climb past several bolts to the top. Big-time runouts. The 5.11d is at the top.

FA: Thomas Koch and Bill Robins, 1986.

GARGOYLE WALL

Almost as fearsome as its name suggests, the Gargoyle Wall is a steep face crossed by a diverse handful of mostly thin cracks. This wall is actually the east side of the Church Buttress. The long approach discourages most climbers, but some great climbing exists, especially in the upper difficulty range.

APPROACH: Follow the approach to The Fin. Routes 1 and 2 are on the west side of the gully BEFORE reaching the stand of Box Elder Trees mentioned in The Fin Approach. Directly across the gully (to the west) of this grove of trees is the start of Motown, route number 3. Continue straight up the gully from the Box Elder trees to reach route 4 through 10. The gully is steep and unstable in places, making hiking unpleasant. The routes are listed left to right, south to north. All parties descending from the Fin will hike down beside the Gargoyle's east-facing walls. See overview on page 220.

DESCENT: When known, the descents are included in the description for each route, or on the topo.

GARGOYLE WALL ROUTES

1. MISSIONARY JAM 5.8 ★
This is the short, perfect hand crack in the slab, on the left and down low in the gully.
FA: Brian and Jonathan Smoot, 1979.

2. MISSIONARY FACE 5.8
This adds a second pitch to Missionary Jam.
FA: Brain Dannemann, Dean and James Garrett, 1986.

3. MOTOWN II 5.9 A3 ★
This route is located between Missionary Jam and Immoral Act. Start with a third-class chimney leading to a tree-filled ledge. Climb a rightward-leaning, 8-inch, right-facing corner until it is possible to pendulum left to a flake (50 feet, A3). Interesting stemming leads to a lieback flake, which culminates with a hand crack (150 feet, 5.8). Continue up flakes and varied climbing, and go right under a broad roof to a corner and belay (90 feet, 5.8). Climb a hand crack and continue right on intricate moves to a large ramp and the end of the climb (65 feet, 5.9). Descend via two, 2-rope rappels from trees at the top of Immoral Act. Bring a selection of pins for the A3 pitch.
FA: Todd Cameron and James Garrett, 1986.

4. IMMORAL ACT 5.8
This ascends right-facing dihedrals on the left side of a smooth, clean section of rock. It is roughly 100 yards up from Missionary Jam. The first two pitches aren't worth much, but the upper dihedrals are nice. Descend by rappelling from trees—bring two ropes.
FA: Mark Smith and Brian Smoot, 1983.

5. SUBMISSION 5.11 A0 ★
A thin lieback left of Confession. A0 at the top of the crack. Hard to place gear.
FA: Dean Hannibal and Bill Robins, 1985.

6. CONFESSION 5.8 A2 R ★★
The right diagonalling, ultra-thin crack on the first pitch has some groundfall potential, so test properly. Take a dozen pieces of thin iron and a few hooks. Medium-to-large cams work well for the belay. Most parties do just the first two pitches, where a rappel from the trees with two ropes reaches the ground. If you go to the top, rappel as for Gargoyle.
FA: Brian and Jonathan Smoot, 1982.

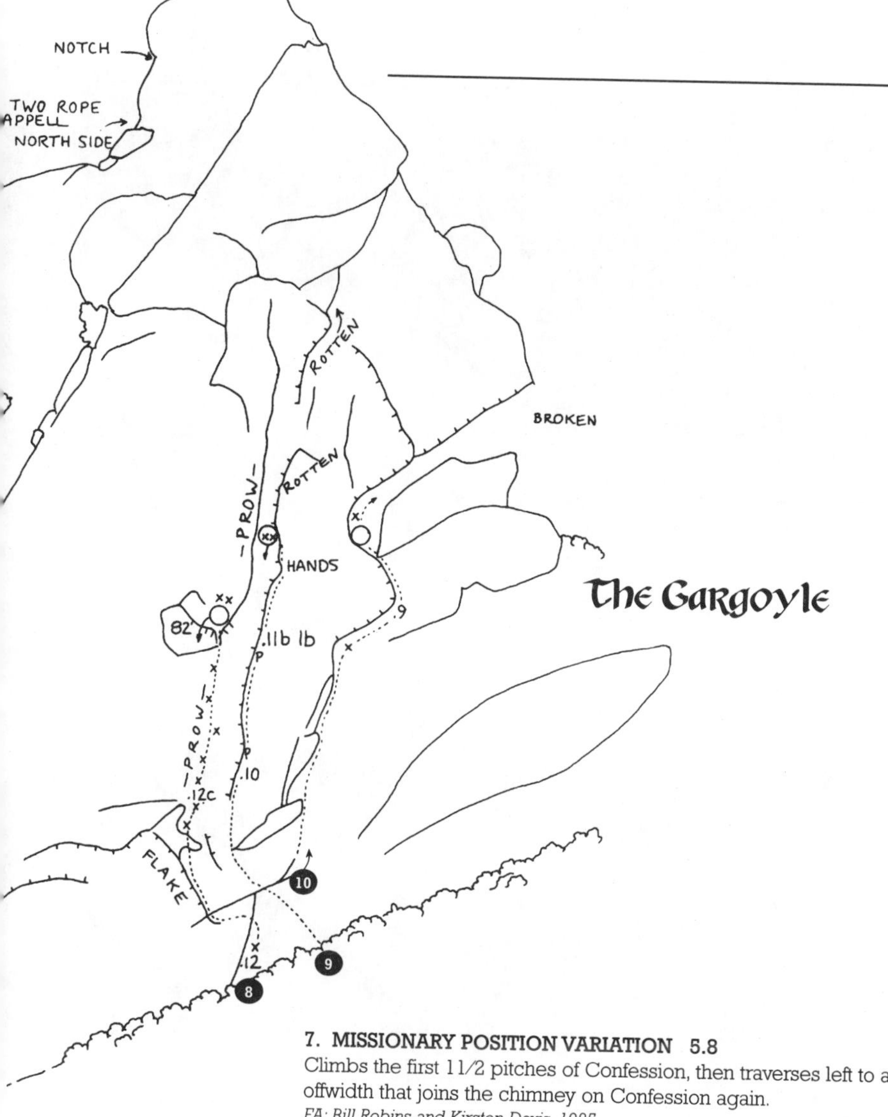

The Gargoyle

7. MISSIONARY POSITION VARIATION 5.8
Climbs the first 1 1/2 pitches of Confession, then traverses left to an offwidth that joins the chimney on Confession again.
FA: Bill Robins and Kirsten Davis, 1985.

8. BIG NEON GLITTER 5.12c ★★★
This scintillating climb is a modern thriller. An airy hand traverse left gets things rolling. Turning the lip is hard, but the face above...! Double ropes or backcleaning methods are recommended to reduce rope drag. Also, bring small- to medium-sized cams for the hand traverse.
FA: John Storm, Douglas Heinrich and Conrad Anker, 1988.

9. GARGOYLE 5.11c or 5.11c A2 ★★
This beautiful right-facing dihedral is great until the rock degrades. Most parties simply climb to the first anchors (5.11c) and rappel off with one rope. If you continue, expect very rotten rock and a 2-rope rappel from the notch (to the north.)
FA: Mark Ward and Jim Knight, 1976.
FFA: pitch one, Bobby Rotert, 1983.

10. CLOISTER 5.9 R
The chimney system right of Gargoyle.
FA: Jim Knight and Bruce Roghaar, 1977.

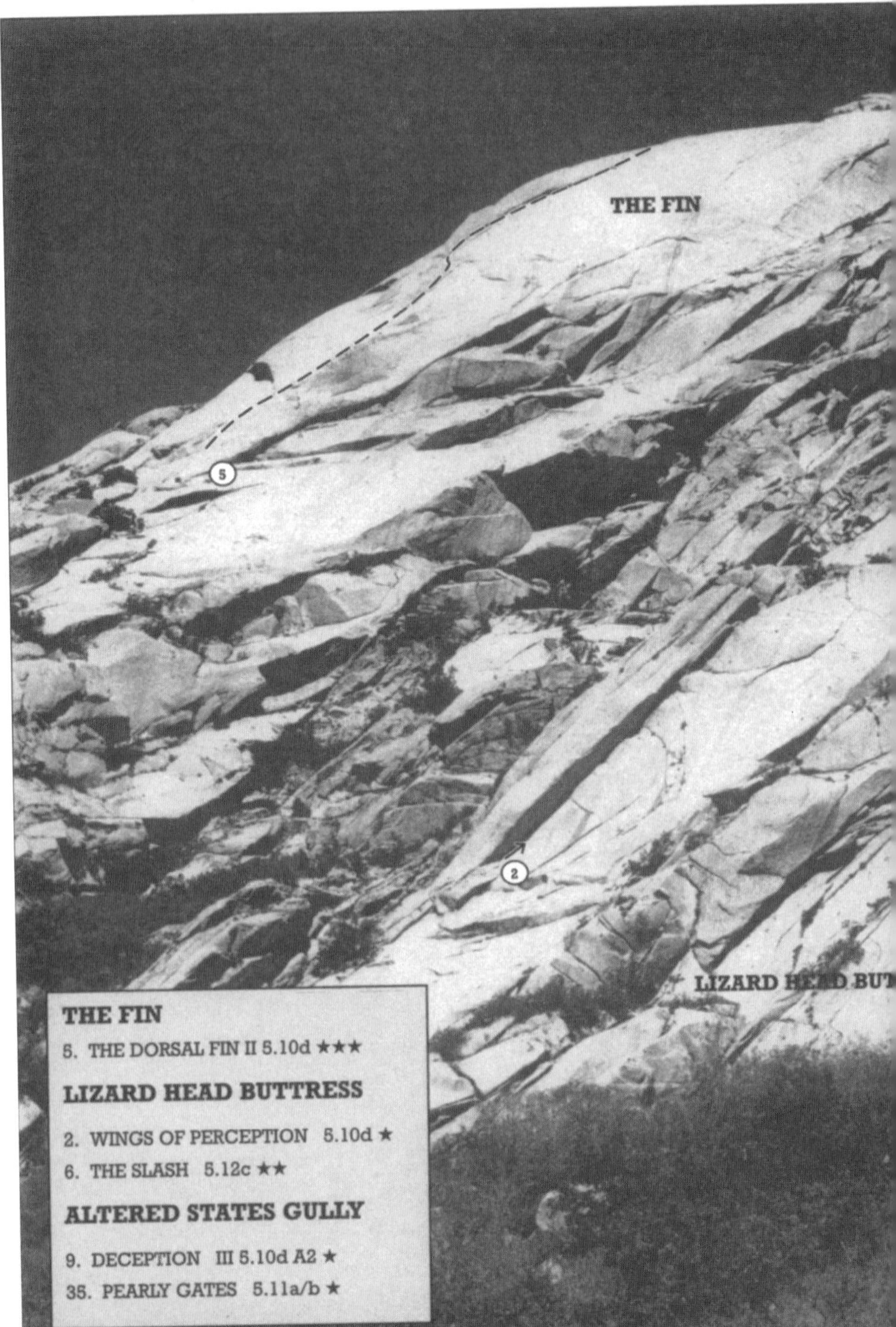
THE FIN
5
2
LIZARD HEAD BUT
THE FIN
5. THE DORSAL FIN II 5.10d ★★★
LIZARD HEAD BUTTRESS
2. WINGS OF PERCEPTION 5.10d ★
6. THE SLASH 5.12c ★★
ALTERED STATES GULLY
9. DECEPTION III 5.10d A2 ★
35. PEARLY GATES 5.11a/b ★

9
35
ALTERED STATES GULLY

INTENSIVE CARE

The slab supreme. From the road, this hunk of granite looks featureless, except for a large dihedral near the western margin of the wall. To imagine climbing such a smooth swath requires audacity, which is just what it took for two young climbers to make the first ascent. Twenty years later, an ascent of Intensive Care is still a feather in one's cap, and only the bold masters of slab technique venture up to this wall. If you want to friction amid a sea of rock, drop anchor here.

APPROACH: Follow the approach to The Fin (see page 258). From the gravelly flat spot mentioned in the Fin approach, continue straight up the gully, passing the Gargoyle Wall on the left (west) and eventually overcoming the brush and loose gravel to reach the base of the large south-facing slab. This is a long, mostly unpleasant walk. See overview on page 220.

DESCENT: The routes on the Intensive Care Slab can all be escaped via an 80 foot rappel from the pine tree at the far right side of the wall.

INTENSIVE CARE ROUTES

1. BEACH COMBER 5.5
The highly-featured face below Intensive Care has one bolt to get you started. The route is 150 feet long. Walk off.
FA: Kirsten Davis and Bill Robins, 1985.

2. LIZARD LIPS 5.7
This southwest-facing slab with two bolts is 100 feet directly east of the route Gargoyle. Smooth, water polished rock.
FA: Bill Robins and Kirsten Davis, 1985.

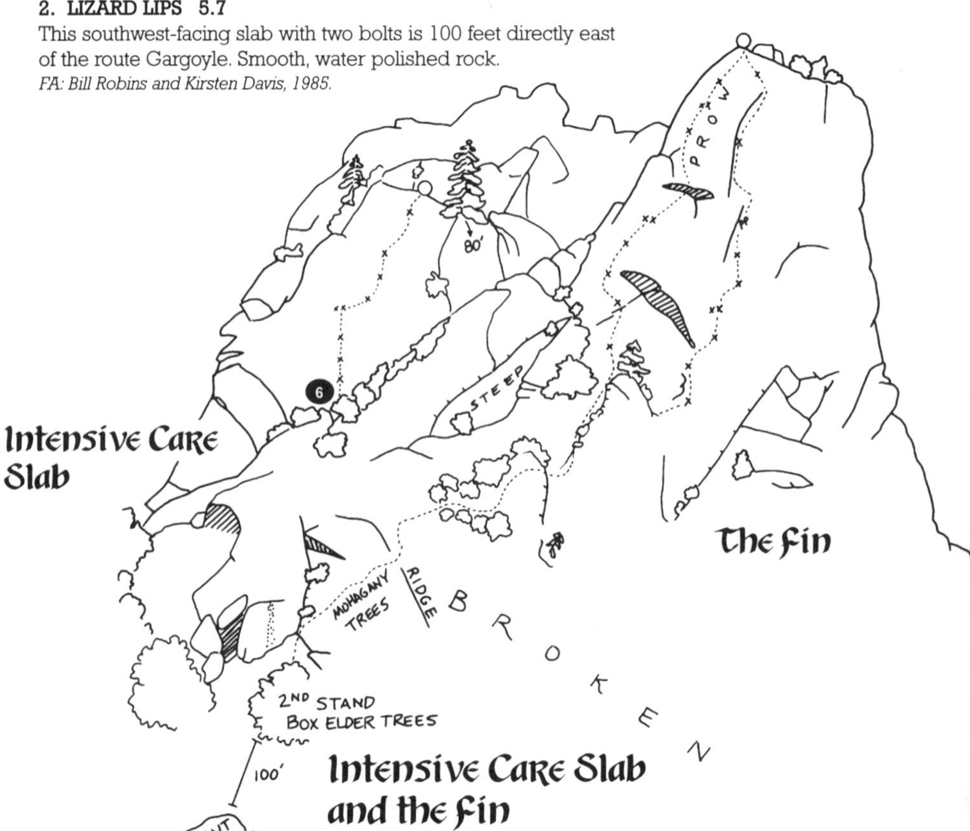

Intensive Care Slab and the Fin
approach and overview

3. A QUESTION OF FAITH 5.11a
Directly above Lizard Lips is an offwidth on an arête. Climb this to a roof (crux) and set a belay. Climb the slab above (5.10). The crux is a leftward hand traverse.
FA: Bill Robins and Kirsten Davis, 1985.

4. CDFT ROUTE 5.7
Climb the dihedral system left of the Intensive Care face in two pitches. Most parties begin the climb just below Intensive Care, however, the first ascent was a link-up that actually started above the gravelly, flat place described in the approach. It traverses the upper margins of Beach Comber's slab and continues into the present day start.
FA: Ralph Tingey and Rich Ream, 1965.

5. BURN UNIT 5.11b ★★★
The first ascent was completed in the heat of the summer, hence the name. Persistent friction climbing is required for this slab left of Intensive Care. Clip the first bolt on that route with a long runner, move left (the traverse requires some up and down adventuring) and follow the dwindling chickenheads to a long holdless section. Above, it's possible to join Intensive Care again at the first belay.
FA: Nolan Wall and Jim Reynolds, 1996.

6. INTENSIVE CARE 5.11a R ★★★
This route took significant effort to establish. One attempt left Mark Ward in the intensive care unit after a long fall. The bolts were drilled on lead from lousy stances, with long runouts up the inexorable slab. QDs, runners and a few nuts are recommended.
FA: Kim Miller and Jim Knight, 1977.

7. SHOCK TRAUMA 5.11b ★★
Start fifteen feet right of Intensive Care. Follow small edges, chickenheads, and an electrifying dike past five bolts to a belay. Step down and right to begin the tenuous second pitch which leads to an offwidth and finally the rappel tree. A 60 meter or two 50 meter ropes are necessary to rappel from the top of the first pitch.
FA: Lance Bateman, Jim Reynolds, and Nolan Wall, 1996.

8. CHICKEN LIPS 5.7
Climb the slab 100 feet right of Intensive Care.
FA: Bill Robins and Kirsten Davis. 1985.

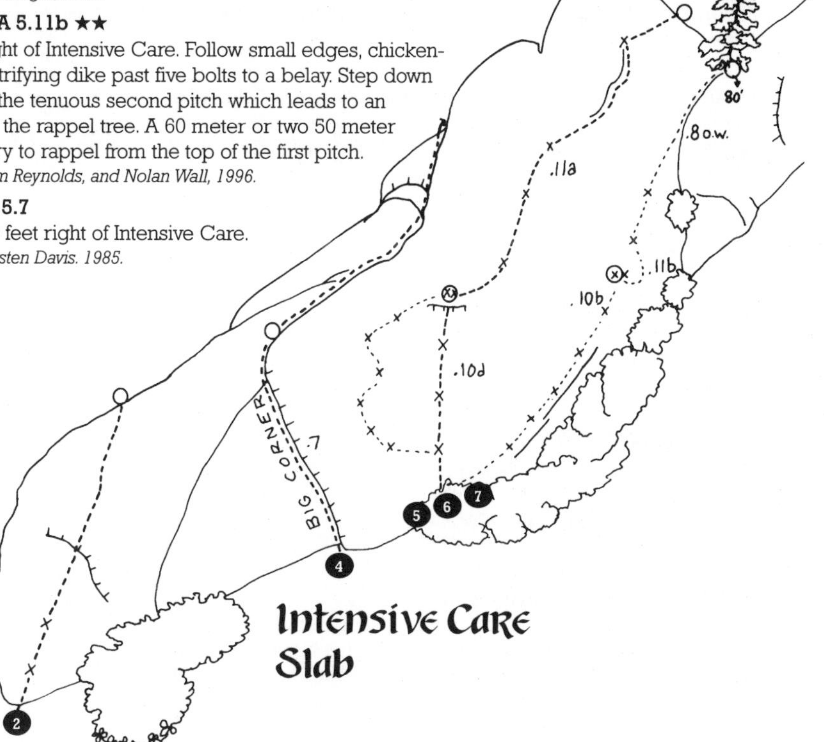

THE FIN

You can get a good view of perhaps the most beautiful buttress in the canyon—the Fin—from around .85 miles up canyon, near the junction of the church archives road with Little Cottonwood Canyon road. This steep backbone of granite offers the highest quality face/slab climbing in the region. Complicated approaches and descents make climbing the Fin at least half-a-day's outing. The access to the Fin is through private property, which means climbers must be amicable to the landowners' wishes.

APPROACH: Park .9 miles up canyon from the neon sign. The Fin resides directly above the archives road. This LDS Church-owned road is strictly off limits. This forces climbers to bushwhack through a quarter-mile of thick, hateful oak brush paralleling the road, to reach a gully that descends just west of The Fin. A trail that begins just below the parking lot for the archives employees (no trespassing), can be met and followed here. Hike up this gully until you reach a gravelly flat place just past the second of three stands of large Box Elder trees. These trees are 100 feet up from an enormous boulder. Behind the flat spot is a large, low-angled corner. Scramble up the corner about ten feet, then traverse up and right, passing mahogany trees to the ridge. Turn the ridge and walk up slabs for 50 feet until a traverse through some small oak brush brings you to the bottom of another set of slabs. On the right side of these slabs, a brush-filled corner is topped by an old gnarled pine tree. Scramble up to this corner on knobs, then follow the corner up to the base of the climbs. Stepping out of the corner into the brush to the left is unpleasant, but much easier. See overview on page 256 for the Fin approach.

DESCENT: Go north 25 feet from the belay in the trees at the top of the Fin and find two bolts at the top of a left-facing corner. Rappel west 80 feet and downclimb another 100 feet to a big tree. One more 82-foot rappel lands you at the base of Intensive Care and the gully home.

THE FIN ROUTES

1. WHEN WE DEAD AWAKEN 5.11d

On the approach march to the Fin, you will pass by this route. It is on the lowest south section of the cliff, 100 feet above the very base of the Fin. A right-angling crack through an overhang leads to a belay/rappel from trees. There is one bolt.

FA: John Rogers and Troy Warburton, 1988.

2. PAY THE KITTY 5.10a

From the base of the second rappel off the Fin routes, go down and south a bit, to a slab nestled between two left-facing corners. Climb past three bolts to a belay. Climb a 5.8 slab to the top. The crux is near the first bolt.

FA: Scott Lunt, Dave Black and Tito Black, 1984.

3. THE FIN ARÊTE II 5.10b ★★★

A beautiful, fun line up the arête of the Fin. Rope drag can be a real drag on the first pitch. The aquiline arête on the third pitch of Dark Horse is a good but runout variation. The last pitch has only one bolt, but is 5.7.

FA: Jonathan and Brian Smoot, 1978.

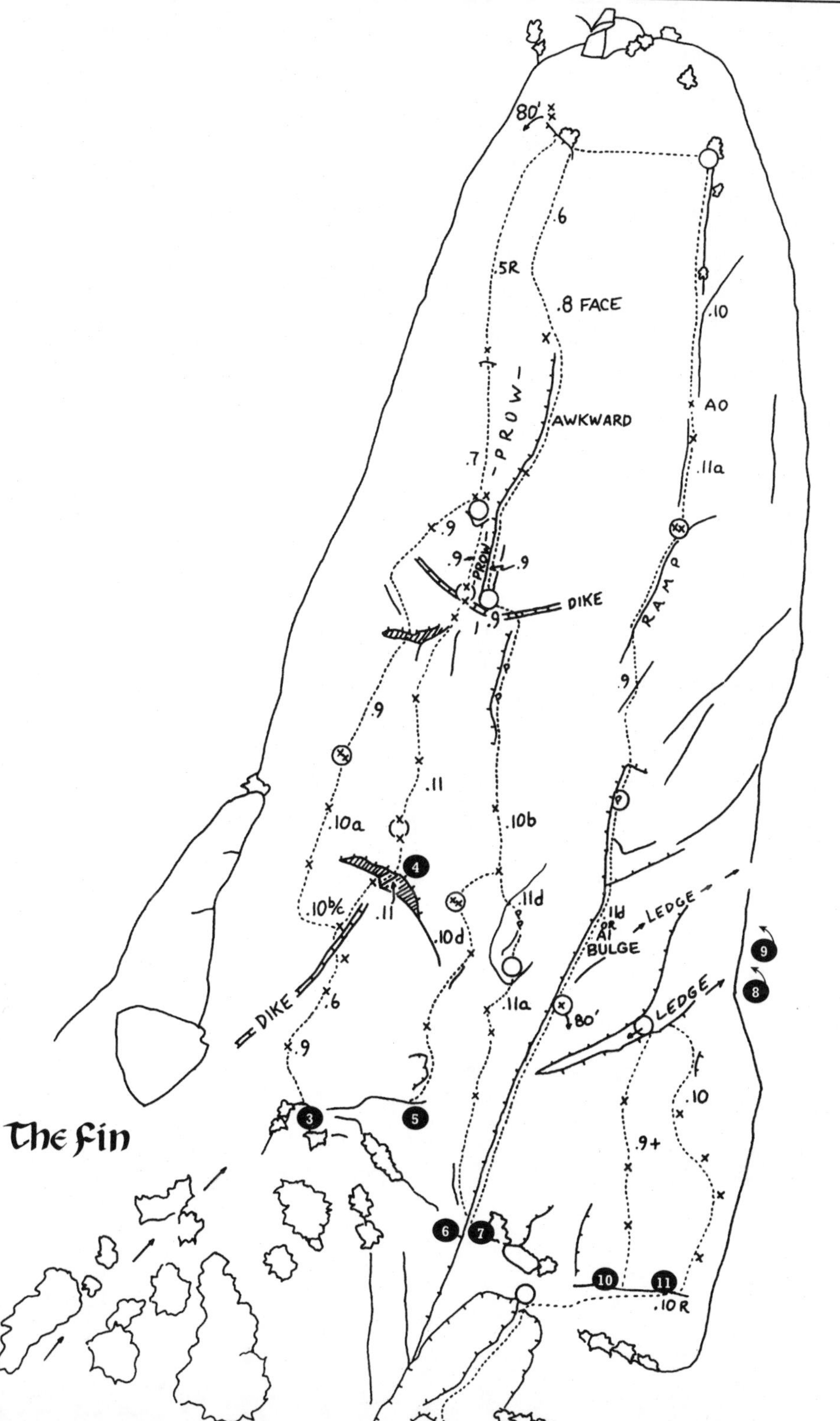
80'
.6
.5R
.8 FACE
.10
AWKWARD
A0
PROW
.7
.11a
.9
.9
PROW
.9
DIKE
RAMP
.9
.9
.9
.11
.10a
.10b
4
.11d
.10b/c
.11
.10d
11d OR A1 BULGE
LEDGE
9
8
DIKE
.6
.11a
80'
LEDGE
.9
.10
3
5
.9+
6
7
10
11
.10R

The Fin

THE FIN ROUTES

4. DARK HORSE II 5.11 R ★★★

Indeed improbable. If you can climb this route, then you're a master of the slab climbing discipline. Long runouts. Some bolts were placed on rappel. Branch off the Fin Arête where it traverses left.

FA: Mark Ward and Kim Miller, 1979.

5. THE DORSAL FIN II 5.10d ★★★

The area's classic. Some 30 years after its first ascent, an ascent of this climb still is a cherished coup. The boldness of the first ascent cannot be overplayed; it marks a milestone in Utah climbing history. One hopes this route will remain an inspiration for all climbers. Bring QDs and a selection of nuts. The final 5.8 section of the route can suffer from rope drag.

FA: George Lowe and Mark McQuarrie, 1965.

6. FINAGLE VARIATION II 5.11d ★

Being tall helps on the crux moves. The first pitch originally was done without the first bolt.

FA: Bret Ruckman and Les Ellison, 1985.

7. THE LATERAL FIN III 5.11d A0 or 5.10 A1 ★★

Only one move remains to go free. The bulge on the second pitch can be avoided by starting on The Ventral Fin and making a long traverse back left, to gain the crack above the bulge. The final pitch is a beautiful thin finger crack/flake that is rated 5.10/11 up to the bolt, then 5.10 again one move higher. Bring a standard rack, leaning towards the thin side.

FA: George Lowe and Bill Conrad, 1966.

8. THE VENTRAL FIN IV 5.10d A3 ★

Bring a hatful of tricks for this one. The first pitch has been done all clean at C2. The third pitch is dangerous for the seconding climber. The final pitch is a beauty, starting with a lasso and culminating with airy face climbing. Bring RURPS to one-inch angle, 15 KBs, 8 LAs, hooks and nuts. At least one climber has suggested that only 6 KBs and 6 LAs are needed, however.

FA: Brian and Jonathan Smoot, 1982.

9. FINS AND NEEDLES 5.12 A0 ★

A fine, radically overhung dihedral with a good finger and hand crack that is just waiting for its first free ascent. It is just right of the first pitch of The Ventral Fin.

FA: Stuart Ruckman and Gordon Douglass, 1986.

10. THAT'S REBOLTING 5.9+

This follows two bolts on the slab below The Lateral Fin's first pitch.

FA: Dana Hauser and Paul Budd, 1984.

11. SNOW QUEENS AND ICE FAIRIES 5.10 R

Pitch one: Climb the slab below the start of The Lateral Fin. Pitch two: Traverse down and right to the start of the second pitch. Traverse right some more and climb the slab above. The seconding climber could be frightened to death. There are four bolts.

FA: Bill Robins and Skeeter Malinski, 1987.

ALTERED STATES GULLY AND ENVIRONS

The Altered States Gully is a wonderful mixture of high-quality rock, below par rock, excellent routes, and second rate routes. More broken than the clean slabs at the Gate Buttress, the lines here are still worthwhile, with the added benefit of few, if any, other climbers. Approaching and climbing in this area may be construed as trespassing. See overview on page 220.

APPROACH: Park .9 miles up canyon from the neon sign, at the junction of the main road and the road leading to the church archives. Two trails head up into the gully and start off the archives road. One is 30 feet beyond the gate, the other 180 feet beyond. The first approach has more brush, but less time on the private road. Begin in a clearing 30 feet from the gate. Follow a small path up to some talus, then to a large pine tree, then directly above the tree. Keep heading up at each clearing until an easy traverse west on big boulders reaches the Altered States Gully just above the route Errant Edge.

The second approach ducks through a bit of brush 180 feet past the gate, and follows a trail up a long clearing, staying to the left. At a quarried boulder, traverse left (west) into the gully. Walk up the gully, passing several big chockstones on the right to the route of choice. When descending, don't forget to traverse back to the quarried boulder.

DESCENT: Several of the routes in this area require two rope rappels. See the topo for specific information.

ALTERED STATES AREA —SHEEP WALL (No topo)

This wall is located above the Lizard Head Wall, and east of The Fin.

APPROACH: From the base of the route Zigzag, beat west through the brush, then turn uphill and force your way through more brush to the base of the wall.

1. A SHEEP AT THE WHEEL 5.7

This is above Lizard Head. Climb the face left of the dihedral on the west-facing wall, below and east of the Fin.

FA: Skeeter and Bill Robins.

2. WHAT, ME WORRY? 5.8 X

Climb the face five feet left of dihedral mentioned above.

FA: Skeeter and Bill Robins.

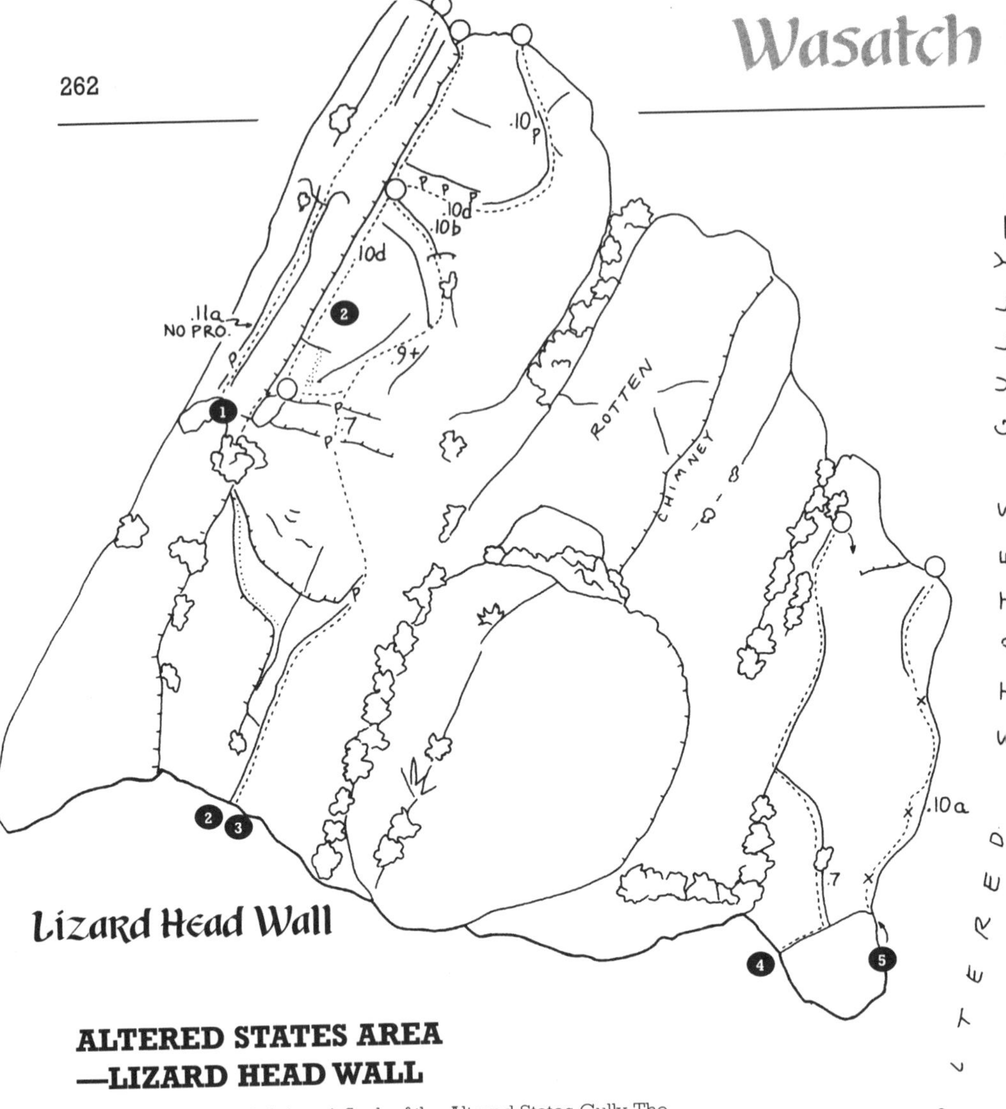

Lizard Head Wall

ALTERED STATES AREA —LIZARD HEAD WALL

This wall forms the left (west) flank of the Altered States Gully. The Lizard Head Wall is south-facing, and showcases a right-leaning corner.

APPROACH: See the approach for the Altered States Gully.

DESCENT: A 75-foot rappel off of a mahogany tree (located down and east from the top of the Lizard Head Wall at the belay for the route The Slash), drops one into the Altered States Gully.

LIZARD HEAD WALL ROUTES

1. ASSUMPTION OF RISK 5.11a X

This route challenges the poorly-protected incipient cracks on the left side of the wall. It certainly will mark the temerity of a climber.

FA: Mark Bennett and Bill Robins, sometime in the 1980's.

2. WINGS OF PERCEPTION 5.10d ★

A great line with an awkward, right-slanting dihedral. Harder than it appears.

FA: Doug Madera and Jeff Butterfield, 1980.

3. ZIGZAG 5.10d ★★
This serpentine route offers some interesting stuff. The third pitch can present rope drag problems, especially toward its end. Double ropes would help.
FA: pitch two, Brad Gilbert and Jeff Allred, 1978.
FA: Les Ellison and Larry Carrol, 1979.

4. SQUEEZE MY LEMON 5.7
A hand and fist crack that becomes cleaner with each ascent. Is this the next Bushwhack Crack?
FA: Dave and Scott Lunt, 1979.

5. ERRANT EDGE 5.10a ★★
Blind protection placements can be obtained on the very right edge—before making the move to reach the second bolt. A thrilling route. A scamper off the back will put you back into the Altered States gully.
FA: Bret and Stuart Ruckman, 1982.

ALTERED STATES GULLY—EAST FACE

Routes 6 through 10 are on the east-facing (left) wall of the gully. There are no topos for these climbs.

APPROACH/DESCENT: See individual route descriptions.

6. THE SLASH 5.12c ★★
Yet another Hong test piece for mutant climbers with thigh-sized forearms. This striking roof crack is the first route on the east face in the gully proper. Two short rappels reach the ground.
FA: Steve Hong and Karin Budding, 1983.

7. HEAVE HO 5.9
Named for inevitable rope drag problems. This starts about 30 feet up the gully from The Slash. Look for a widening slot that is climbed for 30 feet, until a traverse right gains an arching, right-facing dihedral. Once through this section, watch for loose rock. Descend as for The Slash.
FA: Kent Sundberg and Mark Bennett, 1980.

8. STICKY FINGERS 5.10d ★★
Up high in the gully, past the Romance on the Rocks area, is a south-east-facing crack that meanders rightward. Climb up to a mahogany tree, then traverse right past two fixed pins and tie on a good pump. A strong seconding climber is advised.
FA: Steve Carruthers and Lynn Wheeler, 1982.

9. DECEPTION III 5.10d A2 ★
At the head of the gully is a series of cracks leading to two paralleling left-slanting offwidth cracks, which can be readily seen from the road. This south-facing four-pitcher sees little action. Getting to the crack system is a trick, and once there, it's no picnic. Expect some loose rock and runouts. Descend off to the right.
FA: Mark Ward and Hal Throolin, 1979.

10. ADDED DECEPTION III 5.10d or A1
This is a six-pitch, free variation to Deception. Start with Deception's first pitch (5.6). Climb the gully up and left (5.7). A right-facing corner is climbed straight up (5.8). Traverse right to the bottom of the fourth pitch of Deception. Struggle up pitch four of Deception—the right of the two obvious paralleling cracks. A final pitch climbs past two bolts up a steep wall and then traverses off to the right (5.10d). Descend off to the right.
FA: James and Franziska Garrett, 1990.

ALTERED STATES GULLY—WEST FACE

The remaining routes are all on the west-facing (right) wall of the gully.

APPROACH/DESCENT: See information on page 261.

WEST FACE ROUTES

11. CHEAP THRILLS AKA INQUISITION II 5.7
An attractive dihedral that initially is good, but rapidly disintegrates into a grovel with poor rock and chimneys.
FA: Tom Burris and Larry Carrol, 1978.

12. WALK ON AIR 5.11a ★
A strange line with funky protection and hard climbing. A bolt on Cheap Thrills is used to protect the second, rightward traverse. Double ropes are essential.
FA: Les Ellison and Pat Maloney, 1982.

13. AIR EXPRESS 5.11d ★★
A straightened-out version of Walk On Air. One of the premier slab climbing test pieces of the area. The crux is getting to the bolt after Walk on Air traverses left.
FA: Gary Taylor, 1989.

14. ALTERED STATES 5.9 ★★
Start 20 feet right of Cheap Thrills. This is a long, interesting pitch of groove and face work that stays on great rock until the last few feet.
FA: Les Ellison and Steve Carruthers, 1981.

15. ROMANCE ON THE ROCKS 5.10d ★★★
Hold your breath getting to the first bolt. This took a monumental effort to equip, with multiple falls occurring when the first ascensionists drilled bolt #4. The old belay block has given in to gravity and time.
FA: Les Ellison and Dana Hauser, 1980.

16. A BRIGHT, SHINING LIE 5.10c ★★
10 bolts and one pin are needed to protect the expanse between Romance on the Rocks and the last pitch of Magic Circus. Drilling this route on lead involved major whippers.
FA: Chris Begue, Jason Ball, Stan Smigle, 1994.

17. DEL TONGO 5.9 ★
A link up of chickenheads, corners and ledges leads to the bombay chimney on Magic Circus' third pitch. Bring runners for tie-offs.
A recommended alternate start is Latter-Day Sinner.
FA: Bret and Stuart Ruckman, 1980.

18. LATTER-DAY SINNER 5.10a ★
Climb weaknesses that begin 40 feet downhill from the start of Altered States (30 feet uphill from the start of Magic Circus) to join the two bolt belay on Del Tongo. Bring brass-type nuts, a 3½" cam and TCUs.
FA: Alan Bartlett and Shari Schubot, 1984.

19. MAGIC CIRCUS II 5.9 R ★
Three pitches of hocus pocus. The first pitch is tricky to protect, the second pitch is easy, and the third wrestles with the infamous "wizard's chin".
FA: Doug Madera, Jeff Butterfield and Ed Webster, 1980.

20. MARCH OF THE GUMMI BEARS 5.10b ★
Bring medium cams as well as all your friction skills. An easy second pitch gains the two-bolt belay on Del Tongo, where an 80 foot rappel to the ground can be made.
FA: Mike and John Hansen, 1995.

21. PROSCENIUM 5.10a ★★

A fine slab climb that starts on Magic Circus for a few feet, then traverses a ledge right to reach the first bolt. Sort of runout. An easy second pitch gains the two-bolt belay on Del Tongo, where an 80 foot rappel to the ground can be made.

FA: Stuart and Bret Ruckman, 1983.

22. BORROWED TIME 5.10b/c R ★

The first pitch clocks in at 5.9+, with an exciting leftward traverse. The third pitch is scary and potentially dangerous, but the climbing is good. The best descent is to gain the two-bolt anchor at the top of Altered States.

FA: Bret and Stuart Ruckman, 1982.

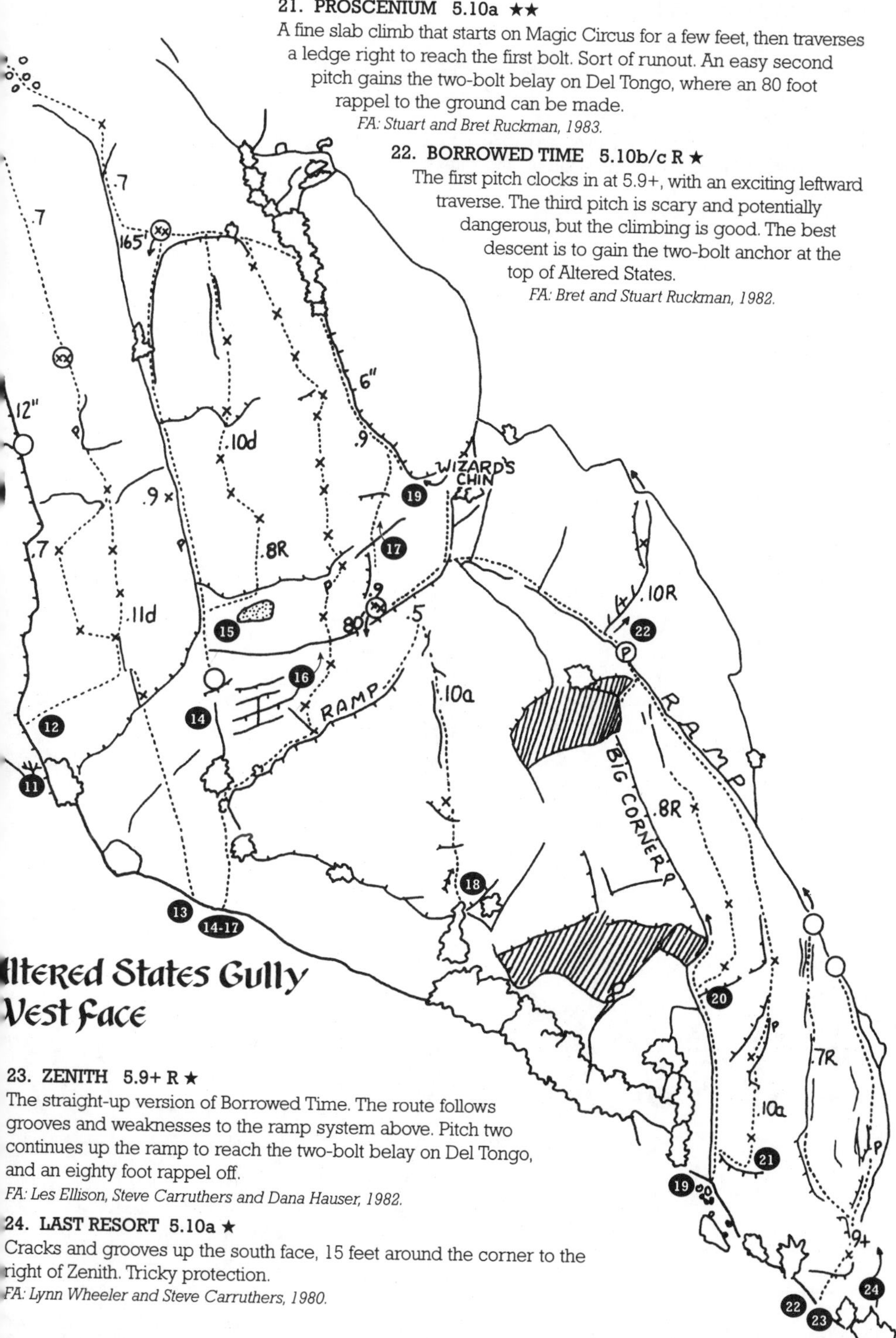

ltered States Gully Vest Face

23. ZENITH 5.9+ R ★

The straight-up version of Borrowed Time. The route follows grooves and weaknesses to the ramp system above. Pitch two continues up the ramp to reach the two-bolt belay on Del Tongo, and an eighty foot rappel off.

FA: Les Ellison, Steve Carruthers and Dana Hauser, 1982.

24. LAST RESORT 5.10a ★

Cracks and grooves up the south face, 15 feet around the corner to the right of Zenith. Tricky protection.

FA: Lynn Wheeler and Steve Carruthers, 1980.

WEST FACE ROUTES

25. EASY SQUEEZE 5.6

The big, obvious, left-facing, low-angled corner filled with several trees.

FA: Les and Gail Ellison, 1986

26. SLEIGHT OF HAND 5.9+ ★

Start in a corner on polished rock, located 20 feet uphill from Discreet Feat (15 feet up the gully from the stand of maple trees). Descent is the same as for Discreet Feat.

FA: Alan Bartlett and Shari Schubot, 1984.

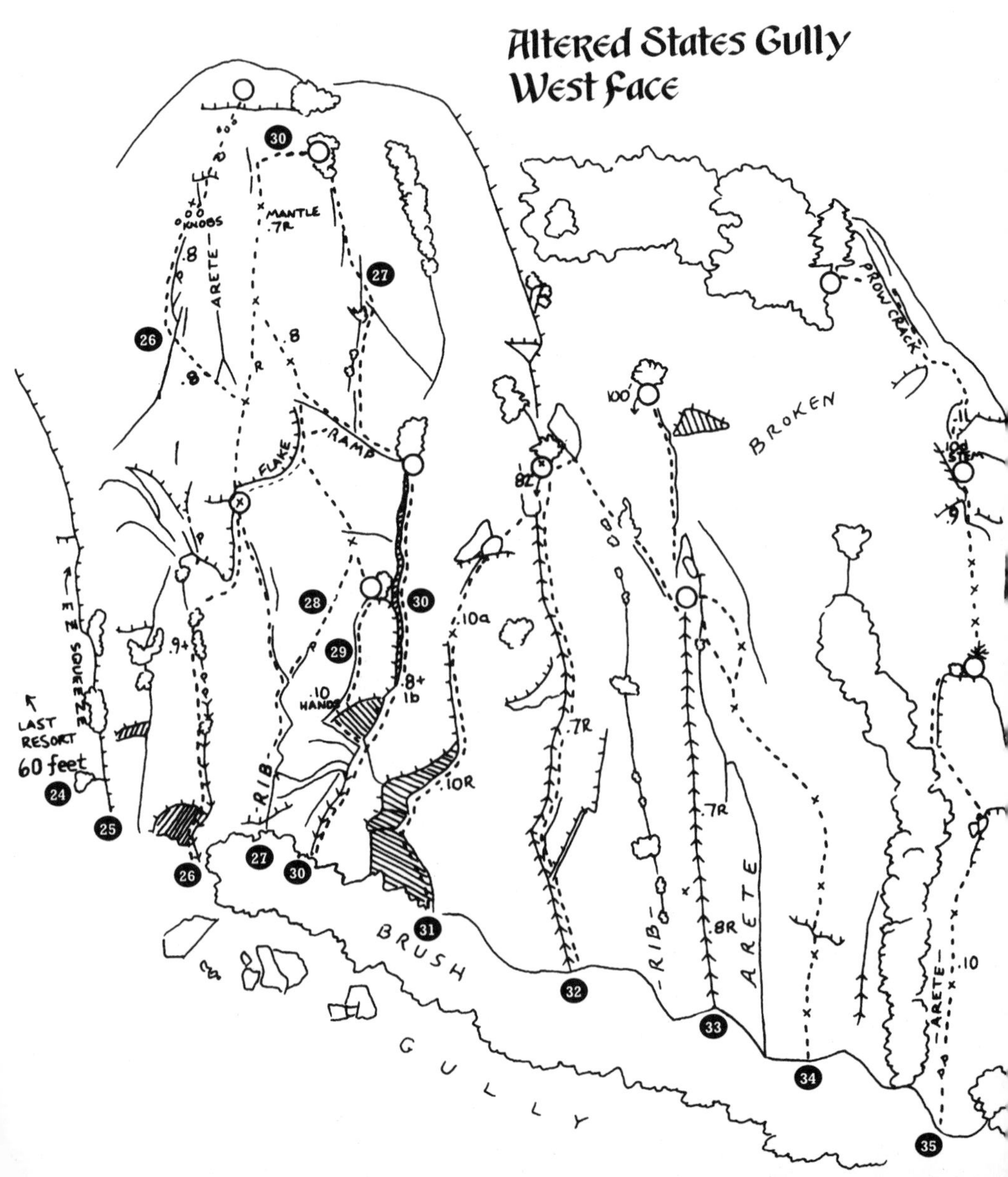

27. DROPPING OUT 5.9+

A series of weaknesses just left of Discreet Feat, eventually crossing that route.

FA: Bill Robins and Les Ellison, 1985.

28. DROPPING OUT VARIATION 5.?

29. EAGLE ROOF 5.10d ★

A crack splitting the roof of Discreet Feat, joins Dropping Out.

FA: Bill Robins and Brian Smoot, 1985.

30. DISCREET FEAT 5.8+R ★

Well hidden behind some trees, the first-pitch dihedral has some discreet moves, and a second pitch has a mantel that is quite a feat. A trampled area just inside the northern termination of a maple grove marks the start.

FA: Gary Olsen and Bret Ruckman, 1980.

31. THOROUGHFLARE 5.10c R ★

An undercling leads to a thoroughly-flaring corner. The final face moves are a bit gritty.

FA: Stuart and Bret Ruckman, 1989.

32. CLUTCHING AT STRAWS 5.7 R ★

A gear battle up a nice, grassy corner system on good rock. Bring mainly smaller nuts.

FA: Unknown

33. SLIP SLIDIN' 5.8 R ★★

Quality climbing up a water groove. Hefty runouts. Large cams are helpful. A traverse left near the top puts one at the belay of Thoroughflare. Rappel off.

FA: Gary Olsen and Bret Ruckman, 1980.

34. ANGEL'S LADDER 5.10d ★★

Thin face climbing. The first pitch has good rock and is quite popular, but the remaining pitches – the same as for Slip Slidin' – are probably not worth it and are not included.

FA: Ken Gygi and Kent Jameson, 1982.

35. PEARLY GATES 5.11a/b ★

A step-over move under the roof is largely dependent on one's stemming span. A good line. Would be worthy of more stars if it had better rock at the top.

FA: Steve Hong, Dave and Tito Black, 1983.

WESTWIND BUTTRESS

Between Altered States Gully and the Thumb is the large Westwind Buttress. It has variable rock quality, and therefore doesn't see as much action as some of the other buttresses. The rock here generally is more weathered, except on its eastern side, and the vegetation on the wall is flourishing.

APPROACH: Follow the approach for The Thumb, except veer off west once you pass the Plumb Line Wall. See overview on pages 220 and 290.

DESCENT: A gully to the west of the routes is probably the best descent except where noted otherwise.

WESTWIND BUTTRESS ROUTES

1. PERSEVERANCE II 5.10d ★

To the west of the main Westwind Buttress is a slab, which serves as the initial pitch of Perseverance. This is a thrash to get to. The final pitch has a dangerous section for the seconding climber.

FA: Kent Jameson, Mike Todd and Ken Gygi, 1982.

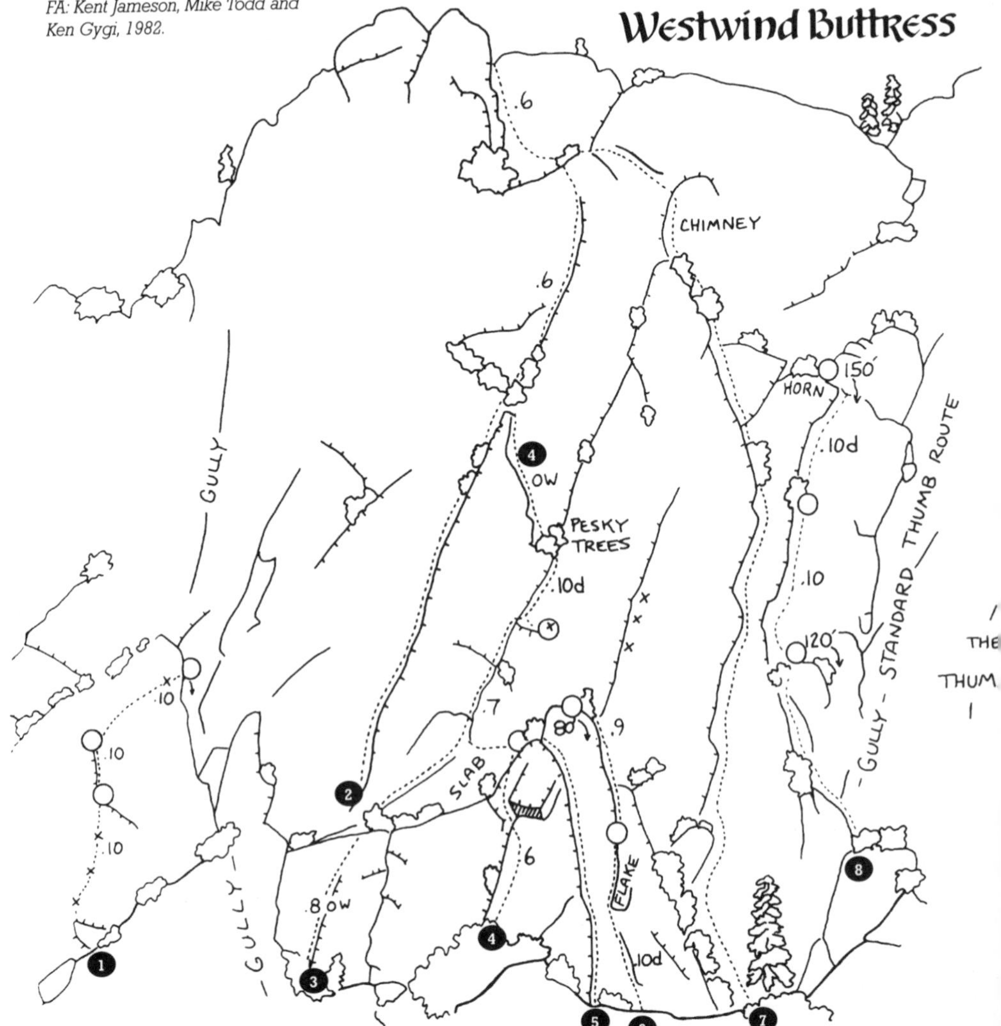

2. BLOWING WIND II 5.7

Not much is going for this route – scrub oak and rotten rock abound.
FA: Don Black, George Lowe and Dave Smith, 1970.

3. TEXTBOOK VARIATION 5.8 ★

FA: Kent Jameson and Pat Manley, 1982.

4. WESTWIND CRACK II 5.10d

Expect some difficult dodging of vegetation at the crux.
FA: Bill Conrod and Paul Anderson.
FFA: Ken Gygi

5. TRUE GRIT VARIATION 5.8

FA: Kent Jameson and Pat Manley, 1982.

6. SACRIFICE 5.10d ★

A thin, east-facing crack with a hanging guillotine flake that is passed on the left. Bring a 4" camming unit. Rappel from the tree.
FA: Lynn Wheeler and Jeff Newsome, 1980.

7. EASTWIND CRACK II 5.8

Follow the obvious feature of the cliff – a right-facing corner on the east side. Take the left line where the corner splits.
FA: George Lowe and Dick Ream, 1967.

8. EXPECT NO MERCY 5.10d ★

Starting on the left side of the Standard Thumb gully is a crack system that leads up and onto the Westwind Buttress. This good crack system is continuous in its grade. Unfortunately, it doesn't get climbed enough to get cleaned out. Two two-rope rappels provide the descent.
FFA: Ed Webster and Jeff Butterfield, 1980.

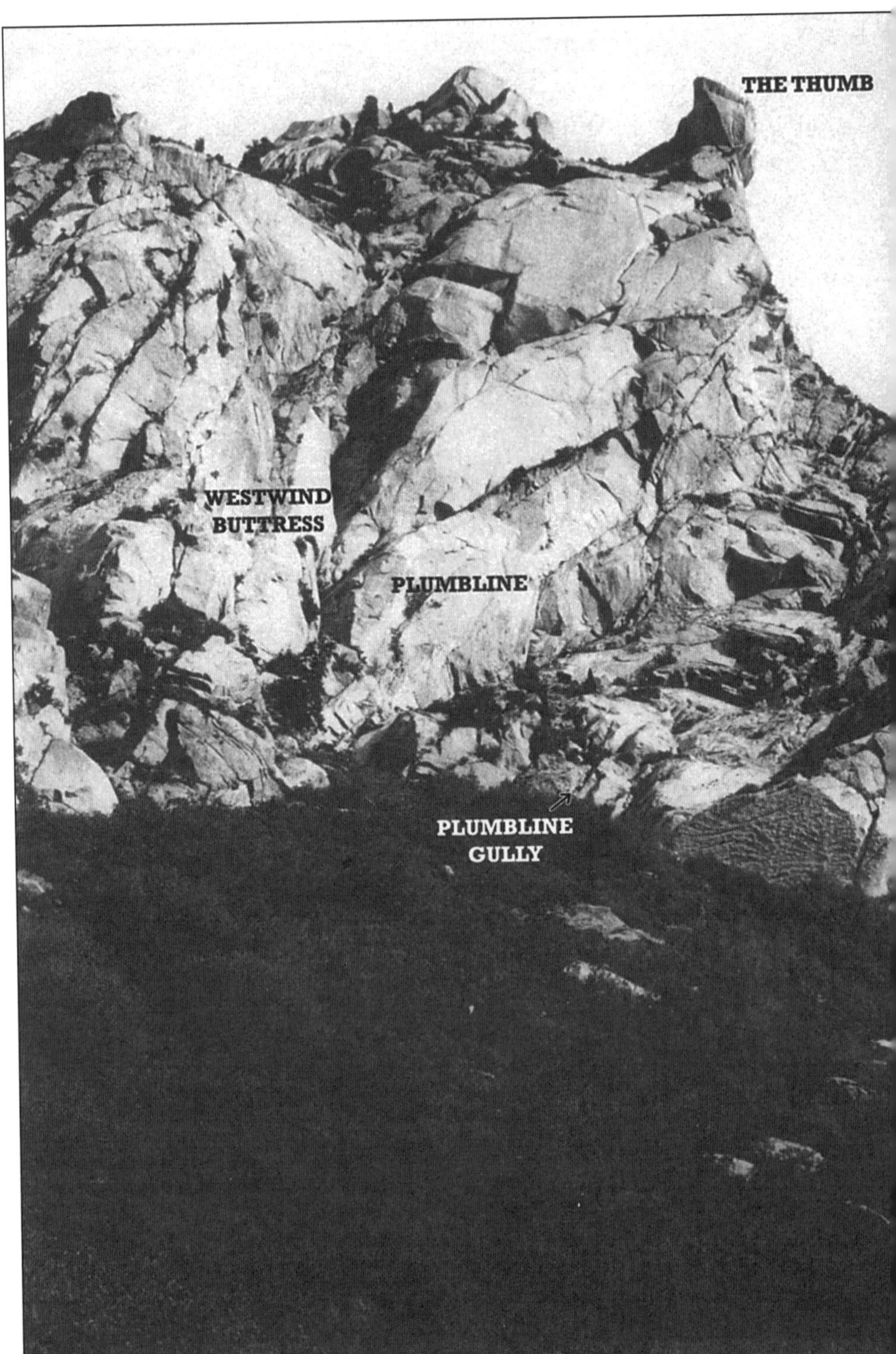
THE THUMB
WESTWIND
BUTTRESS
PLUMBLINE
PLUMBLINE
GULLY

THE THUMB
WESTWIND BUTTRESS
PLUMBLINE
WATERFRONT
WATERFRONT

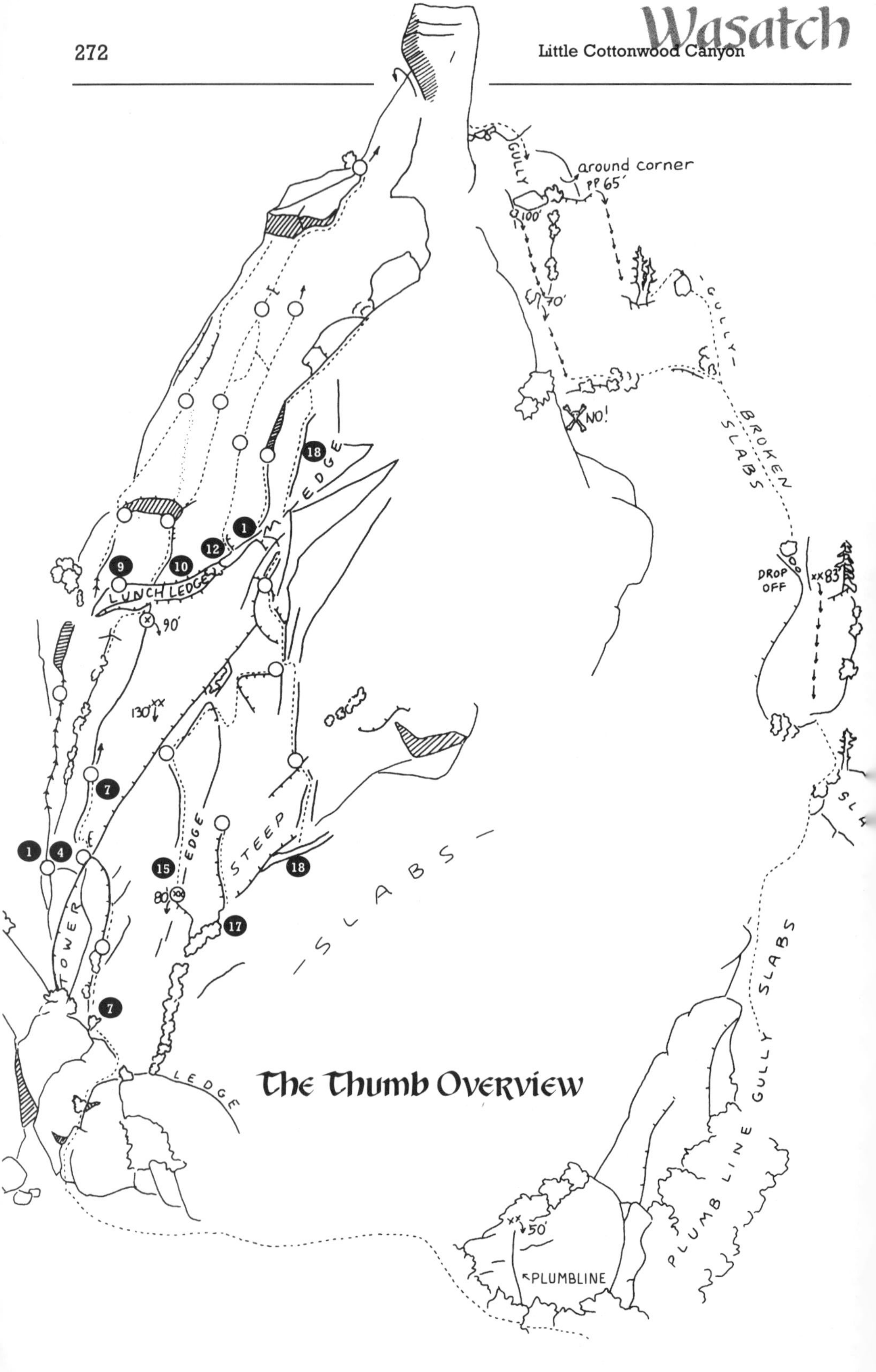

around corner
GULLY
PP 65′
100′
70′
GULLY
BROKEN SLABS
NO!
EDGE
LUNCH LEDGE
90′
130′ XX
DROP OFF
XX 83′
TOWER
EDGE
STEEP
SLABS
SLABS
80′
SLABS
GULLY
LEDGE
PLUMB LINE GULLY SLABS
XX 50′
PLUMBLINE

The Thumb Overview

THE THUMB

This buttress is the largest in the canyon and is distinguished by the thumb-like pinnacle resting atop acres of clean granite. The S-Crack, coupled with the S-Direct, makes for a magnificent eight-pitch route (nine, if the true summit is reached) and is given a grade IV rating. Many of the first ascents on the thumb were climbed prior to 1970, yet even with modern equipment, they still feel committing, and require a full day.

APPROACH: The best view of the The Thumb is at 1.05 up canyon at a bend in the road. However, the approach begins at the Gate Buttress parking area 1.25 miles up canyon from the neon sign.

As you approach the first boulder at the Gate Boulders, follow the path that leads left (west). The trail climbs up and west above the Tower Boulder, along the base of a short slab. Take the lower fork here and follow the trail into the talus. The trail crosses the talus, then continues up and west until it meets the base of The Waterfront. Keep traversing west, under The Waterfront. The trail then climbs up to the Plumb Line Wall. Many Thumb climbers stow their packs in this area, which alleviates the traverse back to the base of The Thumb from this point on the descent. Continuing to The Thumb, the trail climbs up and left (west) for one hundred and fifty feet, then traverses left (west) through the trees and below a slabby cliffband, to the gully at the base of the routes 1 to 12.

Continue up and right for routes 13 to 16. See overview on pages 272 and 290.

DESCENT: See the descent drawing on The Thumb topo. There are two options for the initial rappels. If you choose the western option, it is important to traverse into the gully at the bottom of the second rappel. With the eastern option, the two pin anchor is hidden around a corner on the north side of a ledge. Both descents eventually join and share an eighty foot rappel. Below that point, be careful not to miss the cut-off into the Plumb Line Gully.

THE THUMB ROUTES

1. STANDARD THUMB III 5.7 ★★
The trough pitches above Lunch Ledge "make" the route. Don't get caught too deep in these squeeze chimneys. Be super careful of loose rock on the first four pitches leading up to Lunch Ledge, and seriously consider the Indecent Exposure Variation.
FA: Bob Irvine, Ralph Tingey and Dave Wood, 1962.

2. THE CAVE II 5.7
Climb the Standard Thumb route for three pitches. Instead of traversing right to reach Lunch Ledge, continue following the main gully. Eventually, after numerous chimneys and bushwhacking, you'll emerge on the west ridge.
FA: Ron Perla and "Charlie Brown" Artman.

3. HIGHER EXPECTATIONS 5.9 R
A scary two pitch route that sneaks its way between the Standard Thumb and Indecent Exposure. From the belay at the top of the first pitch of Indecent Exposure, climb the face above passing two shaky pins, a bolt, and some scattered gear placements that take camming devices and stoppers.
FA: Tim Wolfe and Pete Carney, 1987.

THE THUMB ROUTES

4. INDECENT EXPOSURE VARIATION 5.7 ★★

A very highly recommended variation, since this avoids the worst sections of the Standard Thumb route.

FA: unknown.

5. FLABBERGASTER 5.11c ★

Cool moves on chickenheads. Gritty rock.

FA: Bret and Stuart Ruckman, 1990.

6. COYNE CRACK 5.11d ★★

A wincingly hard finger crack.

FA: Leonard Coyne, 1978.

7. S-CRACK III 5.8 A1 or 5.11d A0 or 5.12a ★★

Great! One hell of a bold undertaking for the first ascent. The second pitch can be protected by climbing a crack to the right of the chimney, protecting at its top, then downclimbing and tackling the chimney. The third pitch is highly logistical and can be climbed several ways. The first possibility is rated A.1. Aid up the left-facing corner for 20 feet, pendulum left, then aid up the start of the S-crack to the belay. The second option is 5.11d A.0. Free climb the left-facing corner, pendulum left, then free climb to the belay. The final option is a 5.12a squeaker, that free climbs from the belay past two bolts directly to the bottom of the S-Crack, then frees the S-Crack to the belay. For all of these options, don't get drawn into the bolt line to the right of the left-facing corner, which is an unfinished route. The fourth pitch groove is tricky to protect and wonderfully exposed.

FA: Steve Ellsworth, Mark McQuarrie and Ted Wilson, 1964. FFA: of the steep crack on the third pitch, Greg Lowe, late sixties! FFA: via bolt variation, Drew Bedford, 1986

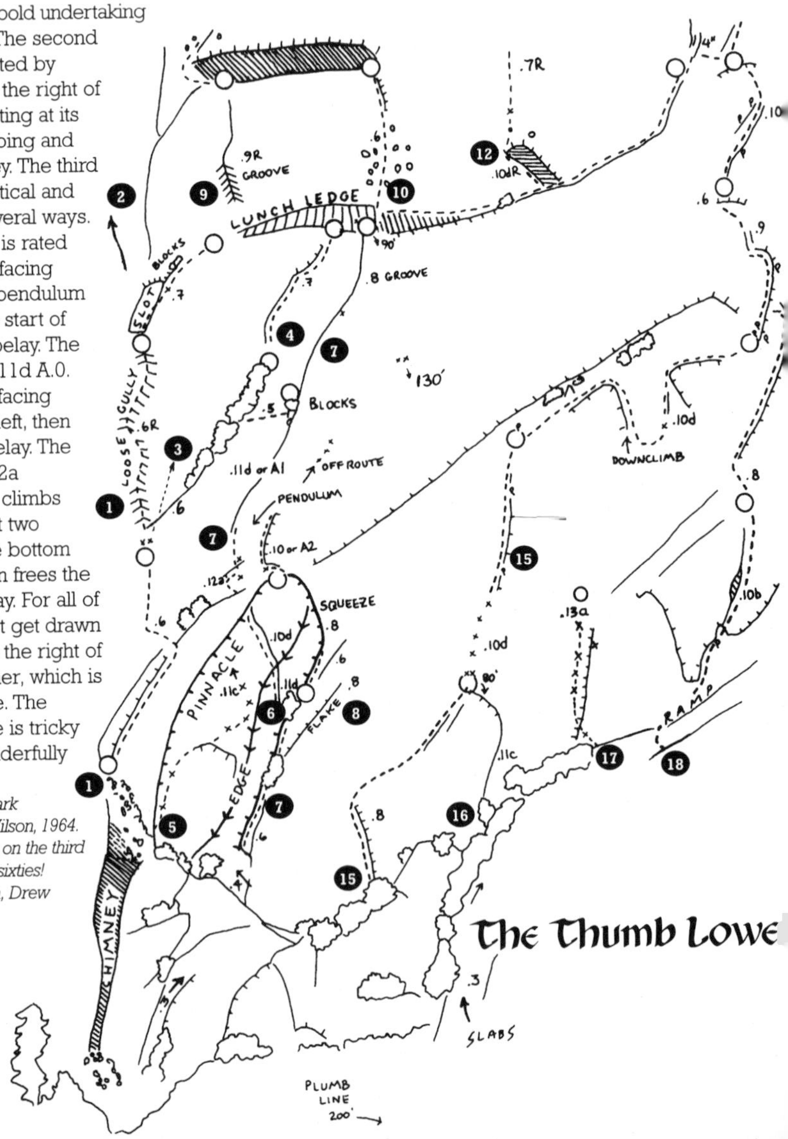

13 ROBBINS CRACK

TO SADDLE AND DESCENT

14 ON N. FACE IS 5.5 SUMMIT PITCH (1 - BOLT)

The Thumb Upper

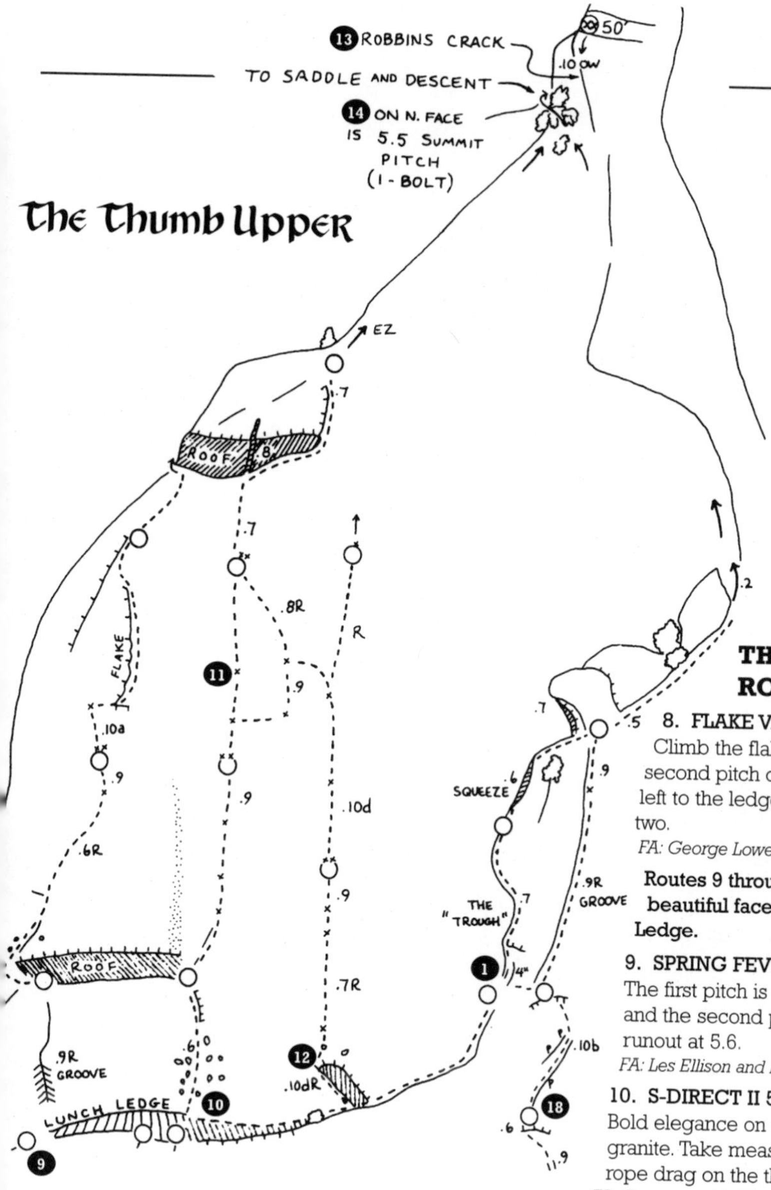

THE THUMB ROUTES

8. FLAKE VARIATION 5.8 R ★
Climb the flake to the right of the second pitch chimney and traverse left to the ledge at the top of pitch two.
FA: George Lowe.

Routes 9 through 12 climb the beautiful face above Lunch Ledge.

9. SPRING FEVER II 5.10a R ★
The first pitch is difficult to protect and the second pitch has a 60-foot runout at 5.6.
FA: Les Ellison and Brian Smoot, 1979.

10. S-DIRECT II 5.9+ R ★★★
Bold elegance on a sea of white granite. Take measures to minimize rope drag on the third, runout pitch.
FA: George and Jeff Lowe, 1967.

11. VARIATION 5.9 R ★
Continue straight above the first bolt of the third pitch; avoiding the traverse. The bolt that protects this variation was not placed by the first ascent party.
FA: Kelly McKeen, Merrill Bitter and Jeff Newsome, 1979, sans bolt..

12. NOB JOB II 5.10d R ★★
Very runout and stimulating. The initial overhang is protected by throwing a second rope over a chickenhead just above.
FA: Mugs Stump and Jack Roberts, 1977.

Routes 13 and 14 climb to the very summit of the Thumb.

13. ROBBINS' CRACK 5.10 ★
This is the offwidth crack on the west side of the Thumb pinnacle. Some large cams are handy.
FA: Royal Robbins and Ted Wilson, 1964.

14. SUMMIT PITCH 5.5 ★★

A one bolt route on the north side of the very summit pinnacle gains the top of the Thumb. A tree near the top of the Robbins' Crack provides an anchor for the fifty foot rappel to the west.

FA: Unknown.

Routes 15 through 18 are located back down on ground level, along the south and east flanks of the Thumb's base.

15. S-MATRIX II 5.10d ★★

Some bolts have been added to the second pitch. The third pitch is uniquely different.

FA: George Lowe, Pete Gibbs and Eric Eliason, 1968.
FFA: Brian Smoot and Mark Rolofson, 1979.

16. SPRING AND FALL 5.11c ★★

A crash course in difficult crack climbing. The first ascent party originally rated this climb 5.10!

FA: Kim Miller and Mark Ward, 1976.

17. MONKEY LIP 5.13a/b ★★

Very strenuous liebacking and face climbing.

FA: lower 5.12c section, Bobby Rotert and Steve Hong, 1982.
FA: of upper section, Dana Hauser, 1990.

18. ROBBINS' ROUTE III 5.10b ★

Four pitches of not-so-good rock. This route was however, the first 5.10 in the canyon. The twin paralleling cracks on the fourth pitch are thrilling and well-protected. The final groove pitch can be bypassed by traversing left into the Standard Thumb route.

FA: Royal Robbins and Ted Wilson, 1964.
FFA: George Lowe and Eric Eliason.

19. A LITTLE RAZZ-MA-TAZZ AND ALL THAT JAZZ 5.11d ★

This is located on the "old" approach to The Thumb. This boulder is hidden in the bushes below the western edge of The Waterfront Buttress. A faint trail heads down slope from here, and the route is in the trees to the west. Follow a hand-to-fist crack splitting a ten-foot roof.

FA: Merrill Bitter, 1981.

PLUMB LINE GULLY

Plumb Line is the striking south-facing crack that is passed on the way to The Thumb. The gully to its right has several routes on its steepest east-facing aspect, and even a couple on the scruffy west face (which is actually the left side of The Waterfront).

APPROACH: The Thumb approach is used to reach Plumb Line and the gully east of Plumb Line. Plumb Line climbs a perfect crack up a steep, featured face and should be easily identified. A short thrash up the gully 100 feet to the east will deposit the climber at Boomerang.

DESCENT: The route Hangman requires a walk down easy slabs to the west, while Gravity's Rainbow and Over the Rainbow Variation require two ropes for the descent. The remaining routes can all be descended with one rope.

PLUMB LINE GULLY ROUTES

1. ACUTE ANGLE VARIATION 5.9 R ★
Makes Plumb Line into a skewed line, but settles more favorably for many.
FA: Les Ellison and Doug Moffat, 1975.

2. PLUMB LINE 5.10a ★★
A great fingertips-to-thin hand crack. Rappel from two bolts at the top. Bring small wireds.
FA: Ted Wilson.
FFA: George Lowe, 1968.

3. ZOT 5.11d/12a R ★
Steep and technical face climbing right of Plumb Line. Three quickdraws and the mindset for a big runout are all you'll need for this knee-quaking lead.
FA: George Rosenthal and Tim Wolfe, 1988.

4. FILTHY GARBAGE 5.6
The wide crack near the right edge of the wall.

5. HANGMAN 5.9+ ★
Climb the flake right of Filthy Garbage via an overhanging hand crack, then slab climb past three closely-spaced bolts to a big ledge. Above the ledge, climb another flake to a belay. A bolt and a bashie protect the moderate prow on the final pitch.
FA: Kent Jameson, Pat Manley and Blayde Boyd, 1982.

6. GOLDLINE ARETE 5.11c ★
A four bolt arête climb above and right of the first pitch of Hangman. Although this climb has cool moves, the unclimbed blank section has forced a disappointingly short route.
FA: Kent Wheeler , Susan Ozaki 1993.

7. OVER THE RAINBOW VARIATION 5.10a ★
Start 70 feet downhill from Gravity's Rainbow. Climb a thin 10-foot flake, move right and into a right-facing corner system, ending at a small mahogany.
FA: Les Ellison and Dana Hauser, 1982.

PLUMB LINE GULLY ROUTES

8. GRAVITY'S RAINBOW II 5.11 A1 ★★

Gravity never sleeps. For those with a penchant for offwidths, grab the first lead—a flake starting 10 feet off the ground. The second pitch has one aid move on a bolt, skirting a blank section of rock. One more pitch leads to the top, where a 150-foot rappel off a mahogany provides escape.

FA: Les Ellison and Hank Armantrout, 1982.

9. BOOMERANG II 5.10a R ★★

The diagonalling finger crack on pitch one is "killer." The second pitch is long and difficult to protect. The descent is a single-rope rappel off a mahogany tree at the top.

FA: Les Ellison and Paul Scannel, 1980.

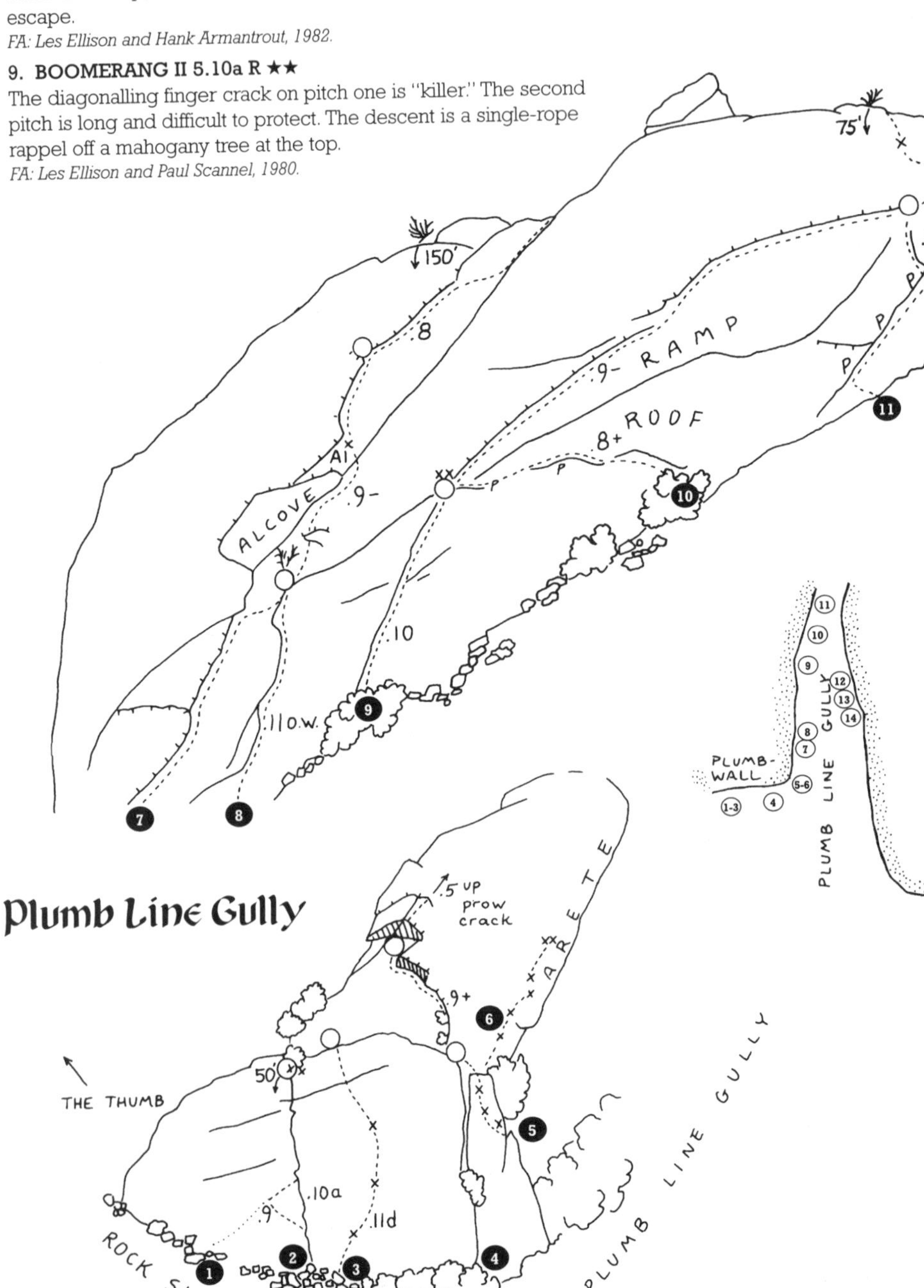

Plumb Line Gully

PLUMB LINE GULLY ROUTES

10. DOWN UNDER VARIATION 5.8+ R

A creative traverse left under a roof avoids the best pitch of Boomerang. It is no less scary following than leading.

FA: Les Ellison and Carl Buckland, 1982.

11. PINCHING CRISCO 5.12a ★

A slime-fest on a hot day. Originally called The Five Thirteen Crack by the first ascent party, this route joins the final section of Boomerang, and shares its descent.

FA: Steve Carruthers and Les Ellison, 1981.
FFA: Drew Bedford, 1985.

Routes 12 to 14 are found on the west-facing wall of the gully. The best descent for these routes is to traverse off to the north (or back toward the top of the gully).

12. FLASHPOINT VARIATION 5.6

As an alternate start, climb the right-slanting dihedral just left of Flash in the Pan.

FA: Les Ellison and Bret Ruckman, 1982.

13. FLASH IN THE PAN 5.8

A thin crack slants leftward and joins a dihedral. Follow this back rightward until a big crack through an overhang is reached. Climb the crack through the overhang and blaze to a belay in blocks and trees.

FA: Bret Ruckman and Les Ellison, 1982.

14. OCTOBERFEST 5.7

Hardly a celebration. This route climbs offwidths just right of Flash in the Pan. Climb a left-facing offwidth corner, jog left a bit and climb another off-width to a roof, which is then turned on its right side. Belay in blocks.

FA: Les Ellison and Gail Ellison, 1982.

THE WATERFRONT

This is a large buttress with a slabby lower section and an ominous overhanging upper section. It is located between the Plumb Line Gully and the Kermit's Wall Area. The upper half of The Waterfront yields few lines on its left, but leans more favorably towards its right end, allowing six routes. The lower half of the cliff is generally slabby, with the routes following steeper, more interesting anomalies.

APPROACH: The approach begins at the Gate Buttress parking area 1.25 miles up canyon from the neon sign. As you approach the first boulder at the Gate Boulders, follow the path that leads left (west). The trail climbs up and west above the Tower Boulder, along the base of a short slab. Take the lower fork here and follow the trail into the talus. The trail crosses the talus, then continues up and west until it meets the base of The Waterfront. In the first major gully to the right of The Waterfront you'll find Disco Duck and Disco Chicken. Both are about 100 feet up on the east face. In the winter, this wet area sometimes freezes up, producing the ice climb Cold Duck. Continue up this gully for another 350 feet to reach the routes on the upper right side of The Waterfront. See overview on pages 220 and 270.

DESCENT: For routes on the middle to left side of The Waterfront, walk west to the Plumb Line gully for descent. For the Disco Duck routes, rappel off bolts with a single rope. An 82 foot rappel just reaches the ground for the Beam Me Up Scotty routes. For routes 16 and 17, rappel off trees on the east side, near the top of Certain Death.

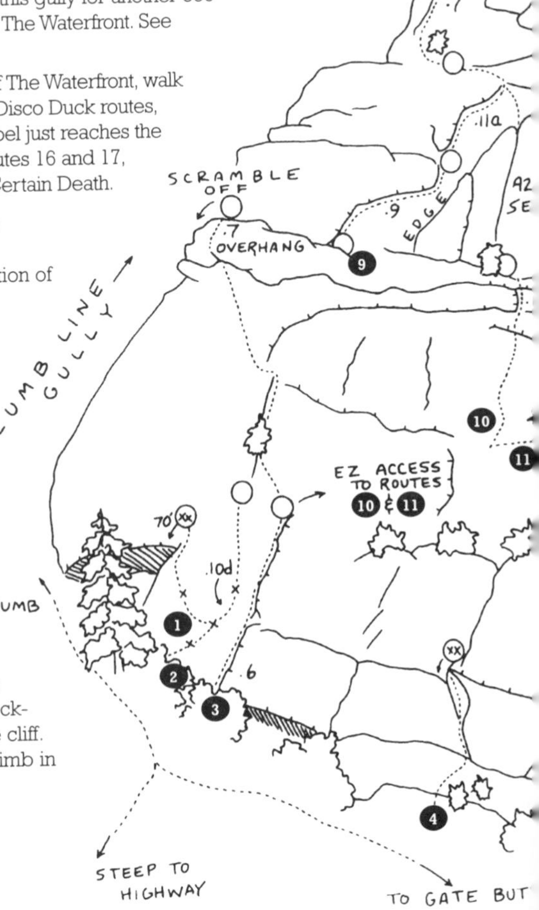

THE LOWER WATERFRONT

The following climbs are on the lower west portion of The Waterfront, just above the base.

THE LOWER WATERFRONT ROUTES

1. ACAPULCO ARETE 5.10b ★
Avoid the crux of Mantles to Mazatlan with this friction variation.
FA: John Maddux and John Hansen, 1995.

2. MANTLES TO MAZATLAN 5.10d ★★
The delicate smears above the abyss usually leave the leader wishing they were sipping suds down south.
FA: Chris Pendleton and Bret Ruckman, 1985.

3. CHICKENHEAD HOLIDAY 5.6 ★
The initial moves getting over the undercut are tricky. This route starts in a recess below a chockstone that impedes travel along the base of the cliff. Chickenhead Holiday was the first recorded climb in Little Cottonwood Canyon.
FA: Ted Wilson and Bob Stout, 1961.

THE LOWER WATERFRONT ROUTES

4. ON THE WATERFRONT 5.12a ★

This route climbs an overhanging crack up the right side of a dagger-like flake. Luckily, a bad bolt can be backed up by a large camming device. There is one big, burly move. The wide crack to the left probably has been climbed, but looks pretty funkadelic.

FA: Unknown.

5. DISCO DUCK 5.10A ★★

An awkward yet endearing animal. Be ready for some blind protection placements and wild chickenhead moves. See inset topo.

FA: Brad Gilbert and Jeff Alred, 1979.

6. DISCO CHICKEN 5.11a R ★

There are two possibilities after the last bolt: going straight up is hard and runout; moving left is more forgiving. Often wet. See inset topo.

FA: Bob Rotert and Tom McMillan, 1982.

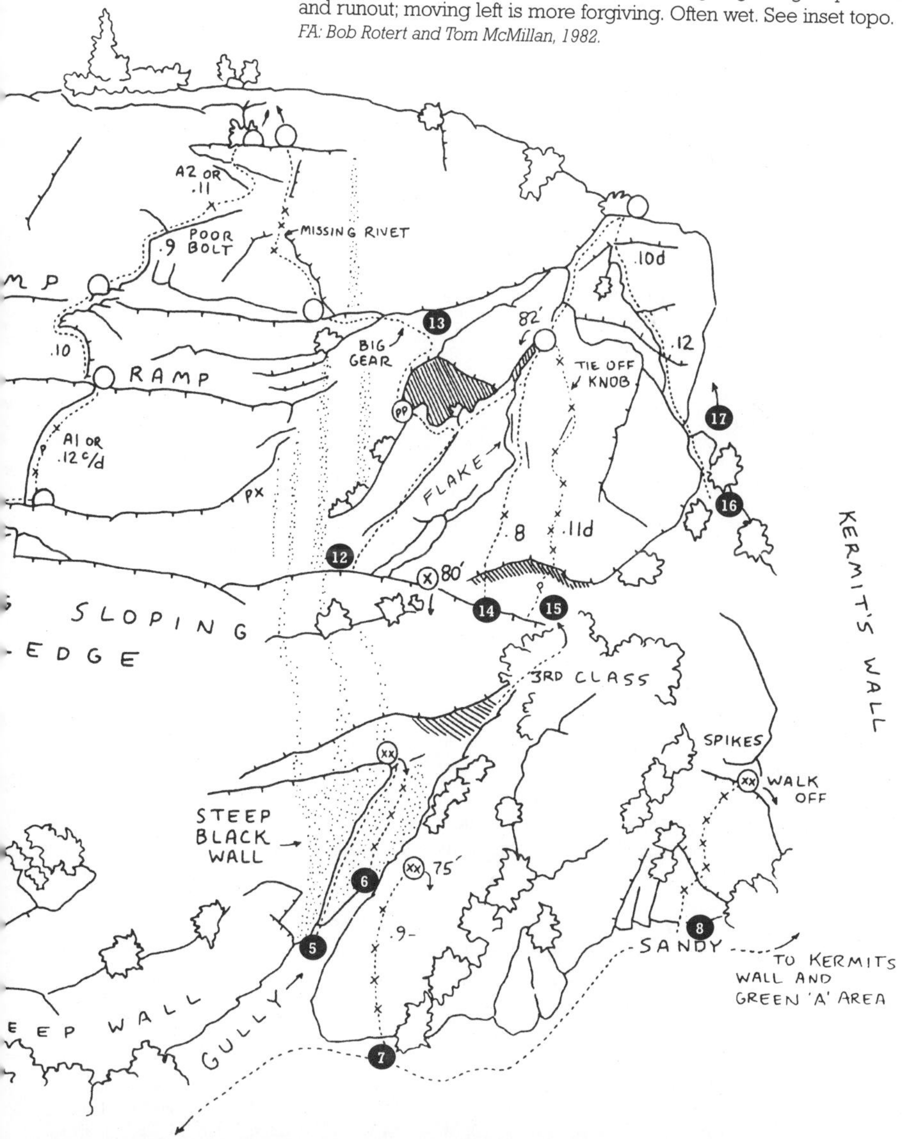

7. COMFORT ZONE 5.9- ★

About 30 feet east of the Disco Duck gully is a slab route with five bolts leading to a two-bolt belay/rappel. This route is 70 feet long and features friction, edges and the occasional chickenhead.

FA: Pat Contor, 1989.

8. BAREFOOT IN BARBADOS 5.10a ★

Halfway between Comfort Zone and the Kermit's Wall Area is a water-polished section of slab with a flat, sandy base. Climb past underclings to a foot intensive slab with five bolts. Walk off.

FA: Bret and Stuart Ruckman sans bolts, 1990.

UPPER WATERFRONT

The next routes are above the slabby mid-section of the cliff. Listed from left to right.

9. FLUID DYNAMICS VARIATION 5.11a ★

The first 5.9 section of this is an old variation to Chickenhead Holiday, first led by Ted Wilson. For Fluid Dynamics, continue with a rightward undercling, avoiding the belay for this 5.9 variation. Difficult protection.

FA: Mark Bennett and Bret Ruckman, 1985.

10. SEAMS LIKE THE SEASHORE III 5.10d A2+

This route explores the seam 100 feet left of Birdland. Mantel a knob and ascend a steep southwest-facing lieback/finger corner crack to a ledge and belay. Ease your way up the seam and join in with Fluid Dynamics to the left. Bring RP's, small angles, leepers and blades.

FA: Will Gilmer and James Garrett, 1985.

11. BIRDLAND or RIPCURL III 5.10 A2 R ★★ or 5.12c/d ★★

The original aid route was known as Birdland, a necky four-pitch line. Although all free now, aid ascents are still common. Climbed via aid or free moves, the final pitch sports difficult climbing off marginal protection. Ripcurl, rated 5.12c/d, is the name of second pitch climbed free—a worthy ascent in its own right.

FA: Jim Collinson, Paul Scannel and Les Ellison, 1980.
FFA: of second pitch (Ripcurl), John Storm, 1986.
FFA: of final pitch, Mark Bennett.

12. WATERFRONT CAVE 5.8

Crawl up the predominant dihedral under the huge roof in two 5.8 pitches.

FA: unknown

13. THE GOLDEN GATE A2+ ★

Traverse left out the big roof from The Cave to an exposed belay. Climb up and left again, making an improbable traverse to gain a belay at the base of the arch. Tricky climbing up and over the arch finishes things off. Bring LAs, baby angles, copperheads and steel nerves.

FA: Cameron Lawson, 1994.

14. JUST HANGING OUT 5.8 ★

A face with a bolt leads to a flake.

FA: Larry Carrol and Tom Burris, 1978.

15. BEAM ME UP SCOTTY 5.11d ★★★

Klingon to an archipelago of chickenheads 30 feet right of Just Hanging Out. This is located on the dominant slab near the right end of The Waterfront. Led from the ground up.

FA: Stuart Ruckman and Gordon Douglass, 1985.

16. UNCERTAIN DEATH (AKA Pope's Nose) 5.12a ★

Cracks on the upper east side with a tenuous face crux. Two pitches.

FA: Mark Ward and Hal Throolin, 1979.
FFA: Bob Rotert and Steve Hong, 1982.

17. CERTAIN DEATH 5.8 R

Offwidth aficionados will flock to this rarely-done offwidth/chimney system on the east face of The Waterfront. Bring protection to 6 inches and expect runouts.

FA: Eric Eliason, Cado Avenali and Pete Lev, 1972.

Kim Csizmazia over easy on Leggo My Eggo, The Egg.

photo: Kennan Harvey.

70'
.8
FLAKE
.9+
.9F
.9
70'
.9
FLAKE
.7
12a

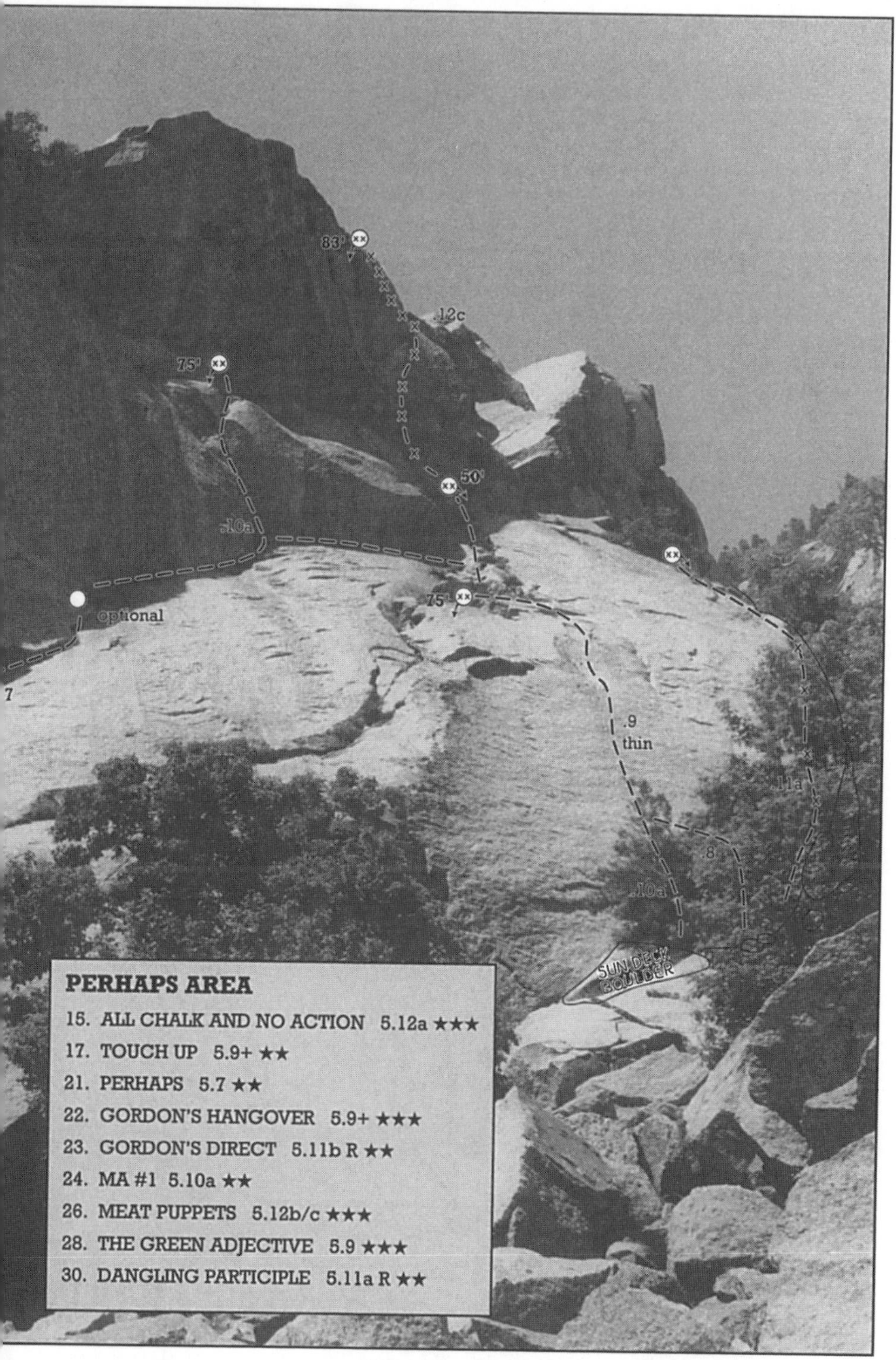
83'
.12c
75'
50'
.10a
optional
75'
7
.9
thin
.11a
8
.10a
SUN DECK BOULDER
PERHAPS AREA
15. ALL CHALK AND NO ACTION 5.12a ★★★
17. TOUCH UP 5.9+ ★★
21. PERHAPS 5.7 ★★
22. GORDON'S HANGOVER 5.9+ ★★★
23. GORDON'S DIRECT 5.11b R ★★
24. MA #1 5.10a ★★
26. MEAT PUPPETS 5.12b/c ★★★
28. THE GREEN ADJECTIVE 5.9 ★★★
30. DANGLING PARTICIPLE 5.11a R ★★

KERMIT'S WALL and PERHAPS AREA

This slabby playground is located on the leftmost (west) abutment of the Green Adjective Gully. Being mostly south-facing and warm, this cliff is amiable for much of the year. Summer shade makes for great afternoon and evening climbing.

APPROACH: Park 1.25 miles up canyon from the neon sign at the obvious pullout on either side of the road. A trail leaves the western (down canyon) end of the parking area and heads north into the trees. As you approach the first boulder at the Gate Boulders, follow the path that leads left (west). The trail climbs up and west above the Tower Boulder, along the base of a short slab, to a slippery lieback between two boulders. Above this challenge, the trail continues straight up, then moves into the boulderfield near the right (east) edge of a large slab. Traverse left (west) on ledges above the slab into the next boulderfield. Walk directly up this talus, roughly paralleling the buttress on the right, until several large boulders form an impass. Cracks and ledges on the right (east) wall of this impass allow for some third class climbing to reach the top of the boulder. Walk directly across the top of this boulder, then straight up through a bit more talus to reach the Sun Deck boulder at the base of The Green Adjective. Or from the top of the boulder walk straight across more talus to reach the bottom of Perhaps. From Perhaps, walk downhill through more talus to reach a flat spot at the base of Kermit's Wall. See overview on page 290.

DESCENT: Single rope rappels work for all routes in this area with the exception of Paranoia Streak and Koyaanisqaatsi. For Paranoia Streak a single rope rappel is possible, but some downclimbing (5.3) is involved. Koyaanisqaatsi requires two ropes or scramble down to the anchors at the top of Paranoia Streak.

KERMIT'S WALL ROUTES

1. BOTTLENECK 5.4

The chimney system on the left side of Kermit's Slab.

FA: Unknown.

2. BEAVER'S CLEAVER 5.10

Somewhat contrived.

FA: Les Ellison and Carl Buckland, 1982.

3. PARANOIA STREAK 5.10c R ★★★

What a route! The fact that it all links together is remarkable. Healthy runouts. Bring gear up to 2 inches for the upper crack.

FA: Bill Cramer and Hank Armantrout, 1982.

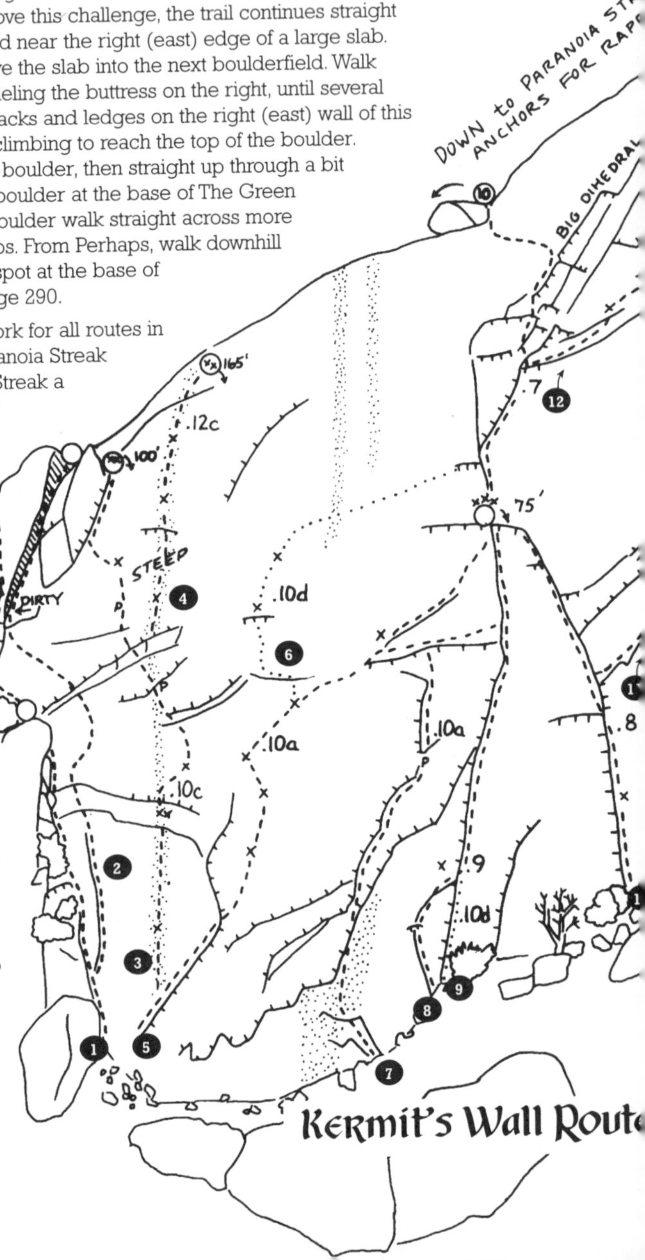

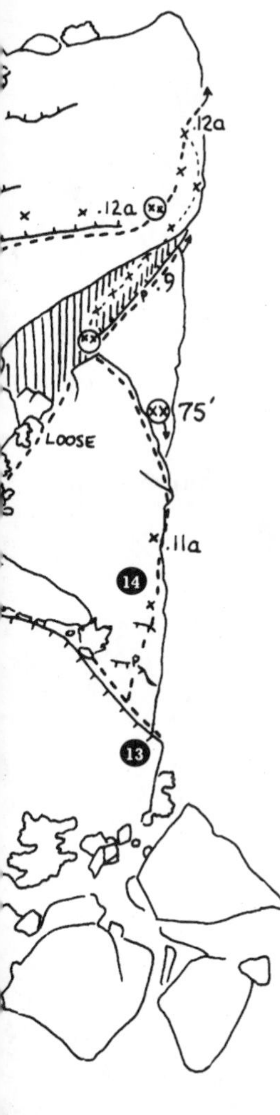

4. KOYAANISQAATSI (Life out of balance) 5.12c ★★
An unusual trick was used on the first ascent: Because the rope weight was such a burden at the crux, an overhand bite was tied into the rope above the top piece of protection, creating a loop of slack. With the advantage of pulling only 15 feet of rope in lieu of 150 feet, and with a greatly-increased fall potential, the first ascent was made.
FA: John Storm, 1987.

5. KERMIT'S WAD 5.10a ★★
A fun route that you'll find yourself doing over and over again. Small nuts and a long runner provide protection in the initial corner.
FA: Unknown.

6. KERMIT'S DIRECT VARIATION 5.10d ★
This offers much steeper face climbing.
FA: Lynn Wheeler and Doug Heinrich, 1982.

7. CENTERFOLD 5.10c R ★
This is often wet. It has fixed protection that should be considered suspect.
FA: Les Ellison and Bill Simmons, 1982.

8. SMITTY'S WET DREAM 5.9 ★★
The slick nature of the rock gives away few holds, but just enough with the correct sequence.
FA: Mark Smith and Brent Jarvis, 1980.

9. LIME LINE VARIATION 5.10d ★
Start 10 feet to the right of Smitty's, in a steep dihedral.
FA: Kent Jameson, Blayde Boyd and Ken Gygi, 1980.

10. CRANIAL PROPHYLACTIC 5.8 ★★
A good finger crack with one touchy move required. The bolt was not added by the first ascent party, but has arrested many a fall.
FA: Kim Miller and Dave Smith, 1976.

11. CINDERBLOCK VARIATION 5.8
A poor way to start Tender Touch because of the loose rock.
FA: Les Ellison, Fred Fisher and Patricia Lambrose, 1978.

12. LEND ME A DIME 5.12a ★★
Many climbers just climb out to the hanging belay, where a 100-foot rappel to the ground is possible. Save some spare change for the unbelievable second pitch, which features imminent exposure and layaways on flexi-flakes (four bolts on the second pitch).
FA: Pat Contor and Gary Taylor, 1989.

13. TENDER TOUCH 5.9
Fifty feet right of Cranial is a flake that leads leftward to a ledge, and eventually to loose blocks. The second pitch continues up the nice corner system until a traverse left (beyond Touch Up's second-pitch flake) is possible.
FA: Les Ellison, Fred Fischer and Pat Lambrose, 1978.

14. REVENGE OF THE NERDS 5.11a R ★
Climb the left side of the arête that forms the left wall of Perhaps. Some moves are right on the edge. The top bolt was placed while hanging on a shaky hook – hence its weird location.
FA: Chris Pendleton and Steve Britt, 1986.

PERHAPS AREA ROUTES

15. ALL CHALK AND NO ACTION 5.12a ★★★

Vertical, well-protected face climbing on clean edges make for a classic test piece.

FA: Stuart Ruckman, 1987.

16. PROJECT

When completed, this climb should be 5.13b.

17. TOUCH UP 5.9+ ★★

This can be pumpy. Remember that a serious swing back into the dihedral on the first-pitch hand traverse is a real possibility if not properly protected. The flake on the second pitch, seemingly a ditto of the first-pitch flake, is airy and balancey.

FA: Mark Bennett and Audrey Huerta, 1980.

18. PERHAPS NOT 5.11c R ★

Go out Touch Up a few moves, then move right and up into the small corner.

FA: Stuart Ruckman, 1987, sans bolts.

19. TEMPORARY SANITY 5.11a ★

This is a direct finish to Tender Touch. TCU's are helpful just before the final bolt. Good moves, fair rock.

FA: Pat Contor and Gary Taylor, 1989.

20. ORIGINAL START TO GORDON'S HANGOVER 5.9+ ★★

Continue straight up the Perhaps corner proper, and join in with Gordon's Hangover.

FA: Don Black and Pete Gibbs, 1974.

21. PERHAPS 5.7 ★★

The first pitch traverses right at the fixed pin on the right wall. This presents the route's crux; it is a good idea to secure some protection in between the fixed pin and the two-bolt belay anchor to avoid a 20-foot pendulum if the second climber should happen to fall. The second pitch is all of 160 feet, and can have heinous rope drag—consider using the optional hanging belay.

FA: Dave Boyd and Dave Smith, 1970.

22. GORDON'S HANGOVER 5.9+ ★★★

Thrilling lieback and jam moves, certain to awaken the senses.

FA: Unknown.

23. GORDON'S DIRECT 5.11b R ★★

A must-do route that requires some insightful climbing. Height is an issue at the crux. A few micro nuts protect the initial moves.

FA: Don Black, Pete Gibbs, 1974.
FFA: Steve Hong, Karin Budding and Steve Carruthers, 1985.

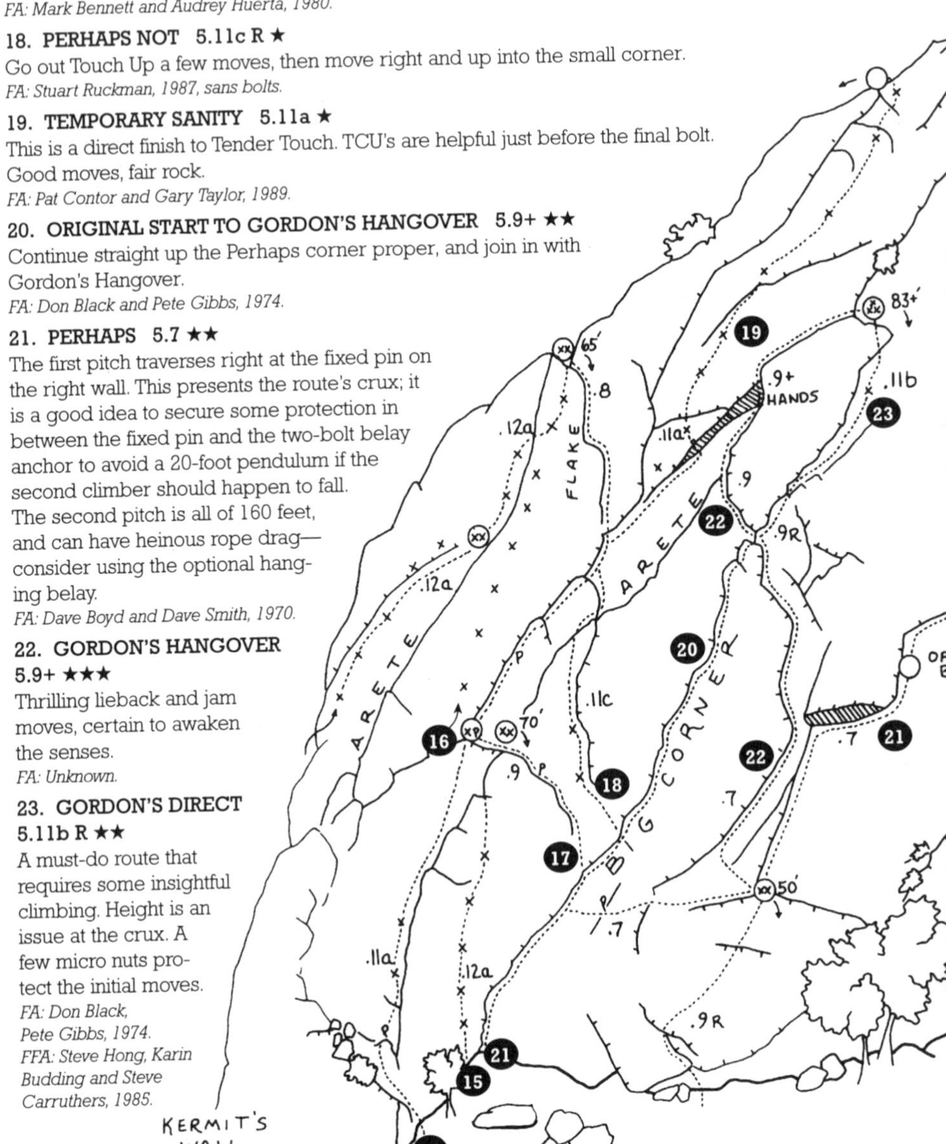

24. MA #1 5.10a ★★

Holds on the left edge of the initial corner help immeasurably. The second pitch, though worthwhile, is only occasionally climbed due to some rotten rock at the top and a more difficult descent.
FA: Rick Bradshaw and Dave Jenkins, 1978.

25. ADVERBIAL TRAVERSE 5.10a ★
Climb up to the first bolt on Meat Puppet, then traverse left underneath the huge headwall to the belay on MA #1. Bring along gear, including medium sized TCUs. A few holds big enough for just one hand are exciting, to say the least.
FA: Andy Howe and Scott Hinton, 1994.

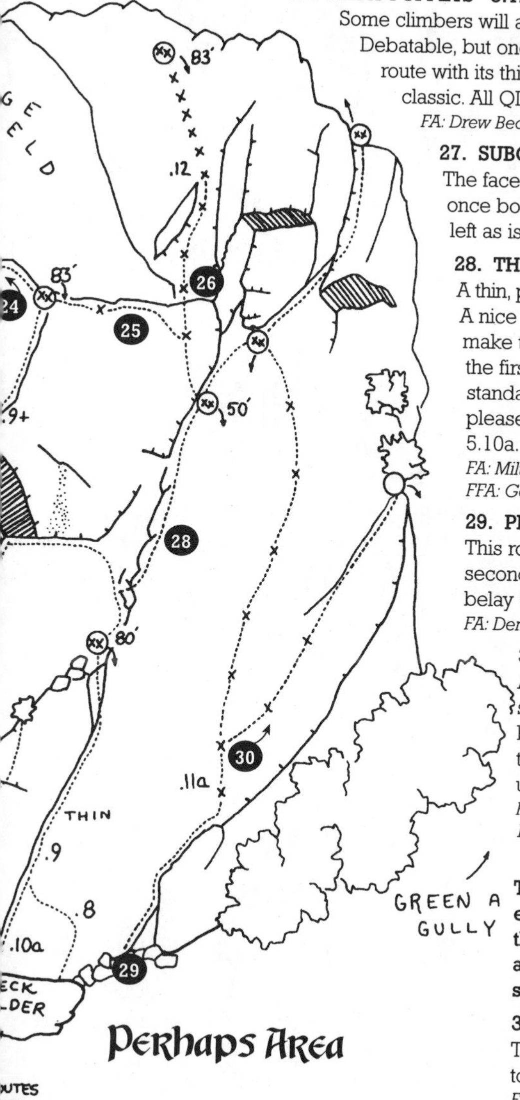

26. MEAT PUPPETS 5.12b/c ★★★
Some climbers will argue that this is the best route in the canyon. Debatable, but one thing everybody agrees upon is that this route with its thin face climbing and exposed position is a classic. All QDs.
FA: Drew Bedford, 1988.

27. SUBORDINATE CLAWS 5.9 R ★
The face immediately left of the Green A. This was once bolted and then chopped; the face should be left as is. Commonly toproped.

28. THE GREEN ADJECTIVE 5.9 ★★★
A thin, pin-scarred crack splitting impeccable granite. A nice porch at its base and southern exposure make this show a sellout. Most climbers merely do the first pitch. It takes small nuts for protection. A standard rack is needed for the rest. No pins, please. The direct start on the first pitch is rated 5.10a. Also, see topo page 292.
FA: Milt Hokanson, Court Richards and Ralph Tingey, 1965.
FFA: George Lowe.

29. PREPOSITIONAL PHRASE 5.11a ★
This route departs from Dangling Participle at its second bolt and heads straight up the face to a belay 60 feet above the first pitch of the Green A.
FA: Dennis Turville.

30. DANGLING PARTICIPLE 5.11a R ★★
A mantel gone awry prompts the name. A seconding climber could potentially take a big swing, especially after unclipping from the second bolt. A mahogany tree 150 feet up provides the belay and rappel.
FA: Ed Webster, Jay Wilson and Susan Patenaude, 1981.

The following two routes are located on an enormous boulder seventy-five feet down the talus from the Sun Deck boulder. They are found on the south face, and can be seen on the approach march.

31. FAT BOY 5.12a ★
This is the left line, the one that doesn't look too bad, until you touch the holds...
FA: Douglas Heinrich, 1995.

32. THE DREAMSCAPE (PROJECT)
The right line on the boulder.

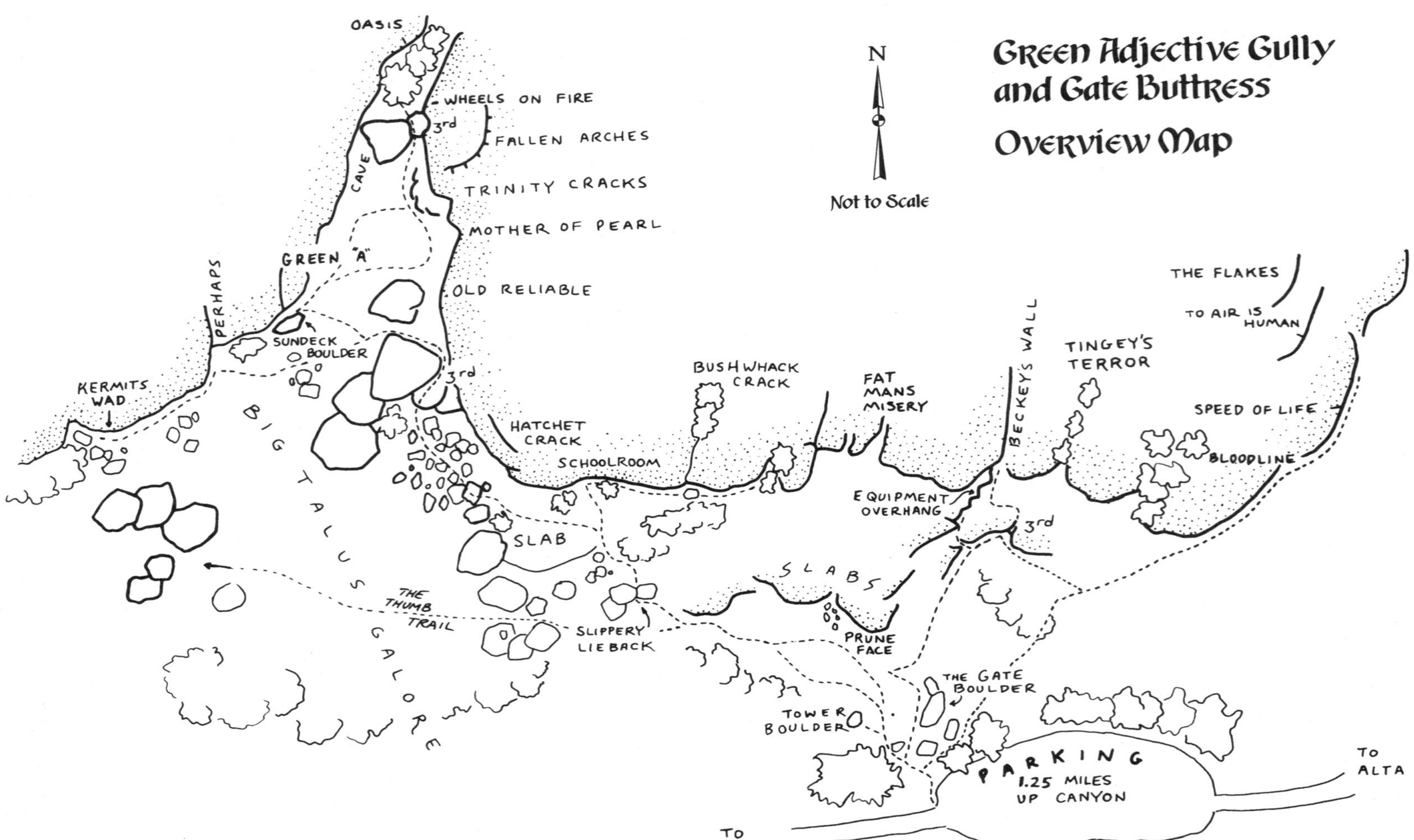
Green Adjective Gully and Gate Buttress Overview Map
N
Not to Scale
OASIS
WHEELS ON FIRE
3rd
FALLEN ARCHES
CAVE
TRINITY CRACKS
MOTHER OF PEARL
GREEN "A"
OLD RELIABLE
PERHAPS
SUNDECK BOULDER
3rd
KERMITS WAD
BIG TALUS GALORE
HATCHET CRACK
SCHOOLROOM
BUSHWHACK CRACK
FAT MANS MISERY
BECKEY'S WALL
TINGEY'S TERROR
THE FLAKES
TO AIR IS HUMAN
SPEED OF LIFE
BLOODLINE
EQUIPMENT OVERHANG
3rd
SLAB
SLABS
THE THUMB TRAIL
SLIPPERY LIEBACK
PRUNE FACE
THE GATE BOULDER
TOWER BOULDER
PARKING
1.25 MILES UP CANYON
TO ALTA
TO

THE GREEN ADJECTIVE GULLY

This gully, with its shade and vertical walls, has a special character. In the summer, this gully provides hours of stupendous climbing before the sun strikes. Most of the routes here are steep—in fact, much steeper and more continuous than most of the Gate Buttress. Therefore, the free climbing is some of the most difficult in the Wasatch.

APPROACH: Follow the approach description for the Kermit's Wall and Perhaps Area, page 286 to the Sun Deck Boulder at the base of The Green Adjective route. From here, a faint trail heads up the left (west) side of the gully. After several hundred feet, the path forks. Continue straight up the left side of the gully for routes 1 to 21. To approach the Green Adjective Gully West Face, cut across to the right (east) side of the gully from here. Continue up the right side of the gully from the base of Catalyst to reach the Trinity Cracks and Wheels on Fire Area. The actual base of Wheels on Fire requires a short section of water polished third class chockstones to be negotiated. See overview on page 290.

DESCENT: It is possible to rappel off all the routes in this area with one rope with the exception of Mother of Pearl, on the Lower West Face, which requires two ropes. However, to avoid making two rappels, many climbers use two ropes to rappel from the top of Nip and Tuck and Old Reliable as well. A scramble down to the top of the Schoolroom Rappel can also be made from the top of these three routes.

For routes on the Lower and Upper East Faces that do not have anchors at their finish, walk down the slabs just west of the top of the gully to reach the anchors at the top of the last pitch of the Green Adjective. From here three single rope rappels reach the ground.

GREEN ADJECTIVE GULLY —LOWER EAST FACE

1. THIS IS ALMOST THE PLACE 5.11d
Struggle with the awkward right-slanting crack 100 feet around the corner from the start of The Green Adjective. Not on topo.
FA: Steve Hong and Karin Budding, 1983.

2. SURPRISE BEGINNING 5.11d ★
The route just left of Stranger Than Friction, with a horrendous start.
FA: Gary Taylor and Susan Ashley, 1988.

3. STRANGER THAN FRICTION 5.10d ★
Flash the initial moves and continue past two more bolts and a pin.
FA: Gary Taylor, Pat Contor, Susan Ashley and Nancy Cohn, 1988.

4. SURPRISE ENDING 5.11b ★
A difficult and quality face route left of the final offwidth pitch of Goodro's Nightmare.
FA: Stuart Ruckman and Gordon Douglass, 1988.

5. GOODRO'S NIGHTMARE 5.8
The highlight of this route is an offwidth. It starts in a right-facing flake.
FA: Jonathan Smoot, Brian Smoot and Terry Lein, 1980.

6. DIVINE INTERVENTION II 5.6 A3 ★★
This explores the zig-zagging ultra-thin cracks on the prow above and right of the final pitch of Goodro's Nightmare. Bring faith, KBs, LAs, and baby angles.
FA: Brian Smoot and Rich Carlston, 1983.

7. CREEP SHOW 5.10 ★
Protection to five inches is mighty handy. Join the Butterfield Route or rig a rappel.
FA: Brian Smoot and Hank Armantrout, 1983.

8. CRASH TEST DUMMY A2+ ★
A wild aid line that comes to grips with the roof above Creep Show. Bring along a selection of KBs, LAs, hooks, and a two foot cheat stick—or have a good lasso arm.
FA: Cameron Lawson, 1994.

9. BUTTERFIELD ROUTE 5.7
FA: Ken Butterfield and partner, 1976.

10. NOSTRUM II 5.8 A2 ★
This route will ready you for Yosemite walls. The first pitch is awkward and has difficult protection. Bring a selection of pins – from knifeblades to baby angles and include some heads.
FA: Lynn Wheeler and Les Ellison, 1980.

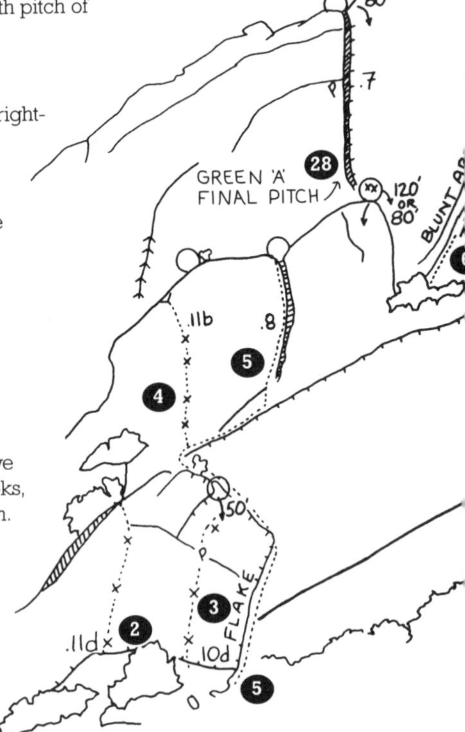

11. BLANK GENERATION II 5.9 A2+ ★★
At the top of the ramp, 30 feet right of the start of Nostrum, climb past two studs and into an ultra-thin crack. More studs, hook moves, head placements and etc., lead up a left-facing dihedral to a belay. From the top of the dihedral carry on to the top of the wall.
FA: Drew Bedford, 1988.

12. HEM LINE A1 TR ★
A difficult aid seam that requires heads, KBs, and hooks. A grade of A3+ has been suggested for the first successful lead. A potential ground fall guards the start.

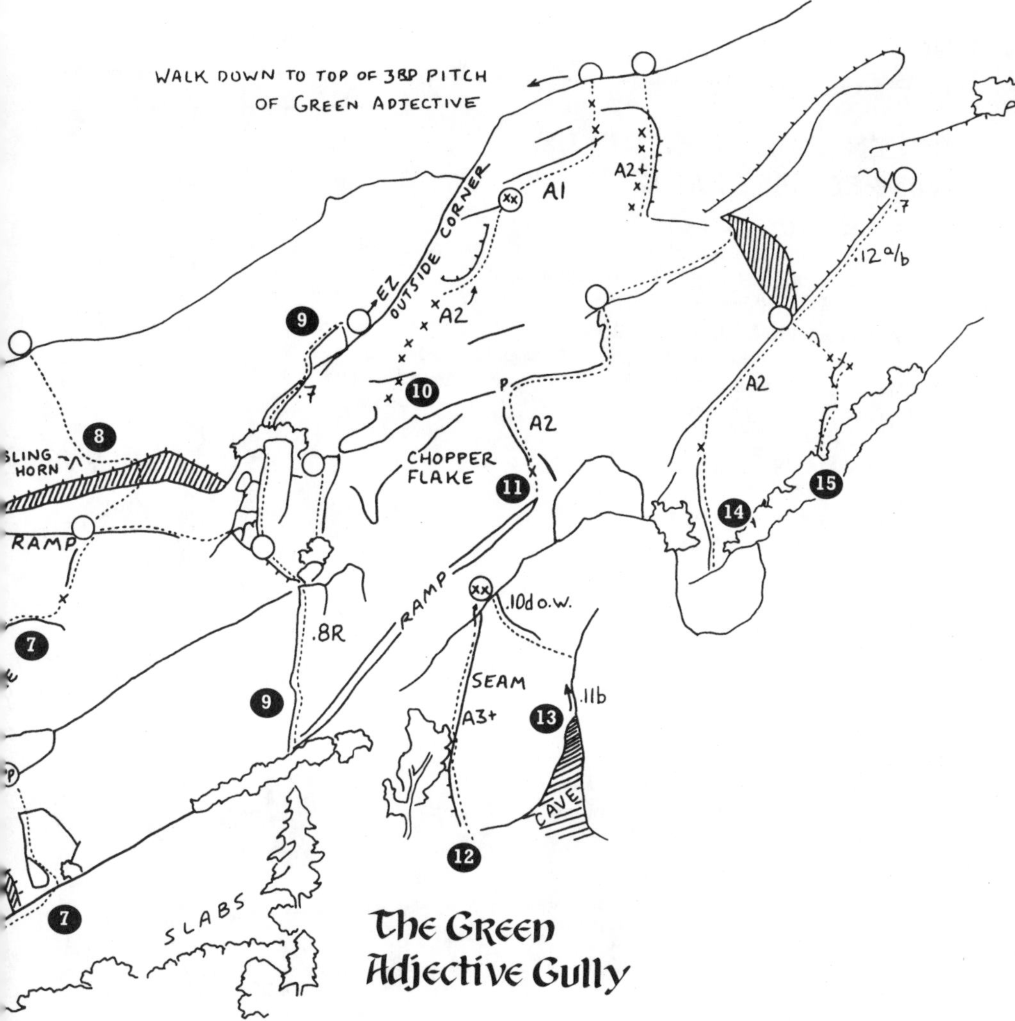

13. STORMY RESURRECTION 5.11b ★

Climb the overhanging thin crack on the west wall of the cave, throw into a stem near its apex, then continue on a hand traverse leftward. The traverse turns offwidth at the top.

FA: unknown

FFA: John Storm and Bret Ruckman, Easter 1986.

14. EVE TRAVERSE 5.12b A2 ★★

Two pitches of diagonalling madness. The first pitch is aid (usually protected with a knifeblade or two), but can be climbed mostly clean once the traverse is reached. The second pitch requires a mastery of thin finger cracks and mucho endurance (or more aid climbing).

FA: Brian Smoot and Jonathan Smoot, 1978.

FFA of second pitch: Lance Bateman and Ben Folsom, 1993.

15. AGAINST THE GRAIN A2+ ★★

A stout undertaking that climbs a direct line to join the first belay of Eve Traverse. A quiver of KBs, LAs, heads and hooks is necessary.

FA: Brandon Prince and Ben Folsom, 1993.

GREEN ADJECTIVE GULLY —UPPER EAST FACE

16. SINSEMILLA CRACK 5.10 ★★

Depending on hand size, this is either a cruise or a bad trip. Most climbers rappel off two pins at the top of the difficult section.

FA: Doug Madera and Jeff Butterfield, 1980.

17. DAWDLING PIGALOTTOS 5.10d ★

Start 5 feet right of the base of the Sinsemilla rappel (i.e. 30 feet from Sinsemilla's start). One full set of cams (with double in the 2" size) and medium nuts are recommended.

FA: Mark Allgood and Jim Kutsko, 1989.

18. FAT WOMAN'S MISERY 5.8

A squeeze.

FA: Rick Wyatt, Brian Smoot and Jonathan Smoot, 1978.

19. A NIGHT AT THE OPERA 5.8 ★

Climb the outside edge of a dihedral right of Fat Woman's Misery. There are five pitches. Bring micro nuts for the first pitch.

FA: Bill Robins and Kristen Davis, 1985.

20. GARDEN SONG 5.10d

Climb the corner right of A Night at the Opera.

FA: Bill Robins and Kristen Davis.
FFA: Bill Robins and Brian Smoot.

21. OASIS 5.11b ★★

There is no oasis on the difficult upper slab.

FA: Jonathon and Brian Smoot, 1982.
FFA: Drew Bedford and Mark Bennett, 1985-6

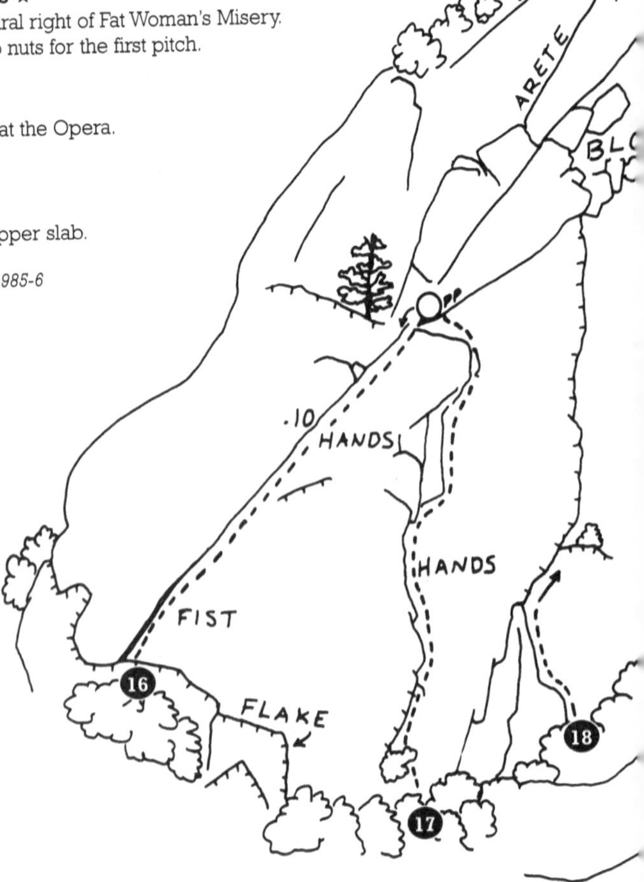

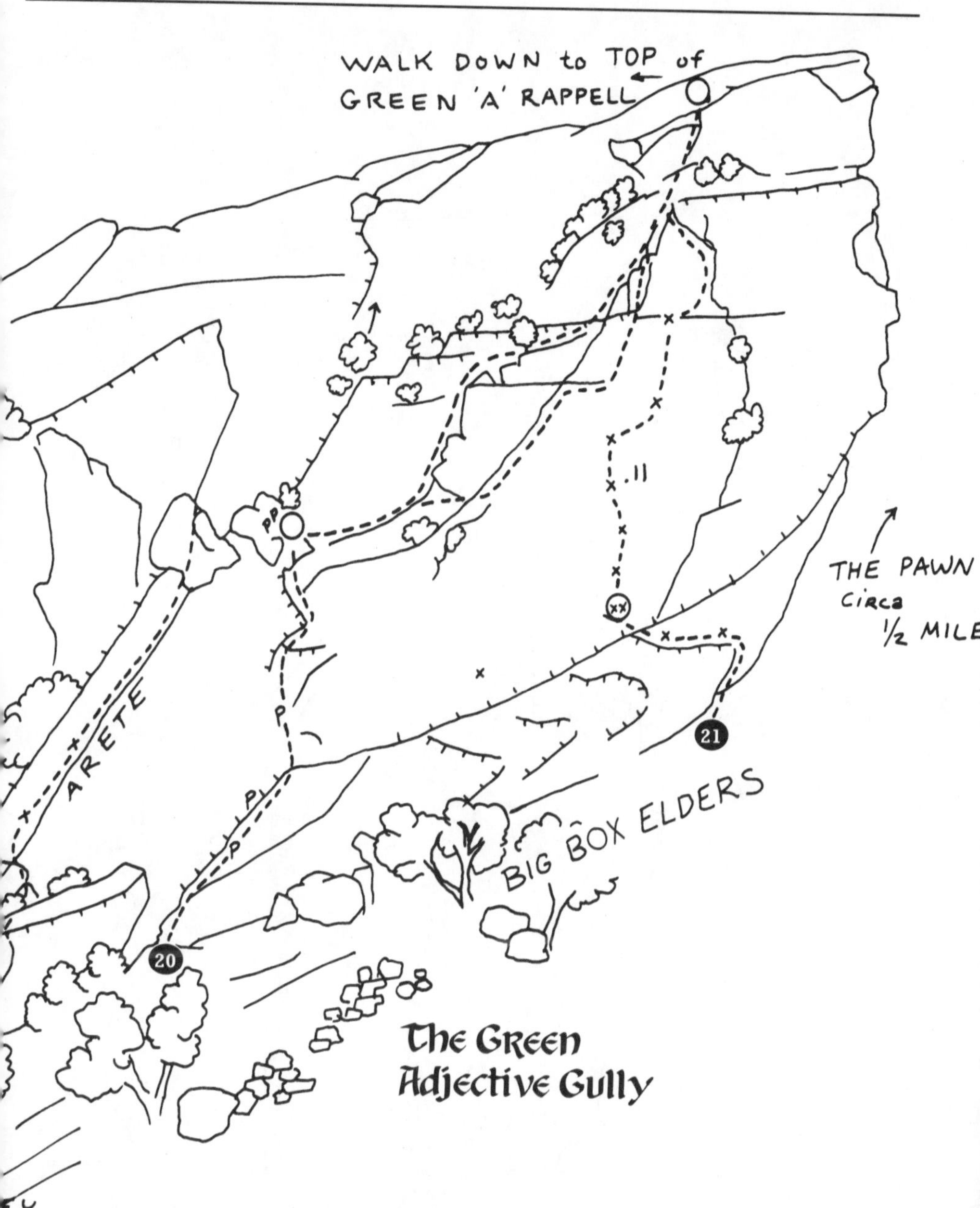

The Green Adjective Gully

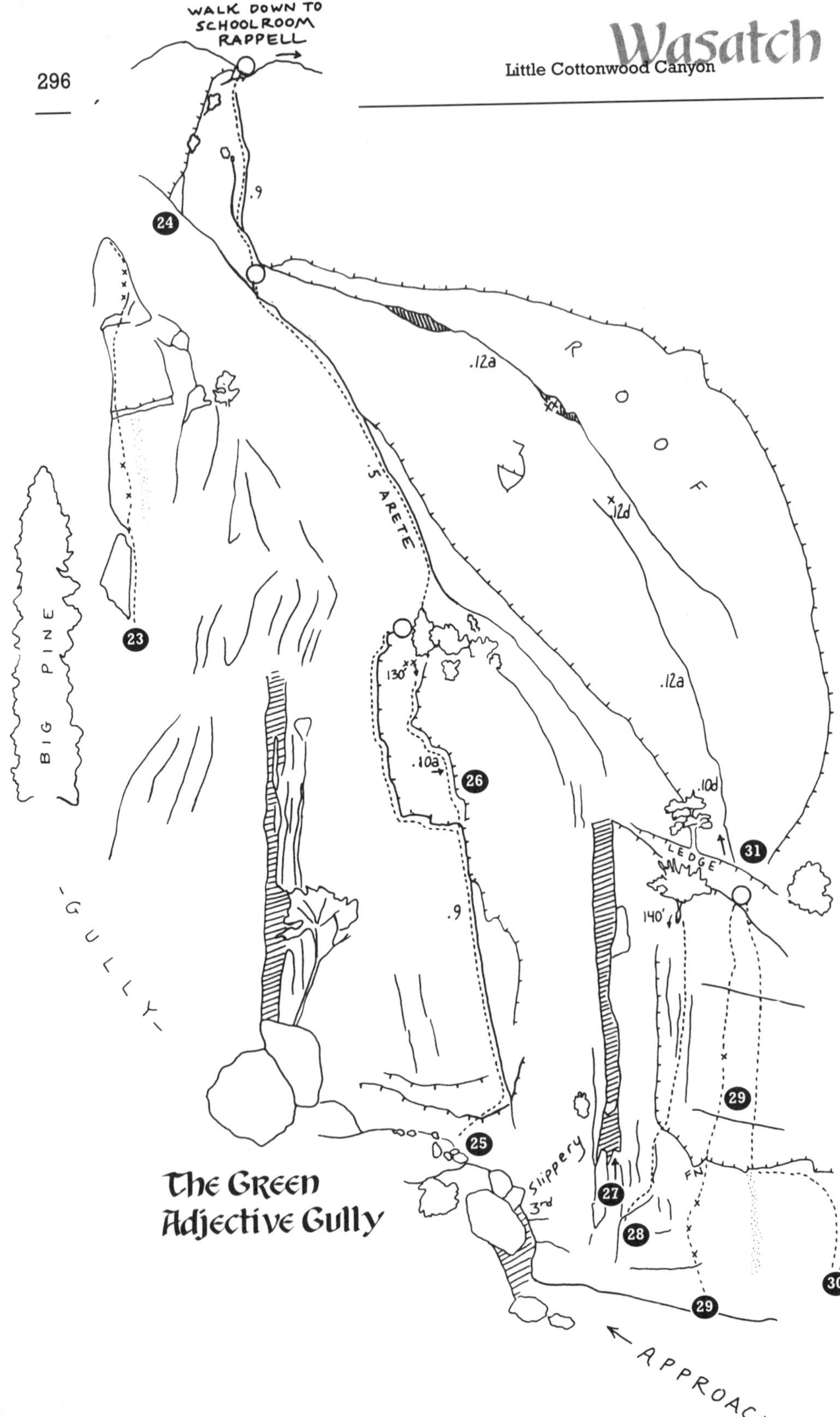

The Green Adjective Gully

THE GREEN ADJECTIVE GULLY —UPPER WEST FACE

UPPER WEST FACE ROUTES

22. NIPPLE REMOVER 5.9
FA: Rick Wyatt and Dave Jenkins, 1978.

23. UNKNOWN 5.11
Little is known about this route.

24. CRAZED AND CONFUSED 5.10a
The harbinger of snafus to come?
FA: Bill Robins, 1985.

25. WHEELS ON FIRE 5.9 ★★
This zingy route is popular despite its long approach. Good rock and continuous climbing.
FA: Lynn Wheeler, Jeff Alred and Brad Gilbert, 1978.

26. WHEELS ON FIRE DIRECT 5.10a ★
Fun liebacking that avoids the leftward traverse on Wheels On Fire.
FA: Mark Smith, Les Ellison and Chris Noble, 1980.

27. SOLO SLOT 5.6
FA: Unknown.

28. VICTORY GARDENS 5.10
Two pins on the face to the right of Solo Slot.
FA: Les Ellison and Tito Black, 1985.

29. PINS, BASHIES, MATCHES AND BEER 5.11b ★
Delicate climbing up weaknesses in the center of the wall. Although some gear is fixed, bring along a healthy selection of small to medium wires and cams.
FA: Jamie Kanzler, Jim Edwards, Cory Andersen, and Randy Kielszewski.

30. ST. ALPHONSO'S PANCAKE BREAKFAST 5.9+
FA: Callum Hudson and Paul Peterson, 1978.

31. FALLEN ARCHES 5.13a/b ★★★
The all-time classic of the Wasatch. Steve Hong says of Fallen Arches, "The nice thing about it is that it is long enough to give you a nice pump, and not one of these short little things that are too hard to leave the ground on!" Because it faces northwest, it doesn't receive much sun until mid-afternoon in the summer. The approach pains can be lessened by doing warm-up climbs along the way.
FA: Mark Ward and Jim Langdon,
FAA: Steve Hong and Bob Rotert, 1985. Done in two pitches.
FAA: Dan Goodwin, 1985. Done in one pitch.

GREEN ADJECTIVE GULLY —LOWER WEST FACE

32. WHY ME? 5.10d

This wide, overhanging crack with a bolt is 80 feet up the ramp from the Trinity Cracks. Belay at a bolt and tree. Bring a 3" or 4" cam.

FA: Dana Hauser, 1989.

33. TRINITY LEFT 5.12d ★★★

Superb, and way up there in difficulty. An unequivocal pump!

FA: Mugs Stump and Randy Trover, 1978.
FFA: Steve Hong, Steve Carruthers and Karin Budding, 1985.

34. CENTER TRINITY (AKA HOLY GHOST) 5.13a ★★★

Gorilla climbing and bizarre sequences must be used if you want to stand a ghost of a chance. Start on Trinity Left.

FA: Jim Dockery and Lynn Wheeler, 1975.
FFA: John Storm, 1988.

35. TRINITY RIGHT (AKA CATWALK) 5.12a ★★★

Again, start on Trinity Left. A lunge for the belay slings isn't uncommon. A second pitch has been added, with two bolts protecting grooves above the hanging belay.

FA: Steve Carruthers and Gary Olsen, 1985.
FFA: Steve Hong, Karin Budding and Steve Carruthers, 1985.
FA second pitch: Steve Carruthers and Glen Burke, 1989.

36. MOTHER OF PEARL 5.11c ★★★

This can be broken into three-, two- or one-pitch ascents. Of course, if done in one 140-foot pitch, it is the hardest. A regular assortment of nuts, with plenty of QD's and runners, will suffice. Small wireds help protect one barn-door lieback section in the middle. This brilliant climb is frequently wet. Start on Looney Tunes.

FA: Les Ellison and Doug Moffat, 1976.
FFA: Merrill Bitter, 1983.

37. LOONEY TUNES 5.11b R ★★

This one is hardly a chuckle. A groundfall is possible until an obvious nut placement 20 feet off the deck is attained and clipped. A 3½" cam works well on the initial moves.

FA: Paul Peterson and Jim Dockery, 1974.
FFA: Brad Gilbert, Lynn Wheeler and Jeff Alred, 1980.

38. BADLANDS 5.12a ★

A strenuous lieback is topped by a 6-1/2-foot stem to a finger crack that passes through a roof.

FA: Drew Bedford and Seth Shaw, 1985.

Rockfall in the winter of '98 eliminated routes 39 to 43.

39. CATALYST 5.10c ★★

A disconcerting undercling starts things off, followed by a strenuous lieback. Rope drag seems inevitable.

FA: Jeff Alred and Les Ellison, 1977.

40. NIP AND TUCK 5.12b ★★

Sporting a powerful layaway section, and tenuous face climbing, this route has metamorphosed from a shaky aid line to a test-piece free line. Bolts and gear.

FA: Les Ellison and Chris Noble, 1979.
FFA: Lance Bateman, 1992.

140'
.11a
.12d
34
.13a
35
.11c
35
.12a
.11c
33
.12a
60'
39
.10a
38
8
65'
36
55'
.12b
.12b/c
.10
40
.11b
37
.10c
39
41

41. OLD RELIABLE 5.10d R ★★
A dicey start with little protection and a bold crux make this a well-respected lead. It is highly recommended, however.
FA: Brad Gilbert and Jeff Alred, 1979.

42. KNUCKLEHEAD 5.10
Start in small left-facing corners 50 feet right of the start of Old Reliable. Climb up cracks on the left side of a bulge. Watch for loose blocks. Rappel from a tree at the top or cruise down to the Schoolroom Rappel. Not on photo/topo.
FA: Drew Bedford, Seth Shaw and Bob Ingle, 1985.

43. KNUCKLEBUSTER 5.9+ ★
Located 70 feet right of Old Reliable. Climb up to a ramp/ledge, then entertain right-facing cracks (with a spike) right of the bulge. This route is characterized by awkward fist jams. Not on photo/topo.
FA: Mark Ward, Jim Knight and Bruce Roghaar.

THE GATE BUTTRESS

This large chunk of granite is crossed by many excellent routes which link together cracks and slabs. Nubbins and crystals provide great friction on some routes while others, like Bushwhack Crack are perfect hand and finger cracks. Numerous routes kick back at a comfortable angle, offering fine beginner terrain, but not at the exclusion of more extreme routes. There are plenty of those as well. Mostly south-facing, this wall basks in the sun, although mornings and evenings are fine, even in the heat of summer.

The traditional gathering spot for climbers to boulder, meet partners, socialize and retreat from the summer heat is the Gate Boulders, at the base of the Gate Buttress. This verdant and shady area is home to boulders that seem designed to be climbed, with hidden buckets, overhangs and perfect edges. The Gate Boulder has a row of bolts across its crown that allow climbers to toprope the fun face climbing on its west side. In the middle of a hot summer day, it is still pleasant beneath the big oaks and maples. In autumn, among the carpet of leaves, it is magic.

Please do your best to keep this area trash free. Preservation of this beautiful grove requires picking up after other people as well as setting them straight when they litter. Remember, this is private land. If climbers take a few seconds to clean up, their precautions will pay off in improved climber/land owner relations. Reducing environmental impact at the Gate Buttress—an imperative—is every user's responsibility. Don't wait for the next person to do it!

"In autumn, among the carpet of leaves,
It is Magic."

photo: Ruckman.

optional
80'
80'
xx
.7
.7
.7
5
3rd
9
10
.5
10

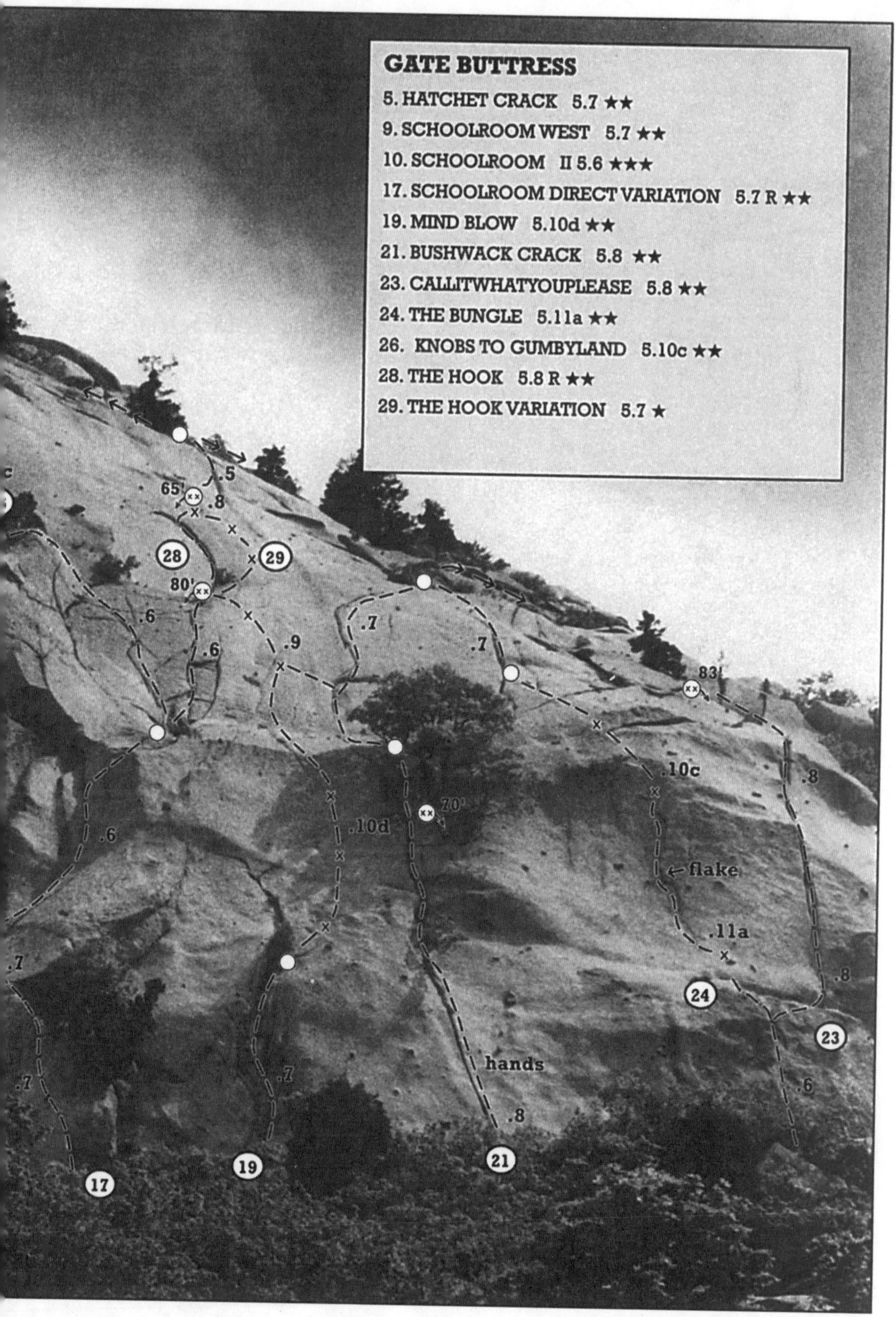
GATE BUTTRESS
5. HATCHET CRACK 5.7 ★★
9. SCHOOLROOM WEST 5.7 ★★
10. SCHOOLROOM II 5.6 ★★★
17. SCHOOLROOM DIRECT VARIATION 5.7 R ★★
19. MIND BLOW 5.10d ★★
21. BUSHWACK CRACK 5.8 ★★
23. CALLITWHATYOUPLEASE 5.8 ★★
24. THE BUNGLE 5.11a ★★
26. KNOBS TO GUMBYLAND 5.10c ★★
28. THE HOOK 5.8 R ★★
29. THE HOOK VARIATION 5.7 ★
65'
80'
70'
83'
28
29
.10c
.10d
.11a
flake
hands
24
23
17
19
21

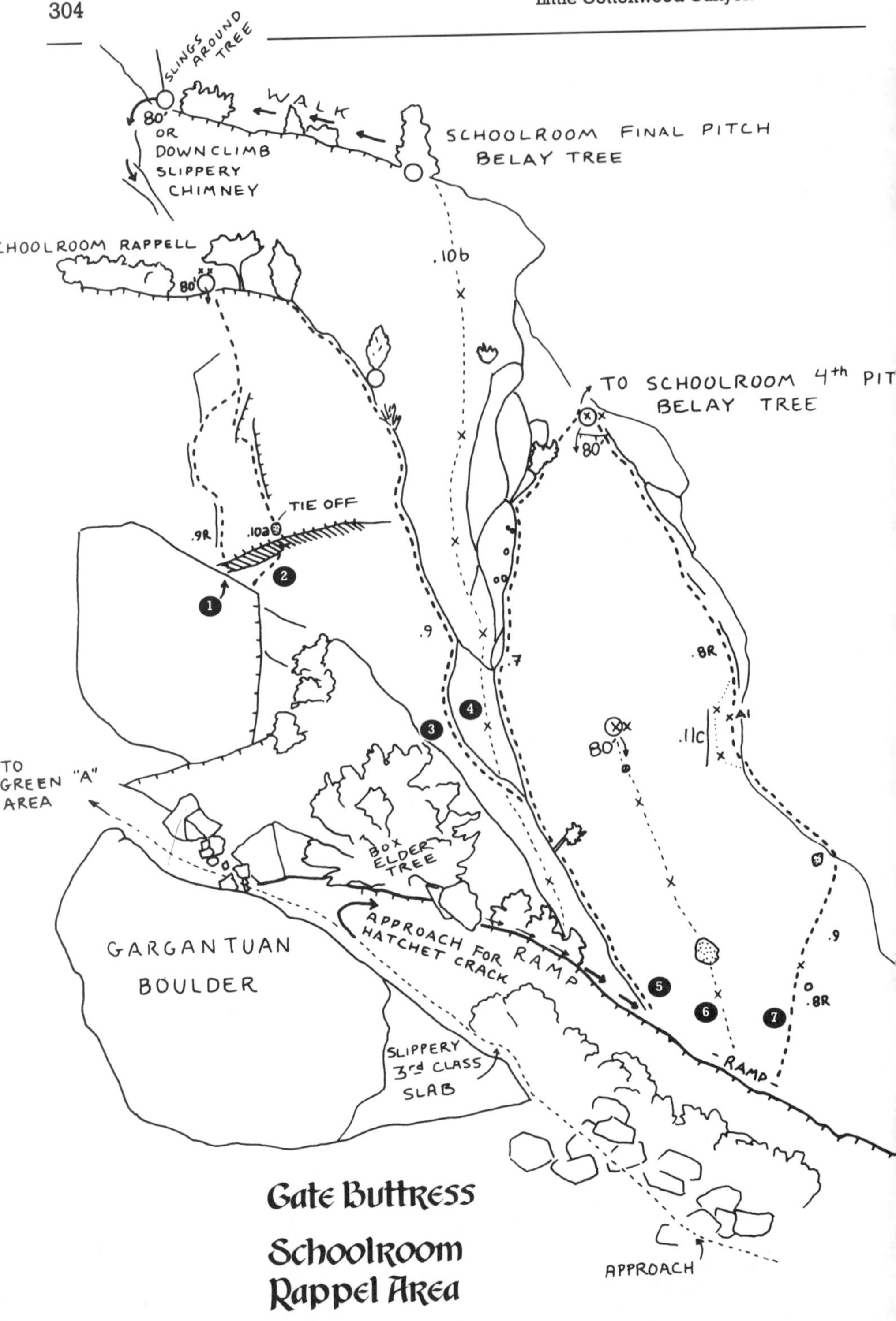

Gate Buttress

Schoolroom Rappel Area

THE GATE BUTTRESS—SCHOOLROOM RAPPEL AREA

Slabs and cracks are the attraction here, linked together by a matrix of good stone, a pleasant angle, and quality lines.

APPROACH: Park 1.25 miles up canyon from the neon sign at obvious pullouts on both sides of the road. A trail leaves the west (down canyon) end of this parking lot and heads north into the trees. As you approach the first boulder at the Gate Boulders, follow the path that leads left (west). The trail climbs up and west above the Tower Boulder, along the base of a short slab, to a slippery lieback between two boulders. Above this challenge, the trail continues straight up then moves left into the boulderfield near the right edge of a large slab. The trail forks above this slab. Continue walking straight above the slab another two hundred feet to reach the base of Schoolroom. Routes 17 to 25 can be reached by walking right (east) along the base of the wall from Schoolroom. To reach routes number 1 to 7, walk west on ledges above the previously mentioned slab to a boulderfield. Walk up the talus until several huge boulders form an impasse. Cracks and ledges on the right (east) side allow for some third class climbing to reach the top of the boulder. Routes 1 and 2 are fifty feet from the boulder, further up the talus on the right. From the boulder, cutting right (east) behind a Box Elder tree and down climbing the ramp reaches the base routes 3 through 7. See overview on page 290.

DESCENT: Use the Schoolroom Rappel for routes 1 through 20 and 26 through 30. From the pine tree atop Schoolroom, walk up and north, toward the Green Adjective Gully on a brushy ledge system to a pine tree. Either do one rappel off the pine or downclimb a crack and chimney to the ledge system below. Anchors here allow an eighty foot rappel to the ground. For climbs 21 through 25 it is best to utilize the Callitwhatyouplease Rappel. Both descents require some downclimbing to reach the anchors. Care should be taken. See topos for rappel locations.

SCHOOLROOM RAPPEL AREA ROUTES

1. THE SCOURGE 5.9 R ★

Hopefully, you won't be caught dicing the first moves when a rope comes whipping down from the rappel station above. This climbs the left grooves. Bring a 3½" camming unit.

FA: Unknown.

2. CHICKEN RODEO 5.10a ★

Tie off a chickenhead, mantel it and continue up grooves to the rappel station. A 2" cam on the undercling is useful.

FA: Unknown.

3. LIZZIE BORDEN 5.9 ★

Climb grooves just left of Hatchet Crack. Bring a 4" camming unit.

FA: Alan Bartlett and Shari Schubot, 1984.

4. THE RUMBA 5.10b ★

Despite the six protection bolts, gear is still recommended. Here and there it is tempting to step into Hatchet Crack.

FA: Unknown.

5. HATCHET CRACK 5.7 ★★

A bulging section provides the crux.

FA: Bill Conrod and Ed Anderson, 1964.

6. PRIMAL SCREAM 5.11d ★

Thin face climbing up tenuous terrain.

FA: Tony Calderone and Michael Taylor, 1996.

7. CORNERSTONE 5.11c R ★ or 5.9 A1 R

The aid move on the original line is off the second bolt. A free variation moves left here, and climbs the face past two more bolts, joining the original line above for the runout climbing to the top.

FA: Gary Olsen, Bret and Stuart Ruckman, 1983.
FFA: Tony Calderone, 1996.

SCHOOLROOM RAPPEL AREA ROUTES

8. SCHOOLROOM WILD WEST 5.11b ★
Climb the weaknesses left of Schoolroom West's initial pitch. A mantle connecting the left incipient crack to the right one is the crux.
FA: Drew Bedford, Conrad Anker, 1986.

9. SCHOOLROOM WEST 5.7 ★★
Very enjoyable – lots of interesting climbing in five pitches.

10. SCHOOLROOM II 5.6 ★★★
The climber will utilize almost all techniques across five pitches of perfect granite. Several traverses can be scary for the following climber, if not protected properly by the leader.
FA: Larry Evans, Dick Ream, Rich Ream and Court Richards, 1964.

11. MANTLE VARIATION 5.9 R
Usually toproped.

12. RECESS VARIATION 5.9+ R
Follow two bolts on the face to the left of the fourth-pitch chimney. Unnecessarily runout.
FA: Lenny Nelson and Tom Oaks, 1989.

13. MOVIE VARIATION 5.8 ★★
Initially intimidating, but really good.

14. THE SCHOOLROOM STREAK 5.12a R ★★
Follow the vein of dark rock directly up the convex face. Bring along your micro technique, and prepare for a wicked mantle.
FA: Tony Calderone and Scott Keller, 1996.

15. SCHOOLROOM ROOF VARIATION 5.6 A1 ★★
Yeehaw! All fixed pins.

16. RISING SUN 5.11c R ★
The start to this is wicked and has seen very few repeats. Be prepared with brass-type nuts.
FFA: Dirk Tyler, 1980.

17. SCHOOLROOM DIRECT VARIATION 5.7 R ★★
The non-trivial traverse left into the second pitch of Schoolroom is runout. The block used just before you make this traverse is expanding, so beware.

18. THE GREAT RIPOFF 5.10b ★
Start up the tree-filled crack 5 feet right of Schoolroom Direct Variation. Climb out right on a flake, then past two bolts to the Schoolroom second-pitch belay. Beware of the second bolt.
FA: Tim Wolfe and Pete Carney.

19. MIND BLOW 5.10d ★★
Get your neurons fired up for this one. Continuously difficult face climbing. The bolts were placed on lead! The second pitch is 5.9 and recommended.
FA: Dave Houser and Jim Downs, 1972.

20. TALUS FOOD 5.12c ★★
Several insatiable mantles lead up to the business on Mind Blow.
FA: Tony Calderone, 1995.

Climbs 21 through 25 best utilize the Five Fingers or Callitwhatyouplease rappels.

21. BUSHWHACK CRACK 5.8 ★★
This is getting harder because the chickenheads are getting greasier. A great introduction to true crack climbing.
FA: Bill Conrod and Paul Anderson, 1965.

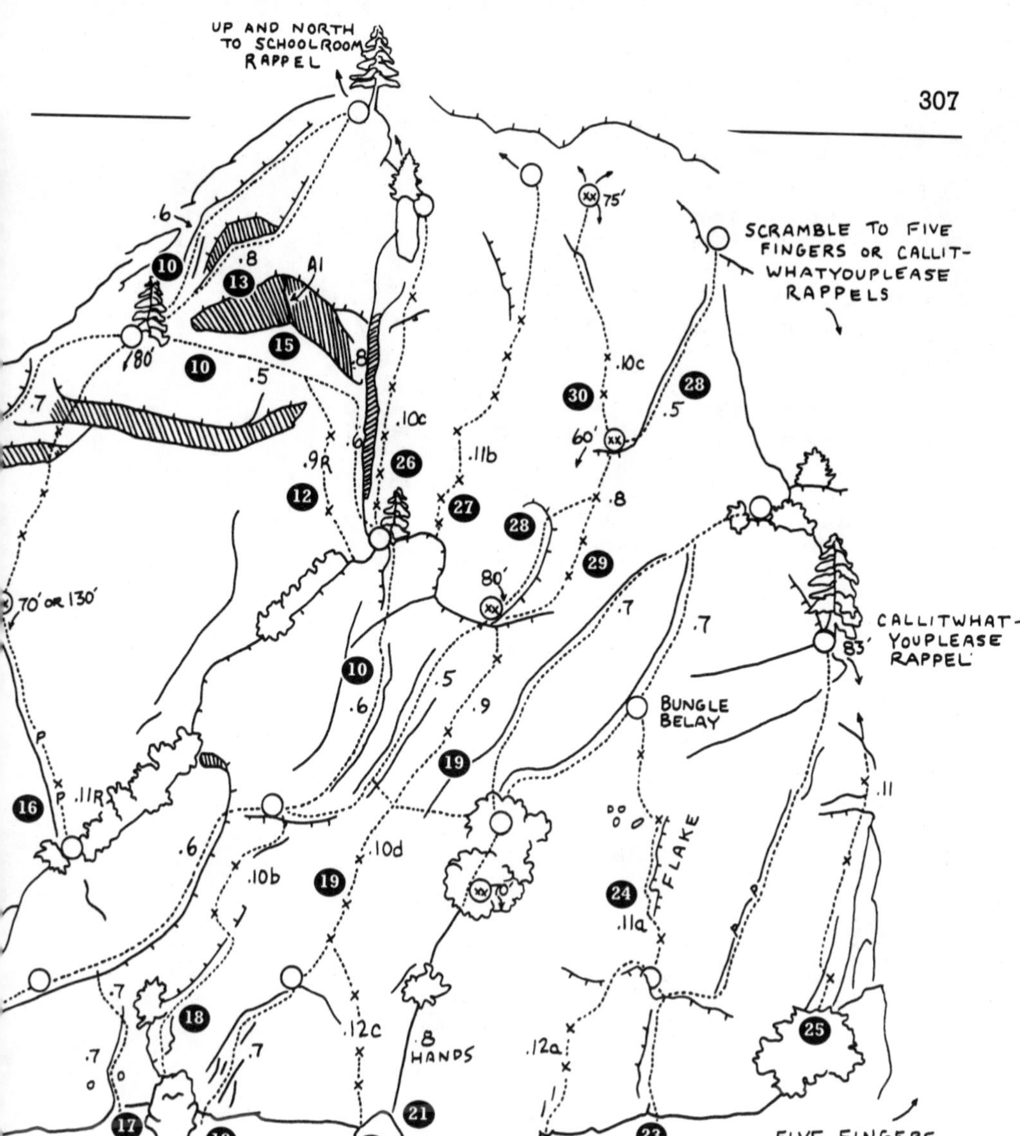

Gate Buttress

Schoolroom Rappel Area

22. CHICKEN LITTLE 5.12a ★
Is the sky falling or are you? Two bolts protect the arcane sequence of thin face climbing. Height-related crux.
FA: Drew Bedford, 1988.

23. CALLITWHATYOUPLEASE 5.8 ★★
Callitaclassic. Bring protection to 3 inches.
FA: George Lowe and Dick Ream, 1966.

24. THE BUNGLE 5.11a ★★
Two distinct cruxes; cool climbing. The first crux is height-dependent. The second is kinda scary.
FA: Dave Houser and Jim Knight, 1971.
FFA: Kim Miller and Mark Ward, 1977.

25. STONE THE CROWS 5.11 R ★★
A chickenhead highstep marks the start.
FA: Alan Bartlett, Dave Black and Tito Black, 1982.

Climbs 26 to 30 can be descended by the Schoolroom Rappel.

26. KNOBS TO GUMBYLAND 5.10c ★★
This is a sweet pitch on good rock. Sometimes wet.
FA: Steve Carruthers and Dana Hauser, 1984.

27. STATE OF CONFUSION 5.11b ★★
Was a pun intended? A challenge even to the adroit slab climber. Somewhat flaky rock, but getting cleaner.
FA: Lynn Wheeler and Tom Carruthers, 1983.

28. THE HOOK 5.8 R ★★
No bolts were used by the klettershoe-shod first ascensionists. The bolts were added later.
FA: Fred Beckey and Layton Kor, 1961

29. THE HOOK VARIATION 5.7 ★
Climb the slab right of the hook on crystals and cool knobs, passing three bolts, to a bolt belay.

30. THE HOOK DIRECT 5.10c R ★
Two bolts protect the most difficult sections and some shaky nuts or TCUs protect the easier exit moves.
FA: Mugs Stump and Jack Roberts, 1977.

The tenuous crux of Mexican Crack. Chris VanDiver leading. Crescent Crack area.

photo: Jeff Baldwin.

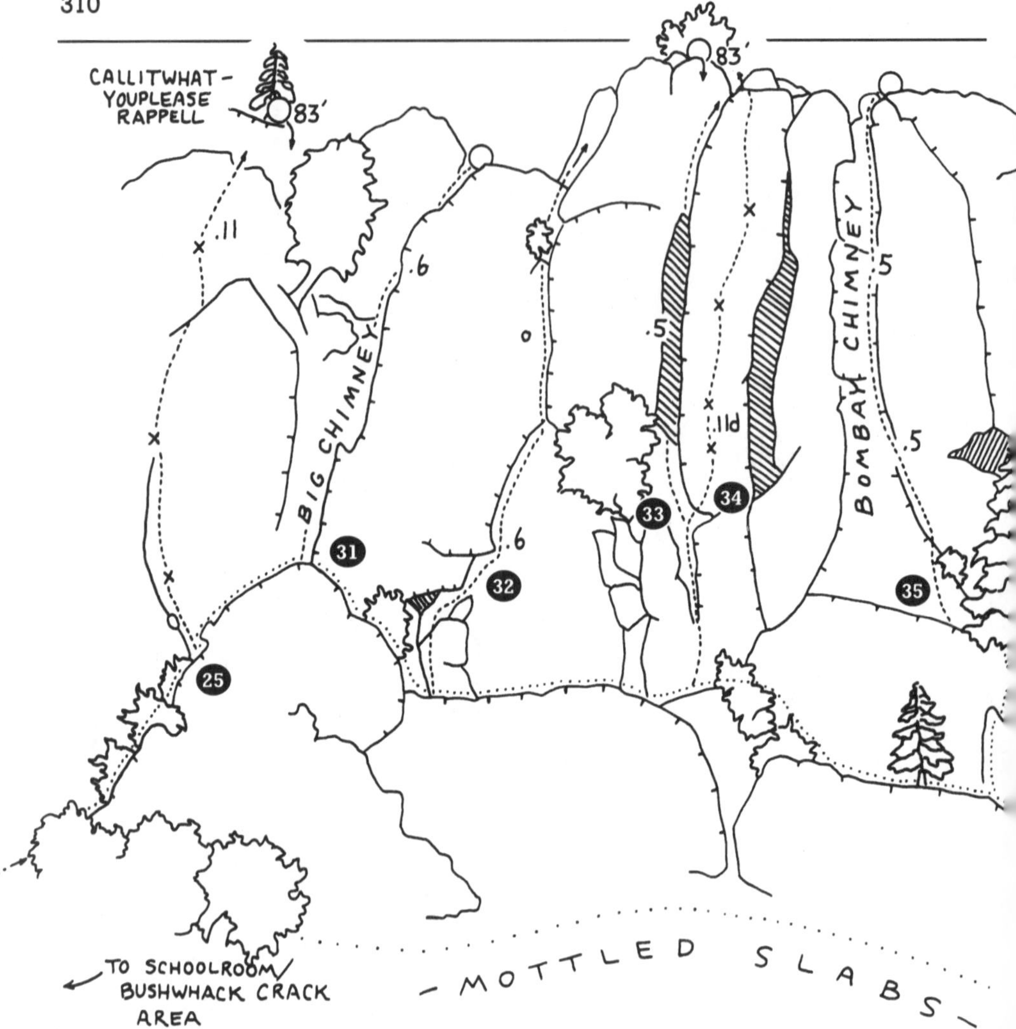

THE GATE BUTTRESS —FIVE FINGERS AREA

The Gate Buttress grows shorter and steeper here, split by numerous cracks and chimneys. The area catches its name from the series of conspicuous vertical cracks located where the buttress changes from south-facing to east-facing.

APPROACH: The easiest way (less scrambling) is the longest, and will be described first. Follow the approach to the base of the route Schoolroom, page 305. Walk east (up canyon) along the base of the wall to a short, brush-filled gully. Walk up this and you'll be at the base of Chicken Chickenhead. Continuing east on a series of ledges, from here access the remaining routes. It is also possible to approach this area more directly. Follow the approach to Prune Face, page 312. About 50 feet left of Prune Face is a series of low angled slabs. Scramble up these via ledges and cracks to access the gully running down from Five Fingers. From the top of the gully, ledges to the left and right will bring you to the desired routes. For both approaches, see overview on page 290.

DESCENT: Climbs 32 to 40 can be descended using the Five Fingers Rappel with one rope. See topo for location of rappel tree.

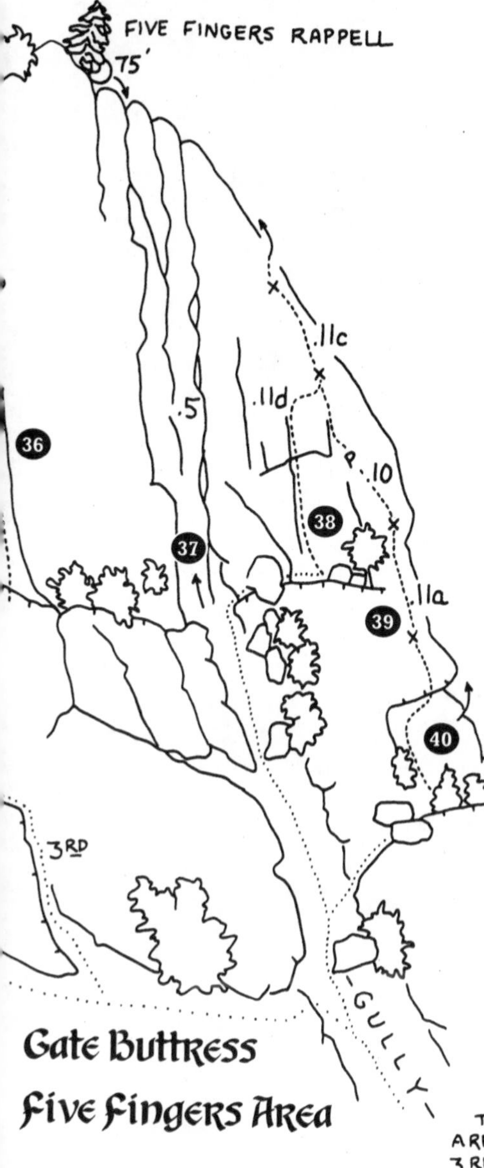

FIVE FINGERS AREA ROUTES

31. CHICKEN CHICKENHEAD 5.6 ★
Named for a shy chickenhead that doesn't stick out as far as the first ascensionist would have liked. Use the Callitwhatyouplease Rappel.
FA: Larry Evans and Rich Ream.

32. THE WALTZ 5.6 ★
Fun. An undercling turns into a lieback which turns into a wide crack.

33. TENDERLOIN 5.5
Simply a chimney.

34. HIGH FIVE 5.11d ★★
You'll be slapping high fives on this intricate, yet pumping, bolt-protected arête.
FA: Stuart and Bret Ruckman, 1990.

35. FAT MAN'S MISERY 5.5 ★
A bit dirty at the bottom, but the bombay chimney is quite good. A short fist crack has been climbed on the left wall of the chimney and is rated 5.10.

36. SCUMBAG CRACK 5.6
An unpleasant squeeze chimney.

37. FIVE FINGERS 5.6 / 5.7
Many possibilities; most of them grooves.
FA: Bob Bruschke, Wilf Bruschke and Ted Wilson, 1960.

38. BITTERFINGERS 5.11d ★★
This essentially climbs the Five Fingers rappel route. There are three ways to do this. One: Climb the hard crack for 15 feet, then swing around right to a small stance (original route). Two: Traverse around the corner 10 feet lower. The third option is the direct start. This route was drilled on lead. Primo thin face climbing.
FA: Merrill Bitter, 1981.

39. BITTERFINGERS DIRECT 5.11a ★★
This variation starts around the corner 20 feet right of the regular start. It joins Bitterfingers at its first bolt and assumes a 5.11d rating from this point on.
FA: Gordon Douglass and Stuart Ruckman, 1988.

40. HORNET'S REST 5.8+ ★★
Start up the crack and right-facing corner system above the top of Half-a-Finger. A long reach and a stimulating rightward undercling lead to the two bolts atop Satan's Corner.
FA: Ted Wilson, Bob Bruschke and Wilf Bruschke.

GATE BUTTRESS—PRUNE FACE

This slab is hidden among the oaks, directly below the Five Finger Area. Expect good quality slab climbing and super-quick access.

APPROACH: Follow the approach information for the Schoolroom Area, page 305. until just above the Tower Boulder. Here the trail forks. The left fork levels out and heads west towards Schoolroom, while the right fork continues straight up the slope. Take the right path, and after a short distance you'll reach a long, narrow slab. This is Prune Face. See overview on page 290.

DESCENT: Scramble down third class ledges to the west, or make a careful eighty foot rappel, aiming for the highest ground, not the base of the routes.

PRUNE FACE ROUTES

41. SHUFFLEBOARD 5.8
Start by climbing up the broken corner left of Iron Grit. Continue above the corner in a crack that arcs out of the gully and returns 50 feet higher.
FA: Conrad Anker, Tito Black and Bob Ingle, sometime in the 1980s.

42. IRON GRIT VARIATION
Start in the corner left of Iron Grit. Climb the corner for a short ways, then traverse right on a steep ramp to join Iron Grit at the third bolt.
FA: Layne Oliver and Fred Durtschi, 1994.

43. IRON GRIT 5.11a ★
Friction past three bolts to join the upper grooves of Prune Face.
FA: Tony Calderone, Fred Durtschi, and Layne Oliver, 1995.

44 . PRUNE FACE 5.9 ★
Climb the right side of the slab past three bolts, traverse left, then move up cracks and grooves to the top. This route was originally led with only one bolt and one pin for fixed protection. A later party, unfortunately, bolted the start.
FA: Drew Bedford and Conrad Anker, sometime in the 1980s.

45. STRAIGHT ON FOR YOU 5.8+ ★★
Start on Prune Face, then continue straight up the face.
FA: Tony Calderone and Dan Giovale, 1995.

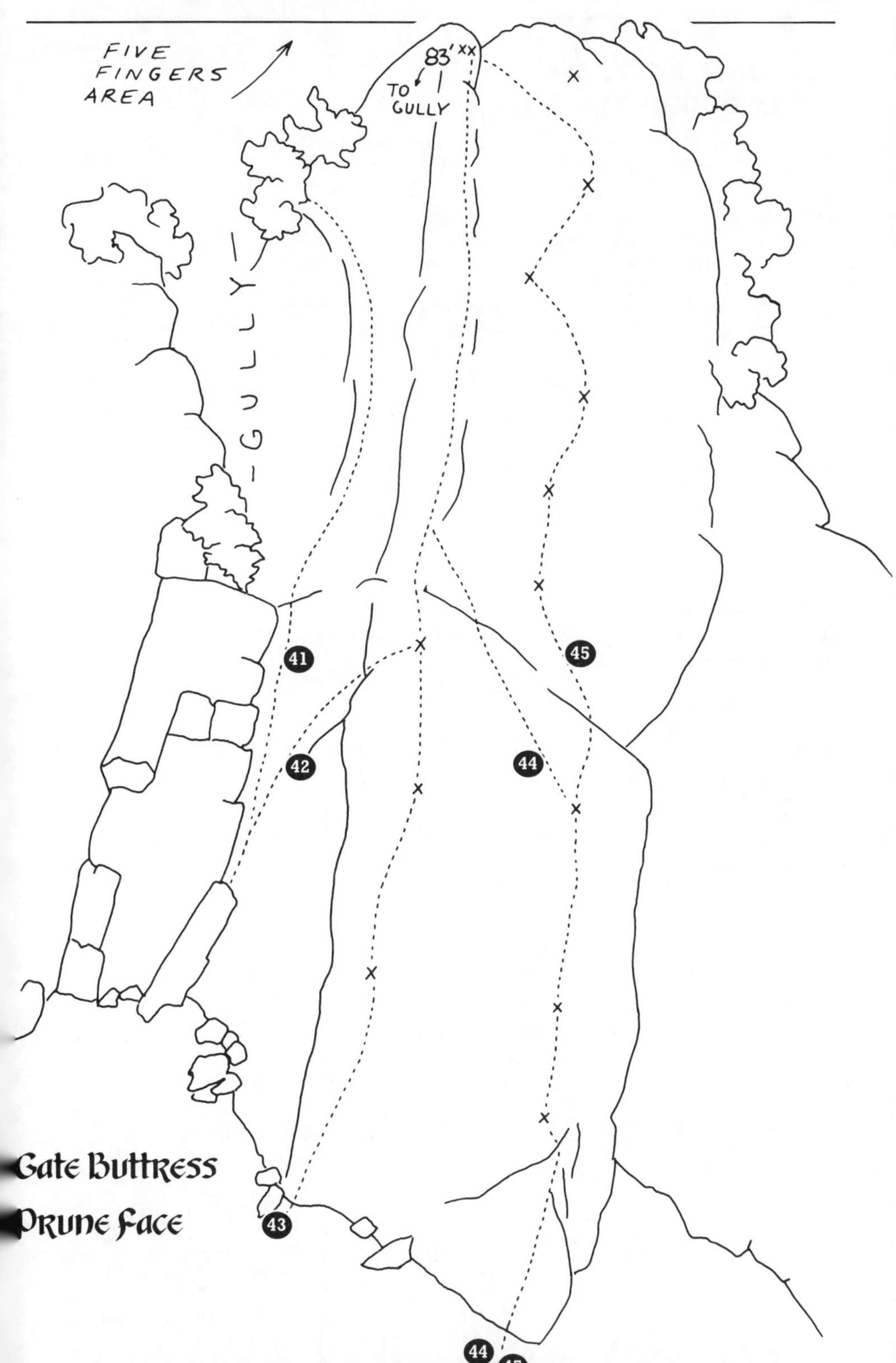
FIVE FINGERS AREA
83' XX
TO GULLY
GULLY
41
42
43
44
45
44
45
Gate Buttress
Prune Face

THE GATE BUTTRESS —THE DIHEDRALS AREA

Many of the routes in this area are steep corner and crack climbs. The rock is excellent, and the routes airy and exposed. With afternoon shade, these climbs are immensely popular.

APPROACH: Park 1.25 miles up canyon from the neon sign at obvious pullouts on either side of the road. A trail leaves the west (down canyon) end of the parking area and heads north into the trees. To reach The Dihedrals and Tarzan area, walk to the upper end of the Gate Boulder (the largest boulder) and follow a trail that leads left (west), then switchbacks east, before heading straight up through the trees. This path ends at twenty feet of third class climbing up a set of double cracks. Above the cracks, a short scramble leads to a ledge system and a traverse left (west). These ledges lead to a short gully and the base of Beckey's Wall. A short third-class chimney near the base of Satan's Corner accesses routes 46 through 54. A short scramble right (east) from the base of Beckey's Wall reaches the belay bolt on Tarzan. See overview on page 290.

An easier alternative to access just the Dihedral Routes (routes 46 to 54) is to stop sixty feet before the slippery double cracks on the main trail, turn left (west) at a small break in the cliff band. From here, follow a ledge around the corner, and scramble up slabs to the base of the routes. See overview on page 290.

DESCENT: All routes can be descended with one rope. Rappel from anchors at the top of each route.

THE DIHEDRALS AREA ROUTES

46. INCUBATOR 5.12c ★
Ridiculously hard climbing with a wild finish.
FA: John Storm and Stuart Ruckman, 1988.

47. CORE SHOT 5.12b ★
Bouldery moves in the corner to the right of Incubator.
FA: Douglas Heinrich and Brian Mecham, 1997.

48. HALF-A-FINGER 5.9+ ★★
Strenuous and bold. Many an aspiring 5.9 climber has lowered off this route! The final "finger" can be climbed on the right or left sides – the left is considered "cooler." The cracks just left of the dihedral also have been climbed, joining the route at the final overhang (5.9).
FA: Dave Boyd and Eric Eliason, 1970.
FFA: Dave Jenkins and Rick Wyatt, 1977.

49. BLACK AND WHITE JOHN AND MARY 5.10c ★★★
Stemming and liebacking, with a new bolt to protect the crux where a manky pin used to be. A respectable lead. The direct start (often wet) is 5.11a R.
FA: Dave Boyd and Eric Eliason, 1970.
FFA: Les Ellison and Larry Carrol, 1979.

50. EQUIPMENT OVERHANG 5.11a ★★★
Face climbing the crackless section is the crux. The final 20 feet also are a tickler. Superb.
FA: Eric Eliason and Dave Raymond, 1970.
FFA: Jack Roberts and Don McCarthy, 1976.

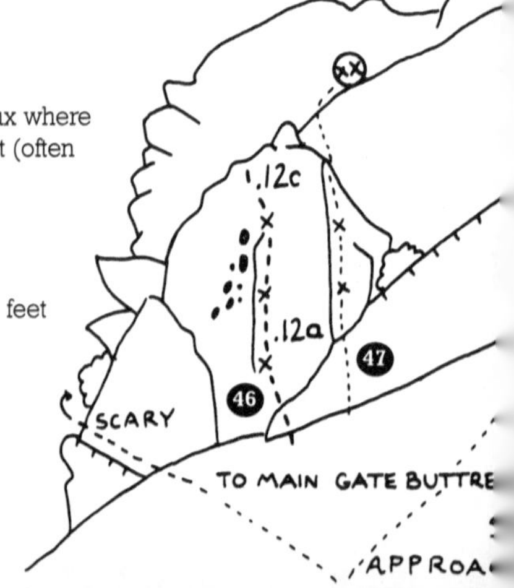

51. EQUIPMENT OVERHANG RIGHT 5.10b ★★★

A runout lieback starts things off, only to be followed by a thin crack with thin pro at the crux. Most climbers move left out of the dihedral, just above the crux, and re-enter five feet higher.

FFA: Jack Roberts and Frank Trummel, 1976.

52. MOTOR SKILLS VARIATION 5.12a ★

Power undercling from Equipment Overhang, then go right to Lisa's Shoulder. There are three bolts.

FA: John Storm, 1988.

53. LISA'S SHOULDER 5.9 R ★★★

This scary climb shouldn't be missed by the solid leader. The upper face is thrilling—small yet positive holds abound. A tingling final sweep up the arête will bring you into Hornet's Rest and the two-bolt belay at the top of Satan's Corner.

FA: Eric Eliason and Dave Raymond, 1969.
FFA: Unknown.

Gate Buttress Dihedrals Area

54. STEM THE TIDE 5.10d R ★★★

The first ascent was in impeccable style. An etude of technical stemming. Bolts have been added where the original pins used to be. There is long fall potential.

FA: Merrill Bitter and Bret Ruckman, 1983.

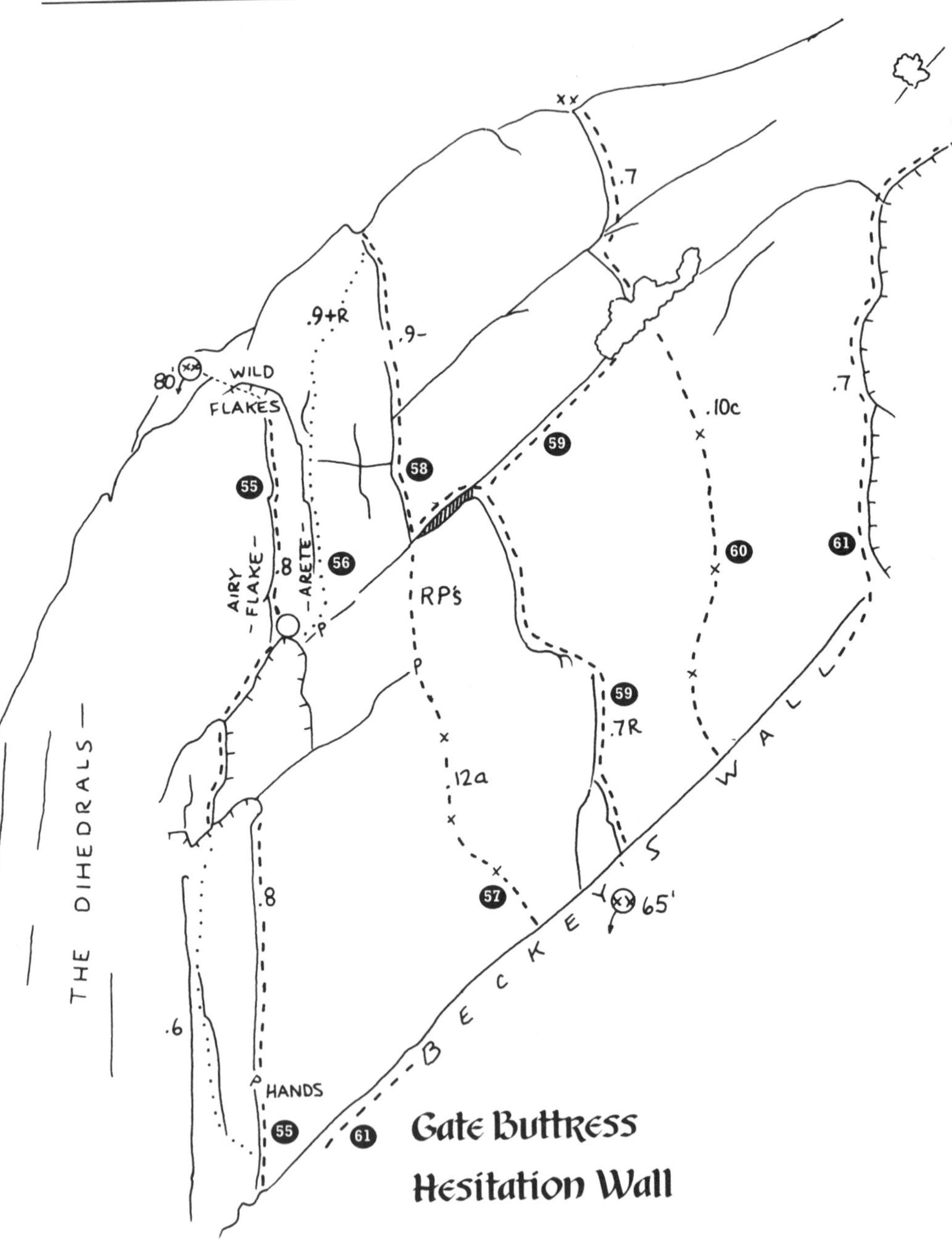

Gate Buttress
Hesitation Wall

THE DIHEDRALS AREA ROUTES

55. SATAN'S CORNER 5.8 ★★★

Climbers agree that this is one of the best routes in the Wasatch. Steep and enthralling crack climbing with a diabolical second pitch exit. A crack to the left provides a 5.6 alternative to the first pitch.

FA: Bob Irvine and Dave Wood, 1962.
FFA: George Lowe and Ed Anderson.

56. FALLEN ANGEL VARIATION 5.9+ R ★

Infrequently done flakes rise straight up the prow above the first pitch belay on Satan's Corner.

FA: George Lowe.

THE GATE BUTTRESS —HESITATION WALL

This is the large east-facing wall that rises above the first pitch of Beckey's Wall.

APPROACH: Follow the approach to the Dihedrals Area.
See overview on page 290.

DESCENT: With one rope you can use the Five Fingers Rappel.

HESITATION WALL ROUTES

57. INDEPENDENT STREAK 5.12a R ★

Micro nuts are necessary to protect the easier climbing above the crux. The crux itself presents a veritable vacuum of holds.

FA: Stuart Ruckman, 1987.

58. HESITATE NO MORE 5.9- R ★

FA: Rick Wyatt and Dave Jenkins, 1978.

59. HESITATION 5.7 R ★

60. FRUIT LOOPS 5.10c R ★★

Getting to the second bolt is potentially hazardous. The bolts were drilled on the lead.

FA: Drew Bedford, Doug Heinrich, 1988.

THE GATE BUTTRESS —BECKEY'S WALL TO TINGEY'S TERROR

The Gate Buttress tips back to a more comfortable angle here, and slab climbing again prevails. Most routes, however, follow clean crack systems that split the faces.

APPROACH: Follow the approach to The Dihedrals, page 314.

DESCENT: For Beckey's Wall routes, and Cheetah, scramble down to the large pine at the top of the Five Fingers Rappel. For Tarzan, two rappels or a scramble east down ledges will get you to the base. For Tingey's Terror and Tingey's Torture, it is best to make a long scramble west to gain the Schoolroom Rappel. See topos pages 303 and 304.

BECKEY'S WALL TO TINGEY'S TERROR ROUTES

61. BECKEY'S WALL 5.7 ★★★

The start has tricky protection. This is probably the best 5.7 in the canyon.

FA: Fred Beckey and Layton Kor, 1961. (In 1996, Fred claimed that the first ascent was made with Rosalyn Stewart, not Layton Kor.)

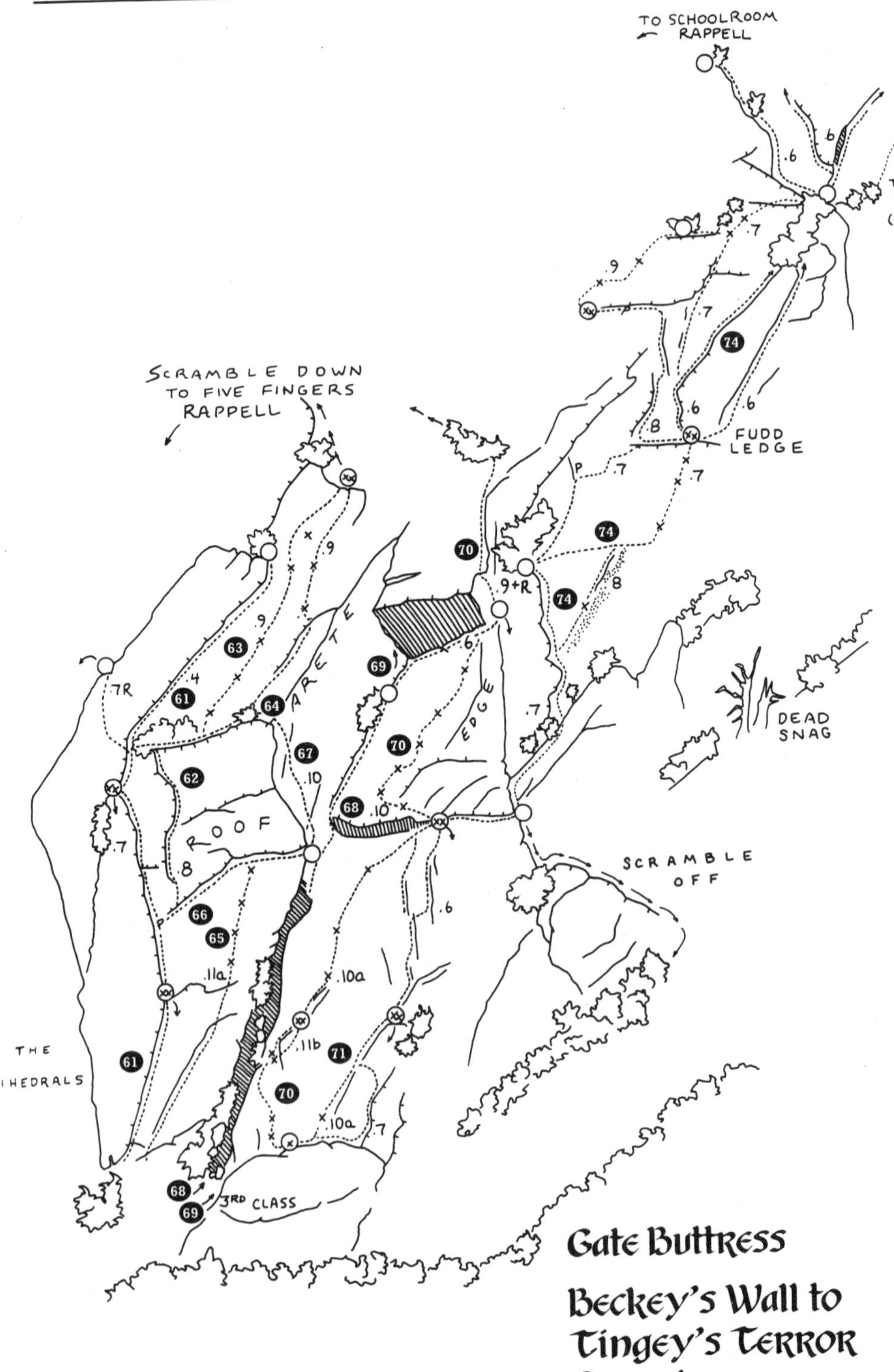

Gate Buttress

Beckey's Wall to Tingey's Terror Overview

BECKEY'S WALL TO TINGEY'S TERROR ROUTES

61. BECKEY'S WALL 5.7 ★★★

The start has tricky protection. This is probably the best 5.7 in the canyon.

FA: Fred Beckey and Layton Kor, 1961. (In 1996, Fred claimed that the first ascent was made with Rosalyn Stewart, not Layton Kor.)

62. FINGERTRIP VARIATION 5.8+ R ★★

An awesome variant up a vertical wall right of the regular dihedral. Micro nuts are useful.

FA: Ron Weber and Ed Anderson, mid 60s.

63. PEBBLES AND BAMBAM 5.9 ★

Follow five bolts directly up the center of the slab that rests above Beckey's Wall. Good, tenuous stuff. Roughly 100 feet above the end of this route is a nice ledge with a right-leaning thin crack above. This route has been named Siesta and rated 5.10a.

FA: Bill Hunt, Joe Wrona, Tom Whipple and Ed Wones.

64. DATE WITH FATE 5.9 ★

Tack on another fun pitch with this flake and bolt protected face.

FA: Gordon Douglass and Stuart Ruckman, 1982.

65. BALONEY ON WHITE 5.11a ★

Four bolts on the face right of Beckey's Wall. Rounded holds are sandwiched between the crux and the roof.

FA: Lynn Watson and Jim Hall, 1988.

66. SPLIT FINGERS 5.11c ★★

The canyon's undercling/lieback test piece. The pretty long runouts were gnarly in the old EBs.

FFA: Brain Smoot, 1979.

67. LUNCH BUCKET VARIATION 5.10 R

Climb up weaknesses above the finish of Split Fingers to the ledge atop the Fingertrip Variation.

FA: Bob Rotert, Mark Rolofson and Les Ellison, 1982.

68. SPLIT PANTS 5.6 ★

One redeeming pitch at the top. There is no convenient escape from the end of this route. It is best to continue up Tingey's Terror.

FA: Dick Ream, Rich Ream and Court Richards, 1962.

69. NEEDLE'S EYE VARIATION 5.7 ★

The brutal squeeze chimney that defines the left side of the Split Pants roof.

FA: Mark McQuarrie and Steve Ellsworth, 1964.

70. CHEETAH 5.11b R ★★

Four pitches. This route epitomizes the canyon's slab routes. The first pitch sees a lot of action, but the third pitch is the most interesting.

FA: Dave and Robert (Tito) Black, 1981.

71. TARZAN 5.7 A0 or 5.10a ★★

A classic crack climb with good protection. Aid or free climb past the first bolt to reach the crack above. If freed, this bouldery move is 5.10a. The Sweet Jane Variation is recommended to avoid the aid and still keep the route rated 5.7.

FA: Lenny Nelson and Jim Booth.

74. TINGEY'S TERROR II 5.7 ★★

A fine route with a fine slab pitch to match. The second lead used to have a reputation for runouts, but unfortunately, a third bolt was added by a party who swears that they were returning the route to the way it was in the 60s. Who knows? Regardless, good climbing prevails.There are many variations to this route. The best descent, unfortunately, is a long scramble west to gain the Schoolroom Rappel. Watch those loose rocks; there are climbers below.

FA: Ralph Tingey, Rick Reese and Dave Wood, 1962.

BECKEY'S WALL TO TINGEY'S TERROR ROUTES

67. LUNCH BUCKET VARIATION 5.10 R

Climb up weaknesses above the finish of Split Fingers to the ledge atop the Fingertrip Variation.

FA: Bob Rotert, Mark Rolofson and Les Ellison, 1982.

68. SPLIT PANTS 5.6 ★

One redeeming pitch at the top. There is no convenient escape from the end of this route. It is best to continue up Tingey's Terror.

FA: Dick Ream, Rich Ream and Court Richards, 1962.

69. NEEDLE'S EYE VARIATION 5.7 ★

The brutal squeeze chimney that defines the left side of the Split Pants roof.

FA: Mark McQuarrie and Steve Ellsworth, 1964.

70. CHEETAH 5.11b R ★★

Four pitches. This route epitomizes the canyon's slab routes. The first pitch sees a lot of action, but the third pitch is the most interesting.

FA: Dave and Robert (Tito) Black, 1981.

71. TARZAN 5.7 A0 or 5.10a ★★

A classic crack climb with good protection. Aid or free climb past the first bolt to reach the crack above. If freed, this bouldery move is 5.10a. The Sweet Jane Variation is recommended to avoid the aid and still keep the route rated 5.7.

FA: Lenny Nelson and Jim Booth.

72. TOURIST VARIATION 5.7 R

Instead of switching cracks on the second pitch, continue straight up, enduring the long runouts. Traverse left under the roof to Split Pants. Poor protection.

73. SWEET JANE VARIATION 5.7 ★

The start eight feet right of Tarzan is recommended to keep Tarzan 5.7.

74. TINGEY'S TERROR II 5.7 ★★ (topo on page 318.)

A fine route with a fine slab pitch to match. The second lead used to have a reputation for runouts, but unfortunately, a third bolt was added by a party who swears that they were returning the route to the way it was in the 60's. Who knows? Regardless, good climbing prevails.There are many variations to this route. The best descent, unfortunately, is a long scramble west to gain the Schoolroom Rappel. Watch those loose rocks; there are climbers below.

FA: Ralph Tingey, Rick Reese and Dave Wood, 1962.

75. TINGEY'S TORTURE III 5.8 ★★

This route, when combined with Tarzan and Tingey's Terror, presents the longest offering on the Gate Buttress. There is a 5.10 variant to the second pitch, if you want some numbers. Like Tingey's Terror, the best descent is a long scramble west to the top of the Schoolroom Rappel; however, it is also possible to rappel east via three 180 foot rappels, down The Flakes. Bring a standard rack including cams from TCU size to large hand size.

FA: Brian Smoot, Todd Gardner, Brandt Saxey, 1996.

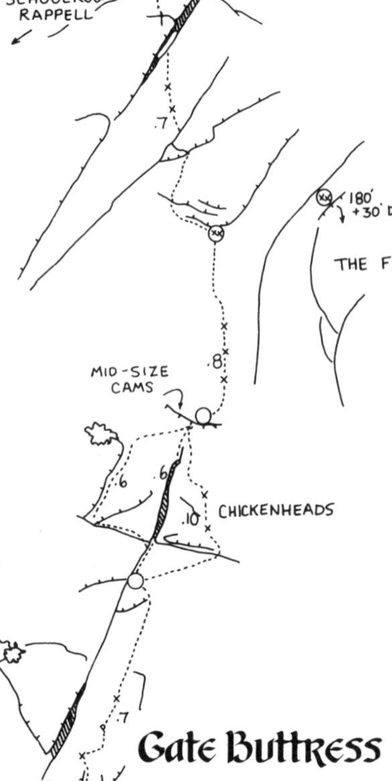

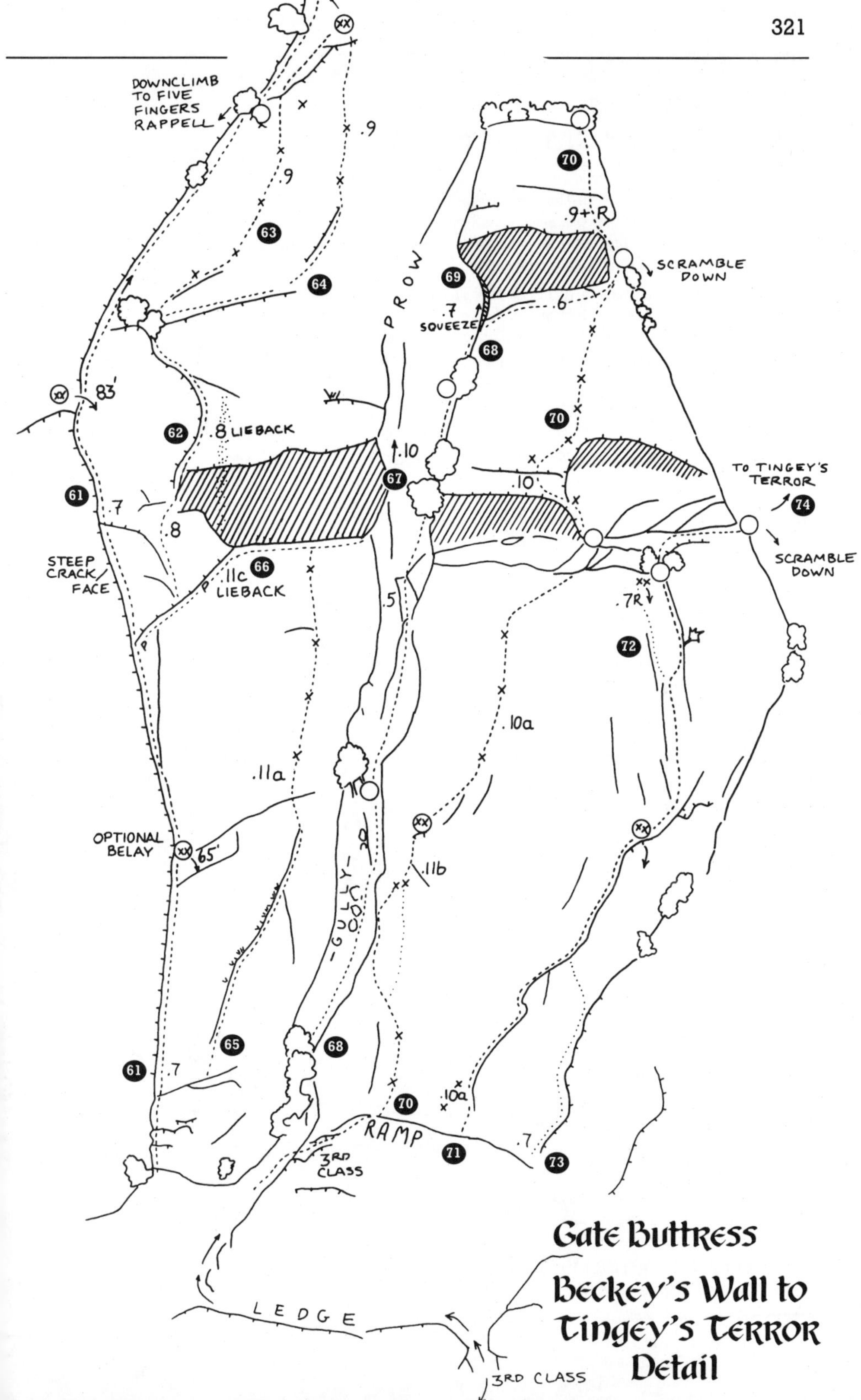

Gate Buttress

Beckey's Wall to Tingey's Terror Detail

GATE BUTTRESS —LOWER EAST GATE BUTTRESS

Steeper rock and thin seams dominate the scenery on these walls. Although lacking the popularity of other Gate Buttress areas, The Lower East Gate Buttress is crossed by numerous high quality routes. Routes 76 through 87 are on the Lower East Gate Buttress, just off of terra firma. The routes higher up and on the east side are referred to as the Upper East Gate Buttress.

APPROACH: Two approaches are possible. The first follows the approach to the Dihedrals, page 314. At the base of the third class double cracks, drop down to the right on a path that heads east (up canyon) along the base of the buttress. The trail grows more prominent as you approach the routes. The second approach follows a trail that starts out faint, then grows into a good path. It leaves the east end of the Inferno Boulder. This is the boulder just east and a bit south of The Gate Boulder. See overview on page 290.

DESCENT: All routes can be descended with one rope. See topos for rappel locations.

LOWER EAST GATE BUTTRESS ROUTES

76. B-POSITIVE 5.11d ★★
Face climbing on cool flakes and small corners.
FA: Drew Bedford.

77. BLOODLINE 5.12b ★★
This is the prominent right-leaning seam, easily visible from the Gate Buttress parking lot. The first move off the block is height-related, and the remainder is relentless.
FA: Drew Bedford, 1987.

78. BLOODDRIVE 5.9
Lieback/undercling the big flake system just right of Bloodline.
FA: Drew Bedford and Ron George, 1988.

79. BLOODSPORT 5.7
Continue out right on Blooddrive, instead of the lieback/undercling flake.
FA: Drew Bedford and Ron George, 1988.

80 PLASMA 5.10a ★
Join into Bloodsport via a thin undercling.
FA: Drew Bedford and Ron George, 1988.

81. SNOWFLAKES 5.11c ★★
A perplexing route that shouldn't be missed.
FA: Les Ellison, Karin Budding and Steve Hong, 1983.

82. PURPLE HORIZONS 5.11d ★★
The right-facing corner just right of Snowflakes has a one-finger cling that is a killer.
FA: Drew Bedford and Bill Sherman, 1983.

83. NARROW HORIZONS 5.12a ★
Tenuous, to say the least.
FA: Drew Bedford and Stewart Middleness.

84. CHRISTOPHER OF THE EVERGLADES 5.11b ★
Bring TCU,s and brass-type nuts.
FA: Chris Begue, Rush Bowers and Kent Wheeler, fall 1991.

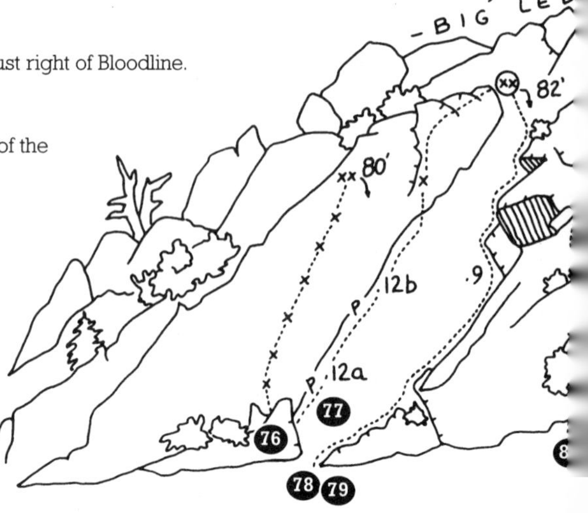

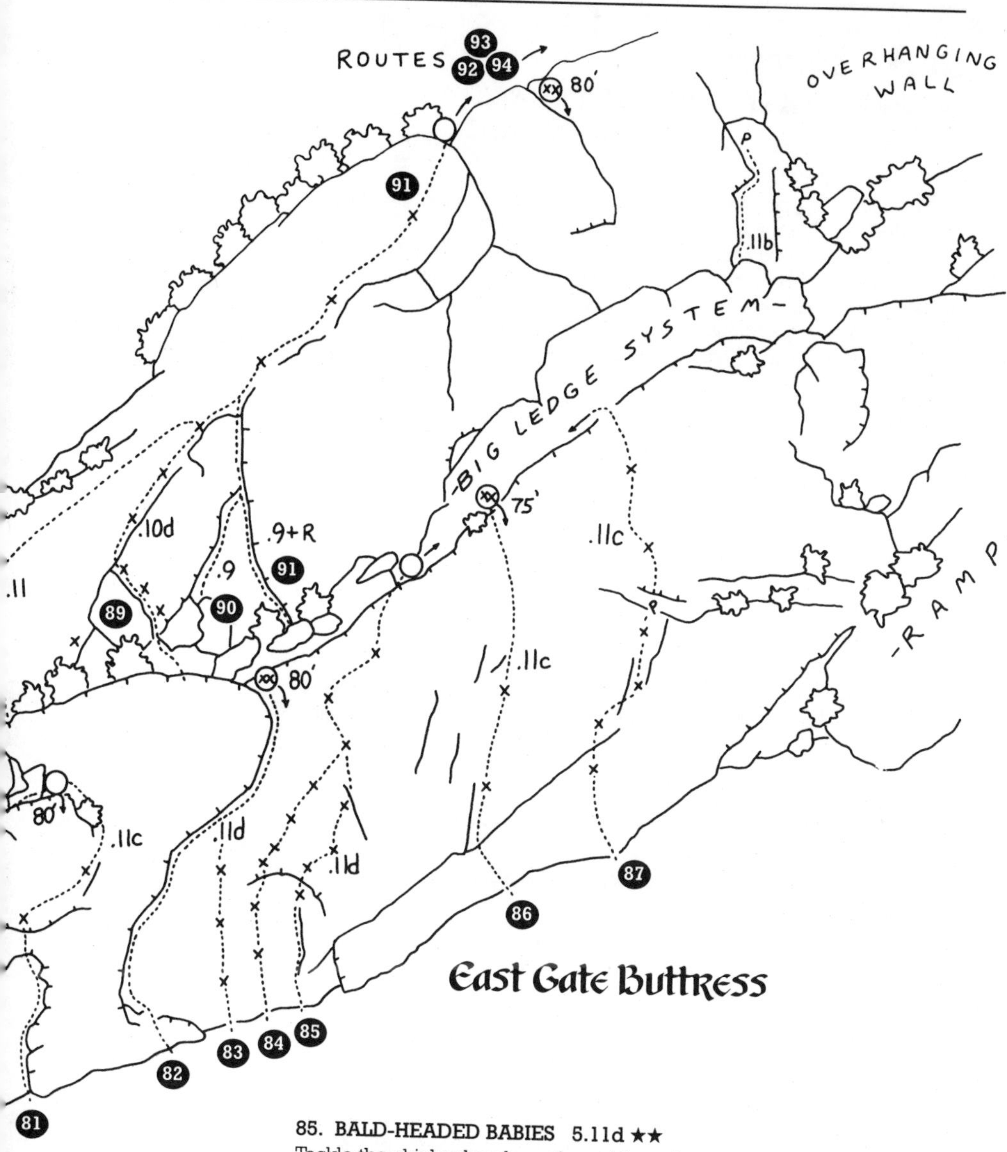

85. BALD-HEADED BABIES 5.11d ★★

Tackle the chickenhead mantle and face above. Seven bolts' worth of drastic measures.

FA: Lynn Wheeler, 1984.

86. SPEED OF LIFE 5.11c R ★★

Superb groove climbing 30 feet uphill from the Purple Horizons corner. Climb past two bolts. Bring brass-type nuts and small TCU's.

FA: Drew Bedford and Dave Casey, 1985.

87. GRAYING AT THE ROUTES 5.11c ★★

Well-protected face climbing. Protect in an undercling at the top of the route (medium nuts) and downclimb to the Speed of Life belay.

FA: Bret and Stuart Ruckman, 1990.

GATE BUTTRESS —UPPER EAST GATE BUTTRESS

The slabs to the right (east) of the mid-pitches of Tingey's Terror have some worthy climbing on them.

APPROACH: Two approaches are possible, neither of which is particularly pleasant. The first approach follows the approach to the Lower East Gate Buttress. From Graying at the Routes, continue walking uphill along the base of the wall to a ramp. Scramble up the ramp until ledge systems allow you to traverse left to gain a big ledge, which is descended to the base of the upper wall. The big ledge is the top of the lower wall.

The second approach follows the trail to The Dihedrals, page 314. At the top of the third class double cracks, continue up the broken gully above. Then work your way uphill and east through uncooperative brush and slabs to the base of the wall.

DESCENT: An 80 foot rappel near the top of Under Fire brings you back to the top of the Lower East Gate Buttress, where a 75 foot rappel reaches the ground.

88. THIS AIN'T NO DISCO 5.11 ★
A wandering route on the right slabs of the Gate Buttress. Joins in with Under Fire. Thin face climbing.
FA: Bill Robins and Kirsten Davis, 1985.

89. TO AIR IS HUMAN 5.10d ★★
This is below The Flakes. Start with a wild hand traverse left and climb a great crystal-strewn arête, joining the slab section of Under Fire. You can opt for the direct start, thus avoiding the hand traverse.
FA: Pat Contor and Gary Taylor, 1988.

90. ONLY HUMAN VARIATION 5.9 ★
Climb the fat crack that eventually joins the Under Fire dihedral.

91. UNDER FIRE 5.10 ★★
Climb the difficult-to-protect corner and enjoy the slab above.
FA: Bill Hunt and John Bird.

92. TRIVIAL PURSUIT 5.7 ★
An alternate start to the first pitch of The Flakes. Small cams are helpful.
FA: Pete Carney and Tim Wolfe.

93. THE FLAKES 5.10b ★★
Quite a grunt to get to and tricky to find. The upper portion of the route, a flake, is either a scary lieback or an offwidth on good rock with great exposure. The route faces east, and is visible from the road 300 yards east of Gate Buttress parking. Approach via a walk and scramble up the east side of Gate Buttress, climbing one of routes 88-92, or climbing Tingey's Terror and traversing east (right) from the top of the third pitch. Any approach involves considerable route finding. From the start of the route, climb a perfect hand/fist crack to the ramp below The Flakes proper (5.6). Jam an elegant thin hands crack up and right, then make some gonzo moves back left and up the fragile flake to the top (5.10b). Bring at least one 4" cam.
FA: Dennis Turville and Lynn Wheeler, early 70's.
FFA: Mark Ward and Randy Wright.

94. WILD THINGS 5.11c ★
A wild route through a roof crack around and to the north of The Flakes (about 100 feet). Bring mostly cams for protection: a set from 2" to 4", with doubles on the 2½" and 3" sizes.
FA: John Storm, 1986.

THE LITTLE COTTONWOOD TOWERS (no topo)

Several granite towers sit way up high on the ridge between Little Cottonwood Canyon and Deaf Smith Canyon. The south faces of these towers tend to be longer and more massive, while the north faces form slabs that drop into the upper reaches of the South Fork of Deaf Smith Canyon. The walls here are more frequently visited by mountain goats than climbers. Expect long, steep approaches followed by routes that require a sense of exploration. A good place to eyeball these towers is from the parking pullout for the Pentapitch Area. The Pawn is the most massive tower, the one with a large dihedral.

GOAT TOWER (no topo)

This tower is located along the ridge to the west of The Pawn.

APPROACH: The first ascent party approached via the ridge separating Little Cottonwood Canyon and the South Fork of Deaf Smith Canyon. Park at a dirt road on the east side of Little Cottonwood Canyon Road, .5 miles south from the junction of Little Cottonwood Canyon Road and Wasatch Blvd. Expect a long dry hike up the ridge with plenty of brush. It may also be possible to reach the descent notch from the approach to The Pawn.

1. Goat Tower 5.7 ★
The only known route climbs a long, distinct water streak that snakes its way down the north face. An easy first pitch is unprotected and leads to a ledge. The second pitch follows bolts to a two-bolt belay. The final pitch has one bolt, a diagonal crack, and a long stretch of easy, unprotected climbing. A 130' rappel to the east reaches a notch and the scramble back to the base of the wall.
FA: Scott Keller, Brian Wieland, 1995.

THE PAWN

Only extremely motivated climbers ever climb the Pawn. Located at the top of the ridge north of Gate Buttress, a full two hours of strenuous hiking is required just to reach the base. Then, up to ten pitches of difficult climbing cap off the day. If the crowds are getting you down, this is your place.

APPROACH: The approach is best made from the Gate Buttress. Follow the approach information for the East Gate Buttress, then follow faint trails and brush, eventually reaching The Pawn. An alternate approach is to follow the Green Adjective Gully approach and continue up the gully and slopes beyond to reach The Pawn. Maybe three routes have been done to date and details are sparse. No route descriptions are included for this area. Explore and enjoy.

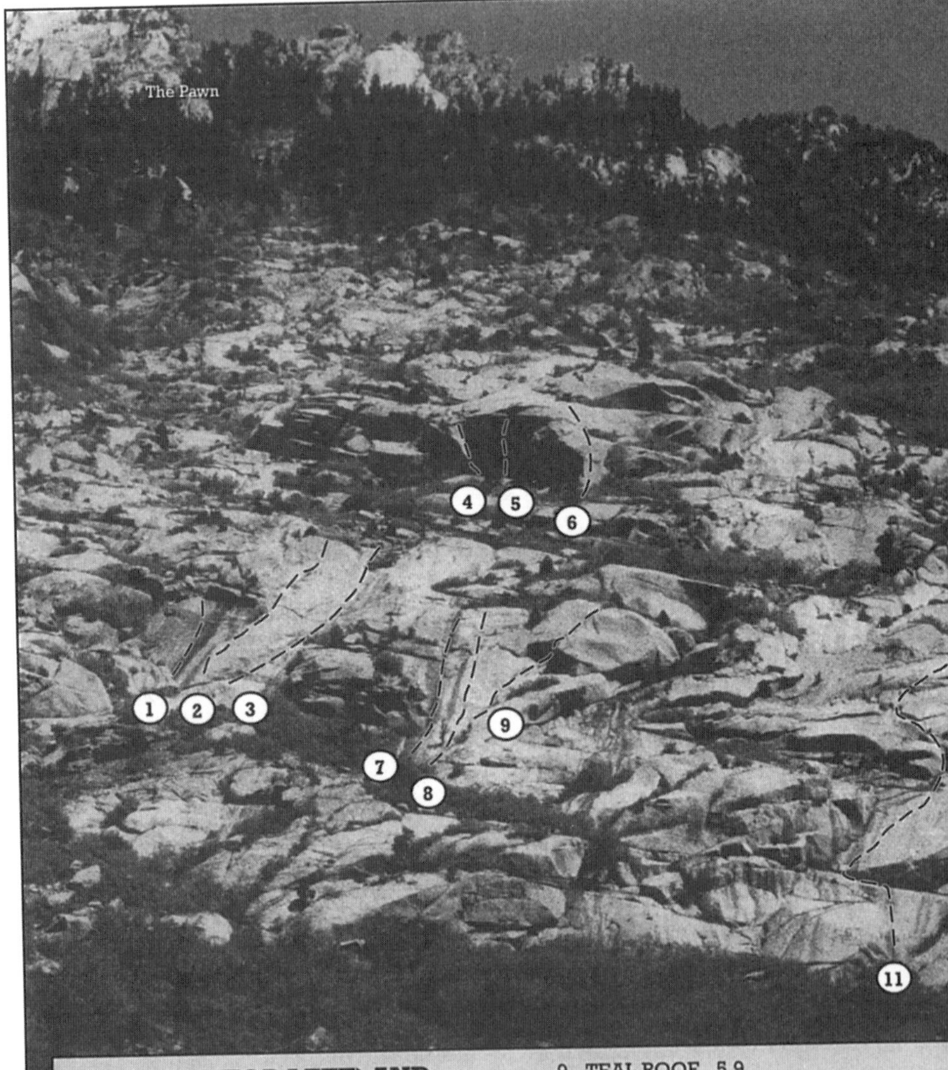

THE PAWN (TOP LEFT) AND BLACKPEELER AREA

1. BLACK DUCK 5.10
2. EIDER DUCK 5.8
3. WINTER DIVERSION 5.6
4. WIDGEONS IN BONDAGE 5.9
5. BRIAN SMOOT MEMORIAL WIDGEON 5.5
6. WIDGEON ARCH 5.6
7. BLUE-WING TEAL 5.10
8. GREEN-WING TEAL 5.10
9. TEAL ROOF 5.9
11. WESTERN GREBE 5.8 ★ or ★★
26. SPORTSMAN'S PARADISE 5.11 ★
32. DUCKS IN BONDAGE 5.10
33. DEBBIE DOES DAFFY 5.10c R
35. FROZEN STOOL 5.12a ★★
39. DUCK WALK 5.9+ ★★
42. DAFFY'S SHAFT 5.10 ★
50. PEELER DIRECT II 5.7 A2 ★★

32
33
26
35
39
50
42

THE BLACK PEELER

One of the last big granite buttresses on the north side of Little Cottonwood Canyon is the Black Peeler, located about 1.8 miles up canyon from the neon sign. The striking southeast side of this buttress sports vertical walls with limited numbers of climbable features. The routes on this side of the cliff are mostly aid climbing on compact rock, and are excellent warmups for big wall climbing. The routes on the lower-angled south face had long been ignored until Bill Robins and company began to develop them in 1985. These aspects contrast the blank southeast face, in that there is a plethora of climbable features. In general, the south face offers bolt-protected slab climbing on good quality rock. Because of the duck theme and the crisscrossing of routes, confusion is common for those trying to figure out south face routes.

APPROACH: Park at a white power plant on the right side of the road, 1.85 miles up canyon from the neon sign (this is located .55 miles beyond the Gate Buttress). Cross the road and walk west on a dirt road until you reach a bombed-out switchback. A trail leads up the west end of this switchback into the scrub oak, and traverses to the base of the cliff, then over to the Western Grebe area. For routes on the Southeast side—The Peeler Face, traverse on this trail for only 100 feet, then set out up the hill. See overview on page 220.

DESCENT: Most rappels in this area require two ropes. See topos for specific rappel locations.

THE BLACK PEELER—SOUTH FACE ROUTES

These are the broken slabs facing the road.
Routes 1 to 45 are included here.

1. BLACK DUCK 5.10
Follows black streaks on the far west end of the south face.
FA: Skeeter Malinski and Bill Robins, 1987.

2. EIDER DUCK 5.8
Ascend the white face right of Black Duck.
FA: Skeeter Malinski and Bill Robins, 1987.

3. WINTER DIVERSION 5.6
This climbs the right side of the Eider Duck slab.
FA: Dave Smith, Guy Toombes, Dennis Turville and Lynn Wheeler, 1969.

4. WIDGEONS IN BONDAGE 5.9
Way up on the west side is a trapezoidal-shaped roof. This climbs the left dihedral of this roof.
FA: Doug Larson and Bill Robins, 1987.

5. BRIAN SMOOT MEMORIAL WIDGEON 5.5
Climb the right dihedral of the roof. (See route #4.)
FA: Doug Larson and Bill Robins, 1987.

6. WIDGEON ARCH 5.6
Climb the slab just right of the trapezoidal roof. (See route #4.)
FA: Doug Larson and Bill Robins, 1987.

7. BLUE-WING TEAL 5.10
Follow black streaks right of a broken section rise about 150 feet right of Eider Duck.
FA: Skeeter Malinski and Bill Robins, 1987.

8. GREEN-WING TEAL 5.10
The white slab just right of Blue-wing Teal.
FA: Doug Larson and Bill Robins, 1987.

9. TEAL ROOF 5.9
Climb the roof crack to the right of Green-wing Teal.
FA: Doug Larson and Bill Robins, 1987.

10. PUFFIN PROMENADE 5.11 ★
Branch off of Western Grebe and climb up a steep black face/corner.
FA: Kirsten Davis and Bill Robins, 1986.

11. WESTERN GREBE 5.8 ★ or ★★
Follows slabs for the full length of the south face. When linked with Bull Dykes And Biker Ducks and Great Grebes, Batman!, this route gets two stars. Another two star linkup: Western Grebe to Fool's Paradise to Dark of the Moon.
FA: Kirsten Davis and Bill Robins, 1985.

The ever enthusiastic Doug Hall leading the ever classic S-Direct, The Thumb.

photo: Kennan Harvey.

THE BLACK PEELER—SOUTH FACE ROUTES

12. PIED-BILLED GREBE 5.8 R

This climbs right of the second pitch of Western Grebe.

FA: Skeeter Malinski and Bill Robins, 1987.

13. WHY A DUCK? 5.8 ★

Good question. Climb the bolt-protected slab six feet right of Western Grebe's first pitch.

FA: Bill Foster, Pete Lenz and Doug Fuller, 1988.

14. VIA DUCK 5.8

A direct start to Why A Duck? Contrived.

FA: Bill Foster, Pete Lenz and Doug Fuller, 1988.

15. JUST DUCKY 5.11

Climb a thin slab above the last pitch of Puffin Promenade.

FA: Bill Robins and Skeeter Malinski, 1987.

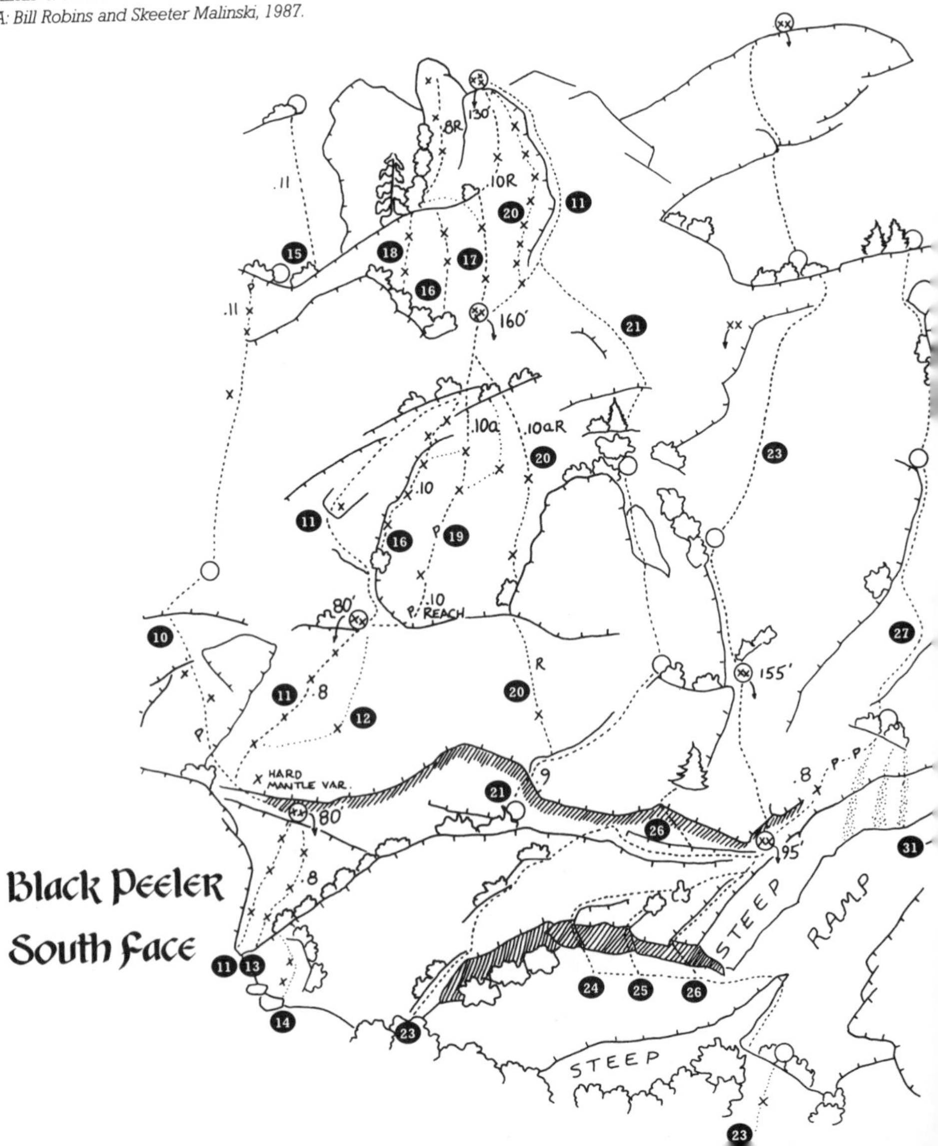

Black Peeler South Face

16. FOOL'S PARADISE 5.10 ★★
Climb the bolt protected dihedral right of the third pitch of Western Grebe, to a belay. The second pitch embarks upon the final slab which leads directly to the pine tree.
FA: Pete Lenz and Doug Fuller.

17. GREAT GREBES, BATMAN! 5.10 R ★★
Sort of runout slab climbing that goes directly up the prow to the rappel station. A few pieces of gear are needed.
FA: Bill Robins and Kirsten Davis, 1985.

18. DARK OF THE MOON 5.10c ★★
Excellent , well-protected, steep friction climbing with nicely spaced chickenheads.
FA: Chris Begue and Scott Keller June, 1995.

19. BULL DYKES AND BIKER DUCKS 5.10 ★
Turn the roof (strongly height-related) and climb the slab above. The final one bolt slab (not on topo) has been called Dancing Duck.
FA: Bill Robins and Skeeter Malinski, 1987.

20. ROLLER DUCKS AND DAIRY QUEENS 5.10a R
Surmount the roof on Viper, then continue up runout slabs and join Western Grebe.
FA: Bill Robins and Skeeter Malinski, 1987.

21. VIPER 5.9
Climb the crack through the roof band that guards the lower section of the cliff. Join a sickle-shaped crack on the fourth pitch.
FA: Kent Christensen, Dick Grow and Dave Smith, 1972.
FFA: Max Townsend, Dave Smith, Lenny Nelson and Marshall Ralph, 1976.

22. MINNESOTA DUCK 5.7
Branch rightward on Viper's final section, instead of joining the sickle-shaped crack Not on topo.
FA: Dan Anton and Bill Robins, 1987.

23. HORNED GREBE 5.8
Wander and meander up rock in the middle of the south face. The direct start to the left makes a lot more sense.
FA: Thomas Koch and Bill Robins, 1985.

24. DUCK BLIND VARIATION 5.10 ★
Climb a flaring, overhanging hand crack to a chickenhead exit.
FA: Kirsten Davis and Bill Robins, 1985.

25. DUCK WADDLE VARIATION 5.11
Climb the steep wall 20 feet left of Sportsman's Paradise via a flaring offwidth.
FA: Thomas Koch and Bill Robins, 1985.

26. SPORTSMAN'S PARADISE 5.11 ★
This route follows two hard, but short roofs separated by easy ground. The first is a hard to protect 5.11, the second is a mini-Separate Reality and is 5.10.
FA: Mark Bennett, Thomas Koch and Bill Robins, 1985.

27. SURF SCOOTER 5.8 R
Branch off Horned Grebe for four uneventful pitches.
FA: Bill Robins and Kirsten Davis, 1985.

28. COOT CONFERENCE 5.8
Climb the left of the right-facing dihedrals on the upper face.
FA: Bill Foster, Michelle Perkins and Bill Robins, 1987.

THE BLACK PEELER SOUTH FACE

29. MISSING DUCK 5.8

Diverge from Duck Soup with a leftward traverse and climb the dihedral above.

FA: Bill Robins and Skeeter Malinski, 1987.

30. DUCK SALAD 5.7

A variation to the final pitch of Missing Duck. Climb the right-branching crack.

FA: Skeeter Malinski and Bill Robins, 1987.

31. DUCK SOUP 5.9+

Traverse in from the left to join the Duck Walk routes.

FA: Kirsten Davis and Bill Robins, 1985.

32. DUCKS IN BONDAGE 5.10

At the top of the Black Peeler is a slab. This is the left line up this slab.

FA: Bill Robins and Skeeter Malinski, 1987.

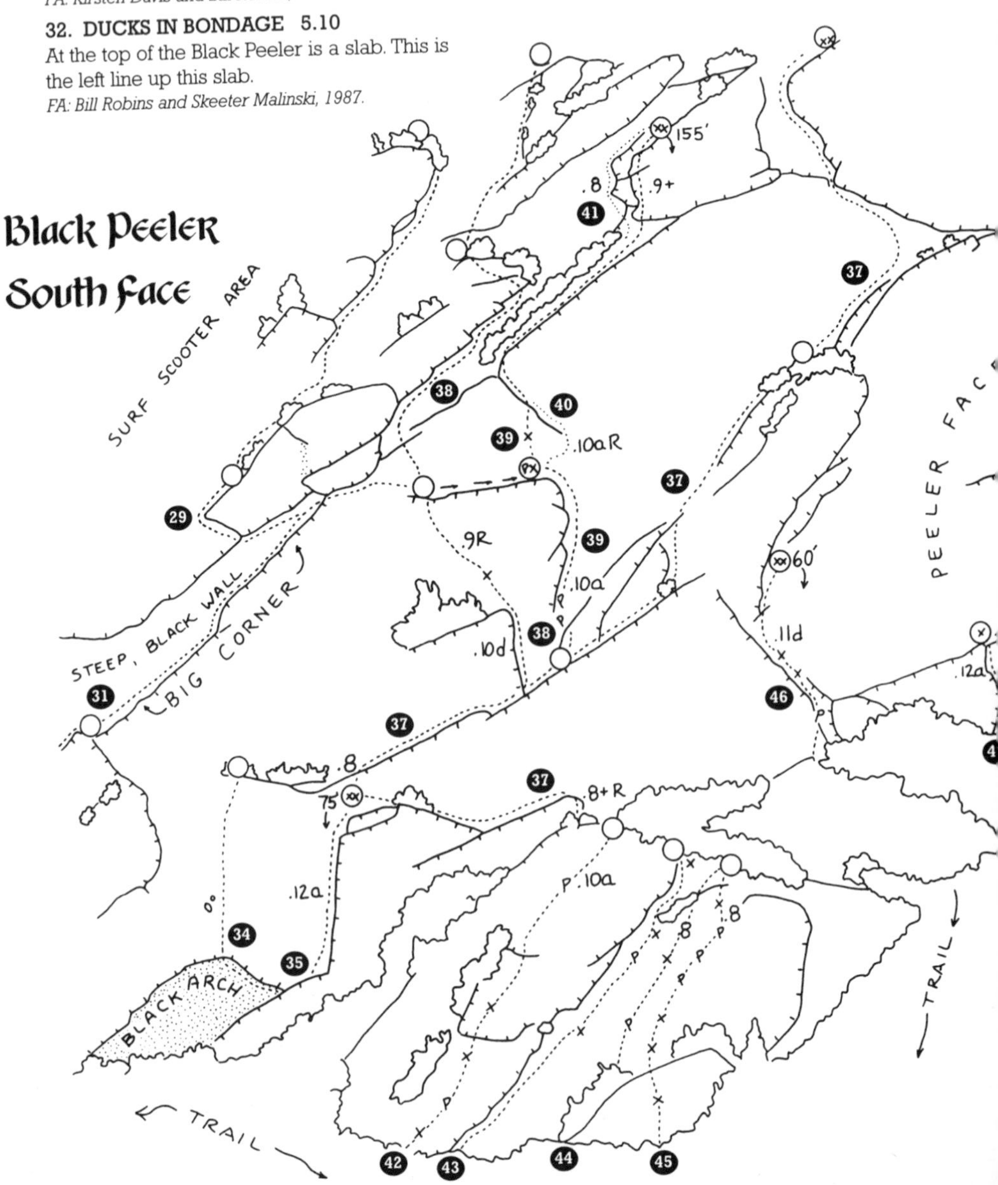

33. DEBBIE DOES DAFFY 5.10c R
This is the right-hand line up the slab. It is runout. (See route #32.)
FA: Bill Robins and Kelly Laakso, 1987.

34. THE BLACK ARCH II A3+ ★★
Just left of Frozen Stool is a prominent black arch. Above the highest point of the arch is an overhanging seam. Gain the seam from the right via easy aid, then follow the seam and slab above to a fixed belay/rappel station. Bring a selection of beaks, heads, hooks, RPs, and wires and some camming devices. The original line used a six-foot extension rod to hook past a blank section, the direct variation of this section requires a 3⁄16" bat hook.
FA: Mark Bennett, Adrian Burgess and Robyn Rogin, 1996.
FA of direct variation: Mark Bennett and Matt Floyd, 1996.

35. FROZEN STOOL 5.12a ★★
Advanced chimney (or stemming) technique in a corner system. Thin.
FA: Eric Eliason and Pete Gibbs, 1969.
FFA: Peter Hunt and Bill Robins, 1985.

36. HORNET A2 ★
An aid line following the corner that begins ten feet right of Frozen Stool. You'll nead the usual bag o' tricks: beaks, blades, heads, small angles, and a hook. This route shares the belay and rappel with Frozen Stool. Not on topo.
FA: Ben Folsom, 1994.

37. BAT WALK 5.9+ ★
The first moves are the crux of the climb—bring a big Friend for protection. A wandering route.
FA: Lenny Nelson and Paul Anderson, 1965.
FFA: Mark Bennett and Bill Robins, 1985.

38. MANDARIN DUCK 5.10d ★
Climb the offwidth or lieback corner and the face above. The final pitch traverses beneath the roof until flakes provide exit.
FA: Thomas Koch, P. Diener, K. Davis and B. Robins, 1986.

39. DUCK WALK 5.9+ ★★
The third pitch dihedral is very nice.
FA: Bill Robins and Kirsten Davis, 1985.

40. DIRTY DUCK VARIATION 5.10a R
Traverse right to a crack, avoiding the bolt-protected groove above.
FA: John Lodgson, Bill Robins and Kirsten Davis, 1985.

41. FUPDUCK VARIATION 5.8
Exit out the left side of the roof.
FA: John Lodgson, Bill Robins and Kirsten Davis, 1985.

42. DAFFY'S SHAFT 5.10 ★
The slabs on the lower right end of the south face (the trail passes directly beneath them) offer several routes. This is the left line, turning an overhang mid-pitch.
FA: Bill Robins and Skeeter Malinski, 1987.

43. WALKING THE DUCK 5.7 R
This follows the right-facing dihedral, the principal feature of the face.
FA: Bill Robins and Skeeter Malinski, 1987.

44. RUDDY DUCK 5.8
Climb the red streak 15 feet right of Walking the Duck.
FA: Bill Robins and Kirsten Davis, 1985.

45. DUCK A L'ORANGE 5.8 ★
Follow fixed pins and bolts on the far right face and crack.
FA: Bill Foster and Bill Robins, 1988.

THE BLACK PEELER—THE PEELER FACE

The awesomely sheer southeast face has long been the main attraction of this buttress.

46. BIRTHDAY ROUTE 5.11d ★
One very blank move onto a sloping chickenhead.
FA: Kirk Andriano, Kirsten Davis, Bill Robins and Skeeter Malinski, 1987.

47. LOST PUPPIES IN TIE DYE 5.12a ★
Climb a short flake/thin-crack 50 left of the start of Black Peeler.
FA: Drew Bedford, 1987.

48. BLACK PEELER III 5.10d A3 ★
This foray up the blank and imposing east face tackles the best line of weakness. It traverses more than it goes up, so it's just as thrilling to second as it is to lead. It can be done hammerless. Bring many brass-type nuts and small stoppers.
FA: Bill Conrod and Steve Ellsworth.

49. THE SERPENT III 5.12a A3 ★
The thin seam left of Peeler Direct. The third pitch flake is way out there—bring a few 4" cams for this section, as well as hooks, heads, and a selection of pins for the rest of the route. Lost Puppies in Tie Dye can be used as the first pitch, if desired.
FA: Drew Bedford and Kurt Fashanpaur, 1988.

50. PEELER DIRECT II 5.7 A2 ★★
All clean, please. Starting off the ramp with dicey bashie and bolt moves, continue up a fine ultra thin crack on marginal nut placements. The standard pre-Valley warmup.
FA: Eric Eliason and Lenny Nelson.

51. RIVETING A1
A rivet ladder provides quick, although less interesting access, to the belay at the base of the Peeler Direct.

52. ORANGUTAN AFTERNOON 5.11a ★
One hundred feet up and right of the start of Black Peeler is a right-slanting overhanging hand crack that leads into a corner system. Either walk off or rappel from trees.
FA: Brian Smoot and Bill Robins, 1987.

53. EZRA THE CATAMITE 5.8
In the broken section right of the Peeler Face, gain a ramp that traverses above Tin Man, and follow the ramp all the way to the top.
FA: Kirk Andriano, Bill Robins and Skeeter Malinski, 1987.

54. BRIGHAM'S BEER 5.10d ★
This is a series of right-facing corners 100 feet left of Tin Man.
FA: Robyn Rogin, Bill Robins and Skeeter Malinski, 1987.

55. BATMAN II 5.10d A2 ★
Start in a peapod-shaped dihedral with a fixed pin, or climb around to the right (5.5). You'll be mumbling "Holy Cow" on the final, very nice pitch.
FA: James Garrett, Mike Schwitter and Steve Kauffmann, 1987.

56. TIN MAN II A4 ★★

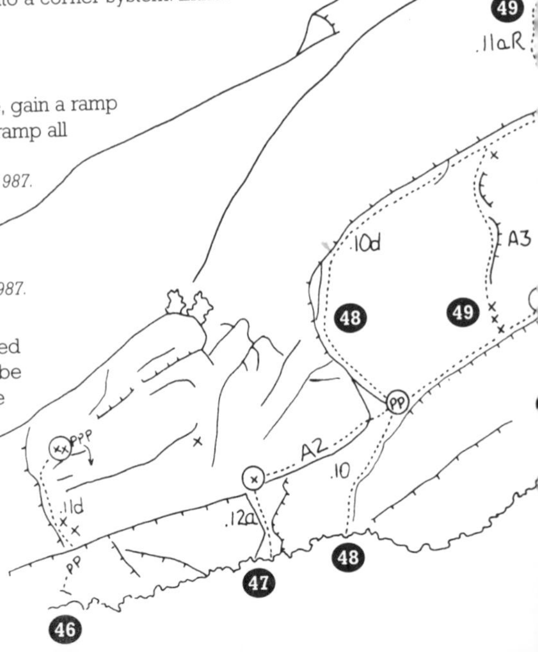

A route with a reputation. A very difficult start poses serious ankle threat. Bring TCUs, stoppers, R.P.s, thin iron, a few small angles, heads, circle heads, and hooks. The flake above the roof is slightly expanding.
FA: Pete Gibbs and Eric Eliason, 1969.

57. SKIN MAN II A3+ ★★
A modern aid route, sure to get under your skin. Include heads, circle heads, KBs, LAs, baby angles, and hooks on your rack. A pendulum left from the last bolt reaches the Tin Man belay anchors. Unfortunately, the second ascent party drilled an optional belay anchor in the middle of the route.
FA: Tim Wagner, 1994.

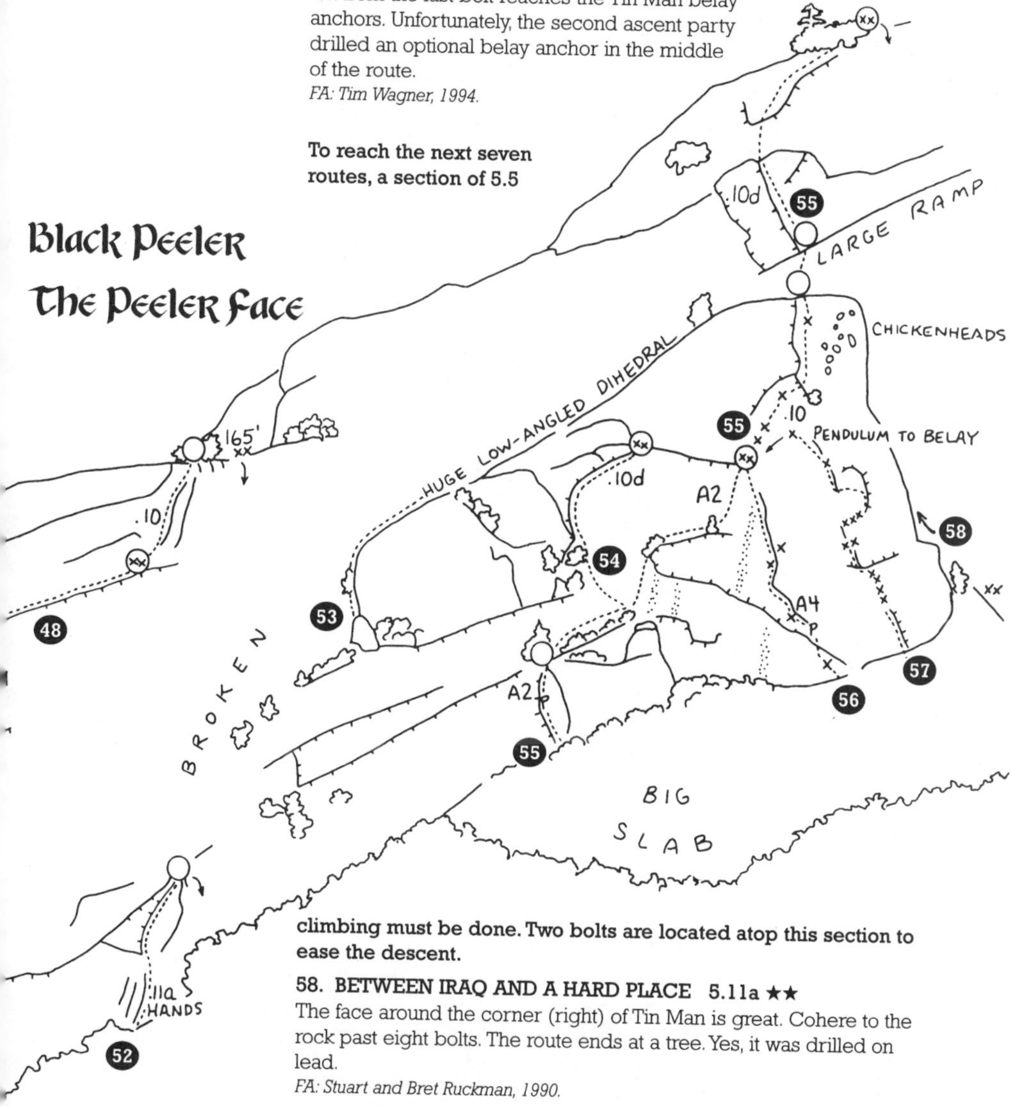

To reach the next seven routes, a section of 5.5 climbing must be done. Two bolts are located atop this section to ease the descent.

Black Peeler
The Peeler Face

58. BETWEEN IRAQ AND A HARD PLACE 5.11a ★★
The face around the corner (right) of Tin Man is great. Cohere to the rock past eight bolts. The route ends at a tree. Yes, it was drilled on lead.
FA: Stuart and Bret Ruckman, 1990.

59. SCIMITAR 5.9 ★
A good two-pitcher. Avoid the trees on pitch two by climbing an incipient crack four feet to the left. The overhang offers some cranker hand jams. Rappel from the top of Iraq. Bring protection up to a 3" cam.
FA: Judy and Bret Ruckman, 1990.

PEELER FACE ROUTES

60. SALT LAKE SYNDROME 5.9 ★

Starting with a vicious looking chimney and leading up into a beautiful hand crack, this route was named for the snobbish attitudes of the late 60s and early 70s. The upper pitches wander up the easy, though runout, slab to a prow and belay. Climb the prow for 20 feet, then run it out to the top (5.7 R). Rappel from bolts.

FA: Paul Horton and Doug Cairns, 1982.

61. MISSING VICKI AND KIRSTEN 5.10

Start on Animal Crackers, then branch off left and climb a steep black dihedral that ends at the two-bolt anchor atop Salt Lake Syndrome.

FA: Brian Smoot and Bill Robins, 1987.

62. ANIMAL CRACKERS 5.9

Climb the ramp-like dihedral for five pitches. A traverse on the fourth pitch gains a dihedral to the west, which is climbed to the top.

FA: Bill Robins, Kirsten Davis and Skeeter Malinski, 1987.

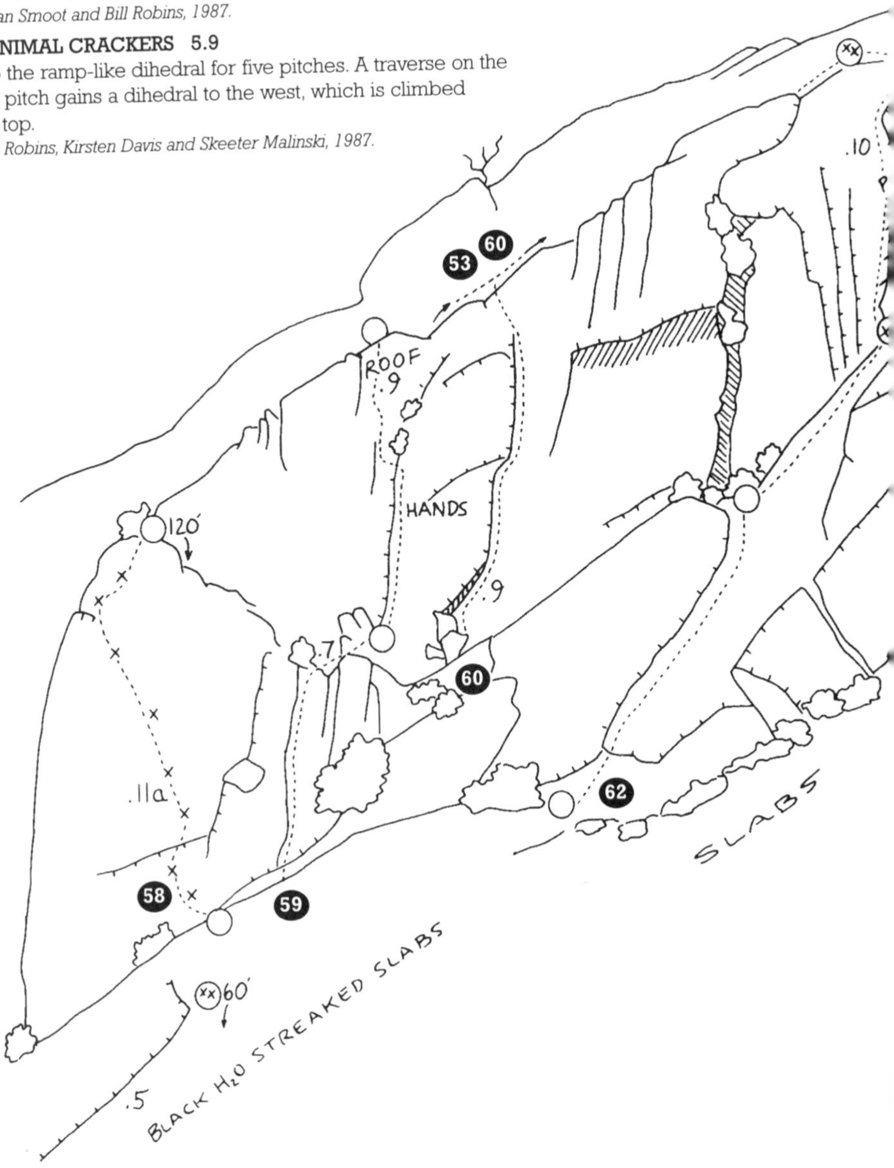

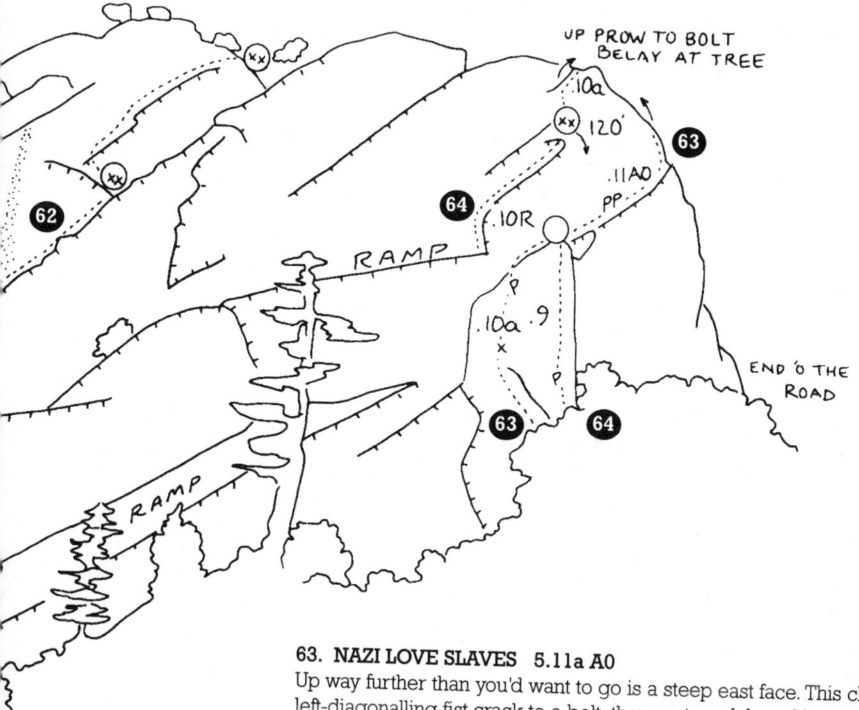

63. NAZI LOVE SLAVES 5.11a A0
Up way further than you'd want to go is a steep east face. This climbs a left-diagonalling fist crack to a bolt, then up to a slab and belay (5.10a). From the belay, angle right on an exposed ramp (5.11 A0). Head straight up an offwidth crack for the third pitch (5.10). Climb the roof and slab above (5.9+).
FA: Bill Robins and Kirk Andriano, 1987.

64. STAG PARTY 5.10c R ★
To start, climb the crack 10 feet right of Nazi Love Slaves past a pin. For the final pitch, climb the thin crack above for 20 feet, traverse left to the prow and up past a bolt to a rappel tree. Bring RPs and small TCUs.
FA: Bill Robins and Mark Bennett, 1987.

LISA FALLS

This popular area offers a smorgasbord of diverse climbing possibilities. From smooth, holdless friction, to clean cracks, and even overhanging jug climbing—it's all here, cooled by the year-round stream. A waterfall down the Lower Slab creates a pleasant atmosphere, with climbs both on the right and left sides. The routes on the Freedom Wall rise out of the stream, and rarely see sunshine, making them perfect in the summer, even on scorcher days. One problem exists, however—that of the rank beginner (usually loiterers turned climbers) getting in above their heads on a route. The slabs look relatively easy, but...

APPROACH: Park 2.8 miles up canyon from the neon sign at large pullouts on either side of a big right hand turn. A good trail heads north through the trees and emerges at the base of a smooth granite slab, split by a waterfall. This first wall is the Lower Slab. To access the Freedom Wall, walk west along the base of the Lower Slab, past the waterfall, to the left edge of the wall. A steep, eroded trail can be followed from here (with some scrambling) to where the canyon levels out above the waterfall. The freedom wall is east-facing and on the left. See overview on page 220.

DESCENT: All of the routes in this area can be descended with one rope.

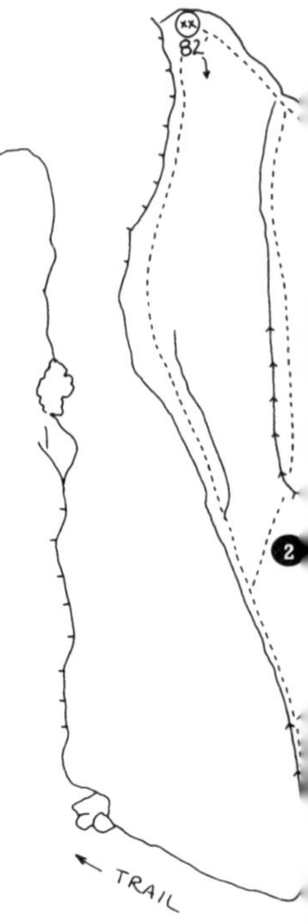

LISA FALLS—LOWER SLAB

1. LISA FALLS LEFT 5.8 R ★
This is mostly unprotected and usually toproped.

2. SWEET SPOT 5.8+ R ★
Step right from Lisa Falls Left to a bolt, then friction to the top. Poor protection and slippery rock.

3. SWEEP LEFT 5.10b ★
Four bolts, glazed rock, and a whole lot of skating.
FA: Tony Calderone and James Preziosi, 1994.

4. END RUN 5.7
Climb just right of the falls.

5. FLEE FLICKER 5.7 ★
Three bolts just right of the falls. Polished rock.

6. FLEETING GLIMPSE 5.8+ ★
Three bolts of slab work leading directly to the belay at the top of the first pitch of Lisa Falls Right.

7. LISA FALLS RIGHT 5.5 ★★
A great route. Follow a rounded right-leaning crack to a ledge. An unprotected mantle above the ledge gains some knobs and a two-bolt belay (5.5). Continue up and right into a shallow dihedral that leads to another bolt belay (5.4). Rappel the route with one rope.

8. LEFTY 5.4
Not much going for this variation.

9. HARD KNOCKS 5.9+ ★
The face left of the dihedral on the second pitch of Lisa Falls Right is protected by one bolt.

10. NEUROTICA 5.5
One short section of finger crack is noteworthy, as is the little roof.

11. SAFETY BLITZ 5.7
The roof and corner above merit an ascent.

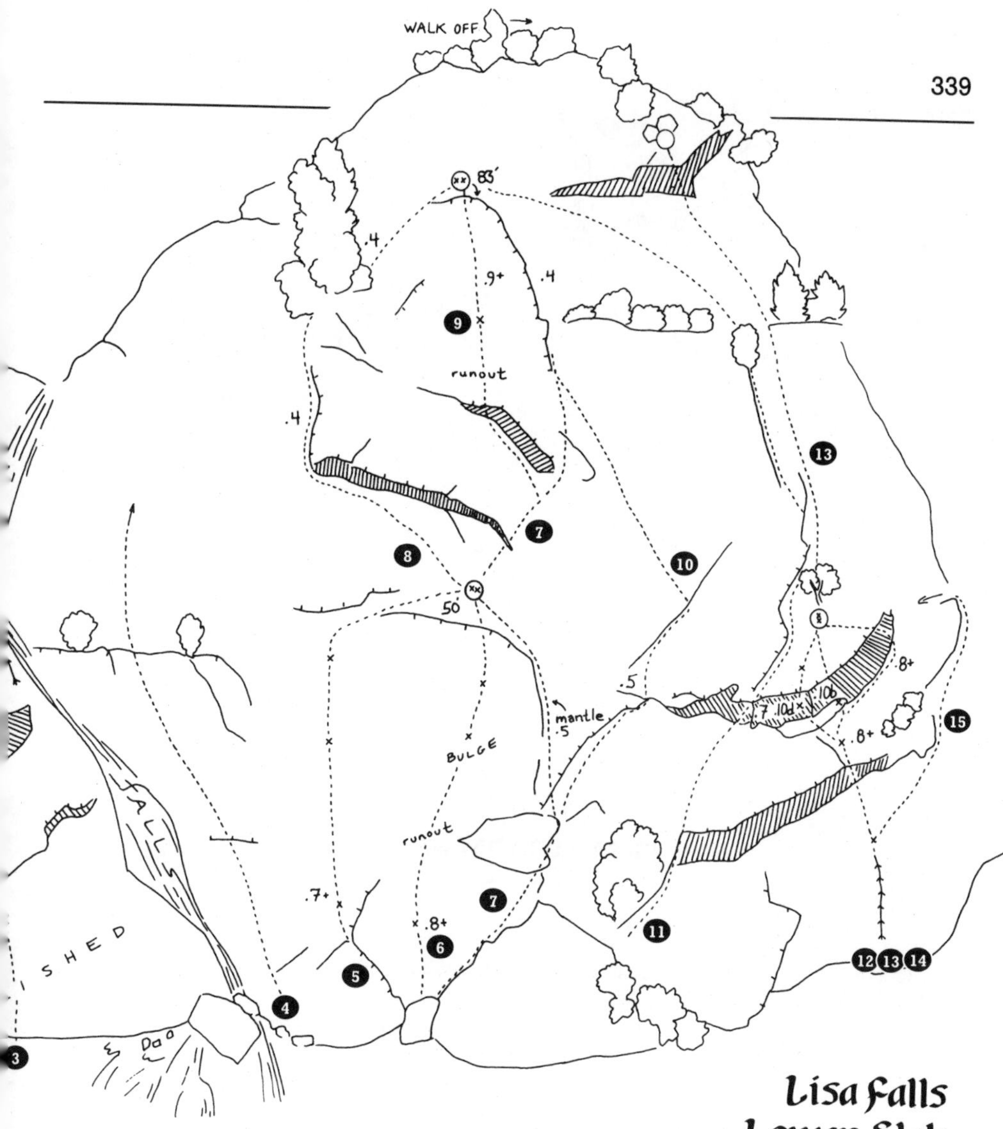

Lisa Falls Lower Slab

12. RODAN 5.10d ★
Pull the roofs directly. Four bolts and a good, eye opening lip sequence.
FA: Jason Ball and Doug Hunter, 1996.

13. UNDER THE SKIRT AND CLIP THE BUSH 5.10b ★
Climb past the first two bolts of Rodan, then move up and right in a finger crack, clip a hidden bolt and step left onto the slab just below the chain anchors.
FA: Tony Calderone and Kevin Standifer, 1992.

14. DRAG QUEEN 5.8+
Continue rightward up the right-trending crack after the hidden bolt on Under the Skirt.
FA: Tony Calderone and Kathy Lagerquist, July 1992

15. WHERE'S WINKY? 5.8 R
Clip the first bolt of Rodan, then launch off to the right.
FA: Jay Knight, Layne Oliver, April 1994.

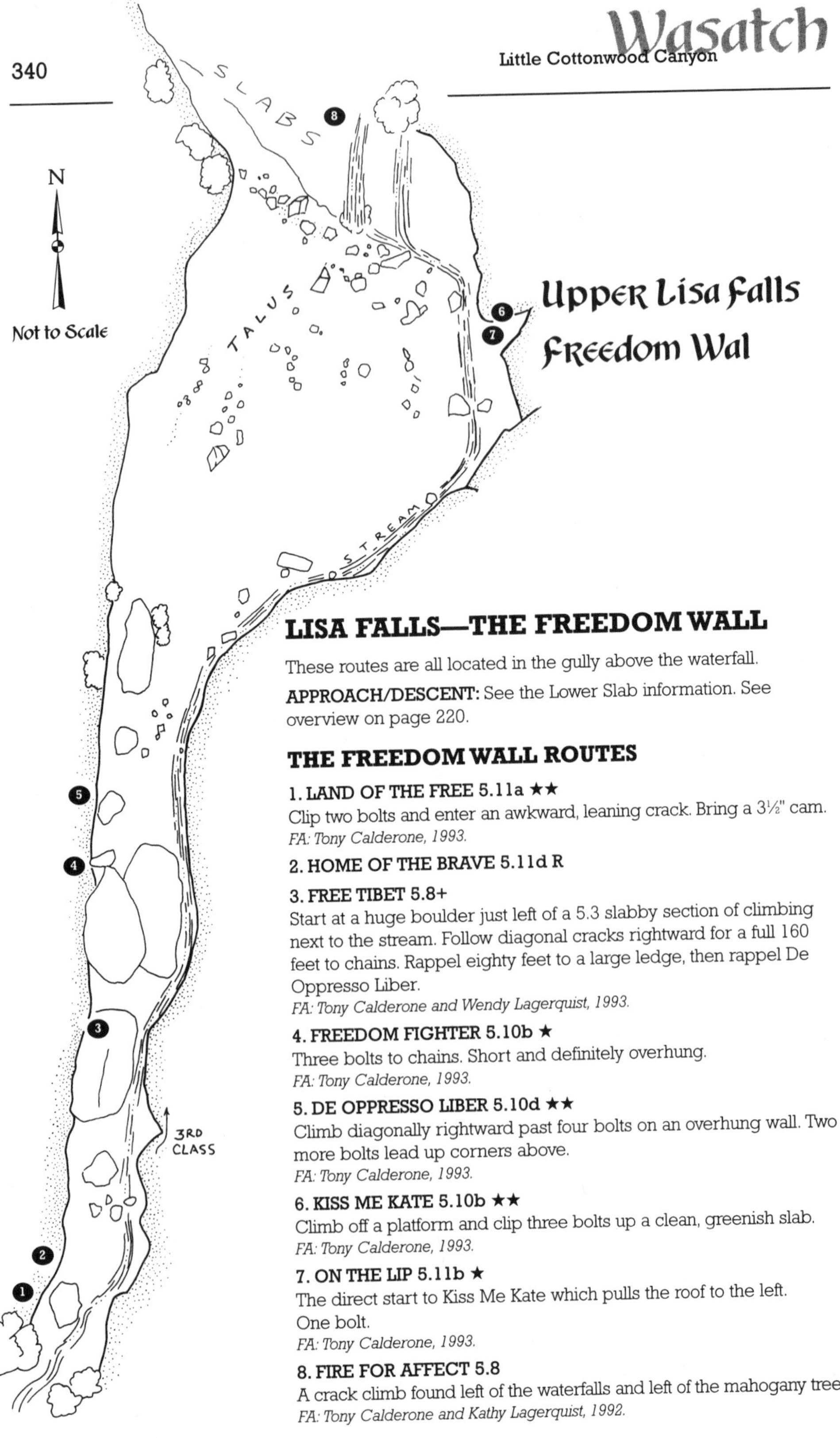

LISA FALLS—THE FREEDOM WALL

These routes are all located in the gully above the waterfall.

APPROACH/DESCENT: See the Lower Slab information. See overview on page 220.

THE FREEDOM WALL ROUTES

1. LAND OF THE FREE 5.11a ★★
Clip two bolts and enter an awkward, leaning crack. Bring a 3½" cam.
FA: Tony Calderone, 1993.

2. HOME OF THE BRAVE 5.11d R

3. FREE TIBET 5.8+
Start at a huge boulder just left of a 5.3 slabby section of climbing next to the stream. Follow diagonal cracks rightward for a full 160 feet to chains. Rappel eighty feet to a large ledge, then rappel De Oppresso Liber.
FA: Tony Calderone and Wendy Lagerquist, 1993.

4. FREEDOM FIGHTER 5.10b ★
Three bolts to chains. Short and definitely overhung.
FA: Tony Calderone, 1993.

5. DE OPPRESSO LIBER 5.10d ★★
Climb diagonally rightward past four bolts on an overhung wall. Two more bolts lead up corners above.
FA: Tony Calderone, 1993.

6. KISS ME KATE 5.10b ★★
Climb off a platform and clip three bolts up a clean, greenish slab.
FA: Tony Calderone, 1993.

7. ON THE LIP 5.11b ★
The direct start to Kiss Me Kate which pulls the roof to the left. One bolt.
FA: Tony Calderone, 1993.

8. FIRE FOR AFFECT 5.8
A crack climb found left of the waterfalls and left of the mahogany tree.
FA: Tony Calderone and Kathy Lagerquist, 1992.

TANNER'S GULCH (no topo)

Many hikers have climbed Dromedary and Sunrise Peaks from this steep gully, especially in the spring when the gully is full of hard, frozen snow. However, the broken cliffs have long been overlooked for rock climbing. So far, only one route exists.

APPROACH: Drive 4.2 miles up LCC and park. A trail leads west and then up into the gully. Expect a 25-minute approach.

DESCENT: Walk off.

1. SKINNY PUPPIES 5.11b ★
This route is hard to locate, but can be found on the first real climbable piece of rock on the right (east) side of Tanner's Gulch. Start in an overhanging dihedral capped by roofs. Diagonal up and left as the crack goes from tight fingers to 1½ inches. Bring a standard rack and some RPs.
FA: Drew Bedford and Ron George.

Randy Trover blazing up The Sting, West Bell Tower.

photo: John Barstow.

THE HELLGATE CLIFFS

Located halfway between Snowbird and Alta, the Hellgate Cliffs afford fine vistas and cooler climbing in the summer. The atmosphere is a welcomed reprieve from the sometimes sweltering temperatures found down canyon. Limestone, highly variable in quality, forms towers on the southern end, and becomes a 400-foot cliff further north.

The rock quality at the Hellgate is unpredictable, and blind trust in holds will likely mean rock falls and leader falls. Do not belay directly under the leader at The Hellgate. While this is a good practice for all climbing, it is especially important here, even on the more popular routes where the occasional off-route hold is still dislodged. A very serious recommendation: bring helmets. Naturally-occurring rockfall is common. The gullies (nicknamed the Tower One Gully, the Shooting Gallery, and The Gully Of Eternal Peril), and the Main Hellgate are particularly bad, especially during the spring. Even walking under the right (east) side of the main cliff can be dangerous. The top of the cliff here is a steep talus slope that looms precariously over the wall. This slope poses serious threats, particularly if mountain goats or hikers are moving around in this area. It is a good idea to look for the mountain goats with binoculars before climbing any routes on this part of the wall. There are sections of The Hellgate that have good rock, however. The best quality stone can be found in the Towers area. In general, the climbing is really fun and the area enjoys moderate popularity.

Mugs Stump and partners made the initial ascents on the cliff, using traditional ground-up style. In 1988, the new ethic of rappel-placed bolts was practiced, and the steepest walls were developed. Offering better protection and, in general, better climbing, this latter group of routes began to draw other climbers. More recently, some Alta locals, inspired by Mugs's ground up efforts, began to explore The Hellgate's Main Wall and Towers with an eye towards naturally protected routes, or mixed bolt and gear routes. These climbs were often led boldly from the ground up. Luckily, these two factions peacefully coexist, and the result is a large number of good routes in one area. The high concentration of climbs in the Towers area means you can tick-off many of the routes without much hassle, all in the beauty of the high Wasatch. Bring a ton of quickdraws, a rack, and two ropes. Once again, the climbing is on private land. Be mindful of this and please keep the area clean. The best season is from June to October. The routes are described from right to left, those that you reach first to those furthest away.

APPROACH: Park off the road at a pullout on the north side, about 7.35 miles up canyon from the neon sign. This pullout is just up canyon from the Hellgate condos. A dirt road diagonals west across the hillside. DO NOT drive up this road. Instead, walk up the dirt road 200 feet to a gully. This gully is just before a chain gate and leads directly up to the Shooting Gallery between Tower Two and Tower Three. To access Tower One more directly, follow the approach gully to a small trail that contours east out of the gully and over to Tower One. This trail is marked by a piece of rebar.

DESCENT: Two-rope rappels from bolts provide the typical descent; otherwise expect a long, loose walk off the shoulder of Flagstaff Peak (not recommended) along an old mining trail that traverses above the cliffs and leads to Alta Central (marshal's office).

Scott Oda, living the good life at Altaworld. Hellgate Area.

photo: Craig Dillon.

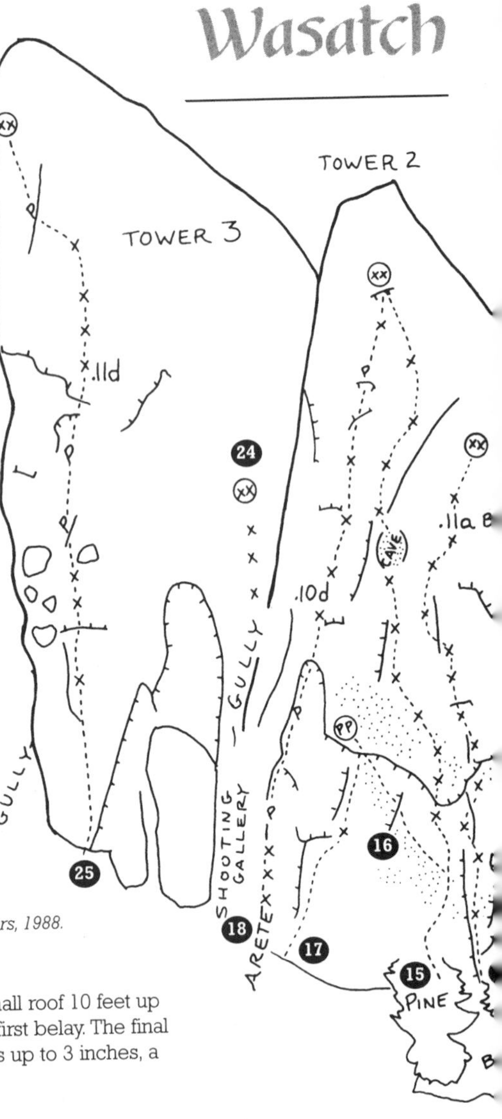

1. HELL IS FOR CHILDREN 5.7 ★

60 feet right of What The Hell, and just right of a right-facing corner is a short, slabby, route on good rock. 5 bolts protect to a chain anchor.

FA: Bill Hunt and Dan Caruso, early post-mid-90's.

TOWER ONE ROUTES

This is the southeast most tower, the one with the shortest approach. Much of the rock is black dolomite. An enormous roof guards the better part of the wall. Shelter From The Storm and Dark Star generally remain dry during rainstorms.

2. WHAT THE HELL 5.7 ★

Start up a crack and follow 3 bolts along an arête to chains.

FA: Franziska and James Garrett, July 1993.

3. CHEAP THRILLS 5.11a ★★

Gear (bring cams up to large hand sized) protects the corner leading to bolts. This first pitch is tricky and a bit scary. The bolted second pitch climbs a narrow black streak on crimpy holds to a white face above.

FA: In bold traditional style, Dave Medera, Pat McInerney and Bill Hunt, 1991.

4. SINBAD 5.11a ★

The compelling V-slot system with roof at the top. Somewhat difficult to protect. The wild crux roof is well-protected. Descend the shooting gallery gully, or walk to the top of Cheap Thrills.

FA: Pitch one, Mark Whitton, Mugs Stump and Tom Carruthers, 1988.
FA: Complete route, Mugs Stump and Bret Ruckman, 1990.

5. SECOND VOYAGE 5.11c ★★

Start in a V-slot just left of the Sinbad start, pull a small roof 10 feet up and climb overhangs and an arête to join Sinbad's first belay. The final moves are overhanging and wild. Bring TCUs, cams up to 3 inches, a few micro nuts and an assortment of wired nuts.

FA: Mugs Stump, 1990.

6. SHELTER FROM THE STORM 5.12a ★★

A great line with wild climbing. Place gear in the finger crack between the first and second bolts. The first pitch is 5.11c/d. The second has seen few attempts, is rated 5.12a, and "should be repeated."

FA: Bill Hunt, Pat McImerney and Dave Medara, 1991.
FA: Pitch two: Bill Hunt, 1994.

7. DARK STAR 5.12a ★★

Climb up the obvious initial corner, move right for a few moves, left to the roof, then begin climbing a series of cracks out a roof to a two-bolt station. Back-cleaning is recommended due to rope drag, especially at the roof. The protection is tricky to place. Despite the wandering line, this route is something of a local (gear) test-piece.

FA: Mugs Stump.
FFA: Mugs Stump 1991.

8. DARK STAR TOO 5.12a/b ★

This is the second pitch of Dark Star Roof. Climb up left of the arête in wild, overhanging pods and wind caves. Remember your leg bars.

FA: Kimber Almond and Janice Almond, Oct. 1995.

9. PANDORA 5.12 a/b ★

Another radically overhung addition to Tower One. Long slings are recommended to help rope drag. Long reaches. Bring gear, including some bigger (fist sized) pieces.
FA: Kimber Almond and Tony Calvert, July 1995.

10. MEDUSSA 5.11b/c ★★★
An excellent route up the dark rock on the left side of the tower. Bring a 1" and 1½" cam and get psyched for the final moves.
FA: Pat McInerney, Scott Lockart and Erik Faul, August, 1993.

11. LITTLE HELLION 5.9 ★★
Starts in Tower One gully and climbs a rib which leads to a long slabby section. Good pockets and edges.
FA: Franziska and James Garrett, August 1993.

TOWER TWO ROUTES

Hellgate Cliffs

This is the middle tower, with the "shooting gallery" gully defining its left side.

12. FALCON CORNER 5.9-
Just left of the Tower One Gully. Nice dihedral moves lead to jugs and a series of semi-pullups, then a delicate step left below the huge block to join Fryable. Long slings and backcleaning help reduce some of the rope drag. Bring gear up to hand-sized cams. Not on topo.
FA: Bill Hunt and Dan Caruso, 1991.

13. FRYABLE 5.9 ★
Start at the crack in the black streak. Cams provide protection for the initial moves. Climb the black streak past two bolts to a right-facing corner/crack that leads one to a neat "sit" belay. Expect some loose rock—hence the name.
FA: Bill Hunt and Kevin Almond, 1991.

TOWER TWO ROUTES

14. DEJA VU 5.11a ★★
Two tricky bulges. Bring some longer draws. Popular.
FA: Gordon Douglass, Frank Ray, Tad Swarner and Gary Olsen,1988.

15. CAVE MAN 5.11d ★
Power first, finesse later. Climb up a face and into a cave. Exit the cave and climb the slab above to the Desp-Arête belay.
FA: Dave Medara, Pat McInernt, and Dave Klein, 1990.

16. THE SHADOW 5.9+ ★★
A very good route with all natural gear and quality moves. The crux bulge is tricky and committing.
FA: Pat McInerny and Dave Medara, 1990.

17. KLEIN'S GIRLS 5.11a
A short route with inobvious holds and one bolt. Bring a 3½ inch cam for the first pocket, wires and smaller cams protect the remainder of the climb.
FA: Dave Medara and Pat McInerny, 1990.

18. DESP-ARÊTE 5.10d ★★
Climb the arête of Tower Two. Great!
FA: Gary Olsen, Stuart Ruckman and Chris Pendleton, 1988.

19. FROM TRILOBITES TO LYCRA TIGHTS 5.11d ★★
Long reaches and good rock. Starts 30 feet up the shooting gallery. Bring small to medium pieces.
FA: Bret Ruckman and Gary Olsen, 1988.

20. NOT BOSCHED UP 5.9+ R ★★
This spooky lead follows a leftward-diagonalling weakness on good rock. The second pin is hidden and route finding seems to be the crux. The climb is two pitches long.
FA: Mugs Stump and Mark Whitton, 1988.

21. THE BIG CHILL 5.10a ★★
Eight bolts protect. A bit runout at the top. Can be used as a direct start to Social Realism.
FA: Mike Vonberg and William Borghetti, 1996.

22. SOCIAL REALISM 5.10a ★★★
The best quality rock on the Hellgate. Although accurately rated, this route keeps coming at you. Bring a few nuts or small cams to protect reaching the first bolt. Beware the possibility of a ledge fall at the sixth bolt. Descend via a single-rope rappel.
FA: Gary Olsen, Chris Pendleton and Stuart Ruckman, 1988.

TOWER THREE ROUTES

23. MON AMI 5.11a ★
This route ascends a line of friendly pockets found way at the top of the shooting gallery on the left wall. There is a single-rope rappel. Bring eight QDs. Not on topo.
FA: Gordon Douglass and Frank Ray, 1988.

24. BLIND FAITH 5.11a ★★
Directly across from Social Realism is a 7 bolt route that has a distinctive "hole" marking the middle of the route. One 50m rope will work for the descent here.
FA: Sean and John Hansen, August, 1995.

25. HEROES ARE ZEROS 5.11d ★★

"Every hero becomes a bore at last."—Ralph Waldo Emerson. Journey up the prow of Tower Three for nearly a rope length. Small wired nuts and 14 QDs are needed. Wild! Watch for loose rock.
FA: Stuart Ruckman and Gary Olsen, 1988.

26. VIRGA 5.11c/d ★★

Starts out of the " Gully of Eternal Peril" on the the north side of Tower Three. Steep, and apparently bare of holds. Your forearm strength likely will evaporate on this one. The route sports all fixed protection (14 bolts).
FA: Stuart Ruckman and Gary Olsen, 1988.

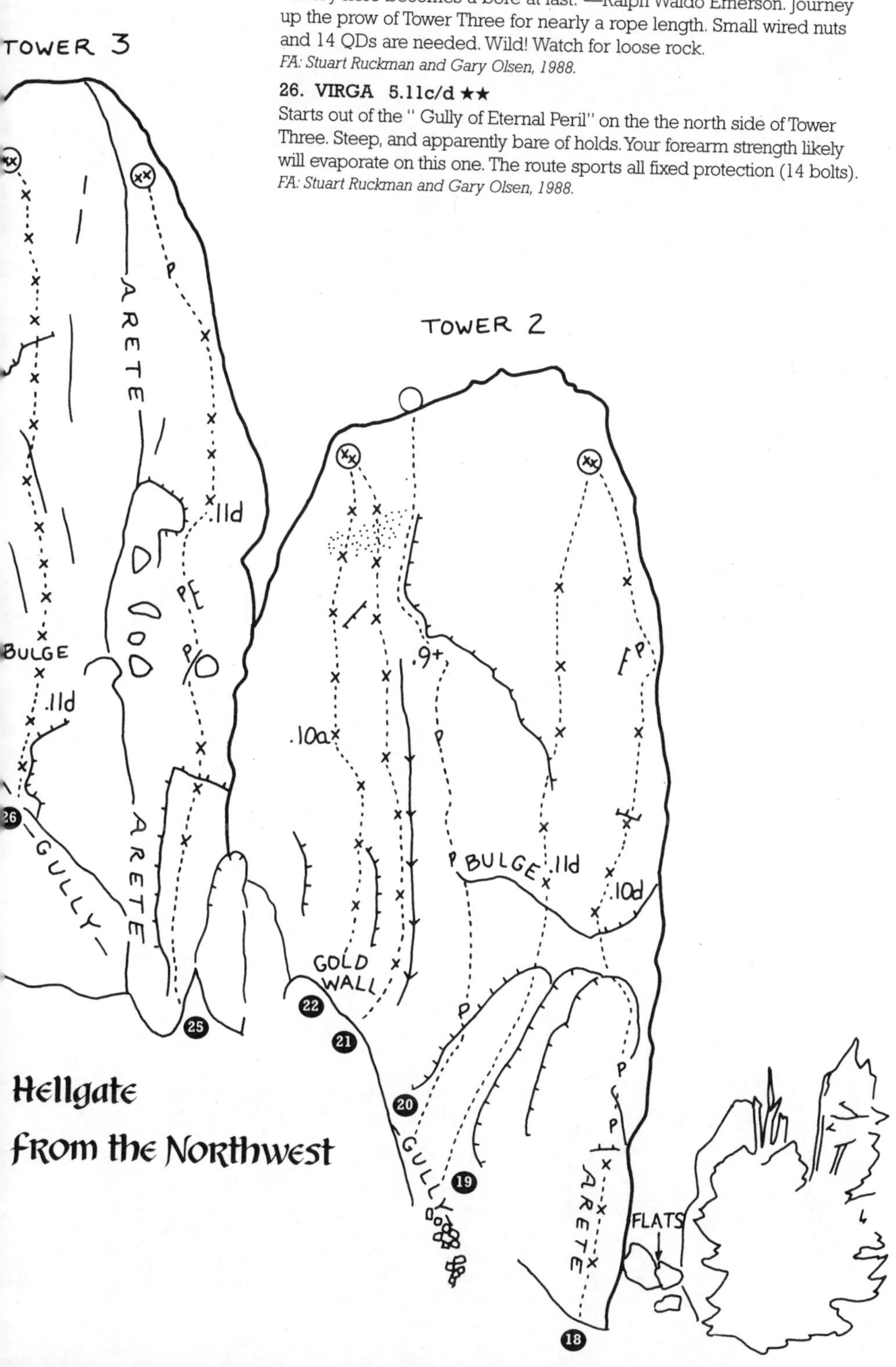

Hellgate
from the Northwest

30
31
32
33
34
35

THE MAIN HELLGATE
27. DEVIL'S DEN II 5.7
28. MARBLEOUS III 5.10d R ★
29. VIRGO III 5.9 R
30. THE DRIP (project)
31. HELL RAISER II 5.10b ★★
32. TILL HELL FREEZES OVER III 5.11b ★★
33. DANTE III 5.10 A3 ★
34. FOSSILS FROM HELL III 5.11a X
35. TEMPTING, ISN'T IT? 5.10a A2 ★
Hellgate Towers →
28
27

MAIN HELLGATE

The common rule among Hellgate locals is to avoid the main wall during the spring because of rockfall. As with all Hellgate climbs, helmets should be worn. When approaching this area, walk quickly under the east end of the wall. See photo on pages 348 and 349.

27. DEVIL'S DEN II 5.7
This takes the apparent line that rises 30 feet right of Marbleous, on the southeast end of the Main Hellgate. Four pitches lead up this ugly gully system.
FA: Mugs Stump, 1975.

28. MARBLEOUS III 5.10d R ★
"A worthy outing." This route climbs the very obvious right-facing, black corner system—the most prominent feature of the wall. The first two pitches are good, with ten feet of rotten rock at the end of pitch two. Pitch three is rotten and runout. Bring an assortment of nuts and up to a 2½" cam. Two 155-foot rappels get one off the top of the third pitch. The first pitch (160 feet) and the second pitch make for a worthwhile climb in their own right; however, pitch two belay needs another bolt. Fixed protection consists of 14 bolts and three pins.
FA: Bret Ruckman and Gary Olsen, 1988.

29. VIRGO III 5.9 R
Climb the crack system 30 feet left of Marbleous. The climb consists of four or five pitches, with one bolt at the crux bulge in the middle of the route. The first three pitches are quite good. The bulge section is runout.
FA: Mugs Stump and Mona Rizzo, 1976.

30. THE DRIP (project)
So far two pitches have been climbed. Pitch one is 5.10a, and pitch two is 5.11. This will be a very good route when completed.

31. HELL RAISER II 5.10b ★★
Starts in right-facing corner 50 feet right of Till Hell Freezes Over. Two bolts protect a right-facing corner on the first pitch leading to a two-bolt anchor (5.8). The second pitch follows eight bolts up a blunt arête. The third pitch traverses left past a bolt and then joins with Till Hell Freezes Over.
FA: James Garrett and George Jamison, July 1995.

32. TILL HELL FREEZES OVER III 5.11b ★★
A four pitch adventure on the main wall. The first pitch is 5.10a hands, the second pitch is 5.11a pockets, a 5.10b edge pitch is third, and the final pitch, at 5.9 is loose. Rap the route or walk off to avoid the loose rock on the first rappel (last pitch). Drilled on lead. James Garrett says, "Most importantly, the climbing is fun."
FA: James and Franziska Garrett, Spring 1994.

33. DANTE III 5.10 A3 ★
Start 60 feet right of Fossils from Hell, to the right of a pedestal. Climb up into a "cave," and up the right-facing corner above to a belay on top of the pedestal. The second pitch climbs the bulging section above into a V-slot, and onto a ledge with one bolt 30 feet higher (165 feet, 5.10 A3). An A2 section ends at the base of the "hooka"—the right-facing corner above. Climb the "hooka" up and out (5.8). This is the most continuous crack system in the bulging middle section of the Main Hellgate.
FA: Mugs Stump and Randy Trover, 1979.

Hellgate Detail

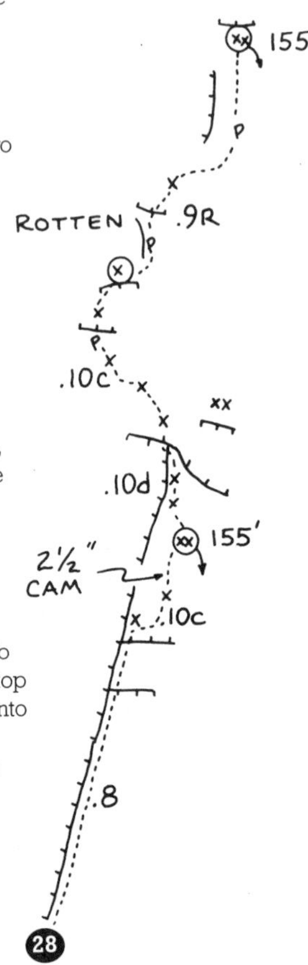

34. FOSSILS FROM HELL III 5.11a X

This route is easily identified as the crack system with the pointed chockstone near its top, on the far west (up hill) side of the Main Hellgate. The climb consists of four pitches with bolt belays at the top of pitches two and three. The second pitch, involving a scary flake, is runout and 5.11a. Be careful of the bird's nest on pitch three. "This climb shouldn't be repeated."

FA: Conrad Anker and Mugs Stump, 1990.

35. TEMPTING, ISN'T IT? 5.10a A2 ★

Someday this will probably go free. This climb starts left of Fossils From Hell and eventually intersects that route midway, then continues up and right of the prow. The first pitch climbs past three bolts on grey rock, then up to a belay below an overhang. Pull the overhang and belay 40 feet higher. Climb gently overhanging face above to a belay at a small ledge with two bolts, right where Fossils From Hell intersects. Continue up more bulges and overhangs, taking the path of least resistance for 130 feet, to a three bolt belay. Three two-rope rappels to the east of the route (two are short, one is long) provide the descent.

FA: Kimber Almond and Tony Calvert, 1996.

Hellgate Detail

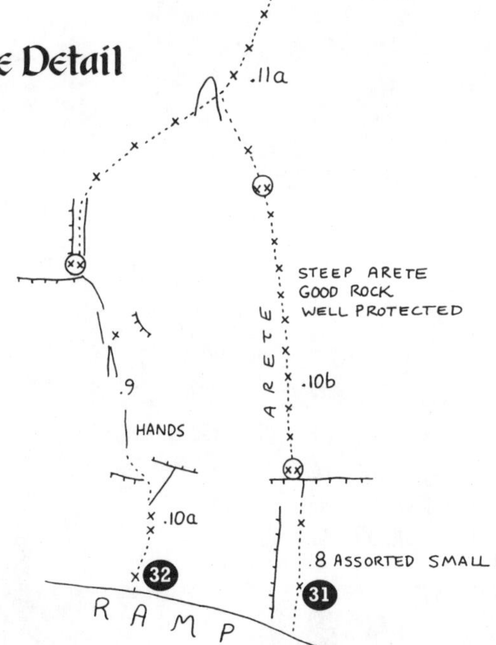

38
Altaworld
ALTAWORLD AND THE CLAMSHELL
36. A CLOUD IN THE SKY 5.10a ★
37. CRACK OF NOON CLUB 5.8 R
38. ALTAWORLD 5.12a ★★

36
37

MAIN SLIDEPATH AREA (no topo)

This area is west of the Main Hellgate wall, and is comprised of some good rock, but suffers from severe rockfall. Approach via the gully below the main avalanche slide path. Stay to the east, then traverse left (west) under the protective lowest overhang. There are no topos for the following routes.

36. DESTINED FOR OBSCURITY 5.9
Pull a bulge and wander up the slab leftwards towards Hell In A Bucket. Bring knifeblades. No anchor.
FA: Loren Glick and Bill Hunt.

37. HELL IN A BUCKET 5.9 ★
Gear with one bolt protects the darker buttress of rock just left of the major gully to the west of Fossils From Hell. Expect runouts on the easier climbing and a long scramble off. Walk up hill and east to meet the East Hellgate Trail.
FA: Bill Hunt and a visiting Swiss climber, 1994.

38. LIGHT IN THE DARKNESS 5.8
The corner 35 feet left of Hell In A Bucket holds some large blocks and a dirty exit.
FA: Bill Hunt, 1994.

39. HEAVEN HELP THE FOOL 5.9 R
One bolt marks a belay stance on the left side of the slide path "bowl." Move right and jam the hand crack to a large belay ledge. The second pitch turns a bulge and leads to a run out 5.9 slab. Two ropes are needed for the descent.
FA: Bill Hunt and Jake Kilgrow, 1996.

THE CLAMSHELL

The Clamshell forms the most easterly white cliffband of the Hellgate Cliffs.

APPROACH: Park in the vicinity of Peruvian Lodge at Alta. Walk to the lowest part of the cliff and follow goat trails west and upward along the cliff base to the whitest, smoothest section of cliff—its furthest uphill side. This route starts just left of a precarious pillar leaning against the base and climbs the slabby, blunt shield of the Clamshell.

DESCENT: Walk off or do a 100 foot rappel from chains.

36. A CLOUD IN THE SKY 5.10a ★
Most people like this climb—good protection. The route has some friable sections. A long, 12 bolt pitch.
FA: James and Franziska Garrett, July 1994.

37. CRACK OF NOON CLUB 5.8 R
100 feet west of the Clamshell is a right-facing, rightward diagonalling corner system. Runout at the start.
FA Dan Caruso.
FFA Craig Dillon, 1992.

The following route is located on a tier above the tower routes. Two approaches are common. The first is to approach from the Clamshell. Walk up and west along a slopey meadow for 500 feet to a south-eastly face with 8 bolts and chain anchors. It is also possible to scramble up the "Shooting Gallery" gully, then continue scrambling up the slope above (taking great care not to knock rocks down).

38. ALTAWORLD 5.12a ★★
Powerful climbing up a slightly overhanging wall with airy moves and good views of Altaworld. One long (60m) rope is needed for the descent, or two 165 foot ropes.
FA: Bill Hunt, 1991.

ALBION BASIN

Albion Basin is the scene of spectacular wildflower displays during July and August. Located at the very head of Little Cottonwood Canyon, this cirque holds considerable amounts of snow until late summer. When the snow finally melts and the ground warms, watch out—the carpet of color is amazing. In the summer, Albion Basin is also home to a campground, which makes it possible to escape even the hottest valley night.

For the climber, bits and pieces of exposed rock are worth checking out, but the eye catcher is the north face of Devil's Castle, which seems to chaperone the entire basin. Climbers have long dreamed of walking up to this face to discover bullet-proof limestone, but all forays found just the opposite. Nowadays, one route exists on Devil's Castle, following a water streak which has worked over the years to scour the loose rock from the face. The remaining climbing in Albion Basin is located on various outcrops, all with the same common theme—cool in summer.

APPROACH: About 8.5 miles up canyon from the neon sign, the highway turns into a dirt road just past the Snowpine Lodge at Alta Ski Resort. Another 2.5 miles up this good dirt road brings you to the Albion Basin Campground. Individual approaches will be described with each wall, and all begin near the campground.

DESCENT: One rope is all that is needed to descend all the routes in this area unless you plan to rappel Black Streak, the Devil's Castle route, which requires two ropes.

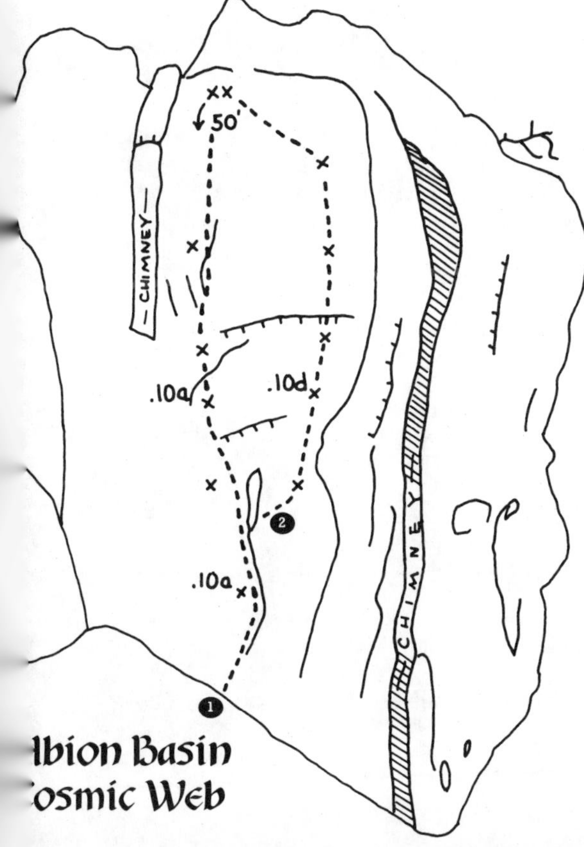

lbion Basin
osmic Web

ALBION BASIN —CATHERINE'S PASS

Several 70-foot, south-facing granite walls are the attraction here, as well as the wildflowers and the solitude.

APPROACH: Follow the approach information for Albion Basin. The turn off for Catherine's Pass parking is .35 miles before the Albion Basin Campground. Hike up the Catherine's Pass trail for three-quarters of a mile until the trail flattens out and meanders through a meadow. To the east of this meadow is Catherine Pass, but to the north are the south-facing walls. Walk up to these and explore on your own.

1. 5.6 TO 5.8 ★
Most routes are between the 5.6 to 5.8 rating, although the steeper ones could be harder. Some are worth leading, others are fun to toprope, so bring a rack. (No topo.)

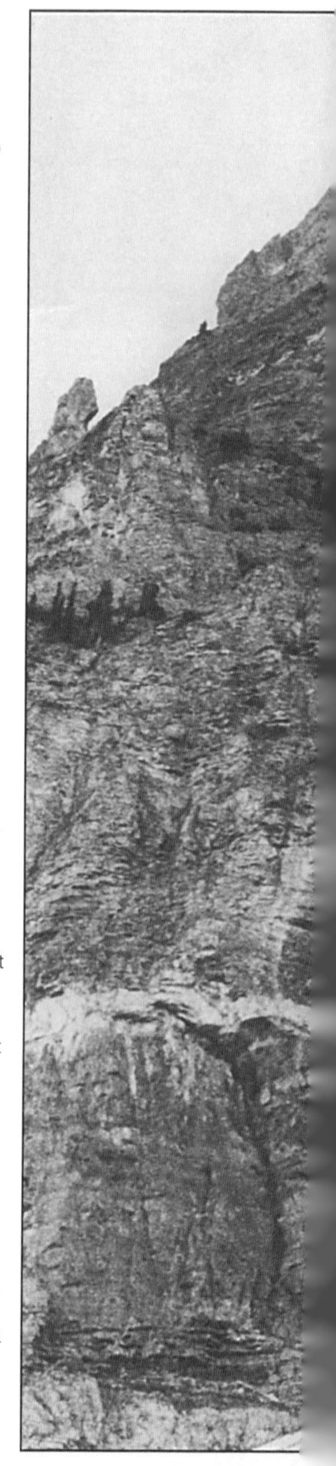

ALBION BASIN—COSMIC WEB

A limestone "pinnacle" to the right of the Point Supreme ski lift at Alta Ski Resort is home to two steep routes, and provides cool climbing even on the hottest days. This is strictly a summertime area. The two routes are right next to one another on the black dolomite (northwest) side of the pinnacle, just left of the prominent chimney system. (See topo on page 355.)

APPROACH: Follow the approach information for Albion Basin. Drive the one-way loop at the campground and park near the outhouse at the south end of the loop. At campsite 15, look east. The small blob of limestone with a striking chimney is the destination. Scamper 150 yards up the hill to the climbs.

DESCENT: Two bolts at the top of the routes allow a quick one rope rappel.

1. COSMIC WEB 5.10b ★★
The left line of bolts. Fun, steep climbing on good holds.
FA: Mark Hadnot, Jim Reynolds and Lance Bateman, 1989.

2. SOUL ASYLUM 5.10d ★
The right bolt line. More pumper and technical than Cosmic Web.
FA: Mark Hadnot and Jim Reynolds, 1990.

ALBION BASIN—DEVIL'S CASTLE

Sitting at 10,860 feet above sea level, and forming the ominous backdrop to Albion Basin, the north-face of Devil's Castle is a familiar sight to hikers and skiers. Climbers have never looked too seriously at the north face because it appeared to be rotten and scary. But luckily, James Garrett had the vision to create a fine route on this face.

APPROACH: Follow the approach information for Albion Basin. Drive to a parking area immediately below the Albion Basin Campground. Follow the Cecret Lake trail as it passes under two ski lifts. After passing under the second ski lift walk circa 600 feet and the road splits just after a nature sign and before a rocky, wet area. Take the left fork and follow this trail to an old mine with a cool, pyramid-shaped overhung outcrop to its right. From here go straight up the steep hill to a talus slope. Follow the talus to the start, which is just right of an obvious cleft and climbs the blackest of the black streaks. Approach time is around 30 minutes.

DESCENT: Although it is possible to rappel the route with two ropes, it isn't recommended due to the potential for rockfall as you pull your ropes, particularly if another party is on the route. The recommended descent is a scramble down the west ridge toward Mt. Sugarloaf.

1. BLACK STREAK 5.11a ★★★
Pitch one: 5.10a, five bolts, two bolt belay. Pitch two: 5.11a, intermixed pins and bolts, eight fixed pieces, pin and medium cams for belay. Pitch three: 5.8, two bolts, more medium cams, two-bolt belay. Pitch four: 200 feet of mostly unpleasant 5.3 climbing to a hidden, two-bolt anchor on a ledge. Pitch five: unknown rating, three bolts and two pins, two-bolt anchor. Pitch six: 5.9+,Forty feet to the right is a cairn.Climb past six bolts above the cairn to the west summit. There is 5.7R section above the second bolt. These final pitches are some of the best on the route. Descend by walking off to the west. Rappelling the route is not recommended due to loose rock. Helmets are advised.
FA: James and Franziska Garrett, late 1980's (sans bolts). Retro-bolted by James Garrett and John Sweeley, 1993.

1
Albion Basin
Devil's Castle
1. BLACK STREAK 5.11a ★★★

LITTLE COTTONWOOD DIVIDE

The ridge that separates Little Cottonwood Canyon from American Fork Canyon and Dry Creek Canyon begins with the summit backbone of Devil's Castle and runs west to its termination among the ramparts of Lone Peak. Along this ridge are many peaks, most of which hover around 11,000 feet above sea level. In the winter these peaks and the drainages below them are the destination of countless powder hounds, searching for the elusive, most-perfect ski run. In the summer, peaks like White Baldy and The Peifferhorn are goals for hikers and climbers alike. While the scenery is unsurpassed, the rock quality along the divide can be frustrating. Subjected to extremes in weathering, the granite here is often fractured into blocks, which can be balanced as precariously as a house of cards. Here and there, though, solid chunks of granite poke through the talus, and it is these formations that lure the climber.

APPROACH: All the approaches begin at the same trailhead. Park at the White Pine Trailhead/Parking Lot, located 5.5 miles up canyon from the neon sign. Follow the Whitepine/Redpine hiking trail to a junction with the White Pine stream, and a fork in the trail. Follow the Red Pine trail to the right, the one that crosses the creek, and eventually rounds the ridge between Red Pine and White Pine. The trail climbs steeply through aspen trees, staying on the west-facing slope of the canyon above the stream. After two and a half miles (from the trailhead), you'll join the creek at a bridge and the trail junction to Maybird Gulch. Approach information from this point is described in each peak's approach section.

DESCENT: Walk-offs are the norm on all routes in this area.

LITTLE COTTONWOOD DIVIDE —WHITE BALDY (no topo)

At 11,321 feet above sea level, White Baldy guards the head of two drainages—White Pine and Red Pine Canyons.

APPROACH: Follow the approach information to reach the Red Pine/Maybird trail junction. From here, continue up the Red Pine trail to Upper Red Pine Lake. White Baldy is the peak to the southeast of the upper lake, and a pass to the south is the next objective—reached via considerable boulderhopping. From the pass, the theory is that you can scramble up the west ridge of White Baldy, until it is possible to drop back down south into the basin below the southeast ridge. Good luck!

DESCENT: Walk off.

1. WEST FACE OF THE SOUTHEAST RIDGE 5.6 ★

A tower located on the southeast ridge is the goal. Climb a dihedral on the west face of this tower for three pitches. The rock is reportedly good.

FA: Paul Horton and Larry Swanson, 1974.

LITTLE COTTONWOOD DIVIDE —THE PFEIFFERHORN (no topo)

Rising at the head of Maybird Gulch and Hogum Fork, the Pfeifferhorn is one of the most dramatic Wasatch summits. While the south slope of this 11,326 foot peak drops away at a kind angle, the north aspects command respect, elevated above the Maybird and Hogum basins.

APPROACH: Follow the approach information to reach the Red Pine/ Maybird trail junction. For route 1, continue to walk up the Red Pine trail to upper Red Pine Lake. A faint path can be followed here up the slopes to the southwest, which gains the East Ridge. All the other routes are approached via the Maybird Gulch Trail. From the end of the trail in Maybird, the way to the Pfeifferhorn is apparent. The North Ridge is accessed via a couloir that descends from a notch low on the ridge. The Northwest Face is approached by scrambling to the low point on the ridge that separates the Maybird and Hogum drainages, and then dropping down into Hogum Fork. From here, traverse the north flank of the Pfeifferhorn to reach the Northwest Face. The approaches all take between three and four hours. Beware of avalanches in winter.

DESCENT: Walk off the East Ridge.

1. EAST RIDGE CLASS 3
The ridge is the usual hiking route, and the most common descent.

2. NORTHEAST FACE
This face is usually climbed in winter, when all the loose blocks are frozen together. As a summer route, it cannot be recommended. Since conditions in the winter vary, no grade has been given. The first ascent climbed a line directly above the lowest point of rock, met the North Ridge, and finished on the North Ridge route.
FA: George Lowe, Court Richards, and Tom Stevenson, 1965.

3. NORTH RIDGE II 5.5 ★
This is the Pfeifferhorn classic, although it is usually climbed during the winter, when loose rock is frozen in place. Summer ascents are possible, but great care needs to be taken, and helmets should be worn. A short vertical step is the crux, and can be passed on either the east or west sides.

4. NORTHWEST FACE II 5.6
Start near the base of the northwest couloir, and climb more or less directly towards the summit. Many variations are possible, but most parties end up somewhere on the North Ridge, just shy of the summit.
FA in winter: Jim Dockery and Hooman Aprin, 1977.

LITTLE COTTONWOOD DIVIDE —HOGUM FORK

Of the many side drainages to Little Cottonwood Canyon, Hogum Fork is the largest, and one of the most remote. Skiers visit these cirques more frequently than hikers, and climbers are rarely seen. The wreckage of an airplane can be found among the cirque's boulders, remnants from a December 15, 1936, airliner crash that killed three crew members and four passengers.

APPROACH: Follow the approach to the Northwest Face of the Pfeifferhorn. Continue west across the broad expanse of the upper bowls of Hogum Fork to access these large east-facing walls. Beware of loose rock. The approach is long and arduous—from four to five hours with a heavy pack.

HOGUM FORK ROUTES

1. APPREHENSION III 5.9

This route climbs the east face of the largest tower, the one with a pyramid shaped summit, and a large overhang at its base. Start just south of the overhang, and climb up and left into a squeeze chimney to a ledge and a belay. From the right side of the ledge climb up and left to a crack system and a belay. Climb the face above to a belay (5.9). Follow a grassy dihedral to a belay under an overhang (5.9). Climb easier rock to the summit.

FA: George Lowe and Dave Smith, 1970.

2. HOGUM'S HEROS III 5.11d ★★★

See topo. A 60 meter rope is advised. This route is located on the tallest buttress on the west side of Hogum Fork, to the right of an obvious triangular-shaped buttress. Pennings says "the route more or less follows the prominent left-facing corner on the prow (right side) of the buttress and is of a fairly serious nature. Get after it!" Descend on the south ridge.

FA: Mike Pennings and John Meisler, 1993.

3. THUNDERBOLT RIDGE II 5.4 ★

This route follows the low-angled ridge to the north of the largest tower. The many gendarmes provide the difficulties, but generally, follow the easiest route staying near the ridgecrest.

FA: Cado Avenali, Dave Hamre, Peter Lev, and (?) Kilpatrick, 1972.

4. HAND JOB II 5.6 ★

To the north of the Thunderbolt Ridge is another big, east-facing wall. Climb up to, and follow, a conspicuous corner on the right side of the wall. The final pitch deposits you on the north summit of Thunder Mountain.

FA: Joel Brown, Dave George, and Max Townsend, 1972.

5. HOGUM'S TRIANGLE WALL I 5.8 ★

The exact location of this route is unknown. Les Ellison and Brian Smoot's guide, WASATCH ROCK CLIMBS, had this to say: "Start at the base of a triangle-shaped wall at the very back of the cirque. This wall is split by several vertical cracks. Climb a set of double cracks on the left. Then climb a short corner to the top."

FA: Brian Smoot.

Hogum's Heros 2

2

HOGUM FORK

2. HOGUM'S HEROS III 5.11d ★★★

Photo by: Doug Hall

LITTLE COTTONWOOD CANYON —SOUTH

All the routes that follow in the Little Cottonwood Section can be found on the south side of the canyon.

COMMITMENT BUTTRESS (no topo)

Commitment Buttress is cool, green and uncrowded. It is the slabby area left of the gully leading to Triangle Wall and directly across the gully from Coalpit Buttress. See overview on page 364.

APPROACH: Park 1.85 miles up canyon from the neon sign. (.6 miles up canyon from the Gate Buttress parking area.) There is an old power plant here, as well as a bridge across the creek. Cross the bridge and walk up the trail to a junction with an old road/trail. Turn left (east) and walk up canyon on this trail for a rough half mile, until you reach an open area where the Commitment Buttress, Triangle Wall, and Coalpit Buttress are visible. A small talus slope/stream bed enters from the right, and 30 feet further up the road are two large angular boulders. Follow this stream bed as it leads to a giant talus slope. Stay to the right of this slope, and walk up white talus that leads into a drainage. Walk up the drainage until a low-angled, broken wall appears on the left side of the gully.

DESCENT: Walk off into the gully below the Triangle Wall.

1. COMMITMENT II 5.6 ★
Walk through the brush about 50 feet left of the gully. A sandy wash at the lowest point of the slab allows a comfortable start. Climb the face above and move left into the large, left-facing corner near the left margin of the wall. Follow this corner to the brushy ledge above (5.6). An alternate start climbs the right edge of the slabs on discontinuous flakes and corners that rise out of the gully. This start has better rock but less protection (5.6). Climb the right edge of the slab to a ledge with a large tree (5.5). A short pitch traverses left and down to the base of a corner (5.3). Climb the corner to a lower-angled slab and belay at a bolt. Climb the slabs to the top. Many variations are possible.
FA: Joel Brown, Dave George and Paul Horton, 1970.

2. DIRECT COMMITMENT VARIATION 5.6 R ★
From the start of the Commitment route, Bushwack up and left to reach a smooth, low-angled slab. Climb up the center of the slab and move into a left-diagonalling, left-facing corner. Climb up the corner and turn the roof at the apex of the corner. Belay at the bolt on Commitment.

TRIANGLE WALL

Steep clean walls, ferns, shade and raspberries make this an ideal setting for summer climbing. The climbing is enhanced by the rugged beauty and the solitude.

APPROACH: Approach as for the Commitment Buttress, but continue straight up the gully to the dominant Triangle Wall. See overview on page 364.

DESCENT: Two ropes are needed for rappels from the tops of all the following routes.

TRIANGLE WALL ROUTES

1. COCO PUFFS 5.6

Climb the slabs to the left of the steep Triangle Wall. The climb stays left of the large chimney separating the main wall from the slabs. Simply follow the path of least resistance to the gully above the main wall. The rappel requires two ropes.

FA: Bill Robins and Kirk Andriano, 1987.

2. DINNER PLATES 5.10

Climb a west-facing slab above the top of Coco Puffs.

FA: Bill Robins and Kirk Andriano, 1987.

3. STRATOSPHERE III 5.10 A3 ★★

A beautiful aid line that tackles the center of the face. The thin corner and roof on pitch 3 is outstanding. A standard clean rack and several hooks should suffice.

FA: James Garrett, Michael Franklin and Seth Shaw, 1986.

4. LESS THAN OR EQUAL TO III 5.8 A2+ ★★

The second pitch turns the amazing roof, complete with big exposure and a thin traverse. The original start climbed the slabs and cracks to the left of the fern gully. A standard aid rack and a few hooks are all that is needed.

FA: James Garrett and Kennan Harvey, 1988.

5. CODE BLUE III 5.11 A2+ ★★

A wild aid pitch that follows the thin crack out a spectacular roof via a series of thin iron placements and a "locked RP." (A #1 RP and a filed down key used in opposition in a shallow hole.) Above the roof some difficult free climbing eventually relents, and a link up with the top of Less Than or Equal To is possible.

FA: Mark Bennett and Ari Greenberg, 1996.

6. A DAY IN SCOTLAND II 5.9 A1 ★

A winter adventure that climbs the gully to the right of the Triangle Wall. The first pitch climbs the gully to a belay under the chockstone. Climb behind this chockstone, then over the next one located a pitch higher. Rappel the route from an alcove at the top of the gully. Beware of avalanches from above.

FA: Bill Robins and Brian Smoot, winter 1986.

7. IONOSPHERE III 5.8 A2+ ★

Mixed climbing follows the path of least resistance up the steep wall to the right (north) of A Day In Scotland gully. The first pitch is a right-angling A2+ pitch. The second pitch diagonals rightward under the huge roof (A2 with one bolt). Ascend the corners above in two more pitches (5.8 and 5.7). Bring heads, KBs, LAs and RPs. Descend by traversing left to A Day In Scotland.

FA: James Garrett, and Rob Brinkerhoff, 1992.

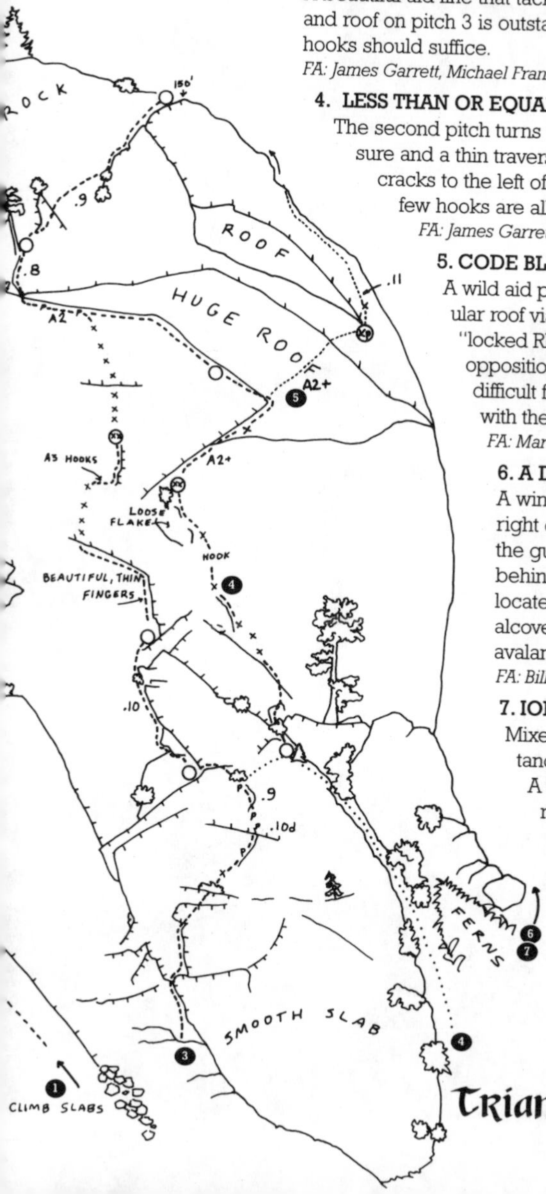

Triangle Wall
2
Commitment Buttress
1
Coalpit Butress

COALPIT BUTTRESS

1. TREE ROUTE II 5.9+ ★
2. DIRECT NORTH FACE III 5.8 A3

PENTAPITCH AREA

5. PENTAPITCH 5.8 ★★★

5

Pentapitch Buttress

Coalpit Buttress

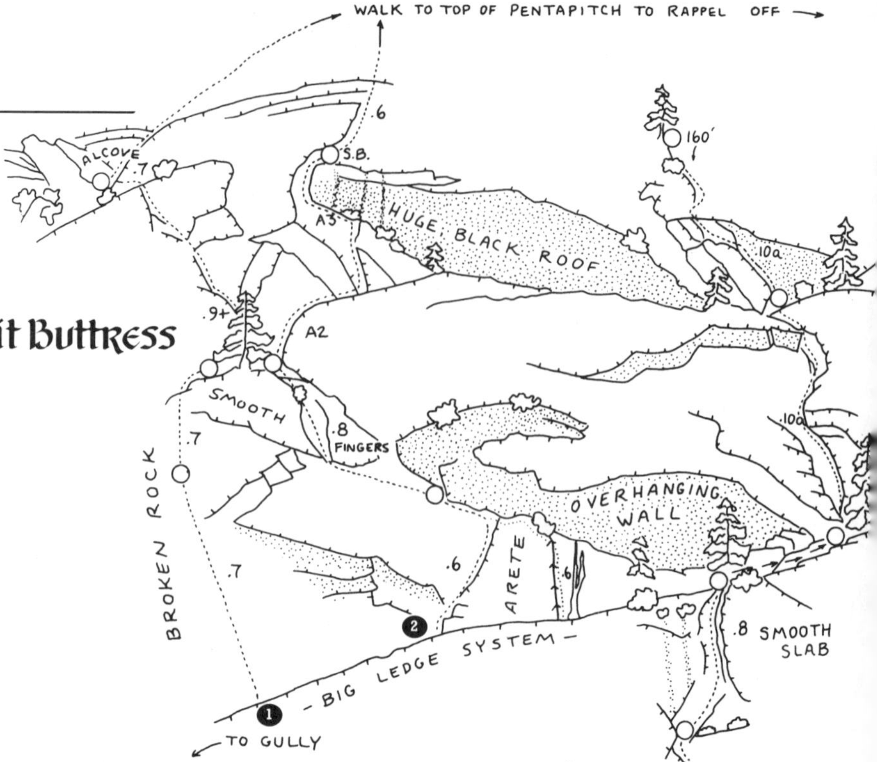

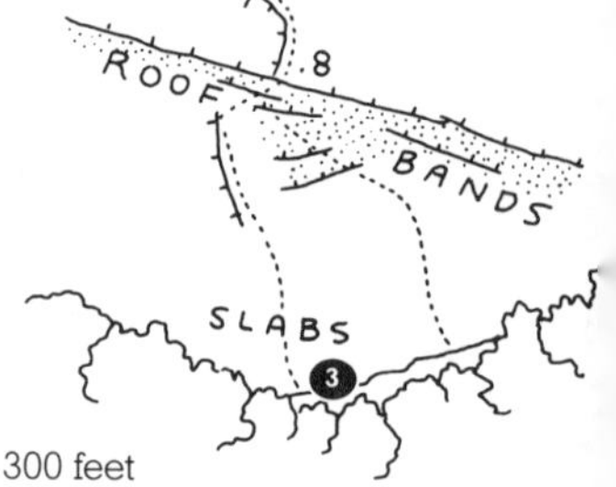

COALPIT BUTTRESS

This north-facing buttress extends west from the Triangle Wall to the Pentapitch Area and the Coalpit gully. In summer, it is shady, cool and never crowded. The buttress is a mixed bag of roofs, slabs and ledges. The result is that the routes wander a bit.

APPROACH: For routes 1 and 2, approach as for the Commitment Buttress, but cut west out of the gully to reach a ledge system that rises upwards to the base of these routes (this ledge system is about 300 feet higher up the gully than the start of the Commitment route). To reach Nanook of the North, follow the approach to the Pentapitch area, then traverse east along the base of the wall. See overview on pages 220 and 364.

DESCENT: For routes 1 and 2, walk west to the top of Pentapitch. A short rappel may be necessary to reach the anchors at the top of Pentapitch. For route 3, see topo. Two ropes are needed.

1. TREE ROUTE II 5.9+ ★

Named for the large pine tree at the second belay ledge. The corners above this pine tree are pleasant. Climb up a broken face for two pitches to reach the pine tree ledge. Most parties start about 100 feet left of the Direct North Face, but it is possible to start just about anywhere.

FA: Ted Wilson and Dave Wood.
FFA: Brian and Jonathan Smoot.

2. DIRECT NORTH FACE III 5.8 A3

Tackle the lefthand edge of the prominent, dark, water-streaked roof located two-thirds of the way up the steep part of the wall. The aid on the third pitch is quite spectacular. Thin pins and a hook are handy.

FA: George Lowe and Mark Mcquarrie.

3. NANOOK OF THE NORTH II 5.10

A somewhat wandering route that links the lower face with the upper. Good exposure on the upper corners with a hand-traverse crux.

FA: Bill Robins and Doug Carson, 1987.

Mike Beck glides up All Chalk and No Action, Perhaps Area.

photo: Jeff Baldwin.

THE PENTAPITCH AREA

The Pentapitch area is popular on summer mornings as it offers cool, northwest-facing climbing on good rock. Quality thin cracks split the slabs here, sometimes for a full pitch, other times linked together by face climbing. The rock is of a finer grain than most areas in Little Cottonwood Canyon and is reminiscent of Yosemite granite. The Pentapitch area is hard to see from the approach trail, however, it is the series of higher angled slabs just east (up canyon) from Coalpit Gulch and the ever pleasant Coalpit stream. See overview on page 364.

APPROACH: Park 1.85 miles up canyon from the neon sign. (.6 miles up canyon from the Gate Buttress parking area.) There is an old power plant here, as well as a bridge across the creek. Cross the bridge and walk up the trail to a junction with an old road/trail. Turn left (east) and walk up canyon on this trail for roughly one quarter mile (you will actually be past the Pentapitch Buttress.) Look for a small path branching off right (south) just past two big pine trees and a flat spot. During runoff, a small stream here flows into a pipe underneath the main trail. Walk up this path as it cuts through the trees and into a boulder field. Diagonal southwest across the boulder field, staying just above the trees, to a small drainage which is followed directly up to the base of Pentapitch.

DESCENT: Pentapitch can be descended via a series of five one rope rappels, or two 155 foot rappels.

THE PENTAPITCH AREA ROUTES

1. PUDGY GUMBIES 5.11d ★★

A good crack up high on the left side of the slabs. The old belay three-fourths of the way up the crack has been removed, so this route may be harder than indicated.

FA: Merrill Bitter and John Higgens, early 80s.

2. ENDLESS TORMENT 5.10b ★★

Improbable. An enjoyable two-pitch (better if done in one long pitch) climb, featuring cracks, friction moves and just enough protection.

FA: Jonathan and Alison Smoot, mid '80s.

3. NEUROMANCER 5.11a ★
Climb the desperate slabs left of the first pitch of Pentapitch. A few small-to-medium stoppers are optional.
FA: Lenny Nelson and Tom Oaks, 1990.

4. JAPANESE TERRACES 5.8 ★
Follow a dihedral system on the upper face's left side.
FA: Dean Hannibal and Chris Montague, 1979.

5. PENTAPITCH 5.8 ★★★
Five (or fewer) pitches on excellent rock. A must-do route.
FA: Rick Reese, Dick Ream, Lloyd Anderson, 1963.

6. FLASHDANCE 5.11c ★★
Free the thin crack branching right on the final pitch. As aid, this is A1. This is the original finish to the Pentapitch route.
FFA: Merrill Bitter and Steve Carruthers, 1983.

7. NUKE THE WHALES 5.10c ★
Climb the right side of the upper slab.
FA: Peter Hunt, Brian Smoot and Bill Robins, 1984.

8. NUBBINS TO NOWHERE 5.10d ★
The name has significance. Good face moves protected by a bolt, leading into lieback corners.
FA: Steve Carruthers and Dana Hauser, 1983.

9. NUBBINS DIRECT 5.10a ★
Tricky climbing on the slab left of Nubbins to Nowhere.
FA: Gary Taylor and Pat Contor, 1989.

10. SASQUATCH 5.9+ ★★★
This is one of the finest cracks in the canyon. This pitch is reminiscent of a Yosemite crack climb.
FA: Lynn Wheeler, Dan Hall and Jim Irvine, 1977.

11. LITTLEFOOT 5.11a ★
Very thin slab climbing right of Sasquatch.
FA: Gary Taylor, Deb Dolf and Jerry Otto, 1989.

12. GINSENG 5.10a ★
Small brass-type nuts protect the initial barndoor moves but require a bit of work to secure. Make sure these nuts are good, because serious injury will be the result if they rip out. The offwidth protects with stoppers in a hidden crack. A recommended alternate finish climbs up the face above the offwidth, past one bolt and a TCU placement, and joins the belay at the top of Sasquatch.
FA: Mike Tea, Roxane Mathews, 1995.

13. LOCH NESS MONSTER 5.10 ★
A two-bolt direct start to Ginseng that is harder than it looks.
FA: Jim Reynolds, Steve Nichol, Jeff Cobabe, 1996.

14. COOL YOUR JETS 5.12a ★★
An overhanging wall on the west side of Coalpit Gully offers cool streamside climbing. Its single route is good, and has seven bolts to protect strenuous liebacks and a delicate face move. Go right after making the delicate face move, find a hidden bolt above a roof and make a final crank to the two-bolt anchor.
FA: Bret and Stuart Ruckman, 1990.

entapitch Area

THE INDUSTRIAL WALL

Cool, shady, and resting comfortably on streamside real estate, The Industrial Wall is a great place to beat the heat. The routes are all bolt protected and demand a unique blend of slab climbing techniques, body positioning, and steep wall savvy. There is even the occasional roof move.

APPROACH: Follow the approach to the Pentapitch Area. From the base of Pentapitch, walk up and right, following the base of the wall until the wall forces you towards the Coalpit stream. Stay above the water on the left (east) side of the gully. A slab section can be made easier by descending down to the edge of the water, then traversing just above the waterline. From here, continue on up the gully, passing the large chockstone on the left, to reach the wall. See overview on page 220.

DESCENT: You can descend all the routes here with one rope.

THE INDUSTRIAL WALL ROUTES

1. MAID IN AMERICA 5.10b ★
A slippery start leads to considerably easier climbing.
FA: Jim Reynolds and Mark Hadnot, 1994.

2. ASSEMBLY LINE 5.7 ★
A more direct line up the lower part of the wall, with consistent climbing, and some noteworthy moves.
FA: Jim Reynolds and Mark Hadnot, 1994.

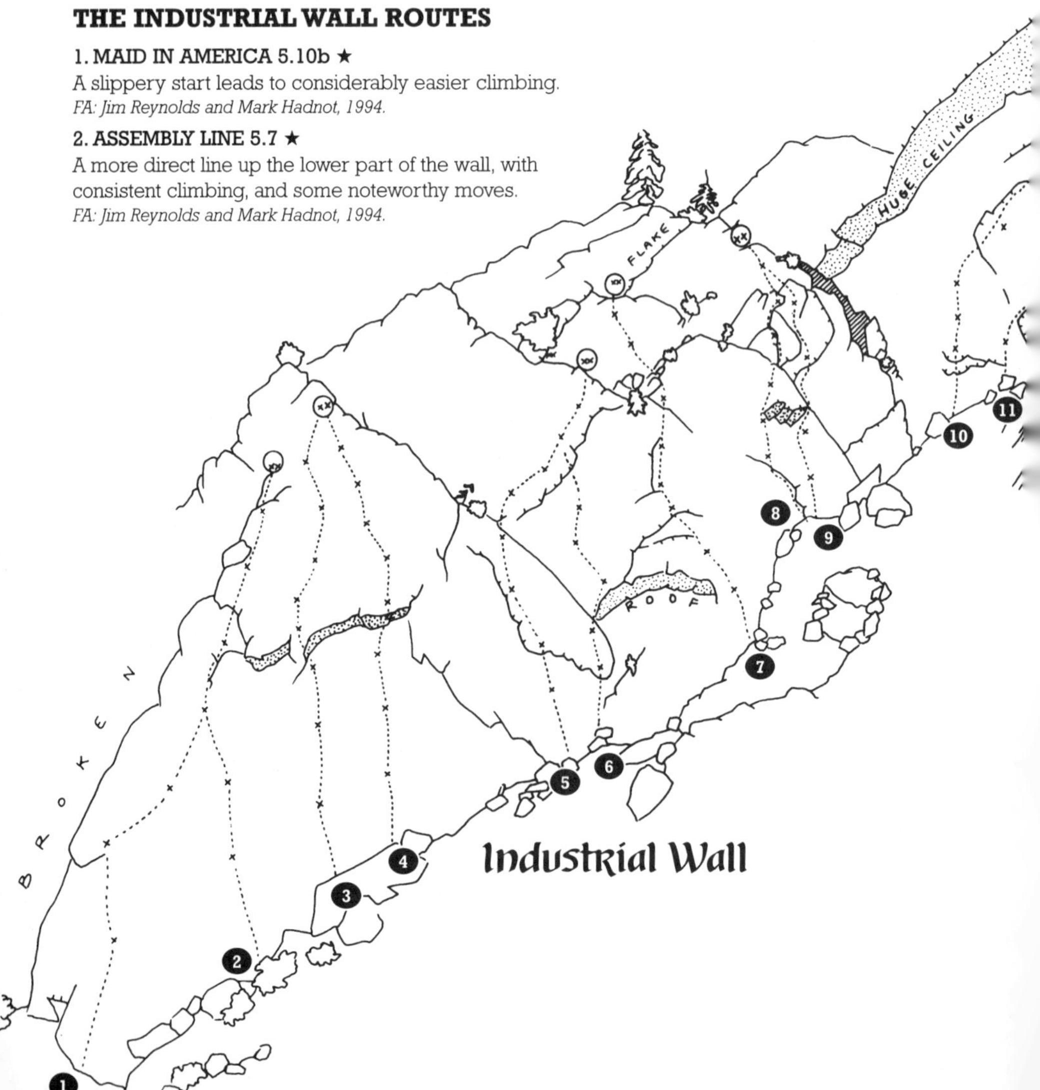

3. WHITE COLLAR REDNECK 5.11b ★★
The mid section of this stout route is guaranteed to knock your socks off. The roof is powerful, but the face above is a real puzzler.
FA: Jim Reynolds, Lance Bateman, Shane Dunleavy, 1994.

4. HIDDEN AGENDA 5.10b ★★
A touchy start and an action packed roof sequence make for a fine package deal.
FA: Jim Reynolds, Mark Hadnot, Shane Dunleavy, 1994.

5. UNION DUES 5.10b ★★★
A syndicate of shuffling moves that extract a high price if not properly executed.
FA: Jim Reynolds and Shane Dunleavy, 1994.

6. BENSON BOLT 5.12b ★
A monument to anorexic holds. Originally an aid route, this rarified line is now a fine free climb.
FA: Tony Calderone, 1994.
FFA: Tony Calderone, 1994.

7. WAGE SLAVE 5.11d ★
A delicate traverse left above the roof keeps the synapses firing. The stopper crux move climbs like a boulder problem.
FA: Steve Nichol and Jim Reynolds, 1994.

8. IGNOMINIOUS DEMISE 5.10b ★
A line of small corners, roofs, and sloping ramps that culminate in a character building spike move. This should clean up with more traffic.
FA: Jim Reynolds and Mark Hadnot, 1994.

9. HOFFA FINGER 5.9 ★★
Roofs and blocks that require liebacking, stemming and jamming. The spike is reminiscent of the final roof on Half-A-Finger.
FA: Jim Reynolds, Mark Hadnot and Jeff Cobabe, 1994.

10. LOADING DOCK 5.9+
Two mini roofs start things rolling with a bouldery move, followed by a long rightward traverse.
FA: Jim Reynolds and Shaun Shakib, 1994.

11. CONVEYOR BELT 5.6
Three well spaced bolts and some benevolent holds should keep you moving upwards.
FA: Jim Reynolds and Mark Hadnot, 1994.

12. BLAST FURNACE 5.9 ★★
A direct line searing the uppermost face. Edges, jugs, high steps and cool moves.
FA: Jim Reynolds, Mark Hadnot and Shaun Shakib, 1994.

13. LIKE A VIRGIN 5.10 X
A nice-looking face roughly 600 feet further up the gulch from the start of Blast Furnace, on the left (east) side. Climb up marginal grooves to a belay in a small cave (5.9+). Exit the right side of the cave, and head towards a roof. Make a 5.10 X mantle to conquer the roof. Not on topo.
FA: Brian Smoot and Bill Robins, 1986.

GREAT WHITE ICICLE AREA
2. OLD UNKNOWN 5.9 R
3. APE INDEX 5.10d ★
4. SLAB X 5.11
5. MOUNTAIN MONKEY SWING II 5.9+
6. MONKEY TALK 5.10 A1
7. ASTAIR 5.12a ★
8. THE RIVER'S EDGE 5.10b ★★
9. DADDY LONG LEGS 5.9- ★
10. TAP 'N STANCE 5.11b
11. TOE SHOES 5.11a ★
12. UNKNOWN 5.9 R
13. SNOW SLAB 5.5 R
14. A CHORUS LINE 5.11b ★★
15. EVENING FALLS 5.10a ★
16. DANCING IN THE MOONLIGHT 5.9+ R ★
4
5
2
3

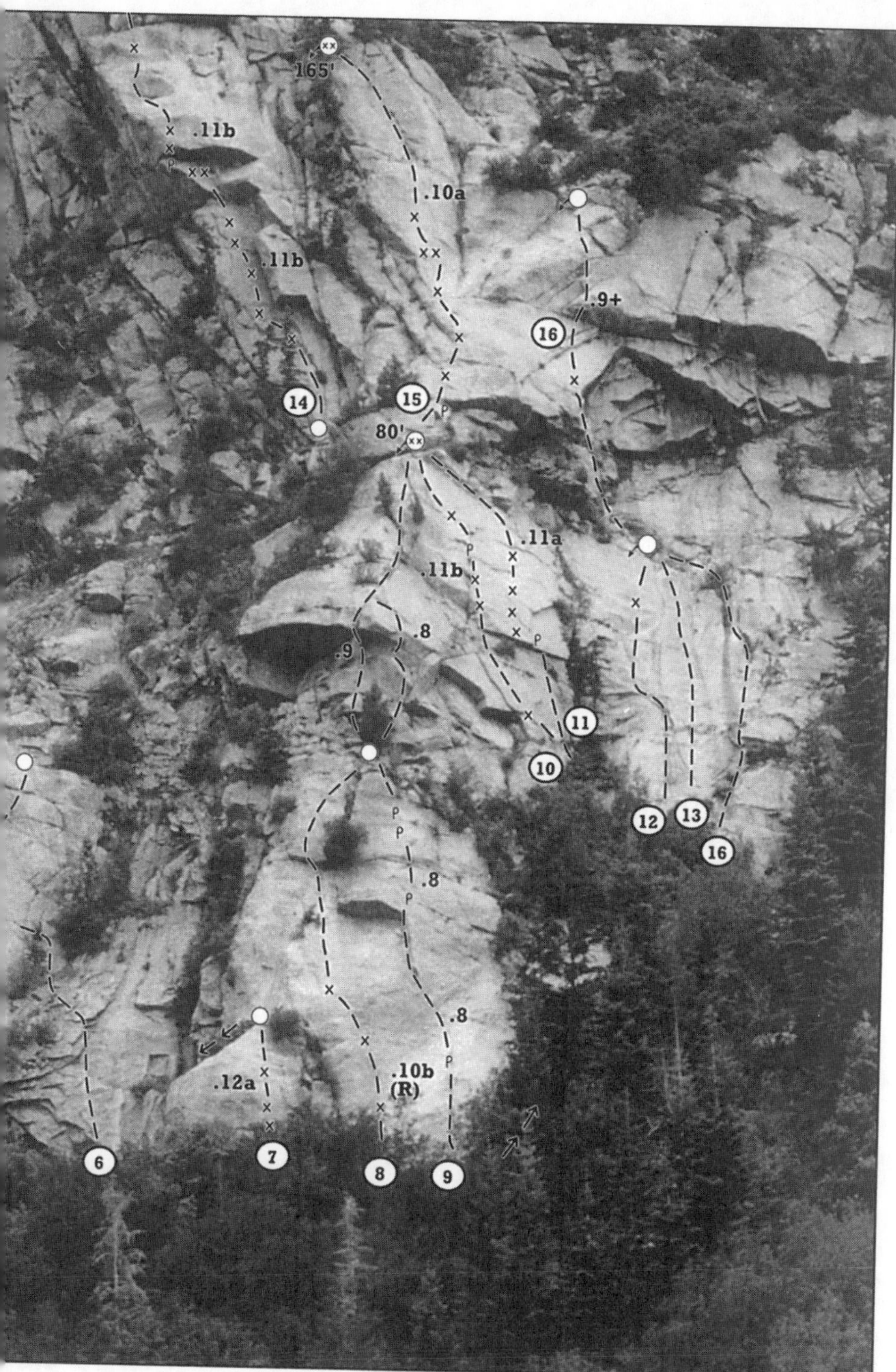
165'
.11b
.10a
.11b
.9+
16
14
15
80'
.11a
.11b
.8
.9
11
10
12
13
16
.8
.8
.12a
.10b
(R)
6
7
8
9

GREAT WHITE ICICLE AREA

Better known for its classic five-pitch ice route—The Great White Icicle—this area also is a pleasant summer hangout. Slab climbing is the principle attraction and like its counterpart, the Pentapitch Area, the rock is a finer-grained variety that provides a bit more bite than the smooth slabs across the canyon.

APPROACH: Park 1.85 miles up canyon from the neon sign. (.6 miles up canyon from the Gate Buttress parking area.) There is an old power plant here, as well as a bridge across the creek. Cross the bridge and go up the trail 100 feet to an overgrown road. Walk down (southwest) on this road 150 feet to a trail on the south side. The trail leads directly to the cliff. The routes are described from left to right. See overview on page 372 and 220.

DESCENT: The shorter routes can be descended with one rope, however the longer lines require two ropes for their rappels.

GREAT WHITE ICICLE—LEFT SIDE ROUTES

1. GRINNING GIBBONS 5.10
This face, protected with two bolts, is located 400 yards up canyon from the waterfall. The bolts lead to a roof, and then to a ledge. (Not on photo.)
FA: Bill Robins and Kirsten Davis.

2. OLD UNKNOWN 5.9 R
This climbs a series of flakes 20 feet left of Ape Index.

3. APE INDEX 5.10d ★
This slab, with two bolts and a long reach, is 100 feet left of the waterfall's base.
FA: Mark Bennett and Bill Robins, 1985.

4. SLAB X 5.11
Two routes tackle the slabs 165 feet above the base of the left side of the waterfall. The one on the left is 5.11, and has two bolts. The prominent right slab has one bolt and an unknown rating.

5. MOUNTAIN MONKEY SWING II 5.9+
A long route that stays just left of the falls for its entirety. Little else is known. Not on photo.
FA: Kirsten Davis and Bill Robins, 1985.

GREAT WHITE ICICLE—LOWER RIGHT SIDE

6. MONKEY TALK 5.10 A1
The route starts at some flakes on a slab. Lieback up flakes and cross easy rock to a crack with a pin. Move left (some aid) to a prow and another crack, which is followed to the top.
FA: Bill Robins and Kirsten Davis, 1985.

7. ASTAIR 5.12a ★
At the right side's lowest point is a steep wall with yellow lichen and three bolts. Short, but fierce.
FA: Bill Robins, Kirsten Davis and Kirk Andriano, 1987.

8. THE RIVER'S EDGE 5.10b ★★
Climb the slab just left of Daddy Long Legs, past several bolts. Shoes that can grip on glass would be advised.
FA: Chris Begue and Win Steere, 1989.

9. DADDY LONG LEGS 5.9- ★
The thin crack on the first pitch is very apparent. Climb past four pins and some exciting friction to a belay at the tree. The second pitch climbs a hand crack through an overhang. A bolt and two pins 50 feet higher provide a good descent. A 5.8 variation climbs the overhang on its right side.
FA: Bill Robins and Mark Bennett, 1985.

Routes 10 to 13, and route 16, are located on two slabs to the right and up the gully 200 feet from the start of Daddy Long Legs.

10. TAP 'N STANCE 5.11b
Follow four bolts and a pin on the left side of the slab. Thin moves are the name of this dance.
FA: Kent Wheeler, Rush Bowers and Chris Begue, 1988.

11. TOE SHOES 5.11a ★
Ten feet right of Tap 'N Stance, turn the roof at a pin, and follow four closely-spaced bolts to a more runout crux. The climbing is intricate, on holds that are just big enough.
FA: Bill Robins, Kirsten Davis, Skeeter Malinski and Cohan, 1987.

The following slab is lower-angled and is 50 feet to the right of Toe Shoes.

12. UNKNOWN 5.9 R
One bolt up high protects the left side of Snow Slab. A flake provides the best access to the bolt.

13. SNOW SLAB 5.5 R
Climb the right side of the slab.
FA: Bill Robins, 1985.

GREAT WHITE ICICLE —WATERFALL UPPER RIGHT SIDE ROUTES

14. A CHORUS LINE 5.11b ★★
Start 20 feet above and to the left of Daddy Long Legs' second-pitch belay, and climb just left of a chimney to an uncomfortable belay (five bolts, 5.11b). Another difficult pitch, protected with bolts and pins, leads to a two-bolt anchor and a 165-foot rappel (5.11b). It is easy to step right into the chimney on the first pitch.
FA: Rush Bowers and Kent Wheeler, 1990.

15. EVENING FALLS 5.10a ★
Climb above and slightly right of the belay atop the second pitch of Daddy Long Legs. A pin and six bolts lead to a diagonalling crack. Some exciting friction moves connect the bolts with the crack. A single-rope rappel is possible if you utilize the adjacent bolts midway up the pitch; otherwise it is a 165-foot rappel.
FA: Chris Begue and Kirsten Davis, 1988.

16. DANCING IN THE MOONLIGHT 5.9+ R ★
The second pitch climbs over some suspect rock, for this reason the preferred descent is to rappel off the tree at the top and diagonal to the two-bolt belay at the top of Tap'N Stance.
FA: Tony Calderone and Wendy Lagerquist, 1992.

PERLA'S RIDGE

Directly south of the Gate Buttress is an arête or ridge flanked by avalanche gullies that rises nearly 2000 feet. With its northerly exposure, it offers cool summer outings and cold and wild winter excursions. The gullies to the sides of this ridge are very active slide paths, especially in the spring. These grade III climbs will consume an entire day. The route descriptions are vague, as there are many variations possible. Aside from the long ridge climb, two short routes can be found along the base of Perla's Ridge. See overview on pages 220 and 377.

APPROACH: Park 1.25 miles up canyon from the neon sign at the obvious Gate Buttress parking area. Approach by crossing the stream on the pipeline 100 yards east of the Gate Buttress parking. For routes 1 and 2, two options exist. Either struggle directly up the slope from here, or walk down canyon along the dirt road to a bridge across the LCC stream. Continue to walk downstream another 500 feet on indistinct trails to the slide path coming down from Perla's. From here, the approach is a cruise up boulders with little or no vegetation. To reach routes 1 and 2, thrash east along the very base of the wall from the approach gully. For routes 3 to 5, continue up the gully. See overview on page 377.

DESCENT: Scramble down the gully to the east back into LCC, or pick your way down into Bell's Canyon.

PERLA'S RIDGE ROUTES

1. LOW BUDGET 5.11c ★

A roof crack can be spotted about 300 feet down and left of Perla's. This is left of the eastern gully flanking Perla's Ridge, and a couple hundred feet lower than Stump the Stars. Climb up to this crack and belay. Climb the hand crack through the roof (5.11c). Bring 1½" and 2" cams.

FA: Steve Carruthers, Kevin Ghean and Lynn Wheeler, 1984.

2. STUMP THE STARS 5.11d ★★

Perla's Ridge is flanked on both sides by gullies. This short crack in a face is located 100 feet up the eastern gully from the base of Perla's. The route is north-facing, obscured by pine trees, and tricky to find. Climb the crack until it thins out, move left into another crack and fight through an overhanging off-fingers crux. Rap anchors now grace the top.

FA: Steve Hong, Karin Budding and Steve Carruthers, 1983.

3. SATYR RIDGE III 5.8 ★

Starting at the base of Perla's Ridge, follow it in its entirety—a full 1800 feet. The majority of the climbing involves 5.4 to 5.5 difficulty.

FA: Ron Perla and Chuck Satterfield, 1964.

4. GROW-MYERS ROUTE III 5.8 ★

Climb the slabs to the right of the ridge. The upper smooth section will challenge your route-finding and belay-setting skills. Expect several pitches of 5.7 and 5.8 climbing, and some runouts.

FA: Richard Grow and Keith Myers, 1972.

5. BOWN-GEORGE ROUTE III 5.6 ★

The slabs to the right of the Grow-Myers route offer easier alternatives if you can find them. Be prepared for long runouts and continuous difficulty.

FA: Joel Bown and David George, 1972.

Perla's Ridge

Low Budget

Stump The Stars

GOAT GULLY

This gully is named for the mountain goats that inhabit the north face of LCC, particularly in the late fall. When driving up the canyon, a teardrop-shaped, orange, west-facing slab—between Perla's Ridge and the Alpenbock Ridge, and directly across the canyon from The Fin—will come into view. This is where Seamin' and Screamline are located. See overview on page 220.

APPROACH: Park at the old gritmill, .55 miles up canyon from the neon sign. DO NOT park in the Wasatch Resort. A long, arduous approach is required, and attempts to avoid private land may prove to be frustrating. However, the best approach is to drop south off the road through the brush to a dirt road. Cross this and head south again to reach the river bed. Walk up the river bed a short distance to a break in the trees, then turn and head uphill (south) through the trees to the base of the wall. A huge boulder blocks the gully just below these routes. This boulder is useful in identifying the correct gully when you're in the river bed. A rivulet cascades along the base of the climbs for much of the year.

DESCENT: Two ropes are needed for all routes on this wall.

GOAT GULLY ROUTES

1. THINK OF SOMETHING STONED 5.10a ★
Five bolts protect this route. A two-rope rappel is necessary.
FA: Kyle Ricketts, Scott Lunt and Wayne Belles, 1988.

2. VEGGIES DELIGHT 5.7
Dirty. The initial rightward diagonalling crack looks OK.
FA: Wayne Belles, Kyle Ricketts and Scott Lunt, 1988.

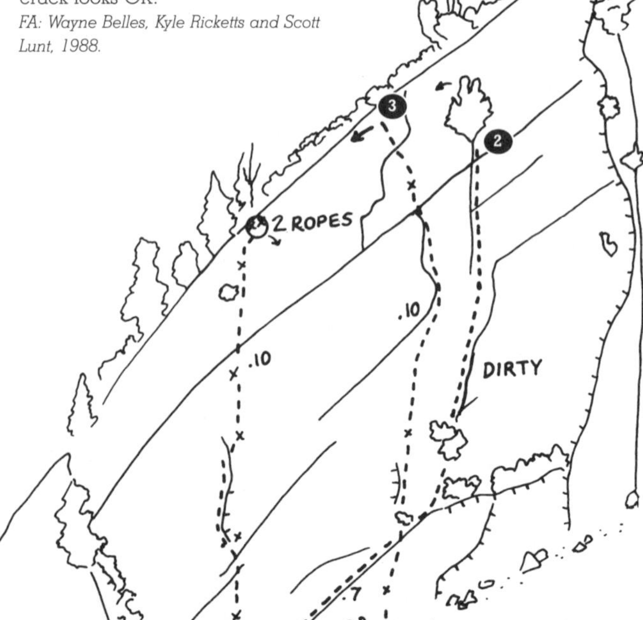

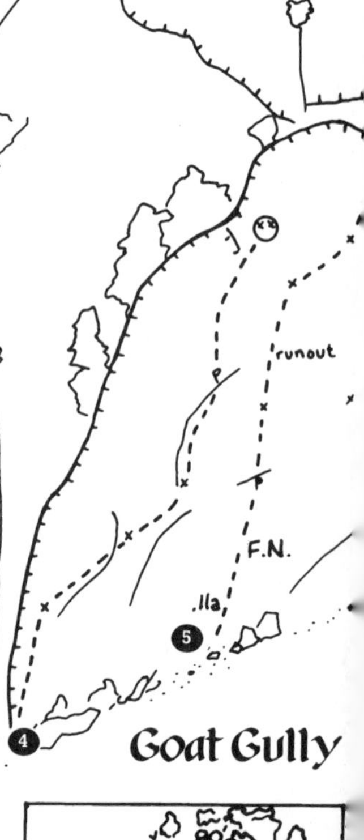

3. VEGGIE COMBO 5.10
The face right of Veggies Delight has a bolt. Climb this face and cross Veggies Delight, continuing past two more bolts to the top. Bring a selection of gear.
FA: Kent Wheeler, Dave Armon and Chris Begue, 1989.

4. SEAMIN' 5.10d R ★
Entertain the seams on the left of the smooth, central section. This was originally lead without bolts; an unknown party added them latter.
FA: sans bolts, Drew Bedford and Hank Armantrout, 1985.

5. SCREAMLINE 5.11a R ★★
"Courage is the art of being the only one who knows you're scared to death."—Earl Wilson. This is the righthand option, with continuously heinous climbing on beautiful rock. In addition to QDs, bring a few medium stoppers, and 3" and 4" cams. A serious lead.
FA: Drew Bedford and Hank Armantrout, 1985.

6. IN TRANSIT 5.8+ ★
Climb the crack eight feet left of Nitro. (See inset.)
FA: Drew Bedford and David Casey, 1985.

7. NITRO 5.10a ★★
This striking set of parallel, west-facing cracks is located further up the Goat Gully, about 200 feet beyond Screamline. Climb the right seam. A variation called Short Fuse (5.7) can start either In Transit or Nitro. Bring micro nuts. (See inset.)
FA: Drew Bedford and David Casey, 1985.

THE RIDGES

Between Goat Gully and the conspicuous Hanging Slab are three granite ridges that rise up from the pine trees to meet the ridge crest between Little Cottonwood Canyon and Bell's Canyon. The furthest east ridge is unnamed, the middle ridge is the Alpenbock Ridge, and the west ridge, the one directly above hanging slab, is Allen's Ridge. See overview on page 382.

APPROACH: Follow the approach described for Hanging Slab (below). From the big slab in the gully (the cutoff to Hanging Slab), continue straight up the gully, then bushwhack west to reach Allen's Ridge. For the Alpenbock Ridge, continue up the gully a bit further, then strike west through the trees to the base of the wall. Both approaches are steep and brushy.

DESCENT: Descend the gully in between the two ridges—some rappels are needed.

1. ALPENBOCK RIDGE III 5.8 ★
This is the next ridge east of Allen's Ridge. Climb this ridge for five pitches to a notch, downclimb or rappel to the west, then climb three more pitches and rejoin the ridge crest. About 45 minutes of 5.3 scrambling leads to the top. The crux is on the first pitch.

2. ALLEN'S RIDGE III 5.8 A0 or 5.8 ★
Climb the ridge rising straight above Hanging Slab. At mid-height, a steep, orange pinnacle can be free climbed on the west or tension traversed on the east.
FA: Dave Allen and Chuck Satterfield, 1965.

HANGING SLAB

Hanging Slab can't be missed. The overhanging cavity at the bottom of the slab was formed when a long-time resident decided to move out. That resident—a colossal boulder—now resides 100 feet down the slope and is home to the canyon's most famous offwidth, Trench Warfare. Hanging Slab is the next wall east of Super Slab. See overview on page 382.

APPROACH: Approach the routes by parking at the Egg parking area .35 miles up canyon from the neon sign. Drop down the embankment, heading south, at any place that looks good and thrash through some brush to a dirt road. Walk up canyon (east) along the dirt road to a powerline pole with two boulders behind it. Drop off the road here, and walk to the right of the boulders to somewhat of a break in the trees, 50 feet down canyon from the boulders. A faint path here leads to the streambed. Walk down the streambed roughly 150 feet to a grove of pine trees on the south side of the riverbed, just past a large boulder. A very faint drainage comes into the river bed 20 feet down canyon (west) from the big boulder, hidden by the eastern most pine trees. Follow this wash as it meanders through the trees, eventually turning and heading east, to a junction with a gully that flows down from the slope above. Walk up this gully to a big slab of granite that blocks the entire gully. At the top of the slab, the trail heads right (west) into the pine trees, then zig-zags up to the base of the enormous boulder. Above the boulder, thrash through a bit of brush to meet the base of the steep, main wall.

DESCENT: Except for Trench Warfare, where a simple step down reaches the ground, the descent is the nasty gully to the east of the routes (The upper reaches of the approach gully).

1. TRENCH WARFARE 5.12d ★★

Completing this six-inch roof crack requires abs of steel and the upside down savvy of a bat. The route travels from west to east on the underside of the gargantuan boulder.

FA: Johnny Woodward, 1995.

2. STEINFELL ROUTE 5.10 ★

Who was Steinfell, anyway? To the left of the cavity is a steep, smooth slab. Climb up to a bolt, traverse right to another bolt, then find a hidden crack and climb it to a belay in bushes. The long slab above can be climbed (5.7), or you can bail out early along a brush-covered ledge.

FA: Kent Christensen, Richard Grow and John Marsh, 1970.
FFA: Jonathan Smoot and Tom Lund, 1977.

3. DIRECT VARIATION 5.9 ★

Climb straight up to the second bolt. This is the logical way to go, despite its lack of protection.

4. CAVITY CHIMNEY 5.9 ★

Or better yet, a route canal. The chimney on the left recess of the cavity joins the final crack of the Steinfell Route.

5. ALPENBOCK 5.8

The right flank of the overhanging recess has some brushy cracks that can be climbed to the brushy ledge system (5.8). Traverse left along this ledge to the top of the Steinfell Route. Meander up the slab above and eventually enter the gully to the east (5.6). Four pitches.

FA: Dick and Rich Ream, Rick Reese, Court Richards and Ted Wilson.

SUPERSLAB

The first immense slab on the south side of LCC looks pretty cool, but actually holds little interest for most rock climbers. However, in winter this may form a film of ice, attracting ice climbers and avalanches. See overview, page 382.

APPROACH: Park at the Temple Quarry Nature Trail parking lot, which is located on highway 209, just before the neon sign at the mouth of the canyon. The best approach appears to be to follow the Nature Trail to its end, drop down into the streambed and walk up canyon until directly below the wall. Thrash upwards, through the brush to the base.

DESCENT: Scramble off to the east or west. Rappels may be necessary.

1. SUPER SLAB 5.4
FA: Fred Beckey and Layton Kor, 1961.

SCRUFFY BAND

The first granite outcrop on the south side of the canyon has a seep above it that freezes during winter and creates a good ice climb known simply as the Scruffy Band. The climb's difficulty varies upon the ice conditions and the line chosen, but generally is in the intermediate to advanced range.

APPROACH: Park at the bus stop/parking lot at the mouth of the canyon. Scruffy Band can be seen directly south across the canyon from here. Walk down the embankment to the parking lot, cross the main road, and continue walking south to join the road that leads to the Temple Quarry parking lot (closed in winter). A trail usually leaves the upper end of this parking lot and wanders through the trees to the base of the route.

CONTACT BUTTRESS

The first granite up high on the south side of the canyon, just left of the granite/quartzite contact. See overview on page 382.

APPROACH: Follow the approach to Superslab, but continue up and west, following the broken slabs and brush to the base of the wall. Expect a 45-minute approach.

DESCENT: Unknown.

1. DIAGONALLY SEEKING SUSAN I 5.10 A2
The Contact Buttress has a leftward diagonalling line on its left half. This climbs that weakness for three pitches (10a, 10b, A2). Bring two ropes, micro nuts and TCUs.
FA: George Jamison and James Garrett, 1988.

2. ESTAMOS PERDIDOS 5.10d R
Located 50 to 100 feet left of the contact. Climb up the brushy face and cracks for three pitches. Bring two ropes.
FA: Bill Robins and Thomas Koch, 1986.

Allens Ridge
Alpenbock Ridge
Goat Gully
Hanging Slab
GOAT GULLY
ALPENBOCK RIDGE
HANGING SLAB
ALLEN'S RIDGE
SUPERSLAB
CONTACT BUTTRESS
1. DIAGONALLY SEEKING SUSAN II 5.10 A2

Contact Buttress

1

Super Slab

Scruffy Band

HUMANE SOCIETY WALL

This is the only quartzite area in LCC. Located on the south side at the mouth of the canyon, The Humane Society's northwest face and gully routes stay cool even on the hottest summer mornings. Overhanging climbing is the draw here—expect square edges, thin seams, technical sequences and mostly fixed protection. Don't leave the rack at home, though. A selection of stoppers and cams is needed on many of the routes. See overview on page 220.

APPROACH: Park at the Temple Quarry Nature Trail parking lot, which is located on highway 209, just before the neon sign at the mouth of the canyon. From the parking lot, take a minute to locate the wall. It is the steepest section of quartzite to the south, just up canyon from a stand of pines that sit atop a talus slope. Note that a smaller talus slope runs down and left (east) from the wall. This is the best approach. From the bathrooms at the parking lot, follow the nature trail a short distance until it is possible to drop down through the trees to the river bed. Walk west down the river bed, keeping the talus slope in view, then thrash through some trees at the most likely location. A small trail here can be picked up. Hop up the talus to the base of the wall. The routes are described from east to west, with the main wall being the furthest west.

DESCENT: All routes can be descended with one rope from anchors at the top.

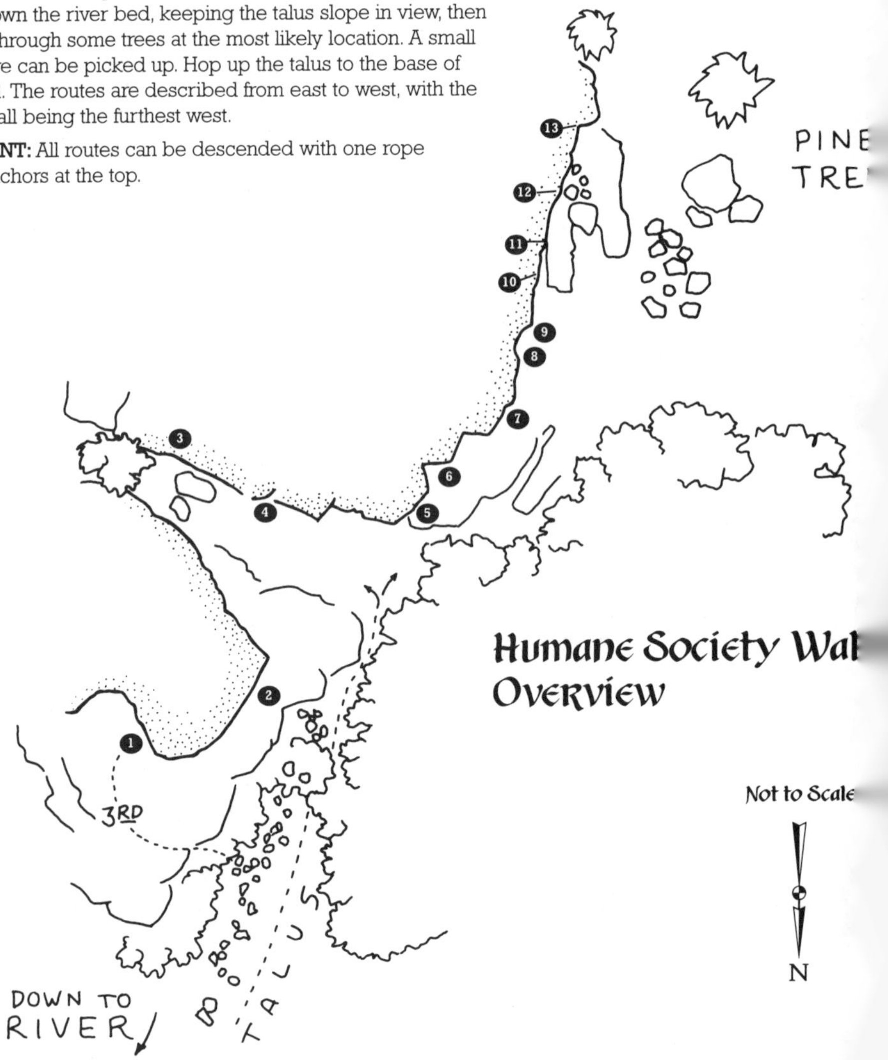

Humane Society Wall Overview

Not to Scale

Seth Shaw on the Little Cottonwood Classic, Fallen Arches, Green Adjective Gully.

photo: Kennan Harvey.

HUMANE SOCIETY WALL ROUTES

1. THOR 5.12a ★★
This climbs the steepest east-facing wall on the lowest chunk of rock. Scramble up ledges to reach the base of the route. Strenuous climbing on small edges with one big move. Five bolts to chains.
FA: Styles Larsen and Shane Saunders, 1993.

2. LICENSE REQUIRED 5.10c ★
A left leaning crack starts things off and a steep finish puts an end to them. Cams or stoppers anchor the belayer at the bottom. Four bolts protect.
FA: Eric Klement and Steve Habovstak, 1993.

3. NO DOGS ALLOWED 5.11c ★
This route is located at the top of the gully, on the south side. Steep at the bottom and sustained near the top. Five bolts to chains—the first bolt is upside down and hard to see.
FA: Eric Klement and Steve Habovstak, 1993.

4. STRAY DOG 5.10 ★
Found near the start of the gully on the south side. A finger crack ends with an awkward hand crack in a notch. The start has shattered rock. Bring a 3" cam and an assortment of nuts, etc. There is a two-bolt anchor.
FA: Steve Habovstak and Eric Klement, 1989.

5. TOPROPE 5.11
The overhanging arête 15 feet right of Stray Dog has anchors on top for toproping.

6. DOG YEARS 5.11? ★
This is the thin corner with a single pin up high, marking an old aid line, just waiting to be free climbed. Looks good and technical.

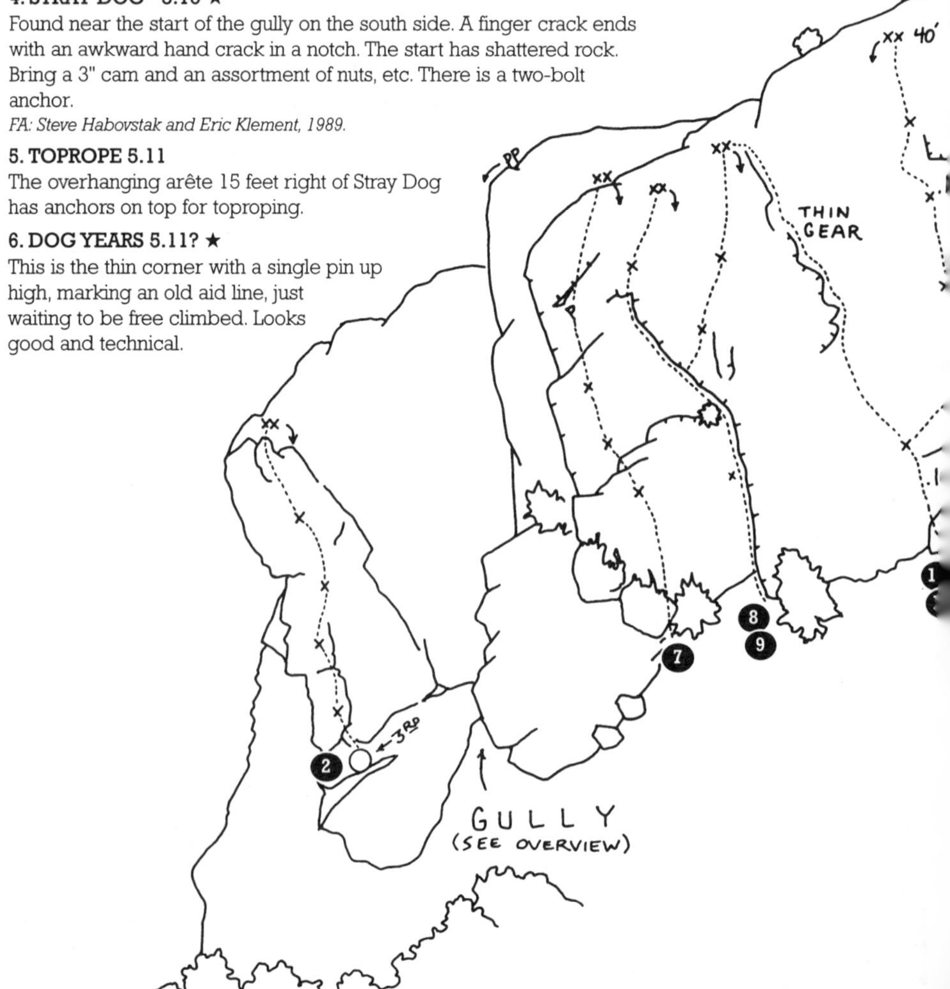

7. THE DOGCATCHER 5.12c ★★

A stick clip is recommended for the first bolt. Burly moves, steep rock, and a few awkward holds send most climbers back to the pound. Runout at the top.

FA: Eric Klement and Steve Habovstak, 1993.

8. ROOFUS VARIATION 5.11b ★

The initial thin moves are protected by a bolt, while the mid section protects well with gear.

FA: Eric Klement and Steve Habovstak, 1993.

9. ROOFUS 5.11 ★★

After the opening difficulties, cut right and tackle the sheer face directly.

FA: Steve Habovstak and Randy Kieliszewski, 1993.

10. HUMANE SOCIETY 5.10b ★

Climb up into a flake-like system that leads to the top. Bring along a selection of thin to medium-sized nuts.

FA: Eric Klement and Steve Habovstak, 1989.

11. FIDO 5.11c ★★

Excellent climbing up the center of the main wall.

FA: Eric Klement and Steve Habovstak, 1989.

12. SICK PUPPIES 5.12b ★★

Most climbers get sickly pumped on this one.

FA: Eric Klement and Steve Habovstak, 1989.

13. PUPPY CHOW 5.10

Climb the right-most corner which protects via a pin and some wired nuts.

FA: Eric Klement and Steve Habovstak, 1989.

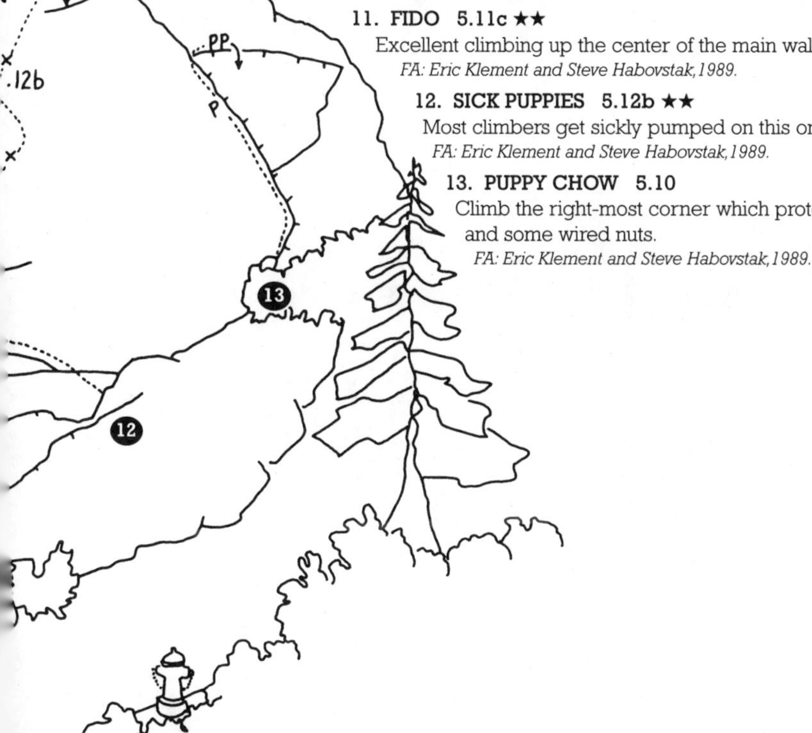

Humane Society Wall

TO THUNDER BOWL
UPPER BELLS
CANYON RESERV
9400'
WATERFALL
DOME
EAST BELL
WATERFALL
7836' x
MIDDLE BELL
TALUS
WEST BELL
FAR WEST
BELL
7259' x
STEEP
SPRING
WATERFALL
LITTLE COTTONWOOD CANYON
Bell's Canyon
overview Map
RIDGE
CROSS STREAM
NO!
WHITE BLDG.
(WATER CATCHMENT)
LITTLE COTTONWOOD RD.
LOWER BELLS
RESERVOIR
(DRAINED)
WASATCH BLVD.
PARK
STONE MTN LANE
WASATCH BLVD.
BELL CANYON
ROAD
CHURCH
3100 E.
DIMPLE DALE RD.
9400 S.
N
Not to Scale

Bell's Canyon

One of the most convincingly beautiful areas in the Wasatch is the broad U-shaped crescent of Bell's Canyon. The glacier did its stuff here, sculpting the granite into impressive cliffs or scouring it down to smooth bedrock planes. With waterfalls, alpine meadows, lakes, Lone Peak, Thunder Mountain, great rock climbing and solitude, is it any wonder the mountain goats reside here?

Along the northern delineation of Bell's Canyon, a whole series of granite towers and domes appear about a mile up the canyon. The first four Bell Towers are distinct and obvious. Further up canyon, however, the domes seem to meld into one another. The rock quality on the towers almost always disappoints the climber at about the two-thirds height. Weathering causes highly-grussified rock, the type that feels like ball bearings no matter how sticky your shoes. The climber should grin and bear it, though, as this is all part of the Bell's experience.

The season for climbing is roughly April through October. Because the towers face south, climbing in the mid-summer may be out of the question, though the quick party can be in the shade along the creek by noontime. At the other extreme, climbers may be caught unprepared for quick-forming summer storms and find themselves fully committed on routes where retreat is nearly impossible. Use your best judgment climbing in Bell's Canyon.

HOW TO GET THERE: Exit off I-15 at the 90th South Exit. Follow 90th South as it bends and joins 9400 South at a stoplight. Continue east towards the mountains on 9400 South to an intersection with Wasatch Blvd. Follow Wasatch Blvd. to the intersection of Wasatch Blvd. and Bell Canyon Road (10040 South). Turn east. Take a quick left on Stone Mountain Lane (10050 South), which is followed with a left at the jog, to the end of the road. See overview on page 388. Park here, but do not block the residents' driveways or ability to turn around. If you have to, park down the road a bit.

APPROACH: The approach takes around 1½ hours and is steep. The approach begins as a dirt road that heads east to the lower Bell's Reservoir. Follow this road despite the initial No Trespassing signs, but please stay on the road and do not litter, or access could be permanently closed. The road continues along the north shore of the drained reservoir, eventually meeting another trail that continues east into the canyon. A level area comes next, and many trails make this section confusing, but try to locate the trail that heads to a stream crossing. After the crossing, the main hiking trail is fairly evident. See overview on page 388.

FAR WEST BELL TOWER

This is the smallest, most westerly of the Bell Towers and therefore has the shortest approach. Like the other Bell Towers, expect some rotten rock and dirty sections.

APPROACH: Follow the How To Get There information for Bell's Canyon. Walk up the Bell's Canyon trail until you are roughly straight across from the West Bell Tower. There, you'll find an unmarked trail leading to the lower Bell's Canyon Falls. Cross the stream (no easy task in the spring) and traverse westerly through the brush to the base of the routes. See overview on page 388.

DESCENT: Two ropes are needed to make the rappels on this wall.

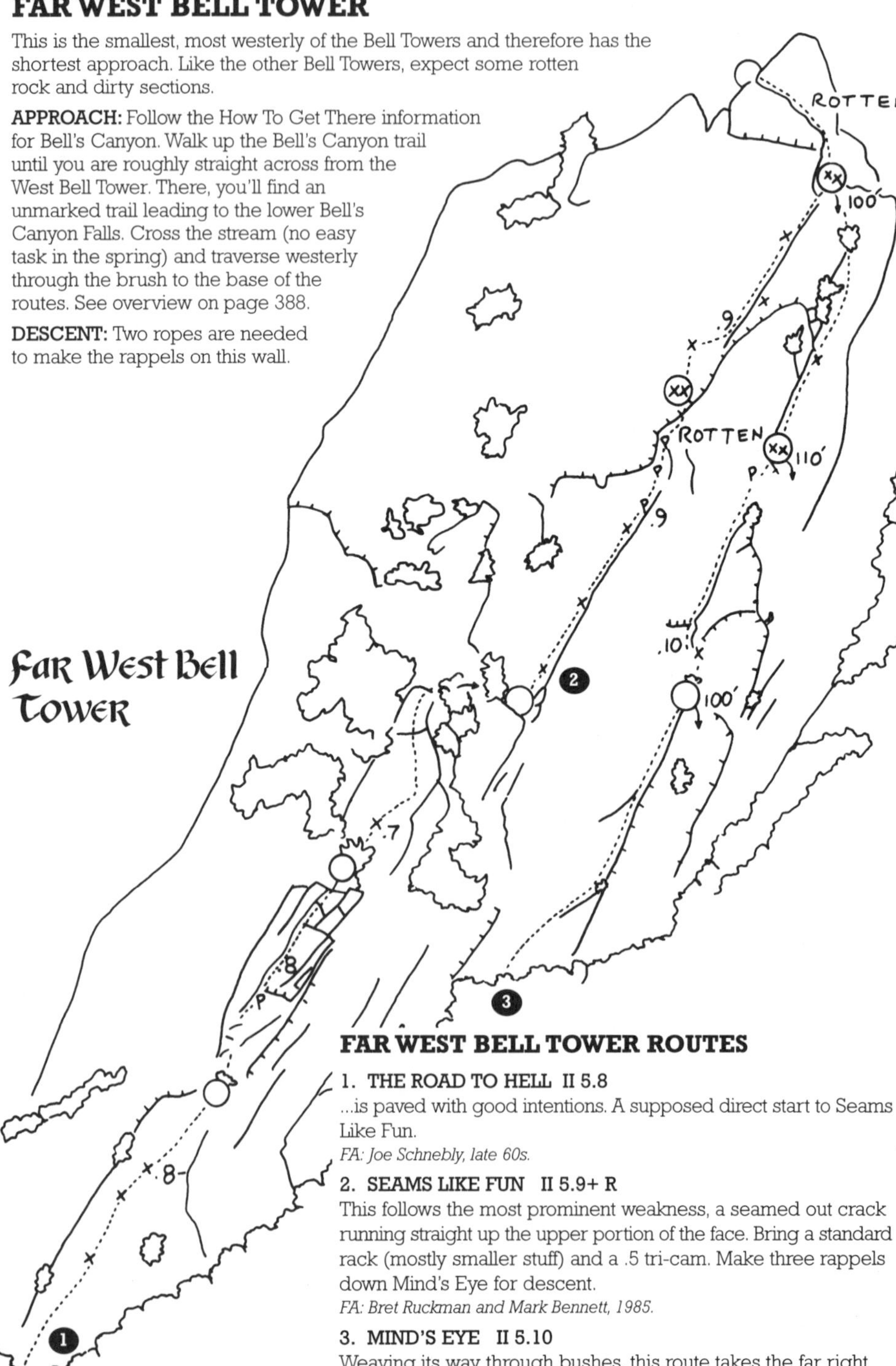

FAR WEST BELL TOWER ROUTES

1. THE ROAD TO HELL II 5.8

...is paved with good intentions. A supposed direct start to Seams Like Fun.

FA: Joe Schnebly, late 60s.

2. SEAMS LIKE FUN II 5.9+ R

This follows the most prominent weakness, a seamed out crack running straight up the upper portion of the face. Bring a standard rack (mostly smaller stuff) and a .5 tri-cam. Make three rappels down Mind's Eye for descent.

FA: Bret Ruckman and Mark Bennett, 1985.

3. MIND'S EYE II 5.10

Weaving its way through bushes, this route takes the far right side of the Far West Bell Tower.

FA: Mark Bennett and Bill Simons, 1985.

The Zion Curtain Pitch, Arm and Hammer, Middle Bell Tower.

photo: John Barstow.

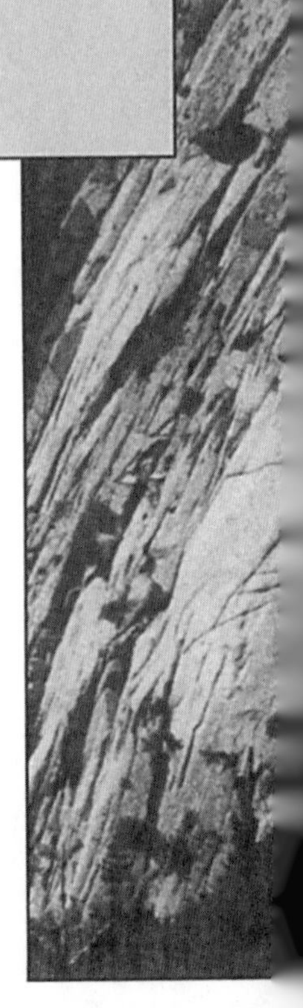

WEST BELL TOWER

1. BECKEY ROUTE II 5.9 R ★★
3. CROWN OF CREATION III 5.10a A2+ ★★
4. LOWE-CONROD ROUTE II 5.9 ★
7. NITTY GRITTY VARIATION II 5.10
8. NITTY GRITTY II 5.8 A2
9. PERTURBATION III 5.11 A3
10. THE STING III 5.9 A3

WEST BELL TOWER

The West Bell Tower has four routes that attract the free climber, as well as a number of mixed routes. Climbs here are generally about four pitches in length, with the rock quality varying from compact and polished to incredibly weathered and rotten. Difficult to poor protection is the norm. George Lowe and Bill Conrod climbed three of the most obvious lines on the Tower in the mid-60s, but today, sadly enough, these routes see little action.

APPROACH: Follow the How To Get There information for Bell's Canyon. Walk up the Bell's Canyon trail until you are roughly straight across from the West Bell Tower. There, you'll find an unmarked trail leading to the lower Bell's Canyon Falls. Cross the stream (no easy task in the spring) and struggle through the brush to the base of the routes. See overview on page 388.

DESCENT: The walk off descent can be made on either side of the tower, but the west side is recommended—be prepared to do full battle with the brush.

WEST BELL TOWER ROUTES

1. BECKEY ROUTE II 5.9 R ★★

A good first pitch has difficult protection. The final pitches follow the obvious corner on the left side of the tower. All pitches are full length.

FA: Fred Beckey, Rich Ream, Larry Evans, Dick Ream, 1963. FFA: Unknown

2. SWEET SOULED SISTER II 5.8 A3 ★

A direct aid start to Crown of Creation. A bag full of heads, hooks, beaks, LAs, KBs, angles, and hangers is needed. Follow the weakness up and right to the junction of the Beckey Route and Crown of Creation.

FA: John Slezak, 1994.

3. CROWN OF CREATION III 5.10a A2+ ★★

Big air and sections of hard aid will leave you feeling like royalty. Bring a good selection of knifeblades, lost arrows, RURPS, baby angles and beaks. The second belay is on expanding rock. The final pitch has some looping of chickenheads on suspect rock. It has been reported that it is possible to rappel the route.

FA: Les Ellison and Terry Lein, 1979.

4. LOWE-CONROD ROUTE II 5.9 ★

The obvious chimney line right of the huge roof. Climb the fine initial pitch of the Beckey Route. The second pitch does a weird traverse right (past the Crown of Creation belay) to gain this obvious chimney line. Large protection is useful. The upper pitches are tricky to protect.

FA: George Lowe, Bill Conrod, 1966.

5. THE NERVE II 5.11a ★★★

The first pitch is beautiful, very challenging climbing up a polished corner. Staying directly in the corner is somewhat harder. The second pitch follows the Lowe-Conrod route to the bolt then traverses 25 feet east to the prow. The third pitch, up a gritty arête, is fun. Two long rappels provide escape. The second rappel anchor is an old bolt and needs to be backed up.

FA: Brian Smoot and Les Ellison, 1983.

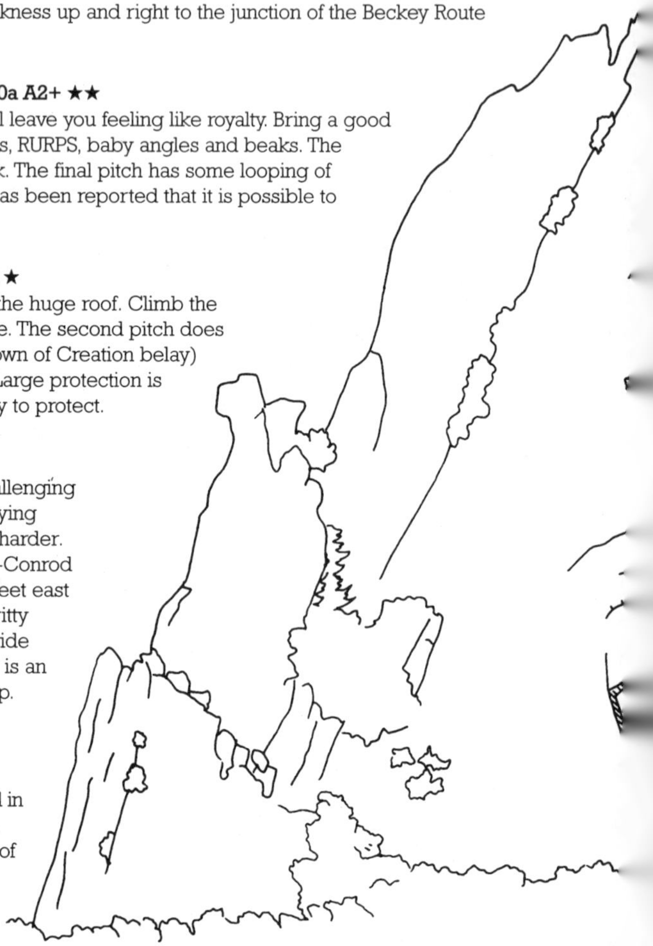

6. TOGA TRAVERSE III 5.10 ★

Who dreamed this one up? An odd route that must have been conceived in a living room over a couple of beers. Climb to the top of the second pitch of the Lowe-Conrod Route. Traverse right 30 feet, move up to a stance at a crack, downclimb 30 feet on chickenheads and jump into the tree-filled alcove (whew!). Continue past Nitty Gritty to a belay (140 feet, 5.9). Climb up a right-sloping corner to a crack, then move right on thin moves to a belay atop a pinnacle (140 feet, 5.10). Downclimb a crack to the right of the pinnacle, then conceive a traverse rightward across Perturbation to the second pitch belay of The Sting (5.8). Traverse down and right on the ramp until you are back on terra firma. (Not on topo.)

FA: Les Ellison, Terry Lein and Brian Smoot, 1978.

7. NITTY GRITTY VARIATION II 5.10

8. NITTY GRITTY II 5.8 A2

This starts left of the lightning-bolt series of roofs near the bottom center of the tower. After the first pitch, the route is very rotten, hence the name.

FA: Bill Conrod and George Lowe, 1967.

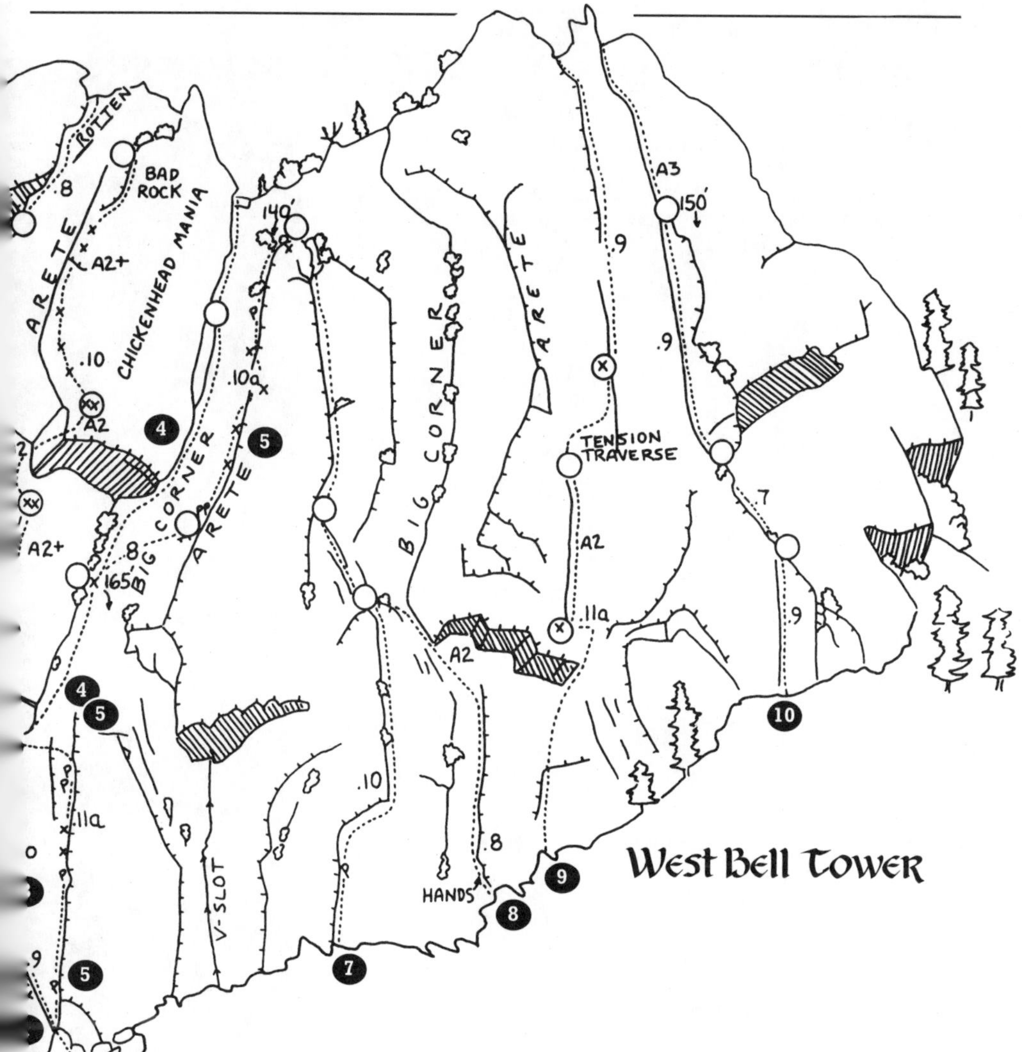

West Bell Tower

9. PERTURBATION III 5.11 A3

Climb straight up the right margin of the lightning bolt series of roofs. Part of pitch two has gone free at 5.11 (bring big protection). The final clencher is the requisite rotten chimney leading to the top.

FA: George Lowe, Bill Conrod, 1967.

FFA: pitch one, Mark Bennett and Bill Robins, 1985.

10. THE STING III 5.9 A3

This offers a captivating first pitch hand crack. Either rappel 150 feet off at the top of the third pitch to a ramp and downclimb (recommended), or aid up the rotten, overhanging crack above (5.8 A3).

FA: Les Ellison and Brian Smoot, 1978.

11. OVER AND UNDER II 5.9 or 5.10

Between the Westbell and Middle Bell Towers is a buttress with a huge arching roof. This route goes up a chimney on the left side of the main face of the buttress. One variation goes all the way up the chimney and over the roof via a surprisingly easy hidden passage. The other variation goes through the tunnel at the top of the chimney and then up easy ground to the top. The approach to this route is awful.

FA: Mark Bennett and Bill Simmons, 1983.

MIDDLE BELL TOWER

The most dominant and beautiful of the Bell Towers is the Middle Bell. It generally features five to six pitches of climbing on steep, difficult terrain. Unlike the West Bell Tower, almost all the routes have been free climbed, stacking the cliff with options for a wide range of abilities. The middle section of the tower has the best granite in the Wasatch, as it has been exposed to less weathering since part of the wall fell off during the recent (thousands of years?) past. The large talus boulders and the white, clean rock display the effects of this huge rock slide. The routes venturing up this section are definitely the best in Bell's Canyon.

APPROACH: Follow the How To Get There information for Bell's Canyon. Walk up the Bell's Canyon trail until you are adjacent to the Middle Bell Tower. Most climbers cut north on an indistinct trail, just after entering a clearing straight across from the central section of the tower. A casual approach across the stream and up the white boulders above takes about 5 minutes and has no bushwhacking. Raspberries may be found in August among the boulders—a tasty treat for thirsty, sun-baked climbers. See overview on page 388.

DESCENT: The gully to the east is the best descent. One rappel is needed. The central slab routes are best descended by rappelling Butcher Knife and Cymbals Of The Sun—two ropes needed.

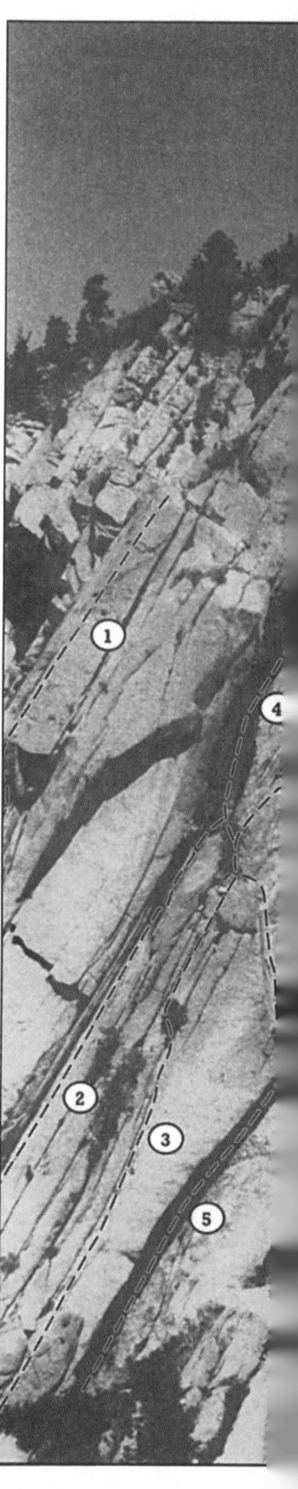

MIDDLE BELL TOWER ROUTES

1. THE GENDARME II 5.9 A2

Look at the west edge of the tower and you'll notice that a chunk of it forms a pinnacle or gendarme. This route climbs up cracks that lead up and over a prominent roof. The rock quality is poor for three pitches up this crack system.

FA: George Lowe and Ted Wilson, 1970.

2. ALLEN-REID VARIATION 5.8 ★

Five cracks slice the face left of "The Great Cleft" (the obvious right-leaning chimney in the lower center of the face). This ascends the left-most of these—the one in the right-facing corner—to the bush belay of the Wilson-Ream. Two pitches.

FA: Dave Allen and John Reid, 1967.

3. LOWE VARIATION 5.8 ★★

Ascend the crack immediately west of "The Great Cleft" to a ledge and belay. This is a good crack and contrasts the bottoming grooves found on the upper face. It is a 165-foot pitch.

FA: George and Jeff Lowe, 1967.

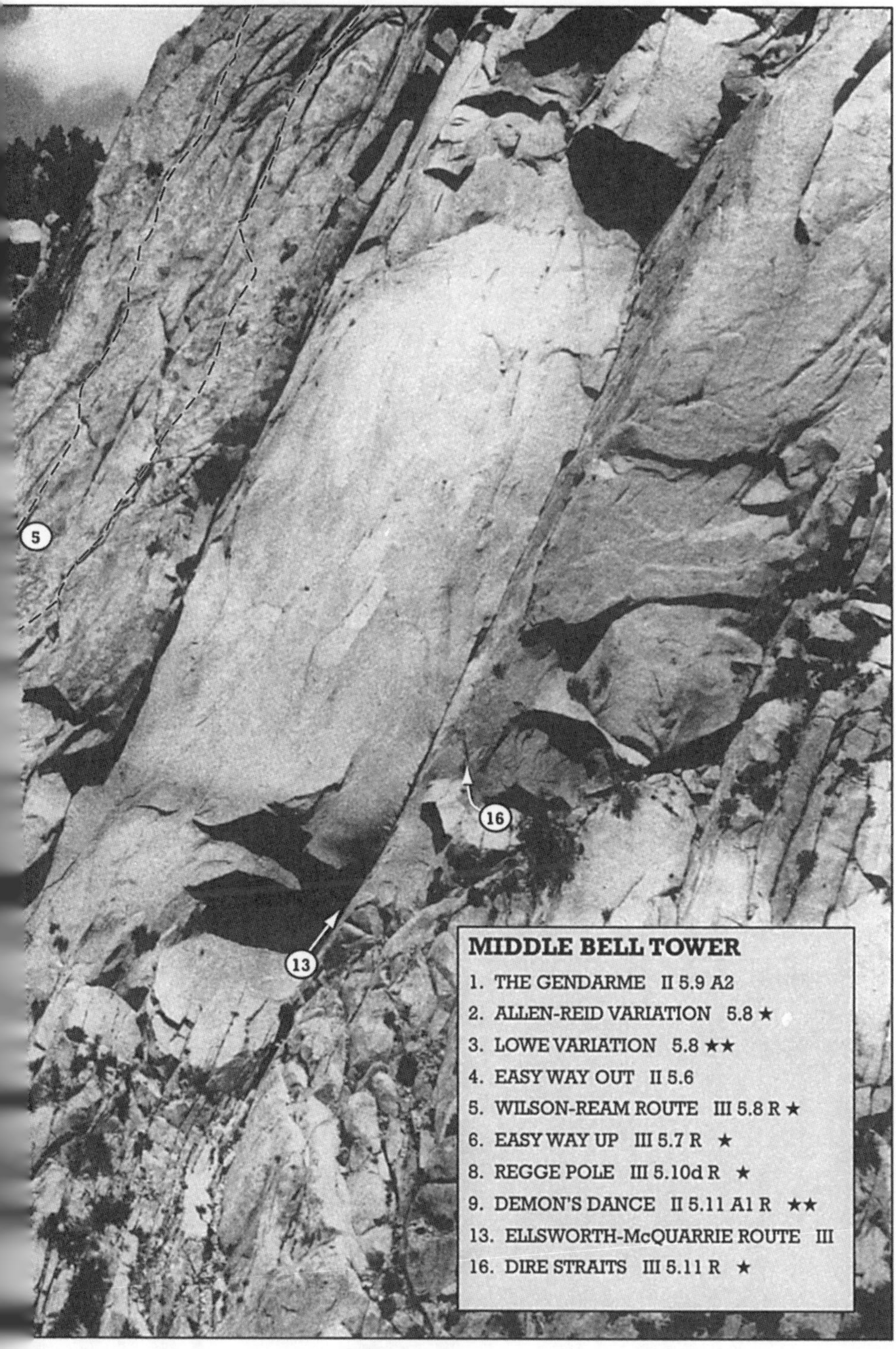

5

16

13

MIDDLE BELL TOWER

1. THE GENDARME II 5.9 A2
2. ALLEN-REID VARIATION 5.8 ★
3. LOWE VARIATION 5.8 ★★
4. EASY WAY OUT II 5.6
5. WILSON-REAM ROUTE III 5.8 R ★
6. EASY WAY UP III 5.7 R ★
8. REGGE POLE III 5.10d R ★
9. DEMON'S DANCE II 5.11 A1 R ★★
13. ELLSWORTH-McQUARRIE ROUTE III
16. DIRE STRAITS III 5.11 R ★

MIDDLE BELL TOWER ROUTES

4. EASY WAY OUT II 5.6

Climb the first pitch of the Wilson-Ream Route and belay to the left about 150 feet up (5.6). Traverse leftward along a ramp system to a chimney (5.5). Continue up this feature for two more ugly pitches to the notch between The Gendarme and the main face (5.6).

FA: John Reid and Dave Allen, 1967.

5. WILSON-REAM ROUTE III 5.8 R ★

The first route on the Middle Bell, this was an impressive and daring undertaking for two lads just getting into the sport. During the first ascent, a weird jog to the right avoided a bottoming "furrow" on the fourth pitch and involved several tension traverses from bolts. Start in The Great Cleft. The final pitches have bad rock.

FA: Rich Ream and Ted Wilson, 1963.
FFA: George Lowe and Max Townsend, 1967.

6. EASY WAY UP III 5.7 R ★

Don't fall into this "sarchasm." Continuous difficulty, tricky route finding, 165+ foot pitches and poor protection may jeopardize the unassuming. The final pitch has terrible rock, including a dangerous rotten chockstone, but the first three are good.

FA: George and Jeff Lowe, 1967.

7. SUNSTROKE VARIATION 5.8+ R

Follow the right cracks and chimneys, avoiding the long fourth-pitch chimney on Easy Way Up. A flake right of the chimney on the first pitch of this variation is recommended. Belay just below a cluster of chickenheads on a ledge on the left. Climb up the face above, using rotten, scary friction to get to the top.

FA: Lenny Nelson and Dave Smith, 1970.

8. REGGE POLE III 5.10d R ★

A physicist's colloquialism or a damned hard route. This crack system defines the left margin of the smooth, central section of the Middle Bell.

FA: George Lowe and Ed Anderson, 1966.
FFA: Jeff Lowe and Jim Langdon, 1971.

9. DEMON'S DANCE II 5.11 A1 R ★★

The left-most of the central slab routes. Two pitches of tantalizing climbing join the other routes at the pedestal ledge. Bring a hook. A reasonable 30 foot runout on the first pitch is what garners the R rating, the rest of the route protects fine.

FA: Brian Smoot and Les Ellison, 1990.

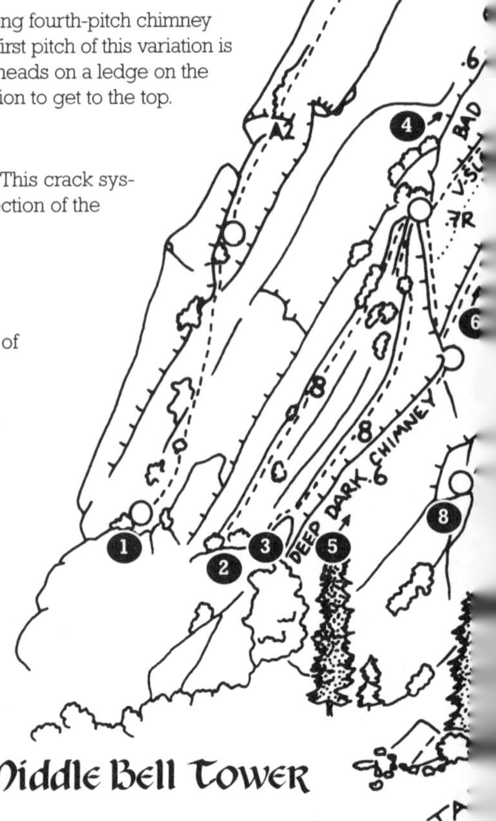

Middle Bell Tower

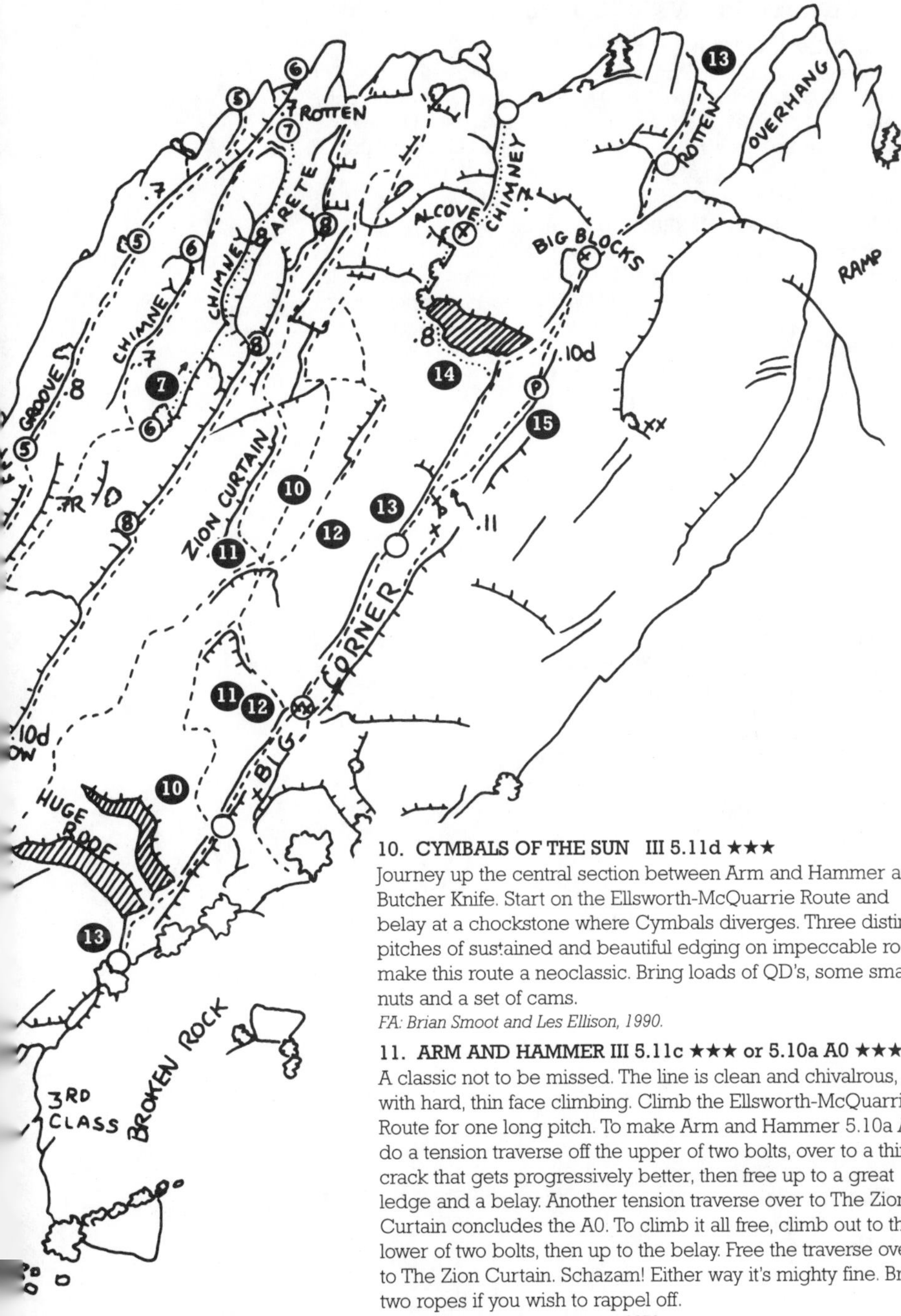

10. CYMBALS OF THE SUN III 5.11d ★★★
Journey up the central section between Arm and Hammer and Butcher Knife. Start on the Ellsworth-McQuarrie Route and belay at a chockstone where Cymbals diverges. Three distinct pitches of sustained and beautiful edging on impeccable rock make this route a neoclassic. Bring loads of QD's, some small nuts and a set of cams.
FA: Brian Smoot and Les Ellison, 1990.

11. ARM AND HAMMER III 5.11c ★★★ or 5.10a A0 ★★★
A classic not to be missed. The line is clean and chivalrous, with hard, thin face climbing. Climb the Ellsworth-McQuarrie Route for one long pitch. To make Arm and Hammer 5.10a A0, do a tension traverse off the upper of two bolts, over to a thin crack that gets progressively better, then free up to a great ledge and a belay. Another tension traverse over to The Zion Curtain concludes the A0. To climb it all free, climb out to the lower of two bolts, then up to the belay. Free the traverse over to The Zion Curtain. Schazam! Either way it's mighty fine. Bring two ropes if you wish to rappel off.
FA: Les Ellison and Russ Jacobs, 1979.
FFA of the first traverse: Merrill Bitter and Bret Ruckman, 1984.
FFA of the second traverse: Drew Bedford, David Casey, Ron George and Karen Kelley, 1985.

MIDDLE BELL TOWER ROUTES

12. BUTCHER KNIFE III 5.11c ★★★

The megaclassic right of Cymbals, again with thanks to the travails of Les Ellison. On pitch two, traverse 10 feet left to the lower of two bolts and then up to a belay. The roof's pitch contrasts the face pitches below—it requires power, which is waning in most climbers at this point. Two ropes are needed for a rappel descent.

FA: Les Ellison and Rick Wyatt, 1982.

13. ELLSWORTH-McQUARRIE ROUTE III 5.7 ★★

One of the obvious plums in Bell's Canyon, picked early by two up-and-comings. The line is hard to miss, following the conspicuous left-facing corner system up to a roof, which is passed to the right. Poor rock on the upper two pitches greatly reduces the fun of an otherwise classic route.

FA: Steve Ellsworth and Mark McQuarrie, 1964.

14. WEST EXIT VARIATION 5.8 ★

Undercling the left side of the roof and set up a belay. Be careful not to get the rope jammed. Continue up to a bolt and then up squalid chimneys to the top. Poor rock.

15. DIRE DIRECT III 5.10d ★★

An exposed line that attacks the mottled face between Ellsworth-McQuarrie and Dire Straits, eventually crossing that route to finish up near the arête.

FA: Scott Keller, Mike Lyons, Brian Wieland, Jake Anderegg, 1996.

16. DIRE STRAITS III 5.11 R ★

A sporty route that wonders up the face right of the Ellsworth-McQuarrie dihedral. Start 50 feet up and right of the start of Ellsworth-McQuarrie.

FA: Mark Rolofson and Les Ellison, 1979.

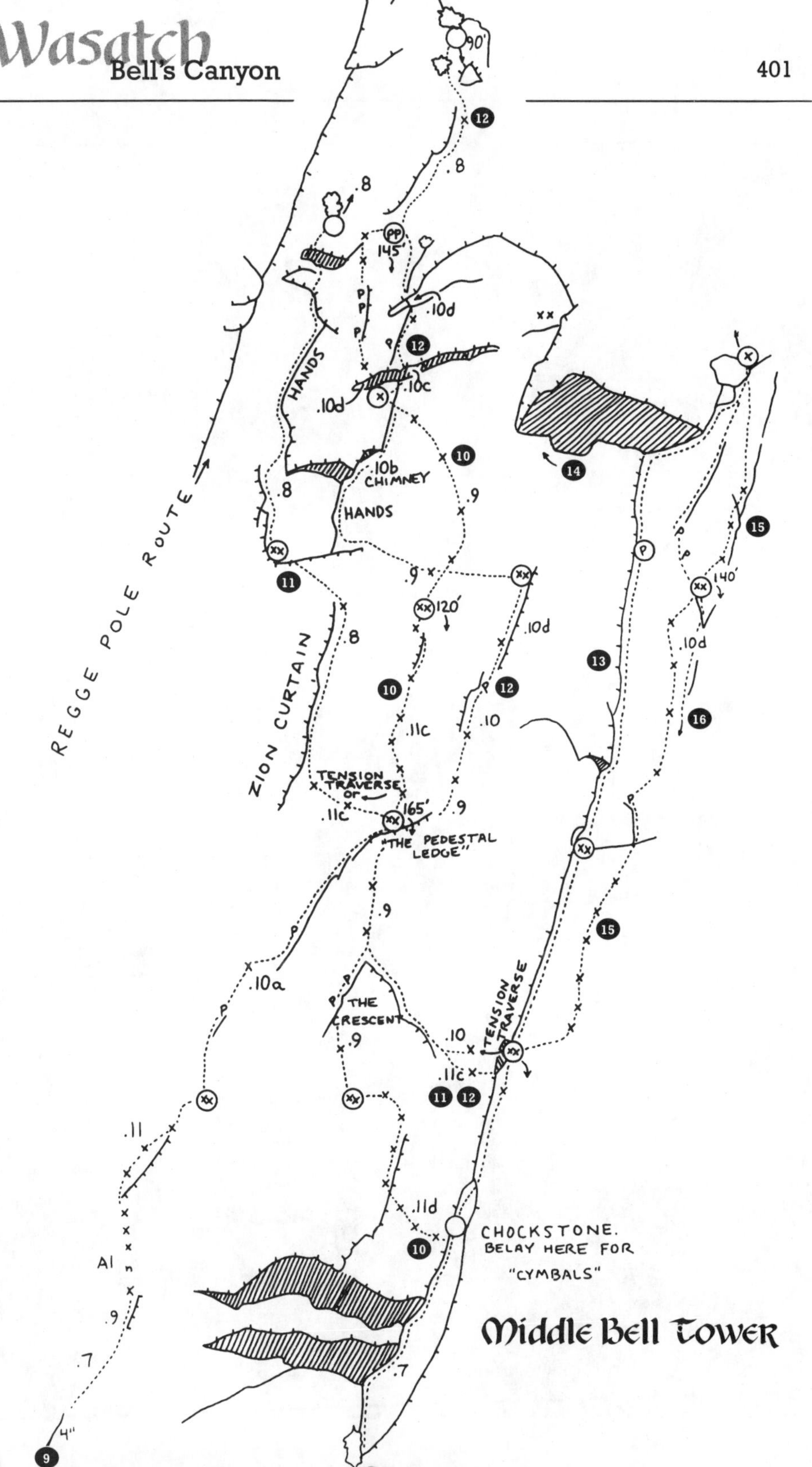
REGGE POLE ROUTE
ZION CURTAIN
HANDS
CHIMNEY
TENSION TRAVERSE or
"THE PEDESTAL LEDGE"
THE CRESCENT
TENSION TRAVERSE
CHOCKSTONE. BELAY HERE FOR "CYMBALS"
90'
145'
120'
165'
140'
.10d
.10c
.10b
.11c
.11d
.10a
A1
4"
Middle Bell Tower

1
2
3

EAST BELL TOWER

East Bell Tower is the easternmost of the "towers," but is less distinctive than the West or the Middle. The angle of the East Bell is a bit more forgiving, and consequently, vegetation is more abundant. The routes tend to be on good rock and are enjoyable.

APPROACH: Follow the How To Get There information for Bell's Canyon. Walk up the Bell's Canyon trail until you are directly across from the tower. Forge the stream. On the opposite bank, convince the brush to let you through and fight your way to the base of the wall. Or, approach as for the Middle Bell Tower and traverse the pine covered slope to the base of the routes (longer, but less brushy). See overview on page 388.

DESCENT: Struggle down the gully to the west, with one rappel.

EAST BELL TOWER ROUTES

1. ROUTE OF ALL EVIL II 5.6 ★★
2. McQUARRIE ROUTE III 5.9+ ★
3. HORTON-JACKSON ROUTE III 5.9

EAST BELL TOWER ROUTES

1. ROUTE OF ALL EVIL II 5.6 ★★

This line is the most popular on the East Bell Tower and offers good, sustained 5.5 to 5.6 climbing for four pitches. Start on the most obvious dihedral system on the left side of the buttress. Basically, the route follows chimneys and cracks up to a perplexing crux roof—which is passed on the right (5.6)—for three pitches. The final pitch continues up the dihedral to the top (5.5).

FA: George Lowe and Mark McQuarrie, 1964.

2. McQUARRIE ROUTE III 5.9+ ★

Starting 40 feet right of the Route of All Evil, this climb tackles the line of dihedrals in the center of the face. Six pitches of varied climbing lead to the top.

FA: George Lowe and Mark McQuarrie, 1964.

FFA: George Lowe and Dave George, early 70s.

3. HORTON-JACKSON ROUTE III 5.9

With moderate climbing for most of the route, the final 5.9 pitch of the adjoined McQuarrie Route seems disproportionately hard. Start 50 feet right of the McQuarrie Route in a chimney/corner below a large pine tree. Climb past the pine to a large, forested ledge. Cracks and corners above join in with the McQuarrie Route and the path home.

FA: Renny Jackson and Paul Horton, 1974.

BELL'S CANYON—WATERFALL DOME (no topo)

An unfortunate name, because this dome actually has little to do with the waterfall. Waterfall Dome is more broken and less steep than the other Towers to the west, yet the views into upper Bell's and Thunder bowl are unsurpassed.

APPROACH: Follow the How To Get There information for Bell's Canyon. Waterfall Dome is located 200 yards north of the upper waterfall on the Bell's Canyon trail. Continue on the trail past the East Bell for a quarter-mile to a stream crossing and a beautiful waterfall (nice lunch spot). Cross the stream on the bridge and continue 200 feet up the trail. A vicious bushwhack north brings one to the base. See overview on page 388.

DESCENT: Unknown.

1. PILZ GRIND II 5.9 R ★

Climb the first pitch of Old Goat. From the far left end of the sandy ledge, climb up via wild mantles on knobs to the left of Old Goat. The protection takes imagination.

FA: Res Von Kanel, Koni Hari and James Garrett.

2. OLD GOAT 5.8 ★

Start at the lowest point of the wall, and climb grooves up and right for 25 feet. Move left to a slanting ramp and continue to a belay at a pine tree. Scramble up easy rock 200 feet to a sandy ledge below the steeper wall above. From the left end of the sandy ledge, climb up and left 20 feet, to the top of a blocky flake. Move left to a thin crack that leads to a right-slanting groove. Climb the groove past a bolt to a belay at the top of the groove system. Continue up the low-angled rock above, staying right of a large chimney, to the top.

FA: Rick Wyatt.

3. THE WATERFALL ROUTE 5.6

From the bolt on Old Goat, traverse right on knobs to a right-slanting crack that forms a ledge, and belay. Climb the converging double cracks above and belay. Climb up crack systems above for 150 feet, then scramble to the top.

FA: Paul Horton and Bill Conrod, 1971.

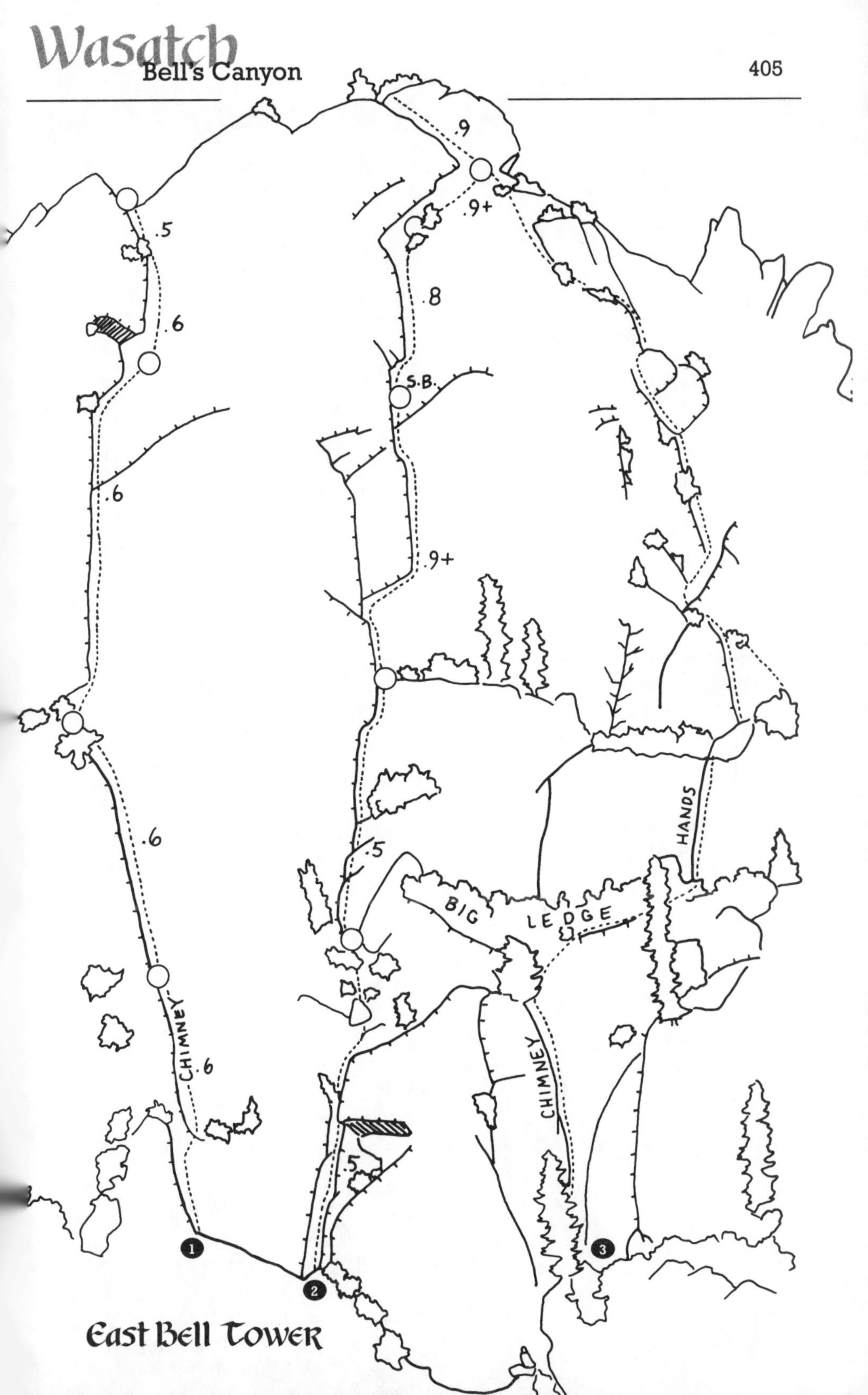
.9
.9+
.5
.8
.6
S.B.
.6
.9+
.6
.5
HANDS
BIG
LEDGE
CHIMNEY
.6
CHIMNEY
.5
1
2
3
East Bell Tower

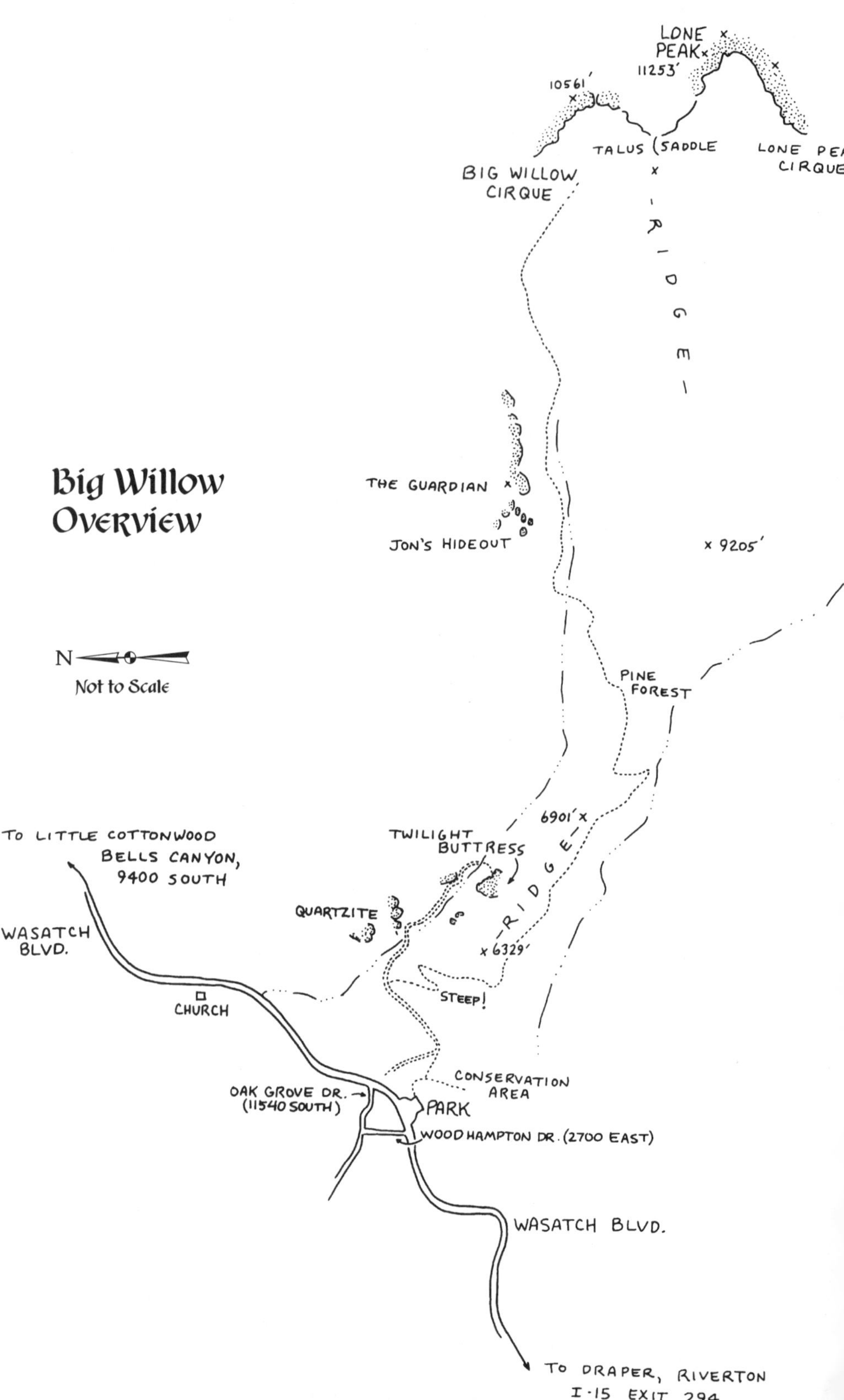
LONE PEAK
11253'
10561'
TALUS
SADDLE
LONE PEAK CIRQUE
BIG WILLOW CIRQUE
RIDGE
Big Willow Overview
N
Not to Scale
THE GUARDIAN
JON'S HIDEOUT
9205'
PINE FOREST
6901'
TO LITTLE COTTONWOOD
BELLS CANYON, 9400 SOUTH
TWILIGHT BUTTRESS
RIDGE
QUARTZITE
WASATCH BLVD.
6329'
STEEP!
CHURCH
CONSERVATION AREA
OAK GROVE DR. (11540 SOUTH)
PARK
WOODHAMPTON DR. (2700 EAST)
WASATCH BLVD.
TO DRAPER, RIVERTON
I-15 EXIT 294

Big Willow Canyon

This steep, scenic, and complicated canyon is the largest drainage on the west slope between Bell's Canyon and Lone Peak. Snow lingers for a long time in upper Big Willow Canyon, sometimes into late summer. A drop of water that melts from snow here begins its journey to the Great Salt Lake in a spectacular and beautifully alpine cirque that graces the upper walls of Big Willow. Rarely visited, this cirque is overshadowed in popularity by its sister to the south—Lone Peak Cirque. As the water cascades down, it passes along the approach to the cirque and several granite towers that feature good rock and patina edges. Further down canyon, at the stream's last hurrah near the mouth, a small granite wall, etched with more of the patina, is home to 18 popular routes that stay cool most of the year.

HOW TO GET THERE: Exit off I-15 at the Draper/Riverton Exit, 12300 South (Highway 71). Turn east on Highway 71 (12300 South). Follow this road which eventually turns into Draper Parkway, then bends to become 1700 East. Look for an intersection (stoplight) with Wasatch Blvd. Turn east on Wasatch and drive towards the mountains. A parking area at the southeast corner of a bend in Wasatch Blvd. is the start for a walk into Big Willow Canyon. This parking is located at roughly 11600 South, 2750 East, on Wasatch Blvd. See overview on page 406. Walk across the field, heading for the far east edge next to the mountain. A steep dirt road cuts northward, across the foot of the mountain and into Big Willow Canyon. See the individual cliff descriptions for approach information from here.

BIG WILLOW QUARTZITE (no topo)

Most climbers visiting Big Willow Canyon are headed to the Twilight Buttress. On the way there, they will pass two quartzite outcrops on the north side of the dirt road. The first outcrop encountered is more broken and shattered, while the second outcrop is composed of two overhanging walls. This lone route climbs the lower of the two overhanging faces.

APPROACH: Follow the approach to the Twilight Buttress and you'll pass right by this route. Some talus on the left (north) side of the road, just below the wall provides brush-free access. See overview on page 406.

DESCENT: A one rope rappel from anchors at the top of the route reaches the ground.

1. HALF-LIGHT 5.10? ★

Follow three bolts on the overhanging east face. The first clip is scary.
FA: Unknown.

BIG WILLOW CANYON —TWILIGHT BUTTRESS

This buttress rests among the pines near the mouth of Big Willow Canyon. The rock is a varnished granite, liberally splattered with edges and solution pockets. Nearby, Big Willow stream runs year round, cooling the north-facing cliffs during the summer. A relatively quick walk up a dirt road, steep face climbs and a sense of solitude create a first-rate climbing experience.

APPROACH: Follow the How To Get There information for Big Willow Canyon. Walk up the dirt road, passing a gate, and enter the canyon. The dirt road crosses the creek, then climbs steeply until it meets the stream again at a water diversion dam or pond. The road ends here, but the approach to the Twilight Buttress traverses southwest through the pines to reach the base of the wall. See overview page 406.

DESCENT: With the exception of For Lorne, one rope is all that is needed to descend from anchors at the top of most of the routes on this wall.

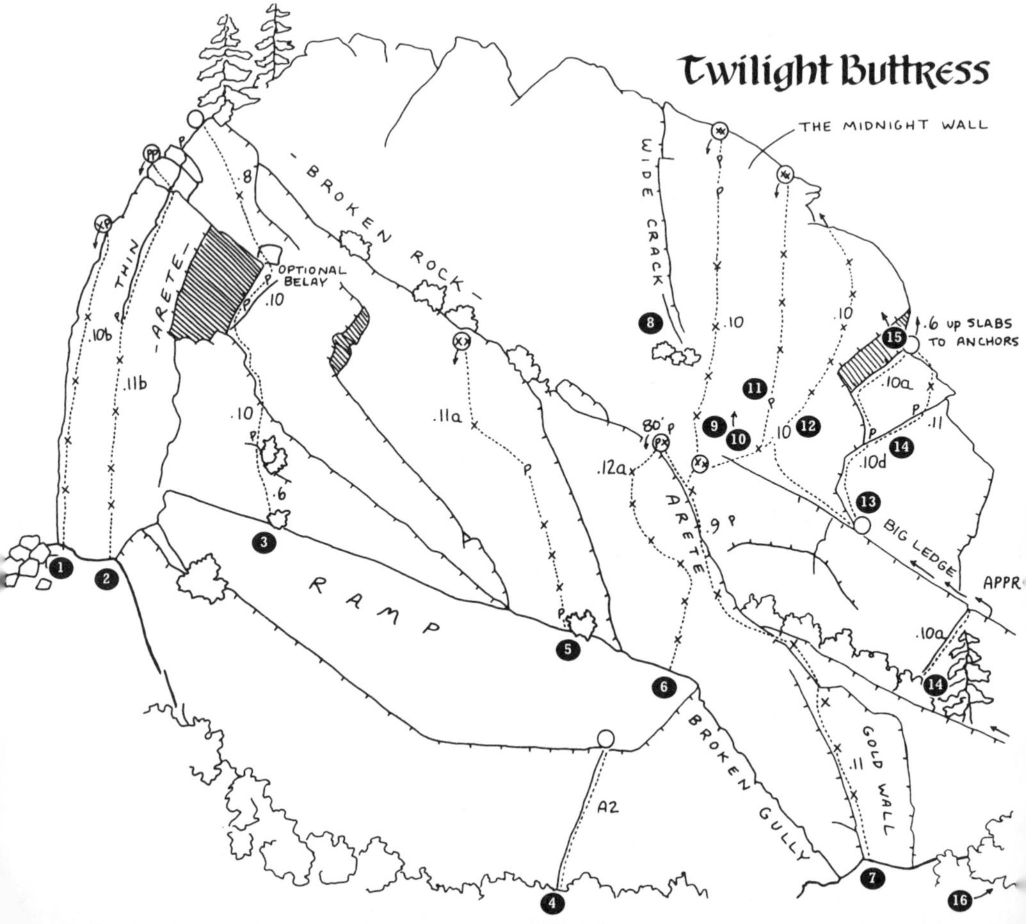

Twilight Buttress

TWILIGHT BUTTRESS ROUTES

1. SUNSET ARÊTE 5.10b ★★
The City of Rocks has come to the Wasatch. The left side of the buttress is vertical and blessed with varnished solution pockets. This fine route climbs the lefthand arête past four bolts.
FA: Ted Coletti, George Rosenthal and Pat Maloney, 1989.

2. EDGE OF NIGHT 5.11b ★★
Climb the patina pockets right of Sunset Arête. Strenuous moves lead to a thin crack. Super good. Bring small to medium nuts and TCU's.
FA: Pat Maloney and James Garrett, 1990.

3. WITHOUT WINGS 5.10 A0 R ★
Climb the corner right of Edge of Night. A sporty runout is at the top.
FA: James and Franziska Garrett, 1990.

4. FREE ME A2
Climb the thin crack on lower north face below the ramp. When will this be free climbed?
FA: George Rosenthal and Ted Coletti, 1990.

5. MYKONOS 5.11a ★
Flash up the vertical face 100 feet right of Sunset Arête.
FA: Stuart and Bret Ruckman, 1990.

6. ROME IN A DAY 5.12a ★★
Begin 30 feet right of Mykonos. A desperate high-step tests your flexibility.
FA: Stuart and Bret Ruckman, 1990.

7. WITHOUT WHEELS 5.11 ★★
The thin right-facing corner at the northwest end of the buttress requires solid stemming technique. Small nuts and TCUs are handy. This route provides the best access to the Midnight Wall.
FA: Pat Maloney and James Garrett, 1990.

8. CRUISING THE FREEWAY 5.10
The crack is 5.8, but getting to it is 5.10.
FA: George Rosenthal and Ted Coletti, 1990.

9. THE NIGHTSTALKER 5.10 ★★
Don't be caught out alone! Climb the face above the belay of Without Wheels. Steep face climbing on good edges may leave one breathless.
FA: George and Marc Rosenthal and Ted Coletti, 1990.

10. NEUTRAL ZONE 5.9
Climb the loose face between The Nightstalker and Up In The Night on all natural gear. Bring TCUs, cams and wireds.
FA: George Rosenthal and Ted Coletti, 1990.

11. UP IN THE NIGHT 5.10 ★★
Edges facilitate some steep climbing right of The Nightstalker. The traverse at the bottom is protected with fixed pins.
FA: Ted Coletti and George Rosenthal, 1990.

12. OUTER SPACE 5.10c ★★
Delirious exposure and a very unoriginal name.
FA: Ted Colletti and George Rosenthal, 1990.

13. ROAM AROUND THE WORLD 5.10d ★★
This route journeys up the zig-zagging corners on the far right side of the buttress. Approach from the west to reach the big sloping ledge at the base. The final roof is great. TCUs should augment a standard rack.
FA: Pat Maloney and James Garrett, 1990.

14. BRINKERHOFF VARIATION 5.11c/d ★
This variation adds a short pitch to the start, joins the original route for the first roof, then continues out the strenuous right-diagonalling crack.
FA: Rob Brinkerhoff, Mel Brown and James Garrett, 1990.

TWILIGHT BUTTRESS ROUTES

15. SPACED OUT A2

Climb Roam Around The World until an airy traverse left past four fixed pins is possible. Bring some TCUs. Belay at the top of Outer Space.
FA: George Rosenthal and Ted Coletti, 1990.

16. MADE IN THE SHADE 5.11b

Not on the topo. This short route climbs a face with three bolts right of the start of Without Wheels.
FA: George Rosenthal and Ted Coletti, 1992.

17. FOR LORNE 5.9 A2

This climb is not on the Twilight Buttress itself, but above and east of it, on the next north-facing buttress in Big Willow Canyon. Start off a slab and climb a 5.9 finger crack to an A2 upper crack. The rappel off is 120 feet.
FA: James Garrett, solo, 1990.

18. COSMIC THING 5.8

This climb is not on the Twilight Buttress. Rather, it is located on a west-facing granite slab, 30 feet above the dirt road, several hundred feet before reaching the concrete contraption (pond) at the end of the road. Climb a steep brown face to a lower-angled slab above. Move past a bolt and belay from the bushes at the top. Rappel 80 feet.
FA: James and Franziska Garrett, 1990.

Brad Jackson leading Trench Warfare,
Hanging Slab, Little Cottonwood Canyon.

photo: Kennan Harvey.

BIG WILLOW CANYON—JON'S HIDEOUT

A series of granite walls, buttresses, and outcrops descend from the north ridge of Big Willow Canyon. The largest of these is known as The Guardian. The smaller walls down canyon from The Guardian have been explored as well, and several fine routes are the result. Solitude and a sense of adventure are the rewards for a long two hour approach.

APPROACH: Follow the How To Get There information for Big Willow Canyon. Follow the directions to the Twilight Buttress to get started, however, instead of simply following the dirt road into the canyon, hike about 300 feet beyond the gate near the bottom of the road until the road flattens out, and turns east into the canyon. Here, blue spray paint on a rock marks a well-hidden trail heading off to the south. Follow this trail as it climbs steeply towards Little Willow Canyon, makes a big lazy traverse, then tops the ridge back into Big Willow Canyon. You'll be able to see The Guardian from the trail, and roughly ¼ mile before you reach The Guardian, turn north on a faint trail that leads directly to a small boulder. A boulder move gains the top of the boulder, and the path which continues up and right (east) to the first outcrop. See overviews on page 406 and below.

DESCENT: Rappel from anchors at the top of each route with one rope.

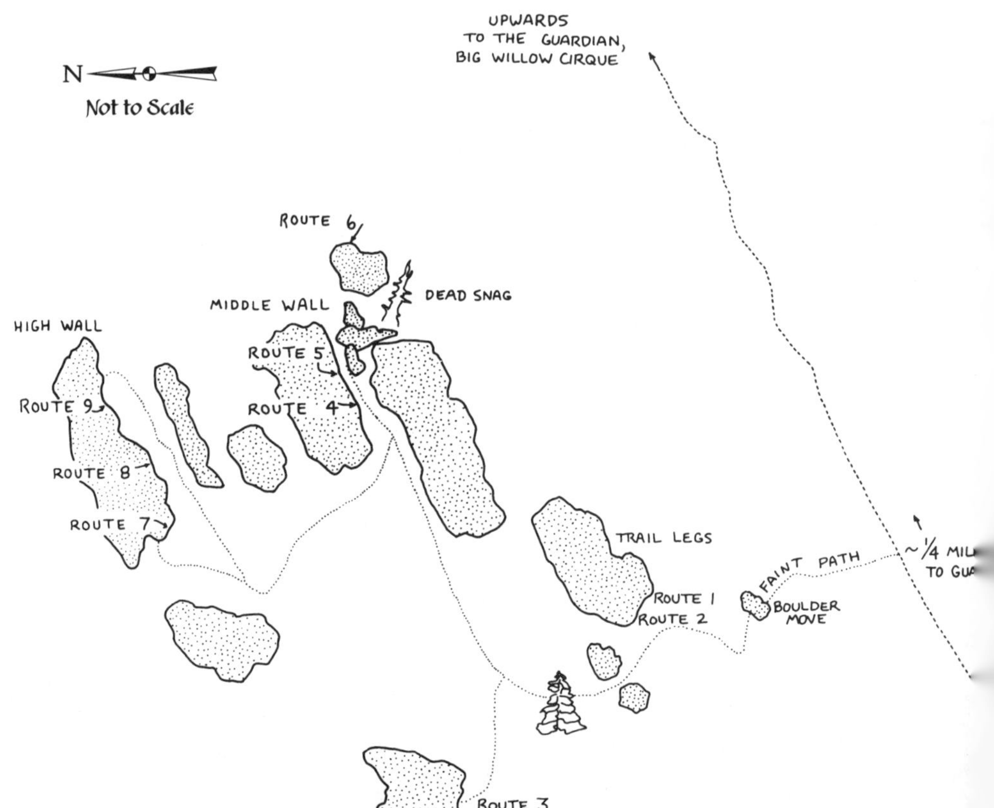

JON'S HIDEOUT ROUTES

1. TRAIL LEGS 5.9 ★
Technical slab climbing to a two-bolt anchor. Six bolts.
FA: Jon Ray, 1990.

2. TRAIL LEGS 2 5.9 ★
More of the same—thin face moves with seven bolts.
FA: Jon and Pam Ray, 1990.

3. PROJECT
Seven bolts at the time of this writing.

4. RIPPED DOEJI 5.10d ★★
A series of patina edges lead to an arête, followed by a few committing face moves. Six bolts to a hanging belay.
FA: Jon Ray, 1990.

5. **PROJECT** Only anchors at the time of this writing.

6. THE NOSTRIL 5.10
Walk east and downhill from Ripped Doeji, passing through a small cave, to find this east-facing route with four bolts.
FA: Randy Kielszewski and Jon Ray, 1990.

7. WALKING SUNDANCE 5.10d ★★
Persistent friction climbing that reaches the top of the highest wall. 17 bolts?!
FA: Jon Ray, 1991.

8. TOOTH DECAY 5.10 ★★
Nice edges and wild chickenheads. Eight bolts.
FA: Jon and Pam Ray, 1991.

9. D-10 5.11d ★★
A technical start is followed by a roof and some very fine face climbing.
FA: Jon Ray, 1991.

BIG WILLOW CANYON—THE GUARDIAN

You will pass by this large granite tower while hiking up the Big Willow trail on the way to Big Willow Cirque. The west face enjoys more weaknesses, but the south face is splotched with patina.

APPROACH: Expect a two to two-and-a-half hour approach. Follow the How To Get There information for Big Willow Canyon. Follow the approach to Jon's Hideout, however, instead of cutting north on the faint trail that leads towards the boulder, continue up canyon on the main hiking trail until you are directly across from The Guardian. This hike has intermittent water for the first three miles. See overview on page 406.

DESCENT: Two ropes are needed to descend from fixed anchors at the top of each route.

The Guardian routes (no topo)

1. THE SWISS EDGE III 5.9 ★★

Climb the west face of the Guardian in four pitches. The first pitch climbs past three bolts and is rated 5.9. The second pitch passes three more bolts to a belay at a pine tree. Four bolts, a pin, and some 5.9 slab climbing comprise the third lead and a pin and three bolts protect the final pitch. Bring along QDs and a light rack including TCUs. Several pitches are a full 165 feet. Three 160 foot rappels down the south face make for a speedy descent.

FA: Franziska and James Garrett, 1990.

The following routes start off a ledge roughly 150 feet above the base of the wall. Either climb a somewhat dirty 5.8 crack/flare pitch to reach the ledge, or climb The Swiss Edge and descend via the three rappels, passing Infidels along the second rappel.

2. JOKER MAN 5.11b ★

You'll need about three sets of brass-type nuts to protect this scary lead. Climb the right-leaning crack to the left of Infidels. Hard mantles onto sloping knobs seem to be the punch line. The climb is 140 feet long, high quality, and shares the anchors with Infidels.

FA: Mike Friedrichs, Mary Ellen Gage, and Jean Roush, 1992.

3. INFIDELS 5.10d ★★

A ten bolt sport route up the south face of The Guardian. This is classic hueco climbing, unlike anything else in the Wasatch. Good rock, good position, and good moves will make a believer out of you.

FA: Mike Friedrichs and Mary Ellen Gage, 1992.

4. DYLAN 5.9 ★

Clip the first bolt on Infidels, then start wandering right across a sea of holes, edges, and patina. All bolts to a two-bolt station.

FA: Mike Friedrichs, Mary Ellen Gage, and Jean Roush, 1992.

Bill Patton feeling the heat on Crosscurrent, Parley's Canyon.

photo: Ruckman

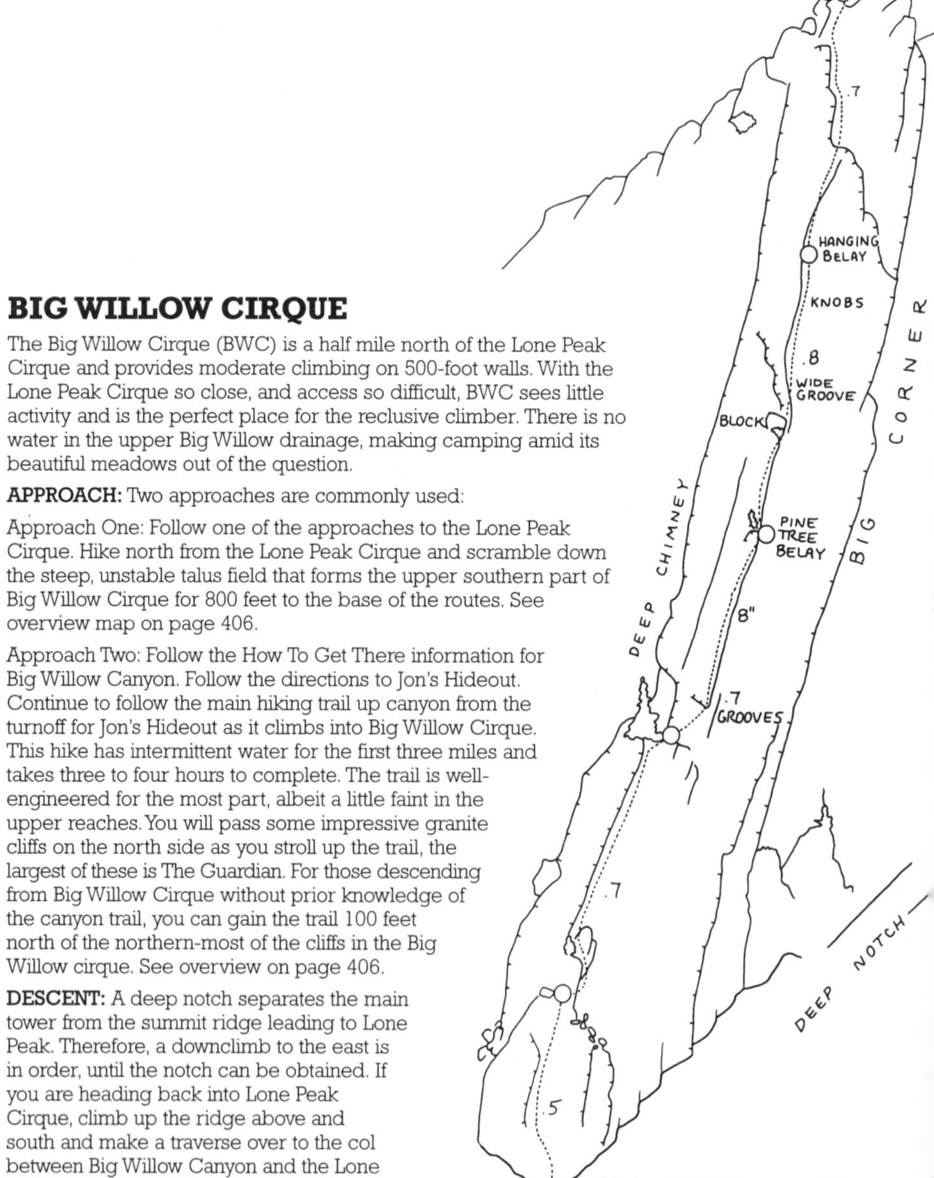

BIG WILLOW CIRQUE

The Big Willow Cirque (BWC) is a half mile north of the Lone Peak Cirque and provides moderate climbing on 500-foot walls. With the Lone Peak Cirque so close, and access so difficult, BWC sees little activity and is the perfect place for the reclusive climber. There is no water in the upper Big Willow drainage, making camping amid its beautiful meadows out of the question.

APPROACH: Two approaches are commonly used:

Approach One: Follow one of the approaches to the Lone Peak Cirque. Hike north from the Lone Peak Cirque and scramble down the steep, unstable talus field that forms the upper southern part of Big Willow Cirque for 800 feet to the base of the routes. See overview map on page 406.

Approach Two: Follow the How To Get There information for Big Willow Canyon. Follow the directions to Jon's Hideout. Continue to follow the main hiking trail up canyon from the turnoff for Jon's Hideout as it climbs into Big Willow Cirque. This hike has intermittent water for the first three miles and takes three to four hours to complete. The trail is well-engineered for the most part, albeit a little faint in the upper reaches. You will pass some impressive granite cliffs on the north side as you stroll up the trail, the largest of these is The Guardian. For those descending from Big Willow Cirque without prior knowledge of the canyon trail, you can gain the trail 100 feet north of the northern-most of the cliffs in the Big Willow cirque. See overview on page 406.

DESCENT: A deep notch separates the main tower from the summit ridge leading to Lone Peak. Therefore, a downclimb to the east is in order, until the notch can be obtained. If you are heading back into Lone Peak Cirque, climb up the ridge above and south and make a traverse over to the col between Big Willow Canyon and the Lone Peak Cirque.

BIG WILLOW CIRQUE ROUTES

A word of caution: the route lines on the photo are only a rendering. Although we did the best we could, the exact path is sometimes a mystery.

1. BASQUE CIRQUE ROUTE II 5.6 ★

Begin 100 feet left of Late Start, on a "tower" to the north of the main (Giggles) tower. Climb a right-facing corner for a long pitch to a belay on the left by a small pine (5.6). Climb a prominent eight-inch crack on the west, then the principal face to a nice belay atop a pedestal (5.6). Continue to the top. This description may not be entirely accurate.

FA: Pete Lev, Cado Avenali and Dave Hamre, 1972.

2. LATE START II 5.8

The left and lowest point of the main tower has some good white rock and is split by several one-to two-inch cracks. Climb these cracks to some pine trees and belay 20 feet higher (5.5). Climb up and right, past a corner, to a pine tree (5.5). Climb weaknesses above to the "dagger-like" beginning of a long, shallow right-facing corner. Belay 20 feet above the "dagger." Climb the corner to a good belay (5.8). Finish off the corner and face climb up and right to the top (5.8).

FA: Kent Jameson, Blayde Boyd and Chip LeCure, 1980.

3. BETTER HOMES AND GARDENS II 5.7

Climb the first two pitches of Giggles, then entertain the cracks within a deep chimney left of the main face of Giggles and belay at a pin. Climb a right-facing corner past a pin, traverse right into a vegetated crack and belay. Cruise up the vegetated crack to the top.

FA: Ron George and James Garrett, 1983.

4. GIGGLES II 5.8 ★★

The BWC classic. Bring a standard rack. See topo.

FA: George Lowe and Jock Glidden, 1972.

5. HIGHWAY OF HOLINESS II 5.7

A solitary pine rises near the right side of the main tower. Climb up to the pine and belay (150 feet, 5.6). Climb a host of cracks up and right to a big belay ledge (5.6). A wide crack system is groveled up to a belay stance (5.5). Climb up the chimney to a stacked block overhang that is passed on the right, and fight through trees to the top (5.7).

FA: Brian Smoot and Steve Aldous, 1982.

6. WHIMPERS II 5.8 ★

A four pitch route that combines dihedral climbing with exposed face traverses and an airy belay ledge. The third pitch climbs from a blocky belay ledge up and right, through a series of improbable overlaps and flakes to a crack in the mottled face. Follow the crack up and right again to reach the exposed belay. Weaknesses above the belay become progressively easier.

FA: Daniel Horton and Art Lang, 1992.

7. LAUGHING ALL THE WAY II 5.8 R ★

A long pitch with some delicate climbing. Continue up the the dihedral, then traverse right to avoid the last vegetated section of the corner. Join Whimpers again at an exposed belay ledge.

FA: Allen Sandersen and Rick Reese, 1995.

8. CLOSE ENCOUNTERS II 5.8

This route is located on the west-facing cliff south of the gully defining the right side of the Giggles tower. Climb a maze of cracks and knobs located 70 feet right of this gully, to a belay at a tree (165 feet, 5.6). Follow cracks until it is possible to traverse right to a pine tree (5.7). Climb widening cracks to a loose block that is passed on the right via flakes (150 feet, 5.8). Scramble to the top. A UFO was sighted on the first ascent as the climbers were pulling onto the summit.

FA: Brian and Jonathan Smoot, 1981.

CIRQUE ROUTES

1. BASQUE CIRQUE ROUTE II 5.6 ★
2. LATE START II 5.8
3. BETTER HOMES AND GARDENS II 5.7
4. GIGGLES II 5.8 ★★
5. HIGHWAY OF HOLINESS II 5.7
6. WHIMPERS II 5.8 ★
7. LAUGHING ALL THE WAY II 5.8 R ★
8. CLOSE ENCOUNTERS II 5.8

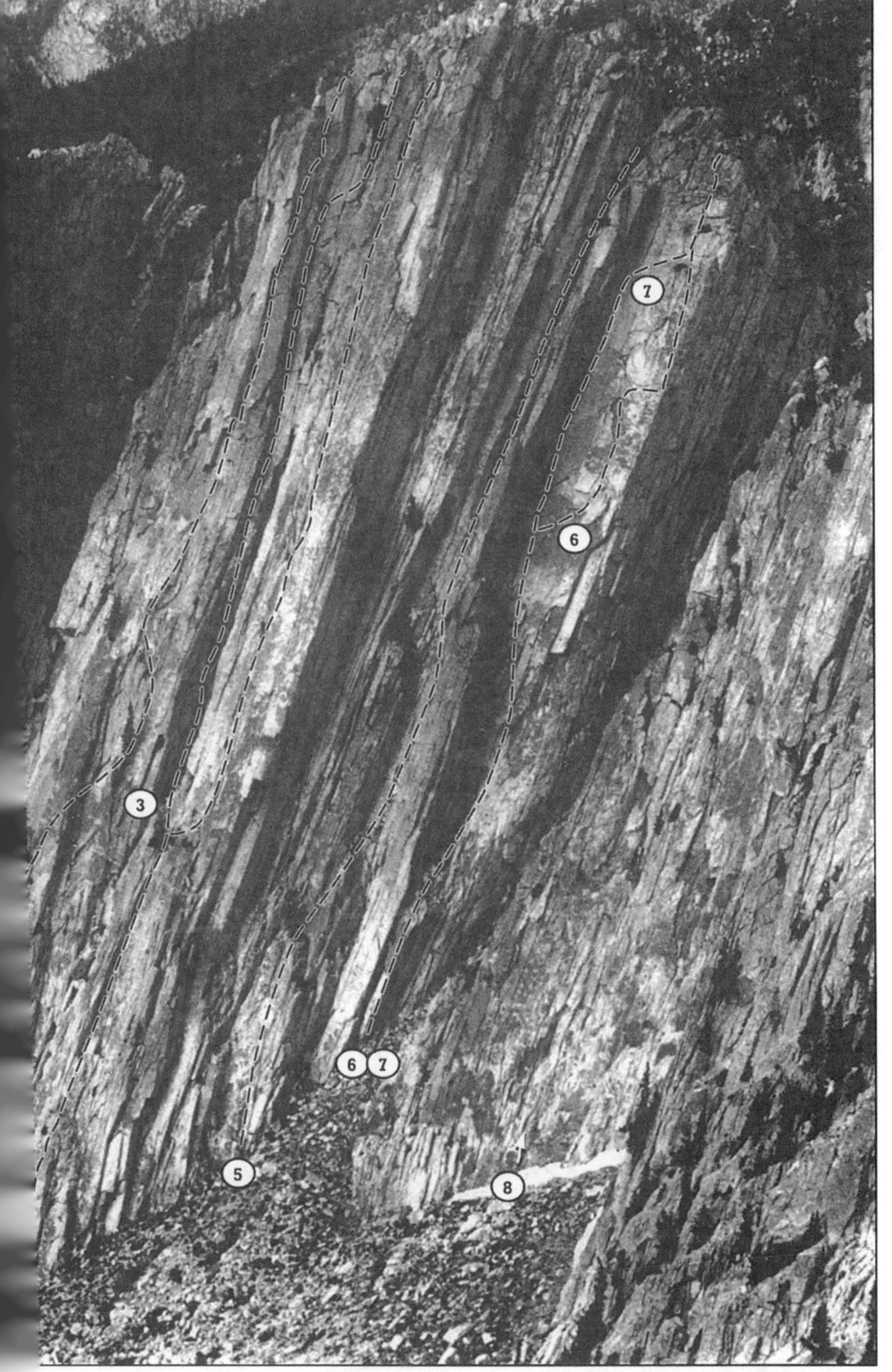

Looking at the Summit Wall, Lone Peak Cirque.

Lone Peak Cirque

At an elevation of 11,253 feet, Lone Peak is the most alpine of the major climbing areas in the Wasatch. Three major cirques surround the peak—earmarks of ice age scouring. The peak is a favorite of peak baggers and climbers alike because of its dramatic summit and superb views of Salt Lake Valley.

The granite in the west cirque is what makes Lone Peak distinctive. It forms steep walls up to 600 feet in height and is fractured by many vertical cracks. In addition to the plentiful cracks, the knobs and solution pockets make for unique climbing situations on apparently blank rock. The walls here are a bit steeper than their Little Cottonwood counterparts, and many of those choice-looking cracks are, in fact, hard-to-protect seams. Most of the routes are four to five pitches in length on generally good rock. Freeze/thaw weathering may produce piles of loose flakes, the so called "house of cards" effect, and require considerable caution when climbing.

It is not uncommon to see mountain goats quietly hanging out on some precarious ledge, or to hear the high-pitched whine of the reticent and elusive pikas. Fortunately, this beautiful and sublime area is protected within the 30,088-acre Lone Peak Wilderness.

The best time to visit the Lone Peak Cirque is mid-June to late August, depending on the duration of the snow fields. Snow melt basically is the only source of water, a fact that limits the climbing/camping to the few months that have conducive temperatures. Of course, the more hardened climbers may choose to carry their own water, do day trips, or ignore numb fingers. As always in the Wasatch, it is recommended that water gathered in the wilderness be treated using a filter or chemicals. By taking plenty of extra water bottles—or at least one larger vessel—you can fill up in the late afternoon when snow melt is at its peak, and have enough for the next day.

GEAR: Bring a fairly broad selection of protection (camming units are especially useful) and plenty of full-length runners. Small micro nuts seem to be particularly useful for protecting seams on the harder routes. Don't forget a rain jacket, as afternoon thunderstorms during the summer are fairly common.

CAMPING: The camping in the cirque is usually on level grassy nooks with boulders at their perimeters. These are beautiful campsites, but will only continue to be so if we "walk softly" and carry out our garbage, bury our excrement, and minimize our impact. By camping on the sandy areas alongside the grassy nooks, we can minimize the trampling of the delicate alpine tundra. We walked a long way to behold this wilderness; let's all do our part to preserve it.

HOW TO GET THERE/APPROACH: We have included descriptions of the two most popular approaches. In general, both approaches are strenuous and involve route finding skills. It is also possible to approach via the Draper Ridge. Hiking guidebooks to the Wasatch generally describe this hike, which is long and quite dry, but less steep.

APPROACH FROM ALPINE: The Alpine approach is the shortest access to Lone Peak. Water can usually be found along the way, and good camping is possible in either of the Hammongogs (a biblical word for meadow). With this approach, it is possible to leave after work, hike to one of the Hammongogs, spend the night, and continue into the cirque early the next day. Untold numbers of parties have become lost going this way, however. The approach information may appear excessive as a result. We've included an aerial schematic map and photos (page 424).

To access the Alpine Approach Trailhead, exit off Interstate15 at Exit 287 (Alpine, Highland and Timpanogos Cave). Drive east to the junction of Utah Highways 92 and 74. There is a Chevron on the north-east corner of the intersection. Turn left and drive north on 74 to Main Street in Alpine. From Main Street, turn right (east) on 100 South. Follow this road a short distance, then make a left (north) on 200 East. Follow 200 East through the three-way stop and continue north until it eventually becomes Grove Drive. Continue on Grove Drive through a sharp, ninety degree rightward curve. About 700 feet beyond (east of) the curve is Aspen Cove Drive. Turn left on this road and follow it until it's possible to turn left again on Aspen Drive. This road dead ends at the start of a dirt road that leads up to the first Hammongog. Park here, or continue driving if you've got a 4x4. (Please park out of the way of the homeowners, even if it means parking back down the road.)

The aerial schematic shows the approach from here. One may encounter route finding cruxes in locating the correct trail out of the First Hammongog, and in choosing the correct gully when leaving the Second Hamongog. See overview page 424.

CORNER CANYON APPROACH This approach has the advantage of being less steep (though longer), and the advantage of a shorter drive to the trailhead when coming from Salt Lake City. However, reliable water is generally not available for most of the hike.

To access the Corner Canyon Trailhead, exit off I-15 at Exit 294 (Draper, Riverton). Turn east on Highway 71 and head toward the mountains. Continue on 71 until the intersection of 1300 East. Turn right (south) on 1300 East, then turn left (east) on Pioneer Road (12300 South.) Follow Pioneer Road to 2000 East where a right turn (south) takes you to the end of the pavement (as of 1997) at Bear Mountain Drive (12550 South). Follow the upper dirt road for 2.7 miles to a large pullout (parking area) on the right side of the road. As of this writing, this road was passable for passenger cars. The hike begins here.

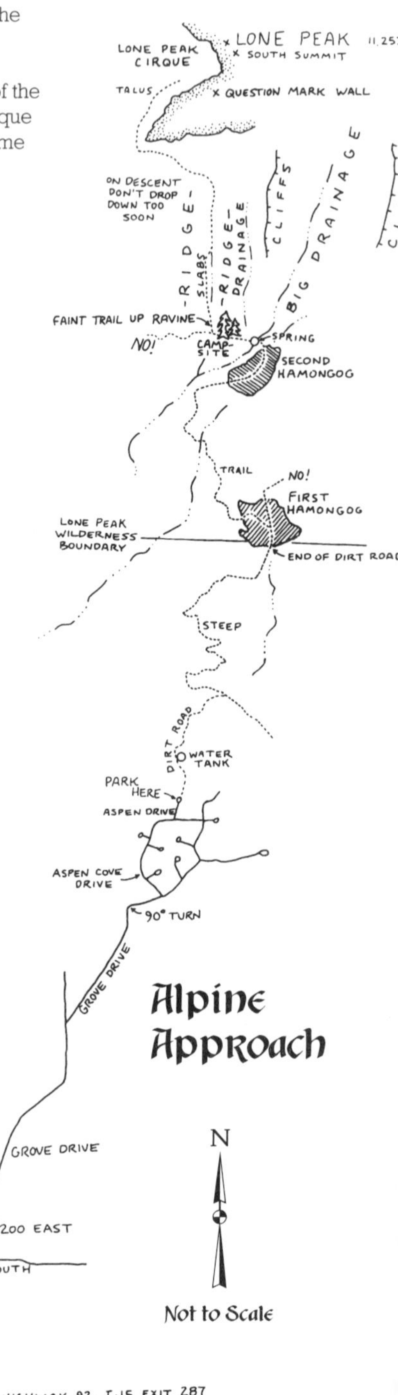

A steep dirt road climbs the hill east of the parking area. Follow this road up to the top of the hill and stop. This is a crux. Descending down the other side of this hill, essentially continuing to follow the dirt road and the most obvious path, is NOT the way to go. Instead, at the top of the hill, turn right and follow a faint trail that stays on the ridge crest, weaving in and out of oak and mahogany trees, but always following the ridge. The ridge you are on DOES NOT lead to Movie Rock, but passes to the south instead. Eventually the trail reaches a viewpoint, at the end of the ridge. From here, the trail climbs steeply up through the oak, heading north up the slope, until it intersects with the Draper Ridge Trail. From here, the path grows increasingly faint, but the destination becomes very clear. One last potential crux exists in the meadow not too far beyond the intersection of the Corner Canyon Trail and the Draper Ridge Trail. In this meadow it is possible to stray too far north. Be on the lookout for paths that head to the right, crossing a small dry streambed. From the meadow to the cirque is about an hour or more.

DESCENT: The easiest descent from the summit back into the cirque is to walk down Collin's Highway (the large ramp system that runs east to west below the Question Mark Wall) and rappel or downclimb Pete's Staircase (see Question Mark Wall topo). It is also possible to scramble down the ridge to the northwest from the summit, and make a more lengthy walk back to the cirque.

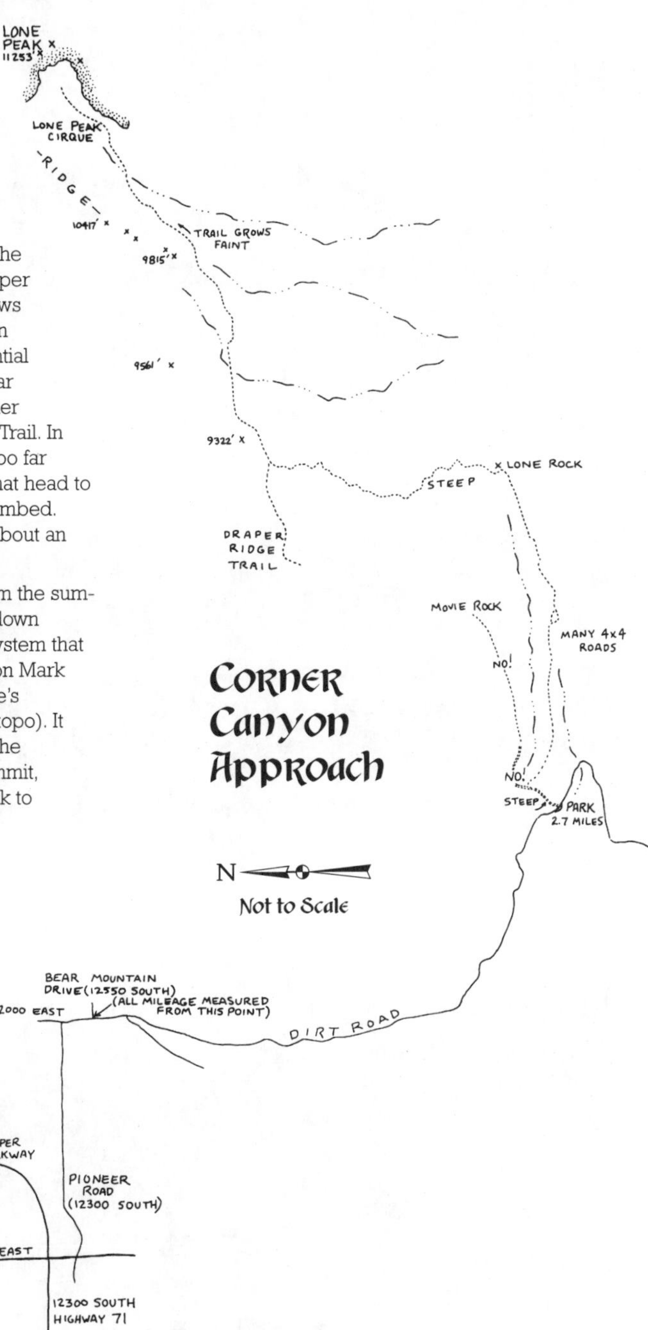

Lone Peak

Pfeifferhorn

amongog

First Hamongog

Approach from Alpine

FLYING BUTTRESS ROUTES

1. LICHEN IT 5.8
2. HOUND'S TOOTH 5.10d A1
3. FLYING BUTTRESS ROUTE II 5.10 ★
4. STORM WATCH II 5.10b/c
5. MOSAIC WALL II 5.10b R ★
6. PENNY ARCADE II 5.9 ★★
7. THE THIN MAN II 5.10a ★

FLYING BUTTRESS

The appropriately-named Flying Buttress appears to help support the summit, and sweeps off left of the pinnacle in a host of dihedrals and inviting rock. In actuality, most of the cracks are seams, and protection is, in large part, nonexistent. The routes described here do have adequate protection, however, and are about three pitches in length.

2 3 4 5 6 7

FLYING BUTTRESS ROUTES

1. LICHEN IT 5.8

The route follows cracks directly below a perched snag on the rim, on the left end of Flying Buttress. Follow the face and chickenheads up for 60 to 70 feet, then follow a corner up to snag. (140 feet, 5.8). Rappel off of a snag.

FA: Allen Sanderson and Dan Baker, 1988.

2. HOUND'S TOOTH 5.10d A1

Start 25 feet left of the Flying Buttress Route in a right-facing corner that holds a seam and several chickenheads, which are located on the lowest right wall. Moving left out of the corner past the pointed flake is A1. Belay 25 feet above a huge block. The second pitch is 5.8.

FA: Allen Sanderson and Dana Tangren, 1990.

3. FLYING BUTTRESS ROUTE II 5.10 ★

About 50 feet left of Mosaic Wall is a chimney. Climb a seam to reach a chimney located behind a flake, then move right to a groove and make moves up past a bolt that leads to another chimney (5.8). An easy pitch leads to a good ledge (5.6). Move left to bolts below a roof. Go to the roof's left edge and continue up a corner above (5.10d).

FA: Fred Beckey, Dan Davis and Ted Wilson, 1962.
FFA: Mark Bennett, Tito Black and Ted Warm, 1985.

4. STORM WATCH II 5.10b/c

Start left of Mosaic Wall in a dihedral. Climb up to a small ledge (150 feet, 5.8). Continue to another ledge, which is right of the top of the third pitch of Flying Buttress (70 feet, 5.6). Fierce jamming and stemming leads to the top (90 feet, 5.10b/c).

FA: Allen Sanderson and Mike Vanderbeck, 1989.

5. MOSAIC WALL II 5.10b R ★

Start by climbing the mosaic of cracks (5.8) up to a ledge at 165 feet (this is the upper of two ledges). Climb the difficult corner above (with tricky protection) to a hanging belay in a crack that is right of the main dihedral (140 feet, 5.10). Continue up this crack and rejoin the main dihedral, then scamper to the rim (5.9). The first pitch alone makes a great pitch, and a two rope-rappel (from a threaded runner) allows escape.

FA: Mark Bennett and Bret Ruckman, 1983.

6. PENNY ARCADE II 5.9 ★★

This route climbs the second big dihedral (with the highly mottled left wall) 100 feet right of Mosaic Wall. It is named for a circular dark spot at mid-height on the wall. Follow an elegant stemming corner to a grassy ledge (140 feet, 5.9). Continue up the corner for 40 feet, then traverse right and follow a face that leads to an offwidth, and finally to a ledge (120 feet, 5.9). Climbing at 5.7 leads to the top. Take RPs for the first pitch and watch for loose rock on the second pitch. Rappel Thin Man.

FA: unknown
Probable FFA: first pitch, Merrill Bitter, Steve and Tom Carruthers, 1982.
First reported ascent of the complete route: Allen Sanderson and Dan Baker, 1988.

7. THE THIN MAN II 5.10a ★

Twenty-five feet right of Penny Arcade, just left of a large boulder, is a lichen-filled slot with loads of flakes. Climb the flakes, swing left and mantel the black knob, then go past a pin to a small ledge (80 feet, 5.8). Climb the corner past a pin to a grassy ledge and a two-pin anchor (70 feet, 5.10a). A short pitch leads up blocks to a belay in blocks (50 feet, 5.7). A right-facing dihedral is ascended to a ledge with a pin/bolt anchor. Two long rappels get one down.

FA: James Garrett and Brian Dannemann, 1985.

Thin finger locks on the Green A, Perhaps area.

photo: Craig Dillon.

9
10
11
12
13
18
17
17
18

SUMMIT WALL ROUTES

8. WEST RIDGE II 5.6
9. TRIPLE OVERHANGS III 5.10a ★★★
10. VERTICAL SMILE III 5.10a ★★★
11. UNDONE BOOK III 5.9+ R ★★★
12. WONDERWALL III 5.9 A3 ★★
13. THE OPEN BOOK III 5.7 ★★

SOUTH SUMMIT WALL ROUTES

17. GOLD WALL II 5.9 ★★
18. FOOL'S GOLD II 5.10c R ★★
19. FREE MEXICAN AIR FORCE II 5.9 A2 ★★

TOM'S THUMB ROUTES

20. LEFT THUMB II 5.8 ★
21. CENTER THUMB II 5.9 ★★

SUMMIT WALL

The routes that line the Summit Wall are among the longest and finest in the Wasatch. Proud lines up steep cracks and corners, they rise directly from the base of the wall to the top with few deviations. Not for the faint of heart, these routes are steep, exposed, sustained and involve the whole spectrum of climbing repertoire—from stems, to jams, to bold faces. The reward however, is topping out within spitting distance of the summit, if not directly upon the summit block. Once there, you can lay on the crowning slab with your shoes off and bask in the sweetness of life!

Summit Wall

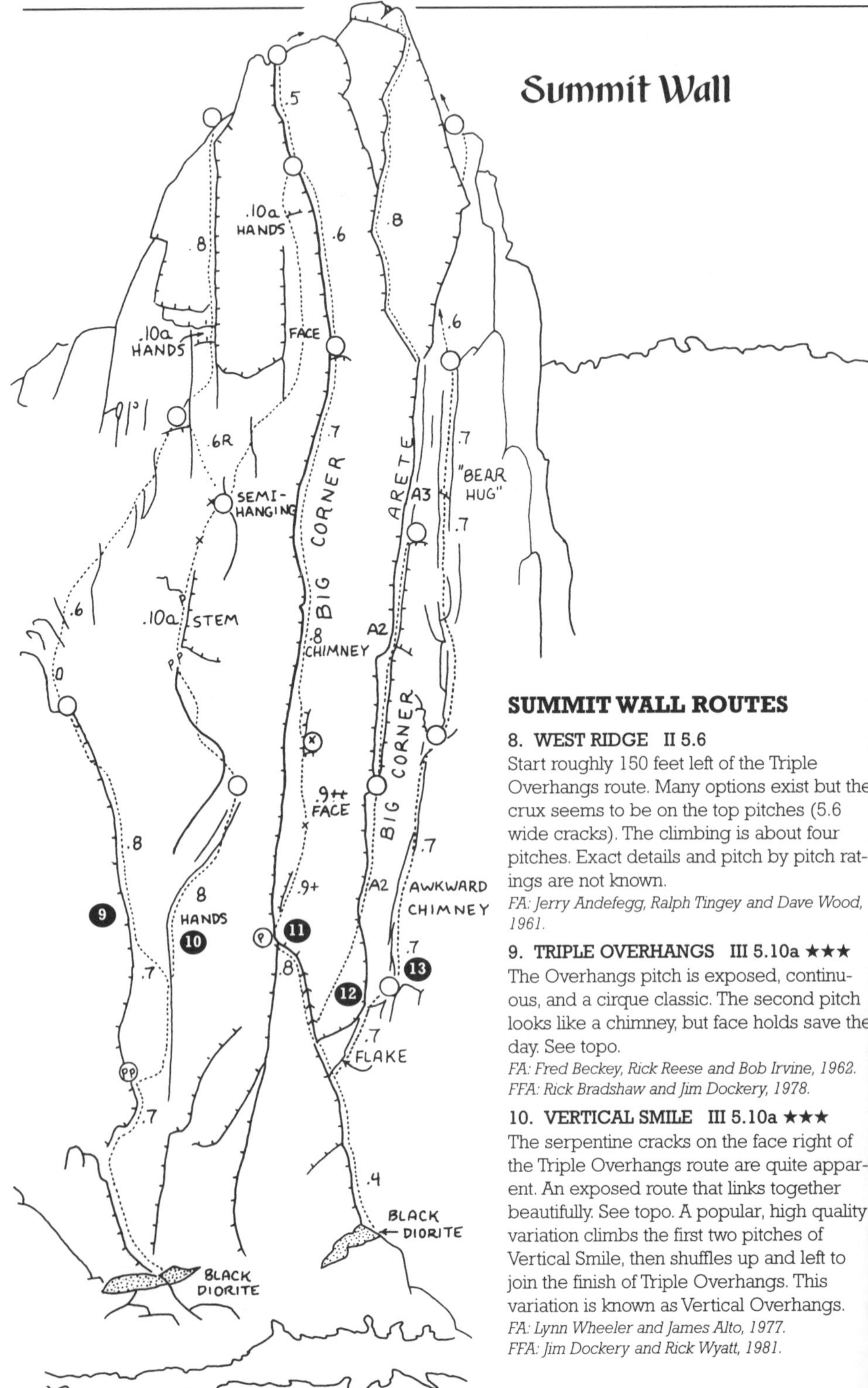

SUMMIT WALL ROUTES

8. WEST RIDGE II 5.6

Start roughly 150 feet left of the Triple Overhangs route. Many options exist but the crux seems to be on the top pitches (5.6 wide cracks). The climbing is about four pitches. Exact details and pitch by pitch ratings are not known.

FA: Jerry Andefegg, Ralph Tingey and Dave Wood, 1961.

9. TRIPLE OVERHANGS III 5.10a ★★★

The Overhangs pitch is exposed, continuous, and a cirque classic. The second pitch looks like a chimney, but face holds save the day. See topo.

FA: Fred Beckey, Rick Reese and Bob Irvine, 1962.
FFA: Rick Bradshaw and Jim Dockery, 1978.

10. VERTICAL SMILE III 5.10a ★★★

The serpentine cracks on the face right of the Triple Overhangs route are quite apparent. An exposed route that links together beautifully. See topo. A popular, high quality variation climbs the first two pitches of Vertical Smile, then shuffles up and left to join the finish of Triple Overhangs. This variation is known as Vertical Overhangs.

FA: Lynn Wheeler and James Alto, 1977.
FFA: Jim Dockery and Rick Wyatt, 1981.

11. UNDONE BOOK III 5.9+ R ★★★

A prime line to the top, taking the right-facing dihedral to the left shoulder of the summit. There is a reason it's called the Undone Book; it lay waiting for the skills of George Lowe to finish the Book. The second pitch is classic, and protection is good for the competent leader armed with TCUs, cams up to 3½", small tri-cams and nuts. Take great care with the block at the end of the second pitch. The rating reflects the incredible skills of George Lowe—modern climbers have suggested a 5.11a rating! See topo.

FA: George Lowe and Ed Anderson, 1967.

12. WONDERWALL III 5.9 A3 ★★

Start up the Undone Book for 30 feet, then follow flakes and cracks rightward, and aid up to a bolt and belay in a small nook on the prow (5.9 A3). The route now is obvious, as it ascends the shallow dihedral above to a killer belay ledge on the right (5.9 A2). A wonderful, thin knifeblade-and-RURP crack leads up the airy prow to a belay in the lower-angled dihedral (A3). The dihedral leads directly to the top (5.8). See topo.

FA: Mark Ward and Randy Wright, 1978.

13. THE OPEN BOOK III 5.7 ★★

Hundreds have enjoyed this moderate route to the summit, with its eye-catching line and varied climbing. A surprising number of accidents have occurred on this route, either by people getting off-route, by heedless beginners taking falls, or by falling rocks. Be prepared for tricky climbing with less protection than you may be accustomed to. See topo.

First attempt: Rick Reese, Ralph Tingey, and Ted Wilson were stormed off within one pitch of the summit.

Probable FA: Tom Spencer and Ron Perla, 1962.

14. THE MERCIFUL TRAVERSE II 5.6 (not on topo)

Follow the southwest ridge to the summit, which intersects the Open Book route on its terminal pitches. The climb has four pitches.

FA: Dick Bell, Calvin Giddings and Alexis Kelner, 1958.

15. THE MERCIFUL DIRECT II 5.8 (not on topo)

Where the Merciful Traverse traverses into the Open Book, a direct variation straight up corners can be taken, adding a 5.8 pitch.

FA: Hal Gribble, Paul Horton and Renny Jackson.

16. AMNESIA II 5.8 (not on topo)

The cleft between the Summit Wall and Gold Wall has loose rock. It rises to the rim just east of the main summit in three or four pitches.

FA: Tom Spencer and partner, 1959.

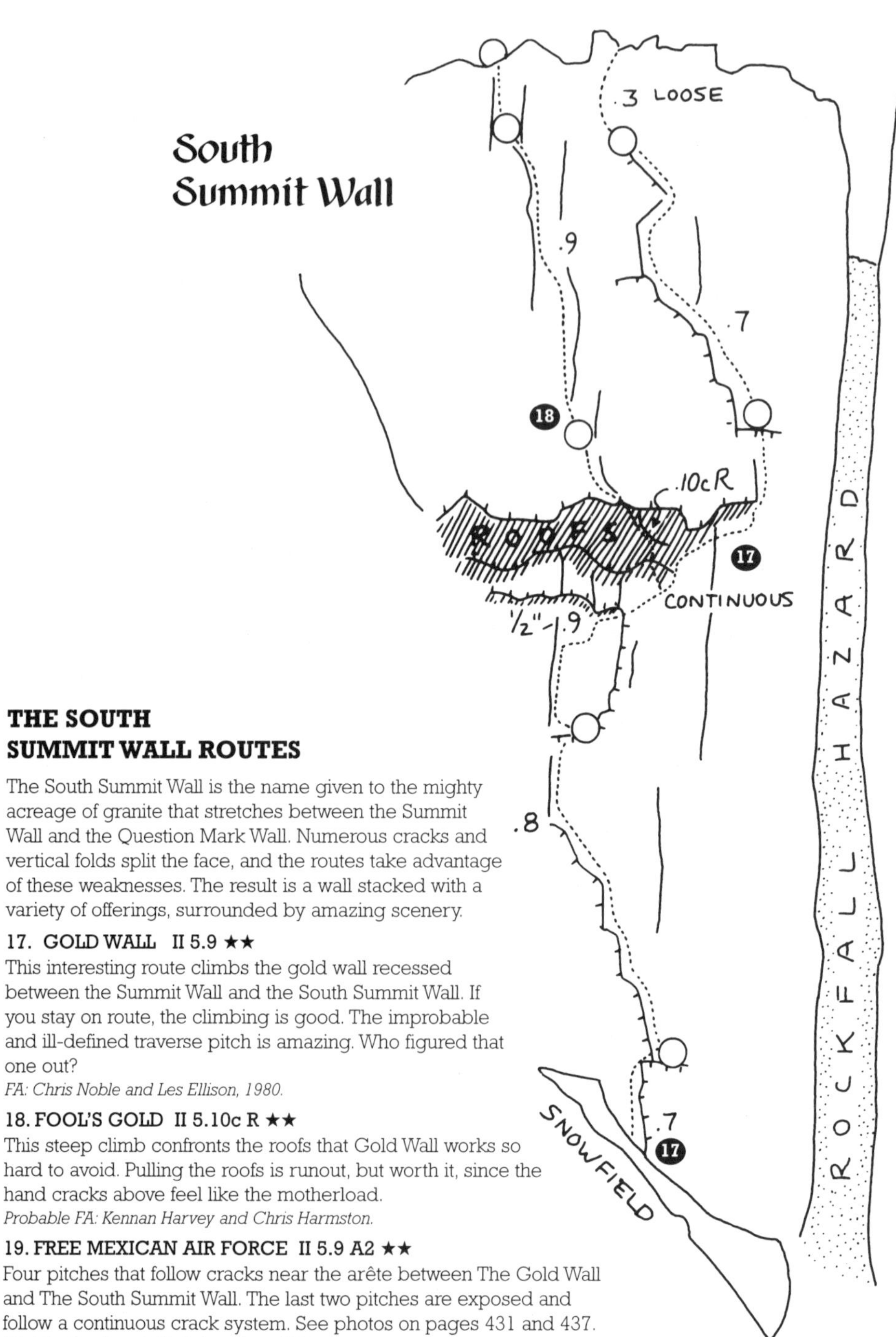

THE SOUTH SUMMIT WALL ROUTES

The South Summit Wall is the name given to the mighty acreage of granite that stretches between the Summit Wall and the Question Mark Wall. Numerous cracks and vertical folds split the face, and the routes take advantage of these weaknesses. The result is a wall stacked with a variety of offerings, surrounded by amazing scenery.

17. GOLD WALL II 5.9 ★★

This interesting route climbs the gold wall recessed between the Summit Wall and the South Summit Wall. If you stay on route, the climbing is good. The improbable and ill-defined traverse pitch is amazing. Who figured that one out?

FA: Chris Noble and Les Ellison, 1980.

18. FOOL'S GOLD II 5.10c R ★★

This steep climb confronts the roofs that Gold Wall works so hard to avoid. Pulling the roofs is runout, but worth it, since the hand cracks above feel like the motherload.

Probable FA: Kennan Harvey and Chris Harmston.

19. FREE MEXICAN AIR FORCE II 5.9 A2 ★★

Four pitches that follow cracks near the arête between The Gold Wall and The South Summit Wall. The last two pitches are exposed and follow a continuous crack system. See photos on pages 431 and 437.

FA: John Slezak and Cindy Ingraham, 1994.

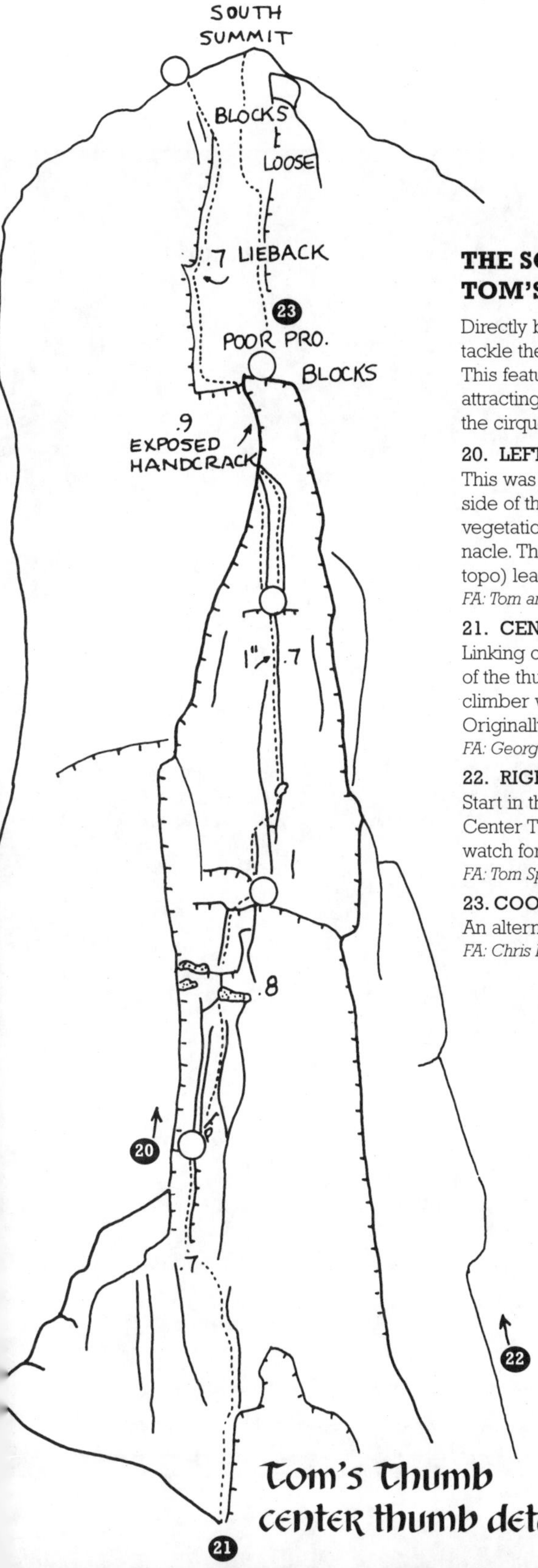

THE SOUTH SUMMIT WALL TOM'S THUMB ROUTES

Directly beneath the south summit, three routes tackle the obelisk that ends just shy of the top. This feature (Tom's Thumb) is very prominent, attracting some of the earliest climbing activity in the cirque.

20. LEFT THUMB II 5.8 ★

This was quite a route for 1959! Follow the left side of the thumb—nice dihedral climbing (some vegetation) for three pitches to the top of the pinnacle. Then, the exit cracks (see Center Thumb topo) lead up and out (5.7).

FA: Tom and Bill Spencer, 1959.

21. CENTER THUMB II 5.9 ★★

Linking cracks and weaknesses on the main face of the thumb, this excellent route challenges the climber with route finding on magnificent rock. Originally rated 5.7! See topo.

FA: George and Jeff Lowe, 1970.

22. RIGHT THUMB II 5.7 ★

Start in the second dihedral system right of the Center Thumb. Chimneys are prevalent, and watch for loose rock. Finish with the exit cracks.

FA: Tom Spencer, Bob Irvine and Ben Peterson, 1959.

23. COORS VARIATION 5.9+

An alternate finish for the Tom's Thumb routes.

FA: Chris Harmston and Freemont Shields, 1996.

Tom's Thumb
center thumb detail

THE SOUTH SUMMIT WALL ROUTES

19. FREE MEXICAN AIR FORCE II 5.9 A2 ★★
20. LEFT THUMB II 5.8 ★
21. CENTER THUMB II 5.9 ★★
22. RIGHT THUMB II 5.7 ★
23. COORS VARIATION 5.9+
24. PHLEGM FATALES II 5.9
25. FLYING CIRCUS II 5.9 R

26. HIGH ANXIETY II 5.8 R ★
27. DREAMS OF KATY II 5.9- R ★
28. SPENCER ROUTE II 5.8
29. INNER VISION II 5.10a
30. TAIVALLISTA II 5.9 A2 ★
31. DEGENERATE CRACK II 5.10b R ★
32. EXPANDING MAN II 5.9 R ★
33. THE GREAT ESCAPE II 5.9+ ★★
34. THE DAGGER II 5.8
35. BELL, GIDDINGS, KELNER ROUTE II 5.10a R
36. ROOF STOPPER 5.10c
37. PETE'S STAIRCASE 5.4 ★★

SOUTH SUMMIT WALL ROUTES

24. PHLEGM FATALES II 5.9

Given the choice, most prefer the femme fatales. Start 5 feet right of Right Thumb, in a right-facing corner that is climbed for 150 feet (5.9). More of the same lead to a belay above a roof (5.9). Climb the crack until it veers sharply right, traverse a bit left to another wide crack. Belay in a broken area (5.8). A chimney with lots of loose rock leads to the top (5.7).

FA: Rick Wyatt and Jim Dockery, 1981.

25. FLYING CIRCUS II 5.9 R

This is located 20 feet right of Phlegm Fatales, and 30 feet left of the huge corner on the Spencer Route. Chimneys dominate the route's first three pitches (5.7/5.8). The final pitch climbs a loose section with poor protection, followed by some stemming, which leads to the redeeming conclusion—a straight-in and exposed crack (150 feet, 5.9).

FA: Mark Smith and Brian Smoot, 1979.

26. HIGH ANXIETY II 5.8 R ★

A distinctive left-facing corner system, starting about 50 feet right of the Right Thumb route, rises the entire length of the wall. Climb the corner for a full pitch to a ledge (5.7). Immediately below the 3-foot roof, a hanging belay from two fixed pins marks the end of the second pitch (165 feet, 5.8). Continue up the corner to the top (150 feet, 5.6).

FA: Les Ellison and Fred Fisher, 1978.

27. DREAMS OF KATY II 5.9- R ★

"Life and love are all a dream." This route is 10 feet right of High Anxiety, and 20 feet left of the huge corner on Spencer Route. Connect sparsely-protected grooves with face climbing up to a deep groove and belay. Perseverance up the chimneys and offwidths leads to a belay atop a chockstone (150 feet, 5.8). Chimney up until chickenheads to the right allow a respite; continue up the face to a block, and then go higher to a belay in a gray dike (5.9-). Yet another chimney, 15 feet to the right, leads to the top (5.8). Cams are useful.

FA: Les Ellison, Rick Wyatt and Steve Carruthers, 1980.

28. SPENCER ROUTE II 5.8

This is the largest left-facing brown corner 100 feet right of Tom's Thumb. It is broken and loose in many sections. A helmet would be a good idea. Basically follow the crack in the corner for 4 pitches to the rim.

FA: Tom and Bill Spencer, 1959.

29. INNER VISION II 5.10a

An imposing route that takes the right margin of the Spencer Route's dihedral through overhangs and diorite bands. An initial pitch leads up to a hand crack (5.2). Then, climb the cracks up a left-facing corner until the crack pinches off. At this point, traverse right 10 feet (an alien quartzite hold is used) to a stance, then climb a crackless, left-facing corner to a hanging belay (140 feet, 5.10a). The third pitch, a ditto of the second, ascends the corner above for 20 feet, makes an improbable traverse right along a gray band of rock, then struggles up 100 feet to another hanging belay (140 feet, 5.9+). A final push, encountering loose rock, will reach the top (150 feet, 5.8).

FA: Les Ellison and Brent Davis, 1982.

30. TAIVALLISTA II 5.9 A2 ★

This route beelines up to a big roof approximately 80 feet below the rim, beginning 100 feet to the right of the Spencer Route. Follow the left-facing corners for almost a full rope-length (150 feet, 5.7). Free moves lead to a roof, which is passed by angling right and using some aid, then another roof leads to a ledgeless belay above its lip (5.9 A2). A brilliant face is climbed to a belay just below the big roof (5.7). Aid moves conquer the ceiling, and some more aid rightward along a diagonalling crack takes the climber to a welcome bolt. Arching back left is a scabrous crack that is followed (with ample rope drag) to the top (5.9, A2). Bring a selection of pins.

FA: Jeff Lowe and Bruce Roghaar, 1970.

31. DEGENERATE CRACK II 5.10b R ★

The most eye-catching crack on the south summit wall. Twenty feet right of Taivallista. Continuously difficult flares with tricky protection keep off the riff-raff. Do what you can to get up to this crack (mostly left-facing grassy corners), then dice your way through the crux (the first 40 feet) and belay (5.10b). More grooves lead to a belay stance (5.9). Corners take the weary climber to the top (5.9).

FA: Mark Ward and Jim Langdon.

32. EXPANDING MAN II 5.9 R ★

"This is the day of the expanding man." The second of the largest left-facing corners right of the Spencer Route. Identify Taivallista's prominent roof, and you'll find this big corner system 50 feet to its right. Climb a long pitch up the corner to a ramp (5.7). A two-inch crack in the right wall allows entry to the corner above, which is followed to a belay below a smooth corner (5.9). Stem up the corner past old fixed pins to a good belay ledge (150 feet, 5.8). Some easy face climbing leads to the top (5.6). Lots of stemming and a paucity of protection.

FA: unknown

FFA: Mark Ward and Randy Wright, 1979.

33. THE GREAT ESCAPE II 5.9+ ★★

Start 30 feet left of a small grove of dwarfed pines at the cliff's base. Look for a small solitary pine below the roof on the first pitch. A fine route that goes hither and yon. See topo.

FA: Brian Smoot and Steve Aldous, 1983.

34. THE DAGGER II 5.8

Start up wide cracks above the small grove of dwarfed pines. A shallow chimney leads to a steep face, then traverse left and follow a thin flake (the dagger) to a grassy ledge (150 feet, 5.8). An overhanging flake leads to an obvious diagonalling crack. Follow this crack and others to a restful ledge (165 feet, 5.8). Continue up the corner to the top (5.8).

FA: Brian Smoot and Steve Aldous, 1982.

35. BELL, GIDDINGS, KELNER ROUTE II 5.10a R

This large, left-facing corner, with a roof at two-thirds height, is located 10 feet right of The Dagger. Climb wide cracks (mostly stemming) to a hard-to-establish belay (150 feet, 5.8). Climb up to the roof, pass it on the left and continue up a hand crack until a big stem left regains The Dagger (125 feet, 5.10a).

FA: Dick Bell, Calvin Giddings and Alexis Kelner, 1958.

FFA: Bret and Stuart Ruckman, 1990.

36. ROOF STOPPER 5.10c

A tenuous route that leads up to a fixed belay/rappel below a long traversing roof. So far this roof section has stopped all attempts to add a second pitch.

FA: Kim Csizmazia and Kennan Harvey, 1996.

37. PETE'S STAIRCASE 5.4 ★★

This broken section of rock serves as an avenue to Collin's Highway, the large easy ramp running beneath the Question Mark Wall. The 5.4 route is circuitous and is easy to make harder. This course is used as a descent for the South Summit Wall routes, in addition to an approach for the Question Mark Wall Routes. One or two rappels from trees usually suit the tired climber better than the downclimbing of Pete's Staircase.

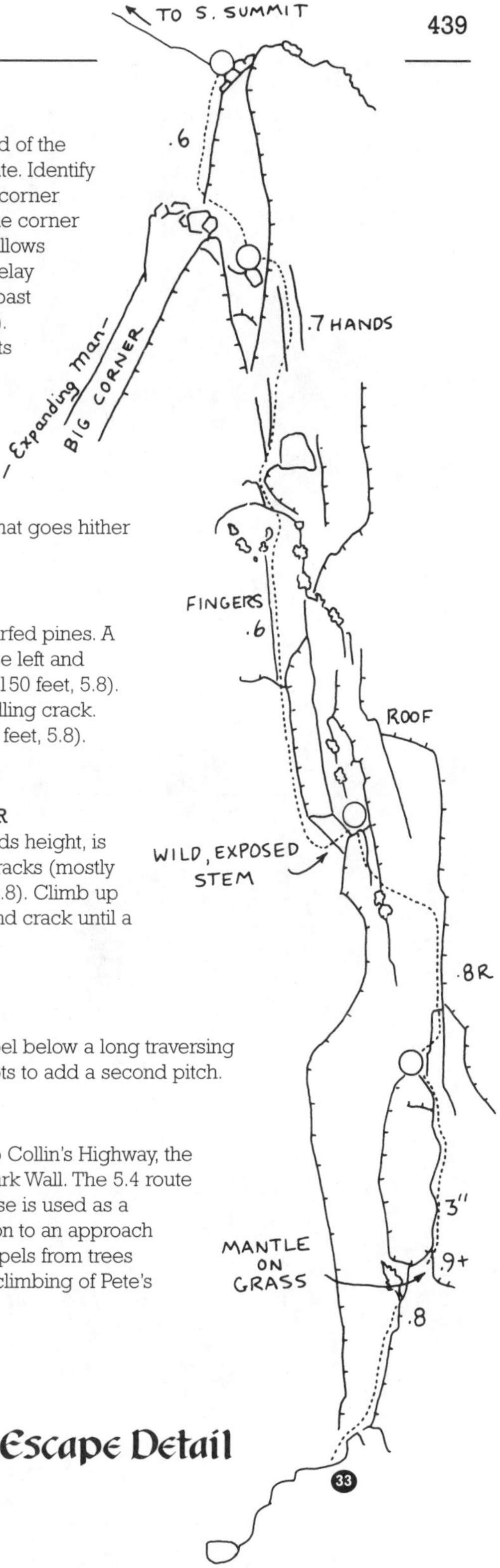

Great Escape Detail

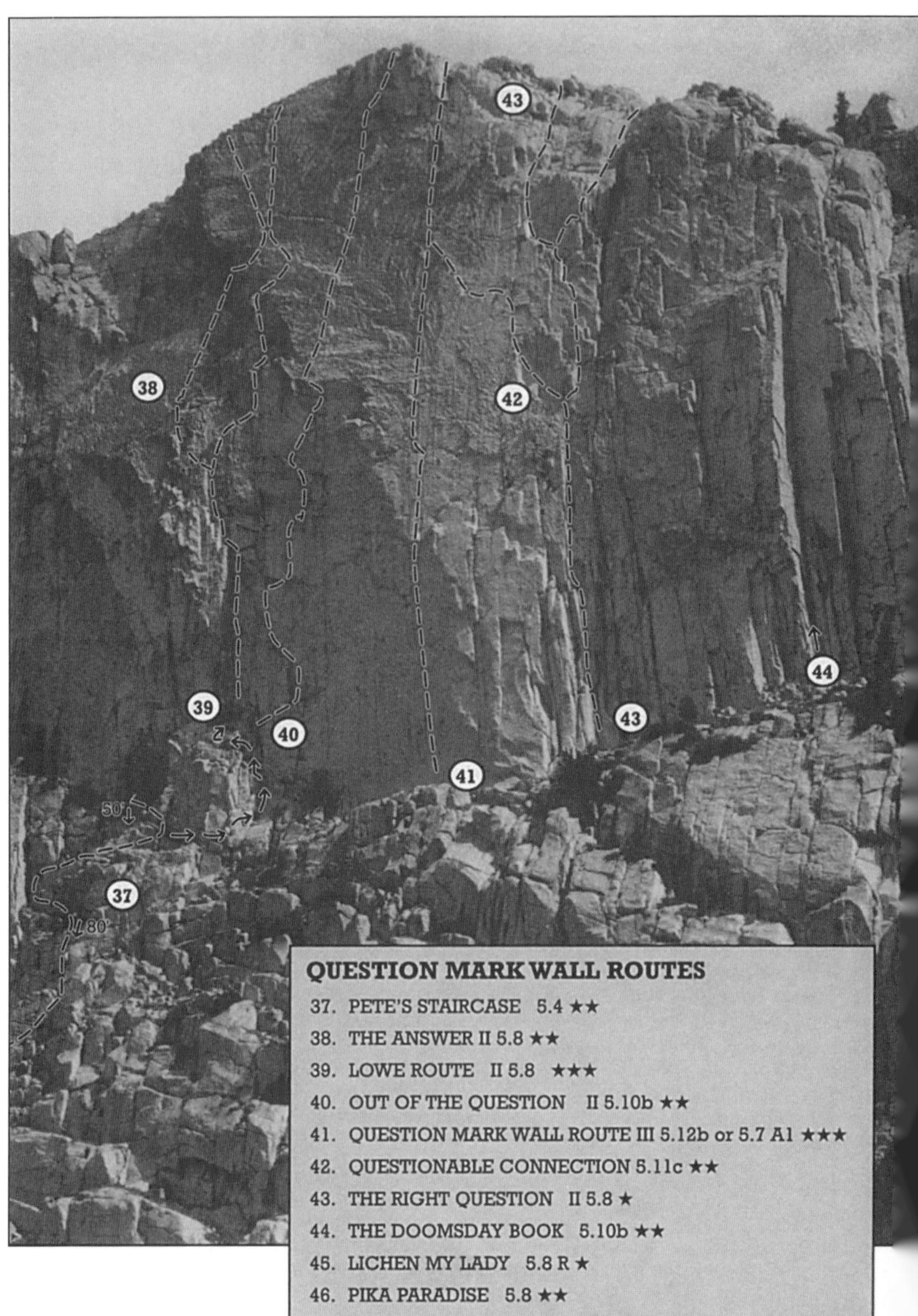

QUESTION MARK WALL ROUTES

37. PETE'S STAIRCASE 5.4 ★★
38. THE ANSWER II 5.8 ★★
39. LOWE ROUTE II 5.8 ★★★
40. OUT OF THE QUESTION II 5.10b ★★
41. QUESTION MARK WALL ROUTE III 5.12b or 5.7 A1 ★★★
42. QUESTIONABLE CONNECTION 5.11c ★★
43. THE RIGHT QUESTION II 5.8 ★
44. THE DOOMSDAY BOOK 5.10b ★★
45. LICHEN MY LADY 5.8 R ★
46. PIKA PARADISE 5.8 ★★
47. BLADERUNNER 5.10c ★★

45
46
47

QUESTION MARK WALL

The most awesome wall in the cirque is the smooth and steep north-facing Question Mark Wall, so named because of the ?-like character located in the upper face. As you move southwest, this wall becomes more featured with dihedrals.

38. THE ANSWER II 5.8 ★★

Exposed face climbing on patina edges and solution pockets. Hand sized protection is needed for the first pitch of the Lowe Route. TCUs and wires protect between the bolts.
FA: Brian and Jonathan Smoot, 1995.

39. LOWE ROUTE II 5.8 ★★★

This is an undeniable classic, with breathtaking exposure and continuous difficulty. The final pitch won't be forgotten. This route starts in a right-facing corner to the left of the smoothest section.
FA: George and Jeff Lowe, 1970.

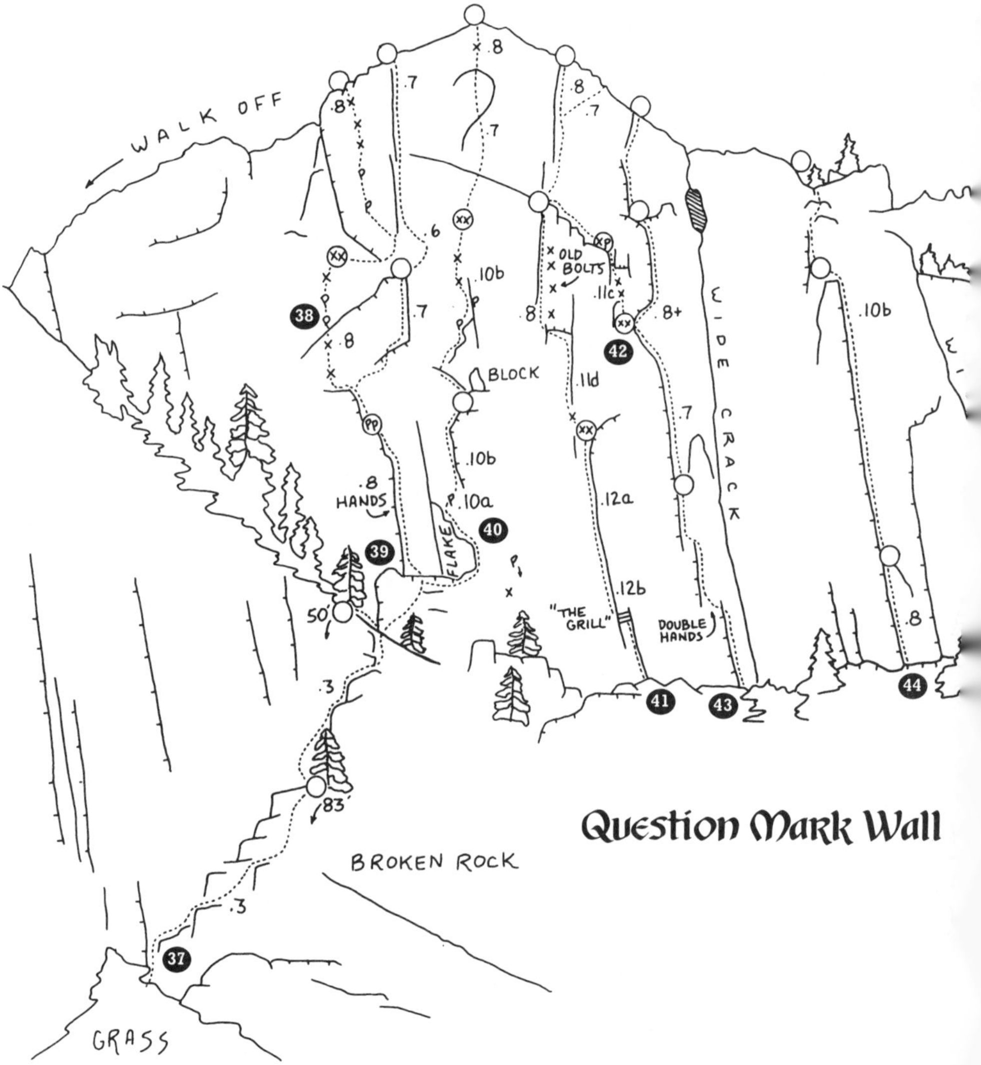

Question Mark Wall

40. OUT OF THE QUESTION II 5.10b ★★

This thriller starts 20 feet right of the Lowe Route on an eight-inch flake. Bring many runners for tieing off protection on the stupendous final pitch.

FA: Stuart and Bret Ruckman, 1990.

41. QUESTION MARK WALL ROUTE III 5.12b or 5.7 A1 ★★★

Several factions of climbing coalesce to form an ultimate route, one with artful nutting, an alpine environment and sustained super-difficulty. Bring two full sets of micro nuts. As an aid route, its ratings are respectively A1, A1 5.7, 5.7; all clean, of course.

FA: Fred Beckey and Dan Davis, 1962.

FFA: Merrill Bitter and Stuart Ruckman, 1989.

42. QUESTIONABLE CONNECTION 5.11c ★★

A difficult link that crosses some airy terrain between The Right Question and the Question Mark Wall Route. TCUs are worth their weight.

FA: Brian Smoot and Steve Aldous, 1996.

43. THE RIGHT QUESTION II 5.8 ★

A fun route located 120 feet to the right of the Question Mark Wall Route. Start in a series of right-facing, left-leaning dihedrals.

FA: Brian Dannamann and James Garrett, 1985.

44. THE DOOMSDAY BOOK 5.10b ★★

The historic book is on display. A large, green, right-facing corner 300 feet right of the Question Mark Wall Route. The vegetation on the first pitch can be bypassed by face climbing on the left. Ticklish moves conclude the difficult second pitch (150 feet, 5.10b).

FA: Bret and Stuart Ruckman, Gary Olsen, 1981.

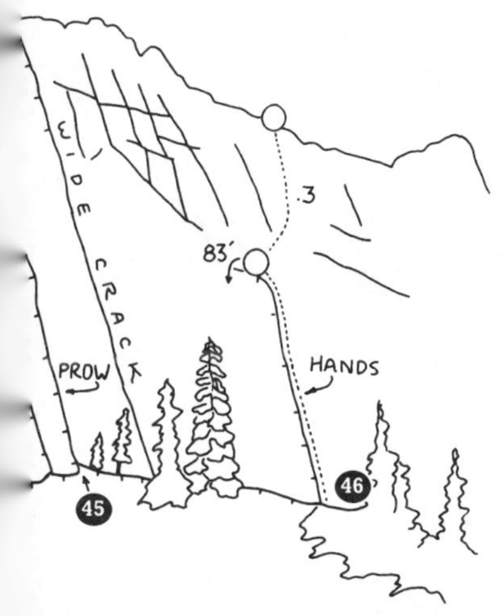

45. LICHEN MY LADY 5.8 R ★

Halfway between Doomsday Book and Pika Paradise is a west-facing prow with a deep cleft on its right side. Climb a knobby, poorly-protected face up to a crack that is followed to a ledge (165 feet, 5.8). Climb cracks on a smooth face past a pin (5.7) and scamper to the top.

FA: Bret and Judy Ruckman, 1985.

46. PIKA PARADISE 5.8 ★★

A nearly perfect right-facing corner starts hard and stays enjoyable (120 feet, 5.8). Large nuts/cams are useful.

FA: Gary Olsen, Stuart and Bret Ruckman, 1981.

CAMP CLIMBS

Toproping and bouldering have been popular pastimes in the cirque for years. A little imagination and a positive attitude will yield many gems, providing an outlet for climbers with energy remaining at the end of the day. While these topropes and boulder problems are not recorded, two leads near camp are certainly worthy of climbing.

Above the furthest meadow to the south is a slabby band of broken cliffs. Bladerunner is the only reported route here.

47. BLADERUNNER 5.10c ★★
This route is hard to locate, but worth the effort. Climb a seam near the right edge of a slab, probably 200 feet above the southernmost meadow (about a 3-minute approach) and below Pika Paradise about 200 feet. Look for pins. Continuous and intricate climbing up several seams makes for a nice, one-pitch route close to camp. Bring small camming devices and nuts. See photo page 441.
FA: James and Franziska Garrett, 1989.

48. THAT THING 5.10c ★
Located on the small, south-facing wall that forms the northern boundary of the cirque. Look for a right-leaning, right-facing corner with a pin. This route climbs a crack just left of the corner and sports a relic pin itself. About 30 feet long.

HYPERFORM WALL

This cliff defines the south side of the cirque below the Question Mark Wall. It is fairly complex, with many arêtes, dihedrals, an undulating base height, and few good landmarks to help locate routes. The standard descent is to walk all the way from the top of the cliff off the easy south side, and re-enter the cirque via the Alpine approach. Other, shorter descents are possible, however. See photo page 446.

49. BOOK OF RHYMES 5.8
The first big open book on the left end of Hyperform Wall is the target. It is easily identified as the large dihedral 50 feet left of a pine-covered ledge half way up the cliff. The route climbs the left margin of the dihedral, staying in crack systems, and eventually traverses right under some nasty-looking blocks to the pine-covered ledge on Thunder Crack. There are two pitches.
FA: Bret Ruckman and Mark Bennett, 1983.

50. THUNDER CRACK 5.9 ★
At the high point of the talus, 100 feet to the right of Book of Rhymes and 100 feet left of Hyperform, a large, broken dihedral leads to the right of a big, pine-populated ledge (5.7). Climb this corner, angling up and left to the pine-covered ledge. On the left side of the wall above, a nice hand-crack bisects a roof and gradually widens to a chimney (5.9).
FA: Lynn Wheeler and Steve Carruthers, 1982.

51. VANDALS TOOK THE HANDLE 5.11a ★★
High quality arête climbing. Climb the first pitch of Thunder Crack to a two-bolt belay. Climb broken rock up and right to the base of a corner system that shoots straight to the ridge. The original route climbed up the corner, traversed left to the arête, then up to a belay. A one bolt variation climbs the arête head on. The last pitch is exposed, intricate, and a pleasure to climb. Three long bolted rappels provide a quick descent.
FA: Mike Friedrichs and James Garrett, 1991.

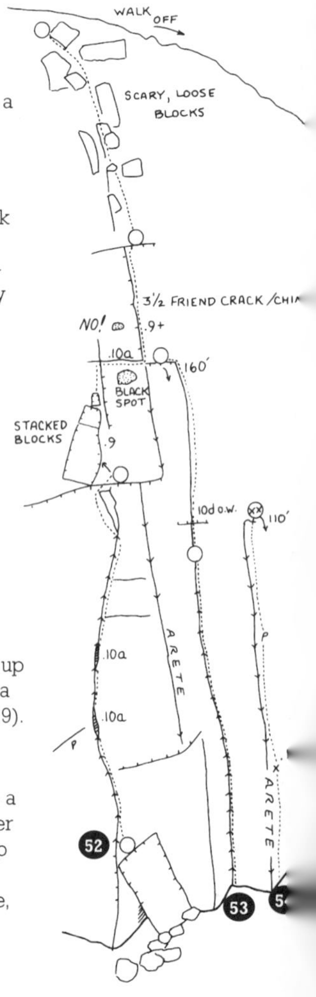

52. HYPERFORM II 5.10b ★★★

Hyperclassic. Above a rectangular boulder is a striking hand-and-finger crack corner that leads to a ledge on an arête. Continuous difficulty-spiced climbing with good rock sets the stage for a command performance. Several large camming devices are useful on the third pitch. See topo.

FA: Dirk Tyler, Lynn Wheeler and Les Ellison, 1978.

53. SUPERFORM II 5.10c ★★

Climb the dihedral system 10 feet right of Hyperform, belaying 15 feet below the roof. Climb up to and out the 6-inch roof crack. Once above the crux roof, face climb the brown rock to the right for relief from the cracks, and belay as for the Hyperform first pitch. Bring those big Friends. See topo.

FA: Merrill Bitter and Steve Carruthers, 1982.

54. MEGAFORM 5.11a R ★★★

Stout. A bolt and a pin protect the arête just right of Superform. Climb thin cracks five feet right of the arête up to the roof, then step left and up past a bolt. Continue up the arête past a pin to a two-bolt belay. Enjoy continuous face climbing on super-good rock. Bring RPs, TCUs, nuts and 3½" and 4" cams for the first 20'. Join Superform or rap off (110 feet). Of historical note, Ted Wilson and Dick Ream climbed 1½ pitches in a crack system to the right of Megaform in '63, turning back because of loose rock. See topo.

FA: Bret Ruckman and Merrill Bitter, 1990.

55. SHADOW OF DEATH II 5.10a ★

A continuous route with wide cracks and rewarding climbing. Start near the top of the talus slope about 100 feet right of Hyperform. A large open book has a perfect hand crack on its left wall. Follow the hand crack to a stance. Continue up wider cracks to a belay beneath a squeeze chimney (5.9+). Climb the squeeze chimney to a belay in an alcove (5.10a). Of the two crack systems above, choose the right, which narrows to fingers above 3 small roofs. At the top of the finger crack, venture left into a wide slot and make your way over blocks to the top (140 feet, 5.10a). Several large camming devices (4") are VERY helpful.

FA: Les Ellison and Pat Maloney, 1983.

56. LONE PINE II 5.8

Named because of the lone pine tree at the top of the route. Start about 40 feet right of Shadow of Death. Climb a right-facing corner system which leads up to a nice ledge (150 feet, 5.7). A shorter pitch leads up cracks in a lower-angled wall to a belay on the left (5.7). Work up the cracks above to the pine tree and belay (5.8). Protection is poor.

FA: Bob Irvine and Rich Ream, 1963. FFA: Leslie Ellison and Steven Carruthers, 1980.

57. OCTOBERFEST 5.11c ★★

A celebration of an enduring Lone Peak season. The first pitch follows a long, straight-in crack with a bolt to protect some mighty thin moves. The second pitch is a fraction easier, and shorter, but every bit as good. Two long rappels reach the ground. The face between Octoberfest and Jolley Green Giant has been climbed on toprope at 5.10d.

FA: Chris Harmston and Freemont Shields, 1996.

50
51
110'
50
49
52
53
54
HYPERFORM WALL ROUTES
49. BOOK OF RHYMES 5.8
50. THUNDER CRACK 5.9 ★
51. VANDALS TOOK THE HANDLE 5.11a ★★
52. HYPERFORM II 5.10b ★★★
53. SUPERFORM II 5.10c ★★
54. MEGAFORM 5.11a R ★★★

HYPERFORM WALL ROUTES

55. SHADOW OF DEATH II 5.10a ★
56. LONE PINE II 5.8
57. OCTOBERFEST 5.11c ★★
58. JOLLEY GREEN GIANT 5.11a ★★★
59. MAIDENFORM II 5.10c ★
60. LATENT STORM II 5.9
61. AGENT ORANGE II 5.9+ ★
62. TAKE IT FOR GRANITE 5.7 ★

58. JOLLEY GREEN GIANT 5.11a ★★★

A classic splitter that cuts a clean swath up the steep north face. Bring along an appetite for fingerlocks, many stoppers, TCUs, some brass-type nuts, and cams up to three inches. Latent Storm makes a great second pitch, or simply rappel off.

FA: Chris Harmson and Freemont Shields, 1996.

59 MAIDENFORM II 5.10c ★

A titillating climb, so to speak. This ascends a prominent and attractive green-orange right-facing dihedral 100 feet west (right) of Shadow of Death. It is located near the western-most edge of the Hyperform Wall. Climb up the corner to a one-foot wide ledge and belay. Continue up the corner to a rightward-diagonalling roof. Traverse under roof and belay at a huge chockstone (60 feet, 5.10c). A 5.7 hand crack leads to the top from the right side of the chockstone.

FA: Karin Budding, Steve Hong and Steve Carruthers, 1983.

60. LATENT STORM II 5.9

Climb Maidenform until you can escape left onto a big ledge (140 feet, 5.9). Traverse left 20 feet to a crack system and reset the belay. Climb the small right-facing corner above to a somewhat dubious belay on a ramp (150 feet, 5.8). Climb left through rotten rock to the top (5.7).

FA: Stuart and Bret Ruckman, 1983.

61. AGENT ORANGE II 5.9+ ★

Forty feet right of Maidenform is an orange-colored acute corner, or "V"-slot, with a large roof to the left. Uninspiring climbing leads to the base of the corner (40 feet, 5.5). Climb the corner in one long pitch, traversing left under a roof to a belay at the chockstone on Maidenform (140 feet, 5.9+). The final pitch of Maidenform now can be ticked off.

FA: Steve Hong, Steve Carruthers and Karin Budding, 1983.

62. TAKE IT FOR GRANITE 5.7 ★

This is a west-facing flat arête located 100 feet right of Agent Orange, near the top of a grassy slope. A broken slot, topped by pine trees, rests to the right. Pick a crack in the ridge and climb 125 feet to a ledge (5.6). Climb the cracks above, veering left to the ridge and up to a steeper fist crack on the north side, which is followed to the top (5.7). Not on photo.

Probable FA: Stuart and Bret Ruckman 1983.

Bouldering

No guide to the Wasatch Mountains would be complete without a mention of the many bouldering areas that local climbers have to choose from. While detailed descriptions of the boulders themselves are beyond the scope of this book, we have provided enough information to get you to the boulders. From there, you're left to your own creative devices.

PETE'S ROCK

Sparse bouldering can be found on the west face, the traverse of the entire southwest face, and on the next outcrop up the hill to the east. See information on page 45.

APPROACH: Follow Wasatch Blvd. to roughly 5500 South. Pete's is the quartzite outcrop with a row of numbers painted along its base. Park in the parking area just east of the boulevard. The approach from the parking area to the base of the wall takes about twenty seconds. See overview on page 34.

BIG COTTONWOOD

Storm Mountain Picnic Area

This is a U.S. Forest service fee area, and you can park inside the picnic area for four dollars per car or park on the main highway and walk in for two dollars per person. The lone boulder was once the site of considerable activity, but this limited rock pales in comparison to the offerings in Little Cottonwood Canyon. Still, if you're in the area to climb, might as well warm up, or cool down.

APPROACH: Park 2.8 miles up canyon from the neon sign. Either walk or drive into the picnic area. The boulder sits directly across from the picnic area host's campsite.

The Black Fence

This tiny crag is popular for bouldering. Eliminate problems are the rage on the short overhanging walls at the base of the crag. One leadable route is here as well (see page 148). This area rests a mere 50 feet from the road, on the north side, just right of a black iron fence.

APPROACH: Park 3.55 miles up canyon from the neon sign (about 1.5 miles up the BCC road from Storm Mountain Picnic Area).

LITTLE COTTONWOOD

Climbers have been bouldering in Little Cottonwood Canyon for years. In fact, the most popular bouldering area, The Gate Boulders, have long been considered the hub of Wasatch rock climbing. Bouldering in the shade of the oaks on a summer evening, or working a problem surrounded by the changing colors of a crisp fall day, are as much a part of the local rock climbing experience as are the crack, face and knob routes on the cliffs above. Recently, local climbers have been exploring for new bouldering areas, often finding gold right off the side of the road. Below is a list of the most convenient bouldering areas in the canyon. See the How To Get There information on page 224 for a description of how to reach Little Cottonwood Canyon.

AREA 1: The Secret Garden

Park .2 miles up canyon from the neon sign. Several high quality boulders live within 100 feet of the road, sheltered by a small grove of oak and maple trees. Additional bouldering can be found by following the path uphill to the infamous "Tiger" boulder. This area can also be accessed from the northeast corner of the bus stop parking lot.

AREA 2: The Cabbage Patch

Park .4 miles up canyon from the neon sign. Two boulders 25 feet from the road, but hidden by trees, provide the bulk of the problems, while several more boulders uphill are worth checking out.

AREA 3: Mile Five Boulders

Park 1.1 miles up canyon from the neon sign. Most of the bouldering is located on or around the prominent Split Boulder. However, several additional boulders are located just down the road and towards the stream.

AREA 4: The Gate Boulders

Park 1.25 miles up canyon from the neon sign at the prominent parking area on both sides of the road. This is the most heavily used bouldering area, and with a wide range of difficulties, mostly good landings, and top-rope anchors on the largest boulder, its popularity is deserved. Follow the trail at the west end of the parking area up into the trees to reach the boulders.

AREA 5: The Swamp Boulders

Park 1.35 miles up canyon from the neon sign, or walk up the road from the Gate Boulders parking area. Walk across a suspended pipe that forms a bridge over the stream. Beyond the stream, continue on the pipe for another 50 feet, then hop off at a path, walk south, crossing another small stream, to an old pavilion. Boulders along the dirt road, both up and down canyon from here, are the attraction. These are the largest boulders in the area, and several of the rocks have bolts on top for anchors.

AREA 6: The Hill

Park 1.55 miles up canyon from the neon sign. A large boulder is right next to the road here, usually propped up (for a joke) with a spindly stick. This is a talus field, so there are a number of boulders, some of them are to the left in the trees.

AREA 7: The Unknown

Park 1.6 miles up canyon from the neon sign. The east face of the boulder right off the road on the river side is the main attraction. Scattered bouldering on the uphill side of the road is also possible.

AREA 8: The Hidden Forest

Park 1.85 miles up canyon from the neon sign. Cross the river on the bridge and follow the path up canyon. This joins another trail which is followed east for several hundred feet to a stand of larger aspen trees. Just past these trees a small trail heads off right (south). Take this trail, hanging a left at the junction to the first of several scattered boulders. This area is in the pine trees and is a good choice for warmer days.

AREA 9: The Campus Boulder

Park 2.6 miles up canyon from the neon sign. A small stream flows past the boulders and crosses under the road. Only a dozen problems exist, but the stream adds a nice ambience.

Index

A

B

C

D

E, F

G, H

I, J, K

N, O

P, Q

R

S

T

U, V

5.2 to 5.5

5.6

5.7

5.8

5.9

5.10

5.10a

5.10b

5.10c

5.10d

5.11

5.11a

5.11b

5.11c

5.11d

5.12

5.12a

5.12b

5.12c

5.12d

5.13

Mixed Free and Aid

Aid Routes